Lincoln Public Library

January 1997

SS

VICTORIAN LOVE STORIES

VICTORIAN LOVE STORIES

AN OXFORD ANTHOLOGY

Edited by

Kate Flint

Oxford   New York

OXFORD UNIVERSITY PRESS

1996

Oxford University Press, Walton Street, Oxford OX2 6DP

Oxford New York
Athens Auckland Bangkok Bogota Bombay
Buenos Aires Calcutta Cape Town Dar es Salaam
Delhi Florence Hong Kong Istanbul Karachi
Kuala Lumpur Madras Madrid Melbourne
Mexico City Nairobi Paris Singapore
Taipei Tokyo Toronto
and associated companies in
Berlin Ibadan

Oxford is a trade mark of Oxford University Press

British Library Cataloguing in Publication Data
Data available

Library of Congress Cataloging in Publication Data
Data available
ISBN 0–19–212330–0

1 3 5 7 9 10 8 6 4 2

Typeset by Graphicraft Typesetters Ltd., Hong Kong
Printed in Great Britain
on acid-free paper by
Bookcraft (Bath) Ltd.
Midsomer Norton, Avon

CONTENTS

v

Contents

INTRODUCTION

Love is a constant theme of Victorian short stories, just as it is a staple of the period's longer fiction. It is represented as both the source of extreme individual happiness, and the grounds for painful division. It provokes humour, melodrama, and subterfuge, treads upon forbidden areas, leads alternatively to undreamed-of happiness or to misery, and acts as a reassuring form of social consolation. Love, in other words, was appropriated by Victorian short-story writers for a number of ends.

For the Victorians, to write of love almost always meant offering some kind of reflection on the position of women within society. The emotion of love was rarely presented as being as lastingly central to men, although the short story's capacity to exploit an expanded moment increasingly offered a medium which emphasized men's emotional vulnerability, and the degree to which fantasy and longing can rule men's private lives. Many of the stories in this volume are by women writers, who perhaps had more sympathy with the escapist needs of their readership, and who, at the same time, could see other possibilities offered by the genre. To choose love as one's subject was, very frequently, to draw on ostensibly unprovocative domestic material, yet the subject of love could easily be turned to pointed social critique, in shorter as well as in longer fictions. The connections between courtship and money, the difficulties faced within conjugal life, the repercussions of former romantic liaisons or indiscretions—the latter two in particular being topics which proliferated in the later decades of the century— provided many opportunities in this respect. They joined with such familiar plot-sustaining devices as obstructive parents, apparent class barriers, and initially mistaken perceptions of the eventual partner in order to interrogate the nature and status of romance and marriage.

Victorian stories dealing with love focus on the period of a woman's life when she appears to be most in charge of her fate. None the less, an individual's apparent claim to personal autonomy—something which many of these stories manifest on the surface—was ultimately subject to both the opportunities available to her within her given class and culture, and the demands of the genre itself. Despite this, the love story provided a vehicle for the imaginative aspirations and desires of a large number of relatively powerless individuals. Countless Victorian novels focus on the romantic fortunes of young girls, taking marriage as their culminating point, and of course this was the staple ingredient of such popular novelette series as *The Princess's Novelettes, The Illustrated Family Novelist*, and the *Dorothy Novelette*. Indeed, their plots were often more or less borrowed from established novelists. There is ample evidence that magazine editors directed their contributors to provide happy endings, and this could apply to short fiction as well as to lengthier works. On 17 July 1855 Dickens wrote to Emily Jolly about the story she had submitted: 'You write to be read, of course. The close of the story is unnecessarily painful—will throw off numbers of persons who would otherwise read it . . . and is so tremendous a piece of severity, that it will defeat your purpose.' She changed it, and 'A Wife's Story' duly appeared in *Household Words* on 15 September that year, with a relatively upbeat (and consequently slightly incongruous) conclusion. Much later in the century, Ella Hepworth Dixon's *The Story of A Modern Woman* (1894), which draws greatly on the author's experience as a freelance writer, shows her heroine having a chapter returned to her by the editor of *Illustrations*, who advises her not to write of 'the truth' of modern life: 'if you don't mind my saying so, there aren't quite enough love scenes between the hero and the heroine. The public like love-scenes . . . I should suggest a thoroughly happy ending. The public like happy endings.'

Yet despite, or very probably because of its popularity as a subject, the treatment of love in fiction was regarded with suspicion throughout the period. Sometimes it was introduced in a way which might cause readers to reflect on the implications of the very book that they held in their hands. The romantically embittered Mrs Pryor in Charlotte Brontë's *Shirley* (1849) speaks vehemently about how writers of love stories seem to know nothing whatsoever of the nature of love, 'nor of marriage; and the false pictures they give of those subjects cannot be too strongly condemned. They are not like reality: they show you only the green tempting surface of the marsh, and give not one faithful or truthful hint of the slough underneath.' At the far end of the century, George Bainton, in *The Wife as Lover and Friend* (1895) complained how frequently romantic fiction culminated at the altar, with no hint of the challenges to follow: ' "They married, and were happy ever afterwards," is a loving tradition, which, though devoutly to be wished, will yet, in too many instances, if dragged into the revealing sunshine of prosaic, everyday life, show how unsubstantial is its origin, and how unreliable its philosophy.' Nor were girls figured as the only victims of love stories. Flora Annie Steel's 'Amor Vincit Omnia' (1898) tells of a young Indian man who is unable to function in the 'real' world because he becomes hooked on the genre.

Certainly a good deal of the romantic fiction which was published readily played to such fears—always assuming (and it would be a rash assumption to make) that the consumers of popular love stories made no distinction between what might happen to them in their own lives, and what happened to the fictional heroines of whom they read. An article on governesses in *Household Words* in 1856 claims that the experience of Jane Eyre as a governess, up to her flight from Thornfield, 'is true. I have known parallel cases, in which, with temptation not less than hers, girls have fought their battles as bravely, as painfully, and as successfully; but, with the final romantic result, no!' Seduction by master or eldest son was a statistically far more likely fate than romantic union for the defenceless employee: a story like Christiana Fraser-Tytler's 'Margaret' (1869) represents a deliberate revision of the plots to be found in such love stories as *Jane Eyre*, showing that a young girl should be able to act with pragmatic common sense (and know her class position).

As the example of 'Margaret' suggests, a good deal of the anxiety which surrounded the corrupting influence of the three-decker romance would have been misplaced in the case of the short story. This is not just true of manifestly didactic pieces like Fraser-Tytler's. The short story offered the opportunity to seize on the heightened sensations provoked by love and to exploit them for emotional effect. Instead of serving the demands of a plot, love becomes the catalyst in an exploration of the emotions aroused both by loyalty and steadfastness (as, say, in Elizabeth Gaskell's 'Right at Last' or Flora Annie Steel's 'Uma Himāvutee') and, more frequently, by loss, grief, and missed opportunities. One further feature of the short story which distinguishes it from longer works is the recurrence of stories which celebrate romantic fulfilment occurring in middle age or even later. Thus in Louisa Parr's

'How it All Happened' (*Good Words*, 1868), a cheerful romance blossoms after a plump 47-year-old woman lends a handkerchief to the man with whom she is uneasily sharing a railway carriage. Margaret Woods's 'Miss Bright-Eyes and Mr Queer' (*Weeping Ferry and Other Stories*, 1898) tells of a couple who first meet at a college ball, tell home truths to each other about the unfavourable impression they make, and are then allowed to meet up again in Switzerland twenty years later. Annie Swan, in *Courtship and Marriage and the Gentle Art of Home-Making* (1893) noted that 'It is beyond question that a love-story has yet the power to charm even sober men and women of middle age, for whom the romance is mistakenly supposed to be over', and such stories as these suggest that middle-aged readers of romance were not just attempting to recapture their youth, but might be looking around them. None the less, holding false expectations based on nostalgic memories provided another favourite theme. The hero of Henry Harland's 'A Sleeveless Errand' (*Mademoiselle Miss*, 1893) keeps his ideal woman in his mind for over twenty years as he stays on as an artist in Paris, and she returns to America. He reads of her husband's death, and sets off in pursuit—only to find that she is unrecognizably fat; for her disappointed part, she discovers he is 'as grey as a rat'. His romantic aspirations are transferred to a girl from Minneapolis whom he has met on the Atlantic crossing.

In conventional romantic fiction there appears to be little heart-searching over how to define 'love', at whatever time of one's life it is encountered. Yet such definitions were, it would seem, increasingly in demand in a wider cultural context. In 1893 Frederick Greenwood published *The Lover's Lexicon. A Handbook for Novelists, Playwrights, Philosophers, and Minor Poets; but especially for the Enamoured*. Under a set of alphabetical headings which run from 'Abhorrence' to 'Wife', and which range through such topics as 'Assignation', 'Blushing', 'Bride', 'Doubts', 'Erotic', 'Flirtation', 'Kiss', 'Old Maids', 'Sweetheart', and 'Temptation'—not to mention 'Love' itself—he compiles sets of quotations which help him to define his themes, and provide a set of ready-made clichés for those who are tempted to write on them. Inevitably, it is found that ''Tis better to have loved and lost than never to have loved at all'. What is it to love? Shakespeare's Silvius, in *As You Like It*, provides the answer:

It is to be all made of sighs and tears;
It is to be all made of faith and service;
It is to be all made of fantasy,
All made of passion and all made of wishes,
All adoration, duty, and observance,
All humbleness, all patience and impatience,
All purity, all trial, all observance.

Nor was Greenwood the only supplier of catch-all definitions. Ellis Ethelmer (Mrs Wolstenholme Elmy)'s *Phases of Love: As It Was; As It Is; As It May Be* (1897) provided useful supportive quotations in the form of chapter headings, from Spenser's 'Love is a celestial harmony | Of likely souls' to George Eliot's 'The first condition of human goodness is something to love'. The Hon. Mrs Lyttelton Gell's *The Most Excellent Way. Words of the Wise on the Life of Love. A Sequence of Meditations* (1898) is a sumptuously produced gift book—blue letterpress, green initial letters and decorations—divided into thirty-six sections, from 'Love, Heaven-born', 'Love, Limitless', 'Love, a Mystery' to 'Love, the Welder', 'Love, the Conqueror', and 'Love, the Interpreter'. Space is left for the owner's personal quotations and reflections.

What is remarkable about these volumes, and others like them, is the fact that their appearance is concentrated in the 1890s. More than ever before, traditional conceptions of marriage were being publicly scrutinized during this period, in particular by novelists and polemicists associated with the New Woman: a woman not afraid to query the sexual ignorance with which many young girls embarked on marriage, and the double standards pertaining in women's and men's sexual relations, nor to press, more widely, for increasing women's educational and employment opportunities. These volumes are responding to, and playing on, an anxiety about the status and implications of love. Such an anxiety is repeatedly addressed in the short stories of the 1890s, the decade which witnessed the flowering of the short-story form, and which also demonstrates the determination of short-story writers to free themselves from certain expectations and conventions surrounding their subject-matter.

This creates something of a problem when putting together an anthology of the Victorian Love Story. The traditional format of the love story—encounter, difficulties, rapturous reunion, and union, or, alternatively, the theme of noble self-sacrifice made in the name of love, or the theme of love that is thwarted by the untimely death of one of the protagonists—is subverted by some of the most innovative, experimental, and interesting short fiction of the period. Some of the most striking stories in this volume, like Ernest Dowson's 'The Statute of Limitations', Ella Darcy's 'The Pleasure-Pilgrim', and Charlotte Mew's 'Some Ways of Love', although they admit the possibility of love, also show how untrustworthy the emotion can be: how non-communication is a more powerful force in determining the direction of some relationships than intimacy. Other notable tales excluded themselves from a book of 'love stories' by their determined repudiation of the very theme. Mary Angela Dickens's 'Another Freak' (1896) is a justifiably angry feminist polemic against men who seduce women and then try to argue their way out of it. Ella Hepworth Dixon's 'One Doubtful Hour' dwells on the obligations felt by a woman to play a flirtatious role and seek a husband: she ends by gassing herself. In George Egerton's 'Virgin Soil', a young girl returns, after five years of marriage, to reprimand her mother about all she did not tell her concerning adult life. Yet more cynical is the treatment of Bob Jennings, in Arthur Morrison's 'A Poor Stick' (*Tales of Mean Streets*, 1894), who remains faithful to his slatternly wife Melier after she runs away with the lodger and the valuables, only to become a figure of fun in his neighbourhood.

The writing of the 1890s, with its stress on troubled relationships, on double standards, and on the need for women to negotiate between a desire for independence and a wish to find an object for their affections, highlights the problems of formulating some kind of understanding as to what, exactly, constitutes love. Parent–child relationships seem to fall outside the genre of the love story, however intense the love manifested in them may be. So, too, do the powerful emotions felt by an individual for a place, although the regret of the colonialist in R. B. Cunninghame-Grahame's 'Higginson's Dream' (1900), who returns to the country he had fallen in love with many years ago to find it utterly changed by the effects of colonization, provides a forceful analogue to the many stories which suggest the dangers of holding in one's head a romantic image of a past encounter with a specific individual. Inadmissible too, although a little less certainly so, would seem to be relationships between humans and animals. Ouida's 'Ruffo and Ruff' (*La Strega and Other Stories*, 1899), for example, is a tear-jerker recording the mutual devotion of a Calabrian boy in England and a dog in a Punch and Judy show, an affecting—or mawkish, depending on one's degree of cynicism—tale of loneliness and dependence. But it is uncomfortably dependent for its effect on the reader's implied distance, even condescension towards the young and the less fortunate, and on the same grounds I am reluctant to admit stories which assume a wry, knowing superiority towards childhood attachments, like Kenneth Grahame's 'Young Adam Cupid' (*The Golden Age*, 1895).

A more awkward question is posed, however, when one asks: where does love end and friendship begin? 'Love, as commonly understood, is the passion between the sexes', wrote A. Burgh and J. J. Spark, in *Marriage a Success. Choice in Wedlock embracing Love, Courtship, etc.* (1891), but I had hoped to find something a little less commonly expressed, to suggest that love was not just a matter of heterosexual romance. But same-sex desire, or passion—if passion and desire are indeed what start to separate love from friendship—are hard to locate, with the exception of the suicidal obsession which drives the senior protagonist in John Francis Bloxam's 'The Priest and the Acolyte' (*Chameleon*, June 1894; reprinted in Brian Reade (ed.), *Sexual Heretics: Male Homosexuality in English Literature from 1850 to 1900*). There are plenty of examples of homosocial bonding, for example in the sentimental representations of male comradeship given by 'John Strange Winter' (the pseudonym of Henrietta Eliza Vaughan Stannard) in *Cavalry Life* (1881) and *Regimental Legends* (1883). A. St John Adcock's 'A Hero in Clay' (*An Unfinished Martyrdom and Other Stories*, 1894) destroys the marvellous statue he has just created, which he thinks 'might make a little noise in the world and yield him some few drops of that fame he had hoped to fill his cup with', because he fears such fame will wreck his friendship with his 'particular crony and brother in Art', but such noble self-sacrifice for the sake of friendship does not necessarily make a love story. Between women, there are not really any more clear-cut romantic liaisons: although lesbian relationships begin to make tentative appearances in a few novels of the 1890s, they almost invariably fail to survive the demands of the heterosexual world, and are—so far as I have been able to discover—surprisingly under-represented in the short-story form.

Love can be redemptive, or it can be futile. It can take place within a very ordinary setting, or the special, intense qualities of love may be more easily evoked in a fantasy land, as we see in the stories by Christina Rossetti and Laurence Housman. Alternatively, other writers, like Anne Thackeray Ritchie, in 'Beauty and the Beast' (*Five Old Friends and a Young Prince*, 1868), and Walter Besant, set out to reshape or debunk traditional fairy-tale romances. Love may give the strength necessary to negotiate the modern world; alternatively, the modern world may prove inimical to close, supportive relationships, as individuals fail to reconcile their personal priorities. Love frequently lets one down, is unsustainable, is based on illusion, and yet, as Virginia Woolf was to point out, at some time or another nine out of ten people passionately want love more than they want anything else.

Necessarily, many of these generalizations hold true for writing about love at any time during the modern period. What is peculiar to the Victorian decades, however, is that new understandings about how relationships might be conducted and represented were developing alongside the emerging genre of the short story: experimentalism, new definitions, new patterns, a refusal of pre-established plots are, by the end of the period, common to both fiction and social forms. Above all, what emerges, perhaps inevitably, from this collection of stories is the fact that love is something defined within the terms of a relationship, not something which obeys any external laws or labellings.

VICTORIAN
LOVE STORIES

GRACE AGUILAR

The Authoress

I

'You surely do not intend acting such a fool's part, Dudley, as that our little world assigns you?' was the address of one friend to another, as they drew their chairs more cosily together, in the little *sanctum* to which they had retreated, after a *tête-à-tête* dinner.

'And what may that be, my good fellow?'

'Why, throw away yourself and your comfortable property on a person little likely to value either one or the other, and certainly worthy of neither—Clara Stanley.'

Granville Dudley coloured highly. 'Oblige me, at least, by speaking of that young lady with respect,' he said; 'however you and your companions may mistake my intentions concerning her.'

'Mistake, my good fellow; your face and tone are confirmation strong. I am sorry for it though, for I would rather see you happy than any man I know.'

'I believe you, Charles; but what is there so terribly opposed to my happiness in an union with Miss Stanley, granting for the moment that I desire it?' Charles Heyward sat silent, and stirred the fire. 'Because she is not rich? nay, I believe, rather the contrary.'

'I do not think you worldly, Granville.'

'Thank you, for doing me but justice. I am perfectly indifferent as to wealth or poverty in a woman. But what is your objection then? She is not superlatively beautiful nor seemingly first-rate in accomplishment; but what then? She is pleasing, unaffected, full of feeling, very domestic, for I seldom meet her out.'

Again were the poker and the blazing coals at variance, and more noisily than before.

'My good friend, you have roused that fire and my curiosity to a most unbearable state of heat. Do speak out. What is the matter with

Miss Stanley, that when I mention the words "feeling" and "domestic",
you look unbelieving as a heretic? Can you say "Nay" to any one thing
I have said?'

'Nay, to them all, Granville Dudley,' exclaimed Heyward, with vehemence. 'It is because you need a most domestic woman for your
happiness, I tell you do not marry Clara Stanley: she is a determined
blue—light, dark, every imaginable shade—a poet, a philosopher, a
preacher—writes for every periodical—lays down the law on all subjects of literature, from a fairy tale to a philosophical treatise or minis-
terial sermon. For heaven's sake! have nothing to do with her. A literary
woman is the very antipodes to domestic happiness. Fly, before your
peace is seriously at stake.'

Granville Dudley looked, and evidently felt disturbed. At first, startled and incredulous, he compelled his friend to reiterate his charge and
its proofs. Nothing loath, Charles Heyward brought forward so many
particulars, so many facts, concerning the lady in question, which, from
his near relationship to the family with whom she lived, he had been
enabled easily to collect, that Granville, unable to disprove or even
contradict one of them, sank back on his chair, almost with a groan.

'Why, my dear sober-minded philosophic friend, you cannot surely
have permitted your heart to escape your wise keeping so effectually in
so short a space of time, that you cannot call it back again with a word?
Cheer up, and be a man. Thank the fates that such a melancholy truth
was discovered before it was too late. I have heard you forswear literary women so often that I could not stand calmly by, and see you run
your head blindfold into such a noose; she is a nice girl enough, and if
she were not so confoundedly clever, might be very bearable.'

'But how is it I never discovered that she is so clever? If it be displayed so broadly, how can she hide it so completely before strangers?'

'She does not display it, Granville. No one would imagine she was
a whit cleverer than other people; she has no pretension, nor airs of
superiority; but she writes, she writes, "there's the rub", and she loves
it too—which is worse still—and a public literary character cannot be
a domestic wife; one who is ever pining for and receiving fame can
never be content with the praise of one; and one who is always creating
imaginary feelings can have none for realities. To speak more plainly,
those who love a thousand times in idea can never love once in reality;

and so I say, Clara Stanley cannot value you sufficiently ever to possess the rich honour of being chosen as your wife. Do not be angry with my bluntness, Granville; I only speak because I love you.'

Granville Dudley was not angry; perhaps it had been better for his happiness if he had been, as then he would not have been so easily convinced by the specious reasoning of his friend. The conversation lasted all that evening, and when Dudley retired to rest, it was with a firm determination to watch Clara Stanley a few weeks longer, and if it really were as Heyward stated, to dismiss her from his thoughts at once, and even quit England for a time, rather than permit a momentary fancy to make him miserable for life.

Now, though Charles Heyward had spoken in the language of the world, he was not by any means a worldly man; nor Granville Dudley, though he had listened and been convinced, unjust or capricious. Unfortunately for Miss Stanley's happiness, Granville's mother had been one of those shallow pretenders to literature which throw such odium upon all its female professors. From his earliest childhood Dudley had been accustomed to regard literature and authorship as synonymous with domestic discord, conjugal disputes, and a complete neglect of all duties, social or domestic. As he grew older, the excessive weakness of his mother's character, her want of judgment and common sense, and— it appeared to his ardent disposition—even of common feelings, struck him more and more; her descriptions of conjugal and maternal love were voted by her set of admirers as perfect; but he could never remember that the practice was equal to the theory. Nay, it did reach his ears, though he banished the thought with horror, that his father's early death might have been averted, had he received more judicious care and tender watchfulness from his literary wife.

Mrs Dudley, however, died before her son's strong affections had been entirely blunted through her apparent indifference; and he therefore only permitted himself to remember her faults as being the necessary consequence of literature and genius encouraged in a woman. He was neither old nor experienced enough, at the time of her death, to distinguish between real genius and true literary aspirings, and their shallow representatives, superficial knowledge and overbearing conceit.

As this was the case, it was not in the least surprising that he should be so easily convinced of the truth and plausibility of Heyward's reasoning, or that Charles Heyward, aware of all which Dudley's youth had endured from literature and authorship in a mother, should be so very eager to save him from their repetition in the closer relationship of wife.

But Clara Stanley was no mere pretender to genius; the wise and judicious training of affectionate parents had saved her from all the irregularities of temper, indecision of purpose, and inconstancy of pursuit which, because they have characterised some wayward ones, are regarded as peculiar to genius. Her earliest childhood had displayed more than common intellect, and its constant companions, keen sensibility and thoughtfulness; a vivid imagination, an intuitive perception of the beautiful, the holy, and the good; an extraordinary memory, and rapid comprehension of every variety of literature, alike prose and poetry, unfolded with her youth, combined with most persevering efforts after improvement in every study which could assist her natural gifts. It was impossible for her parents not to regard her with pride, but it was pride mingled with trembling; for *they* knew, though *she* did not, that even as she was set apart in the capability of *mind* from her fellows, so she was in the capability of *suffering*. Knowing this, their every wish, their every effort, was directed to providing her with a haven of refuge, where that ever-throbbing heart might find its only perfect rest. Taught to regard mental powers, however varied, as subordinate to her duties as a woman, and an English and religious woman, modesty, gentleness, and love marked every word and every action. Few there were, except her own immediate circle and friends, who knew the extent of her mental powers, or the real energy and strength of her character; but countless was the number of those that loved her.

It was not, however, till after her father's death she saw and felt the necessity of making her talents a source of usefulness as well as of pleasure. She was then little more than seventeen, but under the fostering care of an influential literary friend, she was introduced to the periodicals of the day, her productions accepted, and more requested from the same hand.

Though a few years after Mr Stanley's death, however, their pecuniary affairs were so advantageously settled that Clara had no longer any necessity to make literature a profession. Their income was moderate, but it rendered them happily independent.

'Now, now,' was Clara's ardent exclamation, as she clasped her arms about her mother's neck, 'I may concentrate my energies to a better and holier purpose than the mere literature of the day; now I may indulge the dream of effecting *good*, more than the mere amusement of the hour; now I am no longer *bound*. Oh, who in this world is happier or more blessed than I am?'

And as long as she resided under her mother's roof, in the pretty little village which had so long been her home, she was truly happy. Encouraged by the popularity which, through her literary friend, she learned that she had acquired; satisfied that he thought her capable of the work she had attempted, and blessed with a mother for whose sake alone Clara valued fame; for she knew how sweet to maternal affection were the praises of a child.

But this might not last. Before she was one-and-twenty Clara was an orphan, and long, long it was ere she could resume the employments she had so loved, or look forward to anything but loneliness and misery. Every thought, every task was associated with the departed, and could filial love have preserved the vital spark the mother had yet been spared; and had Granville Dudley known Clara in that sad time he would have been compelled to abjure his belief in the incompatibility of literature with woman's duties and affections.

But of such a trial both Granville and Heyward knew nothing; nor, when the latter said that she *loved* her profession, did he imagine the struggle it had been for her to resume it—how completely at first it had been the voice of duty, not of love. Fame had never been to her either incentive or further reward than the mere gratification of the moment, and as a source of pleasure to her mother; and how vain and hollow did fame seem now! But hers was not a spirit to be conquered by deep sorrow. She resumed her employments when health returned, with a bursting heart, indeed, but they brought reward. They drew her from herself for the time being, and energy in seeking to accomplish good gradually followed. The severity of her trial was, however, if possible, heightened by the great change in her mode of life. Her only near relation was an uncle, who lived and moved in one of those circles of high pretension and false merit with which the metropolis abounds. His wife, an ultra-fashionist, lived herself and educated her daughters for the world and its follies alone, inculcating the necessity of *attracting* and *gaining* husbands, but not of keeping them. Exterior accomplishment, superficial conversation, graceful carriage, and fashionable manners were all that were considered needful—and all of feeling or of sentiment rubbed off, as romance much too dreadful to be avowed.

To this family, at the request of her uncle, who actually made the exertion of fetching her himself, Clara removed eight months after her mother's death. Yearning for affection, and knowing little of her relatives, Clara had given imagination vent, and hoped happiness might again be dawning for her. How greatly she was disappointed our readers may judge by the sketch we have given. In their vocabulary, authorship and learning were synonymous with romance and folly; and worse still, as dooming their possessors, unavoidably, to a state of single blessedness, and therefore to be shunned as they would the plague itself. That Clara devoted to her literary pursuits but the same number of hours that one Miss Barclay did to music (that is its mechanical not its mental part), another to oriental or mezzo-tinting, or another to the creation of wax-work, Berlin wool, etc., was not of the least consequence; their horror of blueism was such, that to prevent all supposition of their approval of Clara's mode of life, they never lost an opportunity of bewailing her unfortunate propensity—and of so impressing all who visited at the house with the idea of her great learning and obtrusive wisdom, that the gentle, unpretending manners of the authoress could not weigh against it; and she found herself universally shunned as something too terrible to be defined.

'With all this, I write on, hope on,' she once wrote to an intimate friend; 'struggling to feel that if indeed I accomplish *good*, I shall not live in vain; and my own personal loneliness and sorrow will be of little consequence. But, oh! how different it is to write merely for the good of others, to the same efforts, to the same goal, pursued under the influence of sympathy and affection! Because a woman has *mind*, she is supposed to have no *heart*, and has no occasion therefore for the sweet charities of life; when by her, if possible more than any other, they are imperatively needed. Others may find pleasure or satisfaction in foreign excitement; to her, home is all in all. If there be one to love her there— be it parent, husband, or friend—she heeds no more; the yearnings of her heart are stilled, the mind provides her with unfading flowers, and her lot is as inexpressibly happy as without such domestic ties it is

6

inexpressibly sad. Do not wish me, as you have sometimes done, dear Mary, to love, for it would be unreturned; simply, because it is the general belief that an authoress can have no time, no capability of any emotion save for the creations of her own mind.'

So wrote Clara; though, at the time, she knew not how soon her words would be verified. As soon as the term of mourning had expired, though little inclined for the exertion, she conquered her own shrinking repugnance to asserting and adopting her own rights; and, to the astonishment of Mr and Mrs Barclay, she accepted some of the invitations which courtesy had sent her. Though entered into merely as a duty, society gradually became a source of pleasure, in the discovery that all her aunt's circle were not of the same frivolous kind; and then slowly, but surely, the pleasure deepened into intense enjoyment from the conversation and attentions of Granville Dudley, whom she met constantly, though he did not visit her uncle. Clara was so very unlike her cousins, whose endeavours to gain husbands were somewhat too broadly marked, that Dudley had been irresistibly attracted towards her; a fancy which every interview so strengthened, that he began very seriously to question his own heart as to whether he really was in love.

As Miss Stanley's name was not generally known to the literary world, and the lady, at whose house Granville mostly met her, was herself scarcely aware that she was anything more than an amiable, sensible, and strongly feeling girl, Granville Dudley knew nothing of her claims to literature and authorship till his conversation with Charles Heyward, near the close of the season, revealed them as we have said. The very next time they met, Dudley, half fearfully, half resolutely, led the subject to literature and literati, and drew from Clara's own lips the avowal he dreaded. In the happy state of feeling which his presence always created, she at first imagined he thus spoke from interest and sympathy in all she did; and enthusiastic, as was her wont in conversation with those who she thought understood her, she said more on the subject, its enjoyment and resources, than she had ever done in London. Granville said nothing in reply, which could have chilled her at the time. Yet, when the evening was over, Clara's heart sunk within her; she knew not wherefore, save that a secret foreboding whispered within her *that* conversation had sealed her fate. Dudley would not trust his happiness with her.

At one other party she was to meet him, ere the season closed, and the veriest devotee to balls and *soirées* could not have longed for it more than poor Clara; who looked forward to it as the confirmer or dispenser of her fears. The morning of the day on which it was to take place, little Emily, the youngest of the family, was seized with a violent attack of fever, which increased as evening advanced. It so happened that all the Barclay family who were 'out' were engaged that evening; Mr and Mrs Barclay, and their two elder daughters, at a card and musical *soirée*; the other two, and their brothers, under the *chaperonage* of Mrs Smith, the *gouvernante*, at the ball to which Clara looked forward with so much eagerness. What was to be done? The child could not be left; and without Mrs Smith, what was to become of her sisters? It was impossible for them to go alone, and equally impossible for mother, father, or either sister of the little sufferer, to give up a fashionable party for the dreadful doom of sitting by a sick bed.

Looks and hints of every variety were levelled at Clara, who, with her usual benevolence, had stationed herself close by her little cousin, ever ready to administer kindness or relief. At any other time, she would not have hesitated a moment; but with the restless craving to see Granville Dudley again, the giving up her only chance, for a time at least, was so exquisitely painful, she could not offer to remain. Mrs Barclay, however, seeing hints of no avail, at length directly entreated that, as she was less fond of going out than any one else, she might be glad of the excuse, to give the time to her books and writing, and it would really be doing her (Mrs Barclay) an especial favour if she would stay and nurse Emily. Clara's high spirit, and strong sense of selfish injustice, obtained such unusual dominion, that she had well-nigh proudly refused; but the little sufferer looked in her face so piteously, and entreated her so pleadingly to remain, that, ever awake to the impulse of affection, Miss Stanley consented.

The disappointment was a bitter one, though Clara's strong sense of rectitude caused her to reproach herself for its keenness, as uncalled for. What did Granville Dudley care for her, that she should so think of him? but vain the question. Every backward glance on their intercourse convinced her that he had thought of her, had singled her out, to pay her those attentions, that gentle and winning deference, which, from a man of honour, such as the world designated him, could not be misconstrued. There was one comfort, however, in her not meeting him; if he knew what kept her at home, he would scarcely continue to believe that her only thoughts were of literature and authorship.

Little did she know that, before they departed on their several ways, it was settled in the Barclay parliament that nothing whatever was to be said of little Emily's illness, lest people should fancy it contagious, and send them no more invitations, so closing their chances of matrimony for that season, before it was quite time.

'If Clara is asked for, my dears—which is not at all likely—you can say you know that she could not leave her writing, or correcting a proof, or some such literary business. I leave it to you, Matilda; you are sharp enough, particularly in framing excuses for a rival, whom I know you are glad to get out of your way. Folks say Granville Dudley had a literary mother; he is not likely to wish for a literary wife.'

The young lady answered with a knowing nod; and performed her mission so admirably, that after that evening Granville Dudley disappeared. Power she certainly had to separate him from Clara, but to attach him to herself was not quite so easy. The answer she had given to Granville's inquiries after her cousin was so carelessly natural—that Clara, as an authoress, a literary character, had so many superior claims, that parties and everything else must be secondary, and this followed up by a high encomium on her great talent, she should say genius; but it was, she thought, almost a pity to be so gifted, as it incapacitated her from common sympathies and duties—that it confirmed Granville's previous fears. And while it made him almost turn sick with disappointment and anguish, for it seemed only then he felt how completely she had become a part of himself, he vowed to tear himself from her influence ere it was too late, and the very next morning left London.

'You were right, Heyward. I suppose I shall be a happy man again some day or other, but not now; so do not try to philosophise me into being so.'

'But, my good fellow, perhaps after all we have been frightened at shadows; and, hang it! but I am sorry I said so much at first. That Emily Barclay has been very ill, and was so that eventful night, are facts; and, in my opinion, Clara stayed to nurse her, because the others were all too selfish.'

'A sentimental excuse to obtain time for dear, delightful, solitary musings, or some such thing. It is too late, Heyward; she *is* literary, and so she cannot be domestic. I will not think of her any more.'

This was not quite so easy to do as to say; but Granville Dudley was a man of the world, far too proud and resolute to bow, or seem to bow, beneath feeling, particularly when he believed himself on the point of loving one who was utterly incapacitated from giving him any heart in return. He went abroad, travelled during the remainder of the summer, joined the first Parisian circles in the autumn, and before the year closed was a married man.

II

Eight years have passed, and Clara Stanley is still unmarried; yet she is happy and contented, for she is once more amid the scenes of her childhood; once more the centre of a domestic circle, who vie with each other who can love her best. Two years after she heard of Granville Dudley's marriage, finding a London life less and less suited to her tastes, and not conceiving any actual duty bound her to reside with her uncle's family, she resolved on making her home with an intimate friend of her mother's, who was associated with all the happy memories of her own childhood and youth. Reduced circumstances had lately compelled Mrs Langley to take pupils; a fact which had instantly determined Clara's plans. She was the more desirous for retirement and domestic ties, from the very notoriety which the constant success of her literary efforts had flung around her. She did not disdain or undervalue fame; but all of expressed admiration, all public homage, was so very much more pain than pleasure, that she shrunk from it; longing yet more for some kindly heart on which to rest her own. Let us not be mistaken: it was not for love, in the world's adaptation of the word, she needed; it was a parent's fostering care—a brother's supporting friendship—a sister's sympathy, or one friend to love her for herself, for the qualities of *heart*, not for the labours and capabilities of *mind*. From the time she heard of Dudley's marriage, all thought of individual happiness as a wife faded from her imagination. Her only efforts were to rouse every energy to supply objects of interest and affection, and so prevent the listlessness and despondency too often the fate of disappointed women. This had, at first, been indeed a painfully difficult task; for her heart had whispered it was because she was different from her fellows, because she was what the world termed literary and learned, Granville had shunned her; and a few words, undesignedly and carelessly spoken by Charles Heyward, relative to Dudley's dislike to female literature, from its effect on his mother, confirmed the idea, and made her shrink from her former favourite pursuits. But she, too, had a character to sustain; and once more she compelled herself to work, believing that her talents were lent her to be instruments of good, not to lie unused. And yet, to a character of strong affections and active energies, mental resources, however varied, were not quite sufficient for happiness; and therefore was it she formed and executed the plan we have named.

So seven years had sped, and there was little variation in the life of our heroine for her biographer to record. Her constant prayer was heard. Her name had become a household word, coupled with love, from the pure high feelings and ennobling sympathies which her writings had called forth. Her works had made her beloved and revered, though her person, nay, her very place of residence and all concerning her were, as she desired, utterly unknown. This in itself was happiness, inexpressibly heightened by her present domestic duties, lightening Mrs Langley's household cares; giving part of every day to that lady's pupils; teaching them not only to be accomplished and domestic, but to be *thinkers*; training the *heart*, even more than the mind; making nature alike a temple and a school: all the sweet charities of home were now hers, and her heart was indeed happy and once more at rest.

And was Granville Dudley, then, forgotten? When we say that Clara might have married more than once, and most happily, but that she had refused, simply because she could not permit an unloved reality to usurp the place of a still loved shadow—all doubts, we think, are answered.

Of Granville Dudley she could never hear; all trace of him seemed lost. Within the last few years the newspapers had indeed often teemed with the praises and speeches of a Sir Dudley Granville; but, though the conjunction of names had at first riveted her eye and made her heart turn strangely sick, she banished the thought as folly. It was a Granville Dudley, not a Dudley Granville, whom she had too fondly loved.

Miss Stanley had resided about seven years with Mrs Langley, when application was made to the latter lady to receive the only child of Sir Dudley Granville as her pupil. The child was motherless, and in such very precarious health, that the milder climate of Devonshire had been advised, as, combined with extreme care, the only chance of rearing her to womanhood. Mrs Langley's establishment was full, six being her allotted number, which no persuasion had as yet ever induced her to increase. There was something, however, in the appearance of the little Laura which so unconsciously wore upon Clara, that she could not resist pleading in the child's behalf; and as one of the pupils was to leave the next half year, Mrs Langley acceded. Clara's name, however, had not been mentioned in this transaction. The lady who had the charge of Laura had indeed conversed with her, and had been charmed with her manner; but little imagined she was enjoying the often-coveted honour of conversing with an authoress, and one so popular as Clara Stanley. She said that Laura, though eight years old, literally knew nothing. Lady Granville had been the belle of her time, but one who had the greatest horror of all learning in woman, and in consequence possessing nothing of herself but showy accomplishment, which told in society. She had neglected the poor child, wasted alike her own health and her husband's income in the sole pursuit of pleasure, and hurried herself to an early grave. Laura's health had been so delicate since then, that her father feared to commence her studies, even while he was most anxious she should become a sensible and accomplished woman, with resources for happiness within herself.

'And she shall be, if I can make her so,' was Clara's inward thought, as she looked on the sweet face of the child, and a new chord in her heart was touched she knew not wherefore. It was impossible to analyse the feeling, even to one long accustomed to analysing hearts, and Clara gave it up in despair; but affection and interest alike clung round the child, who gave back all she received. Her weak health prevented her entering into all the routine of the schoolroom, and she became Clara's constant companion and pupil. Repeatedly the artless letters of the child to her doating father teemed with the goodness, the gentleness, the tenderness of Miss Stanley; soon convincing Sir Dudley how quick and ready were her powers of comprehension, and filling his heart with gratitude towards that kind friend, whom he knew not, guessed not was the authoress of the same name whose gentle eloquence in her sex's cause had even now his admiration.

Laura Granville had been with Mrs Langley about eight months, when she became extremely ill, from an epidemic that had suddenly broken out in the village; all Mrs Langley's household were attacked by it in a greater or less degree, but in Laura alone did it threaten to be fatal. Careless of her own fatigue, Clara devoted herself, day and night, to the young sufferer. Her affections had never before been so warmly enlisted; not one of her young friends had ever become so completely part of herself, and as she watched and tended her morning prayers for her recovery, it seemed as if the child must be something nearer to her than in reality she was.

An express had been sent off for Sir Dudley Granville; but, from his having gone unexpectedly to visit a friend in Germany, it was unavoidably delayed on its way, and nearly three weeks elapsed ere the baronet reached Ashford. From the haste with which he had travelled, no account of her progress could reach him; and it was in a state of agony and suspense no words can describe that the father flung himself from his carriage at Mrs Langley's gate, and rushed into her presence.

'Your child lives; is rapidly recovering—may be stronger than she has been yet,' were the first words he heard, for his look and manner were all-sufficient introduction; and the benevolent physician, who had that instant quitted his little patient, grasped Sir Dudley's hand with reassuring pressure. The baronet tried to return it with a smile, but his quivering lip could only gasp forth an ejaculation of thankfulness, and, sinking on a chair, he covered his face with his hand.

'Let me see this incomparable young woman, the preserver of my child!' he passionately exclaimed, as Dr Bernard and Mrs Langley, after describing the progress and crisis of Laura's illness, attributed her unexpected recovery, under Providence, to the incessant care and watchfulness of Miss Stanley, the physician declaring his utmost skill had been, without it, of no avail whatever. Being assured his appearance would not injure Laura, who was, in truth, daily expecting him, he eagerly followed Mrs Langley to the room, and paused a moment on the threshold unobserved.

Laura was sitting up in her little bed, supported by pillows, looking pale and delicate, indeed, but smiling with that joyous animation which, in childhood, is so sure a sign of returning health; and dressing, with the greatest zest, a beautiful doll, which, with its plentifully-supplied wardrobe, lay beside her. Near the bed, and seated by a small table,

covered with books and writings, was Clara, who, by the rapid movement of her pen, and her immovable attention, was evidently deeply
engrossed in her employment. Sir Dudley could not see her face, for it
was bent down, and even its profile turned from him, but a strange thrill
shot through him as he gazed.

'Oh! look, Miss Stanley, how beautiful your work shows, now she is
dressed. How kind you were to make her all these pretty things. I can
do it all but these buttons, will you do them for me?'

Clara laid down her pen with a smile, to comply with the child's
request; and, as she did so, Laura laid her little head caressingly on her
bosom, saying, fondly, 'Dear, dear Miss Stanley, I wish papa would
come; he would thank you for all your goodness much better than I
can.'

'I wish he would come, for your sake and his own, dearest—not to
thank me, though I shall not love you the less for being so grateful,
Laura,' was the reply, in a voice, whose low, musical tones brought
back, as by a flash of light, to Sir Dudley's heart, feelings, thoughts,
memories, of past years, which he thought were hushed for ever.

'Miss Stanley! Clara!—inscrutable Providence!—is it to you I owe my
child?' he exclaimed, springing suddenly forward, and clasping his little
child to his heart—one moment covering Laura's upturned face with
kisses, the next turning his earnest, grateful gaze on the astonished Clara.

For an instant her heart grew faint, for the fatigue of long-continued
nursing had weakened her; nor could she realize in that agitating moment the lapse of ten years, since she had last looked on his face, or
listened to his richly expressive voice. Time had passed over her heart,
leaving its early dream unchanged, and vainly she strove to feel how
long a period had flown. All seemed a thick and traceless mist; but
when she succeeded in shaking off that prostrating weakness, forcing
herself to remember it was Sir Dudley Granville, not Granville Dudley,
who had thus addressed her, still one fact was certain, the object of her
first, her only affection was at her side once more—it was *his* child her
care had saved.

Day after day did Clara Stanley and Sir Dudley Granville pass hours
together by the couch of Laura. Though conscious her secret was still
her own, and grateful that, after the first burst of natural feeling,
Granville's manner to her was only that of an obliged and appreciating

friend, Clara's peculiarly delicate feelings would have kept her from Laura's room during the visits of her father; but the child was restless and uncomfortable whenever she was absent, and Granville so evidently entreated her continued presence, that to keep away was impossible. It was during these pleasant interviews Sir Dudley related the cause of his change of name. He had become, most unexpectedly, the heir to his godfather, Sir William Granville, who had left him all his estates, on the sole condition of his adopting, for himself and his heirs, the name of Granville—Sir Granville Granville, he added, with a smile, was not sufficiently euphonious, and so he had placed the Dudley first, instead of last. He alluded in terms of the warmest admiration to her works, and wondered at his own stupidity in never connecting the Miss Stanley of his Laura's letters with the authoress he had once known. A very peculiar smile beamed on the lips of Clara as he thus spoke, but she did not say its meaning.

One day, some six or seven weeks after Granville's appearance at Ashford, Clara had just comfortably seated herself at her desk, after seeing Laura ensconced in her little pony chaise, when she was startled by hearing Sir Dudley's voice, in accents of unusual seriousness, close beside her.

'Will you tell me, Miss Stanley, how you can possibly contrive to unite so perfectly the literary with the domestic characters? I have watched, but cannot find you fail in either—how is this?'

'Simply, Sir Dudley, because, in my opinion, it is impossible to divide them. Perfect in them, indeed, I am not; but though I know it *is* possible for woman to be domestic without being literary—as we are all not equally endowed by Providence—to my feelings, it is *not* possible to be more than usually gifted without being domestic. The appeal to the heart must come from the heart; and the quick sensibility of the imaginative woman must make her *feel* for others, and *act* for them, more particularly for the loved of home. To *write*, we must *think*, and if we think of duty, we, of all others, must not fail in its performance, or our own words are bitter with reproach. It is from want of thought most failings spring, alike in duty as in feeling. From this want the literary and imaginative woman must be free.'

Granville's eyes never moved from the fair, expressive face of the gentle woman who thus spoke, till she ceased, and then he paced the room in silence; till, seating himself beside her, he besought her to listen to him, and pity and forgive him, and *prove* that she forgave him; and, ere she could reply, he poured forth the tale of his earlier love—how truly he loved her, even when his idle prejudices against literary women caused him to fly from her influence, and enter into a hurried engagement with one, beautiful indeed, but, from having no resources within herself, the mere votaress of pleasure and outward excitement. How bitterly he had repented through seven weary years the misery he had brought upon himself—how constantly he had yearned for a companion of his home and of his mind—and how repeatedly, as he glanced over her pages, where pure fresh feeling breathed in every line, and the love of home and its sacred ties were so forcibly inculcated, he had cursed his own folly. How he had sought to drown thought in a public career, but had still felt desolate; and now that he looked on her again, not only in her own character, but as the preserver of his child, how completely he felt that happiness was gone from him for ever, unless she would give it in herself!

Clara's face was turned from him as he spoke, but, ere he concluded, the quick, bright tears were falling in her lap; and when she tried to meet his glance and speak, her lip so quivered that no words came. It was an effort ere she could tell her tale; but it was told at length, though Granville's ardent gratitude was for the moment checked by her serious rejoinder.

'It is no shame now, dear Granville, to confess how deeply and constantly I have returned your affection; but listen to me, ere you proceed further. I do not doubt what you say, that your prejudices are all removed; but are you certain, quite certain, that a woman who has *resources of mind* as well as of heart can make you happy, as you believe? At one-and-twenty you could have moulded me to what you pleased. I doubt whether I should have written another line, had you not approved of my doing it. At one-and-thirty this cannot be. My character—my habits are formed. I cannot draw back from my literary path, for I feel it accomplishes good. Can I indeed make your happiness as I am? Dearest Granville, do not let feeling alone decide.'

'Feeling! sense! reason! Clara—my own Clara—all speak and have spoken long. Make my child but like yourself, and with two such blessings I dare not picture what life would be—too, too much joy.'

And joy it was. Joy as it seemed. Granville has felt that for once imagination fell short of reality, for his path is indeed one of sunshine; and as Lady Granville, the authoress, continues her path of literary and domestic usefulness, proving to the full how very possible it is for woman to unite the two, and that our great poet* is right when, in contradiction to Moore's shallow theory of the unfitness of genius to domestic happiness, he answered—'It is not because they possess genius that they make unhappy homes, but because they do not possess genius enough. A higher order of mind would enable them to see and feel all the beauty of domestic ties.'

* Wordsworth.

Right at Last

Doctor Brown was poor, and had to make his way in the world. He had gone to study his profession in Edinburgh, and his energy, ability, and good conduct had entitled him to some notice on the part of the professors. Once introduced to the ladies of their families, his prepossessing appearance and pleasing manners made him a universal favourite, and perhaps no other student received so many invitations to dances and evening parties, or was so often singled out to fill up an odd vacancy at the last moment at the dinner-table. No one knew particularly who he was, or where he sprang from; but then he had no near relations, as he had once or twice observed; so he was evidently not hampered with low-born or low-bred connexions. He had been in mourning for his mother when he first came to college.

All this much was recalled to the recollection of Professor Frazer by his niece Margaret, as she stood before him one morning in his study, telling him, in a low, but resolute voice, that the night before Doctor James Brown had offered her marriage—that she had accepted him,—and that he was intending to call on Professor Frazer (her uncle and natural guardian) that very morning, to obtain his consent to their engagement. Professor Frazer was perfectly aware, from Margaret's manner, that his consent was regarded by her as a mere form, for that her mind was made up: and he had more than once had occasion to find out how inflexible she could be. Yet he too was of the same blood, and held to his own opinions in the same obdurate manner. The consequence of which frequently was, that uncle and niece had argued themselves into mutual bitterness of feeling, without altering each other's opinions one jot. But Professor Frazer could not restrain himself on this occasion of all others.

'Then, Margaret, you will just quietly settle down to be a beggar, for that lad Brown has little or no money to think of marrying upon: you that might be my Lady Kennedy, if you would.'

'I could not, uncle.'

'Nonsense, child. Sir Alexander is a personable and agreeable man,—middle aged, if you will—well, a wilful woman maun have her way; but if I had had a notion that this youngster was sneaking into my house to cajole you into fancying him, I would have seen him far enough before I had ever let your aunt invite him to dinner. Aye! you may mutter; but I say no gentleman would ever have come into my house to seduce my niece's affections, without first informing me of his intentions, and asking my leave.'

'Doctor Brown is a gentleman, Uncle Frazer, whatever you may think of him.'

'So you think—so you think. But who cares for the opinion of a love-sick girl? He is a handsome, plausible young fellow, of good address. And I don't mean to deny his ability. But there is something about him I never did like, and now it's accounted for. And Sir Alexander—Well, well! your aunt will be disappointed in you, Margaret. But you were always a headstrong girl. Has this Jamie Brown ever told you who or what his parents were, or where he comes from? I don't ask about his forebears, for he does not look like a lad who has ever had ancestors: and you a Frazer of Lovat! Fie, for shame, Margaret! Who is this Jamie Brown?'

'He is James Brown, Doctor of Medicine of the University of Edinburgh: a good, clever young man, whom I love with my whole heart,' replied Margaret, reddening.

'Hoot! is that the way for a maiden to speak? Where does he come from? Who are his kinsfolk? Unless he can give a pretty good account of his family and prospects, I shall just bid him begone, Margaret, and that I tell you fairly.'

'Uncle' (her eyes were filling with hot indignant tears), 'I am of age; you know he is good and clever; else why have you had him so often to your house? I marry him, and not his kinsfolk. He is an orphan. I doubt if he has any relations that he keeps up with. He has no brothers nor sisters. I don't care where he comes from.'

'What was his father?' asked Professor Frazer, coldly.

'I don't know. Why should I go prying into every particular of his family, and asking who his father was, and what was the maiden name of his mother, and when his grandmother was married?'

'Yet I think I have heard Miss Margaret Frazer speak up pretty strongly in favour of a long line of unspotted ancestry.'

'I had forgotten our own, I suppose, when I spoke so. Simon Lord Lovat is a creditable great-uncle to the Frazers! If all tales be true, he ought to have been hanged for a felon, instead of beheaded like a loyal gentleman.'

'Oh! if you're determined to foul your own nest, I have done. Let James Brown come in; I will make him my bow, and thank him for condescending to marry a Frazer.'

'Uncle,' said Margaret, now fairly crying, 'don't let us part in anger. We love each other in our hearts. You have been good to me, and so has my aunt. But I have given my word to Doctor Brown, and I must keep it. I should love him if he was the son of a ploughman. We don't expect to be rich; but he has a few hundreds to start with, and I have my own hundred a year——'

'Well, well, child, don't cry. You have settled it all for yourself, it seems; so I wash my hands of it. I shake off all responsibility. You will tell your aunt what arrangements you make with Doctor Brown about your marriage, and I will do what you wish in the matter. But don't send the young man in to me to ask my consent. I neither give it nor withhold it. It would have been different if it had been Sir Alexander.'

'Oh, Uncle Frazer, don't speak so. See Doctor Brown, and at any rate—for my sake—tell him you consent. Let me belong to you that much. It seems so desolate at such a time, to have to dispose of myself as if nobody owned or cared for me.'

The door was thrown open, and Doctor James Brown was announced. Margaret hastened away; and, before he was aware, the Professor had given a sort of consent, without asking a question of the happy young man, who hurried away to seek his betrothed; leaving her uncle muttering to himself.

Both Doctor and Mrs Frazer were so strongly opposed to Margaret's engagement, in reality, that they could not help showing it by manner and implication; although they had the grace to keep silent. But Margaret felt even more keenly than her lover that he was not welcome in the house. Her pleasure in seeing him was destroyed by her sense of the coldness with which he was received; and she willingly yielded to his desire of a short engagement; which was contrary to their original plan of waiting until he should be settled in practice in London, and should see his way clear to such an income as would render their marriage a prudent step. Doctor and Mrs Frazer neither objected nor approved. Margaret would rather have had the most vehement opposition than this icy coldness. But it made her turn with redoubled affection to her warm-hearted and sympathizing lover. Not that she had ever discussed her uncle and aunt's behaviour with him. As long as he was apparently unaware of it, she would not awaken him to a sense of it. Besides, they had stood to her so long in the relation of parents, that she felt she had no right to bring in a stranger to sit in judgement upon them.

So it was with rather a heavy heart that she arranged their future *ménage* with Doctor Brown, unable to profit by her aunt's experience and wisdom. But Margaret herself was a prudent and sensible girl. Although accustomed to a degree of comfort in her uncle's house that almost amounted to luxury, she could resolutely dispense with it when occasion required. When Doctor Brown started for London, to seek and prepare their new home, she enjoined him not to make any but the most necessary preparations for her reception. She would herself super-intend all that was wanting when she came. He had some old furniture, stored up in a warehouse, which had been his mother's. He proposed selling it, and buying new in its place. Margaret persuaded him not to do this, but to make it go as far as it could. The household of the newly-married couple was to consist of a Scotchwoman long connected with the Frazer family, who was to be the sole female servant; and of a man whom Doctor Brown picked up in London, soon after he had fixed on a house,—a man named Crawford, who had lived for many years with a gentleman now gone abroad, but who gave him the most excellent character, in reply to Doctor Brown's inquiries. This gentleman had employed Crawford in a number of ways; so that in fact he was a kind of Jack-of-all-trades; and Doctor Brown, in every letter to Margaret, had some new accomplishment of his servant's to relate, which he did with the more fullness and zest, because Margaret had slightly ques-tioned the wisdom of starting in life with a man-servant; but had yielded to Doctor Brown's arguments on the necessity of keeping up a respect-able appearance, making a decent show, &c., to any one who might be inclined to consult him, but be daunted by the appearance of old Christie out of the kitchen, and unwilling to leave a message with one who spoke such unintelligible English. Crawford was so good a carpenter that he could put up shelves, adjust faulty hinges, mend locks, and even went the length of constructing a box of some old boards that had once formed a packing-case. Crawford one day, when his master was too busy to go out for his dinner, improvised an omelette as good as any Doctor Brown had ever tasted in Paris, when he was studying there. In short, Crawford was a kind of Admirable Crichton in his way, and Margaret was quite convinced that Doctor Brown was right in his decision that they must have a man-servant; even before she was respectfully greeted by Crawford as he opened the door to the newly-married couple, when they came to their new home after their short wedding tour.

Doctor Brown was rather afraid lest Margaret should think the house bare and cheerless in its half-furnished state; for he had obeyed her injunctions and bought as little furniture as might be, in addition to the few things he had inherited from his mother. His consulting-room (how grand it sounded!) was completely arranged, ready for stray patients; and it was well calculated to make a good impression on them. There was a Turkey carpet on the floor, that had been his mother's, and was just sufficiently worn to give it the air of respectability which handsome pieces of furniture have, when they look as if they had not just been purchased for the occasion, but are in some degree hereditary. The same appearance pervaded the room: the library-table (bought secondhand, it must be confessed), the bureau—that had been his mother's—the leather chairs (as hereditary as the library-table), the shelves Crawford had put up for Doctor Brown's medical books, a good engraving or two on the walls, gave altogether so pleasant an aspect to the apartment that both Doctor and Mrs Brown thought, for that evening at any rate, that poverty was just as comfortable a thing as riches. Crawford had ventured to take the liberty of placing a few flowers about the room, as his humble way of welcoming his mistress—late autumn flowers, blending the idea of summer with that of winter suggested by the bright little fire in the grate. Christie sent up delicious scones for tea; and Mrs Frazer had made up for her want of geniality as well as she could by a store of marmalade and mutton hams. Doctor Brown could not be easy even in this comfort until he had shown Margaret, almost with a groan, how many rooms were as yet unfurnished, how much remained to be done. But she laughed at his alarm lest she should be disappointed in her new home; declared that she should like nothing better than planning and contriving; that, what with her own talent for upholstery and Crawford's for joinery, the rooms should be furnished as if by magic, and no bills—the usual consequences of comfort—be forthcoming. But with the morning and daylight Doctor Brown's anxiety returned. He saw and felt every crack in the ceiling, every spot on the paper, not for himself, but for Margaret. He was constantly in his own mind, as it seemed, comparing the home he had brought her to with the one she had left. He seemed constantly afraid lest she had repented, or would repent, having married him. This morbid restlessness was the only drawback to their great happiness; and, to do away with it, Margaret was led into expenses much beyond her original intention. She bought this article in preference to that because her husband, if he went shopping with her, seemed so miserable if he suspected that she denied herself the slightest wish on the score of economy. She learnt to avoid taking him out with her when she went to make her purchases, as it was a very simple thing to her to choose the least expensive thing, even though it were the ugliest, when she was by herself, but not a simple painless thing to harden her heart to his look of mortification when she quietly said to the shopman that she could not afford this or that. On coming out of a shop after one of these occasions, he had said—

'Oh, Margaret, I ought not to have married you. You must forgive me—I have so loved you.'

'Forgive you, James!' said she. 'For making me so happy! What should make you think I care so much for rep in preference to moreen? Don't speak so again, please.'

'Oh, Margaret! but don't forget how I ask you to forgive me.'

Crawford was everything that he had promised to be, and more than could be desired. He was Margaret's right hand in all her little household plans, in a way which irritated Christie not a little. This feud between Christie and Crawford was indeed the greatest discomfort in the household. Crawford was silently triumphant in his superior knowledge of London, in his favour upstairs, in his power of assisting his mistress, and in the consequent privilege of being frequently consulted. Christie was for ever regretting Scotland, and hinting at Margaret's neglect of one who had followed her fortunes into a strange country, to make a favourite of a stranger, and one who was none so good as he ought to be, as she would sometimes affirm. But, as she never brought any proof of her vague accusations, Margaret did not choose to question her, but set them down to a jealousy of her fellow-servant which the mistress did all in her power to heal. On the whole, however, the four people forming this family lived together in tolerable harmony. Doctor Brown was more than satisfied with his house, his servants, his professional prospects, and most of all with his little bright energetic wife. Margaret, from time to time, was taken by certain moods of her husband's; but the tendency of these moods was not to weaken her affection, rather to call out a feeling of pity for what appeared to her morbid sufferings and suspicions—a pity ready to be turned into sympathy as soon as she could discover any definite cause for his occasional depression of spirits. Christie did not pretend to like Crawford; but as Margaret quietly declined to listen to her grumblings and discontent on this head, and as Crawford himself was almost painfully solicitous to gain the good opinion of the old Scotchwoman, there was no open rupture between them. On the whole, the popular, successful Doctor Brown was apparently the most anxious person in his family. There could be no great cause for this as regarded his money affairs. By one of those lucky accidents which sometimes lift a man up out of his struggles, and carry him on to smooth unencumbered ground, he made a great step in his professional progress, and their income from this source was likely to be fully as much as Margaret and he had ever anticipated in their most sanguine moments, with the likelihood, too, of a steady increase as the years went on.

I must explain myself more fully on this head.

Margaret herself had rather more than a hundred a year; sometimes, indeed, her dividends had amounted to a hundred and thirty or forty pounds; but on that she dared not rely. Doctor Brown had seventeen hundred remaining of the three thousand left him by his mother; and out of this he had to pay for some of the furniture, the bills for which had not been sent in at the time in spite of all Margaret's entreaties that such might be the case. They came in about a week before the time when the events I am going to narrate took place. Of course they amounted to more than even the prudent Margaret had expected, and she was a little dispirited to find how much money it would take to liquidate them. But, curiously and contradictorily enough—as she had often noticed before—any real cause for anxiety or disappointment did not seem to affect her husband's cheerfulness. He laughed at her dismay over her accounts, jingled the proceeds of that day's work in his pockets, counted it out to her, and calculated the year's probable income from that day's gains. Margaret took the guineas, and carried them upstairs to her own secrétaire in silence; having learnt the difficult art of trying to swallow down her household cares in the presence of her husband. When she came back she was cheerful, if grave. He had taken up the bills in her absence, and had been adding them together.

'Two hundred and thirty-six pounds,' he said, putting the accounts away to clear the table for tea, as Crawford brought in the things. 'Why, I don't call that much. I believe I reckoned on their coming to a great deal more. I'll go into the City to-morrow, and sell out some shares, and set your little heart at ease. Now don't go and put a spoonful less tea in to-night to help to pay these bills. Earning is better than saving, and I am earning at a famous rate. Give me good tea, Maggie, for I have done a good day's work.'

They were sitting in the doctor's consulting-room, for the better economy of fire. To add to Margaret's discomfort, the chimney smoked this evening. She had held her tongue from any repining words; for she remembered the old proverb about a smoky chimney and a scolding wife; but she was more irritated by the puffs of smoke coming over her pretty white work than she cared to show; and it was in a sharper tone than usual that she spoke, in bidding Crawford take care and have the chimney swept. The next morning all had cleared brightly off. Her husband had convinced her that their money matters were going on well; the fire burned briskly at breakfast time, and the unwonted sun shone in at the windows. Margaret was surprised when Crawford told her that he had not been able to meet with a chimney-sweeper that morning, but that he had tried to arrange the coals in the grate so that, for this one morning at least, his mistress should not be annoyed, and, by the next, he would take care to secure a sweep. Margaret thanked him, and acquiesced in all his plans about giving a general cleaning to the room, the more readily because she felt that she had spoken sharply the night before. She decided to go and pay all her bills, and make some distant calls on the next morning; and her husband promised to go into the City and provide her with the money.

This he did. He showed her the notes that evening, locked them up for the night in his bureau; and, lo, in the morning they were gone! They had breakfasted in the back parlour, or half-furnished dining-room. A charwoman was in the front room, cleaning after the sweeps. Doctor Brown went to his bureau, singing an old Scotch tune as he left the dining-room. It was so long before he came back, that Margaret went to look for him. He was sitting in the chair nearest to the bureau, leaning his head upon it, in an attitude of the deepest despondency. He did not seem to hear Margaret's step, as she made her way among rolled-up carpets and chairs piled on each other. She had to touch him on the shoulder before she could rouse him.

'James, James!' she said in alarm.

He looked up at her almost as if he did not know her.

'Oh, Margaret!' he said, and took hold of her hands, and hid his face in her neck.

'Dearest love, what is it?' she asked, thinking he was suddenly taken ill.

'Some one has been to my bureau since last night,' he groaned, without either looking up or moving.

'And taken the money,' said Margaret, in an instant understanding how it stood. It was a great blow; a great loss, far greater than the few extra pounds by which the bills had exceeded her calculations: yet it seemed as if she could bear it better. 'Oh, dear!' she said, 'that is bad; but after all—Do you know,' she said, trying to raise his face, so that she might look into it, and give him the encouragement of her honest loving eyes, 'at first I thought you were deadly ill, and all sorts of dreadful possibilities rushed through my mind,—it is such a relief to find that it is only money—'

'Only money!' he echoed sadly, avoiding her look, as if he could not bear to show her how much he felt it.

'And after all,' she said, with spirit, 'it can't be gone far. Only last night here. The chimney-sweeps—we must send Crawford for the police directly. You did not take the numbers of the notes?' ringing the bell as she spoke.

'No; they were only to be in our possession one night,' he said.

'No, to be sure not.'

The charwoman now appeared at the door with her pail of hot water. Margaret looked into her face, as if to read guilt or innocence. She was a protégée of Christie's, who was not apt to accord her favour easily, or without good grounds; an honest, decent widow, with a large family to maintain by her labour,—that was the character in which Margaret had engaged her; and she looked it. Grimy in her dress—because she could not spare the money or time to be clean—her skin looked healthy and cared-for; she had a straightforward, business-like appearance about her, and seemed in no ways daunted nor surprised to see Doctor and Mrs Brown standing in the middle of the room, in displeased perplexity and distress. She went about her business without taking any particular notice of them. Margaret's suspicions settled down yet more distinctly upon the chimney-sweeper; but he could not have gone far, the notes could hardly have got into circulation. Such a sum could not have been spent by such a man in so short a time, and the restoration of the money was her first, her only object. She had scarcely a thought for subsequent duties, such as prosecution of the offender, and the like consequences of crime. While her whole energies were bent on the speedy recovery of the money, and she was rapidly going over the necessary steps to be taken, her husband 'sat all poured out into his chair', as the Germans say; no force in him to keep his limbs in any attitude requiring the slightest exertion; his face sunk, miserable, and with that foreshadowing of the lines of age which sudden distress is apt to call out on the youngest and smoothest faces.

'What can Crawford be about?' said Margaret, pulling the bell again with vehemence. 'Oh, Crawford!' as the man at that instant appeared at the door.

'Is anything the matter?' he said, interrupting her, as if alarmed into an unusual discomposure by her violent ringing. 'I had just gone round the corner with the letter master gave me last night for the post, and when I came back Christie told me you had rung for me, ma'am. I beg your pardon, but I have hurried so,' and indeed his breath did come quickly, and his face was full of penitent anxiety.

'Oh, Crawford! I am afraid the sweep has got into your master's bureau, and taken all the money he put there last night. It is gone, at any rate. Did you ever leave him in the room alone?'

'I can't say, ma'am; perhaps I did. Yes! I believe I did. I remember now, I had my work to do; and I thought the charwoman was come, and I went to my pantry; and some time after Christie came to me, complaining that Mrs Roberts was so late; and then I knew that he must have been alone in the room. But, dear me, ma'am, who would have thought there had been so much wickedness in him?'

'How was it he got into the bureau?' said Margaret, turning to her husband. 'Was the lock broken?'

He roused himself up, like one who wakens from sleep.

'Yes! No! I suppose I had turned the key without locking it last night. The bureau was closed, not locked, when I went to it this morning, and the bolt was shot.' He relapsed into inactive, thoughtful silence.

'At any rate, it is no use losing time in wondering now. Go, Crawford, as fast as you can, for a policeman. You know the name of the chimney-sweeper, of course,' she added, as Crawford was preparing to leave the room.

'Indeed, ma'am, I'm very sorry, but I just agreed with the first who was passing along the street. If I could have known——'

But Margaret had turned away with an impatient gesture of despair. Crawford went without another word to seek a policeman.

In vain did his wife try and persuade Doctor Brown to taste any breakfast; a cup of tea was all he would try to swallow, and that was taken in hasty gulps, to clear his dry throat, as he heard Crawford's voice talking to the policeman whom he was ushering in.

The policeman heard all, and said little. Then the inspector came. Doctor Brown seemed to leave all the talking to Crawford, who apparently liked nothing better. Margaret was infinitely distressed and dismayed by the effect the robbery seemed to have on her husband's energies. The probable loss of such a sum was bad enough, but there was something so weak and poor in character, in letting it affect him so strongly—to deaden all energy and destroy all hopeful spring, that, although Margaret did not dare to define her feeling, nor the cause of it, to herself, she had the fact before her perpetually, that, if she were to judge of her husband from this morning only, she must learn to rely on herself alone in all cases of emergency. The inspector repeatedly turned from Crawford to Doctor and Mrs Brown for answers to his inquiries. It was Margaret who replied, with terse, short sentences, very different from Crawford's long, involved explanations.

At length the inspector asked to speak to her alone. She followed him into the room, past the affronted Crawford and her despondent husband. The inspector gave one sharp look at the charwoman, who was going on with her scouring with stolid indifference, turned her out, and then asked Margaret where Crawford came from,—how long he had lived with them, and various other questions, all showing the direction his suspicions had taken. This shocked Margaret extremely; but she quickly answered every inquiry; and, at the end, watched the inspector's face closely, and waited for the avowal of the suspicion.

He led the way back to the other room without a word, however. Crawford had left, and Doctor Brown was trying to read the morning's letters (which had just been delivered), but his hands shook so much that he could not see a line.

'Doctor Brown,' said the inspector, 'I have little doubt that your man-servant has committed this robbery. I judge so from his whole manner; and from his anxiety to tell the story, and his way of trying to throw suspicion on the chimney-sweeper, neither whose name nor dwelling can he give; at least, he says not. Your wife tells us he has already been out of the house this morning, even before he went to summon a policeman; so there is little doubt that he has found means for concealing or disposing of the notes; and you say you do not know the numbers. However, that can probably be ascertained.'

At this moment Christie knocked at the door, and, in a state of great agitation, demanded to speak to Margaret. She brought up an additional store of suspicious circumstances, none of them much in themselves, but all tending to criminate her fellow servant. She had expected to find herself blamed for starting the idea of Crawford's guilt, and was rather surprised to find herself listened to with attention by the inspector. This led her to tell many other little things, all bearing against Crawford, which a dread of being thought jealous and quarrelsome had led her to conceal before from her master and mistress. At the end of her story the inspector said:

'There can be no doubt of the course to be taken. You, sir, must give your man-servant in charge. He will be taken before the sitting magistrate directly; and there is already evidence enough to make him be remanded for a week; during which time we may trace the notes, and complete the chain.'

'Must I prosecute?' said Doctor Brown, almost lividly pale. 'It is, I own, a serious loss of money to me; but there will be the further expenses of the prosecution—the loss of time—the——'

He stopped. He saw his wife's indignant eyes fixed upon him; and shrank from their look of unconscious reproach.

'Yes, inspector,' he said, 'I give him in charge. Do what you will. Do what is right. Of course I take the consequences. We take the consequences. Don't we, Margaret?' He spoke in a kind of wild low voice, of which Margaret thought it best to take no notice.

'Tell us exactly what to do,' she said, very coldly and quietly, addressing herself to the policeman.

He gave her the necessary directions as to their attending at the police-office, and bringing Christie as a witness, and then went away to take measures for securing Crawford.

Margaret was surprised to find how little hurry or violence needed to be used in Crawford's arrest. She had expected to hear sounds of commotion in the house, if indeed Crawford himself had not taken the alarm and escaped. But, when she had suggested the latter apprehension to the inspector, he smiled, and told her that when he had first heard of the charge from the policeman on the beat, he had stationed a detective officer within sight of the house, to watch all ingress or egress; so that Crawford's whereabouts would soon have been discovered if he had attempted to escape.

Margaret's attention was now directed to her husband. He was making hurried preparations for setting off on his round of visits, and evidently did not wish to have any conversation with her on the subject of the morning's event. He promised to be back by eleven o'clock; before which time, the inspector had assured them, their presence would not be needed. Once or twice Doctor Brown said, as if to himself, 'It is a miserable business.' Indeed, Margaret felt it to be so; and now that the necessity for immediate speech and action was over, she began to fancy that she must be very hard-hearted—very deficient in common feeling; inasmuch as she had not suffered like her husband, at the discovery that the servant—whom they had been learning to consider as a friend, and to look upon as having their interests so warmly at heart—was, in all probability, a treacherous thief. She remembered all his pretty marks of attention to her, from the day when he had welcomed her arrival at her new home by his humble present of flowers, until only the day before when, seeing her fatigued, he had, unasked, made her a cup of coffee— coffee such as none but he could make. How often had he thought of warm dry clothes for her husband; how wakeful had he been at nights; how diligent in the mornings! It was no wonder that her husband felt this discovery of domestic treason acutely. It was she who was hard and selfish, and thinking more of the recovery of the money than of the terrible disappointment in character, if the charge against Crawford were true.

At eleven o'clock her husband returned with a cab. Christie had thought the occasion of appearing at a police-office worthy of her Sunday clothes, and was as smart as her possessions could make her. But Margaret and her husband looked as pale and sorrow-stricken as if they had been the accused and not the accusers.

Doctor Brown shrank from meeting Crawford's eye, as the one took his place in the witness-box, the other in the dock. Yet Crawford was trying—Margaret was sure of this—to catch his master's attention. Failing that, he looked at Margaret with an expression she could not fathom. Indeed, the whole character of his face was changed. Instead of the calm, smooth look of attentive obedience, he had assumed an insolent, threatening expression of defiance; smiling occasionally in a most unpleasant manner as Doctor Brown spoke of the bureau and its contents. He was remanded for a week; but, the evidence as yet being far from conclusive, bail for his appearance was taken. This bail was offered by his brother, a respectable tradesman, well known in his neighbourhood, and to whom Crawford had sent on his arrest.

So Crawford was at large again, much to Christie's dismay; who took off her Sunday clothes, on her return home, with a heavy heart, hoping, rather than trusting, that they should not all be murdered in their beds before the week was out. It must be confessed, Margaret herself was not entirely free from fears of Crawford's vengeance; his eyes had looked so maliciously and vindictively at her and at her husband, as they gave their evidence.

But his absence in the household gave Margaret enough to do to prevent her dwelling on foolish fears. His being away made a terrible blank in their daily comfort, which neither Margaret nor Christie—exert themselves as they would—could fill up; and it was the more necessary that all should go on smoothly, as Doctor Brown's nerves had received such a shock at the discovery of the guilt of his favourite, trusted servant, that Margaret was led at times to apprehend a serious illness. He would pace about the room at night, when he thought she was asleep, moaning to himself—and in the morning would require the utmost persuasion to induce him to go out and see his patients. He was worse than ever after consulting the lawyer whom he had employed to conduct the prosecution. There was, as Margaret was brought unwillingly to perceive, some mystery in the case; for he eagerly took his letters from the post, going to the door as soon as he heard the knock, and concealing their directions from her. As the week passed away, his nervous misery still increased.

One evening—the candles were not lighted—he was sitting over the fire in a listless attitude, resting his head on his hand, and that supported on his knee—Margaret determined to try an experiment, to see if she could not probe, and find out the nature of the sore that he hid with such constant care. She took a stool and sat down at his feet, taking his hand in hers.

'Listen, dearest James, to an old story I once heard. It may interest you. There were two orphans, boy and girl in their hearts, though they were a young man and young woman in years. They were not brother and sister, and by and by they fell in love; just in the same fond, silly way you and I did, you remember. Well, the girl was amongst her own people, but the boy was far away from his—if indeed he had any alive. But the girl loved him so dearly for himself, that sometimes she thought she was glad that he had no one to care for him but just her alone. Her friends did not like him as much as she did; for, perhaps, they were wise, grave, cold people, and she, I dare say, was very foolish. And they did not like her marrying the boy; which was just stupidity in them, for they had not a word to say against him. But, about a week before the marriage day was fixed, they thought they had found out something—my darling love, don't take away your hand—don't tremble so, only just listen! Her aunt came to her and said: "Child, you must give up your lover; his father was tempted, and sinned, and if he is now

32

alive he is a transported convict. The marriage cannot take place." But the girl stood up and said: "If he has known this great sorrow and shame, he needs my love all the more. I will not leave him, nor forsake him, but love him all the better. And I charge you, aunt, as you hope to receive a blessing for doing as you would be done by, that you tell no one!" I really think that girl awed her aunt, in some strange way, into secrecy. But, when she was left alone, she cried long and sadly, to think what a shadow rested on the heart she loved so dearly, and she meant to strive to lighten the life, and to conceal for ever that she had heard of the burden; but now she thinks. Oh, my husband! how you must have suffered—' as he bent down his head on her shoulder and cried terrible man's tears.

'God be thanked!' he said at length. 'You know all, and you do not shrink from me. Oh, what a miserable, deceitful coward I have been! Suffered! Yes—suffered enough to drive me mad; and if I had but been brave, I might have been spared all this long twelve months of agony. But it is right I should have been punished. And you knew it even before we were married, when you might have drawn back.'

'I could not: you would not have broken off your engagement with me, would you, under the like circumstances, if our cases had been reversed?'

'I do not know. Perhaps I might, for I am not so brave, so good, so strong as you, my Margaret. How could I be? Let me tell you more: We wandered about, my mother and I, thankful that our name was such a common one, but shrinking from every allusion—in a way which no one can understand who has not been conscious of an inward sore. Living in an assize town was torture: a commercial one was nearly as bad. My father was the son of a dignified clergyman, well known to his brethren: a cathedral town was to be avoided, because there the circumstance of the Dean of Saint Botolph's son having been transported, was sure to be known. I had to be educated; therefore we had to live in a town; for my mother could not bear to part from me, and I was sent to a day-school. We were very poor for our station—no! we had no station; we were the wife and child of a convict—for my poor mother's early habits, I should have said. But, when I was about fourteen, my father died in his exile, leaving, as convicts in those days sometimes did, a large fortune. It all came to us. My mother shut herself up, and cried and prayed for a whole day. Then she called me in, and took me into her counsel. We solemnly pledged ourselves to give the money to some charity as soon as I was legally of age. Till then the interest was laid by, every penny of it; though sometimes we were in sore distress for money, my education cost so much. But how could we tell in what way the money had been accumulated?' Here he dropped his voice. 'Soon after I was one-and-twenty, the papers rang with admiration of the unknown munificent donor of certain sums. I loathed their praises. I shrank from all recollection of my father. I remembered him dimly, but always as angry and violent with my mother. My poor, gentle mother! Margaret, she loved my father; and, for her sake, I have tried, since her death, to feel kindly towards his memory. Soon after my mother's death, I came to know you, my jewel, my treasure!'

After a while, he began again. 'But, oh, Margaret! even now you do not know the worst. After my mother's death, I found a bundle of law papers—of newspaper reports about my father's trial. Poor soul! why she had kept them, I cannot say. They were covered over with notes in her handwriting; and, for that reason, I kept them. It was so touching to read her record of the days spent by her in her solitary innocence, while he was embroiling himself deeper and deeper in crime. I kept this bundle (as I thought so safely!) in a secret drawer of my bureau; but that wretch Crawford has got hold of it. I missed the papers that very morning. The loss of them was infinitely worse than the loss of the money; and now Crawford threatens to bring out the one terrible fact, in open court, if he can; and his lawyer may do it, I believe. At any rate, to have it blazoned out to the world—I who have spent my life in fearing this hour! But most of all for you, Margaret! Still—if only it could be avoided! Who will employ the son of Brown, the noted forger? I shall lose all my practice. Men will look askance at me as I enter their doors. They will drive me into crime. I sometimes fear that crime is hereditary! Oh, Margaret! what am I to do?'

'What can you do?' she asked.

'I can refuse to prosecute.'

'Let Crawford go free, you knowing him to be guilty?'

'I know him to be guilty.'

'Then, simply, you cannot do this thing. You let loose a criminal upon the public.'

'But if I do not, we shall come to shame and poverty. It is for you I mind it, not for myself. I ought never to have married.'

'Listen to me. I don't care for poverty; and, as to shame, I should feel it twenty times more grievously if you and I consented to screen the guilty, from any fear or for any selfish motives of our own. I don't pretend that I shall not feel it, when first the truth is known. But my shame will turn into pride, as I watch you live it down. You have been rendered morbid, dear husband, by having something all your life to conceal. Let the world know the truth, and say the worst. You will go forth a free, honest, honourable man, able to do your future work without fear.'

'That scoundrel Crawford has sent for an answer to his impudent note,' said Christie, putting in her head at the door.

'Stay! May *I* write it?' said Margaret.

She wrote:

Whatever you may do or say, there is but one course open to us. No threats can deter your master from doing his duty.

MARGARET BROWN

'There!' she said, passing it to her husband; 'he will see that I know all, and I suspect he has reckoned something on your tenderness for me.'

Margaret's note only enraged, it did not daunt, Crawford. Before a week was out, every one who cared knew that Doctor Brown, the rising young physician, was son of the notorious Brown the forger. All the consequences took place which he had anticipated. Crawford had to suffer a severe sentence; and Doctor Brown and his wife had to leave their house and go to a smaller one; they had to pinch and to screw, aided in all most zealously by the faithful Christie. But Doctor Brown was lighter-hearted than he had ever been before in his conscious life-time. His foot was now firmly planted on the ground, and every step he rose was a sure gain. People did say that Margaret had been seen, in those worst times, on her hands and knees cleaning her own door-step. But I don't believe it, for Christie would never have let her do that. And, as far as my own evidence goes, I can only say, that the last time I was in London, I saw a brass plate with Doctor James Brown upon it, on the door of a handsome house in a handsome square. And as I

35

looked, I saw a brougham drive up to the door, and a lady get out, and go into that house, who was certainly the Margaret Frazer of old days— graver, more portly, more stern I had almost said. But, as I watched and thought, I saw her come to the dining-room window with a baby in her arms, and her whole face melted into a smile of infinite sweetness.

WILLIAM MORRIS

Frank's Sealed Letter

Ever since I can remember, even when I was quite a child, people have always told me that I had no perseverance, no strength of will; they have always kept on saying to me, directly and indirectly, 'Unstable as water, thou shalt not excel'; and they have always been quite wrong in this matter, for of all men I ever heard of, I have the strongest will for good and evil. I could soon find out whether a thing were possible or not to me; then if it were not, I threw it away for ever, never thought of it again, no regret, no longing for that, it was past, and over to me; but if it were possible, and I made up my mind to do it, then and there I began it, and in due time finished it, turning neither to the right hand nor the left, till it was done. So I did with all things that I set my hand to.

Love only, and the wild restless passions that went with it, were too strong for me, and they bent my strong will, so that people think me now a weak man, with no end to make for in the purposeless wanderings of my life.

Yes, my life is purposeless now. I have failed, I know, but I know that I have fought too; I know the weary struggle from day to day, in which, with my loins girded, and my muscles all a-strain, I have fought, while years and years have passed away. I know what they do not, how that Passion trembled in my grasp, shook, staggered: how I grew stronger and stronger; till when, as I stood at last quivering with collected force, the light of victory across my lips and brow, God's hand struck me, and I fell at once, and without remedy; and am now a vanquished man; and really without any object in life, not desiring death any more than life, or life any more than death; a vanquished man, though no coward; forlorn, hopeless, unloved, living now altogether in the past.

I will tell you how I fell, and then I pray you all to pity me, and if you can, love me, and pray for me that I may be forgiven.

37

I said, when I left her that day, that I would forget her, look upon her as if she had never been; coming and going to and from that house, indeed, seeing her often, talking to her, as to any other friendly and accomplished lady; but seeing Mabel, my Mabel, that had been, no more. She was dead, and the twenty years that I had lived with her, man and boy, and little child, were gone—dead too, and forgotten. No shadow of them should rest upon my path, I said. Meantime the world wanted help; I was strong and willing, and would help it. I saw all about me men without a leader, looking and yearning for one to come and help them. I would be that leader, I said; there was no reason for me to be bitter and misanthropical, for I could forget the past utterly, could be another man in short. Why! I never loved that woman there, with her heavy, sweeping, black hair, and dreamily-passionate eyes; that was some one past away long ago. Who knows when he lived? but I am the man that knows, that feels all poetry and art, that can create, that can sympathize with every man and woman that ever lived—even with that cold, proud woman there, without a heart, but with heavy, sweeping hair, and great dreamily-passionate eyes, which might cause a weak man to love her.

Yes, I said so when I left her—nay, even before I left her, for in my agonized pleading I had said words that made her cold, selfish blood run quick enough to speak scornful things to me. 'Mabel!' I said, 'Mabel! think awhile before you turn from me for ever! Am I not good enough for you? Yet tell me, I pray you, for God's sake, what you would have me do? what you would have me make myself, and I will do that thing, make myself such, whatever it is. Think how long I have worshipped you, looked on all the world through your eyes. I loved you as soon as I saw you, even when I was a child, before I had reason almost; and my love and my reason have grown together, till now. Oh! Mabel, think of the things we have talked of together, thought of together! Will you ever find another man who thinks the same as you do in everything? Nay, but you must love me. Such letters you have written me too! Oh! Mabel, Mabel, I know God will never let love like mine go unrequited. You love me, I know, I am sure of it; you are trying me only; let it be enough now, my own Mabel, the only one that loves me. See, do not I love you enough?'

I fell there before her feet. I caught the hem of her garment. I buried my face in its folds; madly I strove to convince myself that she was but trying me, that she could not speak for her deep love, that it was a dream only. Oh! how I tried to wake, to find myself, with my heart beating wildly, and the black night round me, lying on my bed; as often, when a child, I used to wake from a dream of lions, and robbers, and ugly deaths, and the devil, to find myself in the dear room, though it was dark, my heart bounding with the fear of pursuit and joy of escape.

But no dream breaks now, desperate, desperate, earnest. The dreams have closed round me, and become the dismallest reality, as I often used to fear those other dreams might; the walls of this fact are closed round about me now like the sides of an iron chest, hurrying on down some swift river, with the black water above, to the measureless, rolling sea. I shall never any more wake to anything but that.

For listen to what she said, you who are happy lovers. Can you believe it? I can scarce do so myself. I, not looking up from where I lay, felt her lips curl into a cruel smile, as she drew herself from my grasp, and said:

'Listen, Hugh. I call you "Hugh", by the way, not because I am fond of you, but because surnames never seemed to me to express anything; they are quite meaningless. Hugh, I never loved you, never shall, nay, something more. I am not quite sure that I do not hate you, for coming to claim me as a right in this way, and appealing to God against me. Who gave you any right to be lord over me, and question my heart? Why, for this long time I have seen that you would claim me at last, and your "love" which I now cast from me for ever, and trample upon, so—so,—your "love", I say, has been a bitterly heavy burden to me, dogging me up and down, everywhere. You think my thoughts? Yes, verily, you who think yourself the teacher of such an one as I am, have few thoughts of your own to think. What do I want better than you? Why, I want a man who is brave and beautiful. You are a coward and a cripple. Am I trying you? No, Hugh; there is no need for that. I think I know you well enough, weak and irresolute, you will never do anything great. I must marry a great man—

'White honour shall be like a plaything to him,
Borne lightly, a pet falcon on his wrist;

39

> One who can feel the very pulse o' the time,
> Instant to act, to plunge into the strife,
> And with a strong arm hold the rearing world.'

But before she had begun to quote, my life had changed. While I lay there, in I know not what agony, that which I have just said came suddenly across me. I became calm all at once. I began to bend my passion beneath my strong will; the fight I fought so bravely had begun.

I rose up quietly before she began to quote, and when she saw me standing there, so calmly, ay, and looking so brave too, though I was a 'cripple and a coward', she quailed before me, her voice fell, even in the midst of her scornful speech; then I thought, 'so cool, and can quote pretty verses at such a time! Oh! but my revenge is good, and sure too, it is almost as if I killed her, stabbed her to the heart, here in this room.' Then my heart grew quite obedient, and my purpose began to work, so that I could speak with no shadow of passion in my words, and with no forced unnatural calm either. I could seem, and for years and years did seem, to be no hard cold man of the world, no mere calculating machine for gauging God's earth by modern science; but a kindly genial man; though so full of knowledge, yet having room for love too, and enthusiasm, and faith. Ah! they who saw me as such did not see the fight, did not see that bitter passage in the room of the old house at Riston, where the river widens.

I stood there silent for a very short time; then, raising my eyes to hers, said, 'Well, Mabel, I shall go up to London, and see the publishers, and perhaps stay there a day or two, so that I shall probably be back again at Casley by Tuesday; and I daresay I shall find time to walk over to Riston on Wednesday or Thursday, to tell you what we have determined on—goodbye.' She trembled, and turned pale, as I gave her my hand, and said, 'goodbye', in a forced tone, that was in strong contrast to my natural-seeming calmness. She was frightened of me then, already. Good.

So I walked away from Riston to my own house at Casley (which was about two miles from Riston), and got ready to start for London; then, about an hour after I had parted from her, set out again across the fields to the railway, that was five miles from my house. It was on the afternoon of a lovely spring day; I took a book with me, a volume of

poems just published, and my dead friend's manuscript; for my purpose
in going to London was to see to its publication.

Then, looking at that over which so many years of toil and agony of
striving had been spent, I thought of him who wrote it; thought how
admirable he was, how that glorious calm purpose of his shone through
all his restless energy. I thought, too, as I had never done before, of the
many, many ways he had helped me; and my eyes filled with tears, as
I remembered remorsefully the slight return I had given him for his
affection, my forgetfulness of him in the years when I was happy. I
thought of his quiet, successful love, and that sweet wife of his, the poor
widow that was now, who lived at Florence, watching the shadows
come and go on her husband's tomb, the rain that washed it, the sun
and moon that shone on it; then how he had died at Florence, and of
the short letter he had written to me, or rather that had been written,
just before his death, by his wife, from his dictation, and stained with
the many tears of the poor heartbroken lady. Those farewell words that
threw but a slight shadow over the happy days when I loved Mabel, had
more weight now, both for sorrow and consolation; for the thought that
that dead man cared for me surely did me good, made me think more
of the unseen world, less of the terrible earth-world that seemed all
going wrong, and which the unseen was slowly righting.

I had the letter with me at that very time. I had taken it out with the
manuscript, and together with that, another, a sealed letter that came
with it, and which, according to the dying man's wish, I had never yet
opened. I took out both the letters, and turning aside from the path sat
down under a willow by the side of the river, a willow just growing
grey-green with the spring. And there, to the music of the west wind
through the slim boughs, to the very faint music of the river's flow, I
read the two letters, and first the one I had read before.

Dear friend, I am going the last journey, and I wish to say farewell before I
go. My wife's tears fall fast, as she writes, and I am sorry to go, though, I
think, not afraid to die. Two things I want to say to you: the first and least has
to do with my writings; I do not wish them to perish: you know I wrote,
thinking I might do some one good; will you see about this for me? Do you
know, Hugh, I never cared for any man so much as for you: there was something which drew me to you wonderfully; it used to trouble me sometimes to
think that you scarcely cared for me so much; but only sometimes, for I saw

that you knew this, and tried to love me more; it was not your fault that you could not; God bless you for the trying even! When you see my wife, be kind to her; we have had happy talk about you often, thinking what a great man you ought to be. Yet one thing more. I send you with this a sealed enclosure. On the day that you are married to Mabel, or on the day that she dies, still loving you, burn this unopened; but, oh friend, if such a misfortune happen to you, as I scarce dare hint at even, then open it, and read it for the sake of, Frank.

Then I remembered, sadly, how when I read this, I was angry at first, even with the dead man, for his suspicion; only, when I thought of him dying, and how loving he was, my anger quickly sunk into regret for him; not deep anguish, but quiet regret. Ah! what a long time it was since I loved Mabel! how I had conquered my raging passion! Frank will surely applaud my resolution. Dear heart! how wise he was in his loving simplicity.

I looked at the sealed letter; it also was directed in his wife's handwriting; I broke the seal, and saw Frank's writing there; it was written, therefore, some time before his death.

How solemn the wind was through the willow boughs, how solemn the faint sound of the swirls of the lowland river! I read—

O Hugh, Hugh! poor wounded heart! I saw it all along, that she was not worthy of that heart stored up with so much love. I do not ask for that love, dear friend; I know you cannot give it me; I was never jealous of her; and I know, moreover, that your love for her will not be wasted. I think, for my part, that there is One Who gathers up all such wandering love, and keeps it for Himself; think, Hugh, of those many weary hours on the Cross; in that way did they requite His Love then, and how do we requite it now? Should He not then sympathize with all those whose love is not returned?

And, Hugh, sweet friend, I pray you, for Christ's love, never strive to forget the love you bore her in the days when you thought her noble, the noblest of all things, never cast away the gift of memory; never cast it away for your ease, never even for the better serving of God; He will help Himself, and does not want mere deeds; you are weak, and love cannot live without memory. Oh! Hugh! if you do as I pray you, this remembered love will be a very bright crown to you up in Heaven; meantime, may it not be that your love for others will grow, that you will love all men more, and me, perhaps, even much more? And I, though I never see you again in the body till the Day of Doom, will nevertheless be near you in spirit, to comfort you somewhat through the days of your toiling on earth; and now, Frank prays God to bless poor wounded Hugh!

I ceased reading; a dull pain came about my forehead and eyes. What! must I be all alone in my struggle with passion? not even Frank to help me? dear fellow! to think how fond he was of me! I am very very sorry he cannot be with me in this fight; for I must kill her utterly in my memory, and I think, if he knew all, how very noble I thought her, how altogether base she really is, he would be with me after all. Yet, Frank, though I do not do this that you pray me to do, you shall still be my friend, will you not? you shall help me to become more like you, if that is possible in any degree.

So, I determined to forget her; and was I not successful, at first; ah! and for long too? nevertheless, alas! alas! Frank's memory faded with her memory, and I did not feel his spirit by me often, only sometimes, and those were my weakest times, when I was least fit to have him by me; for then my purpose would give in somewhat, and memory would come to me, not clear and distinct, but only as a dull pain about my eyes and forehead; but my strong will could banish that, for I had much work to do, trying to help my fellow-men, with all my heart I thought. I threw myself heart and soul into that work, and joy grew up in my soul; and I was proud to think that she had not exhausted the world for me.

Nor did I shrink once from the sight of her, but came often, and saw her at her father's house at Riston, that the broadening river flows by always; nay, I sat at her wedding, and saw her go up to the altar with firm step, and heard her say her part in the unfaltering music of her rich voice, wherein was neither doubt nor love; and there I prayed that the brave noble-hearted soldier, her husband, might be happy with her, feeling no jealousy of him, pitying him rather; for I did not think that it was in her nature to love any one but herself thoroughly. Yet, what a Queen she looked on that marriage-day! her black hair crowning her so, her great deep eyes looking so full of all slumbering passion as of old, her full lips underneath, whence the music came; and, as she walked there between the grey walls of that Abbey where they were married, the light fell on her through the jewel-like windows, colouring strangely the white and gold of her gorgeous robes. She also seemed, or wished to seem, to have forgotten that spring-day at Riston; at least, she spoke to me when she went away quite kindly, and very calmly: 'Good bye, Hugh, we hear of you already; you will be a great man soon, and a good man you always were, and always will be; and we shall think of you often, and always with pleasure.'

Yet I knew she hated me; oh! her hollow heart! The dull pain came about my forehead and eyes; somehow I could not keep up the farce just then. I spoke bitterly, a smile that I know now I should not have smiled, curling my lip. 'Well done, Mabel! it is a nicely composed parting speech to an old friend; but you were always good at that kind of thing. Forget you? no—you are too handsome for that; and, if I were a painter or sculptor, I would paint you or carve you from memory. As it is, I never forget beautiful faces—good bye.' And I turned away from her a little without giving my hand. She grew pale at first, then flushed bright crimson, like a stormy sky, and turned from me with a scornful devil's glance.

She was gone, and a sharp pang of memory shot through me for a single instant, a warning of my fall which was to be. For a single instant I saw her sitting there, as of old, in the garden hard by the river, under the gold-dropping laburnums, heard her for a single instant singing wildly in her magnificent voice, as of old:

> Wearily, drearily,
> Half the day long,
> Flap the great banners
> High over the stone;
> Strangely and eerily
> Sounds the wind's song,
> Bending the banner-poles.
>
> While, all alone,
> Watching the loophole's spark,
> Lie I, with life all dark,
> Feet tether'd, hands fetter'd
> Fast to the stone,
> The grim walls, square letter'd,
> With prison'd men's groan.
>
> Still strain the banner-poles
> Through the wind's song,

Westward the banner rolls
Over my wrong.

But it was gone directly, that pang; everything, voice, face, and all: like the topmost twigs of some great tree-limb, that, as it rolls round and round, grinding the gravel and mud at the bottom of a flooded river, shows doubtfully for a second, flashing wet in the February sunlight, then, sinking straightway, goes rolling on toward the sea, in the swift steady flow of the flooded river; yet it appears again often, till it is washed ashore at last, who knows where or when?

But for me, these pangs of memory did not come often; nay, they came less and less frequently for long, till at last, in full triumph, as I thought it, I fell.

That marriage-day was more than two years after the day in April that I told you of, when I read the sealed letter; then, for three years after her marriage, I went on working, famous now, with many who almost worshipped me, for the words I had said, the many things I had taught them; and I in return, verily loved these earnestly; yet, round about me clung some shadow that was not the mere dulled memory of what had been, and it deepened sometimes in my drearier moods into fearful doubts that this last five years of my life had been, after all, a mistake, a miserable failure; yet, still I had too much to do to go on doubting for long; so these shadowy doubts had to hold back till, though I knew it not, a whole army of them was marching upon me in my fancied security.

Well, it was Spring-time, just about five years from that day; I was living in London, and for the last few months had been working very hard indeed, writing and reading all day long and every day, often all night long also, and in those nights the hours would pass so quickly that the time between night-fall and dawn scarcely seemed ten minutes long. So I worked, worked so hard, that one day, one morning early, when I saw through my window, on waking about six o'clock, how blue the sky was, even above the London roofs, and remembered how, in the fields all about, it was the cowslip time of the year. I said to myself, 'No work to-day; I will make holiday for once in the sweet spring-time. I will take a book with some tale in it, go into the country, and read it there, not striving particularly to remember it, but enjoying myself only.'

And, as I said this, my heart beat with joy, like a boy's at thought of holiday. So I got up, and as I was dressing, I took up a volume of Shakespeare, and opened it at Troilus and Cressida, and read a line or two just at the place where the parting comes; it almost brought the tears to my eyes. 'How soft-hearted I am this morning,' I said; 'yet I will take this; and read it; it is quite a long time since I read any Shakespeare, and, I think, years and years since I have read Troilus and Cressida.' Yes, I was soft-hearted that morning, and when I looked in the glass and saw my puny deformed figure there, and my sallow thin face, eaten into many furrows by those five years, those furrows that gave a strange grotesque piteousness to the ugly features, I smiled at first, then almost wept for self-pity; the tears were in my eyes again; but I thought, 'I will not spoil my holiday,' and so forbore; then I went out into the streets, with a certain kind of light-heartedness, which I knew might turn any moment into very deep sadness. The bells of a church, that I passed in my way Essex-ward, were ringing, and their music struck upon my heart so, that I walked the faster to get beyond their sound.

I was in the country soon: people called it an ugly country, I knew, that spreading of the broad marsh lands round the river Lea; but I was so weary with my hard work that it seemed very lovely to me then; indeed, I think I should not have despised it at any time. I was always a lover of the sad lowland country. I walked on, my mind keeping up a strange balance between joy and sadness for some time, till gradually all the beauty of things seemed to be stealing into my heart, and making me very soft and womanish, so that, at last, when I was now quite a long way off from the river Lea, and walking close by the side of another little river, a mere brook, all my heart was filled with sadness, and joy had no place there at all; all the songs of birds ringing through the hedges, and about the willows; all the sweet colours of the sky, and the clouds that floated in the blue of it; of the tender fresh grass, and the sweet young shoots of flowering things, were very pensive to me, pleasantly so at first perhaps, but soon they were lying heavy on me, with all the rest of things created; for within my heart rose memory, green and fresh as the young spring leaves. Ah! such thoughts of the old times came about me thronging, that they almost made me faint. I tried hard to shake them off; I noticed every turn of the banks of the little brook, every ripple of its waters over the brown stones, every line of the broad-leaved waterflowers; I went down towards the brook, and, stooping down, gathered a knot of lush marsh-marigolds; then, kneeling on both knees, bent over the water with my arm stretched down to it, till both my hand and the yellow flowers were making the swift-running little stream bubble about them; and, even as I did so, still stronger and stronger came the memories, till they came quite clear at last, those shapes and words of the past days. I rose from the water in haste, and, getting on to the road again, walked along tremblingly, my head bent towards the earth, my wet hand and flowers marking the dust of it as I went. Ah! what was it all, that picture of the old past days.

I see a little girl sitting on the grass, beneath the limes in the hot summertide, with eyes fixed on the far away blue hills, and seeing who knows what shapes there; for the boy by her side is reading to her wondrous stories of knight and lady, and fairy thing, that lived in the ancient days; his voice trembles as he reads—

'And so Sir Isumbras, when he had slain the giant, cut off his head, and came to the town where the Lady Alicia lived, bringing with him that grim thing, the giant's head, and the people pressed all about him at the gate, and brought him to the king, and all the court was there, and the whole palace blazed with gold and jewels. So there, among the ladies, was the Lady Alicia, clothed in black, because she thought that through her evil pride she had caused the death of the good knight and true, who loved her: and when she saw Sir Isumbras with the head of the giant, even before the king, and all, she gave a great cry, and ran before all, and threw her arms round about him.' 'Go on, Hugh,' says the little girl, still looking into the blue distance, 'why do you stop?' 'I was—I was looking at the picture, Mabel,' says the boy. 'Oh! is there a picture of that? let's see it;' and her eyes turn towards him at last. What a very beautiful child she is! 'Not exactly of that,' says Hugh, blushing as their eyes meet, and, when she looks away for a second, drawing his hand across his eyes, for he is soft-hearted, 'not exactly of that, but afterwards, where she crowns him at the tournament; here it is.' 'Oh! that is pretty though; Hugh, I say Hugh!' 'Yes,' says Hugh. 'Go and get me some of the forget-me-not down by the brook there, and some of the pretty white star-shaped flower; I'll crown you too.' Off runs Hugh, directly, carrying the book with him. 'Stop, don't lose the place, Hugh; here, give me the book.' Back he goes, then starts again in a great hurry; the flowers are not easy to get, but they are got somehow; for, Hugh, though deformed, is yet tolerably active, and for her. So, when the flowers come, she weaves them into a crown, blue flowers golden-hearted, and white ones star-shaped, with the green leaves between them.

Then she makes him kneel down, and, looking at the picture in the fairy story-book, places him this way and that, with her smooth brows knit into a puzzled frown; at last she says, 'It wont do, somehow; I can't make it out. I say, Hugh,' she blurts out at last, 'I tell you what, it wont do; you are too ugly.' 'Never mind, Mabel,' he says; 'shall I go on reading again?' 'Yes, you may go on.' Then she sits down; and again her eyes are fixed on the far away blue hills, and Hugh is by her, reading again, only stumbling sometimes, seemingly not so much interested as he was before.

'Poor Hugh!' I said out loud, for strangely, the thing was so strong, that it had almost wrought its own cure; and I found myself looking at my old self, and at her, as at people in a story; yet I was stunned as it were, and knew well that I was incapable of resistance against that memory now. Yes, I knew well what was coming.

I had by this time left the brook, and gone through a little village on the hill above, and on the other side of it; then turned to my right into the forest, that was all about, the quaint hornbeam forest. There, sitting down, I took out the Troilus and Cressida I had brought with me, and began to read, saying to myself (though I did not believe it) that I would cast those memories quite away from me, be triumphantly victorious over them.

Yes, there under the hornbeams I read Troilus and Cressida, the play with the two disappointments in it, Hector dead, and Cressida unfaithful; Troy and Troilus undone. And when I had finished, I thought no more of Troilus and Cressida, or of any one else in the wide world but Mabel.

'O Mabel!' I said, burying my face in the grass as I had before, long ago, in her long robes; 'O Mabel! could you not have loved me? I would have loved you more than any woman was ever loved. Or if you could not love me, why did you speak as you did on that day? I thought you so much above me, Mabel; and yet I could not have spoken so to any one. O Mabel! how will it be between us when we are dead? O Lord! help me, help me! Is it coming over again?'

For as I lay there, I saw again, as clearly as years ago, the room in the old house at Riston, at the noontide of the warm sunny spring weather. The black oak panelling, carved so quaintly, all round the room, whereon, in the space of sunlight that, pouring through the window, lit up the shadowed wall, danced the shadows of the young lime-leaves; the great bay window, with its shattered stone mullions, round which the creepers clung; the rustling of the hard magnolia leaves in the fresh blast of the west wind; the garden, with its clusters of joyous golden daffodils under the acacia-trees, seen through the open window; and beyond that, rolling and flashing in the sun, between its long lines of willows and poplars, the mighty lowland river going to the sea.

And she sat there by the fire-place, where there was no fire burning now. She sat by the cold hearth, with her back to the window, her long hands laid on her knees, bending forward a little, as if she were striving to look through and through something that was far off—there she sat, with her heavy, rolling, purple hair, like a queen's crown above her white temples, with her great slumbrously-passionate eyes, and her full lips underneath, whence the music came. Except that the wind moved a little some of the folds of her dress, she was as motionless and quiet as an old Egyptian statue, sitting out its many thousand years of utter rest, that it may the better ponder on its own greatness; more lifeless far she looked than any one of the grey saints, that hang through rain, and wind, and sunshine, in the porches of the abbey which looks down on the low river waves.

And there was one watched her from near the door, a man with long arms, crooked shoulders, and pale, ugly-featured face, looking out from long, lank, black hair. Yes, his face is pale always; but now it is much paler than usual, as pale almost as the face of a dead man; you can almost hear his heart beat as he stands there; the cold sweat gathers on his brow. Presently he moves towards the lady; he stands before her with one hand raised, and resting on the mantel-shelf. You can see his arm trembling as he does this; he stands so while you might count twenty, she never looking up the while. Then, half-choking, he says, 'Mabel, I want to speak to you, if you please, for a moment'; and she looks round with a calm, unconcerned look at first; but presently a

49

scornful smile begins to flicker about the corners of her mouth. Then that pale man says, 'Ah! I have told you all the rest before'; for he knew the meaning of the flickering smile—and that was five years ago.

And I shall never forget it while I live—never forget those words of hers—never forget a single line of her beautiful, cruel face, as she stood there five years ago. All the world may go by me now; I care not. I cannot work any more. I think I must have had some purpose in coming here; but I forget what it was. I will go back to London, and see if I can remember when I get there—so that day under the hornbeam trees I fell from my steady purpose of five years. I was vanquished then, once and for ever; there was no more fighting for me any more.

And have I ever forgotten it—that day, and the words she spoke? No, not for one moment. I have lived three years since then of bitter anguish. Every moment of that time has been utter pain and woe to me; that is what my life has been these three years. And what death may be like I cannot tell; I dare not even think for fear.

And I have fled from the world; no one of all my worshippers knows what has become of me, and the people with whom I live now, call me a man without a purpose, without a will.

Yes, I wonder what death would be like. The Eure is deep at Louviers I know—deep, and runs very swiftly towards the Seine, past the cloth mills.

Louviers! Louviers! What am I saying? Where am I? O Christ! I hold the sealed letter—Frank's sealed letter, in my hand, the seal just broken. Five years! Eight years! It was but two hours ago that my head lay before her feet; yet I seem to have lived those eight years. Then I have not been famous; have not forgotten; never sat under the hornbeams by Chigwell; and she is sitting there, still perhaps in that same oak room.

How strange it is, fearfully strange, yet true; for here is Frank's letter; here is his manuscript, the ink on it, brown through the years of toil and longing. There close by my side the great river is going to the sea, and the wind goes softly through the willow-boughs this sunny spring afternoon.

And now what shall I do? I know my will is strong, though I failed so in that dream I have awoke from. I know too, 'That a sorrow's crown of sorrow is remembering happier things.' Shall I wear this crown then while I live on earth, or forget, and be brave and strong? Ah! it must be a grand thing to be crowned; and if it cannot be with gold and jewels, or better still, with the river flowers, then must it be with thorns. Shall I wear this or cast it from me? I hear the wind going through the willow-boughs; it seems to have a message for me.

'Good and true, faithful and brave, loving always, and crowned with all wisdom in the days gone by. He was all this and more. Trust your friend Hugh—your friend who loved you so, though you hardly knew it; wear the crown of memory.' Yes, I will wear it; and, O friend! you who sent me this dream of good and evil, help me, I pray you, for I know how bitter it will be. Yes, I will wear it, and then, though never forgetting Mabel, and the things that have been, I may be happy at some time or another.

Yet I cannot see now how that can ever come to pass.

Oh, Mabel! if you could only have loved me.

'Lord, keep my memory green.'

ANTHONY TROLLOPE

Malachi's Cove

On the northern coast of Cornwall, between Tintagel and Bossiney,
down on the very margin of the sea, there lived not long since an
old man who got his living by saving seaweed from the waves, and
selling it for manure. The cliffs there are bold and fine, and the sea beats
in upon them from the north with a grand violence. I doubt whether it
be not the finest morsel of cliff scenery in England, though it is beaten
by many portions of the west coast of Ireland, and perhaps also by spots
in Wales and Scotland. Cliffs should be nearly precipitous, they should
be broken in their outlines, and should barely admit here and there of
an insecure passage from their summit to the sand at their feet. The sea
should come, if not up to them, at least very near to them, and then,
above all things, the water below them should be blue, and not of that
dead leaden colour which is so familiar to us in England. At Tintagel
all these requisites are there, except that bright blue colour which is so
lovely. But the cliffs themselves are bold and well broken, and the
margin of sand at high water is very narrow,—so narrow that at spring-
tides there is barely a footing there.

Close upon this margin was the cottage or hovel of Malachi Trenglos,
the old man of whom I have spoken. But Malachi, or old Glos, as he
was commonly called by the people around him, had not built his house
absolutely upon the sand. There was a fissure in the rock so great that
at the top it formed a narrow ravine, and so complete from the summit
to the base that it afforded an opening for a steep and rugged track from
the top of the rock to the bottom. This fissure was so wide at the
bottom that it had afforded space for Trenglos to fix his habitation on
a foundation of rock, and here he had lived for many years. It was told
of him that in the early days of his trade he had always carried the weed
in a basket on his back to the top, but latterly he had been possessed of
a donkey, which had been trained to go up and down the steep track

52

with a single pannier over his loins, for the rocks would not admit of panniers hanging by his side; and for this assistant he had built a shed adjoining his own, and almost as large as that in which he himself resided.

But, as years went on, old Glos procured other assistance than that of the donkey, or, as I should rather say, Providence supplied him with other help; and, indeed, had it not been so, the old man must have given up his cabin and his independence and gone into the workhouse at Camelford. For rheumatism had afflicted him, old age had bowed him till he was nearly double, and by degrees he became unable to attend the donkey on its upward passage to the world above, or even to assist in rescuing the coveted weed from the waves.

At the time to which our story refers Trenglos had not been up the cliff for twelve months, and for the last six months he had done nothing towards the furtherance of his trade, except to take the money and keep it, if any of it was kept, and occasionally to shake down a bundle of fodder for the donkey. The real work of the business was done altogether by Mahala Trenglos, his granddaughter.

Mally Trenglos was known to all the farmers round the coast, and to all the small tradespeople in Camelford. She was a wild-looking, almost unearthly creature, with wild-flowing, black, uncombed hair, small in stature, with small hands and bright black eyes; but people said that she was very strong, and the children around declared that she worked day and night and knew nothing of fatigue. As to her age there were many doubts. Some said she was ten, and others five-and-twenty, but the reader may be allowed to know that at this time she had in truth passed her twentieth birthday. The old people spoke well of Mally, because she was so good to her grandfather; and it was said of her that though she carried to him a little gin and tobacco almost daily, she bought nothing for herself;—and as to the gin, no one who looked at her would accuse her of meddling with that. But she had no friends and but few acquaintances among people of her own age. They said that she was fierce and ill-natured, that she had not a good word for any one, and that she was, complete at all points, a thorough little vixen. The young men did not care for her; for, as regarded dress, all days were alike with her. She never made herself smart on Sundays. She was generally without stockings, and seemed to care not at all to exercise any of those feminine attractions which might have been hers had she studied to attain them. All days were the same to her in regard to dress; and, indeed, till lately, all days had, I fear, been the same to her in other respects. Old Malachi had never been seen inside a place of worship since he had taken to live under the cliff.

But within the last two years Mally had submitted herself to the teaching of the clergyman at Tintagel, and had appeared at church on Sundays, if not absolutely with punctuality, at any rate so often that no one who knew the peculiarity of her residence was disposed to quarrel with her on that subject. But she made no difference in her dress on these occasions. She took her place on a low stone seat just inside the church door, clothed as usual in her thick red serge petticoat and loose brown serge jacket, such being the apparel which she had found to be best adapted for her hard and perilous work among the waters. She had pleaded to the clergyman when he attacked her on the subject of church attendance with vigour that she had got no church-going clothes. He had explained to her that she would be received there without distinction to her clothing. Mally had taken him at his word, and had gone, with a courage which certainly deserved admiration, though I doubt whether there was not mingled with it an obstinacy which was less admirable.

For people said that old Glos was rich, and that Mally might have proper clothes if she chose to buy them. Mr Polwarth, the clergyman, who, as the old man could not come to him, went down the rocks to the old man, did make some hint on the matter in Mally's absence. But old Glos, who had been patient with him on other matters, turned upon him so angrily when he made an allusion to money, that Mr Polwarth found himself obliged to give that matter up, and Mally continued to sit upon the stone bench in her short serge petticoat, with her long hair streaming down her face. She did so far sacrifice to decency as on such occasions to tie up her black hair with an old shoestring. So tied it would remain through the Monday and Tuesday, but by Wednesday afternoon Mally's hair had generally managed to escape.

As to Mally's indefatigable industry there could be no manner of doubt, for the quantity of seaweed which she and the donkey amassed between them was very surprising. Old Glos, it was declared, had never collected half what Mally gathered together; but then the article was becoming cheaper, and it was necessary that the exertion should be greater. So Mally and the donkey toiled and toiled, and the seaweed came up in heaps which surprised those who looked at her little hands and light form. Was there not some one who helped her at nights, some fairy, or demon, or the like? Mally was so snappish in her answers to people that she had no right to be surprised if ill-natured things were said of her.

No one ever heard Mally Trenglos complain of her work, but about this time she was heard to make great and loud complaints of the treatment she received from some of her neighbours. It was known that she went with her plaints to Mr Polwarth; and when he could not help her, or did not give her such instant help as she needed, she went—ah, so foolishly! to the office of a certain attorney at Camelford, who was not likely to prove himself a better friend than Mr Polwarth.

Now the nature of her injury was as follows. The place in which she collected her seaweed was a little cove;—the people had come to call it Malachi's Cove from the name of the old man who lived there;—which was so formed, that the margin of the sea therein could only be reached by the passage from the top down to Trenglos's hut. The breadth of the cove when the sea was out might perhaps be two hundred yards, and on each side the rocks ran out in such a way that both from north and south the domain of Trenglos was guarded from intruders. And this locality had been well chosen for its intended purpose.

There was a rush of the sea into the cove, which carried there large, drifting masses of seaweed, leaving them among the rocks when the tide was out. During the equinoctial winds of the spring and autumn the supply would never fail; and even when the sea was calm, the long, soft, salt-bedewed, trailing masses of the weed, could be gathered there when they could not be found elsewhere for miles along the coast. The task of getting the weed from the breakers was often difficult and dangerous,—so difficult that much of it was left to be carried away by the next incoming tide.

Mally doubtless did not gather half the crop that was there at her feet. What was taken by the returning waves she did not regret; but when interlopers came upon her cove, and gathered her wealth,—her grandfather's wealth, beneath her eyes, then her heart was broken. It was this interloping, this intrusion, that drove poor Mally to the

Camelford attorney. But, alas, though the Camelford attorney took Mally's money, he could do nothing for her, and her heart was broken!

She had an idea, in which no doubt her grandfather shared, that the path to the cove was, at any rate, their property. When she was told that the cove, and sea running into the cove, were not the freeholds of her grandfather, she understood that the statement might be true. But what then as to the use of the path? Who had made the path what it was? Had she not painfully, wearily, with exceeding toil, carried up bits of rock with her own little hands, that her grandfather's donkey might have footing for his feet? Had she not scraped together crumbs of earth along the face of the cliff that she might make easier to the animal the track of that rugged way? And now, when she saw big farmer's lads coming down with other donkeys,—and, indeed, there was one who came with a pony; no boy, but a young man, old enough to know better than rob a poor old man and a young girl,—she reviled the whole human race, and swore that the Camelford attorney was a fool.

Any attempt to explain to her that there was still weed enough for her was worse than useless. Was it not all hers and his, or, at any rate, was not the sole way to it his and hers? And was not her trade stopped and impeded? Had she not been forced to back her laden donkey down, twenty yards she said, but it had, in truth, been five, because Farmer Gunliffe's son had been in the way with his thieving pony? Farmer Gunliffe had wanted to buy her weed at his own price, and because she had refused he had set on his thieving son to destroy her in this wicked way.

'I'll hamstring the beast the next time as he's down here!' said Mally to old Glos, while the angry fire literally streamed from her eyes.

Farmer Gunliffe's small homestead,—he held about fifty acres of land, was close by the village of Tintagel, and not a mile from the cliff. The sea-wrack, as they call it, was pretty well the only manure within his reach, and no doubt he thought it hard that he should be kept from using it by Mally Trenglos and her obstinacy.

'There's heaps of other coves, Barty,' said Mally to Barty Gunliffe, the farmer's son.

'But none so nigh, Mally, nor yet none that fills 'emselves as this place.'

Then he explained to her that he would not take the weed that came up close to hand. He was bigger than she was, and stronger, and would get it from the outer rocks, with which she never meddled. Then, with scorn in her eye, she swore that she could get it where he durst not venture, and repeated her threat of hamstringing the pony. Barty laughed at her wrath, jeered her because of her wild hair, and called her a mermaid.

'I'll mermaid you!' she cried. 'Mermaid, indeed! I wouldn't be a man to come and rob a poor girl and an old cripple. But you're no man, Barty Gunliffe! You're not half a man.'

Nevertheless, Bartholomew Gunliffe was a very fine young fellow as far as the eye went. He was about five feet eight inches high, with strong arms and legs, with light curly brown hair and blue eyes. His father was but in a small way as a farmer, but, nevertheless, Barty Gunliffe was well thought of among the girls around. Everybody liked Barty,—excepting only Mally Trenglos, and she hated him like poison.

Barty, when he was asked why so good-natured a lad as he perse-cuted a poor girl and an old man, threw himself upon the justice of the thing. It wouldn't do at all, according to his view, that any single per-son should take upon himself to own that which God Almighty sent as the common property of all. He would do Mally no harm, and so he had told her. But Mally was a vixen,—a wicked little vixen; and she must be taught to have a civil tongue in her head. When once Mally would speak him civil as he went for weed, he would get his father to pay the old man some sort of toll for the use of the path.

'Speak him civil?' said Mally. 'Never; not while I have a tongue in my mouth!' And I fear old Glos encouraged her rather than otherwise in her view of the matter.

But her grandfather did not encourage her to hamstring the pony. Hamstringing a pony would be a serious thing, and old Glos thought it might be very awkward for both of them if Mally were put into prison. He suggested, therefore, that all manner of impediments should be put in the way of the pony's feet, surmising that the well-trained donkey might be able to work in spite of them. And Barty Gunliffe, on his next descent, did find the passage very awkward when he came near to Malachi's hut, but he made his way down, and poor Mally saw the lumps of rock at which she had laboured so hard pushed on one side or rolled out of the way with a steady persistency of injury towards herself that almost drove her frantic.

'Well, Barty, you're a nice boy,' said old Glos, sitting in the door-way of the hut, as he watched the intruder.

'I ain't a doing no harm to none as doesn't harm me,' said Barty. 'The sea's free to all, Malachi.'

'And the sky's free to all, but I musn't get up on the top of your big barn to look at it,' said Mally, who was standing among the rocks with a long hook in her hand. The long hook was the tool with which she worked in dragging the weed from the waves. 'But you ain't got no justice, nor yet no sperrit, or you wouldn't come here to vex an old man like he.'

'I didn't want to vex him, nor yet to vex you, Mally. You let me be for a while, and we'll be friends yet.'

'Friends!' exclaimed Mally. 'Who'd have the likes of you for a friend? What are you moving them stones for? Them stones belongs to grand-father.' And in her wrath she made a movement as though she were going to fly at him.

'Let him be, Mally,' said the old man; 'let him be. He'll get his punishment. He'll come to be drowned some day if he comes down here when the wind is in shore.'

'That he may be drowned then!' said Mally, in her anger. 'If he was in the big hole there among the rocks, and the sea running in at half-tide, I wouldn't lift a hand to help him out.'

'Yes, you would, Mally; you'd fish me up with your hook like a big stick of seaweed.'

She turned from him with scorn as he said this, and went into the hut. It was time for her to get ready for her work, and one of the great injuries done her lay in this,—that such a one as Barty Gunliffe should come and look at her during her toil among the breakers.

It was an afternoon in April, and the hour was something after four o'clock. There had been a heavy wind from the north-west all the morning, with gusts of rain, and the sea-gulls had been in and out of the cove all the day, which was a sure sign to Mally that the incoming tide would cover the rocks with weed.

The quick waves were now returning with wonderful celerity over the low reefs, and the time had come at which the treasure must be seized, if it was to be garnered on that day. By seven o'clock it would be growing dark, at nine it would be high water, and before daylight the crop would be carried out again if not collected. All this Mally understood very well, and some of this Barty was beginning to understand also.

As Mally came down with her bare feet, bearing her long hook in her hand, she saw Barty's pony standing patiently on the sand, and in her heart she longed to attack the brute. Barty at this moment, with a common three-pronged fork in his hand, was standing down on a large rock, gazing forth towards the waters. He had declared that he would gather the weed only at places which were inaccessible to Mally, and he was looking out that he might settle where he would begin.

'Let 'un be, let 'un be,' shouted the old man to Mally, as he saw her take a step towards the beast, which she hated almost as much as she hated the man.

Hearing her grandfather's voice through the wind, she desisted from her purpose, if any purpose she had had, and went forth to her work. As she passed down the cove, and scrambled in among the rocks, she saw Barty still standing on his perch; out beyond, the white-curling waves were cresting and breaking themselves with violence, and the wind was howling among the caverns and abutments of the cliff.

Every now and then there came a squall of rain, and though there was sufficient light, the heavens were black with clouds. A scene more beautiful might hardly be found by those who love the glories of the coast. The light for such objects was perfect. Nothing could exceed the grandeur of the colours,—the blue of the open sea, the white of the breaking waves, the yellow sands, or the streaks of red and brown which gave such richness to the cliff.

But neither Mally nor Barty were thinking of such things as these. Indeed they were hardly thinking of their trade after its ordinary forms. Barty was meditating how he might best accomplish his purpose of working beyond the reach of Mally's feminine powers, and Mally was resolving that wherever Barty went she would go farther.

And, in many respects, Mally had the advantage. She knew every rock in the spot, and was sure of those which gave a good foothold, and sure also of those which did not. And then her activity had been made perfect by practice for the purpose to which it was to be devoted. Barty, no doubt, was stronger than she, and quite as active. But Barty could not jump among the waves from one stone to another as she could do, nor was he as yet able to get aid in his work from the very force of the water as she could get it. She had been hunting seaweed in that cove since she had been an urchin of six years old, and she knew every hole and corner and every spot of vantage. The waves were her friends, and she could use them. She could measure their strength, and knew when and where it would cease.

Mally was great down in the salt pools of her own cove,—great, and very fearless. As she watched Barty make his way forward from rock to rock, she told herself, gleefully, that he was going astray. The curl of the wind as it blew into the cove would not carry the weed up to the northern buttresses of the cove; and then there was the great hole just there,—the great hole of which she had spoken when she wished him evil.

And now she went to work, hooking up the dishevelled hairs of the ocean, and landing many a cargo on the extreme margin of the sand, from whence she would be able in the evening to drag it back before the invading waters would return to reclaim the spoil.

And on his side also Barty made his heap up against the northern buttresses of which I have spoken. Barty's heap became big and still bigger, so that he knew, let the pony work as he might, he could not take it all up that evening. But still it was not as large as Mally's heap. Mally's hook was better than his fork, and Mally's skill was better than his strength. And when he failed in some haul Mally would jeer him with a wild, weird laughter, and shriek to him through the wind that he was not half a man. At first he answered her with laughing words, but before long, as she boasted of her success and pointed to his failure, he became angry, and then he answered her no more. He became angry with himself, in that he missed so much of the plunder before him.

The broken sea was full of the long straggling growth which the waves had torn up from the bottom of the ocean, but the masses were carried past him, away from him,—nay, once or twice over him; and then Mally's weird voice would sound in his ear, jeering him. The gloom among the rocks was now becoming thicker and thicker, the tide was beating in with increased strength, and the gusts of wind came with quicker and greater violence. But still he worked on. While Mally worked he would work, and he would work for some time after she was driven in. He would not be beaten by a girl.

The great hole was now full of water, but of water which seemed to be boiling as though in a pot. And the pot was full of floating masses,— large treasures of seaweed which were thrown to and fro upon its surface, but lying there so thick that one would seem almost able to rest upon it without sinking.

Mally knew well how useless it was to attempt to rescue aught from the fury of that boiling caldron. The hole went in under the rocks, and the side of it towards the shore lay high, slippery, and steep. The hole, even at low water, was never empty; and Mally believed that there was no bottom to it. Fish thrown in there could escape out to the ocean, miles away,—so Mally in her softer moods would tell the visitors to the cove. She knew the hole well. Poulnadioul she was accustomed to call it; which was supposed, when translated, to mean that this was the hole of the Evil One. Never did Mally attempt to make her own of weed which had found its way into that pot.

But Barty Gunliffe knew no better, and she watched him as he endeavoured to steady himself on the treacherously slippery edge of the pool. He fixed himself there and made a haul, with some small success. How he managed it she hardly knew, but she stood still for a while watching him anxiously, and then she saw him slip. He slipped, and recovered himself;—slipped again, and again recovered himself.

'Barty, you fool!' she screamed, 'if you get yourself pitched in there, you'll never come out no more.'

Whether she simply wished to frighten him, or whether her heart relented and she had thought of his danger with dismay, who shall say? She could not have told herself. She hated him as much as ever,—but she could hardly have wished to see him drowned before her eyes.

'You go on, and don't mind me,' said he, speaking in a hoarse, angry tone.

'Mind you!—who minds you?' retorted the girl. And then she again prepared herself for her work.

But as she went down over the rocks with her long hook balanced in her hands, she suddenly heard a splash, and, turning quickly round, saw the body of her enemy tumbling amidst the eddying waves in the pool. The tide had now come up so far that every succeeding wave washed into it and over it from the side nearest to the sea, and then ran down again back from the rocks, as the rolling wave receded, with a noise like the fall of a cataract. And then, when the surplus water had retreated for a moment, the surface of the pool would be partly calm, though the fretting bubbles would still boil up and down, and there was ever a simmer on the surface, as though, in truth, the caldron were heated. But this time of comparative rest was but a moment, for the succeeding breaker would come up almost as soon as the foam of the preceding one had gone, and then again the waters would be dashed upon the rocks, and the sides would echo with the roar of the angry wave.

Instantly Mally hurried across to the edge of the pool, crouching down upon her hands and knees for security as she did so. As a wave receded, Barty's head and face was carried round near to her, and she could see that his forehead was covered with blood. Whether he were alive or dead she did not know. She had seen nothing but his blood, and the light-coloured hair of his head lying amidst the foam. Then his body was drawn along by the suction of the retreating wave; but the mass of water that escaped was not on this occasion large enough to carry the man out with it.

Instantly Mally was at work with her hook, and getting it fixed into his coat, dragged him towards the spot on which she was kneeling. During the half minute of repose she got him so close that she could touch his shoulder. Straining herself down, laying herself over the long bending handle of the hook, she strove to grasp him with her right hand. But she could not do it; she could only touch him.

Then came the next breaker, forcing itself on with a roar, looking to Mally as though it must certainly knock her from her resting-place, and destroy them both. But she had nothing for it but to kneel, and hold by her hook.

What prayer passed through her mind at that moment for herself or for him, or for that old man who was sitting unconsciously up at the cabin, who can say? The great wave came and rushed over her as she lay almost prostrate, and when the water was gone from her eyes, and the tumult of the foam, and the violence of the roaring breaker had passed by her, she found herself at her length upon the rock, while his body had been lifted up, free from her hook, and was lying upon the slippery ledge, half in the water and half out of it. As she looked at him, in that instant, she could see that his eyes were open and that he was struggling with his hands.

'Hold by the hook, Barty,' she cried, pushing the stick of it before him, while she seized the collar of his coat in her hands.

Had he been her brother, her lover, her father she could not have clung to him with more of the energy of despair. He did contrive to hold by the stick which she had given him, and when the succeeding wave had passed by, he was still on the ledge. In the next moment she was seated a yard or two above the hole, in comparative safety, while Barty lay upon the rocks with his still bleeding head resting upon her lap.

What could she do now? She could not carry him; and in fifteen minutes the sea would be up where she was sitting. He was quite insensible, and very pale, and the blood was coming slowly,—very slowly,—from the wound on his forehead. Ever so gently she put her hand upon his hair to move it back from his face; and then she bent over his mouth to see if he breathed, and as she looked at him she knew that he was beautiful.

What would she not give that he might live? Nothing now was so precious to her as his life,—as this life which she had so far rescued from the waters. But what could she do? Her grandfather could scarcely get himself down over the rocks, if indeed he could succeed in doing so much as that. Could she drag the wounded man backwards, if it were only a few feet, so that he might lie above the reach of the waves till further assistance could be procured?

She set herself to work and she moved him, almost lifting him. As she did so she wondered at her own strength, but she was very strong at that moment. Slowly, tenderly, falling on the rocks herself so that he might fall on her, she got him back to the margin of the sand, to a spot which the waters would not reach for the next two hours.

Here her grandfather met them, having seen at last what had happened from the door.

'Dada,' she said, 'he fell into the pool yonder, and was battered against the rocks. See there at his forehead.'

'Mally, I'm thinking that he's dead already,' said old Glos, peering down over the body.

'No, dada; he is not dead; but mayhap he's dying. But I'll go at once up to the farm.'

'Mally,' said the old man, 'look at his head. They'll say we murdered him.'

63

'Who'll say so? Who'll lie like that? Didn't I pull him out of the hole?'

'What matters that? His father'll say we killed him.'

It was manifest to Mally that whatever any one might say hereafter, her present course was plain before her. She must run up the path to Gunliffe's farm and get necessary assistance. If the world were as bad as her grandfather said, it would be so bad that she would not care to live longer in it. But be that as it might, there was no doubt as to what she must do now.

So away she went as fast as her naked feet could carry her up the cliff. When at the top she looked round to see if any person might be within ken, but she saw no one. So she ran with all her speed along the headland of the corn-field which led in the direction of old Gunliffe's house, and as she drew near to the homestead she saw that Barty's mother was leaning on the gate. As she approached she attempted to call, but her breath failed her for any purpose of loud speech, so she ran on till she was able to grasp Mrs Gunliffe by the arm.

'Where's himself?' she said, holding her hand upon her beating heart that she might husband her breath.

'Who is it you mean?' said Mrs Gunliffe, who participated in the family feud against Trenglos and his granddaughter. 'What does the girl clutch me for in that way?'

'He's dying then, that's all.'

'Who is dying? Is it old Malachi? If the old man's bad, we'll send some one down.'

'It ain't dada; it's Barty! Where's himself? where's the master?' But by this time Mrs Gunliffe was in an agony of despair, and was calling out for assistance lustily. Happily Gunliffe, the father, was at hand, and with him a man from the neighbouring village.

'Will you not send for the doctor?' said Mally. 'Oh, man, you should send for the doctor!'

Whether any orders were given for the doctor she did not know, but in a very few minutes she was hurrying across the field again towards the path to the cove, and Gunliffe with the other man and his wife were following her.

As Mally went along she recovered her voice, for their step was not so quick as hers, and that which to them was a hurried movement,

allowed her to get her breath again. And as she went she tried to explain
to the father what had happened, saying but little, however, of her own
doings in the matter. The wife hung behind listening, exclaiming every
now and again that her boy was killed, and then asking wild questions
as to his being yet alive. The father, as he went, said little. He was
known as a silent, sober man, well spoken of for diligence and general
conduct, but supposed to be stern and very hard when angered.

As they drew near to the top of the path the other man whispered
something to him, and then he turned round upon Mally and stopped
her.

'If he has come by his death between you, your blood shall be taken
for his,' said he.

Then the wife shrieked out that her child had been murdered, and
Mally, looking round into the faces of the three, saw that her grandfather's words had come true. They suspected her of having taken the
life, in saving which she had nearly lost her own.

She looked round at them with awe in her face, and then, without
saying a word, preceded them down the path. What had she to answer
when such a charge as that was made against her? If they chose to say
that she pushed him into the pool and hit him with her hook as he lay
amidst the waters, how could she show that it was not so?

Poor Mally knew little of the law of evidence, and it seemed to her
that she was in their hands. But as she went down the steep track with
a hurried step,—a step so quick that they could not keep up with her,—
her heart was very full,—very full and very high. She had striven for
the man's life as though he had been her brother. The blood was yet not
dry on her own legs and arms, where she had torn them in his service.
At one moment she had felt sure that she would die with him in that
pool. And now they said that she had murdered him! It may be that he
was not dead, and what would he say if ever he should speak again?
Then she thought of that moment when his eyes had opened, and he
had seemed to see her. She had no fear for herself, for her heart was
very high. But it was full also,—full of scorn, disdain, and wrath.

When she had reached the bottom, she stood close to the door of the
hut waiting for them, so that they might precede her to the other group,
which was there in front of them, at a little distance on the sand.

'He is there, and dada is with him. Go and look at him,' said Mally.

The father and mother ran on stumbling over the stones, but Mally remained behind by the door of the hut.

Barty Gunliffe was lying on the sand where Mally had left him, and old Malachi Trenglos was standing over him, resting himself with difficulty upon a stick.

'Not a move he's moved since she left him,' said he; 'not a move. I put his head on the old rug as you see, and I tried 'un with a drop of gin, but he wouldn't take it,—he wouldn't take it.'

'Oh, my boy! my boy!' said the mother, throwing herself beside her son upon the sand.

'Haud your tongue, woman,' said the father, kneeling down slowly by the lad's head, 'whimpering that way will do 'un no good.'

Then having gazed for a minute or two upon the pale face beneath him, he looked up sternly into that of Malachi Trenglos.

The old man hardly knew how to bear this terrible inquisition.

'He would come,' said Malachi; 'he brought it all upon hisself.'

'Who was it struck him?' said the father.

'Sure he struck hisself, as he fell among the breakers.'

'Liar!' said the father, looking up at the old man.

'They have murdered him!—they have murdered him!' shrieked the mother.

'Haud your peace, woman!' said the husband again. 'They shall give us blood for blood.'

Mally, leaning against the corner of the hovel, heard it all, but did not stir. They might say what they liked. They might make it out to be murder. They might drag her and her grandfather to Camelford gaol, and then to Bodmin, and the gallows; but they could not take from her the conscious feeling that was her own. She had done her best to save him,—her very best. And she had saved him!

She remembered her threat to him before they had gone down on the rocks together, and her evil wish. Those words had been very wicked; but since that she had risked her life to save his. They might say what they pleased of her, and do what they pleased. She knew what she knew.

Then the father raised his son's head and shoulders in his arms, and called on the others to assist him in carrying Barty towards the path. They raised him between them carefully and tenderly, and lifted their burden on towards the spot at which Mally was standing. She never moved, but watched them at their work; and the old man followed them, hobbling after them with his crutch.

When they had reached the end of the hut she looked upon Barty's face, and saw that it was very pale. There was no longer blood upon the forehead, but the great gash was to be seen there plainly, with its jagged cut, and the skin livid and blue round the orifice. His light brown hair was hanging back, as she had made it to hang when she had gathered it with her hand after the big wave had passed over them. Ah, how beautiful he was in Mally's eyes with that pale face, and the sad scar upon his brow! She turned her face away, that they might not see her tears; but she did not move, nor did she speak.

But now, when they had passed the end of the hut, shuffling along with their burden, she heard a sound which stirred her. She roused herself quickly from her leaning posture, and stretched forth her head as though to listen; then she moved to follow them. Yes, they had stopped at the bottom of the path, and had again laid the body on the rocks. She heard that sound again, as of a long, long sigh, and then, regardless of any of them, she ran to the wounded man's head.

'He is not dead,' she said. 'There; he is not dead.'

As she spoke Barty's eyes opened, and he looked about him.

'Barty, my boy, speak to me,' said the mother.

Barty turned his face upon his mother, smiled, and then stared about him wildly.

'How is it with thee, lad?' said his father. Then Barty turned his face again to the latter voice, and as he did so his eyes fell upon Mally.

'Mally!' he said, 'Mally!'

It could have wanted nothing further to any of those present to teach them that, according to Barty's own view of the case, Mally had not been his enemy; and, in truth, Mally herself wanted no further triumph. That word had vindicated her, and she withdrew back to the hut.

'Dada,' she said, 'Barty is not dead, and I'm thinking they won't say anything more about our hurting him.'

Old Glos shook his head. He was glad the lad hadn't met his death there; he didn't want the young man's blood, but he knew what folk would say. The poorer he was the more sure the world would be to trample on him. Mally said what she could to comfort him, being full of comfort herself.

She would have crept up to the farm if she dared, to ask how Barty was. But her courage failed her when she thought of that, so she went to work again, dragging back the weed she had saved to the spot at which on the morrow she would load the donkey. As she did this she saw Barty's pony still standing patiently under the rock; so she got a lock of fodder and threw it down before the beast.

It had become dark down in the cove, but she was still dragging back the seaweed, when she saw the glimmer of a lantern coming down the pathway. It was a most unusual sight, for lanterns were not common down in Malachi's Cove. Down came the lantern rather slowly,—much more slowly than she was in the habit of descending, and then through the gloom she saw the figure of a man standing at the bottom of the path. She went up to him, and saw that it was Mr Gunliffe, the father.

'Is that Mally?' said Gunliffe.

'Yes, it is Mally; and how is Barty, Mr Gunliffe?'

'You must come to 'un yourself, now at once,' said the farmer. 'He won't sleep a wink till he's seed you. You must not say but you'll come.'

'Sure I'll come if I'm wanted,' said Mally.

Gunliffe waited a moment, thinking that Mally might have to prepare herself, but Mally needed no preparation. She was dripping with salt water from the weed which she had been dragging, and her elfin locks were streaming wildly from her head; but, such as she was, she was ready.

'Dada's in bed,' she said, 'and I can go now if you please.'

Then Gunliffe turned round and followed her up the path, wondering at the life which this girl led so far away from all her sex. It was now dark night, and he had found her working at the very edge of the rolling waves by herself, in the darkness, while the only human being who might seem to be her protector had already gone to his bed.

When they were at the top of the cliff Gunliffe took her by her hand, and led her along. She did not comprehend this, but she made no attempt to take hand from his. Something he said about falling on the cliffs, but it was muttered so lowly that Mally hardly understood him. But in truth the man knew that she had saved his boy's life, and that he had injured her instead of thanking her. He was now taking her to his heart, and as words were wanting to him, he was showing his love after this silent fashion. He held her by the hand as though she were a child, and Mally tripped along at his side asking him no questions.

When they were at the farm-yard gate he stopped there for a moment.

'Mally, my girl,' he said, 'he'll not be content till he sees thee, but thou must not stay long wi' him, lass. Doctor says he's weak like, and wants sleep badly.'

Mally merely nodded her head, and then they entered the house. Mally had never been within it before, and looked about with wondering eyes at the furniture of the big kitchen. Did any idea of her future destiny flash upon her then, I wonder? But she did not pause here a moment, but was led up to the bedroom above stairs, where Barty was lying on his mother's bed.

'Is it Mally herself?' said the voice of the weak youth.

'It's Mally herself,' said the mother, 'so now you can say what you please.'

'Mally,' said he, 'Mally, it's along of you that I'm alive this moment.'

'I'll not forget it on her,' said the father, with his eyes turned away from her. 'I'll never forget it on her.'

'We hadn't a one but only him,' said the mother, with her apron up to her face.

'Mally, you'll be friends with me now?' said Barty.

To have been made lady of the manor of the cove for ever, Mally couldn't have spoken a word now. It was not only that the words and presence of the people there cowed her and made her speechless, but the big bed, and the looking-glass, and the unheard-of wonders of the chamber, made her feel her own insignificance. But she crept up to Barty's side, and put her hand upon his.

'I'll come and get the weed, Mally; but it shall all be for you,' said Barty.

'Indeed, you won't then, Barty dear,' said the mother; 'you'll never go near the awsome place again. What would we do if you were took from us?'

'He mustn't go near the hole if he does,' said Mally, speaking at last in a solemn voice, and imparting the knowledge which she had kept to herself while Barty was her enemy; ''specially not if the wind's any way from the nor'rard.'

'She'd better go down now,' said the father.

Barty kissed the hand which he held, and Mally, looking at him as he did so, thought that he was like an angel.

'You'll come and see us to-morrow, Mally?' said he.

To this she made no answer, but followed Mrs Gunliffe out of the room. When they were down in the kitchen the mother had tea for her, and thick milk, and a hot cake,—all the delicacies which the farm could afford. I don't know that Mally cared much for the eating and drinking that night, but she began to think that the Gunliffes were good people,—very good people. It was better thus, at any rate, than being accused of murder and carried off to Camelford prison.

'I'll never forget it on her—never,' the father had said.

Those words stuck to her from that moment, and seemed to sound in her ears all the night. How glad she was that Barty had come down to the cove,—oh, yes, how glad! There was no question of his dying now, and as for the blow on his forehead, what harm was that to a lad like him?

'But father shall go with you,' said Mrs Gunliffe, when Mally prepared to start for the cove by herself. Mally, however, would not hear of this. She could find her way to the cove whether it was light or dark.

'Mally, thou art my child now, and I shall think of thee so,' said the mother, as the girl went off by herself.

Mally thought of this, too, as she walked home. How could she become Mrs Gunliffe's child; ah, how?

I need not, I think, tell the tale any further. That Mally did become Mrs Gunliffe's child, and how she became so the reader will understand; and in process of time the big kitchen and all the wonders of the farm-house were her own. The people said that Barty Gunliffe had married a mermaid out of the sea; but when it was said in Mally's hearing I doubt whether she liked it; and when Barty himself would call her a mermaid she would frown at him, and throw about her black hair, and pretend to cuff him with her little hand.

Old Glos was brought up to the top of the cliff, and lived his few remaining days under the roof of Mr Gunliffe's house; and as for the cove and the right of seaweed, from that time forth all that has been supposed to attach itself to Gunliffe's farm, and I do not know that any of the neighbours are prepared to dispute the right.

A Day of Days

Mr Herbert Moore, a gentleman of the highest note in the scientific world, and a childless widower, finding himself at last unable to reconcile his sedentary habits with the management of a household, had invited his only sister to come and superintend his domestic affairs. Miss Adela Moore had assented the more willingly to his proposal as by her mother's death she had recently been left without a formal protector. She was twenty-five years of age, and was a very active member of what she and her friends called society. She was almost equally at home in the best company of three great cities, and she had encountered most of the adventures which await a young girl on the threshold of life. She had become rather hastily and imprudently engaged, but she had eventually succeeded in disengaging herself. She had spent a summer or two in Europe, and she had made a voyage to Cuba with a dear friend in the last stage of consumption, who had died at the hotel in Havana. Although by no means perfectly beautiful in person she was yet thoroughly pleasing, rejoicing in what young ladies are fond of calling an *air*; that is, she was tall and slender, with a long neck, a low forehead, and a handsome nose. Even after six years of the best company, too, she still had excellent manners. She was, moreover, mistress of a very pretty little fortune, and was accounted clever without detriment to her amiability and amiable without detriment to her wit. These facts, as the reader will allow, might have ensured her the very best prospects; but he has seen that she had found herself willing to forfeit her prospects and bury herself in the country. It seemed to her that she had seen enough of the world and of human nature, and that a period of seclusion might yield a fine refreshment. She had begun to suspect that for a girl of her age she was unduly old and wise—and, what is more, to suspect that others suspected as much. A great observer of life and manners, so far as her opportunities went, she conceived that it behoved

71

her to organise the results of her observation into principles of conduct and belief. She was becoming—so she argued—too impersonal, too critical, too intelligent, too contemplative, too just. A woman had no business to be so just. The society of nature, of the great expansive skies and the primeval woods, would check the morbid development of her brain-power. She would spend her time in the fields and merely vegetate; walk and ride, and read the old-fashioned books in Herbert's library.

She found her brother established in a very pretty house, at about a mile's distance from the nearest town, and at about six miles' distance from another town, the seat of a small but ancient college, before which he delivered a weekly lecture. She had seen so little of him of late years that his acquaintance was almost to make; but there were no barriers to break down. Herbert Moore was one of the simplest and least aggressive of men, and one of the most patient and conscientious of students. He had had a vague notion that Adela was a young woman of extravagant pleasures, and that, somehow, on her arrival, his house would be overrun with the train of her attendant revellers. It was not until after they had been six months together that he became aware that his sister led almost an ascetic life. By the time six more months had passed Adela had recovered a delightful sense of youth and *naïveté*. She learned, under her brother's tuition, to walk—nay, to climb, for there were great hills in the neighbourhood—to ride and to botanise. At the end of a year, in the month of August, she received a visit from an old friend, a girl of her own age, who had been spending July at a watering-place, and who was now about to be married. Adela had begun to fear that she had declined into an almost irreclaimable rusticity and had rubbed off the social facility, the 'knowledge of the world' for which she was formerly distinguished; but a week spent in intimate conversation with her friend convinced her not only that she had not forgotten much that she had feared, but had also not forgotten much that she had hoped. For this, and other reasons, her friend's departure left her slightly depressed. She felt lonely and even a little elderly—she had lost another illusion. Laura Benton, for whom a year ago she had entertained a serious regard, now impressed her as a very flimsy little person, who talked about her lover with almost indecent flippancy.

Meanwhile, September was slowly running its course. One morning Mr Moore took a hasty breakfast and started to catch the train for

Slowfield, whither a scientific conference called him, which might, he said, release him that afternoon in time for dinner at home, or might, on the other hand, detain him till the night. It was almost the first time during the term of Adela's rustication that she had been left alone for several hours. Her brother's quiet presence was inappreciable enough; yet now that he was at a distance she felt a singular sense of freedom: a return of that condition of early childhood when, through some domestic catastrophe, she had for an infinite morning been left to her own devices. What should she do? she asked herself, with the smile that she reserved for her maidenly monologues. It was a good day for work, but it was a still better one for play. Should she drive into town and call on a lot of tiresome local people? Should she go into the kitchen and try her hand at a pudding for dinner? She felt a delectable longing to do something illicit, to play with fire, to discover some Bluebeard's closet. But poor Herbert was no Bluebeard; if she were to burn down his house he would exact no amends. Adela went out to the verandah, and, sitting down on the steps, gazed across the country. It was apparently the last day of summer. The sky was faintly blue; the woody hills were putting on the morbid colours of autumn; the great pine-grove behind the house seemed to have caught and imprisoned the protesting breezes. Looking down the road toward the village, it occurred to Adela that she might have a visit, and so human was her mood that if any of the local people were to come to her she felt it was in her to humour them. As the sun rose higher she went in and established herself with a piece of embroidery in a deep bow-window, in the second story, which, betwixt its muslin curtains and its external framework of high-creeping plants, commanded most insidiously the principal approach to the house. While she drew her threads she surveyed the road with a deepening conviction that she was destined to have a caller. The air was warm, yet not hot; the dust had been laid during the night by a gentle rain. It had been from the first a source of complaint among Adela's new friends that she was equally gracious to all men, and, what was more remarkable, to all women. Not only had she dedicated herself to no friendships, but she had committed herself to no preferences. Nevertheless, it was with an imagination by no means severely impartial that she sat communing with her open casement. She had very soon made up her mind that, to answer the requirements of the hour, her visitor must be of a sex as different as possible from her own; and as, thanks to the few differences in favour of any individual she had been able to discover among the young males of the country-side, her roll-call in this her hour of need was limited to a single name, so her thoughts were now centred upon the bearer of that name, Mr Weatherby Pynsent, the Unitarian minister. If instead of being Miss Moore's story this were Mr Pynsent's, it might easily be condensed into the simple statement that he was very far gone indeed. Although affiliated to a richer ceremonial than his own she had been so well pleased with one of his sermons, to which she had allowed herself to lend a tolerant ear, that, meeting him some time afterward, she had received him with what she considered a rather knotty doctrinal question; whereupon, gracefully waiving the question, he had asked permission to call upon her and talk over her 'difficulties'. This short interview had enshrined her in the young minister's heart; and the half a dozen occasions on which he had subsequently contrived to see her had each contributed another candle to her altar. It is but fair to add, however, that, although a captive, Mr Pynsent was as yet no captor. He was simply an honourable young parson, who happened at this moment to be the most sympathetic companion within reach. Adela, at twenty-five years of age, had both a past and a future. Mr Pynsent reminded her of the one and gave her a foretaste of the other.

So, at last, when, as the morning waned toward noon, Adela descried in the distance a man's figure treading the grassy margin of the road, and swinging his stick as he came, she smiled to herself with some complacency. But even while she smiled she became conscious that her heart was beating quite idiotically. She rose, and, resenting her gratuitous emotion, stood for a moment half resolved to see no one at all. As she did so she glanced along the road again. Her friend had drawn nearer, and as the distance lessened she began to perceive that he was not her friend. Before many moments her doubts were removed; the gentleman was a stranger. In front of the house three roads went their different ways, and a spreading elm, tall and slim, like the feathery sheaf of a gleaner, with an ancient bench beneath it, made an informal *rond-point*. The stranger came along the opposite side of the highway, and when he reached the elm stopped and looked about him, as if to verify some direction that had been given him. Then he deliberately crossed over. Adela had time to see, unseen, that he was a robust young man, with a bearded chin and a soft white hat. After the due interval Becky the maid came up with a card somewhat rudely superscribed in pencil:

THOMAS LUDLOW,
New York

Turning it over in her fingers, Adela saw the gentleman had made use of the reverse of a pasteboard abstracted from the basket on her own drawing-room table. The printed name on the other side was dashed out; it ran: *Mr Weatherby Pynsent.*

'He asked me to give you this, ma'am,' said Becky. 'He helped himself to it out of the tray.'

'Did he ask for me by name?'

'No, ma'am; he asked for Mr Moore. When I told him Mr Moore was away, he asked for some of the family. I told him you was all the family, ma'am.'

'Very well,' said Adela, 'I will go down.' But, begging her pardon, we will precede her by a few steps.

Tom Ludlow, as his friends called him, was a young man of twenty-eight, concerning whom you might have heard the most various opinions; for, as far as he was known (which, indeed, was not very far), he was at once one of the best liked and one of the best hated of men. Born in one of the lower walks of New York life, he still seemed always to move in his native element. A certain crudity of manner and aspect proved him to belong to the great vulgar, muscular, popular majority. On this basis, however, he was a sufficiently good-looking fellow: a middle-sized, agile figure, a head so well shaped as to be handsome, a pair of inquisitive, responsive eyes, and a large, manly mouth, constituting the most expressive part of his equipment. Turned upon the world at an early age, he had, in the pursuit of a subsistence, tried his head at everything in succession, and had generally found it to be quite as hard as the opposing substance; and his person may have been thought to reflect this experience in an air of taking success too much for granted. He was a man of strong faculties and a strong will, but it is doubtful whether his feelings were stronger than he. People liked him for his directness, his good-humour, his general soundness and serviceableness, and disliked him for the same qualities under different names; that

75

is, for his impudence, his offensive optimism, his inhuman avidity for facts. When his friends insisted upon his noble disinterestedness, his enemies were wont to reply it was all very well to ignore, to suppress, one's own sensibilities in the pursuit of knowledge, but to trample on the rest of mankind at the same time betrayed an excess of zeal. Fortunately for Ludlow, on the whole, he was no great listener, and even if he had been, a certain plebeian thick-skinnedness would always have saved his tenderer parts; although it must be added that, if, like a genuine democrat, he was very insensitive, like a genuine democrat, too, he was unexpectedly pound. His tastes, which had always been for the natural sciences, had recently led him to the study of fossil remains, the branch cultivated by Herbert Moore; and it was upon business connected with this pursuit that, after a short correspondence, he had now come to see him.

As Adela went to him he came out from the window, where he had been looking at the lawn. She acknowledged the friendly nod which he apparently intended for a greeting.

'Miss Moore, I believe,' said Ludlow.

'Miss Moore,' said Adela.

'I beg your pardon for this intrusion, but as I have come from a distance to see Mr Moore, on business, I thought I might venture either to ask at headquarters how he may most easily be reached, or even to give you a message for him.' These words were accompanied with a smile under the influence of which it had been written on the scroll of Adela's fate that she was to descend from her pedestal.

'Pray make no apologies,' she said. 'We hardly recognise such a thing as intrusion in this simple little place. Won't you sit down? My brother went away only this morning, and I expect him back this afternoon.'

'This afternoon? indeed. In that case I believe I'll wait. It was very stupid of me not to have dropped a word beforehand. But I have been in the city all summer long, and I shall not be sorry to squeeze a little vacation out of this business. I'm tremendously fond of the country, and I have been working for many months in a musty museum.'

'It's possible that my brother may not come home until the evening,' Adela said. 'He was uncertain. You might go to him at Slowfield.'

Ludlow reflected a moment, with his eyes on his hostess. 'If he does return in the afternoon, at what hour will he arrive?'

'Well, about three.'

'And my own train leaves at four. Allow him a quarter of an hour to come from town and myself a quarter of an hour to get there (if he would give me his vehicle back). In that case I should have about half an hour to see him. We couldn't do much talk, but I could ask him the essential questions. I wish chiefly to ask him for some letters—letters of recommendation to some foreign scientists. He is the only man in this country who knows how much I know. It seems a pity to take two superfluous—that is, possibly superfluous—railway-journeys of an hour apiece; for I should probably come back with him, don't you think so?' he asked, very frankly.

'You know best,' said Adela. 'I am not particularly fond of the journey to Slowfield, even when it's absolutely necessary.'

'Yes; and then this is such a lovely day for a good long ramble in the fields. That's a thing I haven't had since I don't know when. I guess I'll remain.' And he placed his hat on the floor beside him.

'I am afraid, now that I think of it,' said Adela, 'that there is no train until so late an hour that you would have very little time left on your arrival to talk with my brother, before the hour at which he himself might have determined to start for home. It's true that you might induce him to stop over till the evening.'

'Dear me! I shouldn't want to do that. It might be very inconvenient for Mr Moore, don't you see? Besides, I shouldn't have time. And then I always like to see a man in his home—or at some place of my own; a man, that is, whom I have any regard for—and I have a very great regard for your brother, Miss Moore. When men meet at a half way house neither feels at his ease. And then this is such an attractive country residence of yours,' pursued Ludlow, looking about him.

'Yes, it's a very pretty place,' said Adela.

Ludlow got up and walked to the window. 'I want to look at your view,' he remarked. 'A lovely little spot. You are a happy woman, Miss Moore, to have the beauties of nature always before your eyes.'

'Yes, if pretty scenery can make one happy, I ought to be happy.' And Adela was glad to regain her feet and stand on the other side of the table, before the window.

'Don't you think it can?' asked Ludlow, turning round. 'I don't know, though; perhaps it can't. Ugly sights can't make you unhappy, necessarily. I have been working for a year in one of the narrowest, darkest, dirtiest, busiest streets in New York, with rusty bricks and muddy gutters for scenery. But I think I can hardly set up to be miserable. I wish I could! It might be a claim on your benevolence.' As he said these words he stood leaning against the window-gutter, outside the curtain, with folded arms. The morning light covered his face, and, mingled with that of his radiant laugh, showed Adela that his was a nature very much alive.

'Whatever else he may be,' she said to herself, as she stood within the shade of the other curtain, playing with the paper-knife, which she had plucked from the table, 'I think he is honest. I am afraid he isn't a gentleman—but he isn't a bore.' She met his eye, freely, for a moment. 'What do you want of my benevolence?' she asked, with an abruptness of which she was perfectly conscious. 'Does he wish to make friends,' she pursued, tacitly, 'or does he merely wish to pay me a vulgar compliment? There is bad taste, perhaps, in either case, but especially in the latter.' Meanwhile her visitor had already answered her.

'What do I want of your benevolence? Why, what does one want of any pleasant thing in life?'

'Dear me, if you never have anything pleasanter than that!' our heroine exclaimed.

'It will do very well for the present occasion,' said the young man, blushing, in a large masculine way, at his own quickness of repartee.

Adela glanced toward the clock on the chimney-piece. She was curious to measure the duration of the acquaintance with this breezy invader of her privacy, with whom she so suddenly found herself bandying jokes so personal. She had known him some eight minutes.

Ludlow observed her movement. 'I am interrupting you and detaining you from your own affairs,' he said; and he moved toward his hat. 'I suppose I must bid you good-morning.' And he picked it up.

Adela stood at the table and watched him cross the room. To express a very delicate feeling in terms comparatively crude, she was loath to see him depart. She divined, too, that he was very sorry to go. The knowledge of this feeling on his side, however, affected her composure but slightly. The truth is—we say it with respect—Adela was an old hand. She was modest, honest and wise; but, as we have said, she had a past—a past of which importunate swains in the guise of morning-callers had been no inconsiderable part; and a great dexterity in what may be called outflanking these gentlemen was one of her registered accomplishments. Her liveliest emotion at present, therefore, was less one of annoyance at her companion than of surprise at her own mansuetude, which was yet undeniable. 'Am I dreaming?' she asked herself. She looked out of the window, and then back at Ludlow, who stood grasping his hat and stick, contemplating her face. Should she give him leave to remain? 'He is honest,' she repeated; 'why should I not be honest for once? I am sorry you are in a hurry,' she said, aloud.

'I am in no hurry,' he answered.

Adela turned her face to the window again, and toward the opposite hills. There was a moment's pause.

'I thought *you* were in a hurry,' said Ludlow.

Adela shifted her eyes back to where they could see him. 'My brother would be very glad that you should stay as long as you like. He would expect me to offer you what little hospitality is in my power.'

'Pray, offer it then.'

'That is very easily done. This is the parlour, and there, beyond the hall, is my brother's study. Perhaps you would like to look at his books and collections. I know nothing about them, and I should be a very poor guide. But you are welcome to go in and use your discretion in examining what may interest you.'

'This, I take it, would be but another way of separating from you.'

'For the present, yes.'

'But I hesitate to take such liberties with your brother's things as you recommend.'

'Recommend? I recommend nothing.'

'But if I decline to penetrate into Mr Moore's sanctum, what alternative remains?'

'Really—you must make your own alternative.'

'I think you mentioned the parlour. Suppose I choose that.'

'Just as you please. Here are some books, and if you like I will bring you some periodicals. There are ever so many scientific papers. Can I serve you in any other way? Are you tired by your walk? Would you like a glass of wine?'

'Tired by my walk?—not exactly. You are very kind, but I feel no immediate desire for a glass of wine. I think you needn't trouble yourself about scientific periodicals either. I am not exactly in the mood to read.' And Ludlow pulled out his watch and compared it with the clock. 'I am afraid your clock is fast.'

'Yes,' said Adela; 'very likely.'

'Some ten minutes. Well, I suppose I had better be walking.' And, coming toward Adela, he extended his hand.

She gave him hers. 'It is a day of days for a long, slow ramble,' she said.

Ludlow's only rejoinder was his hand-shake. He moved slowly toward the door, half accompanied by Adela. 'Poor fellow!' she said to herself. There was a summer-door, composed of lattices painted green, like a shutter; it admitted into the hall a cool, dusky light, in which Adela looked pale. Ludlow pushed its wings apart with his stick, and disclosed a landscape, long, deep, and bright, framed by the pillars of the porch. He stopped on the threshold, swinging his cane. 'I hope I shall not lose my way,' he said.

'I hope not. My brother will not forgive me if you do.'

Ludlow's brows were slightly contracted by a frown, but he contrived to smile with his lips. 'When shall I come back?' he asked, abruptly.

Adela found but a low tone—almost a whisper—at her command to answer—'Whenever you please.'

The young man turned round, with his back to the bright doorway, and looked into Adela's face, which was now covered with light. 'Miss Moore,' said he, 'it's very much against my will that I leave you at all!'

Adela stood debating within herself. After all, what if her companion should stay with her? It would, under the circumstances, be an adventure; but was an adventure necessarily a criminal thing? It lay wholly with herself to decide. She was her own mistress, and she had hitherto been a just mistress. Might she not for once be a generous one? The reader will observe in Adela's meditation the recurrence of this saving clause 'for once'. It was produced by the simple fact that she had begun the day in a romantic mood. She was prepared to be interested; and now that an interesting phenomenon had presented itself, that it stood before her in vivid human—nay, manly—shape, instinct with reciprocity, was she to close her hand to the liberality of fate? To do so would be only to expose herself the more, for it would imply a gratuitous insult to human nature. Was not the man before her redolent of good intentions, and was that not enough? He was not what Adela had been used to call a gentleman; at this conviction she had arrived by a rapid diagonal, and now it served as a fresh starting-point. 'I have seen all the gentlemen can show me' (this was her syllogism): 'let us try something new! I see no reason why you should run away so fast, Mr Ludlow,' she said, aloud.

'I think it would be the greatest piece of folly I ever committed!' cried the young man.

'I think it would be rather a pity,' Adela remarked.

'And you invite me into your parlour again? I come as *your* visitor, you know. I was your brother's before. It's a simple enough matter. We are old friends. We have a solid common ground in your brother. Isn't that about it?'

'You may adopt whatever theory you please. To my mind it is indeed a very simple matter.'

'Oh, but I wouldn't have it too simple,' said Ludlow, with a genial smile.

'Have it as you please!'

Ludlow leaned back against the doorway. 'Look here, Miss Moore; your kindness makes me as gentle as a little child. I am passive; I am in your hands; do with me what you please. I can't help contrasting my fate with what it might have been but for you. A quarter of an hour ago I was ignorant of your existence; you were not in my programme. I had no idea your brother had a sister. When your servant spoke of "Miss Moore", upon my word I expected something rather elderly— something venerable—some rigid old lady, who would say, "exactly", and "very well, sir", and leave me to spend the rest of the morning tilting back in a chair on the piazza of the hotel. It shows what fools we are to attempt to forecast the future.'

'We must not let our imagination run away with us in any direction,' said Adela, sententiously.

'Imagination? I don't believe I have any. No, madam'—and Ludlow straightened himself up—'I live in the present. I write my programme from hour to hour—or, at any rate, I will in the future.'

'I think you are very wise,' said Adela. 'Suppose you write a programme for the present hour. What shall we do? It seems to me a pity

to spend so lovely a morning indoors. There is something in the air—
I can't imagine what—which seems to say it is the last day of summer.
We ought to commemorate it. How should you like to take a walk?'
Adela had decided that, to reconcile her aforesaid benevolence with the
proper maintenance of her dignity, her only course was to be the perfect hostess. This decision made, very naturally and gracefully she played
her part. It was the one possible part; and yet it did not preclude those
delicate sensations with which so rare an episode seem charged: it simply legitimated them. A romantic adventure on so conventional a basis
would assuredly hurt no one.

'I should like a walk very much,' said Ludlow; 'a walk with a halt at
the end of it.'

'Well, if you will consent to a short halt at the beginning of it,' Adela
rejoined, 'I will be with you in a very few minutes.' When she returned,
in her little hat and jacket, she found her friend seated on the steps of
the verandah. He arose and gave her a card.

'I have been requested, in your absence, to hand you this.'

Adela read with some compunction the name of Mr Weatherby
Pynsent.

'Has he been here?' she asked. 'Why didn't he come in?'

'I told him you were not at home. If it wasn't true then, it was going
to be true so soon that the interval was hardly worth taking account of.
He addressed himself to me, as I seemed from my position to be quite
in possession; that is, I put myself in his way, as it were, so that he had
to speak to me: but I confess he looked at me as if he doubted my word.
He hesitated as to whether he should confide his name to me, or whether
he should ring for the servant. I think he wished to show me that he
suspected my veracity, for he was making rather grimly for the doorbell
when I, fearing that once inside the house he might encounter the living
truth, informed him in the most good-humoured tone possible that I
would take charge of his little tribute, if he would trust me with it.'

'It seems to me, Mr Ludlow, that you are a strangely unscrupulous
man. How did you know that Mr Pynsent's business was not urgent?'

'I didn't know it! But I knew it could be no more urgent than mine.
Depend upon it, Miss Moore, you have no case against me. I only
pretend to be a man; to have admitted that sweet little cleric—isn't he
a cleric, eh?—would have been the act of an angel.'

Adela was familiar with a sequestered spot, in the very heart of the fields, as it seemed to her, to which she now proposed to conduct her friend. The point was to select a goal neither too distant nor too near, and to adopt a pace neither too rapid nor too slow. But although Adela's happy valley was at least two miles away, and they had dawdled immensely over the interval, yet their arrival at a certain little rustic gate, beyond which the country grew vague and gently wild, struck Adela as sudden. Once on the road she felt a precipitate conviction that there could be no evil in an excursion so purely pastoral and no guile in a spirit so deeply sensitive to the influences of nature, and to the melancholy aspect of incipient autumn, as that of her companion. A man with an unaffected relish for small children is a man to inspire young women with a confidence; and so, in a less degree, a man with a genuine feeling for the unsophisticated beauties of a casual New England landscape may not unreasonably be regarded by the daughters of the scene as a person whose motives are pure. Adela was a great observer of the clouds, the trees, and the streams, the sounds and colours, the transparent airs and blue horizons of her adopted home; and she was reassured by Ludlow's appreciation of these modest phenomena. His enjoyment of them, deep as it was, however, had to struggle against the sensuous depression natural to a man who has spent the summer looking over dry specimens in a laboratory, and against an impediment of a less material order—the feeling that Adela was a remarkably attractive woman. Still, naturally a great talker, he uttered his various satisfactions with abundant humour and point. Adela felt that he was decidedly a companion for the open air—he was a man to make use even to abuse, of the wide horizon and the high ceiling of nature. The freedom of his gestures, the sonority of his voice, the keenness of his vision, the general vivacity of his manners, seemed to necessitate and to justify a universal absence of resisting surfaces. They passed through the little gate and wandered over empty pastures, until the ground began to rise, and stony surfaces to crop through the turf; when, after a short ascent, they reached a broad plateau, covered with boulders and shrubs, which lost itself on one side in a short, steep cliff, whence fields and marshes stretched down to the opposite river, and on the other, in scattered clumps of cedar and maple, which gradually thickened and multiplied, until the horizon in that quarter was purple with mild masses of forest.

Here was both sun and shade—the unobstructed sky, or the whispering dome of a circle of trees which had always reminded Adela of the stone-pines of the Villa Borghese. Adela led the way to a sunny seat among the rocks which commanded the course of the river, where the murmuring cedars would give them a kind of human company.

'It has always seemed to me that the wind in the trees is always the voice of coming changes,' Ludlow said.

'Perhaps it is,' Adela replied. 'The trees are for ever talking in this melancholy way, and men are for ever changing.'

'Yes, but they can only be said to express the foreboding of coming events—that is what I mean—when there is someone there to hear them; and more especially someone in whose life a change is, to his knowledge, about to take place. Then they are quite prophetic. Don't you know Longfellow says so?'

'Yes, I know Longfellow says so. But you seem to speak from your own inspiration.'

'Well, I rather think I do.'

'Is there some great change hanging over you?'

'Yes, rather an important one.'

'I believe that's what men say when they are going to be married,' said Adela.

'I am going to be divorced, rather. I am going to Europe.'

'Indeed! soon?'

'To-morrow,' said Ludlow, after an instant's pause.

'Oh!' exclaimed Adela. 'How I envy you!'

Ludlow, who sat looking over the cliff and tossing stones down into the plain, observed a certain inequality in the tone of his companion's two exclamations. The first was nature, the second art. He turned his eyes upon her, but she had directed hers away into the distance. Then, for a moment, he retreated within himself and thought. He rapidly surveyed his position. Here was he, Tom Ludlow, a hard-headed son of toil; without fortune, without credit, without antecedents, whose lot was cast exclusively with vulgar males, and who had never had a mother, a sister, nor a well-bred sweetheart, to pitch his voice for the feminine tympanum, who had seldom come nearer an indubitable lady than, in a favouring crowd, to receive a mechanical 'thank you' (as if he were a policeman) for some accidental assistance: here he found himself up to his neck in a sudden pastoral with a young woman who was evidently altogether superior. That it was in him to enjoy the society of such a person (provided, of course, she were not a chit) he very well knew; but he had never happened to suppose that he should find it open to him. Was he now to infer that this brilliant gift was his—the gift of which is called in the relation between the sexes success? The inference was at least logical. He had made a good impression. Why else should an eminently discriminating girl have fraternised with him at such a rate? It was with a little thrill of satisfaction that Ludlow reflected upon the directness of his course. 'It all comes back to my old theory that a process can't be too simple. I used no arts. In such an enterprise I shouldn't have known where to begin. It was my ignorance of the regular way that saved me. Women like a gentleman, of course; but they like a man better.' It was the little touch of nature he had detected in Adela's tone that set him thinking; but as compared with the frankness of his own attitude it betrayed after all no undue emotion. Ludlow had accepted the fact of his adaptability to the idle mood of a cultivated woman in a thoroughly rational spirit, and he was not now tempted to exaggerate its bearings. He was not the man to be intoxicated by a triumph after all possibly superficial. 'If Miss Moore is so wise—or so foolish—as to like me half an hour for what I am, she is welcome,' he said to himself. 'Assuredly,' he added, as he glanced at her intelligent profile, 'she will not like me for what I am not.' It needs a woman, however, far more intelligent than (thank heaven!) most women are—more intelligent, certainly, than Adela was—to guard her happiness against a clever man's consistent assumption of her intelligence; and doubtless it was from a sense of this general truth that, as Ludlow continued to observe his companion, he felt an emotion of manly tenderness. 'I wouldn't offend her for the world,' he thought. Just then Adela, conscious of his contemplation, looked about; and before he knew it, Ludlow had repeated aloud, 'Miss Moore, I wouldn't offend you for the world.'

Adela eyed him for a moment with a little flush that subsided into a smile. 'To what dreadful impertinence is that the prelude?' she inquired.

'It's a prelude to nothing. It refers to the past—to any possible displeasure I may have caused you.'

'Your scruples are unnecessary, Mr Ludlow. If you had given me

offence, I should not have left you to apologise for it. I should not have
left the matter to occur to you as you sat dreaming charitably in the
sun.'

'What would you have done?'

'Done? nothing. You don't imagine I would have scolded you—or
snubbed you—or answered you back, I take it. I would have left undone—what, I can't tell you. Ask yourself what I *have* done. I am sure
I hardly know myself,' said Adela, with some intensity. 'At all events,
here I am sitting with you in the fields, as if you were a friend of many
years. Why do you speak of offence?' And Adela (an uncommon accident with her) lost command of her voice, which trembled ever so
slightly. 'What an odd thought! why should you offend me? Do I seem
so open to that sort of thing?' Her colour had deepened again, and her
eyes had brightened. She had forgotten herself, and before speaking
had not, as was her wont, sought counsel of that staunch conservative,
her taste. She had spoken from a full heart—a heart which had been
filling rapidly, since the outset of their walk, with a feeling almost passionate in its quality, and which that little puff of the actual conveyed
in Mr Ludlow's announcement of his departure had caused to overflow.
The reader may give this feeling whatever name he chooses. We will
content ourselves with saying that Adela had played with fire so effectually that she had been scorched. The slight violence of the speech just
quoted may represent her sensation of pain.

'You pull one up rather short, Miss Moore,' said Ludlow. 'A man
says the best he can.'

Adela made no reply—for a moment she hung her head. Was she to
cry out because she was hurt? Was she to thrust her injured heart into
a company in which there was, as yet at least, no question of hearts?
No! here our reserved and contemplative heroine is herself again. Her
part was still to be the youthful woman of the world, the perfect young
lady. For our own part, we can imagine no figure more engaging than
this civilised and disciplined personage under such circumstances; and
if Adela had been the most accomplished of coquettes she could not
have assumed a more becoming expression than the air of judicious
consideration which now covered her features. But having paid this
generous homage to propriety, she felt free to suffer in secret. Raising
her eyes from the ground, she abruptly addressed her companion.

'By the way, Mr Ludlow, tell me something about yourself.'

Ludlow burst into a laugh. 'What shall I tell you?'

'Everything.'

'Everything? Excuse me, I'm not such a fool. But do you know that's a very tempting request you make? I suppose I ought to blush and hesitate; but I never yet blushed or hesitated in the right place.'

'Very good. There is one fact. Continue. Begin at the beginning.'

'Well, let me see. My name you know. I am twenty-eight years old.'

'That's the end,' said Adela.

'But you don't want the history of my babyhood, I take it. I imagine that I was a very big, noisy, ugly baby—what's called a "splendid infant". My parents were poor, and of course, honest. They belonged to a very different set—or "sphere", I suppose you call it—from any you probably know. They were working people. My father was a chemist, in a small way of business, and I suspect my mother was not above using her hands to turn a penny. But although I don't remember her, I am sure she was a good, sound woman; I feel her occasionally in my own sinews. I myself have been at work all my life, and a very good worker I am, let me tell you. I am not patient, as I imagine your brother to be—although I have more patience than you might suppose—but I don't let go easily. If I strike you as very egotistical, remember 'twas you began it. I don't know whether I am clever, and I don't much care; that's a kind of metaphysical, sentimental, vapid word. But I know what I want to know, and I generally manage to find it out. I don't know much about my moral nature; I have no doubt I am beastly selfish. Still, I don't like to hurt people's feelings, and I am rather fond of poetry and flowers. I don't believe I am very "high-toned", all the same. I should not be at all surprised to discover I was prodigiously conceited; but I am afraid the discovery wouldn't cut me down much. I am remarkably hard to keep down, I know. Oh, you would think me a great brute if you knew me. I shouldn't recommend anyone to count too much on my being of an amiable disposition. I am often very much bored with people who are fond of me—because some of them are, really; so I am afraid I am ungrateful. Of course, as a man speaking to a woman, there's nothing for it but to say I am very low; but I hate to talk about things you can't prove. I have got very little "general culture", you know, but first and last I have read a great many books—and, thank heaven, I remember things. And I have some tastes, too. I am very fond of music. I have a good young voice of my own; *that* I can't help knowing; and I am not one to be bullied about pictures. I know how to sit on a horse, and how to row a boat. Is that enough? I am conscious of a great inability to say anything to the point. To put myself in a nutshell, I am a greedy specialist—and not a bad fellow. Still, I am only what I am—a very common creature.'

'Do you call yourself a very common creature because you really believe yourself to be one, or because you are weakly tempted to disfigure your rather flattering catalogue with a great final blot?'

'I am sure I don't know. You show more subtlety in that one question than I have shown in a whole string of affirmations. You women are strong on asking embarrassing questions. Seriously, I believe I *am* second-rate. I wouldn't make such an admission to every one though. But to you, Miss Moore, who sit there under your parasol as impartial as the muse of history, to you I owe the truth. I am no man of genius. There is something I miss; some final distinction I lack; you may call it what you please. Perhaps it's humility. Perhaps you can find it in Ruskin, somewhere. Perhaps it's delicacy—perhaps it's imagination. I am very vulgar, Miss Moore. I am the vulgar son of vulgar people. I use the word, of course, in its literal sense. So much I grant you at the outset, but it's my last concession!'

'Your concessions are smaller than they sound. Have you any sisters?'

'Not a sister; and no brothers, nor cousins, nor uncles, nor aunts.'

'And you sail for Europe to-morrow?'

'To-morrow, at ten o'clock.'

'To be away how long?'

'As long as I can. Five years, if possible.'

'What do you expect to do in those five years?'

'Well, study.'

'Nothing but study?'

'It will all come back to that, I guess. I hope to enjoy myself considerably, and to look at the world as I go. But I must not waste time; I am growing old.'

'Where are you going?'

'To Berlin. I wanted to get some letters of introduction from your brother.'

'Have you money? Are you well off?'

'Well off? Not I, heaven forgive me! I am very poor. I have in hand a little money that has just come to me from an unexpected quarter: an old debt owing my father. It will take me to Germany and keep me for six months. After that I shall work my way.'

'Are you happy? Are you contented?'

'Just now I am pretty comfortable, thank you.'

'But shall you be so when you get to Berlin?'

'I don't promise to be contented; but I am pretty sure to be happy.'

'Well,' said Adela, 'I sincerely hope you will succeed in everything.'

'Thank you, awfully,' said Ludlow.

Of what more was said at this moment no record may be given here. The reader has been put into possession of the key of our friends' conversation; it is only needful to say that in this key it was prolonged for half an hour more. As the minutes elapsed Adela found herself drifting further and further away from her anchorage. When at last she compelled herself to consult her watch and remind her companion that there remained but just time enough for them to reach home in antici- pation of her brother's arrival, she knew that she was rapidly floating seaward. As she descended the hill at her companion's side she felt herself suddenly thrilled by an acute temptation. Her first instinct was to close her eyes upon it, in the trust that when she should open them again it would have vanished; but she found that it was not to be so uncompromisingly dismissed. It pressed her so hard that before she walked a mile homeward she had succumbed to it, or had at least given it the pledge of that quickening of the heart which accompanies a bold resolution. This little sacrifice allowed her no breath for idle words, and she accordingly advanced with a bent and listening head. Ludlow marched along, with no apparent diminution of his habitual buoyancy of mien, talking as fast and loud as at the outset. He risked a prophecy that Mr Moore would not have returned, and charged Adela with a comical message of regrets. Adela had begun by wondering whether the approach of their separation had wrought within him any sentimen- tal depression at all commensurate with her own, with that which sealed her lips and weighed upon her heart; and now she was debating as to whether his express declaration that he felt 'awfully blue' ought neces- sarily to remove her doubts. Ludlow followed up this declaration with a very pretty review of the morning, and a leave-taking speech which, whether intensely sincere or not, struck Adela as at least in very good taste. He might be a common creature—but he was certainly a very uncommon one. When they reached the garden-gate it was with a fluttering heart that Adela scanned the premises for some accidental sign of her brother's presence. She felt that there would be an especial fitness in his not having returned. She led the way in. The hall table was bare of his usual hat and overcoat, his silver-headed stick was not in the corner. The only object that struck her was Mr Pynsent's card, which she had deposited there on her exit. All that was represented by that little white ticket seemed a thousand miles away. She looked for Mr Moore in his study, but it was empty.

As Adela went back from her quest into the drawing-room she simply shook her head at Ludlow, who was standing before the fire-place; and as she did so she caught her reflection in the mantel-glass. 'Verily,' she said to herself, 'I have travelled far.' She had pretty well unlearned her old dignities and forms, but she was to break with them still more completely. It was with a singular hardihood that she prepared to redeem the little pledge which had been extorted from her on her way home. She felt that there was no trial to which her generosity might now be called which she would not hail with enthusiasm. Unfortunately, her generosity was not likely to be challenged; although she nevertheless had the satisfaction of assuring herself at this moment that, like the mercy of the Lord, it was infinite. Should she satisfy herself of her friend's? or should she leave it delightfully uncertain? These had been the terms of what has been called her temptation, at the foot of the hill.

'Well, I have very little time,' said Ludlow; 'I must get my dinner and pay my bill and drive to the train.' And he put out his hand.

Adela gave him her own, without meeting his eyes. 'You are in a great hurry,' she said, rather casually.

'It's not I who am in a hurry. It's my confounded destiny. It's the train and the steamer.'

'If you really wished to stay you wouldn't be bullied by the train and the steamer.'

'Very true—very true. But *do* I really wish to stay?'

'That's the question. That's exactly what I want to know.'

'You ask difficult questions, Miss Moore.'

'Difficult for me—yes.'

'Then, of course, you are prepared to answer easy ones.'

'Let me hear what you call easy.'

'Well then, do you wish me to stay? All I have to do is to throw down my hat, sit down, and fold my arms for twenty minutes. I lose my train and my ship. I remain in America, instead of going to Europe.'

'I have thought of all that.'

'I don't mean to say it's a great deal. There are attractions on both sides.'

'Yes, and especially on one. It *is* a great deal.'

'And you request me to give it up—to renounce Berlin?'

'No; I ought not to do that. What I ask of you is whether, if I *should* so request you, you would say "yes".'

'That *does* make the matter easy for you, Miss Moore. What attractions do you hold out?'

'I hold out nothing whatever, sir.'

'I suppose that means a great deal.'

'A great deal of absurdity.'

'Well, you are certainly a most interesting woman, Miss Moore—a charming woman.'

'Why don't you call me irresistible at once, and bid me good morning?'

'I don't know but that I shall have to come to that. But I will give you no answer that leaves you at an advantage. Ask me to stay—order me to stay, if that suits you better—and I will see how it sounds. Come, you must not trifle with a man.' He still held Adela's hand, and now they were looking watchfully into each other's eyes. He paused, waiting for an answer.

'Goodbye, Mr Ludlow,' said Adela. 'God bless you!' And she was about to withdraw her hand; but he held it.

'Are we friends?' said he.

Adela gave a little shrug of her shoulders. 'Friends of three hours!'

Ludlow looked at her with some sternness. 'Our parting could at best hardly have been sweet,' said he; 'but why should you make it bitter, Miss Moore?'

'If it's bitter, why should you try to change it?'

'Because I don't like bitter things.'

Ludlow had caught a glimpse of the truth—that truth of which the reader has had a glimpse—and he stood there at once thrilled and annoyed. He had both a heart and a conscience. 'It's not my fault,' he murmured to the latter; but he was unable to add, in all consistency, that it was his misfortune. It would be very heroic, very poetic, very chivalric, to lose his steamer, and he felt that he could do so for sufficient cause—at the suggestion of a fact. But the motive here was less than a fact—an idea; less than an idea—a mere guess. 'It's a very pretty little romance as it is,' he said to himself. 'Why spoil it? She's a different sort from any I have met, and just to have seen her like this—that is enough for me!' He raised her hand to his lips, pressed them to it, dropped it, reached the door, and bounded out of the garden gate.

WILKIE COLLINS

The Captain's Last Love

I

'The Captain is still in the prime of life,' the widow remarked. 'He has given up his ship; he possesses a sufficient income, and he has nobody to live with him. I should like to know why he doesn't marry.'

'The Captain was excessively rude to Me,' the widow's younger sister added, on her side. 'When we took leave of him in London, I asked if there was any chance of his joining us at Brighton this season. He turned his back on me as if I had mortally offended him; and he made me this extraordinary answer: "Miss! I hate the sight of the sea." The man has been a sailor all his life. What does he mean by saying that he hates the sight of the sea?'

These questions were addressed to a third person present—and the person was a man. He was entirely at the mercy of the widow and the widow's sister. The other ladies of the family—who might have taken him under their protection—had gone to an evening concert. He was known to be the Captain's friend, and to be well acquainted with events in the Captain's later life. As it happened, he had reasons for hesitating to revive associations connected with those events. But what polite alternative was left to him? He must either inflict disappointment, and, worse still, aggravate curiosity—or he must resign himself to circumstances, and tell the ladies why the Captain would never marry, and why (sailor as he was) he hated the sight of the sea. They were both young women and handsome women—and the person to whom they had appealed (being a man) followed the example of submission to the sex, first set in the garden of Eden. He enlightened the ladies, in the terms that follow:

II

The British merchantman, *Fortuna*, sailed from the port of Liverpool (at a date which it is not necessary to specify) with the morning tide. She was bound for certain islands in the Pacific Ocean, in search of a cargo of sandal-wood—a commodity which, in those days, found a ready and profitable market in the Chinese Empire.

A large discretion was reposed in the Captain by the owners, who knew him to be not only trustworthy, but a man of rare ability, carefully cultivated during the leisure hours of a seafaring life. Devoted heart and soul to his professional duties, he was a hard reader and an excellent linguist as well. Having had considerable experience among the inhabitants of the Pacific Islands, he had attentively studied their characters, and had mastered their language in more than one of its many dialects. Thanks to the valuable information thus obtained, the Captain was never at a loss to conciliate the islanders. He had more than once succeeded in finding a cargo, under circumstances in which other captains had failed.

Possessing these merits, he had also his fair share of human defects. For instance, he was a little too conscious of his own good looks—of his bright chestnut hair and whiskers, of his beautiful blue eyes, of his fair white skin, which many a woman had looked at with the admiration that is akin to envy. His shapely hands were protected by gloves; a broad-brimmed hat sheltered his complexion in fine weather from the sun. He was nice in the choice of his perfumes; he never drank spirits, and the smell of tobacco was abhorrent to him. New men among his officers and his crew, seeing him in his cabin, perfectly dressed, washed, and brushed until he was an object speckless to look upon—a merchant-captain soft of voice, careful in his choice of words, devoted to study in his leisure hours—were apt to conclude that they had trusted themselves at sea under a commander who was an anomalous mixture of a schoolmaster and a dandy. But if the slightest infraction of discipline took place, or if the storm rose and the vessel proved to be in peril, it was soon discovered that the gloved hands held a rod of iron; that the soft voice could make itself heard through wind and sea from one end of the deck to the other; and that it issued orders which the greatest fool on board discovered to be orders that had saved the ship. Throughout his professional life, the general impression that this variously gifted man produced on the little world about him was always the same. Some few liked him; everybody respected him; nobody understood him. The Captain accepted these results. He persisted in reading his books and protecting his complexion, with this result: his owners shook hands with him, and put up with his gloves.

The *Fortuna* touched at Rio for water, and for supplies of food which might prove useful in case of scurvy. In due time the ship rounded Cape Horn, favoured by the finest weather ever known in those latitudes by the oldest hand on board. The mate—one Mr Duncalf—a boozing, wheezing, self-confident old sea-dog, with a flaming face and a vast vocabulary of oaths, swore that he didn't like it. 'The foul weather's coming, my lads,' said Mr Duncalf. 'Mark my words, there'll be wind enough to take the curl out of the Captain's whiskers before we are many days older!'

For one uneventful week, the ship cruised in search of the islands to which the owners had directed her. At the end of that time the wind took the predicted liberties with the Captain's whiskers; and Mr Duncalf stood revealed to an admiring crew in the character of a true prophet.

For three days and three nights the *Fortuna* ran before the storm, at the mercy of wind and sea. On the fourth morning the gale blew itself out, the sun appeared again towards noon, and the Captain was able to take an observation. The result informed him that he was in a part of the Pacific Ocean with which he was entirely unacquainted. Thereupon, the officers were called to a council in the cabin.

Mr Duncalf, as became his rank, was consulted first. His opinion possessed the merit of brevity. 'My lads, this ship's bewitched. Take my word for it, we shall wish ourselves back in our own latitudes before we are many days older.' Which, being interpreted, meant that Mr Duncalf was lost, like his superior officer, in a part of the ocean of which he knew nothing.

The remaining members of the council, having no suggestions to offer, left the Captain to take his own way. He decided (the weather being fine again) to stand on under an easy press of sail for four-and-twenty hours more, and to see if anything came of it.

Soon after night-fall, something did come of it. The look-out forward hailed the quarter-deck with the dreadful cry, 'Breakers ahead!' In less than a minute more, everybody heard the crash of the broken water. The *Fortuna* was put about, and came round slowly in the light wind. Thanks to the timely alarm and the fine weather, the safety of the vessel was easily provided for. They kept her under short sail; and they waited for the morning.

The dawn showed them in the distance a glorious green island, not marked in the ship's charts—an island girt about by a coral-reef, and having in its midst a high-peaked mountain which looked, through the telescope, like a mountain of volcanic origin. Mr Duncalf, taking his morning draught of rum and water, shook his groggy old head, and said (and swore): 'My lads, I don't like the look of that island.' The Captain was of a different opinion. He had one of the ship's boats put into the water; he armed himself and four of his crew who accompanied him; and away he went in the morning sunlight to visit the island.

Skirting round the coral-reef, they found a natural breach, which proved to be broad enough and deep enough not only for the passage of the boat, but of the ship herself if needful. Crossing the broad inner belt of smooth water, they approached the golden sands of the island, strewed with magnificent shells, and crowded by the dusky islanders— men, women, and children, all waiting in breathless astonishment to see the strangers land.

The Captain kept the boat off, and examined the islanders carefully. The innocent simple people danced, and sang, and ran into the water, imploring their wonderful white visitors by gestures to come on shore. Not a creature among them carried arms of any sort; a hospitable curiosity animated the entire population. The men cried out, in their smooth musical language, 'Come and eat!' and the plump black-eyed women, all laughing together, added their own invitation, 'Come and be kissed!' Was it in mortals to resist such temptations as these? The Captain led the way on shore, and the women surrounded him in an instant, and screamed for joy at the glorious spectacle of his whiskers, his complexion, and his gloves. So, the mariners from the far north were welcomed to the newly-discovered island.

III

The morning wore on. Mr Duncalf, in charge of the ship, cursing the island over his rum and water, as a 'beastly green strip of a place, not laid down in any Christian chart', was kept waiting four mortal hours before the Captain returned to his command, and reported himself to his officers as follows:

He had found his knowledge of the Polynesian dialects sufficient to make himself in some degree understood by the natives of the new island. Under the guidance of the chief he had made a first journey of exploration, and had seen for himself that the place was a marvel of natural beauty and fertility. The one barren spot in it was the peak of the volcanic mountain, composed of crumbling rock; originally no doubt lava and ashes, which had cooled and consolidated with the lapse of time. So far as he could see, the crater at the top was now an extinct crater. But, if he had understood rightly, the chief had spoken of earthquakes and eruptions at certain bygone periods, some of which lay within his own earliest recollections of the place.

Adverting next to considerations of practical utility, the Captain announced that he had seen sandal-wood enough on the island to load a dozen ships, and that the natives were willing to part with it for a few toys and trinkets generally distributed amongst them. To the mate's disgust, the *Fortuna* was taken inside the reef that day, and was anchored before sunset in a natural harbour. Twelve hours of recreation, beginning with the next morning, were granted to the men, under the wise restrictions in such cases established by the Captain. That interval over, the work of cutting the precious wood and loading the ship was to be unremittingly pursued.

Mr Duncalf had the first watch after the *Fortuna* had been made snug. He took the boatswain aside (an ancient sea-dog like himself), and he said in a gruff whisper: 'My lad, this here ain't the island laid down in our sailing orders. See if mischief don't come of disobeying orders before we are many days older.'

Nothing in the shape of mischief happened that night. But at sunrise the next morning a suspicious circumstance occurred; and Mr Duncalf whispered to the boatswain: 'What did I tell you?' The Captain and the chief of the islanders held a private conference in the cabin; and the

Captain, after first forbidding any communication with the shore until his return, suddenly left the ship, alone with the chief, in the chief's own canoe.

What did this strange disappearance mean? The Captain himself, when he took his seat in the canoe, would have been puzzled to answer that question. He asked, in the nearest approach that his knowledge could make to the language used in the island, whether he would be a long time or a short time absent from his ship.

The chief answered mysteriously (as the Captain understood him) in these words: 'Long time or short time, your life depends on it, and the lives of your men.'

Paddling his light little boat in silence over the smooth water inside the reef, the chief took his visitor ashore at a part of the island which was quite new to the Captain. The two crossed a ravine, and ascended an eminence beyond. There the chief stopped, and silently pointed out to sea.

The Captain looked in the direction indicated to him, and discovered a second and a smaller island, lying away to the south-west. Taking out his telescope from the case by which it was slung at his back, he narrowly examined the place. Two of the native canoes were lying off the shore of the new island; and the men in them appeared to be all kneeling or crouching in curiously chosen attitudes. Shifting the range of his glass, he next beheld a white-robed figure, tall and solitary—the one inhabitant of the island whom he could discover. The man was standing on the highest point of a rocky cape. A fire was burning at his feet. Now he lifted his arms solemnly to the sky; now he dropped some invisible fuel into the fire, which made a blue smoke; and now he cast other invisible objects into the canoes floating beneath him, which the islanders reverently received with bodies that crouched in abject submission. Lowering his telescope, the Captain looked round at the chief for an explanation. The chief gave the explanation readily. His language was interpreted by the English stranger in these terms:

'Wonderful white man! the island you see yonder is a Holy Island. As such it is *Taboo*—an island sanctified and set apart. The honourable person whom you notice on the rock is an all-powerful favourite of the gods. He is by vocation a Sorcerer, and by rank a Priest. You now see him casting charms and blessings into the canoes of our fishermen, who kneel to him for fine weather and great plenty of fish. If any profane person, native or stranger, presumes to set foot on that island, my otherwise peaceful subjects will (in the performance of a religious duty) put that person to death. Mention this to your men. They will be fed by my male people, and fondled by my female people, so long as they keep clear of the Holy Isle. As they value their lives, let them respect this prohibition. Is it understood between us? Wonderful white man! my canoe is waiting for you. Let us go back.'

Understanding enough of the chief's language (illustrated by his gestures) to receive in the right spirit the communication thus addressed to him, the Captain repeated the warning to the ship's company in the plainest possible English. The officers and men then took their holiday on shore, with the exception of Mr Duncalf, who positively refused to leave the ship. For twelve delightful hours they were fed by the male people, and fondled by the female people, and then they were mercilessly torn from the flesh-pots and the arms of their new friends, and set to work on the sandal-wood in good earnest. Mr Duncalf superintended the loading, and waited for the mischief that was to come of disobeying the owners' orders with a confidence worthy of a better cause.

IV

Strangely enough, chance once more declared itself in favour of the mate's point of view. The mischief did actually come; and the chosen instrument of it was a handsome young islander, who was one of the sons of the chief.

The Captain had taken a fancy to the sweet-tempered intelligent lad. Pursuing his studies in the dialect of the island, at leisure hours, he had made the chief's son his tutor, and had instructed the youth in English by way of return. More than a month had passed in this intercourse, and the ship's lading was being rapidly completed—when, in an evil hour, the talk between the two turned on the subject of the Holy Island.

'Does nobody live on the island but the Priest?' the Captain asked.

The chief's son looked round him suspiciously. 'Promise me you won't tell anybody!' he began very earnestly.

The Captain gave his promise.

99

'There is one other person on the island,' the lad whispered; 'a person to feast your eyes upon, if you could only see her! She is the Priest's daughter. Removed to the island in her infancy, she has never left it since. In that sacred solitude she has only looked on two human beings—her father and her mother. I once saw her from my canoe, taking care not to attract her notice, or to approach too near the holy soil. Oh, so young, dear master, and, oh, so beautiful!' The chief's son completed the description by kissing his own hands as an expression of rapture.

The Captain's fine blue eyes sparkled. He asked no more questions; but, later on that day, he took his telescope with him, and paid a secret visit to the eminence which overlooked the Holy Island. The next day, and the next, he privately returned to the same place. On the fourth day, fatal Destiny favoured him. He discovered the nymph of the island.

Standing alone upon the cape on which he had already seen her father, she was feeding some tame birds which looked like turtle-doves. The glass showed the Captain her white robe, fluttering in the sea-breeze; her long black hair falling to her feet; her slim and supple young figure; her simple grace of attitude, as she turned this way and that, attending to the wants of her birds. Before her was the blue ocean; behind her rose the lustrous green of the island forest. He looked and looked until his eyes and arms ached. When she disappeared among the trees, followed by her favourite birds, the Captain shut up his telescope with a sigh, and said to himself: 'I have seen an angel!'

From that hour he became an altered man; he was languid, silent, interested in nothing. General opinion, on board his ship, decided that he was going to be taken ill.

A week more elapsed, and the officers and crew began to talk of the voyage to their market in China. The Captain refused to fix a day for sailing. He even took offence at being asked to decide. Instead of sleeping in his cabin, he went ashore for the night.

Not many hours afterwards (just before daybreak), Mr Duncalf, snoring in his cabin on deck, was aroused by a hand laid on his shoulder. The swinging lamp, still alight, showed him the dusky face of the chief's son, convulsed with terror. By wild signs, by disconnected words in the little English which he had learnt, the lad tried to make the mate understand him. Dense Mr Duncalf, understanding nothing, hailed the second officer, on the opposite side of the deck. The second officer was young and intelligent; he rightly interpreted the terrible news that had come to the ship.

The Captain had broken his own rules. Watching his opportunity, under cover of the night, he had taken a canoe, and had secretly crossed the channel to the Holy Island. No one had been near him at the time, but the chief's son. The lad had vainly tried to induce him to abandon his desperate enterprise, and had vainly waited on the shore in the hope of hearing the sound of the paddle announcing his return. Beyond all reasonable doubt, the infatuated man had set foot on the shores of the tabooed island.

The one chance for his life was to conceal what he had done, until the ship could be got out of the harbour, and then (if no harm had come to him in the interval) to rescue him after nightfall. It was decided to spread the report that he had really been taken ill, and that he was confined to his cabin. The chief's son, whose heart the Captain's kindness had won, could be trusted to do this, and to keep the secret faithfully for his good friend's sake.

Towards noon, the next day, they attempted to take the ship to sea, and failed for want of wind. Hour by hour, the heat grew more oppressive. As the day declined, there were ominous appearances in the western heaven. The natives, who had given some trouble during the day by their anxiety to see the Captain, and by their curiosity to know the cause of the sudden preparations for the ship's departure, all went ashore together, looking suspiciously at the sky, and reappeared no more. Just at midnight, the ship (still in her snug berth inside the reef) suddenly trembled from her keel to her uppermost masts. Mr Duncalf, surrounded by the startled crew, shook his knotty fist at the island as if he could see it in the dark. 'My lads, what did I tell you? That was a shock of earthquake.'

With the morning the threatening aspect of the weather unexpectedly disappeared. A faint hot breeze from the land, just enough to give the ship steerage-way, offered Mr Duncalf a chance of getting to sea. Slowly the *Fortuna*, with the mate himself at the wheel, half sailed, half drifted into the open ocean. At a distance of barely two miles from the island the breeze was felt no more, and the vessel lay becalmed for the rest of the day.

At night the men waited their orders, expecting to be sent after their Captain in one of the boats. The intense darkness, the airless heat, and a second shock of earthquake (faintly felt in the ship at her present distance from the land) warned the mate to be cautious. 'I smell mischief in the air,' said Mr Duncalf. 'The Captain must wait till I am surer of the weather.'

Still no change came with the new day. The dead calm continued, and the airless heat. As the day declined, another ominous appearance became visible. A thin line of smoke was discovered through the telescope, ascending from the topmost peak of the mountain on the main island. Was the volcano threatening an eruption? The mate, for one, entertained no doubt of it. 'By the Lord, the place is going to burst up!' said Mr Duncalf. 'Come what may of it, we must find the Captain tonight!'

V

What was the lost Captain doing? and what chance had the crew of finding him that night?

He had committed himself to his desperate adventure, without forming any plan for the preservation of his own safety; without giving even a momentary consideration to the consequences which might follow the risk that he had run. The charming figure that he had seen haunted him night and day. The image of the innocent creature, secluded from humanity in her island-solitude, was the one image that filled his mind. A man, passing a woman in the street, acts on the impulse to turn and follow her, and in that one thoughtless moment shapes the destiny of his future life. The Captain had acted on a similar impulse, when he took the first canoe he found on the beach, and shaped his reckless course for the tabooed island.

Reaching the shore while it was still dark, he did one sensible thing—he hid the canoe so that it might not betray him when the daylight came. That done, he waited for the morning on the outskirts of the forest.

The trembling light of dawn revealed the mysterious solitude around him. Following the outer limits of the trees, first in one direction, then in another, and finding no trace of any living creature, he decided on penetrating to the interior of the island. He entered the forest.

An hour of walking brought him to rising ground. Continuing the ascent, he got clear of the trees, and stood on the grassy top of a broad cliff which overlooked the sea. An open hut was on the cliff. He cautiously looked in, and discovered that it was empty. The few household utensils left about, and the simple bed of leaves in a corner, were covered with fine sandy dust. Night-birds flew blundering out of inner cavities in the roof, and took refuge in the shadows of the forest below. It was plain that the hut had not been inhabited for some time past.

Standing at the open doorway and considering what he should do next, the Captain saw a bird flying towards him out of the forest. It was a turtle-dove, so tame that it fluttered close up to him. At the same moment the sound of sweet laughter became audible among the trees. His heart beat fast; he advanced a few steps and stopped. In a moment more the nymph of the island appeared, in her white robe, ascending the cliff in pursuit of her truant bird. She saw the strange man, and suddenly stood still; struck motionless by the amazing discovery that had burst upon her. The Captain approached, smiling and holding out his hand. She never moved; she stood before him in helpless wonderment—her lovely black eyes fixed spell-bound on his face: her dusky bosom palpitating above the fallen folds of her robe; her rich red lips parted in mute astonishment. Feasting his eyes on her beauty in silence, the Captain after a while ventured to speak to her in the language of the main island. The sound of his voice, addressing her in the words that she understood, roused the lovely creature to action. She started, stepped close up to him, and dropped on her knees at his feet.

'My father worships invisible deities,' she said softly. 'Are you a visible deity? Has my mother sent you?' She pointed as she spoke to the deserted hut behind them. 'You appear,' she went on, 'in the place where my mother died. Is it for her sake that you show yourself to her child? Beautiful deity, come to the Temple—come to my father!'

The Captain gently raised her from the ground. If her father saw him, he was a doomed man.

Infatuated as he was, he had sense enough left to announce himself plainly in his own character, as a mortal creature arriving from a distant land. The girl instantly drew back from him with a look of terror.

'He is not like my father,' she said to herself; 'he is not like me. Is

103

he the lying demon of the prophecy? Is he the predestined destroyer of our island?'

The Captain's experience of the sex showed him the only sure way out of the awkward position in which he was now placed. He appealed to his personal appearance.

'Do I look like a demon?' he asked.

Her eyes met his eyes; a faint smile trembled on her lips. He ventured on asking what she meant by the predestined destruction of the island. She held up her hand solemnly, and repeated the prophecy.

The Holy Island was threatened with destruction by an evil being, who would one day appear on its shores. To avert the fatality the place had been sanctified and set apart, under the protection of the gods and their priest. Here was the reason for the taboo, and for the extraordinary rigour with which it was enforced. Listening to her with the deepest interest, the Captain took her hand and pressed it gently.

'Do I feel like a demon?' he whispered.

Her slim brown fingers closed frankly on his hand. 'You feel soft and friendly,' she said with the fearless candour of a child. 'Squeeze me again. I like it!'

The next moment she snatched her hand away from him; the sense of his danger had suddenly forced itself on her mind. 'If my father sees you,' she said, 'he will light the signal fire at the Temple, and the people from the other island will come here and put you to death. Where is your canoe? No! It is daylight. My father may see you on the water.' She considered a little, and, approaching him, laid her hands on his shoulders. 'Stay here till nightfall,' she resumed. 'My father never comes this way. The sight of the place where my mother died is horrible to him. You are safe here. Promise to stay where you are till night-time.'

The Captain gave his promise.

Freed from anxiety so far, the girl's mobile temperament recovered its native cheerfulness, its sweet gaiety and spirit. She admired the beautiful stranger as she might have admired a new bird that had flown to her to be fondled with the rest. She patted his fair white skin, and wished she had a skin like it. She lifted the great glossy folds of her long black hair, and compared it with the Captain's bright curly locks, and longed to change colours with him from the bottom of her heart. His dress was a wonder to her; his watch was a new revelation. She rested her head on his shoulder to listen delightedly to the ticking, as he held the watch to her ear. Her fragrant breath played on his face, her warm supple figure rested against him softly. The Captain's arm stole round her waist, and the Captain's lips gently touched her cheek. She lifted her head with a look of pleased surprise. 'Thank you,' said the child of nature simply. 'Kiss me again; I like it. May I kiss you?' The tame turtle-dove perched on her shoulder as she gave the Captain her first kiss, and diverted her thoughts to the pets that she had left, in pursuit of the truant dove. 'Come,' she said, 'and see my birds. I keep them on this side of the forest. There is no danger, so long as you don't show yourself on the other side. My name is Aimata. Aimata will take care of you. Oh, what a beautiful white neck you have!' She put her arm admiringly round his neck. The Captain's arm held her tenderly to him. Slowly the two descended the cliff, and were lost in the leafy solitudes of the forest. And the tame dove fluttered before them, a winged messenger of love, cooing to his mate.

VI

The night had come, and the Captain had not left the island.

Aimata's resolution to send him away in the darkness was a forgotten resolution already. She had let him persuade her that he was in no danger, so long as he remained in the hut on the cliff; and she had promised, at parting, to return to him while the Priest was still sleeping, at the dawn of day.

He was alone in the hut. The thought of the innocent creature whom he loved was sorrowfully as well as tenderly present to his mind. He almost regretted his rash visit to the island. 'I will take her with me to England,' he said to himself. 'What does a sailor care for the opinion of the world? Aimata shall be my wife.'

The intense heat oppressed him. He stepped out on the cliff, towards midnight, in search of a breath of air.

At that moment, the first shock of earthquake (felt in the ship while she was inside the reef) shook the ground he stood on. He instantly thought of the volcano on the main island. Had he been mistaken in supposing the crater to be extinct? Was the shock that he had just felt a warning from the volcano, communicated through a submarine connection between the two islands? He waited and watched through the hours of darkness, with a vague sense of apprehension, which was not to be reasoned away. With the first light of daybreak he descended into the forest, and saw the lovely being whose safety was already precious to him as his own, hurrying to meet him through the trees.

She waved her hand distractedly, as she approached him. 'Go!' she cried; 'go away in your canoe before our island is destroyed!'

He did his best to quiet her alarm. Was it the shock of earthquake that had frightened her? No: it was more than the shock of earthquake—it was something terrible which had followed the shock. There was a lake near the Temple, the waters of which were supposed to be heated by subterranean fires. The lake had risen with the earthquake, had bubbled furiously, and had then melted away into the earth and been lost. Her father, viewing the portent with horror, had gone to the cape to watch the volcano on the main island, and to implore by prayers and sacrifices the protection of the gods. Hearing this, the Captain entreated Aimata to let him see the emptied lake, in the absence of the Priest. She hesitated; but his influence was all-powerful. He prevailed on her to turn back with him through the forest.

Reaching the farthest limit of the trees, they came out upon open rocky ground which sloped gently downward towards the centre of the island. Having crossed this space, they arrived at a natural amphitheatre of rock. On one side of it, the Temple appeared, partly excavated, partly formed by a natural cavern. In one of the lateral branches of the cavern was the dwelling of the Priest and his daughter. The mouth of it looked out on the rocky basin of the lake. Stooping over the edge, the Captain discovered, far down in the empty depths, a light cloud of steam. Not a drop of water was visible, look where he might.

Aimata pointed to the abyss, and hid her face on his bosom. 'My father says,' she whispered, 'that it is your doing.'

The Captain started. 'Does your father know that I am on the island?'

She looked up at him with a quick glance of reproach. 'Do you think I would tell him, and put your life in peril?' she asked. 'My father felt the destroyer of the island in the earthquake; my father saw the coming destruction in the disappearance of the lake.' Her eyes rested on him with a loving languor. 'Are you indeed the demon of the prophecy?'

she said, winding his hair round her finger. 'I am not afraid of you, if you are. I am a creature bewitched; I love the demon.' She kissed him passionately. 'I don't care if I die,' she whispered between the kisses, 'if I only die with you!'

The Captain made no attempt to reason with her. He took the wiser way—he appealed to her feelings.

'You will come and live with me happily in my own country,' he said. 'My ship is waiting for us. I will take you home with me, and you shall be my wife.'

She clapped her hands for joy. Then she thought of her father, and drew back from him in tears.

The Captain understood her. 'Let us leave this dreary place,' he suggested. 'We will talk about it in the cool glades of the forest, where you first said you loved me.'

She gave him her hand. 'Where I first said I loved you!' she repeated, smiling tenderly as she looked at him. They left the lake together.

VII

The darkness had fallen again; and the ship was still becalmed at sea.

Mr Duncalf came on deck after his supper. The thin line of smoke, seen rising from the peak of the mountain that evening, was now succeeded by ominous flashes of fire from the same quarter, intermittently visible. The faint hot breeze from the land was felt once more. 'There's just an air of wind,' Mr Duncalf remarked. 'I'll try for the Captain while I have the chance.'

One of the boats was lowered into the water—under command of the second mate, who had already taken the bearings of the tabooed island by daylight. Four of the men were to go with him, and they were all to be well-armed. Mr Duncalf addressed his final instructions to the officer in the boat.

'You will keep a look-out, sir, with a lantern in the bows. If the natives annoy you, you know what to do. Always shoot natives. When you get anigh the island, you will fire a gun and sing out for the Captain.'

'Quite needless,' interposed a voice from the sea. 'The Captain is here!'

Without taking the slightest notice of the astonishment that he had caused, the commander of the *Fortuna* paddled his canoe to the side of the ship. Instead of ascending to the deck, he stepped into the boat, waiting alongside. 'Lend me your pistols,' he said quietly to the second officer, 'and oblige me by taking your men back to their duties on board.' He looked up at Mr Duncalf and gave some further directions. 'If there is any change in the weather, keep the ship standing off and on, at a safe distance from the land, and throw up a rocket from time to time to show your position. Expect me on board again by sunrise.'

'What!' cried the mate. 'Do you mean to say you are going back to the island—in that boat—all by yourself?'

'I am going back to the island,' answered the Captain, as quietly as ever; 'in this boat—all by myself.' He pushed off from the ship, and hoisted the sail as he spoke.

'You're deserting your duty!' the old sea-dog shouted, with one of his loudest oaths.

'Attend to my directions,' the Captain shouted back, as he drifted away into the darkness.

Mr Duncalf—violently agitated for the first time in his life—took leave of his superior officer, with a singular mixture of solemnity and politeness, in these words:

'The Lord have mercy on your soul! I wish you good-evening.'

VIII

Alone in the boat, the Captain looked with a misgiving mind at the flashing of the volcano on the main island.

If events had favoured him, he would have removed Aimata to the shelter of the ship on the day when he saw the emptied basin of the lake. But the smoke of the Priest's sacrifice had been discovered by the chief; and he had despatched two canoes with instructions to make inquiries. One of the canoes had returned; the other was kept in waiting off the cape, to place a means of communicating with the main island at the disposal of the Priest. The second shock of earthquake had naturally increased the alarm of the chief. He had sent messages to the Priest, entreating him to leave the island, and other messages to Aimata suggesting that she should exert her influence over her father, if he hesitated. The Priest refused to leave the Temple. He trusted in his gods and his sacrifices—he believed they might avert the fatality that threatened his sanctuary.

Yielding to the holy man, the chief sent reinforcements of canoes to take their turn at keeping watch off the headland. Assisted by torches, the islanders were on the alert (in superstitious terror of the demon of the prophecy) by night as well as by day. The Captain had no alternative but to keep in hiding, and to watch his opportunity of approaching the place in which he had concealed his canoe. It was only after Aimata had left him as usual, to return to her father at the close of evening, that the chances declared themselves in his favour. The fire-flashes from the mountain, visible when the night came, had struck terror into the hearts of the men on the watch. They thought of their wives, their children, and their possessions on the main island, and they one and all deserted their Priest. The Captain seized the opportunity of communicating with the ship, and of exchanging a frail canoe which he was ill able to manage, for a swift-sailing boat capable of keeping the sea in the event of stormy weather.

As he now neared the land, certain small sparks of red, moving on the distant water, informed him that the canoes of the sentinels had been ordered back to their duty.

Carefully avoiding the lights, he reached his own side of the island without accident, and guided by the boat's lantern, anchored under the cliff. He climbed the rocks, advanced to the door of the hut, and was met, to his delight and astonishment, by Aimata on the threshold.

'I dreamed that some dreadful misfortune had parted us for ever,' she said; 'and I came here to see if my dream was true. You have taught me what it is to be miserable; I never felt my heart ache till I looked into the hut and found that you had gone. Now I have seen you, I am satisfied. No! you must not go back with me. My father may be out looking for me. It is you that are in danger, not I. I know the forest as well by dark as by daylight.'

The Captain detained her when she tried to leave him.

'Now you *are* here,' he said, 'why should I not place you at once in safety? I have been to the ship; I have brought back one of the boats. The darkness will befriend us—let us embark while we can.'

She shrank away as he took his hand. 'You forget my father!' she said.

'Your father is in no danger, my love. The canoes are waiting for him at the cape. I saw the lights as I passed.'

With that reply he drew her out of the hut and led her towards the sea. Not a breath of the breeze was now to be felt. The dead calm had returned—and the boat was too large to be easily managed by one man alone at the oars.

'The breeze may come again,' he said. 'Wait here, my angel, for the chance.'

As he spoke, the deep silence of the forest below them was broken by a sound. A harsh wailing voice was heard, calling:

'Aimata! Aimata!'

'My father!' she whispered; 'he has missed me. If he comes here you are lost.'

She kissed him with passionate fervour; she held him to her for a moment with all her strength.

'Expect me at daybreak,' she said, and disappeared down the landward slope of the cliff.

He listened, anxious for her safety. The voices of the father and daughter just reached him from among the trees. The priest spoke in no angry tones; she had apparently found an acceptable excuse for her absence. Little by little, the failing sound of their voices told him that they were on their way back together to the Temple. The silence fell again. Not a ripple broke on the beach. Not a leaf rustled in the forest. Nothing moved but the reflected flashes of the volcano on the mainland over the black sky. It was an airless and an awful calm.

He went into the hut, and laid down on his bed of leaves—not to sleep, but to rest. All his energies might be required to meet the coming events of the morning. After the voyage to and from the ship, and the long watching that had preceded it, strong as he was he stood in need of repose.

For some little time he kept awake, thinking. Insensibly the oppression of the intense heat, aided in its influence by his own fatigue, treacherously closed his eyes. In spite of himself, the weary man fell into a deep sleep.

He was awakened by a roar like the explosion of a park of artillery. The volcano on the main island had burst into a state of eruption. Smoky flame-light overspread the sky, and flashed through the open doorway of the hut. He sprang from his bed—and found himself up to his knees in water.

Had the sea overflowed the land?

He waded out of the hut, and the water rose to his middle. He looked round him by the lurid light of the eruption. The one visible object within the range of view was the sea, stained by reflections from the blood-red sky, swirling and rippling strangely in the dead calm. In a moment more, he became conscious that the earth on which he stood was sinking under his feet. The water rose to his neck; the last vestige of the roof of the hut disappeared.

He looked round again, and the truth burst on him. The island was sinking—slowly, slowly sinking into volcanic depths, below even the depth of the sea! The highest object was the hut, and that had dropped inch by inch under water before his own eyes. Thrown up to the surface by occult volcanic influences, the island had sunk back, under the same influences, to the obscurity from which it had emerged!

A black shadowy object, turning in a wide circle, came slowly near him as the all-destroying ocean washed its bitter waters into his mouth. The buoyant boat, rising as the sea rose, had dragged its anchor, and was floating round in the vortex made by the slowly-sinking island. With a last desperate hope that Aimata might have been saved as *he* had been saved, he swam to the boat, seized the heavy oars with the strength of a giant, and made for the place (so far as he could guess at it now) where the lake and the Temple had once been.

He looked round and round him; he strained his eyes in the vain attempt to penetrate below the surface of the seething dimpling sea. Had the panic-stricken watchers in the canoes saved themselves, without an effort to preserve the father and daughter? Or had they both been suffocated before they could make an attempt to escape? He called to her in his misery, as if she could hear him out of the fathomless depths, 'Aimata! Aimata!' The roar of the distant eruption answered him. The mounting fires lit the solitary sea far and near over the sinking island. The boat turned slowly and more slowly in the lessening vortex. Never again would those gentle eyes look at him with unutterable love! Never again would those fresh lips touch his lips with their fervent kiss! Alone, amid the savage forces of Nature in conflict, the miserable mortal lifted his hands in frantic supplication—and the burning sky glared down on him in its pitiless grandeur, and struck him to his knees in the boat. His reason sank with his sinking limbs. In the merciful frenzy that succeeded the shock, he saw her afar off, in her white robe, an angel poised on the waters, beckoning him to follow her to the brighter and the better world. He loosened the sail, he seized the oars; and the faster he pursued it, the faster the mocking vision fled from him over the empty and endless sea.

IX

The boat was discovered, on the next morning, from the ship.

All that the devotion of the officers of the *Fortuna* could do for their unhappy commander was done on the homeward voyage. Restored to his own country, and to skilled medical help, the Captain's mind by slow degrees recovered its balance. He has taken his place in society again—he lives and moves and manages his affairs like the rest of us. But his heart is dead to all new emotions; nothing remains in it but the sacred remembrance of his lost love. He neither courts nor avoids the society of women. Their sympathy finds him grateful, but their attractions seem to be lost on him; they pass from his mind as they pass from his eyes—they stir nothing in him but the memory of Aimata.

'Now you know, ladies, why the Captain will never marry, and why (sailor as he is) he hates the sight of the sea.'

CHRISTIANA FRASER-TYTLER

Margaret

I

Then Nature said, 'A lovelier flower
On earth was never sown:
This child I to myself will take,
She shall be mine, and I will make
A Lady of my own.'

WORDSWORTH

The small station of Islesworth sees but little of traffic or travellers. It is situated on a branch-line traversing one of the most retired districts of England; and saving for two or three months in summer, when hospitalities are exchanged between the few country houses of this shire and their neighbours of other counties, trade is pronounced to be very 'flat', even by the all-important dignitaries of the place.

If there is one moment, however, to which the Islesworth world looks forward more than another, it is that which falls forty-five minutes after mid-day; for then the 'Express' from Lydford steams through the tunnel and disemburdens itself of all that is to be expected, for that day at least, of beauty, fashion, or celebrity.

In winter, bankers, lawyers, and tradesmen monopolise entirely the three first-class carriages which are left to their disposal; but now, the London season being over, the season for Islesworth is supposed to have begun.

'She's coming, sir: she's rounding the Lighthouse down,' says a porter, as he jumps from the rails on to the platform, and gives himself a shake preparatory to the exertions of the hour. 'She'll be here in less than no time, for the steam's well on.'

The man whom he addresses with so much respect is in livery, and a coachman; but then he is servant at Walcombe Manor, and as such takes a high standing in Islesworth and its neighbourhood.

'Hope the young 'ooman 'll look sharp, that's all,' was the rejoinder; 'for the roan mare won't stand not much longer here.'

As he spoke he flung the reins to an ostler who was lounging near, and passed through the garden-gate on to the platform, where he arrived just in time to see the 'Zephyr' slacken speed, as the train entered the tunnel. In a moment everything was bustle and excitement. Cries of 'Islesworth, Islesworth!' 'Tickets!' 'Any luggage, sir?' and the snorts of the engine,—all seemed combining to make as much of the occasion as could be made.

John Marley, our friend in livery, though perhaps the least demonstrative of the group, is evidently not successful in the object of his search. 'Bless me soul!' he mutters to himself as he peers into each window, 'they're all ladies and gents to-day—the girl's not here, not a bit of her!'

His gaze into the carriages was so earnest and continuous, that he knocked up against some one, before he saw what he was about, and thus put a limit to his own career. He lifted his hat with a thousand apologies, for a slight figure in black addressed him.

'Can you tell me, sir, if this is Islesworth?' she said, 'and whether there is any way of getting to Walcombe from here?'

'Bless me soul! if it ain't the young person as is to be the young lady's maid! there bean't no difference now-a-days 'twixt the gents and common folk!' This was an aside: but having sufficiently recovered his equanimity, he replied in his most courteous of manners, 'Yes, Miss, I think as I can tell you, having been with Mr Seymour these fifteen years; and if you'll get up there, Miss,' pointing to the dog-cart, 'I'll get your box all right in less than no time.'

John Marley was true to his word, and in 'less than no time,' he was seated beside Margaret Ansted, the trunk having been safely lodged on the seat behind.

'There's a good eight miles to drive,' he said, 'and I hopes as you have plenty of coverings: the wind's not so warm as it might be, and on them hills it's keenish.'

'I did not think it was cold,' answered a quiet voice from beneath a thick veil; 'but there were a great many people in the carriage, and I am so glad to get into the air.'

As she spoke, she threw up the crape which fell over her face, and ventured to take her first look at her companion, and the surrounding country. Her study in physiognomy satisfied her, for there was a rough heartiness and warmth about the whole expression of Marley's face, which made her feel that she could trust him. The country, too, looking as it did its very best on a fine day in the end of July, could not have failed to please her eye; and had it not been for a quick beating at her heart, and a tingling of heat to her cheek that was not altogether natural, I think that Margaret would for a time have been almost happy. She fell into a day-dream, in which home and the widowed mother she had left played a prominent part; but, feeling that this was dangerous ground if she was to keep up appearances before Marley and the strange faces towards which she was moving, she turned her thoughts to another parting, interesting enough to hold her attention for the time, and yet having about it nothing of tenderness as far at least as she herself was concerned.

Lovely as she was, Margaret had in her native village for long been the 'cynosure of neighbouring eyes'; and one ardent swain had only that morning done his best to persuade her to remain near the home of her birth, but as his wife.

'I would try to be more worthy of you, Margaret, if you would but give me the chance. How shall I see you when you are gone to this strange place that's so different from the village where you've been happy? I can't think you like it, Margaret; and you're not meant to work, more fit to be a queen! I believe it's for your mother that you do it all; and I would be so proud to help her! I'm not so badly off now, dear, or I would not ask you to have me. I have my 90*l.* a-year now, and maybe it will soon be 100*l.*; leastways, if Mr Strangeman leaves the bank.'

But Margaret would not be moved from her resolve.

'Good-bye, John,' she said, decidedly, as she gave him her hand and stepped into the train; 'I like going': and then, with something very like a sob in her voice as the train began slowly to move out, 'John, I'd do almost anything for one who'd be kind to mother!'

Poor John! those words were light and food to him for many a long day to come. Hope throws many a halo round common words like these.

Margaret was roughly awakened from her reverie by a swerve of the dog-cart as they turned into a straight narrow road, running almost at right angles with the one they had left. It was much more shady than the main road, and the hedge-rows were filled with fern and blossoms.

'Are we near the house?' she asked, timidly, looking through the thick foliage for a first sight of her new home.

Almost before Marley could answer, another turn to the left had taken them through high iron gates, past a lodge, and into an avenue of stately elms. At the end of the avenue, surrounded by trees still more venerable, stood a picturesque building in the Elizabethan style, not high or massive, but still imposing, for it appeared to cover a very large tract of ground.

An exclamation of pleasure and astonishment escaped Margaret's lips at the sight so novel and unexpected.

'I thought it would be grand,' she said, 'but not beautiful like this.' Then her voice sank, for the dog-cart stopped at a back-door, and Marley was at the bell, pulling vigorously.

A page came to the rescue, and to his care the new-comer was intrusted.

'Here's Miss Ansted; and you get her summut hot, for it's a cold drive she's had in the east wind, and she's not over strong, if I'm not much mistaken.'

Through a passage into a still-room, from the still-room into a lobby, and from the lobby into another passage; Margaret thought the labyrinth would never end. But it did end, and the presence of the house-keeper had to be faced. She was very kind in her manner, and shook Margaret's hand warmly; and Mrs Burton had some strength of character, shown in her steady determination not to change from the good old rules of her own time. These good old rules, indeed, induced her to treat with equal civility and attention the scullery-maids of the back kitchen, and the pampered London footmen, and fine maids who came across her path, causing thereby much dissatisfaction, but at the same time much happiness.

Whilst Margaret sipped slowly at the cup of tea placed before her— slowly, not because it was distasteful to her after the long journey, but more that she feared the unknown which was to come after—the door opened brusquely, and a high shrill voice, accompanied by a rustle of silk, broke upon the silence with,—

'*Tenez! des fleurs pour mademoiselle! et vous!*' glancing at Margaret. '*Ah, c'est Miss Ansted! mais, mon Dieu, qu'elle est jeune!*' Then, in English, which was even less intelligible to the bewildered girl, she continued addressing her: 'You had long journey? No, not so much long, I suppose. I do not love the railway, Miss Ansted; it gives me pain in the heart very bad! Shall you come up? By this way, if you please. *Ah, mes jolies roses pour les cheveux de mademoiselle!*'

The excitable little woman whisked a bunch of red roses off the table, and ran upstairs with swift pattering steps, which Margaret found it difficult to keep pace with.

'First to your proper room, or first to miladi? *Ce m'est égale! Eh?*'

Margaret, who went on the principle that the sooner a disagreeable duty is accomplished the better, chose the latter alternative.

'You rest here then,' said Mathilde, 'and I will go tell to miladi you are come.'

A dreadful pause of ten minutes, and my lady was pronounced to be at liberty, and waiting in her boudoir. She was seated at her writing-table, with innumerable small notes spread out before her. In person, she was rather prepossessing than otherwise; for her figure was tall and slender, her features good, and her hair beautifully black and wavy. But in mind Lady Katharine was somewhat of an anomaly; for, vacillating and weak to a degree, she could still be obstinate and ill-tempered when, as she thought, occasion required it.

Moreover, having no gifts of intellect or understanding of her own, she yet possessed at times the art of carrying on a semblance of their existence. She rose as Margaret entered, and stood before her in full-blown dignity.

'I am glad to see you looking so well, Margaret Ansted; you seem quite equal to the duties which lie before you.'

This was a set sentence, which accosted each new-comer to Walcombe, and after its delivery, in majestic tones, Lady Katharine sank into her arm-chair and resumed her every-day language and manner.

'Let us see,' she continued, putting the points of her taper fingers together, and opening and closing them as she went on. 'Let us see how it is all to be managed.' Then a long ramble followed, the point of which was that her second daughter, Maud, was to be Margaret's mistress, and that little Eveline, in the absence of her governess, was to be under her charge. 'Next week,' said my lady, 'you will walk every day with her, either after luncheon or at five o'clock, just as she wishes. Miss Leigh will be away for six weeks.'

Here Lady Katharine sighed, crossed her white hands helplessly, and, putting her head on one side, fixed her eyes steadfastly on Margaret's face. She was too well bred to have purposely put any one to inconvenience; but it was a habit with her to victimise the nearest object with a prolonged stare, when, as was often the case, her thoughts had no object whatsoever of their own.

At this time she may have been in a great degree excused, for a face such as Margaret's does not meet one at every turn. The excitement of the moment, and the faint blush, which Lady Katharine's scrutinising gaze had called forth, all tended to heighten her wonted beauty; and the soft, black dress, fitting closely to her figure, and encircling the long, white throat, completed a picture which, I think, no artist would have passed by unnoticed. Her soft, brown hair was coiled in smooth plaits round the classical head, just as she had worn it from her childhood; and her whole bearing was more that of the high-born lady than of the village maiden.

Margaret's next encounter was to be with her 'own young lady', Miss Maud; and Mathilde escorted her to the bedroom door, introducing her, in a rapid succession of words, as '*La jeune fille, votre femme-de-chambre, Mademoiselle!*'

Mathilde evidently contemplated a little patronising in this quarter. Not so with the young mistress.

'How do you do?' she said. 'I hope you are not very tired? How strange you must feel here. It is your first place, is it not?' And in the interval between this time and dinner, she managed to make Margaret feel for the first time, a little at her ease. In the tedious process of hairdressing, especially, Maud's patience was quite wonderful. 'Never mind how often you pull it down,' she said. 'I will take a book, and then you can try it over and over again; no one can do my hair well the first time.'

Margaret felt certain that with such a mistress everything upstairs must go smoothly. As to the life below, she was not so sure. Mathilde had not taken her fancy; and it was a decided blow when she found that the flighty little Frenchwoman was to share her room at night, in addition to being her constant companion by day.

II

> One praised her ankles, one her eyes,
> One her dark hair and lovesome mien;
> So sweet a face, such angel grace,
> In all that land had never been.
>
> TENNYSON

A week had passed, and with it all the strangeness and uncertainty of the new life.

Margaret had formed her own idea of each member of the large household, and was steering her course accordingly. Mathilde, whom on further acquaintance, she disliked more and more, she could not well avoid, but with the other servants this was less difficult; and, at the cost of being pronounced 'proud' and 'stuck-up', she managed to spend but little time out of the work-room.

And now the next week, of which Lady Katharine had spoken, had been entered upon; and John Marley, having driven a white, shrinking, obsequious, little governess to the station, the entire charge of 'Miss Eveline' devolved upon Margaret.

It was with a feeling of relief that she emerged from mazes of tarlatan and Mathilde's incessant chatter, to the lovely gardens and shrubberies which surrounded the house.

Little Eveline, who had succumbed immediately under the charm of Margaret's manner, skipped along by her side, eager to show all the beauties and curiosities of home. Having no play-fellows of her own age, this child was wise beyond her years, and had at times a grave and almost calculating expression, which surprised Margaret in the extreme. She chattered on of family affairs and arrangements in a way that her companion neither liked to encourage nor repress. Beginning by the subject of her dress, one which was, I fear, very near her heart, the little oracle proceeded to go over the list of visitors who were expected on the following day.

'First,' she said, 'there is Sir John Saul and Lady Saul, and a Miss Saul, with a nose like this (pressing her hand on the point of her own until it became quite flat), but we must not say anything'; and here she sank her voice to a whisper, and then, with the accomplished air of a little actress, mimicked her mother's voice to perfection; 'for Miss Saul is a most amiable young person, and a most desirable friend for our girls. Maud, my dear, make Clara Saul as much at home amongst us as possible; we think that she is a very desirable friend for you all.'

'Maud hates her,' continued Eveline, quite regardless of Margaret's astonishment and reproaches; 'and so does Kate for that matter; but she thinks a rich wife would be very nice for Hastings, and so she makes a fuss, and takes her to her room, and lets her pull about her dressing-case, which I mayn't ever do—no, nor Maud either! Hastings comes home to-morrow, you know, dear old boy! You can't think, Margaret, how nice the house is when he is here!'

Margaret was quite sure that Mr Hastings' arrival would make no change so far as she herself was concerned; but she knew that Miss Maud was looking forward to her brother's return, and she could not help taking an interest in all that concerned one who had been so kind and forbearing throughout all her ignorance and mistakes.

The list of names was soon run through, and on the next afternoon at the same time Eveline and Margaret set out for their second constitutional together.

'Shall we go beyond the garden, Miss Evy?' said Margaret, who was longing for the scent and shade of hedgerows, such as surrounded her own home.

'Yes! that we will,' returned the little girl, 'for I'm sick to death of the gardens, and mamma said we might go into the lanes whenever we liked.'

They had just settled themselves in a shady corner with the purpose of making wreaths of the wild roses and ferns around them, when the sound of carriage-wheels was heard in the distance, and Eveline sprang to her feet, exclaiming,—

'I am *sure* that is Hastings! He always drives so fast when he is coming home.'

Margaret rose, and had only time to collect the flowers they had gathered and to tie on her bonnet, when, dashing round the corner, came the same dog-cart which had brought her to Walcombe the week before. Little Eveline was off in an instant to meet it, but before she had gone twenty yards, the horse was reined up, and Margaret saw the big brother jump down with a—

'Hullo, Evy, you here! and just as rosy as ever. Did you come to meet me? and where is that lazy Maud?'

Margaret could not help hearing the conversation which followed, though she would willingly have been deaf to some of the questions and answers which were exchanged.

'Who is staying here, Evy? Who is that with you? You have not sent away Miss Leigh?'

To which Evy replied in a very loud whisper, 'That is Maud's and my *maid*! is she not pretty? and she is so kind and nice: look at the wreaths we have been making! One is for Maudy's hair, because you have come.'

No answer was given to the question, but Hastings looked at Margaret as if he did think her very pretty, and said, 'He was sure she must be very nice.'

Which last sentence brought the colour with a rush to Margaret's pale face, and made her, as it always did, look prettier than ever.

'You'll come with me in the dog-cart, won't you?' said Hastings, 'there is plenty of room for both.'

Evy was enchanted; but Margaret said, quietly, 'Thank you, sir, I will walk,' and stepped aside.

'No, no, that will not do,' both Eveline and her brother answered at the same time; 'if you will not come in the dog-cart we will all walk; it is only a step. Take my portmanteau to the back-door, Marley, and I will give them a surprise at home.'

Margaret did not like this arrangement, but she felt that anything would be better than arriving at the house in Mr Hastings' dog-cart; and so tried to fall behind and let the brother and sister have the conversation to themselves. But even this was not to be allowed her; Eveline caught hold of her by the dress, and told her to 'walk quicker, and listen to what Hastings is telling me.' And when the little lady had once made up her mind, no ordinary means could move her from her determination.

Moreover, Hastings Seymour being a gentleman, could not think of allowing any woman, but especially such a ladylike and pretty one, to carry anything while he was there to do it for her. So the discarded cloaks, and even some of the wreaths of ivy and bunches of roses, were transferred to his care; and it was only as they neared the house that Margaret's respectful entreaties to have them restored were regarded.

'Here are your flowers,' said he, placing them carefully one by one in her apron; 'but I must have one for my button; which shall it be?'

Margaret looked appealingly at Eveline, who came to the rescue.

'Here, take this one! you must come in now and see mamma.'

Hastings, somewhat dissatisfied, took the flower from his little sister's hand and turned slowly towards the house. Not, however, before he had cast a look behind him at Margaret's retreating figure. 'Fancy,' he muttered to himself as he opened the door, 'Fancy *that* girl going in by the back way! She's more fit to come in here than many who do it and are welcome.'

Margaret meanwhile had reached her own room and was preparing for tea, a time which above all others she dreaded. The butler, fat, snobbish, and in every way repulsive, had made himself most odious to the poor girl, in the short week since her arrival.

His attentions, which would at any time have been distasteful to her, became more so by the seasons which he chose for their display.

Many was the blush which his coarse jests and fulsome compliments brought to Margaret's cheek; and neither her quiet and dignified behaviour, nor Mrs Burton's presence and protection, seemed in the present instance to constitute any sufficient check on his insolence. Nor was this all; Mathilde, who was ugly, ambitious, and a coquette, did not at all approve of this country belle who carried everything before her, and she showed her spite on every possible occasion, and in the most marked manner.

'What a nice walk you had with Mr Hastings, Marguerite! Oh, Mademoiselle Evy took you there, did she? Miss Evy is very clever, but not so clever like that, Marguerite!'

Too indignant to attempt a defence, Margaret remained perfectly unmoved; but Mathilde's tongue was not so easily silenced.

'Are you coming to tea? or shall Mr Barnes bring you it?' (Barnes was the obnoxious butler.) 'Perhaps you like better that Mr Hastings bring it, eh?'

This was more than Margaret could stand.

'Mathilde,' said she, turning from the glass where she had been smoothing her silky brown hair, with a look of stern displeasure in her face, 'if it pleases you to make jokes like these, be kind enough to confine yourself to those who are my equals. I am quite sure there is more harm in talking in this way, than in the unfortunate circumstance of Mr Hastings having stopped to speak to Miss Evy when I was with her.'

As she spoke she opened the door, and left Mathilde in a state of anger, surprise, and jealousy. Neither complimentary nor ornamental were the words she uttered as she smoothed her ruffled plumes, preparatory to a downward flight.

Two days after this, fresh fuel was added to the fire of Mathilde's indignation by the news, imparted to her through Miss Seymour, of Margaret's promotion to a higher office than herself. Miss Leigh had resigned her situation on account of illness in her family, and Lady Katharine was too much occupied with her houseful of visitors to think of beginning a search for a new governess.

'Why not let Margaret try and teach her for a month, mamma?' Maud had suggested. 'I am sure she is more fit for it than Miss Leigh. And Evy is only eight! She has plenty of time before her; and in the meanwhile you can look out for a governess.'

Lady Katharine's indolence made her at once fall in with any plan which could save her the slightest trouble, and Margaret was with some difficulty persuaded into undertaking the task.

It was not without much trepidation that on this evening she entered the room where Mathilde had already betaken herself for the night; and it was with great satisfaction that she discovered that her companion's fury had taken the form of sulkiness, and that she was already in bed, and pretended to be asleep.

On the following morning little Eveline's studies began. During the few days that had passed since Miss Leigh's departure, the child had been running wild as the constant attendant of her brother, and even Margaret's company had been at a discount. Consequently, there had been no walks, no wreath-making, and no taunts on the subject of 'Mr Hastings', from Mathilde, of whose presence her new duties happily relieved her. But an hour of lessons had not been fully accomplished when a knock was heard at the schoolroom door, and a beaming, sunburnt face looked in.

'When will you have done, Evy?'

'Oh, I don't know, I'm sure!' She tossed her long hair back with a profound sigh, and looked at Margaret as if her fate depended on the answer.

'My lady said we must work for an hour and a half, sir.'

'Did she? Bother lessons!' was the reply. 'You never did so many lessons before, Evy—how is it? But after this hour and a half you are to come out immediately. Mr Agnew has brought all his photographing things, and you are to be done, and Margaret. Don't forget, now. You are both to come; Mr Agnew asks it as a great favour.'

Without waiting for an answer, Hastings shut the door and went whistling down the passage.

Margaret little knew that her face, seen at prayers that morning, had created such a sensation among the guests present, that every one was awaiting with impatience her arrival on the lawn. Mr Agnew, a photographer by habit, and an artist by nature, was to perpetuate the lovely face, and little Eveline was to be an accessory only to the picture: an accessory, but at the same time indispensable, for nothing would have induced Margaret to enter the charmed circle scattered on the grass, otherwise than in attendance on her little pupil. They came out of the house hand in hand, Eveline chatting gaily, and Margaret looking timidly at the gay group before her.

Hastings met them half-way; and, with a feeling of compassion for her extreme shyness, led Margaret straight to the spot where Mr Agnew had placed his camera.

'Here is one,' he said, smiling, and looking round for Eveline, who had been captured by Lady Saul: 'the other is on the way.'

Mr Agnew instinctively took off his hat to Margaret, and hoped she did not very much mind the trouble of sitting to him for a few moments. The white apron, he said, must come off; but in every other respect the dress was perfect.

'Evy! Evy, come here! don't keep us waiting!' And Eveline, released, came with a bound to the spot, and settled herself on the grass at Margaret's feet.

'It must be the other way,' said Mr Agnew, coming from beneath his black covering: 'will you sit there?' turning to Margaret, and spreading a rug for her on the grass; 'and Eveline must stand up, with her frock filled with flowers. Seymour, get some roses, will you?—not red ones; and some very long grass.'

Hastings came back with both hands full, and choosing a pale, pink rose from the bunch, he gave it to Margaret. 'She must have one in her hand, Agnew?' he said, raising his voice; then, in a lower tone, 'It looks so nice like that.' He stood for a moment lost in admiration of the picture, and quite forgetful of the little sister who was to complete it.

'Hastings, here, put my flowers in! How shall I hold them? like that?'

'Yes, darling; that is very jolly; but where is your hair gone? bring some to the front; there, that's all right!'

Mr Agnew went for a last look before commencing operations. As he did so, Margaret, who thought the picture was about to be taken, and felt the hand which held the rose tremble, laid the flower against her lips.

'That is *lovely*!' said Hastings: 'do keep it like that!'

'No! no!' interrupted the artist; 'that hides the mouth, and will never do! Hold it a little lower; there, just so!'

'I was afraid of moving, sir,' said Margaret, drawing a long breath previous to the ordeal; and then the photograph was taken.

The sitters got up gladly, and wandered into the shrubbery. 'Don't go far, please,' said Mr Agnew, who was deep in the mysteries of his black box; 'I shall want you again presently.'

'I suppose it is spoilt, Miss Evy!' Margaret exclaimed, in a tone of dismay; but she had very soon cause to alter her opinion. When they returned to the lawn, after an interval of a few moments, a crowd was gathered round the artist, who held his production triumphantly above them all.

'How lovely!' 'How well she has sat!' 'Nothing could be finer than that head!' 'Her mouth is quite perfect!' 'And the expression!' 'You *have* got a *chef d'œuvre*, Mr Agnew!' 'And dear little Evy, too!'

Such were the remarks which greeted Margaret's ear as she approached anew the scene of action. This was in the early days of photography; the success, therefore, was the more remarkable. Again and again were Margaret and her pupil placed in position, and every time with a satisfactory result.

'Thank you,' said Mr Agnew, as he packed up his apparatus; 'you are the best subject, in every way, that I have ever had: you shall have copies of all, in a day or two.'

In the meanwhile Miss Saul, Kate and Maud Seymour, and their brother, were standing a little apart, engaged in discussing the heroine of the day.

'I cannot quite see *what* you find to admire so very much in her,' said Miss Saul, peevishly. 'Her features are good, certainly; but she is not well suited for her situation, is she?'

'She is indescribably superior to it, if you mean that,' returned Maud. 'Mamma intends keeping her permanently as nursery governess to Eveline.'

'You would not notice her in London, for instance,' observed Miss Saul, who had never been noticed anywhere; 'but people are made such a fuss with down here in the country.'

'In country or town,' said Hastings, warmly, 'I, for one, have never seen any one half so pretty.'

'And she is as good as she is beautiful,' added Maud, as they turned towards the house, where luncheon put an end to the discussion.

III

For me I thank the saints I am not great,
For if there ever come a grief to me
I cry my cry in silence, and have done.

TENNYSON

For about three weeks an incessant round of gaiety was the order of the day at Walcombe.

Picnics, boating and riding, emptied the house during the day, and Margaret saw but little of Eveline, and still less of the other members of the family. Day after day she would watch from the schoolroom window the gay groups dispersing on their different ways; and at times a feeling of restlessness and loneliness would seize her, for which she could not altogether account; perhaps the absence of regular occupation, consequent upon her little pupil's many holidays, may have been in some small degree the cause. For the week which immediately followed her promotion, and Mr Agnew's day of triumph in the garden, Margaret observed that morning after morning three horses were brought round, on which rode Miss Saul, Hastings Seymour, and one of his sisters. Strange it was, that at these times especially the sense of loneliness would steal through the open schoolroom window, and touch Margaret, in passing, with its phantom hand.

She was no longer, of course, expected to attend on Maud; but the privilege had been retained to her of helping her mistress of the week before, to dress, when a ride was in prospect.

'I hate having Mathilde about me, Margaret! but of course you are only rising to your right place now; you were quite thrown away as a maid: but I miss you terribly.'

'Thank you, Miss Maud, for saying so: I shall always like to do anything for you that I can.'

Margaret gave whip and gloves into Maud's hands as she spoke, and held the door open until she was out of sight. Then she went slowly back to the schoolroom to await Eveline's appearance, and stood with a book in her hand beside the open window. A footstep at the door startled her, and she turned round. Hastings Seymour it was who looked in.

'Good morning, Margaret! I suppose I must call you Miss Ansted now, eh?'

'No, thank you, sir; I am always called Margaret: did you come for Miss Eveline, sir?'

'Yes—well, no—not exactly. Mr Agnew gave me these photographs for you, and I thought you would like to have them as soon as possible. You don't mind my coming in here; do you, Margaret?'

'Thank you, sir,' replied Margaret, evading a direct answer, but glancing uneasily at the door. 'Will you be so kind as to thank the gentleman for me, sir? Mother——' she was going to say, 'will like so much to have them'; but an idea that it would be presumption in the extreme to converse with Mr Hastings on any point not directly in question, seized her, and she stopped at the first word.

'Well, I must go, I suppose; you won't speak to me, so it is no use staying here. It is very hard that you won't finish that sentence, Margaret; is it any use asking?'

'It was nothing sir, indeed, which could at all concern you.'

'Well, there is one thing which you *can* grant, and it does concern me, very, very nearly': Hastings' dark eyes were fixed upon Margaret, and she felt rooted to the spot. 'I only want one of these, Margaret; this one, with the rose! Mr Agnew offered me one, and I would not take it until I had got your permission; you will not be so cruel as to refuse such a little thing?'

The tone of his voice was so supplicating that Margaret was for an instant on the point of giving way. 'It is only a picture,' she said to herself; 'Miss Evy is in it, and Mr Agnew will give it himself if I do not.' But in a moment she had thrust the idea from her, and drawing herself up, she replied in as cool a voice as she could command,—

'Mr Hastings, I do not know what you mean by this; the pictures are not mine to give away, and if they were, I should not so far forget myself as to give one to you. The horses have come round, sir, I think.'

She held the door open for him, her face averted, and a look which he might well mistake for anger in her soft, grey eyes.

'Thank you for making me remember myself,' said Hastings, stiffly; 'I will not trouble you any more;' and he strode down the passage, and the next moment was standing by his horse.

Burning with agitation, and, as she tried to say to herself, anger, Margaret sat down by the window, and leaned her head against the wall. A hum of voices was going on below, and a few words here and there reached her ear.

'Why have you made this sudden plan? Can't your friend wait for you? Do stay till to-morrow, and the Sauls will be going too! You could . . .'. Here the wind carried away the sound, or the speaker lowered her voice, for Margaret heard no further. Curiosity made her stand up to see who was speaking, but she did so cautiously, from a vague fear that Hastings might look up and believe her to be watching him.

Lady Katharine was standing by her son's side, with her hand on his shoulder, evidently trying to detain him until her eloquence should have had full play. But he released himself almost impatiently from her hold, and sprang into the saddle.

'Why don't you come, Maud? Is Miss Saul ready?'

Then he turned back to his mother, as if to atone for his churlish behaviour of the moment before, and stooped his face to be kissed.

'Forgive me, mother! I am in a bad temper to-day. Oh, yes! I will go to the Sauls. No, I won't come back at present, I think, mother. But I will write in a day or two, and you'll send my things?'

Then the horses' heads were turned, and they rode slowly away. Hastings' hat was pulled down low on his forehead, and he did not look up at the schoolroom window as he passed.

The morning seemed very long. Eveline's lessons were hard and troublesome, and everything and everybody seemed to have taken a wrong turn. One thing alone was as Margaret would have wished, and that was that she had no time left her for thought. Between the monotonous repetitions of the French verb, Hastings' voice, at times almost beseeching, then so changed and formal, forced itself upon her ear and distracted her attention; but she struggled against it again and again, and applied herself vigorously to the task before her. Lessons over, however, there was a lull, for Eveline drove out with Lady Katharine, and Margaret was left to her own resources.

'I must write to mother,' she said to herself; and the little desk that had been fitted up by loving hands, was brought out and placed on the table.

Margaret sat down, pen in hand, but it was hard to bring her mind to bear on the subject of the proposed letter. Quick as lightning her thoughts flew back to the days when writing had been her greatest trial, and when no punishment was so dreaded as the reproachful look which met her when the refractory pen insisted on making a crooked 'S', or an 'N' with a long tail to it! Then she passed to that time so full of sunshine and happiness, when her father—the arduous duties of a schoolmaster being over for the day—would bring his learned books into the garden, and call his little daughter to his feet; not to teach her, save by his example; not to converse with her, for his studies were at such times above her understanding; but just to feel that she was there, to know that at any moment he could lay his hand upon her head or shoulder. Then there had come days less bright, less peaceful, when not sorrow itself, but the shadow it casts before, had laid its finger upon them; when the father had grown wayward, the strong man feeble, the meek spirit fretful, and all men saw that the end was drawing near.

One day in early March he passed away from them for ever; and Margaret, her mother, and a child-sister, had been left alone.

'I must work, mother,' she had said, when, after the first burst of sorrow, a lull had come, forcing upon them the future with its dismal prospects. 'If we stay here we must beg or starve; and I could not live to beg, mother!'

So the angel of the house had taken to herself wings, and was gaining for the loved ones at home the wherewithal to eat, and drink, and to be clothed.

As the past, with all its memories, came upon her, Margaret's head sank lower upon the table; and thoughts of the present, with its dawning troubles, acted as the last drop in the already full cup. 'What would mother say?' she sobbed to herself; 'what have I done? He meant nothing —perhaps, he meant nothing! And now he will despise me; but what could I do? I wanted to do what is right, I am sure—I am sure I did!'

Wearied at length by her sorrow, she laid her throbbing head upon her hands and fell asleep; and so the letter was touched no more on that day. For the next thing of which she was conscious was the sound of a window being closed beside her. Very gently indeed it had been closed, but day-sleep is not heavy, and Margaret awoke with a start.

'Poor child!' said a kind voice, and the speaker laid her hand on her shoulder, 'What is it? Have you got into trouble already? it is a sad house for that!'

'Oh, Miss Maud!' exclaimed Margaret, rising from her seat, 'how idle I have been! I came to write to mother, and I have been asleep instead.'

'Asleep *all* the time?' Maud smiled, but looked tenderly at the flushed face and swollen eyes. 'What is the matter? tell me, Margaret.'

Now, whether it was that kindness coming at such a time was more than Margaret could bear, or whether it was that this voice and manner reminded her of another voice and manner which had been haunting her all day, and was in great measure the cause of her present troubles, I know not. But this I know, that once more tears came thick and fast, all the thicker and faster because she knew that only in part could the reason be made known to the patient friend who waited beside her.

'I don't know how it was,' she said, at length, 'one trouble brings back another, and I was thinking of old days, and all that, Miss Maud.'

'Don't call me "Miss Maud" *now*, Margaret. For the present I am only your friend; we cannot tell our troubles to each other if you say that. You should have heard my brother, to-day, on the subject of equality——he speaks so well, and whatever he takes up he is so eager about. Miss Saul was quite taken by surprise, for she said she had never seen him so vehement and abusive about anything. And yet he is not at all a radical. Poor, dear boy! neither papa nor mamma understand him: there, he has gone away so suddenly to-day, and, of course, there must be some reason for it. Mamma has worried him, I am sure, about something, though she is so devoted to him and means to be so kind.'

Margaret's heart beat so loudly that she feared Maud's hearing it; but speak she could not.

'So you see every one has troubles, Margaret; have they not?'

'Oh, yes, Miss Maud; indeed every one has.'

'There you are, at it again! Do drop that "Miss", just for half-an-hour! Remember, you are Evy's governess now; and, besides, you must always do as you are told. Come and help me to take off my habit, will you? We have had such a long ride!'

As they passed through the cool dark passages a door was standing open, at which Maud paused.

'I was to take some things which Hastings left here: it was so unlike him to go off like that! His portmanteau is to be sent now, and these must be put in it.'

Maud searched all the drawers, but unsuccessfully.

'I believe he said it was in the drawer of the dressing-table.'

She pulled it out, and took a pocket-book from the furthest corner. 'I suppose this is his idea of concealment!' she said, laughing. 'I wonder if there is any money in it! if so, I will not give it to Barnes to pack; it shall go by the first opportunity. I have not the smallest faith in that man!'

Maud opened the pocket-book, but as she did so a sudden gust of wind emptied it of all that was not solid, and the contents were scattered on the floor.

'Careless boy! fancy leaving things about like this! Will you give me that, Margaret? There, close to your feet!'

Margaret stooped to pick up a small crumpled envelope, which had fluttered to the door. It was not closed, and her eyes fell involuntarily on its contents. With a trembling hand she gave it into Maud's extended one, for it contained the remains of a withered rose.

'Thank you, Margaret. That is all, I think. Let us go; there is a draught here.'

And whether from the quivering of the poor hand, or from the strong resemblance which this rose bore to the rose of the picture in the garden, Maud may then have guessed a little of the secret she was afterwards to learn, Margaret never knew. One thing was certain, that from that day the sister spoke no more of her brother's sudden departure, and breathed no word to her, or to others, of the hope of his return.

'It is so good for him to go about a little, papa; he can be so much at home when he has left College,' she said, when discussions were raised as to why Hastings should not come back at once. 'There is no one here at present for him to entertain; we can undertake everybody, I am sure.'

'There is young Temple!' said Mr Seymour, looking up from his newspaper.

But Maud seemed to think she could include his amusement in her undertaking without putting herself to any extra inconvenience whatsoever.

So a fortnight passed, and Hastings was not recalled. Neither did there seem any prospect of his return for the present; for a plan was proposed and finally settled by which the whole family, Eveline excepted, was to leave home on a visit of ten days at least to Lady Katharine's relations. Let it not be supposed, however, that in the meanwhile either Margaret or Hastings was in a happy, or by any means settled, state of mind. The latter fêted, and made much of by the Saul family at large, and Miss Saul in particular, did not feel in the smallest degree compensated for his voluntary exile from home. And Margaret was, if possible, growing daily more anxious, more divided between inclination and duty, between right and wrong.

If it had really to come to that dreadful pass, that Mr Hastings had thought of her as he should never have allowed himself to think of one so beneath him in birth and station, then there was but one way open; she must leave Walcombe at once. But if it was only his way,—his manner,—if he had meant nothing, and she was taking it for much,—what then? Was she to throw up prospects, such as could never be hers again? And if she did so, what could she give to her mother as a sufficient reason? Mr Hastings had only asked her for a picture!—only kept a dead rose! and was that, after all, *the* rose?

But still she failed to convince herself, and the vexed question weighed night and day upon her mind. A morning came, however, which decided it at one stroke.

'Here's a letter for you,' said Mathilde, tossing one across the table at Margaret, as she sat down to breakfast with her little pupil; and the Frenchwoman eyed suspiciously, first the letter and then the face of the recipient. But Margaret, knowing that to read it before those black eyes was to make it public at once, put it without any comment into her pocket, and looked at it no more until breakfast was over, and Mathilde and Eveline gone, when with a sinking heart, she tore open the envelope in the sanctuary of the schoolroom window.

IV

I love thee not, I love thee not! away!
Here's no more courage in my soul to say,
'Look in my face and see.'

ELIZ. BARRETT BROWNING

What that letter said no one except Hastings and Margaret ever knew; but, in half-an-hour from the time of its arrival, the latter had resigned her situation in Lady Katharine's presence.

'Are you not comfortable, Margaret? What is it that annoys you? You surely cannot know what you are doing!'

'Oh, my lady,' said the poor girl, 'I do, indeed, know what I am doing, better than any one else can know! But I must go, my lady; there is no choice—indeed there is not! When can you spare me to go back to mother? I know it is too much to ask, but if I might go soon?'

'*Certainly* not before we leave home next week. Of course I must now take Miss Eveline with me; but it is most inconvenient, most disobliging and absurd of you, I should say.'

Margaret's pale face showed no sign of emotion—anger is so much easier to bear than tenderness when the heart is breaking. And so she left the room without having what Miss Seymour and Lady Katharine would have called 'a scene', and took refuge again in the schoolroom, with the purpose of carrying out to the full the bitter task which had come upon her.

'O God!' she said, falling on her knees to seek that comfort which she felt could now alone avail her, 'O God, help me to do what is right—not what I wish, but what is right!'

Then she rose, and the desk was once more brought out, and the pen taken in hand. And the first letter was easy enough to write.

'I am coming home to you, mother dearest,' she wrote; 'I am not ill, and I have done nothing which could displease you; neither have I displeased my mistress, or any one here. But I must come home, mother, and when I see you I will tell you all I can.'

But Margaret knew that she could never, never tell, even to her mother, the story of her life, which had begun and ended in the few short weeks of their separation.

And still the bitterest drop of all was to be taken; for that Hastings' letter must be answered she had now quite decided.

'If I take no notice of it,' she said to herself, 'he will think I have not courage to answer him, and he deserves that I should behave well by him as he has behaved by me; he shall not think I treat his love lightly, though it can never, never, be mine.'

She could not trust herself to read his letter again before she wrote. All those passionate words of love, all those sacrifices which he said would be no sacrifice if she only were to be the reward! if she would only say she cared for him a little—ever so little! He who was so far beneath her in everything—in everything except the cursed distinctions of rank and wealth—all those promises that no opposition should move him—no threats change his determination—all those vows of eternal fidelity—of protection and shelter in the outset, and then of reconciliation, complete and universal at last, 'Because Maud loves you, and she influences them all: it would be but a short trial, Margaret, compared with the happiness it would bring!' All the threats of despair, of blighted hopes, and blasted prospects, and ruin, at times hinting at self-destruction itself! All these, Margaret knowing her own weakness, forebore to read, until the stiff, cold, formal answer had been written.

There it lay. So neat, so stiff, so carefully worded, and so cold, that when she read it over, and suffered doubly in herself every pang which it would cause, she could not doubt that power from above had been given her to accomplish that for which she had prayed. Then it was folded, placed in an envelope, and sealed, without a sigh of regret, without a pause of hesitation, without one tear.

Poor little Margaret! all active suffering, even, did not end for her until Walcombe had closed its doors upon her for ever. The last days were so harassing in their restlessness, in their grief at the coming separation from Maud and little Eveline, who had been so true and so fond; and in the additional weight of trouble which endless questionings, and taunts, and surmises, as to her departure brought upon her—these last days, I say, were so stormy, that the only two of the household who could be said to see things in their true light, Maud Seymour and the poor little victim herself, longed for the day which would release both, and put an end to much that was now so wearisome and heart-breaking.

Thursday was the day fixed for Margaret's departure; and on the Wednesday evening, as she sat lonely and miserable in the same window which had witnessed all her struggles, a gentle tap was heard at the door, and her faithful friend entered.

'Come out, dear. I must have a talk with you to-night—it is our last chance.'

Margaret rose, and, without a word, moved into the adjoining room and fetched her bonnet.

'I am ready,' she said, feeling at this time no shame at the desired omission of '*Miss* Maud,' a point in happier days so often disputed.

Silently they left the house and passed into the dark quiet shrubberies, where nature seemed resting after the weary heat of a long day.

'Give me your hand, Margaret, and promise me something! That you will not blame yourself for anything that has happened. You have done quite right, dear—you have saved him from making promises which he would never have been allowed to keep, and both from greater misery. You have behaved nobly—like a true, brave, strong-hearted girl as you are, and God will bless you for it; He will make it up to you in some way, I am sure.'

Before Margaret could answer, before she could find words to tell Maud, that though she had acted rightly to the best of her knowledge, she had yet been too late to save the promises and misery of which she spoke, a rustling in the trees startled them both, and Hastings himself stood beside them. In a moment he was on his knees at Margaret's feet, holding her hands in his in a convulsive grasp.

'You shall not move until you say you love me; until you have promised to be my wife!'

He buried his face in the folds of her dress, and his whole frame shook with emotion.

Poor Margaret! she did not speak or move. The power even of disengaging herself from the passionate grasp seemed to have left her. But Maud knew that the trial must be short if she was to pass through it once more triumphant, and came to her aid with a voice and manner admitting of no resistance.

'Hastings, are you a gentleman or a madman? Leave go, I tell you, directly! Go home, Margaret, and I will follow you.'

She took both his hands, and held them in hers, almost as firmly as he had held Margaret's, until the slim figure had been lost in the darkness. One struggle for release he made, and then he stood stunned and passive.

'I cannot stay longer, dear,' said Maud, when half-an-hour had slipped by, 'but I will send some one else to talk to you; you must think of him as a brother now: he will be so sorry for you, Hastings! But make me one promise—never, never to speak like that to Margaret again! You don't know how cruel it is, Hastings, or you would not do it—indeed, you would not. Now, promise! on your honour.'

'Very well, Maud, on my honour. But you don't know how hard it is,—how bitter it is! I have been here night after night since I got her letter, always hoping, always fearing, to meet her. Once I saw her at the window, just once; and night after night I go back, thinking that the next night I may see her. I couldn't stay at Camworth, of course—how could I when the thought of this was maddening me? I believe I *am* a madman, Maud!'

She drew him to a garden-seat, kissed his forehead, and left him. In a few moments Harrington Temple was at his side, comforting, scolding, pitying, and laughing at him in turn.

'I shall be your brother soon, Hastings, so listen to me and be patient. I would do anything for you, if it was only for Maud's sake. Come, and let us talk it over; but, first, where on earth do you spring from?'

After this there is little of story to be told.

Margaret left Walcombe, once more under the care of good John Marley, and twelve hours from the time of her last trial in the garden she was at her mother's side, her arms clasped round her neck, and her face hidden in her shoulder.

'You look very pale, my darling. Have you been ill? or is it home you have been sickening for? May I send for John to come and see you, Margaret? he will be so glad, dear.'

'No, no, mother! he must not come: you must tell him not to think of that any more; we'll be everything to each other now, mother dearest.'

Years have passed, and Hastings Seymour is married. Not to Miss Saul, nor to an heiress, but to a clergyman's daughter—a good little wife, with a white face, fair hair, and a kindly smile. She has won his love so far, that he is said to be a devoted husband; but I think there is a little corner-stone in his heart which has never yet been turned over— a little spot of consecrated ground, to which he has never led his wife, saying, 'Come, dear, and see.'

Perhaps he will some day. When the grass is greener on it: when pink roses and forget-me-nots, which still bloom there, have hung their heads and passed away.

Maud is married, and to Harrington Temple. She is happy as she deserves, for her life is spent in deeds of usefulness and words of love. And she has, perhaps, proved herself to have been better able than any one else to sympathise in poor Hastings' troubles; for she holds as her nearest and truest friend, one, who according to worldly judgment, is far beneath her notice.

If you could but see this friend, when Maud's little ones are clamouring round her; when the mother is telling stories of her childhood, and of the happy Walcombe days; I think you would recognise, by the animated though sad expression, and by the features, still unchanged, of this gentle friend, the heroine of old days, the brave, true, and loyal Margaret.

Her hair is still smooth and abundant; her figure and movements as graceful as before; but the first flush of life and its excitements has passed over her, and a pallor has settled on the calm face, which no mention of old days has power to remove.

One of the group there is who claims, and receives, from this sweet friend a larger share of love than all the others. He is rosy, with fat, dimpled cheeks, and curly hair; and the little one's name is Hastings.

CHRISTINA ROSSETTI

Hero

Oh, wad some power the giftie gie us!

BURNS

If you consult the authentic map of Fairyland (recently published by Messrs Moon, Shine, and Co.) you will notice that the emerald-green line which indicates its territorial limit, is washed towards the south by a bold expanse of sea, undotted by either rocks or islands. To the north-west it touches the work-a-day world, yet is effectually barricaded against intruders by an impassable chain of mountains; which, enriched throughout with mines of gems and metals, presents on Man-side a leaden sameness of hue, but on Elf-side glitters with diamonds and opals as with ten thousand fire-flies. The greater portion of the west frontier is, however, bounded, not by these mountains, but by an arm of the sea, which forms a natural barrier between the two countries; its eastern shore peopled by good folks and canny neighbours, gay sprites, graceful fairies, and sportive elves; its western by a bold tribe of semi-barbarous fishermen.

Nor was it without reason that the first settlers selected this fishing-field, and continued to occupy it, though generation after generation they lived and died almost isolated. Their swift, white-sailed boats ever bore the most delicate freights of fish to the markets of Outerworld—and not of fish only; many a waif and stray from Fairyland washed ashore amongst them. Now a fiery carbuncle blazed upon the sand; now a curiously-wrought ball of gold or ivory was found imbedded amongst the pebbles. Sometimes a sunny wave threw up a rose-coloured winged shell or jewelled starfish; sometimes a branch of unfading seaweed, exquisitely perfumed. But though these treasures, when once secured, could be offered for sale and purchased by all alike, they were never, in the first instance, discovered except by children or innocent young

138

maidens; indeed, this fact was of such invariable occurrence, and children were so fortunate in treasure-finding, that a bluff mariner would often, on returning home empty-handed from his day's toil, despatch his little son or daughter to a certain sheltered stretch of shingle, which went by the name of 'the children's harvest-field'; hoping by such means to repair his failure.

Amongst this race of fishermen was none more courageous, hospitable, and free-spoken than Peter Grump the widower; amongst their daughters was none more graceful and pure than his only child Hero, beautiful, lively, tender-hearted, and fifteen; the pet of her father, the pride of her neighbours, and the true love of Forss, as sturdy a young fellow as ever cast a net in deep water, or rowed against wind and tide for dear life.

One afternoon Hero, rosy through the splashing spray and sea-wind, ran home full-handed from the harvest-field.

'See here, father!' she cried, eagerly depositing a string of sparkling red beads upon the table: 'see, are they not beautiful?'

Peter Grump examined them carefully, holding each bead up to the light, and weighing them in his hand.

'Beautiful indeed!' echoed Forss, who unnoticed, at least by the elder, had followed Hero into the cottage. 'Ah, if I had a sister to find me fairy treasures, I would take the three months' long journey to the best market of Outerworld, and make my fortune there.'

'Then you would rather go the three months' journey into Outerworld than come every evening to my father's cottage?' said Hero, shyly.

'Truly I would go to Outerworld first, and come to you afterwards,' her lover answered, with a smile; for he thought how speedily on his return he would have a tight house of his own, and a fair young wife, too.

'Father,' said Hero presently, 'if, instead of gifts coming now and then to us, I could go to Giftland and grow rich there, would you fret after me?'

'Truly,' answered honest Peter, 'if you can go and be Queen of Fairyland, I will not keep you back from such eminence'; for he thought, 'my darling jests; no one ever traversed those mountains or that inland sea, and how should her little feet cross over?'

But Hero, who could not read their hearts, said within herself, 'They do not love me as I love them. Father should not leave me to be fifty kings; and I would not leave Forss to go to Fairyland, much less Outerworld.'

Yet from that day forward Hero was changed; their love no longer seemed sufficient for her; she sought after other love and other admiration. Once a lily was ample head-dress, now she would heighten her complexion with a wreath of gorgeous blossoms; once it was enough that Peter and Forss should be pleased with her, now she grudged any man's notice to her fellow-maidens. Stung by supposed indifference, she suffered disappointment to make her selfish. Her face, always beautiful, lost its expression of gay sweetness; her temper became capricious, and instead of cheerful airs she would sing snatches of plaintive or bitter songs. Her father looked anxious, her lover sad; both endeavoured, by the most patient tenderness, to win her back to her former self; but a weight lay on their hearts when they noticed that she no longer brought home fairy treasures, and remembered that such could be found only by the innocent.

One evening Hero, sick alike of herself and of others, slipped unnoticed from the cottage, and wandered seawards. Though the moon had not yet risen, she could see her way distinctly, for all Fairycoast flashed one blaze of splendour. A soft wind bore to Hero the hum of distant instruments and songs, mingled with ringing laughter; and she thought, full of curiosity, that some festival must be going on amongst the little people; perhaps a wedding.

Suddenly the music ceased, the lights danced up and down, ran to and fro, clambered here and there, skurried round and round with irregular precipitate haste, while the laughter was succeeded by fitful sounds of lamentation and fear. Hero fancied some precious thing must have been lost, and that a minute search was going on. For hours the commotion continued, then gradually, spark by spark, the blaze died out, and all seemed once more quiet; yet still the low wail of sorrow was audible.

Weary at length of watching, Hero arose; and was just about to turn homewards, when a noisy, vigorous wave leaped ashore, and deposited something shining at her feet.

She stooped. What could it be?

It was a broad, luminous shell, fitted up with pillows and an awning. On the pillows and under the scented canopy lay fast asleep a little creature, butterfly-winged and coloured like a rose-leaf. The fish who should have piloted her had apparently perished at his post, some portion of his pulp still cleaving to the shell's fluted lip; while unconscious of her faithful adherent's fate, rocked by wind and wave, the Princess Royal of Fairyland had floated fast asleep to Man-side. Her disappearance it was which had occasioned such painful commotion amongst her family and affectionate lieges; but all their lamentations failed to rouse her; and not till the motion of the water ceased did she awake to find herself, vessel and all, cradled in the hands of Hero.

During some moments the two stared at each other in silent amazement; then a suspicion of the truth flashing across her mind, Princess Fay sat upright on her couch and spoke,—

'What gift shall I give you that so I may return to my home in peace?'

For an instant Hero would have answered, 'Give me the love of Forss'; but pride checked the words, and she said, 'Grant me, wherever I am, to become the supreme object of admiration.'

Princess Fay smiled, 'As you will,' said she; 'but to effect this you must come with me to my country.'

Then, whilst Hero looked round for some road which mortal feet might traverse, Fay uttered a low, bird-like call. A slight frothing ensued, at the water's edge, close to the shingle, whilst one by one mild, scaly faces peered above the surface, and vigorous tails propelled their owners. Next, three strong fishes combining themselves into a raft, Hero seated herself on the centre back, and holding fast her little captive, launched out upon the water.

Soon they passed beyond where mortal sailor had ever navigated, and explored the unknown sea. Strange forms of seals and porpoises, marine snails and unicorns contemplated them with surprise, followed reverentially in their wake, and watched them safe ashore.

But on Hero their curious ways were lost, so absorbed was she by ambitious longings. Even after landing, to her it seemed nothing that her feet trod on sapphires, and that both birds and fairies made their nests in the adjacent trees. Blinded, deafened, stultified by self, she passed unmoved through crystal streets, between fountains of rainbow, along corridors carpeted with butterflies' wings, up a staircase formed from a single tusk, into the opal presence-chamber, even to the foot of the carnelian dormouse on which sat enthroned Queen Fairy.

Till the Queen said, 'What gift shall I give you, that so my child may be free from you and we at peace?'

Then again Hero answered, 'Grant me, wherever I am, to become the supreme object of admiration.'

Thereat a hum and buzz of conflicting voices ran through the apartment. The immutable statutes of Fairycourt enacted that no captured fairy could be set free except at the price named by the captor; from this necessity not even the blood-royal was exempt, so that the case was very urgent; on the other hand, the beauty of Hero, her extreme youth, and a certain indignant sorrow which spoke in her every look and tone, had enlisted such sympathy on her side as made the pigmy nation loth to endow her with the perilous pre-eminence she demanded.

'Clear the court,' shrilled the usher of the golden rod, an alert elf, green like a grasshopper. Amid the crowd of non-voters Hero, bearing her august prisoner, retired from the throne-room.

When recalled to the assembly an imposing silence reigned, which was almost instantly broken by the Queen. 'Maiden,' she said, 'it cannot be but that the dear ransom of my daughter's liberty must be paid. I grant you, wherever you may appear, to become the supreme object of admiration. In you every man shall find his taste satisfied. In you one shall recognise his ideal of loveliness, another shall bow before the impersonation of dignity. One shall be thrilled by your voice, another fascinated by your wit and inimitable grace. He who prefers colour shall dwell upon your complexion, hair, eyes; he who worships intellect shall find in you his superior; he who is ambitious shall feel you to be a prize more august than an empire. I cannot ennoble the taste of those who look upon you: I can but cause that in you all desire shall be gratified. If sometimes you chafe under a trivial homage, if sometimes you are admired rather for what you have than for what you are, accuse your votaries,—accuse, if you will, yourself, but accuse not me. In consideration, however, of your utter inexperience, I and my trusty counsellors have agreed for one year to retain your body here, whilst in spirit you at will become one with the reigning object of admiration. If at the end of the year you return to claim this pre-eminence as your own proper attribute, it shall then be unconditionally granted: if, on the contrary, you then or even sooner desire to be released from a gift whose sweetness is alloyed by you know not how much of bitter shortcoming and disappointment, return, and you shall at once be relieved of a burden you cannot yet estimate.'

So Hero quitted the presence, led by spirits to a pleasance screened off into a perpetual twilight. Here, on a rippling lake, blossomed lilies. She lay down among their broad leaves and cups, cradled by their interlaced stems, rocked by warm winds on the rocking water; she lay till the splash of fountains, and the chirp of nestlings, and the whisper of spiced breezes, and the chanted monotone of an innumerable choir, lulled to sleep her soul, lulled to rest her tumultuous heart, charmed her conscious spirit into a heavy blazing diamond,—a glory by day, a lamp by night, and a world's wonder at all times.

Let us leave the fair body at rest, and crowned with lilies, to follow the restless spirit, shrined in a jewel, and cast ashore on Man-side.

No sooner was this incomparable diamond picked up and carried home than Hero's darling wish was gratified. She outshone every beauty, she eclipsed the most brilliant eyes of the colony. For a moment the choicest friend was superseded, the dearest mistress overlooked. For a moment—and this outstripped her desire—Peter Grump forgot his lost daughter and Forss his lost love. Soon greedy admiration developed into greedy strife: her spark kindled a conflagration. This gem, in itself an unprecedented fortune, should this gem remain the property of a defenceless orphan to whom mere chance had assigned it? From her it was torn in a moment: then the stronger wrested it from the strong, blows revenged blows, until, as the last contender bit the dust in convulsive death, the victor, feared throughout the settlement for his brute strength and brutal habits, bore off the prize toward the best market of Outerworld.

It irked Hero to nestle in that polluted bosom and count the beatings of that sordid heart; but when, at the end of the three months' long journey, she found herself in a guarded booth, enthroned on a cushion of black velvet, by day blazing even in the full sunshine, by night needing no lamp save her own lustre; when she heard the sums running up from thousands into millions which whole guilds of jewellers, whole caravans of merchant princes, whole royal families clubbed their resources to offer for her purchase, it outweighed all she had undergone of disgust and tedium. Finally, two empires, between which a marriage was about to be contracted and a peace ratified, outbid all rivals and secured the prize.

Princess Lily, the august bride-elect, was celebrated far and near for courteous manners and delicate beauty. Her refusal was more gracious, her reserve more winning, than the acquiescence or frankness of another. She might have been more admired, or even envied, had she been less loved. If she sang, her hearers loved her; if she danced, the lookers-on loved her; thus love forestalled admiration, and happy in the one she never missed the other.

Only on her wedding-day, for the first time, she excited envy; for in her coronet appeared the inestimable jewel, encircling her sweet face with a halo of splendour. Hero eclipsed the bride, dazzled the bridegroom, distracted the queen-mother, and thrilled the whole assembly. Through all the public solemnities of the day Hero reigned supreme: and when, the state parade being at length over, Lily unclasped her gems and laid aside her cumbrous coronet, Hero was handled with more reverential tenderness than her mistress.

The bride leaned over her casket of treasures and gazed at the inestimable diamond. 'Is it not magnificent?' whispered she.

'What?' said the bridegroom: 'I was looking at you.'

So Lily flushed up with delight, and Hero experienced a shock. Next the diamond shot up one ray of dazzling momentary lustre; then lost its supernatural brilliancy, as Hero quitted the gem for the heart of Lily.

Etiquette required that the young couple should for some days remain in strict retirement. Hero now found herself in a secluded palace, screened by the growth of many centuries. She was waited on by twenty bridesmaids only less noble than their princess; she was worshipped by her bridegroom and reflected by a hundred mirrors. In Lily's pure heart she almost found rest: and when the young prince, at dawn, or lazy noon, or mysterious twilight—for indeed the process went on every day and all day—praised his love's eyes, or hair, or voice, or movements, Hero thought with proud eagerness of the moment when, in her own proper person, she might claim undisputed pre-eminence.

The prescribed seclusion, however, drew to a close, and the royal pair must make their entrance on public life. Their entrance coincided with another's exit.

Melice Rapta had for three successive seasons thrilled the world by her voice, and subdued it by her loveliness. She possessed the demeanour of an empress, and the winning simplicity of a child, genius and modesty, tenderness and indomitable will. Her early years had passed in obscurity, subject to neglect, if not unkindness; it was only when approaching womanhood developed and matured her gifts that she met with wealthy protectors and assumed their name: for Melice was a foundling.

No sooner, however, did her world-wide fame place large resources at her command, than she anxiously sought to trace her unknown parentage; and, at length, discovered that her high-born father and plebeian mother—herself sole fruit of their concealed marriage—were dead. Once made known to her kindred, she was eagerly acknowledged by them; but rejecting more brilliant offers, she chose to withdraw into a private sphere, and fix her residence with a maternal uncle, who, long past the meridian of life, devoted his energies to botanical research and culture.

So, on the same evening, Lily and her husband entered on their public duties, and Melice took leave for ever of a nation of admirers.

When the prince and princess appeared in the theatre, the whole house stood up, answering their smiles and blushes by acclamations of welcome. They took their places on chairs of state under an emblazoned canopy, and the performance commenced.

A moonless night: three transparent ghosts flit across the scene, bearing in their bosoms unborn souls. They leave behind tracks of light from which are generated arums. Day breaks—Melice enters; she washes her hands in a fountain, singing to the splash of the water; she plucks arums, and begins weaving them into a garland, still singing.

Lily bent forward to whisper something to her husband; but he raised his hand, enforcing 'Hush!' as through eyes and ears his soul drank deep of beauty. The young wife leaned back with good-humoured acquiescence; but Hero?

In another moment Hero was singing in the unrivalled songstress, charming and subduing every heart. The play proceeded; its incidents, its characters developed. Melice outshone, outsang herself; warbling like a bird, thrilling with entreaty, pouring forth her soul in passion. Her voice commanded an enthusiastic silence, her silence drew down thunders of enthusiastic applause. She acknowledged the honour with majestic courtesy; then, for the first time, trembled, changed colour: would have swept from the presence like a queen, but merely wept like a woman.

It was her hour of supreme triumph.

Next day she set out for her uncle's residence, her own selected home.

Many a long day's journey separated her from her mother's village, and her transit thither assumed the aspect of a ceremonial progress. At every town on her route orations and emblems awaited her; whilst from the capital she was quitting, came, pursuing her, messages of farewell, congratulation, entreaty. Often an unknown cavalier rode beside her carriage some stage of the journey; often a high-born lady met her on the road, and, taking a last view of her countenance, obtained a few more last words from the most musical mouth in the world.

At length the goal was reached. The small cottage, surrounded by its disproportionately extensive garden, was there; the complex forcing-houses, pits, refrigerators, were there; Uncle Treeh was there, standing at the open door to receive his newly-found relative.

Uncle Treeh was rather old, rather short, not handsome; with an acute eye, a sensitive mouth, and spectacles. With his complexion of sere brown, and his scattered threads of white hair, he strikingly resembled certain plants of the cactus tribe, which, in their turn, resemble withered old men.

All his kind face brightened with welcome as he kissed his fair niece, and led her into his sitting-room. On the table were spread for her refreshment the choicest products of his gardens: ponderous pineapples, hundred-berried vine clusters, currants large as grapes and sweet as honey. For a moment his eyes dwelt on a human countenance with more admiration than on a vegetable; for a moment, on comparing Melice's complexion with an oleander, he awarded the palm to the former.

But a week afterwards, when Melice, leaning over his shoulder, threatened to read what he was writing, Treeh looked good-naturedly conscious, and, abandoning the letter to her mercy, made his escape into a neighbouring conservatory.

She read as follows:—

My Friend,—

You will doubtless have learned how my solitude has been invaded by my sister's long-lost daughter, a peach-coloured damsel, with commeline eyes, and hair darker than chestnuts. For one whole evening I suspended my beloved toils and devoted myself to her: alas! next day, on revisiting Lime Alley, house B, pot 37, I found that during my absence a surreptitious slug had devoured three shoots of a tea-rose. Thus nipped in the bud, my cherished nursling seemed to upbraid me with neglect; and so great was my vexation, that, on returning to company, I could scarcely conceal it. From that hour I resolved that no mistaken notions of hospitality should ever again seduce me from the true aim of my existence. Nerved by this resolution, I once more take courage; and now write to inform you that I am in hourly expectation of beholding pierce the soil (loam, drenched with liquid manure) the first sprout from that unnamed alien seed, which was brought to our market, three months ago, by a seafaring man of semi-barbarous aspect. I break off to visit my hoped-for seedling.

At this moment the door, hastily flung open, startled Melice, who, looking up, beheld Treeh, radiant and rejoicing, a flowerpot in his hand. He hurried up to her, and, setting his load on the table, sank upon his knees. 'Look!' he cried.

'Why, uncle,' rejoined Melice, when curious examination revealed to her eyes a minute living point of green, 'this marvel quite eclipses me!'

A pang of humiliation shot through Hero, an instantaneous sharp pang; the next moment she was burrowing beneath the soil in the thirsty sucking roots of a plant not one-eighth of an inch high.

Day by day she grew, watched by an eye unwearied as that of a lover. The green sheath expanded fold after fold, till from it emerged a crumpled leaf, downy and notched. How was this first-born of an unknown race tended; how did fumigations rout its infinitesimal foes, whilst circles of quicklime barricaded it against the invasion of snails! It throve vigorously, adding leaf to leaf and shoot to shoot: at length, a minute furry-bud appeared.

Uncle Treeh, the most devoted of foster-fathers, revelled in ecstasy; yet it seemed to Hero that his step was becoming feebler, and his hand more tremulous. One morning he waited on her as usual, but appeared out of breath and unsteady: gradually he bent more and more forward, till, without removing his eyes from the cherished plant, he sank huddled on the conservatory floor.

Three hours afterwards hurried steps and anxious faces sought the old man. There, on the accustomed spot, he lay, shrunk together, cold, dead; his glazed eyes still riveted on his favourite nursling.

They carried away the corpse—could Treeh have spoken he would have begged to lie where a delicate vine might suck nourishment from his remains—and buried it a mile away from the familiar garden; but no one had the heart to crush him beneath a stone. The earth lay lightly upon him; and though his bed was unvisited by one who would have tended it—for Melice, now a wife, had crossed the sea to a distant home—generations of unbidden flowers, planted by winds and birds, blossomed there.

During one whole week Hero and her peers dwelt in solitude, uncared for save by a mournful gardener, who loved and cherished the vegetable family for their old master's sake. But on the eighth day came a change: all things were furbished up, and assumed their most festive aspect; for the new owners were hourly expected.

The door opened. A magnificently attired lady, followed by two children and a secondary husband, sailed into the narrow passage, casting down with her robe several flower-pots. She glanced around with a superior air, and was about to quit the scene without a word, when the gardener ventured to remark, 'Several very rare plants, madam.'

'Yes, yes,' she cried, 'we knew his eccentric tastes, poor dear old man!' and stepped doorwards.

One more effort: 'This, madam,' indicating Hero, 'is a specimen quite unique.'

'Really,' said she; and observed to her husband as she left the house, 'These useless buildings must be cleared away. This will be the exact spot for a ruin: I adore a ruin!'

A ruin?—Hero's spirit died in the slighted plant. Was it to such taste as this she must condescend? such admiration as this she must court? Merely to receive it would be humiliation. A passionate longing for the old lost life, the old beloved love, seized her; she grew tremulous, numbed: 'Ah,' she thought, 'this is death!'

A hum, a buzz, voices singing and speaking, the splash of fountains, airy laughter, rustling wings, the noise of a thousand leaves and flower-cups in commotion. Sparks dancing in the twilight, dancing feet, joy and triumph; unseen hands loosing succous, interlacing stalks from their roots beneath the water; towing a lily-raft across the lake, down a tortuous inland creek, through Fairy-harbour, out into the open sea.

On the lily-raft lay Hero, crowned with lilies, at rest. A swift tide was running from Fairycoast to Man-side: every wave heaving her to its silver crest bore her homewards; every wind whistling from the shore urged her homewards. Seals and unicorns dived on either hand, unnoticed. All the tumbling porpoises in the ocean could not have caught her eye.

At length, the moon-track crossed, she entered the navigable sea. There all was cold, tedious, dark; not a vessel in sight, not a living sound audible. She floated farther: something black loomed through the obscurity; could it be a boat? yes, it was certainly a distant boat; then she perceived a net lowered into the water; then saw two fishermen kindle a fire, and prepare themselves to wait, it might be for hours. Their forms thrown out against the glare struck Hero as familiar: that old man, stooping more than his former wont; that other strong and active figure, not so broad as in days of yore;—Hero's heart beat painfully: did they remember yet? did they love yet? was it yet time?

Nearer and nearer she floated, nearer and nearer. The men were wakeful, restless; they stirred the embers into a blaze, and sat waiting. Then softly and sadly arose the sound of a boat-song:—

PETER GRUMP

If underneath the water
  You comb your golden hair
With a golden comb, my daughter,
  Oh, would that I were there.
If underneath the wave
You fill a slimy grave,
Would that I, who could not save,
  Might share.

FORSS

If my love Hero queens it
  In summer Fairyland,
  What would I be
  But the ring on her hand?
Her cheek when she leans it
  Would lean on me:—
Or sweet, bitter-sweet,
  The flower that she wore

When we parted, to meet
On the hither shore
Anymore? nevermore.

Something caught Forss's eye; he tried the nets, and finding them heavily burdened began to haul them in, saying, 'It is a shoal of white fish; no, a drift of white seaweed';—but suddenly he cried out: 'Help, old father! it is a corpse, as white as snow!'

Peter ran to the nets, and with the younger man's aid rapidly drew them in. Hero lay quite still, while very gently they lifted the body over the boat-side, whispering one to another: 'It is a woman—she is dead!' They laid her down where the fire-light shone full upon her face—her familiar face.

Not a corpse, O Peter Grump: not a corpse, O true Forss, staggering as from a death-blow. The eyes opened, the face dimpled into a happy smile; with tears, and clinging arms, and clinging kisses, Hero begged forgiveness of her father and her lover.

I will not tell you of the questions asked and answered, the return home, the wonder and joy which spread like wildfire through the colony. Nor how in the moonlight Forss wooed and won his fair love; nor even how at the wedding danced a band of strangers, gay and agile, recognised by none save the bride. I will merely tell you how in after years, sitting by her husband's fireside, or watching on the shingle for his return, Hero would speak to her children of her own early days. And when their eyes kindled while she told of the marvellous splendour of Fairyland, she would assure them, with a convincing smile, that only home is happy: and when, with flushed cheeks and quickened breath, they followed the story of her brief pre-eminence, she would add, that though admiration seems sweet at first, only love is sweet first, and last, and always.

MARY BRADDON

Her Last Appearance

CHAPTER I

HER TEMPTATION

'He is a scoundrel,' said the gentleman.

'He is my husband,' answered the lady.

Not much in either sentence, yet both came from bursting hearts and lips passion-pale.

'Is that your answer, Barbara?'

'The only answer God and man will suffer me to give you.'

'And he is to break your heart, and squander your earnings on his low vices—keep you shut up in this shabby lodging, while all the town is raving about your beauty and your genius—and you are to have no redress, no escape?'

'Yes,' she answered, with a look that thrilled him, 'I shall escape him—in my coffin. My wrongs will have redress—at the day of judgment.'

'Barbara, he is killing you.'

'Don't you think that may be the greatest kindness he has ever shown me?'

The gentleman began to pace the room distractedly. The lady turned to the tall narrow glass over the chimney-piece, with a curious look, half mournful, half scornful.

She was contemplating the beauty which was said to have set the town raving.

What did that tarnished mirror show her? A small pale face, wan and wasted by studious nights and a heavy burden of care, dark shadows about dark eyes. But such eyes! They seemed, in this cold light of day, too black and large and brilliant for the small white face; but at night, in the lamplit theatre, with a patch of rouge under them, and the fire of genius burning in them, they were the most dazzling, soul-ensnaring eyes man had ever seen; or so said the cognoscenti, Horace Walpole among them; and Mrs Barbara Stowell was the last fashion at Covent Garden Theatre.

It was only her second season on those famous boards, and her beauty and talent still wore the bloom of novelty. The town had never seen her by daylight. She never drove in the Ring, or appeared at a fashionable auction, or mystified her admirers at a masquerade in the Pantheon, or drank whey in St James's Park—in a word, she went nowhere,—and the town had invented twenty stories to account for this secluded existence. Yet no one had guessed the truth, which was sadder than the most dismal fiction that had floated down the idle stream of London gossip. Barbara Stowell kept aloof from the world for three reasons,—first, because her husband was a tyrant and a ruffian, and left her without a sixpence; secondly, because her heart was broken; thirdly, because she was dying.

This last reason was only known to herself. No stethoscope had sounded that aching breast—no stately physician, with eye-glass and gold-headed cane, and chariot and footman, had been called in to testify in scientific language to the progress of the destroyer; but Barbara Stowell knew very well that her days were numbered, and that her span of life was of the briefest.

She was not in the first freshness of her youth. Three years ago she had been a country parson's daughter, leading the peacefullest, happiest, obscurest life in a Hertfordshire village—when, as ill luck would have it, she came to London to visit an aunt who was in business there as a milliner, and at this lady's house met Jack Stowell, an actor of small parts at Covent Garden—a cold-hearted rascal with a fine person, a kind of surface cleverness which had a vast effect upon simple people, and ineffable conceit. He had the usual idea of the unsuccessful actor, that his manager was his only enemy, and that the town was languishing to see him play Romeo, and Douglas, and the whole string of youthful heroes. His subordinate position soured him; and he sought consolation from drink and play, and was about as profligate a specimen of his particular genus as could be found in the purlieus of Bow Street. But he knew how to make himself agreeable in society, and passed for a 'mighty pretty fellow'. He had the art of being sentimental too on occasion, could cast up his eyes to heaven and affect a mind all aglow with honour and manly feeling.

Upon this whitened sepulchre Barbara wasted the freshness of her young life. He was caught by her somewhat singular beauty, which was rather that of an old Italian picture than of a rustic Englishwoman. Beauty so striking and peculiar would make its mark, he thought. With such a Juliet he could not fail as Romeo. He loved her as much as his staled and withered heart was capable of loving, and he foresaw his own advantage in marrying her. So, with a little persuasion, and a great many sweet speeches stolen from the British Drama, he broke down the barriers of duty, and wrung from the tearful, blushing girl a hasty consent to a Fleet marriage, which was solemnized before she had time to repent that weak moment of concession.

The milliner was angry, for she had believed Mr Stowell her own admirer, and although too wise to think of him as a husband, wished to retain him as a suitor. The Hertfordshire parson was furious, and told his daughter she had taken the first stage to everlasting destruction without his knowledge, and might go the rest of the way without his interference. She had a step-mother who was very well disposed to widen the breach, and she saw little hope of reconciliation with a father who had never erred on the side of fondness. So she began the world at twenty years of age, with Jack Stowell for her husband and only friend. In the first flush and glamour of a girlish and romantic love, it seemed to her sweet to have him only, to have all her world of love and hope bound up in this one volume.

This fond and foolish dream lasted less than a month. Before that moon which had shone a pale crescent in the summer sky of her wedding night had waxed and waned, Barbara knew that she was married to a drunkard and a gambler, a brute who was savage in his cups, a profligate who had lived amongst degraded women until he knew not what womanly purity meant, a wretch who existed only for self-gratification, and whose love for her had been little more than the fancy of an hour.

He lost no time in teaching her all he knew of his art. She had real genius, was fond of study, and soon discovered that he knew very little. She had her own ideas about all those heroines of which he only knew the merest conventionalities and traditions. She sat late into the night studying, while he was drinking and punting in some low tavern. Her sorrows, her disappointments, her disgusts drove her to the study of the drama for consolation, and temporary forgetfulness. These heroines of tragedy, who were all miserable, seemed to sympathize with her own misery. She became passionately fond of her art before ever she had trodden the stage.

Jack Stowell took his wife to Rich, and asked for an engagement. Had Barbara been an ordinary woman, the manager would have given her a subordinate place in his troupe, and a pittance of twenty shillings a week. But her exceptional beauty struck the managerial eye. He had half a dozen geniuses in his company, but their good looks were on the wane. This young face, these Italian eyes, might attract the town—and the town had been leaning a little towards the rival house lately.

'I'll tell you what, Stowell,' said the manager, 'I should like to give your wife a chance. But to take any hold upon the public she must appear in a leading part. I couldn't trust her till she has learnt the A B C of her profession. She must try her wings in the provinces.'

They were standing at noontide on the great stage at Covent Garden. The house was almost in darkness, and the vast circle of boxes shrouded in linen wrappings had a ghostly look that chilled Barbara's soul. What a little creature she seemed to herself in that mighty arena! Could she ever stand there and pour out her soul in the sorrows of Juliet, or the Duchess of Malfi, or Isabella, as she had done so often before the looking-glass in her dingy lodging?

'Jack,' she said, as they were walking home—he had been unusually kind to her this morning,—'I can't tell you what an awful feeling that great, dark, cold theatre gave me. I felt as if I were standing in my tomb.'

'That shows what a little goose you are,' retorted Jack, contemptuously; 'do you think anybody is going to give you such a big tomb as that?'

Mrs Stowell appeared at the Theatre Royal, Bath, and tried her wings, as the manager called it, with marked success. There could be no doubt that she had the divine fire, a genius and bent so decided that her lack of experience went for nothing; and then she worked like a slave, and threw her soul, mind, heart—her whole being—into this new business of her life. She lived only to act. What else had she to live for, with a husband who came home tipsy three or four nights out of the seven, and whose infidelities were notorious?

She came to London the following winter, and took the town by storm. Her genius, her beauty, her youth, her purity, were on every tongue. She received almost as many letters as a prime minister in that first season of success; but it was found out in due time that she was inaccessible to flattery, and the fops and fribbles of her day ceased their persecutions.

Among so many who admired her, and so many who were eager to pursue, there was only one who discovered her need of pity and pitied her.

This was Sir Philip Hazlemere, a young man of fashion and fortune—neither fop nor fribble, but a man of cultivated mind and intense feeling.

He saw, admired, and, ere long, adored the new actress; but he did not approach her, as the others did, with fulsome letters which insulted her understanding, or costly gifts which offended her honour. He held himself aloof, and loved in silence—for the instinct of his heart told him that she was virtuous. But he was human, and his sense of honour could not altogether stifle hope. He found out where she lived, bought over the lodging-house keeper to his interest, and contrived to learn a great deal more than the well-informed world knew about Barbara Stowell.

He was told that her husband was a wretch, and ill-used her; that this brilliant beauty, who shone and sparkled by night like a star, was by daylight a wan and faded woman, haggard with sorrow and tears. If he had loved her before, when the history of her life was unknown to him, he loved her doubly now, and, taking hope from all that made her life hopeless, flung honour to the winds and determined to win her.

Could she be worse off, he asked himself, than she was now—the slave of a low-born profligate—the darling of an idle, gaping crowd—scorned and neglected at home, where a woman should be paramount? He was rich and his own master—there was all the bright glad world before them. He would take her to Italy, and live and die there for her sake, content and happy in the blessing of her sweet companionship. He had never touched her hand, never spoken to her; but he had lived for the last six months only to see and hear her, and it seemed to him that he knew every thought of her mind, every impulse of her heart. Had he not seen those lovely eyes answer his fond looks sometimes, as he hung over the stage box, and the business of the scene brought her near him, with a tender intelligence that told him he was understood?

If John Stowell should petition for a divorce, so much the better, thought Philip. He could then make his beloved Lady Hazlemere, and let the world see the crowning glory of his life. He was so deeply in love that he thought it would be everlasting renown to have won Barbara. He would go down to posterity famous as the husband of the loveliest woman of his time; like that Duke of Devonshire, of whom the world knows so little except that he had a beautiful duchess.

One day Sir Philip Hazlemere took courage—emboldened by some new tale of Jack Stowell's brutality,—and got himself introduced to the presence of his beloved. She was shocked at first, and very angry; but his deep respect melted her wrath, and for the first time in her life Barbara learnt how reverential, how humble, real love is. It was no bold seducer who had forced himself into her presence, but a man who pitied and honoured her, and who would have deemed it a small thing to shed his blood for her sake.

He was no stranger to her, though she had never heard his voice till to-day. She had seen him in the theatre—night after night, and had divined that it was some stronger feeling than love of the drama which held him riveted to the same spot, listening to the same play, however often it might be repeated in the shifting repertoire of those days.

She knew that he loved her, and that earnest look of his had touched her deeply. What was it now for her, who had never known a good man's love, to hear him offer the devotion of a lifetime, and sue humbly for permission to carry her away from a life which was most abject misery!

Her heart thrilled as she heard him. Yes, this was true love—this was the glory and grace of life which she had missed. She could measure the greatness of her loss now that it was too late. She saw what pitiful tinsel she had mistaken for purest gold. But, though every impulse of her heart drew her to this devoted lover, honour spoke louder than feeling, and made her marble. On one only point she yielded to her lover's pleading. She did not refuse him permission to see her again. He might come sometimes, but it must be seldom, and the hour in which he should forget the respect due to her as a true and loyal wife would be the hour that parted them for ever.

'My life is so lonely!' she said, self-excusingly, after having accorded this permission; 'it will be a comfort to me to see you now and then for a brief half-hour, and to know that there is some one in this great busy world who pities and cares for me.'

She had one reason for granting Sir Philip's prayer, which would have well-nigh broken his heart could he have guessed it. This was her inward conviction that her life was near its close. There was hardly time for temptation between the present hour and the grave. And every day seemed to carry her further from the things and thoughts of earth. Her husband's cruelties stung less keenly than of old; his own degradation, which had been the heaviest part of her burden, seemed further away from her, as if he and she lived in different worlds. Her stage triumphs, which had once intoxicated her, now seemed unreal as the pageant of a dream. Yes, the ties that bind this weak flesh to earthly joys and sufferings were gradually loosening. The fetters were slipping off this weary clay.

CHAPTER II

HER AVENGER

Sir Philip showed himself not undeserving Barbara's confidence. He came to the sordid London lodging—a caravansera which had housed wandering tribes of shabby-genteel adventurers for the last twenty years, and whose dingy panelling seemed to exhale an odour of poverty. He brought his idol hothouse flowers and fruits—the weekly papers—those thin little leaflets which amused our ancestors—a new book now and then—and the latest news of the town—that floating gossip of the clubs, which Walpole was writing to Sir Horace Mann. He came and sat beside her, as she worked at her tambour frame, and cheered her by a tenderness too reverent to alarm. In a word, he made her happy.

If she were slowly fading out of life, he did not see the change, or guess that this fair flower was soon to wither. He saw her too frequently to perceive the gradual progress of decay. Her beauty was of an ethereal type, to which disease lent new charms.

One day he found her with an ugly bruise upon her forehead; she had tried to conceal it with the loose ringlets of her dark hair, but his quick eye saw the mark. When pressed hard by his solicitous questioning, she gave a somewhat lame account of the matter. She had been passing from the sitting-room to her bedchamber last night, when a gust of wind extinguished her candle, and she had fallen and wounded herself against the edge of the chest of drawers. She crimsoned and faltered as she tried to explain this accident.

'Barbara, you are deceiving me!' cried Sir Philip. 'It was a man's clenched fist left that mark. You shall not live with him another day.'

And then came impassioned pleading which shook her soul—fond offers of a sweet glad life in a foreign land—a divorce—a new marriage —honour—station.

'But dishonour first,' said Barbara. 'Can the path of shame ever lead to honour? No, Sir Philip, I will not do evil that good may come of it.'

No eloquence of her lover's could move her from this resolve. She was firm as the Bass Rock, he passionate as the waves that beat against it. He left her at last, burning with indignation against her tyrant.

'God keep and comfort you,' he cried at parting. 'I will not see you again till you are free.'

These words startled her, and she pondered them, full of alarm. Did he mean any threat against her husband? Ought she to warn Jack Stowell of his danger?

Sir Philip Hazlemere and John Stowell had never yet crossed each other's path. The surest place in which not to find the husband was his home. But now Sir Philip was seized with a sudden fancy for making Mr Stowell's acquaintance—or at any rate for coming face to face with him in some of his favourite haunts. These were not difficult to discover. He played deep and he drank hard, and his chosen resort was a disreputable tavern in a narrow court out of Long Acre, where play and drink were the order of the night, and many a friendly festivity had ended in a bloody brawl.

Here on a December midnight, when the pavements about Covent Garden were greasy with a thaw, and the link-boys were reaping their harvest in a thick brown fog, Sir Philip resorted directly the play was over, taking one Captain Montagu, a friend and confidant, with him. A useful man this Montagu, who knew the theatres and most of the actors—among them, Jack Stowell.

'The best of fellows,' he assured Sir Philip, 'capital company.'

'That may be,' replied Sir Philip, 'but he beats his wife, and I mean to beat him.'

'What, Phil, are you going to turn Don Quixote and fight with windmills?'

'Never mind my business,' answered Philip; 'yours is to bring me and this Stowell together.'

They found Mr Stowell engaged at faro with his own particular friends in a private room—a small room at the back of the house, with a window opening on to the leads, which offered a handy exit if the night's enjoyment turned to peril. The mohawks of that day were almost as clever as cats at climbing a steep roof or hanging on to a gutter.

Captain Montagu sent in his card to Mr Stowell, asking permission to join him with a friend, a gentleman from the country. Jack knew that Montagu belonged to the hawk tribe, but scented a pigeon in the rural stranger, and received the pair with effusiveness. Sir Philip had disguised himself in a heavy fur-bordered coat and a flaxen periwig, but Mr Stowell scanned him somewhat suspiciously notwithstanding. His constant attendance in the stage box had made his face very familiar to the Covent Garden actors, and it was only the fumes of brandy punch which prevented Stowell's recognition of him.

The play was fast and furious. Sir Philip, in his character of country squire, ordered punch with profuse liberality, and lost his money with a noisy recklessness, vowing that he would have his revenge before the night was out. Montagu watched him curiously, wondering what it all meant.

So the night wore on, Sir Philip showing unmistakable signs of intoxication, under which influence his uproariousness degenerated by-and-by into a maudlin stupidity. He went on losing money with a sleepy placidity that threw Jack Stowell off his guard, and tempted that adventurer into a free indulgence in certain manœuvres which under other circumstances he would have considered to the last degree dangerous.

What was his astonishment when the country squire suddenly sprang to his feet and flung half a tumbler of punch in his face!

'Gentlemen,' cried Stowell, wiping the liquor from his disconcerted countenance, 'the man is drunk, as you must perceive. I have been grossly insulted, but am too much a gentleman to take advantage of the situation. You had better get your friend away, Captain Montagu, while his legs can carry him, if they are still capable of that exertion. We have had enough play for to-night.'

'Cheat! swindler!' cried Sir Philip. 'I call my friend to witness that you have been playing with marked cards for the last hour. I saw you change the pack.'

'It's a lie!' roared Jack.

'No, it isn't,' said Montagu, 'I've had my eye on you.'

'By God! gentlemen, I'll have satisfaction for this,' cried Jack, drawing his sword a very little way out of its scabbard.

'You shall,' answered Sir Philip, 'and this instant. I shall be glad to see whether you are as good at defending your own cur's life as you are at beating your wife.'

'By heaven, I know you now!' cried Jack. 'You are the fellow that sits in the stage box night after night and hangs on my wife's looks.'

Sir Philip went to the door, locked it, and put the key in his pocket, then came back with his rapier drawn.

Montagu and the other men tried to prevent a fight, but Sir Philip was inexorably bent on settling all scores on the spot, and Stowell was savage in his cups and ready for anything. Preliminaries were hurried through—a table knocked over and a lot of glasses broken; but noise was a natural concomitant of pleasure in this tavern, and the riot awakened no curiosity in the sleepy drawer waiting below.

A space was cleared, and the two men stood opposite each other, ghastly with passion; Sir Philip's assumed intoxication thrown off with his fur-bordered coat, John Stowell considerably the worse for liquor.

The actor was a skilled swordsman, but his first thrusts were too blindly savage to be effective. Sir Philip parried them easily, and stood looking at his antagonist with a scornful smile which goaded Stowell to madness.

'I'll wager my wife and you have got up this play between you,' he said. 'I ought to have known there was mischief on foot. She's too meek and pretty-spoken not to be a ——'

The word he meant to say never passed his lips, for a sudden thrust in tierce from Philip Hazlemere's sword pierced his left lung and silenced him for ever.

'When I saw the mark of your fist on your wife's forehead this morning, I swore to make her a widow to-night,' said Sir Philip, as the actor fell face downward on the sanded floor.

The tavern servants were knocking at the door presently. Jack Stowell's fall had startled even their equanimity. Tables and glasses might be smashed without remark—they only served to swell the reckoning,—but the fall of a human body invited attention. Captain Montagu opened the window, and hustled his friend out upon the slippery leads below it, and, after some peril to life and limb in the hurried descent, Sir Philip Hazlemere found himself in Long Acre, where the watchman was calling 'Past four o'clock, and a rainy morning.'

CHAPTER III
HER FAREWELL SIGH

Before next evening the town knew that Jack Stowell the actor had been killed in a tavern brawl. Captain Montagu had bribed Mr Stowell's friends to keep a judicious silence. The man had been killed in fair fight, and no good could come of letting the police know the details of his end. So when the Bow Street magistrate came to hold his interrogatory, he could only extort a confused account of the fatal event. There had been a row at faro, and Stowell and another man, whose name nobody present knew, had drawn their swords and fought. Stowell had fallen, and the stranger had escaped by a window before the tavern people came to the rescue. The tavern people had seen the stranger enter the house, a man with flaxen hair, and a dark green riding coat trimmed with gray fur, but they had not seen him leave. The magistrate drew the general conclusion that everybody had been drunk, and the examination concluded in a futile manner, which in these days would have offered a fine opening for indignation leaders in the daily papers, and letters signed 'Fiat Justitia', or 'Peckham Rye'; but which at that easygoing period provoked nobody's notice, or served at most to provide Walpole with a paragraph for one of his immortal epistles.

Sir Philip called at Mrs Stowell's, and was told that she was ill, and keeping her room. There was a change of pieces announced at Covent Garden, and the favourite was not to appear 'until to-morrow se'nnight, in consequence of a domestic affliction.'

Sir Philip sent his customary offerings of hothouse fruits and flowers to Mrs Stowell's address, but a restraining delicacy made him keep aloof while the actor's corpse lay at his lodgings, and the young widow was still oppressed with the horror of her husband's death. She might suspect his hand, perhaps, in that untimely end. Would she pity and pardon him, and understand that it was to redress her wrongs his sword had been drawn? Upon this point Sir Philip was hopeful. The future was full of fair promises. There was only a dreary interval of doubt and severance to be endured in the present.

The thought that Barbara was confined to her room by illness did not alarm him. It was natural that her husband's death should have agitated and overwhelmed her. The sense of her release from his tyranny would soon give her hope and comfort. In the meanwhile Sir Philip counted the hours that must pass before her reappearance.

The appointed night came, and the play announced for representation was Webster's 'Duchess of Malfi, concluding with the fourth Act': 'the Duchess by Mrs Stowell'. They were fond of tragedies in those days, the gloomier the better. Covent Garden was a spacious charnel-house for the exhibition of suicide and murder.

Sir Philip was in his box before the fiddlers began to play. The house was more than half empty, despite the favourite's reappearance after her temporary retirement, despite the factitious interest attached to her as the widow of a man who had met his death under somewhat myste-rious circumstances a week ago. There was dire weather out of doors— a dense brown fog. Some of the fog had crept in at the doors of Covent Garden Theatre, and hung like a pall over pit and boxes.

The fiddlers began the overture to Gluck's 'Orpheus and Eurydice'. Philip Hazlemere's heart beat loud and fast. He longed for the rising of the curtain with an over-mastering impatience. It was more than a week since he had seen Barbara Stowell; and what a potent change in both their destinies had befallen since their last meeting! He could look at her now with triumphant delight. No fatal barrier rose between them. He had no doubt of her love, or of her glad consent to his prayer. In a little while—just a decent interval for the satisfaction of the world—she would be his wife. The town would see her no more under these garish lights of the theatre. She would shine as a star still, but only in the calm heaven of home.

The brightness of the picture dispelled those gloomy fancies which the half-empty theatre and its dark mantle of fog had engendered.

The curtain rose, and at last he saw her. The lovely eyes were more brilliant than ever, and blinded him to the hollowness of the wan cheek. There was a thrilling tragedy in her every look which seemed the very breath and fire of genius. The creature standing there, pouring out her story of suffering, was wronged, oppressed; the innocent, helpless victim of hard and bloody men. The strange story, the strange character, seemed natural as she interpreted it. Sir Philip listened with all his soul in his ears, as if he had never seen the gloomy play before—yet every line was familiar to him. The Duchess was one of Barbara's greatest creations.

He hung with rapt attention on every word, and devoured her pale loveliness with his eyes, yet was eager for the play to be over. He meant to lie in wait for her at the stage door, and accompany her home to her lodgings, and stay with her just long enough to speak of their happy future, and to win her promise to be his wife so soon as her weeds could be laid aside. He would respect even idle prejudice for her sake, and wait for her while she went through the ceremony of mourning for the husband who had ill-used her.

The play dragged its slow length along to the awful fourth act, with its accumulated horrors—the wild masque of madmen, the tomb-maker, the bellman, the dirge, the executioners with coffin and cords. Barbara looked pale and shadowy as a spirit, a creature already escaped from earthly bondage, for whom death could have no terrors. Thinly as the house was occupied, the curtain fell amidst a storm of applause. Sir Philip stood looking at the dark-green blankness, as if that dying look of hers had rooted him to the spot, while the audience hurried out of the theatre, uneasy as to the possibility of hackney coaches or protecting link-boys to guide them through the gloom.

He turned suddenly at the sound of a sigh close behind him—a faint and mournful sigh, which startled and chilled him.

Barbara was standing there, in the dress she had worn in that last scene—the shroud-like drapery which had so painfully reminded him of death. She stretched out her hands to him with a sad, appealing gesture. He leaned eagerly forward, and tried to clasp them in his own, but she withdrew herself from him with a shiver, and stood, shadow-like, in the shadow of the doorway.

'Dearest!' he exclaimed, between surprise and delight, 'I was coming round to the stage door. I am most impatient to talk to you, to be assured of your love, now that you are free to make me the most blessed of men. My love, I have a world of sweet words to say to you. I may come, may I not? I may ride home with you in your coach?'

The lights went out suddenly while he was talking to her, breathless in his eagerness. She gave one more faint sigh, half pathetic, half tender, and left him. She had not blessed him with a word, but he took this gentle silence to mean consent.

He groped his way out of the dark theatre, and went round to the stage door. He did not present himself at that entrance, but waited discreetly on the opposite side of the narrow street, till Barbara's coach should be called. He had watched for her thus, in a futile, aimless manner, on many a previous night, and was familiar with her habits.

There were a couple of hackney coaches waiting in the street under the curtain of fog. Presently a link-boy came hurriedly along with his flaring torch, followed by a breathless gentleman in a brown coat and wig of the same colour. The link-boy crossed the road, and the gentleman after him, and both vanished within the theatre.

Sir Philip wondered idly what the breathless gentleman's business could be.

He waited a long time, as it appeared to his impatience, and still there was no call for Mrs Stowell's hackney coach. A group of actors came out and walked away on the opposite pavement, talking intently. The gentleman in brown came out again, and trotted off into the fog, still under guidance of the link-boy. The stage doorkeeper appeared on the threshold, looked up and down the street, and seemed about to extinguish his dim oil lamp and close his door for the night. Sir Philip Hazlemere ran across the street just in time to stop him.

'Why are you shutting up?' he asked; 'Mrs Stowell has not left the theatre, has she?'

It seemed just possible that he had missed her in the fog.

'No, poor thing, she won't go out till to-morrow, and then she'll be carried out feet foremost.'

'Great God! what do you mean?'

'It's a sad ending for such a pretty creature,' said the doorkeeper with a sigh, 'and it was that brute's ill usage was at the bottom of it. She's been sickening of a consumption for the last three months—we all of us knew it; and when she came in at this door to-night I said she looked fitter for her coffin than for the stage. And the curtain was no sooner down than she dropped all of a heap, with one narrow streak of dark blood oozing out of her lips and trickling down her white gown. She was gone before they could carry her to her dressing-room. They sent for Dr Budd, of Henrietta Street, but it was too late; she didn't wait for the doctors to help her out of this world.'

Yes, at the moment when he had looked into that shadow face, seen those sad eyes looking into his with ineffable love and pity, Barbara's troubled soul had winged its flight skyward.

AMELIA B. EDWARDS

The Story of Salome

A few years ago, no matter how many, I, Harcourt Blunt, was travelling with my friend Coventry Turnour, and it was on the steps of our hotel that I received from him the announcement that he was again in love.

'I tell you, Blunt,' said my fellow-traveller, 'she's the loveliest creature I ever beheld in my life.'

I laughed outright.

'My dear fellow,' I replied, 'you've so often seen the loveliest creature you ever beheld in your life.'

'Ay, but I am in earnest now for the first time.'

'And you have so often been in earnest for the first time! Remember the innkeeper's daughter at Cologne.'

'A pretty housemaid, whom no training could have made presentable.'

'Then there was the beautiful American at Interlachen.'

'Yes; but—'

'And the bella Marchesa at Prince Torlonia's ball.'

'Not one of them worthy to be named in the same breath with my imperial Venetian. Come with me to the Merceria and be convinced. By taking a gondola to St Mark's Place we shall be there in a quarter of an hour.'

I went, and he raved of his new flame all the way. She was a Jewess— he would convert her. Her father kept a shop in the Merceria—what of that? He dealt only in costliest Oriental merchandise, and was as rich as a Rothschild. As for any probable injury to his own prospects, why need he hesitate on that account? What were 'prospects' when weighed against the happiness of one's whole life? Besides, he was not ambitious. He didn't care to go into Parliament. If his uncle, Sir Geoffrey, cut him off with a shilling, what then? He had a moderate independence of which no one living could deprive him, and what more could any reasonable man desire?

I listened, smiled, and was silent. I knew Coventry Turnour too well to attach the smallest degree of importance to anything that he might say or do in a matter of this kind. To be distractedly in love was his normal condition. We had been friends from boyhood; and since the time when he used to cherish a hopeless attachment to the young lady behind the counter of the tart-shop at Harrow, I had never known him 'fancy-free' for more than a few weeks at a time. He had gone through every phase of no less than three *grandes passions* during the five months that we had now been travelling together; and having left Rome about eleven weeks before with every hope laid waste, and a heart so broken that it could never by any possibility be put together again, he was now, according to the natural course of events, just ready to fall in love again.

We landed at the traghetto San Marco. It was a cloudless morning towards the middle of April, just ten years ago. The Ducal Palace glowed in the hot sunshine; the boatmen were clustered, gossiping, about the quay; the orange-vendors were busy under the arches of the piazzetta; the *flâneurs* were already eating ices and smoking cigarettes outside the cafés. There was an Austrian military band, strapped, buckled, moustachioed, and white-coated, playing just in front of St Mark's; and the shadow of the great bell-tower slept all across the square.

Passing under the low round archway leading to the Merceria, we plunged at once into that cool labyrinth of narrow, intricate, and picturesque streets, where the sun never penetrates—where no wheels are heard, and no beast of burden is seen—where every house is a shop, and every shop-front is open to the ground, as in an Oriental bazaar—where the upper balconies seem almost to meet overhead, and are separated by only a strip of burning sky—and where more than three people cannot march abreast in any part. Pushing our way as best we might through the motley crowd that here chatters, cheapens, buys, sells, and perpetually jostles to and fro, we came presently to a shop for the sale of Eastern goods. A few glass jars, filled with spices and some pieces of stuff, untidily strewed the counter next the street; but within, dark and narrow though it seemed, the place was crammed with costliest merchandise. Cases of gorgeous Oriental jewelry; embroideries and fringes of massive gold and silver bullion; precious drugs and spices; exquisite toys in filigree; miracles of carving in ivory, sandal-wood, and amber; jewelled yataghans; scimitars of state, rich with 'barbaric pearl and gold'; bales of Cashmere shawls, China silks, India muslins, gauzes, and the like, filled every inch of available space from floor to ceiling, leaving only a narrow lane from the door to the counter, and a still narrower passage to the rooms beyond the shop.

We went in. A young woman who was sitting reading on a low seat behind the counter, laid aside her book, and rose slowly. She was dressed wholly in black. I cannot describe the fashion of her garments. I only know that they fell about her in long, soft, trailing folds, leaving a narrow band of fine cambric visible at the throat and wrists; and that, however graceful and unusual this dress may have been, I scarcely observed it, so entirely was I taken up with admiration of her beauty.

For she was indeed very beautiful—beautiful in a way I had not anticipated. Coventry Turnour, with all his enthusiasm, had failed to do her justice. He had raved of her eyes—her large, lustrous, melancholy eyes,—of the transparent paleness of her complexion, of the faultless delicacy of her features; but he had not prepared me for the unconscious dignity, the perfect nobleness and refinement, that informed her every look and gesture. My friend requested to see a bracelet at which he had been looking the day before. Proud, stately, silent, she unlocked the case in which it was kept, and laid it before him on the counter. He asked permission to take it over to the light. She bent her head, but answered not a word. It was like being waited upon by a young Empress.

Turnour took the bracelet to the door and affected to examine it. It consisted of a double row of gold coins linked together at intervals by a bean-shaped ornament studded with pink coral and diamonds. Coming back into the shop he asked me if I thought it would please his sister, to whom he had promised a remembrance of Venice.

'It is a pretty trifle,' I replied; 'but surely a remembrance of Venice should be of Venetian manufacture. This, I suppose, is Turkish.'

The beautiful Jewess looked up. We spoke in English; but she understood, and replied.

'*E Greco, signore,*' she said coldly.

At this moment an old man came suddenly forward from some dark counting-house at the back—a grizzled, bearded, eager-eyed Shylock, with a pen behind his ear.

'Go in, Salome—go in, my daughter,' he said hurriedly. 'I will serve these gentlemen.'

She lifted her eyes to his for one moment—then moved silently away, and vanished in the gloom of the room beyond.

We saw her no more. We lingered awhile looking over the contents of the jewel-cases; but in vain. Then Turnour bought his bracelet, and we went out again into the narrow streets, and back to the open daylight of the Gran' Piazza.

'Well,' he said breathlessly, 'what do you think of her?'

'She is very lovely.'

'Lovelier than you expected?'

'Much lovelier. But—'

'But what?'

'The sooner you succeed in forgetting her the better.'

He vowed, of course, that he never would and never could forget her. He would hear of no incompatibilities, listen to no objections, believe in no obstacles. That the beautiful Salome was herself not only unconscious of his passion and indifferent to his person, but ignorant of his very name and station, were facts not even to be admitted on the list of difficulties. Finding him thus deaf to reason, I said no more.

It was all over, however, before the week was out.

'Look here, Blunt,' he said, coming up to me one morning in the coffee-room of our hotel just as I was sitting down to answer a pile of home-letters; 'would you like to go on to Trieste to-morrow? There, don't look at me like that—you can guess how it is with me. I was a fool ever to suppose she would care for me—a stranger, a foreigner, a Christian. Well, I'm horribly out of sorts, anyhow—and—and I wish I was a thousand miles off at this moment!'

We travelled on together to Athens, and there parted, Turnour being bound for England, and I for the East. My own tour lasted many months longer. I went first to Egypt and the Holy Land; then joined an exploring party on the Euphrates; and at length, after just twelve months of Oriental life, found myself back again at Trieste about the middle of

April in the year following that during which occurred the events I have just narrated. There I found that batch of letters and papers to which I had been looking forward for many weeks past; and amongst the former, one from Coventry Turnour. This time he was not only irrecoverably in love, but on the eve of matrimony. The letter was rapturous and extravagant enough. The writer was the happiest of men; his destined bride the loveliest and most amiable of her sex; the future a paradise; the past a melancholy series of mistakes. As for love, he had never, of course, known what it was till now.

And what of the beautiful Salome?

Not one word of her from beginning to end. He had forgotten her as utterly as if she had never existed. And yet how desperately in love and how desperately in despair he was 'one little year ago!' Ah, yes; but then it *was* 'one little year ago'; and who that had ever known Coventry Turnour would expect him to remember *la plus grande des grandes passions* for even half that time?

I slept that night at Trieste and went on next day to Venice. Somehow I could not get Turnour and his love-affairs out of my head. I remembered our visit to the Mercería. I was haunted by the image of the beautiful Jewess. Was she still so lovely? Did she still sit reading in her wonted seat by the open counter, with the gloomy shop reaching away behind, and the cases of rich robes and jewels all around?

An irresistible impulse prompted me to go to the Mercería and see her once again. I went. It had been a busy morning with me, and I did not get there till between three and four o'clock in the afternoon. The place was crowded. I passed up the well-remembered street, looking out on both sides for the gloomy little shop with its unattractive counter; but in vain. When I had gone so far that I thought I must have passed it, I turned back. House by house I retraced my steps to the very entrance, and still could not find it. Then, concluding I had not gone far enough at first, I turned back again till I reached a spot where several streets diverged. Here I came to a stand-still, for beyond this point I knew I had not passed before.

It was now evident that the Jew no longer occupied his former shop in the Mercería, and that my chance of discovering his whereabouts was exceedingly slender. I could not inquire of his successor, because I could not identify the house. I found it impossible even to remember what trades were carried on by his neighbours on either side. I was ignorant of his very name. Convinced, therefore, of the inutility of making any further effort, I gave up the search, and comforted myself by reflecting that my own heart was not made of adamant, and that it was, perhaps, better for my peace not to see the beautiful Salome again. I was destined to see her again, however, and that ere many days had passed over my head.

A year of more than ordinarily fatiguing Eastern travel had left me in need of rest, and I had resolved to allow myself a month's sketching in Venice and its neighbourhood before turning my face homeward.

As, therefore, it is manifestly the first object of a sketcher to select his points of view, and as no more luxurious machine than a Venetian gondola was ever invented for the use of man, I proceeded to employ the first days of my stay in endless boatings to and fro; now exploring all manner of canals and canaletti; now rowing out in the direction of Murano; now making for the islands beyond San Pietro Castello, and in the course of these pilgrimages noting down an infinite number of picturesque sites, and smoking an infinite number of cigarettes.

It was, I think, about the fourth or fifth day of this pleasant work, when my gondolier proposed to take me as far as the Lido. It wanted about two hours to sunset, and the great sandbank lay not more than three or four miles away; so I gave the word, and in another moment we had changed our route and were gliding farther and father from Venice at each dip of the oar.

Then the long, dull, distant ridge that had all day bounded the shallow horizon rose gradually above the placid level of the Lagune; assumed a more broken outline; resolved itself into hillocks and hollows of tawny sand; showed here and there a patch of parched grass and tangled brake; and looked like the coasts of some inhospitable desert beyond which no traveller might penetrate. My boatman made straight for a spot where some stakes at the water's edge gave token of a landing-place; and here, though with some difficulty, for the tide was low, ran the gondola aground. I landed. My first step was among graves.

'*E'l Cimiterio Giudaico, signore*,' said my gondolier, with a touch of his cap.

The Jewish cemetery! The *ghetto* of the dead! I remembered now to have read or heard long since how the Venetian Jews, cut off in death as in life from the neighbourhood of their Christian rulers, had been buried from immemorial time upon this desolate waste. I stooped to examine the headstone at my feet. It was but a shattered fragment, crusted over with yellow lichens, and eaten away by the salt sea air. I passed on to the next, and the next.

Some were completely matted over with weeds and brambles; some were half-buried in the drifting sand; of some only a corner remained above the surface. Here and there a name, a date, a fragment of emblematic carving or part of a Hebrew inscription, was yet legible; but all were more or less broken and effaced.

Wandering on thus among graves and hillocks, ascending at every step, and passing some three or four glassy pools overgrown with gaunt-looking reeds, I presently found that I had reached the central and most elevated part of the Lido, and that I commanded an uninterrupted view on every side. On the one hand lay the broad, silent Lagune bounded by Venice and the Euganean hills—on the other, stealing up in long, lazy folds, and breaking noiselessly against the endless shore, the blue Adriatic. An old man gathering shells on the seaward side, a distant gondola on the Lagune, were the only signs of life for miles around.

Standing on the upper ridge of this narrow barrier, looking upon both waters, and watching the gradual approach of what promised to be a gorgeous sunset, I fell into one of those wandering trains of thought in which the real and unreal succeed each other as capriciously as in a dream.

I remembered how Goethe here conceived his vertebral theory of the skull—how Byron, too lame to walk, kept his horse on the Lido, and here rode daily to and fro—how Shelley loved the wild solitude of the place, wrote of it in *Julian and Maddalo*, and listened perhaps from this very spot, to the mad-house bell on the island of San Giorgio. Then I wondered if Titian used sometimes to come hither from his gloomy house on the other side of Venice, to study the gold and purple of these western skies—if Othello had walked here with Desdemona—if Shylock was buried yonder, and Leah whom he loved 'when he was a bachelor'.

And then in the midst of my reverie, I came suddenly upon another Jewish cemetery.

Was it indeed another, or but an outlying portion of the first? It was evidently another, and a more modern one. The ground was better kept. The monuments were newer. Such dates as I had succeeded in deciphering on the broken sepulchres lower down were all of the four-teenth and fifteenth centuries; but the inscriptions upon these bore ref-erence to quite recent interments.

I went on a few steps farther. I stopped to copy a quaint Italian couplet on one tomb—to gather a wild forget-me-not from the foot of another—to put aside a bramble that trailed across a third—and then I became aware for the first time of a lady sitting beside a grave not a dozen yards from the spot on which I stood.

I had believed myself so utterly alone, and was so taken by surprise, that for the first moment I could almost have persuaded myself that she also was 'of the stuff that dreams are made of'. She was dressed from head to foot in deepest mourning; her face turned from me, looking towards the sunset; her cheek resting in the palm of her hand. The grave by which she sat was obviously recent. The scant herbage round about had been lately disturbed, and the marble headstone looked as if it had not yet undergone a week's exposure to wind and weather.

Persuaded that she had not observed me, I lingered for an instant looking at her. Something in the grace and sorrow of her attitude, something in the turn of her head and the flow of her sable draperies, arrested my attention. Was she young? I fancied so. Did she mourn a husband?—a lover?—a parent? I glanced towards the headstone. It was covered with Hebrew characters; so that, had I even been nearer, it could have told me nothing.

But I felt that I had no right to stand there, a spectator of her sorrow, an intruder on her privacy. I proceeded to move noiselessly away. At that moment she turned and looked at me.

It was Salome.

Salome, pale and worn as from some deep and wasting grief, but more beautiful, if that could be, than ever. Beautiful, with a still more spiritual beauty than of old; with cheeks so wan, and eyes so unutter-ably bright and solemn, that my very heart seemed to stand still as I looked upon them. For one second I paused, half fancying, half hoping that there was recognition in her glance; then, not daring to look or linger longer, turned away. When I had gone far enough to do so without discourtesy, I stopped and looked back. She had resumed her former attitude, and was gazing over towards Venice and the setting sun. The stone by which she watched was not more motionless.

The sun went down in glory. The last flush faded from the domes and bell-towers of Venice; the northward peaks changed from rose to purple, from gold to grey; a scarcely perceptible film of mist became all at once visible upon the surface of the Lagune; and overhead, the first star trembled into light. I waited and watched till the shadows had so deepened that I could no longer distinguish one distant object from another. Was that the spot? Was she still there? Was she moving? Was she gone? I could not tell. The more I looked, the more uncertain I became. Then, fearing to miss my way in the fast-gathering twilight, I struck down towards the water's edge and made for the point at which I had landed.

I found my gondolier fast asleep, with his head on a cushion and his bit of gondola-carpet thrown over him for a counterpane. I asked if he had seen any other boat put off from the Lido since I left? He rubbed his eyes, started up, and was awake in a moment.

'*Per Bacco, signore*, I have been asleep,' he said apologetically; 'I have seen nothing.'

'Did you observe any other boat moored hereabouts when we landed?'

'None, signore.'

'And you have seen nothing of a lady in black?'

He laughed and shook his head.

'*Consolatevi, signore*,' he said, archly; 'she will come to-morrow.'

Then, seeing me look grave, he touched his cap, and with a gentle '*Scusate, signore*,' took his place at the stern, and there waited. I bade him row to my hotel; and then, leaning dreamily back, folded my arms, closed my eyes, and thought of Salome.

How lovely she was! How infinitely more lovely than even my first remembrance of her! How was it that I had not admired her more that day in the Merceria? Was I blind, or had she become indeed more beautiful? It was a sad and strange place in which to meet her again. By whose grave was she watching? By her father's? Yes, surely by her father's. He was an old man when I saw him, and in the course of nature had not long to live. He was dead: hence my unavailing search in the Merceria. He was dead. His shop was let to another occupant. His stock-in-trade was sold and dispersed.

And Salome—was she left alone? Had she no mother?—no brother?—no lover? Would her eyes have had that look of speechless woe in them if she had any very near or dear tie left on earth? Then I thought of Coventry Turnour, and his approaching marriage. Had he ever really loved her? I doubted it. 'True love', saith an old song, 'can ne'er forget'; but he had forgotten, as though the past had been a dream. And yet he was in earnest while it lasted,—would have risked all for her sake, if she would have listened to him. Ah, if she *had* listened to him!

And then I remembered that he had never told me the particulars of that affair. Did she herself reject him, or did he lay his suit before her father? And was he rejected only because he was a Christian? I had never cared to ask these things while we were together; but now I would have given the best hunter in my stables to know every minute detail connected with the matter.

Pondering thus, travelling over the same ground again and again, wondering whether she remembered me, whether she was poor, whether she was, indeed, alone in the world, how long the old man had been dead, and a hundred other things of the same kind,—I scarcely noticed how the watery miles glided past, or how the night closed in. One question, however, recurred oftener than any other: How was I to see her again?

I arrived at my hotel; I dined at the *table d'hôte*; I strolled out after dinner to my favourite café in the piazza; I dropped in for half an hour at the Fenice, and heard one act of an extremely poor opera; I came home restless, uneasy, wakeful; and sitting for hours before my bedroom fire, asked myself the same perpetual question—How was I to see her again?

Fairly tired out at last, I fell asleep in my chair, and when I awoke the sun was shining upon my window.

I started to my feet. I had it now. It flashed upon me, as if it came with the sunlight. I had but to go again to the cemetery, copy the inscription upon the old man's tomb, ask my learned friend, Professor Nicolai of Padua, to translate it for me, and then, once in possession of names and dates, the rest would be easy.

In less than an hour, I was once more on my way to the Lido.

I took a rubbing of the stone. It was the quickest way, and the surest;

for I knew that in Hebrew everything depended on the pointing of the characters, and I feared to trust my own untutored skill.

This done, I hastened back, wrote my letter to the professor, and despatched both letter and rubbing by the midday train.

The professor was not a prompt man. On the contrary, he was a preeminently slow man; dreamy, indolent, buried in Oriental lore. From any other correspondent one might have looked for a reply in the course of the morrow; but from Nicolai of Padua it would have been folly to expect one under two or three days. And in the meanwhile? Well, in the meanwhile there were churches and palaces to be seen, sketches to be made, letters of introduction to be delivered. It was, at all events, of no use to be impatient.

And yet I was impatient—so impatient that I could neither sketch, nor read, nor sit still for ten minutes together. Possessed by an uncontrollable restlessness, I wandered from gallery to gallery, from palace to palace, from church to church. The imprisonment of even a gondola was irksome to me. I was, as it were, impelled to be moving and doing; and even so, the day seemed endless.

The next was even worse. There was just the possibility of a reply from Padua, and the knowledge of that possibility unsettled me for the day. Having watched and waited for every post from eight to four, I went down to the traghetto of St Mark's, and was there hailed by my accustomed gondolier.

He touched his cap and waited for orders.

'Where to, signore?' he asked, finding that I remained silent.

'To the Lido.'

It was an irresistible temptation, and I yielded to it; but I yielded in opposition to my judgment. I knew that I ought not to haunt the place. I had resolved that I would not. And yet I went.

Going along, I told myself that I had only come to reconnoitre. It was not unlikely that she might be going to the same spot about the same hour as before; and in that case I might overtake her gondola by the way, or find it moored somewhere along the shore. At all events, I was determined not to land. But we met no gondola beyond San Pietro Castello; saw no sign of one along the shore. The afternoon was far advanced; the sun was near going down; we had the Lagune and the Lido to ourselves.

My boatman made for the same landing-place, and moored his gondola to the same stake as before. He took it for granted that I meant to land; and I landed. After all, however, it was evident that Salome could not be there, in which case I was guilty of no intrusion. I might stroll in the direction of the cemetery, taking care to avoid her, if she were anywhere about, and keeping well away from that part where I had last seen her. So I broke another resolve, and went up towards the top of the Lido. Again I came to the salt pools and the reeds; again stood with the sea upon my left hand and the Lagune upon my right, and the endless sandbank reaching on for miles between the two. Yonder lay the new cemetery. Standing thus I overlooked every foot of the ground. I could even distinguish the headstone of which I had taken a rubbing the morning before. There was no living thing in sight. I was, to all appearance, as utterly alone as Enoch Arden on his desert island.

Then I strolled on a little nearer and a little nearer still; and then, contrary to all my determinations, I found myself standing upon the very spot, beside the very grave, which I had made up my mind on no account to approach.

The sun was now just going down—had gone down, indeed, behind a bank of golden-edged cumuli—and was flooding earth, sea, and sky with crimson. It was at this hour that I saw her. It was upon this spot that she was sitting. A few scant blades of grass had sprung up here and there upon the grave. Her dress must have touched them as she sat there—her dress—perhaps her hand. I gathered one, and laid it carefully between the leaves of my note-book.

At last I turned to go, and, turning, met her face to face!

She was distant about six yards, and advancing slowly towards the spot on which I was standing. Her head drooped slightly forward; her hands were clasped together; her eyes were fixed upon the ground. It was the attitude of a nun. Startled, confused, scarcely knowing what I did, I took off my hat, and drew aside to let her pass.

She looked up—hesitated—stood still—gazed at me with a strange, steadfast, mournful expression—then dropped her eyes again, passed me without another glance, and resumed her former place and attitude beside her father's grave.

I turned away. I would have given worlds to speak to her; but I had not dared, and the opportunity was gone. Yet I might have spoken. She looked at me—looked at me with so strange and piteous an expression in her eyes—continued looking at me as long as one might have counted five. . . . I might have spoken. I surely might have spoken! And now—ah! now it was impossible. She had fallen into the old thoughtful attitude, with her cheek resting on her hand. Her thoughts were far away. She had forgotten my very presence.

I went back to the shore, more disturbed and uneasy than ever. I spent all the remaining daylight in rowing up and down the margin of the Lido, looking for her gondola—hoping, at all events, to see her put off—to follow her, perhaps, across the waste of waters. But the dusk came quickly on, and then darkness; and I left at last without having seen any farther sign or token of her presence.

Lying awake that night, tossing uneasily upon my bed, and thinking over the incidents of the last few days, I found myself perpetually recurring to that long, steady, sorrowful gaze which she fixed upon me in the cemetery. The more I thought of it, the more I seemed to feel that there was in it some deeper meaning than I, in my confusion, had observed at the time. It was such a strange look—a look almost of entreaty, of asking for help or sympathy; like the dumb appeal in the eyes of a sick animal. Could this really be? What, after all, more possible than that, left alone in the world—with, perhaps, not a single male relation to advise her—she found herself in some position of present difficulty, and knew not where to turn for help? All this might well be. She had even, perhaps, some instinctive feeling that she might trust me. Ah! if she would indeed trust me. . . .

I had hoped to receive my Paduan letter by the morning delivery; but morning and afternoon went by as before, and still no letter came. As the day began to decline, I was again on my way to the Lido; this time for the purpose, and with the intention, of speaking to her. I landed, and went direct to the cemetery. It had been a dull day. Lagune and sky were both one uniform leaden grey, and a mist hung over Venice.

I saw her from the moment I reached the upper ridge. She was walking to and fro among the graves, like a stately shadow. I had felt confident, somehow, that she would be there; and now, for some reason that I could not have defined for my life, I felt equally confident that she expected me.

Trembling and eager, yet half dreading the moment when she should discover my presence, I hastened on, printing the loose sand at every noiseless step. A few moments more, and I should overtake her, speak to her, hear the music of her voice—that music which I remembered so well, though a year had gone by since I last heard it. But how should I address her? What had I to say? I knew not. I had no time to think. I could only hurry on till within some ten feet of her trailing garments; stand still when she turned, and uncover before her as if she were a queen.

She paused and looked at me, just as she had paused and looked at me the evening before. With the same sorrowful meaning in her eyes; with even more than the same entreating expression. But she waited for me to speak.

I did speak. I cannot recall what I said; I only know that I faltered something of an apology—mentioned that I had had the honour of meeting her before, many months ago; and, trying to say more—trying to express how thankfully and proudly I would devote myself to any service however humble, however laborious, I failed both in voice and words, and broke down utterly.

Having come to a stop, I looked up and found her eyes still fixed upon me.

'You are a Christian?' she said.

A trembling came upon me at the first sound of her voice. It was the same voice; distinct, melodious, scarce louder than a whisper—and yet it was not quite the same. There was a melancholy in the music, and if I may use a word which, after all, fails to express my meaning, a *remoteness*, that fell upon my ear like the plaintive cadence in an autumnal wind.

I bent my head, and answered that I was.

She pointed to the headstone of which I had taken a rubbing a day or two before.

'A Christian soul lies there,' she said, 'laid in earth without one Christian prayer—with Hebrew rites—in a Hebrew sanctuary. Will you, stranger, perform an act of piety towards the dead?'

'The Signora has but to speak,' I said. 'All that she wishes shall be done.'

'Read one prayer over this grave; and trace a cross upon this stone.'

'I will.'

She thanked me with a gesture, slightly bowed her head, drew her outer garment more closely round her, and moved away to a rising ground at some little distance. I was dismissed. I had no excuse for lingering—no right to prolong the interview—no business to remain there one moment longer. So I left her there, nor once looked back till I had reached the last point from which I knew I should be able to see her. But when I turned for that last look, she was no longer in sight.

I had resolved to speak to her, and this was the result. A stranger interview never, surely, fell to the lot of man! I had said nothing that I meant to say—had learnt nothing that I sought to know. With regard to her circumstances, her place of residence, her very name, I was no wiser than before. And yet I had, perhaps, no reason to be dissatisfied. She had honoured me with her confidence, and entrusted to me a task of some difficulty and importance. It now only remained for me to execute that task as thoroughly and as quickly as possible. That done, I might fairly hope to win some place in her remembrance—by and by, perhaps, in her esteem.

Meanwhile, the old question rose again—whose grave could it be? I had settled this matter so conclusively in my own mind from the first, that I could scarcely believe even now that it was not her father's. Yet that he should have died a secret convert to Christianity was incredible. Whose grave could it be? A lover's? A Christian lover's? Alas! it might be. Or a sister's? In either of these cases, it was more than probable that Salome was herself a convert. But I had no time to waste in conjecture. I must act, and act promptly.

I hastened back to Venice as fast as my gondolier could row me; and as we went along I promised myself that all her wishes should be carried out before she visited the spot again. To secure at once the services of a clergyman who would go with me to the Lido at early dawn and there read some portion, at least, of the burial service; and at the same time to engage a stonemason to cut the cross;—to have all done before she, or anyone, should have approached the place next day, was my especial object. And that object I was resolved to carry out, though I had to search Venice through before I laid my head upon my pillow.

I found a clergyman without difficulty. He was a young man occupying rooms in the same hotel, and on the same floor as myself. I had met him each day at the *table d'hôte*, and conversed with him once or twice in the reading-room. He was a North-countryman, had not long since taken orders, and was both gentlemanly and obliging. He promised in the readiest manner to do all that I required, and to breakfast with me at six next morning, in order that we might reach the cemetery by eight.

To find my stonemason, however, was not so easy; and yet I went to work methodically enough. I began with the Venetian Directory; then copied a list of stonemasons' names and addresses; then took a gondola *a due remi* and started upon my voyage of discovery.

But a night's voyage of discovery among the intricate back *canaletti* of Venice is no very easy and no very safe enterprise. Narrow, tortuous, densely populated, often blocked by huge hay, wood, and provision barges, almost wholly unlighted, and so perplexingly alike that no mere novice in Venetian topography need ever hope to distinguish one from another, they baffle the very gondoliers, and are a *terra incognita* to all but the dwellers therein.

I succeeded, however, in finding three of the places entered on my list. At the first I was told that the workman of whom I was in quest was working by the week somewhere over by Murano, and would not be back again till Saturday night. At the second and third, I found the men at home, supping with their wives and children at the end of the day's work; but neither would consent to undertake my commission. One, after a whispered consultation with his son, declined reluctantly. The other told me plainly that he dared not do it, and that he did not believe I should find a stonemason in Venice who would be bolder than himself.

The Jews, he said, were rich and powerful; no longer an oppressed people; no longer to be insulted even in Venice with impunity. To cut a Christian cross upon a Jewish headstone in the Jewish Cemetery, would be 'a sort of sacrilege', and punishable, no doubt, by the law. This sounded like truth; so, finding that my rowers were by no means confident of their way, and that the *canaletti* were dark as the catacombs, I prevailed upon the stonemason to sell me a small mallet and a couple of chisels, and made up my mind to commit the sacrilege myself.

With this single exception, all was done next morning as I had planned to do it. My new acquaintance breakfasted with me, accompanied me to the Lido, read such portions of the burial service as seemed proper to him, and then, having business in Venice, left me to my task. It was by no means an easy one. To a skilled hand it would have been, perhaps, the work of half-an-hour; but it was my first effort, and rude as the thing was—a mere grooved attempt at a Latin cross, about two inches and a half in length, cut close down at the bottom of the stone, where it could be easily concealed by a little piling of the sand—it took me nearly four hours to complete. While I was at work, the dull grey morning grew duller and greyer; a thick sea-fog drove up from the Adriatic; and a low moaning wind came and went like the echo of a distant requiem. More than once I started, believing that she had surprised me there—fancying I saw the passing of a shadow—heard the rustling of a garment—the breathing of a sigh. But no. The mists and the moaning wind deceived me. I was alone.

When at length I got back to my hotel, it was just two o'clock. The hall-porter put a letter into my hand as I passed through. One glance at that crabbed superscription was enough. It was from Padua. I hastened to my room, tore open the envelope, and read these words:—

CARO SIGNORE,—The rubbing you send is neither ancient nor curious, as I fear you suppose it to be. It is a thing of yesterday. It merely records that one Salome, the only and beloved child of a certain Isaac Da Costa, died last Autumn on the eighteenth of October, aged twenty-one years, and that by the said Isaac Da Costa this monument is erected to the memory of her virtues and his grief.

I pray you, *caro signore*, to receive the assurance of my sincere esteem.

NICOLO NICOLAI

The letter dropped from my hand. I seemed to have read without understanding it. I picked it up; went through it again, word by word; sat down; rose up; took a turn across the room; felt confused, bewildered, incredulous.

Could there, then, be two Salomes? or was there some radical and extraordinary mistake?

I hesitated; I knew not what to do. Should I go down to the Merceria, and see whether the name of Da Costa was known in the *quartier?* Or find out the registrar of births and deaths for the Jewish district? Or call upon the principal rabbi, and learn from him who this second Salome had been, and in what degree of relationship she stood towards the Salome whom I knew? I decided upon the last course. The chief rabbi's address was easily obtained. He lived in an ancient house on the Giudecca, and there I found him—a grave, stately old man, with a grizzled beard reaching nearly to his waist.

I introduced myself and stated my business. I came to ask if he could give me any information respecting the late Salome da Costa who died on the 18th of October last, and was buried on the Lido.

The rabbi replied that he had no doubt he could give me any information I desired, for he had known the lady personally, and was the intimate friend of her father.

'Can you tell me,' I asked, 'whether she had any dear friend or female relative of the same name—Salome?'

The rabbi shook his head.

'I think not,' he said. 'I remember no other maiden of that name.'

'Pardon me, but I know there was another,' I replied. 'There was a very beautiful Salome living in the Merceria when I was last in Venice, just this time last year.'

'Salome da Costa was very fair,' said the rabbi; 'and she dwelt with her father in the Merceria. Since her death, he hath removed to the neighbourhood of the Rialto.'

'This Salome's father was a dealer in Oriental goods,' I said, hastily.

'Isaac da Costa is a dealer in Oriental goods,' replied the old man very gently. 'We are speaking, my son, of the same persons.'

'Impossible!'

He shook his head again.

'But she lives!' I exclaimed, becoming greatly agitated. 'She lives. I have seen her. I have spoken to her. I saw her only last evening.'

'Nay,' he said, compassionately, 'this is some dream. She of whom you speak is indeed no more.'

'I saw her only last evening,' I repeated.

'Where did you suppose you beheld her?'

'On the Lido.'

'On the Lido?'

'And she spoke to me. I heard her voice—heard it as distinctly as I hear my own at this moment.'

The rabbi stroked his beard thoughtfully, and looked at me. 'You think you heard her voice!' he ejaculated. 'That is strange. What said she?'

I was about to answer. I checked myself—a sudden thought flashed upon me—I trembled from head to foot.

'Have you—have you any reason for supposing that she died a Christian?' I faltered.

The old man started and changed colour.

'I—I—that is a strange question,' he stammered. 'Why do you ask it?'

'Yes or no?' I cried wildly. 'Yes or no?'

He frowned, looked down, hesitated.

'I admit,' he said, after a moment or two,—'I admit that I may have heard something tending that way. It may be that the maiden cherished some secret doubt. Yet she was no professed Christian.'

'*Laid in earth without one Christian prayer; with Hebrew rites; in a Hebrew sanctuary!*' I repeated to myself.

'But I marvel how you come to have heard of this,' continued the rabbi. 'It was known only to her father and myself.'

'Sir,' I said solemnly, 'I know now that Salome da Costa is dead; I have seen her spirit thrice, haunting the spot where . . .'

My voice broke. I could not utter the words.

'Last evening at sunset,' I resumed, 'was the third time. Never doubting that—that I indeed beheld her in the flesh, I spoke to her. She answered me. She—she told me this.'

The rabbi covered his face with his hands, and so remained for some time, lost in meditation. 'Young man,' he said at length, 'your story is strange, and you bring strange evidence to bear upon it. It may be as you say; it may be that you are the dupe of some waking dream—I know not.'

He knew not; but I . . . Ah! I knew only too well. I knew now why she had appeared to me clothed with such unearthly beauty. I understood now that look of dumb entreaty in her eyes—that tone of strange remoteness in her voice. The sweet soul could not rest amid the dust of its kinsfolk, 'unhousel'd, unanointed, unanealed', lacking even 'one Christian prayer' above its grave. And now—was it all over? Should I never see her more?

Never—ah! never. How I haunted the Lido at sunset for many a month, till Spring had blossomed into Autumn, and Autumn had ripened into Summer; how I wandered back to Venice year after year at the same season, while yet any vestige of that wild hope remained alive; how my heart has never throbbed, my pulse never leaped, for love of mortal woman since that time—are details into which I need not enter here. Enough that I watched and waited; but that her gracious spirit appeared to me no more. I wait still, but I watch no longer. I know now that our place of meeting will not be here.

THOMAS HARDY

The Son's Veto

I

To the eyes of a man viewing it from behind, the nut-brown hair was a wonder and a mystery. Under the black beaver hat, surmounted by its tuft of black feathers, the long locks, braided and twisted and coiled like the rushes of a basket, composed a rare, if somewhat barbaric, example of ingenious art. One could understand such weavings and coilings being wrought to last intact for a year, or even a calendar month; but that they should be all demolished regularly at bedtime, after a single day of permanence, seemed a reckless waste of successful fabrication.

And she had done it all herself, poor thing. She had no maid, and it was almost the only accomplishment she could boast of. Hence the unstinted pains.

She was a young invalid lady—not so very much of an invalid—sitting in a wheeled chair, which had been pulled up in the front part of a green enclosure, close to a band-stand, where a concert was going on, during a warm June afternoon. It had place in one of the minor parks or private gardens that are to be found in the suburbs of London, and was the effort of a local association to raise money for some charity. There are worlds within worlds in the great city, and though nobody outside the immediate district had ever heard of the charity, or the band, or the garden, the enclosure was filled with an interested audience sufficiently informed on all these.

As the strains proceeded many of the listeners observed the chaired lady, whose back hair, by reason of her prominent position, so challenged inspection. Her face was not easily discernible, but the aforesaid cunning tress-weavings, the white ear and poll, and the curve of a cheek which was neither flaccid nor sallow, were signals that led to the

186

expectation of good beauty in front. Such expectations are not infre-
quently disappointed as soon as the disclosure comes; and in the present
case, when the lady, by a turn of the head, at length revealed herself,
she was not so handsome as the people behind her had supposed, and
even hoped—they did not know why.

For one thing (alas! the commonness of this complaint), she was less
young than they had fancied her to be. Yet attractive her face unquestionably was, and not at all sickly. The revelation of its details came
each time she turned to talk to a boy of twelve or thirteen who stood
beside her, and the shape of whose hat and jacket implied that he belonged to a well-known public school. The immediate bystanders could
hear that he called her 'Mother'.

When the end of the recital was reached, and the audience withdrew,
many chose to find their way out by passing at her elbow. Almost all
turned their heads to take a full and near look at the interesting woman,
who remained stationary in the chair till the way should be clear enough
for her to be wheeled out without obstruction. As if she expected their
glances, and did not mind gratifying their curiosity, she met the eyes of
several of her observers by lifting her own, showing these to be soft,
brown, and affectionate orbs, a little plaintive in their regard.

She was conducted out of the gardens, and passed along the pavement till she disappeared from view, the schoolboy walking beside her.
To inquiries made by some persons who watched her away, the answer
came that she was the second wife of the incumbent of a neighbouring
parish, and that she was lame. She was generally believed to be a woman
with a story—an innocent one, but a story of some sort or other.

In conversing with her on their way home the boy who walked at
her elbow said that he hoped his father had not missed them.

'He have been so comfortable these last few hours that I am sure he
cannot have missed us,' she replied.

'*Has*, dear mother—not *have*!' exclaimed the public-school boy, with
an impatient fastidiousness that was almost harsh. 'Surely you know
that by this time!'

His mother hastily adopted the correction, and did not resent his
making it, or retaliate, as she might well have done, by bidding him to
wipe that crumby mouth of his, whose condition had been caused by
surreptitious attempts to eat a piece of cake without taking it out of the

pocket wherein it lay concealed. After this the pretty woman and the boy went onward in silence.

That question of grammar bore upon her history, and she fell into reverie, of a somewhat sad kind to all appearance. It might have been assumed that she was wondering if she had done wisely in shaping her life as she had shaped it, to bring out such a result as this.

In a remote nook in North Wessex, forty miles from London, near the thriving county-town of Aldbrickham, there stood a pretty village with its church and parsonage, which she knew well enough, but her son had never seen. It was her native village, Gaymead, and the first event bearing upon her present situation had occurred at that place when she was only a girl of nineteen.

How well she remembered it, that first act in her little tragi-comedy, the death of her reverend husband's first wife. It happened on a spring evening, and she who now and for many years had filled that first wife's place was then parlour-maid in the parson's house.

When everything had been done that could be done, and the death was announced, she had gone out in the dusk to visit her parents, who were living in the same village, to tell them the sad news. As she opened the white swing-gate and looked towards the trees which rose westward, shutting out the pale light of the evening sky, she discerned, without much surprise, the figure of a man standing in the hedge, though she roguishly exclaimed as a matter of form, 'Oh, Sam, how you frightened me!'

He was a young gardener of her acquaintance. She told him the particulars of the late event, and they stood silent, these two young people, in that elevated, calmly philosophic mind which is engendered when a tragedy has happened close at hand, and has not happened to the philosophers themselves. But it had its bearing upon their relations.

'And will you stay on now at the Vicarage, just the same?' asked he.

She had hardly thought of that. 'Oh, yes—I suppose!' she said. 'Everything will be just as usual, I imagine?'

He walked beside her towards her mother's. Presently his arm stole round her waist. She gently removed it; but he placed it there again, and she yielded the point. 'You see, dear Sophy, you don't know that you'll stay on; you may want a home; and I shall be ready to offer one some day, though I may not be ready just yet.'

'Why, Sam, how can you be so fast! I've never even said I liked 'ee; and it is all your own doing, coming after me!'

'Still, it is nonsense to say I am not to have a try at you like the rest.' He stooped to kiss her a farewell, for they had reached her mother's door.

'No, Sam; you sha'n't!' she cried, putting her hand over his mouth. 'You ought to be more serious on such a night as this.' And she bade him adieu without allowing him to kiss her or to come indoors.

The vicar just left a widower was at this time a man about forty years of age, of good family, and childless. He had led a secluded existence in this college living, partly because there were no resident landowners; and his loss now intensified his habit of withdrawal from outward observation. He was still less seen than heretofore, kept himself still less in time with the rhythm and racket of the movements called progress in the world without. For many months after his wife's decease the economy of his household remained as before; the cook, the house-maid, the parlour-maid, and the man out-of-doors performed their duties or left them undone, just as Nature prompted them—the vicar knew not which. It was then represented to him that his servants seemed to have nothing to do in his small family of one. He was struck with the truth of this representation, and decided to cut down his establishment. But he was forestalled by Sophy, the parlour-maid, who said one evening that she wished to leave him.

'And why?' said the parson.

'Sam Hobson has asked me to marry him, sir.'

'Well—do you want to marry?'

'Not much. But it would be a home for me. And we have heard that one of us will have to leave.'

A day or two after she said: 'I don't want to leave just yet, sir, if you don't wish it. Sam and I have quarrelled.'

He looked up at her. He had hardly ever observed her before, though he had been frequently conscious of her soft presence in the room. What a kitten-like, flexuous, tender creature she was! She was the only one of the servants with whom he came into immediate and continuous relation. What should he do if Sophy were gone?

Sophy did not go, but one of the others did, and things went on quietly again.

When Mr Twycott, the vicar, was ill, Sophy brought up his meals to him, and she had no sooner left the room one day than he heard a noise on the stairs. She had slipped down with the tray, and so twisted her foot that she could not stand. The village surgeon was called in; the vicar got better, but Sophy was incapacitated for a long time; and she was informed that she must never again walk much or engage in any occupation which required her to stand long on her feet. As soon as she was comparatively well she spoke to him alone. Since she was forbidden to walk and bustle about, and, indeed, could not do so, it became her duty to leave. She could very well work at something sitting down, and she had an aunt a seamstress.

The parson had been very greatly moved by what she had suffered on his account, and he exclaimed, 'No, Sophy; lame or not lame, I cannot let you go. You must never leave me again!'

He came close to her, and, though she could never exactly tell how it happened, she became conscious of his lips upon her cheek. He then asked her to marry him. Sophy did not exactly love him, but she had a respect for him which almost amounted to veneration. Even if she had wished to get away from him she hardly dared refuse a personage so reverend and august in her eyes, and she assented forthwith to be his wife.

Thus it happened that one fine morning, when the doors of the church were naturally open for ventilation, and the singing birds fluttered in and alighted on the tie-beams of the roof, there was a marriage-service at the communion-rails, which hardly a soul knew of. The parson and a neighbouring curate had entered at one door, and Sophy at another, followed by two necessary persons, whereupon in a short time there emerged a newly-made husband and wife.

Mr Twycott knew perfectly well that he had committed social suicide by this step, despite Sophy's spotless character, and he had taken his measures accordingly. An exchange of livings had been arranged with an acquaintance who was incumbent of a church in the south of London, and as soon as possible the couple removed thither, abandoning their pretty country home, with trees and shrubs and glebe, for a narrow, dusty house in a long, straight street, and their fine peal of bells for the wretchedest one-tongued clangour that ever tortured mortal ears. It was all on her account. They were, however, away from every one who had known her former position; and also under less observation from without than they would have had to put up with in any country parish.

Sophy the woman was as charming a partner as a man could possess, though Sophy the lady had her deficiencies. She showed a natural aptitude for little domestic refinements, so far as related to things and manners; but in what is called culture she was less intuitive. She had now been married more than fourteen years, and her husband had taken much trouble with her education; but she still held confused ideas on the use of 'was' and 'were', which did not beget a respect for her among the few acquaintances she made. Her great grief in this relation was that her only child, on whose education no expense had been and would be spared, was now old enough to perceive these deficiencies in his mother, and not only to see them but to feel irritated at their existence.

Thus she lived on in the city, and wasted hours in braiding her beautiful hair, till her once apple cheeks waned to pink of the very faintest. Her foot had never regained its natural strength after the accident, and she was mostly obliged to avoid walking altogether. Her husband had grown to like London for its freedom and its domestic privacy; but he was twenty years his Sophy's senior, and had latterly been seized with a serious illness. On this day, however, he had seemed to be well enough to justify her accompanying her son Randolph to the concert.

II

The next time we get a glimpse of her is when she appears in the mournful attire of a widow.

Mr Twycott had never rallied, and now lay in a well-packed cemetery to the south of the great city, where, if all the dead it contained had stood erect and alive, not one would have known him or recognized his name. The boy had dutifully followed him to the grave, and was now again at school.

Throughout these changes Sophy had been treated like the child she was in nature though not in years. She was left with no control over anything that had been her husband's beyond her modest personal income. In his anxiety lest her inexperience should be overreached he had safeguarded with trustees all he possibly could. The completion of the boy's course at the public school, to be followed in due time by Oxford and ordination, had been all previsioned and arranged, and she really had nothing to occupy her in the world but to eat and drink, and make a business of indolence, and go on weaving and coiling the nut-brown hair, merely keeping a home open for the son whenever he came to her during vacations.

Foreseeing his probable decease long years before her, her husband in his lifetime had purchased for her use a semi-detached villa in the same long, straight road whereon the church and parsonage faced, which was to be hers as long as she chose to live in it. Here she now resided, looking out upon the fragment of lawn in front, and through the railings at the ever-flowing traffic; or, bending forward over the window-sill on the first floor, stretching her eyes far up and down the vista of sooty trees, hazy air, and drab house-façades, along which echoed the noises common to a suburban main thoroughfare.

Somehow, her boy, with his aristocratic school-knowledge, his grammars, and his aversions, was losing those wide infantine sympathies, extending as far as to the sun and moon themselves, with which he, like other children, had been born, and which his mother, a child of nature herself, had loved in him; he was reducing their compass to a population of a few thousand wealthy and titled people, the mere veneer of a thousand million or so of others who did not interest him at all. He drifted further and further away from her. Sophy's *milieu* being a suburb of minor tradesmen and under-clerks, and her almost only companions the two servants of her own house, it was not surprising that after her husband's death she soon lost the little artificial tastes she had acquired from him, and became—in her son's eyes—a mother whose mistakes and origin it was his painful lot as a gentleman to blush for. As yet he was far from being man enough—if he ever would be—to rate these sins of hers at their true infinitesimal value beside the yearning fondness that welled up and remained penned in her heart till it should be more fully accepted by him, or by some other person or thing. If he had lived at home with her he would have had all of it; but he seemed to require so very little in present circumstances, and it remained stored.

Her life became insupportably dreary; she could not take walks, and had no interest in going for drives, or, indeed, in travelling anywhere.

Nearly two years passed without an event, and still she looked on that suburban road, thinking of the village in which she had been born, and whither she would have gone back—O how gladly!—even to work in the fields.

Taking no exercise, she often could not sleep, and would rise in the night or early morning and look out upon the then vacant thoroughfare, where the lamps stood like sentinels waiting for some procession to go by. An approximation to such a procession was indeed made early every morning about one o'clock, when the country vehicles passed up with loads of vegetables for Covent Garden market. She often saw them creeping along at this silent and dusky hour—waggon after waggon, bearing green bastions of cabbages nodding to their fall, yet never falling, walls of baskets enclosing masses of beans and peas, pyramids of snow-white turnips, swaying howdahs of mixed produce—creeping along behind aged night-horses, who seemed ever patiently wondering between their hollow coughs why they had always to work at that still hour when all other sentient creatures were privileged to rest. Wrapped in a cloak, it was soothing to watch and sympathize with them when depression and nervousness hindered sleep, and to see how the fresh green-stuff brightened to life as it came opposite the lamp, and how the sweating animals steamed and shone with their miles of travel.

They had an interest, almost a charm, for Sophy, these semirural people and vehicles moving in an urban atmosphere, leading a life quite distinct from that of the daytime toilers on the same road. One morning a man who accompanied a waggon-load of potatoes gazed rather hard at the house-fronts as he passed, and with a curious emotion she thought his form was familiar to her. She looked out for him again. His being an old-fashioned conveyance, with a yellow front, it was easily recognizable, and on the third night after she saw it a second time. The man alongside was, as she had fancied, Sam Hobson, formerly gardener at Gaymead, who would at one time have married her.

She had occasionally thought of him, and wondered if life in a cottage with him would not have been a happier lot than the life she had accepted. She had not thought of him passionately, but her now dismal situation lent an interest to his resurrection—a tender interest which it is impossible to exaggerate. She went back to bed, and began thinking. When did these market-gardeners, who travelled up to town so regularly at one or two in the morning, come back? She dimly recollected seeing their empty waggons, hardly noticeable amid the ordinary day-traffic, passing down at some hour before noon.

It was only April, but that morning, after breakfast, she had the window opened, and sat looking out, the feeble sun shining full upon her. She affected to sew, but her eyes never left the street. Between ten and eleven the desired waggon, now unladen, reappeared on its return journey. But Sam was not looking round him then, and drove on in a reverie.

'Sam!' cried she.

Turning with a start, his face lighted up. He called to him a little boy to hold the horse, alighted, and came and stood under her window.

'I can't come down easily, Sam, or I would!' she said. 'Did you know I lived here?'

'Well, Mrs Twycott, I knew you lived along here somewhere. I have often looked out for 'ee.'

He briefly explained his own presence on the scene. He had long since given up his gardening in the village near Aldbrickham, and was now manager at a market-gardener's on the south side of London, it being part of his duty to go up to Covent Garden with waggon-loads of produce two or three times a week. In answer to her curious inquiry, he admitted that he had come to this particular district because he had seen in the Aldbrickham paper, a year or two before, the announcement of the death in South London of the aforetime vicar of Gaymead, which had revived an interest in her dwelling-place that he could not extinguish, leading him to hover about the locality till his present post had been secured.

They spoke of their native village in dear old North Wessex, the spots in which they had played together as children. She tried to feel that she was a dignified personage now, that she must not be too confidential with Sam. But she could not keep it up, and the tears hanging in her eyes were indicated in her voice.

'You are not happy, Mrs Twycott, I'm afraid?' he said.

'O, of course not! I lost my husband only the year before last.'

'Ah! I meant in another way. You'd like to be home again?'

'This is my home—for life. The house belongs to me. But I understand——' She let it out then. 'Yes, Sam. I long for home—*our* home!

I *should* like to be there, and never leave it, and die there.' But she remembered herself. 'That's only a momentary feeling. I have a son, you know, a dear boy. He's at school now.'

'Somewhere handy, I suppose? I see there's lots on 'em along this road.'

'O no! Not in one of these wretched holes! At a public school—one of the most distinguished in England.'

'Chok' it all! of course! I forget, ma'am, that you've been a lady for so many years.'

'No, I am not a lady,' she said sadly. 'I never shall be. But he's a gentleman, and that—makes it—O how difficult for me!'

III

The acquaintance thus oddly reopened proceeded apace. She often looked out to get a few words with him, by night or by day. Her sorrow was that she could not accompany her one old friend on foot a little way, and talk more freely than she could do while he paused before the house. One night, at the beginning of June, when she was again on the watch after an absence of some days from the window, he entered the gate and said softly, 'Now, wouldn't some air do you good? I've only half a load this morning. Why not ride up to Covent Garden with me? There's a nice seat on the cabbages, where I've spread a sack. You can be home again in a cab before anybody is up.'

She refused at first, and then, trembling with excitement, hastily finished her dressing, and wrapped herself up in cloak and veil, afterwards sidling downstairs by the aid of the handrail, in a way she could adopt on an emergency. When she had opened the door she found Sam on the step, and he lifted her bodily on his strong arm across the little forecourt into his vehicle. Not a soul was visible or audible in the infinite length of the straight, flat highway, with its ever-waiting lamps converging to points in each direction. The air was fresh as country air at this hour, and the stars shone, except to the north-eastward, where there was a whitish light—the dawn. Sam carefully placed her in the seat, and drove on.

They talked as they had talked in old days, Sam pulling himself up now and then, when he thought himself too familiar. More than once she said with misgiving that she wondered if she ought to have in-dulged in the freak. 'But I am so lonely in my house,' she added, 'and this makes me so happy!'

'You must come again, dear Mrs Twycott. There is no time o' day for taking the air like this.'

It grew lighter and lighter. The sparrows became busy in the streets, and the city waxed denser around them. When they approached the river it was day, and on the bridge they beheld the full blaze of morning sunlight in the direction of St Paul's, the river glistening towards it, and not a craft stirring.

Near Covent Garden he put her into a cab, and they parted, looking into each other's faces like the very old friends they were. She reached home without adventure, limped to the door, and let herself in with her latch-key, unseen.

The air and Sam's presence had revived her: her cheeks were quite pink—almost beautiful. She had something to live for in addition to her son. A woman of pure instincts, she knew there had been nothing really wrong in the journey, but supposed it conventionally to be very wrong indeed.

Soon, however, she gave way to the temptation of going with him again, and on this occasion their conversation was distinctly tender, and Sam said he never should forget her, notwithstanding that she had served him rather badly at one time. After much hesitation he told her of a plan it was in his power to carry out, and one he should like to take in hand, since he did not care for London work: it was to set up as a master greengrocer down at Aldbrickham, the county-town of their native place. He knew of an opening—a shop kept by aged people who wished to retire.

'And why don't you do it, then, Sam?' she asked with a slight heart-sinking.

'Because I'm not sure if—you'd join me. I know you wouldn't—couldn't! Such a lady as ye've been so long, you couldn't be a wife to a man like me.'

'I hardly suppose I could!' she assented, also frightened at the idea.

'If you could,' he said eagerly, 'you'd on'y have to sit in the back parlour and look through the glass partition when I was away some-times—just to keep an eye on things. The lameness wouldn't hinder that. . . . I'd keep you as genteel as ever I could, dear Sophy—if I might think of it!' he pleaded.

'Sam, I'll be frank,' she said, putting her hand on his. 'If it were only myself I would do it, and gladly, though everything I possess would be lost to me by marrying again.'

'I don't mind that! It's more independent.'

'That's good of you, dear, dear Sam. But there's something else. I have a son. . . . I almost fancy when I am miserable sometimes that he is not really mine, but one I hold in trust for my late husband. He seems to belong so little to me personally, so entirely to his dead father. He is so much educated and I so little that I do not feel dignified enough to be his mother. . . . Well, he would have to be told.'

'Yes. Unquestionably.' Sam saw her thought and her fear. 'Still, you can do as you like, Sophy—Mrs Twycott,' he added. 'It is not you who are the child, but he.'

'Ah, you don't know! Sam, if I could, I would marry you, some day. But you must wait a while, and let me think.'

It was enough for him, and he was blithe at their parting. Not so she. To tell Randolph seemed impossible. She could wait till he had gone up to Oxford, when what she did would affect his life but little. But would he ever tolerate the idea? And if not, could she defy him?

She had not told him a word when the yearly cricket-match came on at Lord's between the public schools, though Sam had already gone back to Aldbrickham. Mrs Twycott felt stronger than usual: she went to the match with Randolph, and was able to leave her chair and walk about occasionally. The bright idea occurred to her that she could casually broach the subject while moving round among the spectators, when the boy's spirits were high with interest in the game, and he would weigh domestic matters as feathers in the scale beside the day's victory. They promenaded under the lurid July sun, this pair, so wide apart, yet so near, and Sophy saw the large proportion of boys like her own, in their broad white collars and dwarf hats, and all around the rows of great coaches under which was jumbled the *débris* of luxurious luncheons; bones, pie-crusts, champagne-bottles, glasses, plates, napkins, and the family silver; while on the coaches sat the proud fathers and mothers; but never a poor mother like her. If Randolph had not appertained to these, had not centred all his interests in them, had not

197

cared exclusively for the class they belonged to, how happy would things have been! A great huzza at some small performance with the bat burst from the multitude of relatives, and Randolph jumped wildly into the air to see what had happened. Sophy fetched up the sentence that had been already shaped; but she could not get it out. The occasion was, perhaps, an inopportune one. The contrast between her story and the display of fashion to which Randolph had grown to regard himself as akin would be fatal. She awaited a better time.

It was on an evening when they were alone in their plain suburban residence, where life was not blue but brown, that she ultimately broke silence, qualifying her announcement of a probable second marriage by assuring him that it would not take place for a long time to come, when he would be living quite independently of her.

The boy thought the idea a very reasonable one, and asked if she had chosen anybody? She hesitated; and he seemed to have a misgiving. He hoped his stepfather would be a gentleman? he said.

'Not what you call a gentleman,' she answered timidly. 'He'll be much as I was before I knew your father;' and by degrees she acquainted him with the whole. The youth's face remained fixed for a moment; then he flushed, leant on the table, and burst into passionate tears.

His mother went up to him, kissed all of his face that she could get at, and patted his back as if he were still the baby he once had been, crying herself the while. When he had somewhat recovered from his paroxysm he went hastily to his own room and fastened the door.

Parleyings were attempted through the keyhole, outside which she waited and listened. It was long before he would reply, and when he did it was to say sternly at her from within: 'I am ashamed of you! It will ruin me! A miserable boor! a churl! a clown! It will degrade me in the eyes of all the gentlemen of England!'

'Say no more—perhaps I am wrong! I will struggle against it!' she cried miserably.

Before Randolph left her that summer a letter arrived from Sam to inform her that he had been unexpectedly fortunate in obtaining the shop. He was in possession; it was the largest in the town, combining fruit with vegetables, and he thought it would form a home worthy even of her some day. Might he not run up to town to see her?

She met him by stealth, and said he must still wait for her final answer. The autumn dragged on, and when Randolph was home at Christmas for the holidays she broached the matter again. But the young gentleman was inexorable.

It was dropped for months; renewed again; abandoned under his repugnance; again attempted; and thus the gentle creature reasoned and pleaded till four or five long years had passed. Then the faithful Sam revived his suit with some peremptoriness. Sophy's son, now an under-graduate, was down from Oxford one Easter, when she again opened the subject. As soon as he was ordained, she argued, he would have a home of his own, wherein she, with her bad grammar and her ignor-ance, would be an encumbrance to him. Better obliterate her as much as possible.

He showed a more manly anger now, but would not agree. She on her side was more persistent, and he had doubts whether she could be trusted in his absence. But by indignation and contempt for her taste he completely maintained his ascendency; and finally taking her before a little cross and altar that he had erected in his bedroom for his private devotions, there bade her kneel, and swear that she would not wed Samuel Hobson without his consent. 'I owe this to my father!' he said.

The poor woman swore, thinking he would soften as soon as he was ordained and in full swing of clerical work. But he did not. His educa-tion had by this time sufficiently ousted his humanity to keep him quite firm; though his mother might have led an idyllic life with her faithful fruiterer and greengrocer, and nobody have been anything the worse in the world.

Her lameness became more confirmed as time went on, and she sel-dom or never left the house in the long southern thoroughfare, where she seemed to be pining her heart away. 'Why mayn't I say to Sam that I'll marry him? Why mayn't I?' she would murmur plaintively to her-self when nobody was near.

Some four years after this date a middle-aged man was standing at the door of the largest fruiterer's shop in Aldbrickham. He was the proprietor, but to-day, instead of his usual business attire, he wore a neat suit of black; and his window was partly shuttered. From the railway-station a funeral procession was seen approaching: it passed his door and went out of the town towards the village of Gaymead. The man, whose eyes were wet, held his hat in his hand as the vehicles moved by; while from the mourning coach a young smooth-shaven priest in a high waistcoat looked black as a cloud at the shopkeeper standing there.

LUCY CLIFFORD

The End of Her Journey

CHAPTER I

Mrs Edward Archerson was not an attractive little woman, but she had a thousand a-year of her own, and people generally supposed that that was why 'Teddy A.', as his friends called him, had rather suddenly married her. He was known to be hard up and tolerably in debt, he had done nothing at the Bar, and it seemed unlikely that he ever would do much. At Cambridge he had been exceedingly popular, played an excellent hand at whist, and took a very mild degree. After he came to London, his rooms being pretty and his landlady obliging, he felt that it would be utter folly not to entertain; so he entertained a good deal. There was a bailiff downstairs one evening, while Teddy upstairs was giving one of his most successful parties, and after that things came to a crisis.

'Something will have to be done, or I shall bust up,' he said to himself. 'Must turn over a new leaf and be respectable, for this sort of thing can't go on.' And it didn't go on. He turned over the new leaf, to a certain extent, and became moderately respectable, openly laughing at himself all the time. Then, perhaps, thinking it was no use doing things by halves, he suddenly became very respectable indeed, married Mildred Benson after a short engagement, and settled down to hard work, routine, and the ways of domesticity. His wife was a good gentle little soul with a pale face, rather pathetic grey eyes, and a quantity of dull fair hair done up in very neat plaits. In manner she was quiet, seldom talked much, and was perhaps a little too tame; for it was absolutely certain— and that you knew directly you looked at her—that she would never make herself disagreeable to any one, come what might. Moreover, she was one of those women who weep when they would do wiser to scorn. She was immoderately in love with Teddy when she married him, that was quite evident to every one, except perhaps to Teddy—a clinging worshipping love that expected little, exacted nothing, and satisfied itself in giving all, consciously asking no return. Teddy, it was also equally evident, was only very moderately in love with her, and, as a natural consequence, took her love for him as a fact that was pleasant but not of much importance. Still he was an attentive husband, he thought it good form to be attentive to his wife; besides, he was a gentleman, and there are some little evidences of being a gentleman that he thought a man should never forget to give. So on the whole they got on very well together, and if there was not much billing and cooing there was never any bickering.

At first after their marriage they went out a good deal. Teddy took his wife to parties, and sometimes to a theatre; but he never noticed what she wore, or with whom she talked, or took much interest in what she did or said. Once they spent a day on the river—a whole day; but it was so long before evening time he would never repeat the experiment, though she enjoyed it enormously, so she said.

'The river is all very well, but it doesn't do with your wife,' Teddy thought to himself. 'She is horribly in the way, and makes everything feel played out.' After a time Teddy said he was tired of parties, and made excuses. It also became known in the family that he was disappointed at not having any little ones, for he had always been devoted to children; but he got over that after a few years. Then almost suddenly he took to staying a good deal at his club, and encouraging his wife to have her pretty cousin on a visit.

'It will be more fun for you to take Amy about than to go alone,' he said, 'and a relief to me; for I may often have to stay late at chambers for the next few months. I hate to feel that you are waiting when I can't get back to dinner or in time to take you out anywhere.'

'But I would always rather stay at home when you can't go out,' his wife answered. 'I only care for parties for the pleasure of going with you.'

'Yes, dear; but it looks better for one of us to be seen about—shows we are in the swim, and gives an air of prosperity to the house. Besides, I like to think that you are enjoying yourself, and not moping at home while I am wiring away over some difficult business.'

'Could you not bring your work home sometimes, Teddy?' It was quite a bright idea, she thought; but he gave his head a good professional shake.

'Oh, no, my dear, that would never do. Be as bad as a woman's home-made gown, which Charlie's wife said she could tell at a glance, do you remember? No, Millie, go and enjoy yourself, and don't trouble your head about me, there's a good girl.' After that Mrs Archerson always went about alone, or with her pretty cousin Amy, and Teddy's evenings were free.

It was astonishing how well and quickly Teddy got on; perhaps his wife's money helped, but his quick eyes and charming manner probably did a great deal more. No one knew how it was, but in less than no time, as things go in his profession, all manner of good work fell to him; he was a busy man, prosperous and rising. Yet, in spite of his increasing means, he steadily refused to add to his expenditure, or to launch out in any way. And still he let his wife go out as much as she pleased (though she only pleased because he wished it), while he spent his evenings at his chambers or his club. Sometimes he stayed so late at the club that he did not return till next morning. Then Guy Forbes, Teddy's particular friend, set up a bachelor establishment at Richmond, and Teddy took to going to him once a week, always dining and sleeping, so that his wife did not see him at all till the next evening. It did him good, he said, the air of Richmond was quite different from that of Kensington, which had never really agreed with him; he was afraid he might get headaches if he did not have an occasional change. She bore it very well, but a time came in which the little woman's lip would sometimes quiver and her eyes fill with tears—nay, she would now and then shut herself up, and when she reappeared it looked very much as if she had been having a good cry.

'Don't you wish Edward would come out with us a little oftener, Mildred?' Amy asked one day. 'I know I shouldn't like it if I had a husband, and he left me to my own devices every evening.'

'He has so much to do—it is very difficult to leave his work; and when he can he finds whist a greater rest than parties, especially when he can get change of air too. It is very good of him to let us go about together as we do, dear Amy. Some husbands expect their wives to stay at home.'

'That is all very well; but I should like a man who enjoyed taking me about himself.'

'He doesn't care for parties. He said the other day that he had quite outgrown them.'

'Was he very much in love when you were married?' Amy asked presently. Mrs Archerson reflected for a moment, and did not appear to like the question, for she answered, a little distantly:

'Oh, I don't know. I suppose so, or he would not have married me. Let us talk of something else, dear—people don't always show what they feel, or how much they feel. At any rate, they can't be always showing it, you know; it would be very tiresome and undignified.'

That evening, after dinner, Amy wanted to write a letter for the late post—rather a long one, she said—and went upstairs to begin it. The Archersons stayed in the dining-room, lingering over the dessert; and something made Mrs Archerson ask her husband:

'Did you love me very much when you married me, Teddy?' He got up rather quickly, and went to the fire-place to light a cigarette.

'Yes, I suppose so, dear. What on earth makes you suddenly ask?' She got up and stood beside him on the hearthrug.

'I was thinking—Amy told me to-day that Kate gets a letter from Herbert every morning. You used only to write to me once a week.'

'Not a letter-writing man,' he laughed, with an air of relief.

She looked up at him with a long, tender look, and an expression in her grey eyes that for the moment made her whole face different. Then she spoke in a low voice, that almost trembled:

'I know you—liked me, of course,' she said, humbly; 'but—were you ever really in love with me—were you———'

'Yes, dear, of course,' he interrupted, looking at the end of his cigarette; 'don't get nervous about it. Don't you remember how we used to hang about in the woods at Chilworth?'

'Yes, I do,' she answered; and his words carried conviction enough to her simple heart. 'But do you care for me still—for me at all?' she went on nervously, determined to have the matter out and her fears set at rest; 'or are you tired———'

He turned round, put down his cigarette, and looked back at her, into her eyes.

'What do you mean?' he asked, in an anxious, eager voice, as though he knew of some reason for her questioning. But her manner changed suddenly, she was so unused to excitement; she had always despised it. And now she felt foolish, almost guilty of something—she did not know of what.

'You don't seem to care much,' she said softly. 'You never seem to like being with me. You never take me out——'

'Too busy, my dear child. Lots of men make their wives do the going-out alone, while they grind at their work.'

'Ah, but you never seem to care what I do or say, or anything about me. You are very kind in many ways, I know; but you never seem to—to—I sometimes wonder if I were very, very ill, whether you——' But she broke down helplessly in what she wanted to say; she was not good at making out a case.

'You silly little woman,' he laughed, and put his arm round her waist and kissed her in a kindly affectionate manner that had nothing of the lover in it—'what is the matter? I expect very few people spoon after five or six years of marriage,' he added.

'It is not that,' she answered hurriedly, half-ashamed; 'but if I could only know that you ever loved me, that you really love me still?' She said it almost as an entreaty, longing for his answer. He looked at her again—at her eyes, that had a strange fear and tenderness in them to-night; he remembered swiftly how often they were dull and expressionless, and wondered at it—at her pale face and thin commonplace figure. An almost sad look came over him for a moment, while he answered:

'I should be a brute if I did not love you, Mildred. You are a good little soul—a thousand times too good for me.' And then Teddy smoked his cigarette intently, as if to steady himself after what he felt had been almost a scene. 'I'll tell you what,' he said, when he had enjoyed a few minutes' thoughtful smoking, 'I'll get stalls and take you both to the play to-morrow, you and Amy. It is a long time since we went anywhere; a little spree will cheer us up and do us good, eh?' He went back to the table and helped himself to the claret, and she followed him mechanically. She had a way of 'pattering' after him, as he called it, that worried him sometimes; it was like a cat, a gentle, affectionate cat, but still it worried him. They both sat down to the table again; she considering the question about the play.

'I thought you were going to Richmond to-morrow?' she said.

'Never mind; I'll throw Guy over for once. Some claret, darling?' It was quite an age since he had called her darling; it made her heart feel like a feather as she heard it. What a goose she had been! He was just as fond of her as other men were of their wives, only he was not

205

demonstrative. Dear Teddy, he was so much taken up with his work that he had little time to think of other things; and when he had, it was so natural that he should try to get as thorough a change as possible. She pushed her glass towards him.

'Yes, some claret'—and then a servant entered.

'If you please, sir,' the maid said, 'a man has come with this card-case; he says he found it in Sisterton Road, Clapham, last night.' Teddy knocked the claret jug against his wife's glass, and stained the table-cloth.

'Yes—well—how does he know it's mine?'

'He says he found the address on the cards inside; and he wants to know if there's any reward?'

'But you were not at Clapham last night, Edward, were you?' Mrs Archerson asked. She generally called him Edward before the servants; she thought it sounded better.

'Here's half-a-crown—far more than it's worth—an old card-case and half-a-dozen pasteboards. Confound him! No, dear,' he said when the servant had left the room. 'I suppose it was picked up at the club or somewhere, and dropped again there.'

'Yes, that must have been it. But how odd that it should have been lost twice in one day,' she answered innocently.

'Perhaps the beggar who found it first was disgusted at its not being something better, and threw it away.'

'Yes, perhaps that was it,' she laughed. 'Do you know, Teddy dear, your hand quite trembled when Janet brought it in. That was how you spilt the wine.'

'Too many cigarettes, they make one nervous. I am glad we are going to the play to-morrow. We might have a little dinner somewhere first, be a treat for Amy. What do you say?'

'Yes,' she answered gratefully.

Then he looked at her again. She was a good little soul, he thought; but it was impossible to help being a little bored by her, she was so curiously lacking in charm.

'Then that's agreed. Now I must go out, unfortunately.' He looked at his watch, and there was a tone of relief in his voice. 'Don't sit up for me, dear. Good-night.' As if he reproached himself for his critical thoughts of a minute before, or as if some half-tender remembrance

overtook him, he stopped for a moment by the doorway and looked
back at her. 'Don't be foolish again,' he said. 'I would do anything to
make you happy, Millie dear.'

CHAPTER II

Nearly a year had passed. It was the end of October, and the Archersons
had come back to town. Teddy Archerson was more devoted than ever
to his work, his whist, and his bachelor friend at Richmond. He had
been thoroughly restless in the North; even the shooting when it began
did not engross him as it had formerly. The fact was, he told his wife,
that, in spite of its being vacation-time, there were many things that
needed his presence in town—things concerning the great case of
Willoughby v. Conyers, on which he was among the junior counsel
retained, and so on. Once or twice he grew so anxious about his work
that he ran up to town for a few days, and left Mildred down in Fifeshire.
It was a very wet season, and she could stay indoors and do needle-
work; but he grew impatient in a country-house in bad weather, and a
little spell of work would do him good, he said.

After they were back at Kensington again he seemed to care less and
less for society, his friends almost lost sight of him, except in a professional sense. Even when those with whom he had formerly been most
intimate asked him and his wife to cosy little winter-season dinners he
generally made excuses, though he was always glad when Mildred found
courage to go alone. He was very good to her. He was getting on so
well, was so successful in all he undertook, that he made their single-
horse a pair, and gave her a brougham as a supplement to the victoria
she had always had; it was much nicer than jobbing, he said, especially
as she went about a good deal alone. On her birthday, too, he gave her
quite a beautiful diamond bracelet; and his manner was always gentle,
it was sometimes oddly deferential. But he never seemed happy, nay,
even content, to be much in her society. Anything he could do for her
comfort, anything she wanted, or he fancied she wanted, he was ready
enough to give her, though he always refused to take a larger house or
to live on a more expensive scale; but being with her made him impatient or restless or absent—in short, he always seemed as if he wished
he were somewhere else. At last, in spite of his presents and gentleness,

try as she would, it was no good, she could not satisfy herself with her own excuses and arguments any longer, she grew restless and unhappy. Other women's husbands could take them out or stay at home contented and happy; and why not hers? She was not very pretty or clever or fascinating, but Edward had known what she was when he married her. Besides, lots of women not one whit better than she had devoted husbands. She felt that he was anxious, over-anxious, to be kind; she could not remember that he had ever said a single cross word to her; but virtually she lived alone.

She sat and thought it over for the thousandth time one afternoon early in December. She looked round the room—a trim, well-kept room, with everything in its place, everything pretty and carefully arranged, and yet that somehow lacked coziness. It looked as if it had never been untidy, as if no one had ever sat there dreaming a day-dream or dozing in the twilight, or telling little confidential stories over its crackling fire. She wondered why Teddy always looked so uncomfortable, so like a stranger in it. She could not tell. Beside her was a little tea-table, and on it a tray with a cup and saucer and a plate with two slices of thin bread-and-butter. It told much to discerning eyes. No charming woman has one solitary cup brought in for her afternoon tea; she knows how unlikely it is that she will drink it alone, and a second cup is put ready. Somebody is sure to come—some merry little married woman whose husband will not be at home that day; some happy girl who has been shopping, or forlorn bachelor who remembers that her tea is sure to be good, her talk bright, and her sympathy certain, and who thinks how pleasantly she will make an hour pass before he betakes himself to his club. But cosy chats of this sort were unknown to Mrs Archerson. She was a little dull to the married woman, she had no attraction for girls, and men felt strange and awkward with her. They never quite knew what to talk about; she did not care for books or politics, she never contrived to be in the swing of the gossip of the moment; moreover she had some old-fashioned prejudices she felt it a duty to stand by, that made her rather difficult to get along with. Just as people were trying to be a little intimate with her they found they had to pick and choose carefully their subjects of conversation. It was told of her by a cousin of Teddy's that she had stated openly that she seldom read books, unless they were religious, when it was a duty to read them; or historical,

when it was instructive. Poetry she did not care for unless it rhymed
and flowed very easily; and novels as a rule she considered immoral.
Was not the 'Vicar of Wakefield' a story of seduction? and were the
scenes between the Knight and the Jewess in 'Ivanhoe' fit for modest
women to read? If she had had daughters they would have read neither
till matrimony had overtaken them. As for modern novels, she left
them alone, perhaps to her profit, and certainly to the development of
her natural gravity.

At parties, where she saw most of life and gathered the majority of
her ideas, she merely stood in a crowd with the rest, saying now and
then a word or two to this person or that, noticing the gowns of her
friends, and wondering how it was that others contrived to look so
much more lively than herself. Altogether she had little enough material to form lively talk for her own tea-table. The result was that at five
o'clock Mrs Archerson was generally alone. Her callers left cards or
came early, and having stayed a quarter of an hour went away with an
air of having fulfilled a duty. There are some people who seem born to
put others through minor moral exercises; Mildred was one of them.
And yet meanwhile deaf and dumb the woman's soul lived within its
prison, unconsciously beating against its bars, longing to escape, wondering and weeping at its own limits, its own blindness, its own inca-
pacity, having no power at all except to suffer without seeing the reason
of it, or knowing any remedy.

But it was not yet time for her lonely tea; never did she allow herself
to venture upon it before five. She felt that the mistress of a household
had no business to humour herself, for upon her depended the examples
of method and punctuality that were so important to every member of
it. And yet, how dull and weary she felt! And how much—for women
are comforted by small things—a cup of tea, and a cosy creeping nearer
to the fire, or perhaps a love-story, or the playing of a few snatches on
the piano, would have brightened things. But this never dawned upon
her. She sat, and dreamily waited—for nothing; her thoughts dwelling
on the one subject that engrossed them always now, going over it again
and again, always coming to a *cul de sac*, and turning wearily back once
more. Presently, woman-like, she looked down at her dress; it was
good enough, but not too well made: another woman would probably
have called it dowdy. At her throat there was some soft lace, badly

arranged; it had not the picturesque touch that other fingers would have
given it, or the prim fashioning that would have suited her perfectly, if
she had but known how to manage it. She raised her eyes to the mantel-
shelf; there was a tiny Dresden china clock on it. She thought for a
moment vaguely of the housemaid, and wished she dusted more carefully. There were some little cut crystal vases full of yellow roses, though
it was winter-time. She had told Teddy once, in a longing voice, that
she had seen a bowl of them at Christmas-time at Mrs Stanley's; and the
next day he had ordered a florist to send her some every week. It was
very good of him; but she remembered how once, a few months after
they were married, he had brought her home half-a-dozen snowdrops,
and she had kissed them every morning when she changed the water.
It was not possible to kiss flowers sent from a florist's. And then her
eyes fell on Teddy's portrait, smiling down on her as he himself never
smiled. Her breast swelled, a lump rose in her throat, as she wondered
of what it was that he had been thinking—of whom, that he had looked
so happy, when that portrait was taken, so unconstrained, so thoroughly
light-hearted. It had not been taken very long; yet it was years since she
had seen that look on his face when he was alone with her. She felt as
if she depressed him now, as if she were a duty, a part of his routine of
life, a relation, a something he had to take care of and look after, but
his sweetheart, his wife, the woman of his heart—no, never. It was all
right, perhaps; many men grew absorbed in their work after they were
married, and merely took their wives in with the matter-of-course part
of their lives. And yet all the women she knew, even the women with
far less easy-going generous husbands than hers, were on a better footing than she—a footing that meant greater happiness, that was altogether more satisfying to their hearts and their womanly dignity. She
put her face down on her hands for a moment, and shutting out the
room and the memory of the last few years, thought over the time of
her engagement. It had been a very happy one, for she had been very
much in love, and unsophisticated enough to take it for granted that
Teddy was also. It never entered her head that her money could have
had anything to do with her marriage. It simply never occurred to
Mildred to suspect any one—much less her own husband—of meanness
or untruth. Yet now, looking back, she felt as if he could not have cared
very much; she remembered that he had not seemed very eager even

when he proposed. He had written to her once a week—religiously once a week; but his letters had not been very full of endearment. They had satisfied her at the time, but now they seemed to have been almost cold; for since her marriage she had once or twice been shown other girls' love-letters—they were vastly different from Teddy's to her. She sat and wondered, then suddenly rose, went to the glass over the china shelf at the end of the room and looked at herself, long and sorrowfully. And then she dimly understood it all. She was a woman who would never win any man's intense love—a woman to marry for peace and quietness—one whom a man might be certain would never cause him a moment's uneasiness—but not a woman with whom to fall in love. She looked at her soft and yet dull grey eyes, her only tolerable complexion, her lips that lacked form and colour—at her slim figure that had no roundness, at her own youth that had none of the flush and sunniness of youth. For a moment something like despair overtook her, and then a quick thankfulness that Teddy was so engrossed with his work and whist. Perhaps it would never strike him, perhaps he would never see at all what she saw plainly. In future she would try to accept the inevitable, to be content with what she had; for she felt that it was impossible to get more, it was not in her to provoke it. It was perhaps lucky that Teddy did not go out oftener—did not care for women's society. Who knows but what, seeing the difference, he might—but she could not even think of that! If Teddy were to care for another woman she should die. His neglect, his carelessness, his scant love-making, his absorption in his work—all these she could endure. After all, was it not something to be his, to bear his name, to live beneath the same roof, to have all the affection and care he could spare time or remembered to give her? But if he had cared or were to care for any one else, it would kill her. It was a happy thing for her that women were not attractive to him, that he troubled so little about them.

It was five o'clock. She stopped her thinking as a matter of course, a little brass kettle was brought in, and after waiting a minute for the water to boil up over the spirit lamp, she made tea, then while it was drawing took up her knitting and worked, glad that some little part of the day's routine had claimed her attention. Suddenly there came a cheering sound that caused her to look up expectingly—the sound of the visitors' bell; and then there entered a pretty little woman, lively, and with plenty to say. It was quite a novelty to see anyone so late in the afternoon; Mildred's face almost brightened into a laugh, she was so glad and surprised.

'I thought I should find you,' Mrs Carew said, sitting down and preparing for a cosy chat. She had known Mildred for years—ever since her marriage; and had always rather gone out of her way to be cordial. 'Yes, I am longing for some tea,' she added, as the second cup was brought in. She pulled off her glove ready for some hot tea-cake, and then, seeing that there was none, put it on again. Tea-cake was just one of those things that Mrs Archerson would not have, Mrs Carew thought; but it was too cold for bread-and-butter. 'I have been shopping all the afternoon and am so tired,' she said, putting her two little feet on the fender—'and so cold,' she added, with an apologetic laugh for making herself so much at home.

'Shopping is very tiring,' Mildred remarked.

'Oh dear, yes, very; and I always have to do mine in a hurry. I never have time for anything. I often wish our grandmothers could come back and see what busy lives women have nowadays. It would astonish them.'

'I suppose they went about less than we do,' Mildred said thoughtfully.

'Far less. It is a mere miracle that they did not get covered with moss, on the principle of the stone that never rolls. But they must have had an easy time. I wish I had been born a grandmother.'

'I dare say they found plenty to do, after all,' Mildred answered. 'They looked after their homes better than we do.'

'Made jam and dusted their own china. I am glad we don't. They took more trouble about their homes it is true, but with less success; and they took very little trouble about their dress.'

'But their dress was very pretty. Why, we copy it now!'

'Oh, yes, occasionally. But they always looked precisely the same, and all alike; and we are always looking different, which adds to our charm,' Mrs Carew laughed, 'and prevents our husbands from getting tired of us, as our grandpapas often did of our grandmammas.'

Mrs Archerson thought the remark was not a very nice one, but she was too much interested in the subject to mind.

'Do you think,' she asked slowly, 'that anything one wears or does has any effect on one's husband—say three years after marriage?'

'Of course it has. Three years! Why, it has an effect thirty years after. I often think that it is a woman's own fault if he changes or grows tired of her. It is terrible to a man always to see the same thing before his eyes. She should take care not to become monotonous, not even to herself, for fear of growing stupid!'

'But how is she to avoid growing monotonous to herself? She can't make herself into somebody else to avoid getting tired of herself,' Mildred said. She was becoming quite excited in the conversation, feeling as if every moment Mrs Carew might accidentally give her some recipe by which Teddy could be turned into a devoted husband.

'She can change—she can alter her dress, her amusements, her everything. Men grow tired of women who are always the same, just as they would tire of the same dinner every day. Besides, it would be so dull to one's self to be always the same; one would know so little, and be so narrow. Surely it is better to change with life, which is always changing?'

'I think men grow tired of their wives because they are there, and under their control—because with marriage all the romance and necessity for love-making comes to an end,' Mildred said.

'But wives are not entirely under their control,' Mrs Carew laughed. 'And the romance and all the rest of it does not come to an end with marriage—unless the woman chooses. Let us be thankful for our station in life, my dear. The men much lower down beat their wives; and the men a little lower down—the second-rate men, and half-educated—have notions about keeping their wives in order, and treat them as puppets of which they must pull the strings. But that is over as far as the majority of us are concerned. I think wives now have a very good time; they do pretty much as they like. Men like pleasant companions; and if a woman only knows how to look nice and be nice, she has nothing to complain of.'

'I don't believe in Women's Rights,' Mildred said nervously.

'Neither do I,' answered Mrs Carew. 'But I believe in having a good time. And if we are only nice to our husbands, and take care not to be always the same, that's the fatal thing, we get an excellent time. I know I do—get my own way and fight Charlie as much as I like on various topics, and all the time am proud to feel that he is the stronger of the two, even if he does give way. We all like strong men, you know.'

'Yes—when they love us,' Mildred answered.

'Ah,' Mrs Carew said, with a little mock sigh—'yes, when they love us. It is a terrible thing to reflect how much we women depend for happiness on our affections. If we are only well-loved all the world is ours, and anyone else who pleases may have fame and wealth and everything life has to give, but that is not worth sixpence to one of us, unless we have also love. It is horrible! Give me some more tea—may I have another cup?' And then poor Mildred's aching heart found courage to put the question she longed to ask all women she met.

'Is your husband as fond of you as ever—I don't mean is he kind only; but is he fond of you?'

'As much in love as the day we married—just. I mean him to remain so till the day I die.'

'But if he altered—if he grew careless?'

'Ah, I should nip that sort of thing in the bud, for fear of getting my heart broken,' she added.

'But how would you nip it in the bud?' asked Mrs Archerson eagerly.

'I can't tell you at this moment,' Mrs Carew said, with an air of consideration; 'but I should do it—or run away'—and seeing Mrs Archerson look shocked, she added 'or die.' There was nothing to shock her principles in the idea of dying, Mrs Carew thought.

'Teddy is so much taken up with his work,' Mrs Archerson said.

'He is getting on. How proud you must be!' And she looked up with a sympathetic glow on her pretty face, but it reflected none on Mildred's. 'His name is always in the paper now. What lovely roses! You must have some kind friend at Nice who sends them?'

'No; they came from the florist's.'

'How very extravagant! Charlie would give me a little wigging if I indulged in such luxuries.'

'I don't; it is Teddy. He ordered them, and told Brooks to send enough every week to fill the glasses; he knows I like flowers.'

'I call that being an attentive husband,' Mrs Carew said, arranging her cloak-clasp and preparing to go.

'So he is,' Mildred answered in a grateful voice, while her heart reproached her with all her discontent—'the best and the most generous in the world.'

'By-the-way, were you going on to the Palace yesterday?'

'No. Why?'

'Oh, Charlie said he saw you at Clapham.'

'At Clapham?' Mrs Archerson looked up in surprise.

'Yes, he saw Mr Archerson, and thought you were with him; but you had your back turned, and he only saw your bonnet—or hat, I think he said,' Mrs Carew answered, wondering vaguely, now that it was too late, whether she had been indiscreet; but still something made her go on. 'He said you were on the platform at Clapham, but he did not see you at the Palace, though he looked out for you. He went down to the meeting. Perhaps, after all, he was mistaken,' she added, trying to patch up any mischief she might have done.

'Perhaps so; or perhaps Teddy met some one he knew,' Mrs Archerson said, slowly and naturally enough. But swift as an arrow her thoughts went back to that evening, many months ago now, when the man brought the card-case he had found at Clapham—and from that moment Mrs Archerson was not only an unhappy but a jealous woman. With jealousy too there came its wisdom, or its artfulness. She said nothing to her friend—nay, she seemed to suddenly brighten—and was so lively that when Mrs Carew went home she told her husband Teddy A.'s wife was a nice little thing; it was a shame Teddy didn't take her about more.

'She's rather slow, you know, darling,' Mr Carew answered. 'And then, she always looks so dowdy.'

'I know,' his wife answered triumphantly. 'I tried to give her a hint of that to-day. I told you men were all susceptible to pretty clothes.'

'Indeed! That's your sole reason for wearing them, I suppose?'

'Of course, and because I like you to admire me; and—oh, by-the-way, Charlie, she wasn't at Clapham yesterday. Are you certain there was some one with him?'

'Certain. You were not such a goose as to tell her so?'

'Yes, I did; but I don't think I made any mischief. She said he had probably met some one.'

'Well, perhaps he had. Teddy has toned down of late years. Still, when a man has married for money he is not always such a pattern of virtue as if——'

'As if he had married for love, as you did?'

'Precisely.'

'Then it is a great pity that she was not a pauper, as I was, poor thing.'

'Don't be too sure. You may have been an heiress unawares, and I may have known it beforehand.' At which his wife laughed, and said she only wished it were true. And then they went merrily down to their cosy little dinner, while Mrs Archerson at Kensington was looking blankly at her lonely meal, and wondering if she could get two or three mouthfuls down just to deceive the servants. Ten minutes before she had received a telegram saying that her husband was detained and could not be back to dinner.

Teddy came home late that night, but Mildred was still up—an unusual thing for her; she looked so pale and worn that he noticed it.

'You should have gone to bed,' he said anxiously. 'You know you are not strong enough to be up late at nights. Besides, it worries me to think you are waiting for me.'

'I wanted to finish my work. Besides, I don't see very much of you now, Edward.'

He winced a little. Moreover he always felt uneasy if she called him Edward when they were alone. It was absurd, but it gave him an idea that things were not quite right.

'No, you don't, I am afraid. Somehow I never have any time now.'

'Have you been at work all the evening?'

'Well—no, dear, not precisely at work; but I have been occupied.'

'Mrs Carew came to-day. She says you must be getting on, for she is always seeing your name in the papers.'

'That's all right,' he answered cheerfully.

'I looked for it this morning, but I did not see it. Were you in any case yesterday?'

'Yesterday—let me see. Well, no, not yesterday, dear. I was in chambers all day looking through a brief with Wilson.'

She looked up at him keenly.

'All day?' she asked, and saw him wince.

'Nearly all day. I had an engagement in the afternoon. Why do you ask?'

For a moment she hesitated, tempted to tell him her suspicions. But it is the curse of jealousy that it cannot be straightforward, and she fenced. Something seemed to close her lips. She grew silent and miserable—so miserable that she became thin and pale, and more and more dejected. But tears and dejection, especially when they cannot be accounted for, win no man's heart; and Teddy, though he was sorry enough, and anxious too, felt his feet hurry faster and faster from her, day by day. At last she looked so ill he grew alarmed. 'She wants more excitement,' he thought. 'It's dull for her alone all day at Kensington.' He pondered over matters a bit, and then a bright thought struck him. 'I'll tell you what it is, Millie,' he said, 'you want a thorough change. You ought to get away from all this fog and brick and mortar. How would you like to go to Rome for a month or two, or to Nice or Mentone? You were always fond of travelling.'

'With you, Edward?' she asked eagerly.

'Well, no. You see it would be utterly impossible for me to get away. Mrs Carew would miss my name in the paper every morning. But you might take Amy with you. I dare say she would be delighted. I should be rather on my beam ends at Nice or Mentone, though of course I could get over to Monte Carlo every day; but I don't suppose you would approve of that, or care about staying there.'

'I should care about staying anywhere with you,' she answered quickly.

'Couldn't manage it, dear—not even for a day. Too many things coming on.'

'Then let me stay,' she said. 'I would far rather stay at home.'

'You shall do as you like; but I would rather that you went.'

'Do you want to get rid of me, Teddy?'

'No, of course not. Why should I want to get rid of you?' he asked. But after that he did not press her to go. 'She is only a little moped,' he thought. 'I am away a good deal, and she hasn't many resources. I wish she would go to Mentone for a few months, it would do her a world of good; and I might be able to run out and fetch her at Easter.'

But Mrs Archerson did not mean to go. She stayed at home with eyes that watched and ears that tried to hear, and a heart that ached sorely, with a feeling that a strange drama was being played almost in her presence, but the curtain of the theatre was down so that she could not see, and she was dazed and could not comprehend. She knew instinctively that the end would come of all this terrible suspense, that some day, some moment when she least expected it, the curtain would be thrust aside, and all things made plain. She waited, dreading what she might lift her eyes to see.

CHAPTER III

The great case of Willoughby v. Conyers came on in January. Teddy went off in good time on the morning of the trial. His wife remembered afterwards with a sort of dazed wondering that when he reached the street door he hesitated, and turning back looked in at her, saying 'Good-bye, Millie. Keep up your courage.' Courage for what? It was like the ringing of the prompter's bell to an actor about to play a part in an unknown play. She watched him out of sight, but he did not know, he never looked back; she knew that he forgot her as soon as the door that divided them closed behind him. It had never struck her before that when that door closed it left her a prisoner and made him a free man.

As Teddy vanished in the distance she went back to the fire, and sat thinking over the one ceaseless subject of all her thoughts. What did it mean, her husband's absences, his excuses, his almost elaborate efforts to be kind? She no longer for a moment supposed that he spent all his evenings at his chambers or his club, or went twice a week to see a bachelor friend at Richmond. There was some other woman. For a long time she did not dare to think it, but now she felt it and knew it—some woman who had won him from her. And the odd thing was, that she did not blame him much; it put a sick dread in her heart, while all things grew dim before her eyes; it made her unspeakably miserable, and yet hardly angry at all. Since that afternoon when she had looked hope-lessly at her own face she had understood all that Teddy felt, struggle against it as he would; it said something for her courage that she dared thus far to face the truth. Besides, she loved Teddy too well to be angry with him—the great love was greater than all feelings of anger and pride, than all those that go to make up indignation and self-assertion. It was as a calamity, the greatest that could overtake her, that she dreaded what might come—there might be pain too great to bear, and yet she able to do nothing but bow her head. Other women who loved less might rage and storm with all the fury of jealousy and the burden of insult; it was not in her to do that—not yet, at any rate—as she sat there staring the idea of what might come blankly in the face. Before the reality all her feelings might change—she did not know, she could not tell. She only did know that if she might but have Teddy's deep true love, such as other men gave other women, for just one hour—just one

hour to see his face and hear his voice all full of tender love for her—
of lover's love, and not mere dutiful affection—if she might but feel his
dear arms round her and rest her head on his shoulder for even one
single moment, while he stooped whispering foolish love-words to her,
and then she had to die, no matter how terrible and lonely a death, she
could yet bless fate for its goodness and bountifulness to her. It was odd
how the misery of the last few months had brought the unsuspected
passion in her nature to the surface—passion she held down and hid,
but could not kill. A little while since she had been an even-humoured,
humdrum woman; but all the time hidden somewhere there had been in
her heart a little spark of fire that lately had been fanned and fanned by
cold and bitter winds until it had leaped into flame—flame that withal
was subdued by the gentleness of her nature. She was stupid with going
over and over and over the same thing again and again; she could think,
even of it, actively no more, but sat by the fire, blankly staring at it, the
everlasting subject on which she for ever speculated. She tried to rouse
herself, and went to the window. The postman was in the street, she
went back to her seat by the fire and listened to his knocks. They made
her realize that she was very lonely; the simple homely sound seemed
to come into an empty room, and to find just one woman sitting by the
fire. She heard his footsteps faintly on the pavement, and followed him
in thought from house to house. Then he stopped before the gate; she
knew when he pushed it open; she heard him come up the steps and
drop something into the letter-box. The servant would bring it in a
moment—more than one letter, she thought, judging from the sound.
She shivered and drew nearer to the fire; there is nothing so chilly as
misery.

A note and two printed things—circulars, from the look of the
wrappers—were brought in. She put them down on her lap and looked
round the room again, as if to take farewell of the familiar objects
before the play she had been waiting for ceased to be a play and turned
into a living reality. Then she opened the note. It was a dinner invitation from the Paton-Greenes'. She wondered listlessly if Teddy would
go, and began to think again. Presently she took up the circulars. One
was about the Kensington Bazaar. She had been asked to assist in it. She
would get Amy to make some things: perhaps Amy would like to come
up for it and stay a bit. But no, she did not think just now that she could

bear to have anyone staying with her. She wanted to be alone, to think over the great problem that was for ever perplexing her. She opened the other circular: it was about cottage homes for destitute children, an appeal for subscriptions, a list of patrons and donors. She put it down and began to think once more. The Dresden clock struck ten. Teddy was in his wig and gown, looking bright and handsome. He would be a judge some day, of course. Already he talked of applying for silk, and would probably do so in a couple of years. It was so certain that his career would be a triumph; how odd it was that she did not care! But she cared for nothing save that one thing that she felt was for ever denied her.

The fire was burning hollow. She stirred it, and made a blaze; and mechanically taking up the circular about cottage homes, began reading down the list of donors of small sums. Suddenly she started to her feet, her heart stood still, and quick as lightning it flashed through her that everything was about to be made plain. There, half-way down the page, was—

Mrs Edward Archerson, 3, Sisterton Road, Clapham. £3 3s.

Her own name, and at Clapham! It was in the Sisterton Road that the man had found the card-case; she remembered it perfectly. There were not two Mrs Edward Archersons, there could not be; there were no Archersons in London except themselves. Teddy had often said so in the first years of their marriage. Then suddenly it seemed as if a storm had overtaken the lonely woman standing there helpless and alone.

'Oh, what shall I do!' she cried—'what shall I do! It will break my heart.' She walked about the room in a frenzy of misery, wringing her hands and wishing that she could die. She was mad, or blind, or foolish. It was a nightmare, an evil dream. She stopped quickly and snatched up the paper and looked at it again, half expecting to see that it had vanished. But no, it was clear enough, and she was wide awake. Oh, if Teddy would only come back—if she could but telegraph to him or devise some way of getting at him, to beg him to clear up this mystery! She could not wait till evening time. Then, as if a wind had swept over her, the vehemence died away, the old quiet nature asserted itself, and she sat down calm and still, perhaps half-stunned, to think things over and decide what she would do. She folded her hands and looked blankly towards the window, as she had before the postman; she thought of him for a moment, and the difference his coming had made. She realized that she had regained the senses that had seemed to be going a few minutes since; but the calmness that was overtaking her was the calmness of despair. For before that story was told she knew what it was, and what the end must be. Once more she looked at the name and address. Yes, it was spelt properly—it was the same, the very same; there was no mistake at all. She put it, together with the one about the Kensington Bazaar, into her pocket. In every corner of the room the face of the unknown woman at Clapham seemed to be shaping itself in a blurred mocking manner. She could not see what it was like, only that there was a look upon it that would drive her out of the world. The clock struck half-past ten. Teddy was in Court, full of his case; and she—for a moment she put her hands over her face and shuddered.

'It is no good waiting or flinching,' she thought. 'I will know what it all means. I will see her. I must and will.'

She rang the bell, and waited nervously for it to be answered. It was the beginning of what she was going to do. She was curious to hear her own voice, to judge how she would play her part.

'I am going out,' she said to the servant. 'Tell Rice that I shall want the carriage in half-an-hour.'

She went upstairs and dressed, feeling as if she were a person in a dream pretending to be some one who was awake. She pushed her hair back from her forehead, and put on a veil that tied with two ends under her chin. When she was ready she sat down for a moment and considered. It was a desperate thing that she was about to do, but she was determined to have all doubts set at rest, and above all she was determined to see the woman who bore her name. As if she had decided on some plan of action, she got up after a few minutes and rang the bell again.

'Marks,' she said, 'I shall not want the carriage. I am going to walk.'

She was very calm. No one would have suspected that she was playing a part in a tragedy. Her face was merely the face of a woman setting about the commonplace routine of her daily life. She went slowly downstairs and out of the house. As she left it she turned to look back, and recognised with a quick throb how much she had loved her home. She had perhaps never wholly realised this before, it had merely been a part of her life; but now she felt that it was about to be wrenched away, to become a separate thing, a memory that would for ever be an ache and pain, a bit of the past that had nothing to do with the present.

She went on towards the Addison-road Station. She had never been to Clapham; she had thought of it as a junction at which everyone took fresh trains and no one knew whither the old ones went. Oh, yes! there was Clapham Common. Admiral Somers had once lived there. She remembered how, when he used to dine with her father, he always left at ten o'clock, always remarking in precisely the same tone that he had a long way to drive. How strange it was to think of him now, while she was walking perhaps to the end of the world—to the end of all it held for her. There was a cold wintry wind; she shuddered as it swept past her, it seemed as if it would bear off all the life left in her. Oh, if it could! if it would! If she had only died yesterday—last night, in that dream that kept coming back, all confused and broken, as if it were struggling to make itself clear, to show her that it had had some bearing on all this!

She tried to rouse herself a little, wondering if it were after all but an evil dream. Surely no waking woman could feel as she did—so strange and dazed that she could do and was doing she hardly knew what, but waited half-curiously to see. Afterwards, when the calm came in which she sat and thought all things over, it seemed to her that she had suffered more during that morning of uncertainty and dread than in all the after hours. It was pain so great that it stupefied all other senses, and drove her onwards without consideration of any sort.

There was a train ready to start from Addison Road; she found an empty carriage, and, incapable of thinking more, turned and looked aimlessly out of window. There were the squalid dreary backs of houses—she wondered if the people who lived within were ever happy?—the ugly unkept gardens, with the clothes hanging out to dry, or the crooked dirty lines, where they had been hung, left forgotten. The gardens were worse than the houses, and she looked up at the windows again. She could see into some of the rooms, corners of beds, backs of toilet-glasses, now and then a cheap ornament, and she recoiled a little. It was all so tawdry—the tawdriness of the lower middle-class, that knows not how to make the best of poverty as even the poorest poor of other countries do, and that never for a moment has dreamt of making itself picturesque. A patch of green came, a bank of gravel, an open space, a few distant trees; she looked at them all, glad of the lull that had come into her heart, and speculating idly how long it would last.

A few minutes more and she was at Clapham Junction. It was quite odd to go outside the station and not down among the passages. She enquired of a porter for Sisterton Road. It was a long way off, he said; he didn't quite know how far. So she took a cab and told the man to drive her to it; and when at last he stopped at the end of the Road, she felt more than ever as if everything was a dream and the waking far away somewhere beyond the world. She walked slowly down the Road—No. 3 was at the other end. For a moment she almost stopped her dreamy state to wonder what to do next. But she was too intent on her object to trouble about details. Besides, she had the Bazaar circular; that would serve as an excuse. She was quite accustomed to going on charity missions, and was not likely to betray herself. There were some shops to pass; she saw herself reflected in one of the plate-glass windows. Her prim bonnet with the veil tied under her chin, the comfortable fur-trimmed cloak, the quiet self-possessed air—all helped to make her appear quite a model charitable lady out on a subscription-hunt.

She stopped before the house at last. There were some dark evergreens in boxes at the windows, a little shining brass knocker to the olive-green door. It looked like a cosy, well-kept house, and her heart sank as she beheld it. Even from the outside she fancied that it had an air of Teddy. A young maid-servant answered Mildred's knock, and stared at her in blank surprise, as though she were wholly unused to visitors. Yes, Mrs Archerson was at home.

'Will you ask if I can see her? I will not keep her long. It is on business,' she added hurriedly; for the servant hesitated.

'Well, I'll see.' And, half-unwillingly, she showed the way into a little drawing-room on the ground-floor—a pretty room, all curtains and flowers, brass ornaments, and Japanese screens with storks on them. And there, on a little table facing the doorway, in a crimson plush frame, was a portrait of Teddy. All hope died out of Mildred's life as she beheld it. It was true, then, true—true. On the mantel-shelf was another portrait—a little smiling one, like that she had at home. She understood now of what he had been thinking when the happy look came over his face, and for a moment she was bitterly angry and indignant. She would denounce him to the shameless woman for whose sake he had been so false, and leave the house; she felt that it was unfit for her feet to stand in, and—but, while she was still defiant, the door opened, and there appeared a woman with a slight round figure, and a face on which there was nothing shameless, nor any consciousness of wrong.

She was five or six-and-twenty, perhaps, the woman who entered, but she looked so young that Mildred, remembering her own two or three additional years, felt as if old age had suddenly fastened upon her. A girl, in fact, whom one only called a woman because there was about her a certain sedateness as of one who had domestic responsibilities, and a distinct and defined place in the world. She had blue eyes—tender eyes, with a dreamy look in them, as though they remembered much; and golden-brown hair, twisted in soft coils round her head, different enough from poor Mildred's dull plaits.

'You wanted to see me?' she asked. Mildred's lips quivered, but made no sound. For a moment it seemed as if she were tottering, though the calm face betrayed nothing. 'May I ask why you wish to see me?' There was some surprise in the voice, perhaps a little nervousness. Mildred, pulling the circular concerning the Bazaar from her pocket, tried to remember her part.

'I ought to apologise, but I believe you take an interest in things that help women and children; and there is to be a Bazaar——' An air of relief spread over the other's face, a happy smile came to her lips, as she interrupted, almost gaily:

'Oh, yes, indeed I do, a great deal of interest; but I never go to Bazaars or take stalls, or do anything of the sort, if that is what you wish to ask.'

'No,' Mildred answered, 'I did not want that. I——' She stopped almost with a gasp; but the girl, suspecting nothing, took the circular, and holding it between her two dimpled hands, glanced quickly down it. On the third finger of her left hand there was a pile of rings; the bottom one was a wedding-ring. It fascinated Mildred like a snake.

'But this is for Kensington. Why should you come to us at Clapham?'

'It does not matter where they live, if——' She tried to think of the words to say, but they were like a lesson long forgotten, and impossible to repeat correctly.

'How did you get my address?' the girl asked, puzzled. 'And how did you know that I was interested in charities? I never did anything in public in my life, and I don't want to do anything. Do tell me how you got my name.'

'I found it in a list of donors to cottage homes for children,' Mildred said, looking at the face before her as though she would remember it through all eternity. It was such a happy face; it looked as if there could never have been a cloud on it, never a single tear in those soft eyes.

'Oh, yes, I know. I gave the money, but did not mean my name to appear; and I was so vexed when——' She stopped, and followed the eyes that, with a sad, almost wild look in them, had turned from her face to Teddy's portrait on the table.

'Is that your husband?' Mildred asked slowly, in a low voice, with bated breath. The answer came quickly and firmly.

'Yes, that is my husband.'

'Mr Edward Archerson?'

'Yes.' The speaker looked up, and then her lips closed as if she were prepared to resent any more questions. For a moment they looked at each other in silence; then, with a faltering voice, Mildred spoke—

'I did—I did not know his wife lived here. I thought she lived elsewhere. Please forgive me,' she added hurriedly; for she saw the colour rising on the girl's face, and the idea was taking possession of her that Teddy might have been deceiving two women—that two would have to suffer. 'Please forgive me,' she repeated, 'I know him well. I have known him for years,' she added. The girl rose, and stood looking Mildred straight in the face.

'What do you mean? Did you come on purpose? What business have you to intrude here asking questions? Did you come on purpose?' she repeated, almost breathlessly.

'Yes, I came on purpose,' Mildred said, in the same low voice in which she had previously spoken; it seemed as if she had no strength to raise it.

'May I ask why?' The words were meant to be defiant, but there was a note of coming fear in the voice.

'Because there is one woman to whom this is a matter of life and death,' Mildred answered, so calmly that she might well be taken for a person outside the desperate scene that seemed to be going on somewhere else rather than in the room in which they stood—two women, each with a part that meant her life's whole history. They stood looking at each other for a moment gravely and silently. The girl's face had lost its flush, and slowly turned ashy white. But otherwise she took no notice of Mildred's answer. When she spoke again each word seemed to be dragged from her.

'You say you have known him for years,' she said. 'Did you know that—he—was married?'

'Yes, I knew that he was married.'

'Do you know his wife?' The question was almost whispered.

'Yes, I know his wife,' came the calm, unflinching answer. The girl waited a moment, but the inexplicable woman before her seemed like some strange automaton, and did not offer to speak of her own accord.

'Well?—do you know her well?' There was a change in Mildred's voice then.

'Yes, I know her well,' she said, bitterly; 'better than anyone else in the world knows her.'

'You are her friend?'

'Yes, I suppose so.'

'When did you find this out?'

'Just before I started—an hour ago.'

'Then she cannot know yet! Oh, don't tell her! don't tell her!' the woman who had taken Mildred's place cried, putting her hands out entreatingly. 'Don't tell her. He says she is so gentle and good, it would break her heart. I would rather die, I think, than that she should know;' and, suddenly resting her face down on the edge of the velvet-covered shelf, she sobbed bitterly. The words took Mildred altogether aback, but her heart grew cold and hard as she watched her rival—her rival, and no dupe—and, apart from all other feelings, the remembrance of a marriage ceremony with a choral service filled her full of indignation.

'You are very considerate,' she said, in a grinding voice; 'it is most kind.' The girl raised her head quickly, and brushed her tears away.

'You don't understand,' she said, almost fiercely. 'Wait, and in a moment I will tell you. You must let me get calm—you say you know him—and her?'

'Yes, I know them well.'

'Then you know that he married her for her money. He did not love her. She is very gentle and good, but he does not love her; he never did, and he always loved me—always.' She clasped her hands together, and said the last words with a tenderness of which Mildred knew her own voice to be incapable. In that tone alone lay half the reason of everything.

'Always?'

'Yes, always. He loved me before he had ever seen her.'

Mildred looked at her half-bewildered, incapable of taking in all the bitterness of those last words; but her thoughts went back to the early days of her married life, to all the little endearments and foolish names and sweet nonsense of the time. It had all been a make-believe, then— a sham, a mockery.

'Why did not he marry you, if he loved you before he even saw her?' she asked.

'I was poor, I had no money at all. I was just a little drawing-mistress, and he was poor too, and very much in debt. One day he told me that it was of no use going on, it couldn't be; that he must have money, and could only get it by marrying. I was angry, he wanted to go, and I let him. We were both wrong, for I let him go, though I knew he loved me; but what could I do?' she asked, still speaking eagerly, as though for dear life. 'I was alone too,' she went on; 'there was no one else in the world, and I was so very, very miserable I thought my heart would break. And yet I was angry, too, and gave up all my pupils, and moved so that he might not find me. I only wanted never, never to see him again——'

'Well?'

'And then we met, and—and I had nearly died in the two years and more between. It was like Heaven meeting him again; and though he tried to hide it, it was no good—I saw that he loved me just the same. Oh, you cannot think what it was to meet—the misery, the joy of it; and he told me that his wife was good and gentle, but she had no lilt, no go—she loved him in an even, passionless manner, as a school-girl loves, not as I did, as I do! He is just my life!' she exclaimed, with flushed cheeks and eyes that had lost their dreaminess, and flashed as she looked up—'just my life, and light, and love, and all the world, as I am his.'

'Yes,' Mildred said calmly, 'go on. It is better to tell me all. I know them both, remember.'

'And he had no child, and, try as he would to help it, his wife was so little to him, he could not take her into his life; his heart was empty save for me; it ached for me; and I was alone and loved him. We went on meeting and parting—it was maddening! and at last he made me come to him. "His wife should never know", he said. You must not think—you are her friend, that is why I wish you to know all this—that he does not care for her; he does. But he does not love her; it is just affection——'

'And for her money.'

'Her money was a great deal to him once—he married her for it; but now he is rich, and it is nothing to him. It is that he fears to grieve her; it is because he knows how gentle and good she is——'

'While he is unfaithful to her every hour of his life——' Mildred said. She had listened to the story as if it were all a dream—a story that concerned some other person—some one she had known and remembered. She could not grasp the fact that it was her own history that she was hearing and living through. The girl looked up quickly at Mildred's last words, and spoke again, as she had all through, in a voice that came from the innermost depths of her soul.

'There are some people,' she said, and Mildred, looking back at her, thought while she listened how blue her eyes were. It was odd how Mildred dallied with her knowledge and her anguish that morning, though it wrecked all her happiness; dallied with it and put it a little way from her, and looked at it curiously as a thing for which she could put off grieving, though she knew that there would never be another hour in her life that would not bear the bitter fruit of this. 'There are some people,' the girl said, 'who have lives that go out to meet each other—ours did. They have met, and can never be parted. She lives there his wife in name and before the world by virtue of a marriage ceremony, but I am the wife of his heart, his soul, his innermost self; and as for wronging her——'

'Does he suppose she will never know?' Mildred asked. She had hardly heard the last words.

'She will never know if he and I can help it. How is she to know? I use his name, but that is all. I could not bear not to do that. I go nowhere, know no one, we seldom go out together; the name is not in the Directory, it is by the merest accident that it is in that list, and I shall instantly have it withdrawn; it is in no other place at all. How is she to know? We shall keep our secret. Oh, he would not let her know for the wide world.' She went forward a step or two and put her hand on Mildred's arm, but the latter shrank away. 'Oh, if you love her,' she pleaded, not heeding the movement, 'and have any regard for him; if you have a woman's heart, and know what it is to love—be silent. What good will telling her do? It will not make his heart go from me to her. You cannot love as you will. Remember that. Let her keep her poor happiness; she will never find out what a ghost it is. I, loving him, can understand, and dread to think what she would suffer if she knew——'

'You said she was cold.'

'Yes, she is cold—she has no fire, no abandon, no passion; but she is good and gentle, and loves him truly in her own way. Surely, knowing her, you understand; for I, who have never even seen her, can——'

'Oh, yes, I can understand,' Mildred said, with a long weary sigh, and eyes turned towards the door. For one moment she wondered foolishly if she would be a dead woman when she went out of that room. Then she asked one more question. 'Does it never strike you that you are making him wicked, dragging him down, the man you say you love so much better than she does—and that you are doing her a terrible wrong?'

'No, I am not making him wicked,' the girl answered gravely, in the tone of one who was certain; 'and I am not doing her a terrible wrong. He did her that when he married her for her money, and he knows it now. Yet, after all, remember her money bought her the man of her heart, though she does not know that that was the price of him. She will spend her life with him, possessing his affection and regard, bearing his name, sharing his public triumphs. That he never loved her she will never know. Is it not better than if she had never married, had not had the blessedness of being his, of seeing his face every day of her life?' There was something in her voice that was almost eloquence, that paralysed more and more the woman who listened, that seemed to send farther and farther away all the life left in her.

'But she is his wife.' It was a forlorn argument, but there was nothing else to say.

'No,' the other said, contradicting it as a statement she could not and would not allow; '*I* am his wife. Marriage is not a mere ceremony. It is the joining of two lives that for ever become one. I am the woman of his heart. That is my justification. If I were not I should be infamous. But I am not infamous; for I am his wife, body and soul, bound faster than any ceremony in all the world could bind. As for making him wicked'—and a smile that was almost scornful came for a moment to her face—'I do not, I—oh, I wonder if you understand! Are you married? I do not even know your name. Tell me who you are, and———' The handle rattled for a moment, then the door opened, and there entered a little fair-haired child of two or three years old.

'Mammy, darling,' he said. 'Nurse says am I to go out?'

'Yes, darling; and baby too.'

'Baby's fast asleep,' he answered, looking at the strange lady. Mildred stared at him with a long fixed gaze, as one standing at the gate of hell might turn to see a far-off glimpse of the Heaven for ever denied her. Then she went a step forward towards the door, like some hunted creature seeking instinctively a hiding-place somewhere in the dark, away from everything. How she had longed for children—for a little one to hold in her arms while her husband stooped to kiss it; she knew, too, that he had longed for them. He had them now, and the woman before her was their mother.

'He is so like his father,' the girl said tenderly. 'Teddy, dear, do you love papa?'

'Yes, very much,' the child answered, never once taking his eyes off Mildred; and then shyly turning to avoid her, he ran out of the room. On his way he brushed against her dress, she shivered and shrank back— her husband's child, his and another woman's! The woman looked up as the door closed.

'Do you understand now?' she asked. 'You cannot take him from me, for I am a part of his life. She is a woman outside it.'

'Are you never jealous of her? Do you never wish that she were dead?' Mildred asked, desperately, looking back at her, for she still stood with her face towards the door.

'Dead! No, I could not be so cruel; for life is sweet, even at its worst. And jealous! Why should I be jealous?' the other answered, almost sadly. 'I do not think I am ever jealous. I have his life's best

love; why should I grudge her poor heart the little happiness it sometimes gets?'

'May heaven forgive you!' Mildred said, with a sense of awakening
life, of returning pain, and of what all this would mean to her.

'Tell me who you are!' the girl cried, going forward and trying to see
clearly the pale face and grey eyes of the strange woman who had
wrung from her the story of her life. 'Tell me who you are!—*you*
cannot be his wife!—you could not have borne this if you had been.'

'No, I am not his wife,' Mildred answered; and her whole soul felt
the lie to be a truth.

'Do you love her so much, that you feel it thus keenly?'

'It is so terrible, so much worse than death for her.'

'She will never know, unless you tell her. If you are really her friend—
if you know what love is—Are you married?' she asked, in her impatient, earnest voice.

'I—I am alone in the world, I think.'

'As I was till I loved him, and he me.'

'Had you no friends, no relations, no one to prevent——'

'No, no one. We came to England, my father and I, when I was
little; he speculated, and I was left at school. He died, and I came to
London and lived alone, giving lessons. That is my history. There is
none to whom I need give account of myself, if that is what you mean.
I am his, and he is all I have in the world—he and the children. But
before you go,' she pleaded, putting her hand on the door to keep
Mildred back for a moment, 'promise me you will not tell her. You will
do no good; think how much misery you would cause her. I will make
him entreat you too——' Then Mildred hesitated.

'I will be silent on one condition,' she answered slowly—'that you
are, too—that you never tell him of this.'

'But I never had a secret from him yet in my life. I could not bear
to have one. Remember, nothing can part us—not joy, or sorrow, or
shame, or anything in the world; it is too late for that. You cannot part
us; you will do no good by telling her.'

'Nor you by telling him,' Mildred said, and opened the door.

'If you will promise not to tell her—if that is the only price of your
silence—then I will keep your visit a secret from him,' the girl said,
giving way, since it was the only alternative.

'Very well. Now let me go,' Mildred answered, in a dreamy, miserable voice; and at last she dragged herself to the street-door. For a moment she stopped, wondering almost wildly where she could go. There was no place in the world for her. No one had any need of her. And while she still hesitated she heard the sound of the child's voice above, and the patter-patter of his footsteps coming down the stairs. She looked up once more, with a look of such unspeakable anguish that it wrung an exclamation from her rival.

'Oh, come back———' she cried. But Mildred heard no more, only the sound of the child's joyous voice, as with a scared face she hurried into the street.

CHAPTER IV

Teddy came home to dinner that night. His case was going well, he was in excellent spirits, and ran gaily upstairs to the drawing-room. He felt that something had happened the moment he opened the door. Mildred was lying on the sofa, worn and white. She did not attempt to rise as he entered.

'Why what's the matter?' he asked. 'I thought you would be glad to see me back.'

'Yes,' she answered gently, 'but till half-an-hour ago I thought you were going to dine out. I am resting—it is only a headache,' she added. 'Why didn't you go to your dinner?'

'Had a telegram putting me off. So I instantly telegraphed to you. Did you get it?'

'Yes.'

'I thought you would be glad to see me,' he repeated, resenting mentally his dreary home-coming. 'You are generally glad when I dine at home.'

'Yes,' she said again. She could not say any more, for all the time she heard ringing in her ears, 'You cannot take him from me'; and the infinite pity of her heart kept adding, 'and there are the children.' The anger, the sense of insult, of injury, all that had died away. She was no coward, and unflinchingly faced the whole story. Above all, she saw its hopelessness. There was only one ending, and she knew it. She was like a woman waiting to die. She had a strange power of realising things from another's point of view; it was only from her own that she was narrow; but when mentally she looked from Teddy's she saw clearly, judged herself from it and understood, and did not wonder much. Only there was this great bitterness—it was all done in ignorance, a result of the strange fetters that seemed to bind her body and soul. If she could only once have broken away from them, and have found the voice that was never hers save in the secret recesses of her heart, where, as if in an iron chamber from which it gave no outward sign, a restless fire burnt that made a still agony of life—if just once she had dared to put into words that which she knew well she could never have said at all, for before it reached her lips it would have become distorted, and her voice uncertain and husky. It was no use. For ever before his eyes and in his thoughts she must be the woman she seemed, without charm, or passion, or excitement. His judgment was just; she knew and felt her own narrowness, the narrowness of her outward self, and had no power to help it. It was as if there dwelt in her some other soul besides the one she showed to the world and lived by—some soul that told her of the dulness of its mate, of the unattractiveness of her face and form, of the commonplaceness of her words and gestures, of the bands that bound down her heart, so that even from its depths there came only lukewarm utterances while it vainly longed to find the voice that should have been its natural one. Oh! it was terrible to have that absolute knowledge of self, with the consciousness of the uselessness and hopelessness of striving against it; to know that she had no power to be other than she seemed, to appear other than the woman she looked. A common thing enough, perhaps; for many have secret souls with which to feel, and working ones with which to make themselves felt and known. And if they are judged according to the latter, is it not fair enough in these days, in which it matters little what a man is, but only what he does?

'Have you been out to-day?' Teddy asked, looking round the room with a sense of some defect in its arrangement. It had not the air of restfulness that a woman strong in the characteristics of her sex makes the place to which her husband comes home after his work.

'Yes,' she said once more. There was something choking her, she could not talk. 'You cannot take him from me,' was still ringing in her ears. There were no other words in the world. But as she watched him round the room she thought it was true what her rival had said—she had 'no lilt, no go'. The other woman would have run to meet him, and putting her arms round his neck, looked up into his face with loving eyes and tender words upon her lips. Never in her brightest days had Mildred had courage enough for that sort of thing; she had seemed indifferent, perhaps, but in reality she had been shy and awkward, even with Teddy. She realised this, too, now that all things were too late. Even if to-day had been a year ago, and all the terrible story she had heard untold, it would never have occurred to her to ask Teddy about his work; she had always waited meekly to be told what it pleased him to tell her. The other woman, she knew surely, and he remembered, would have asked him a dozen eager questions—would have lived through the case, laughing at the good points made on his side, vexed at those made on the other. To his wife Teddy hardly mentioned it at all, it never occurred to him that she would be interested in it. He put it away from him as much as possible, in order to talk to her in the manner he thought she would like best.

'By the way,' he said presently, 'I was lunching with Bolton to-day. He gave the medical evidence on our side. I told him about you—that I was anxious to see you regularly set up. He says the real thing for you is a sea-voyage.'

'Yes? To the end of the world?' she asked, getting up and standing listlessly by the fire.

'Well, no, we won't send you quite so far as that; but a brilliant idea struck me all at once to-day. You know George is at Malta. It is a nice place—not too far; you could always race back by Italy, if you were in a hurry to get home again. I should not mind your going out there alone, with Marks, in the P. & O. You would be all right once on board. It is not a long voyage—rather more than a week—but quite long enough to do you good. You would like Malta; there's plenty always going on there. You like George and his wife, and I know they would be awfully glad to see you.'

Teddy had evidently made up his mind that he had hit upon the right thing for her. George was his elder brother.

'Yes, it will do very well,' she answered. 'Let me go at once,' she added. 'I meant to tell you when you came home to-night that I wanted to go somewhere. I don't care where it is, so that it is a long way off. How soon can I go?' There was something in her words and tone that went to his guilty heart like a knife. It was the tone that might have been hers had she known all, and was breaking her heart, he thought. The fire blazed up, and he saw her face plainly. Either the firelight exaggerated its paleness and weariness, or she had altered much since yesterday.

'Is anything the matter? You look so ill—so different,' he said.

'Oh, I am neuralgic, I suppose.' But her voice trembled, her eyes filled with tears. He felt that he was somehow, though how he did not know, responsible for her sorrowfulness; that it was not all neuralgia or mere low spirits, as she would have him believe; and he hated himself for the part he had played. Had she not given him her all in the world—that poor little soul whom he had never once loved truly, but had used merely as a stepping-stone to that which was his now, but a few years since had been far enough away. He felt that he was a scoundrel, and wished with all his heart that in days that were gone he had had courage enough to be honest.

'You will be better soon, dear,' he said gently. 'You want cheering up a bit; you have not been anywhere lately.' And going forward he stooped to kiss her. She pushed him away, almost with a shudder.

'Oh, don't, don't,' she cried, 'I cannot bear it—I cannot, indeed.' He looked at her in surprise. Usually she had been demurely eager for the caresses that he had half-grudged her.

'What is the matter, Mildred?' he asked, facing the worst.

'I am ill,' she answered, cowering away from him. 'I cannot go on living this life. Let me go away.' Then suddenly a flood of memories swept over her, as she looked at him bending down, as she felt his breath upon her cheek—her handsome, clever husband, of whom she had been so proud. She thought of the days they had spent together, days in which she had never dreamt of all that now must evermore divide them. She thought of all his tenderness and gentleness, for he had been very tender and gentle to her; and she divined that at heart he had been grateful and often self-reproachful. He need not have married her; but it was not his fault that he had not been in love with her. Did not many men marry for money, just as he had, and soon grow careless and callous? He had never done that. Perhaps it was all her fault. And yet it was not her fault; for she could not help not being pretty and lovable, like that other woman. She put her arms gently round his neck and kissed him. She had seldom had courage to do so much before uncoaxed, though he was her own husband. 'You must forgive me,' she said, in the low weary voice that had become natural to her, 'I am not well; let me go away, and soon, as soon as possible. I shall be better then. Now I am worn out, and tired of everything.'

'All right, dear,' he said, thankful that the scene was blowing over. 'You shall start for Malta as soon as we can get you off. Now we'll have dinner—there's the gong—so we have just made it up in time. We had better have some champagne to pick us up. Come along.' He pulled her arm through his, and almost dragged her downstairs, in laughing, good-humoured fashion. She would be better when she once got away, he thought. The voyage was an excellent idea. How lucky it was he had spoken to Bolton. She could not help this sort of thing, he supposed; still, it was trying when a man had been hard at work all day. But she had never been so foolish before; it was evident that she was out of health. It was very bad luck that the little girl at Clapham had tele-graphed that she had a headache too, and was obliged to go to bed. He had so longed to go to her—he had been looking forward to it all day—his darling, his pretty one; and he thought of her even in that one moment with a love that outweighed all that he had ever felt for the fragile woman on his arm since the day when he had first set eyes on her.

Teddy and his wife were standing on board the P. & O. at Southamp-ton. He had come down to see her off. They had lunched together downstairs, and Teddy had quite won over the captain, who knew him by reputation, and was delighted to make his acquaintance. There were a good many passengers, the captain said, and when they were within two or three days of Gibraltar Mrs Archerson would find everything delightful—weather warm, sea smooth, and every one friendly.

'By the way, you stop at Gibraltar, Millie, probably for a few hours,' Teddy said, as they took a last walk up and down the deck, 'so you may be able to go ashore and have a look at the big guns and the orange-trees. I remember George writing home when he stopped on his way to India, and saying it was all big guns and orange-trees.'

'Yes,' she answered. She could only think of him, just of him whom she was about to leave, and not of any place in the world. But he rattled on:

'Lucky little woman you are to get away into the sunshine, while your unfortunate husband stays behind, and slaves——' She turned round quickly; it seemed as if some words rose to her lips, but if so, they were left unsaid. He misunderstood the action. 'Of course, I sha'n't slave really,' he said, consolingly. 'I dare say I shall manage to take things pretty easily.'

'Oh, yes,' she said, with a long sigh. She had no words to talk with, no thoughts that she dared put into words. She was living through a crisis in which everything but a silent struggle for self-control was impossible. She shivered suddenly—it was all so terrible, and she was so utterly alone in her suffering. He thought she was trembling, and, stopping, adjusted her furs closer round her neck, while she submitted half-bewildered. For a passing moment he vaguely guessed that she was going through some terrible ordeal, and his heart smote him. He pulled her hand through his arm and drew her a little closer to him as they resumed their walk.

'You will soon be in the sunshine,' he said. 'You will get rather too much of it at Malta. They say there isn't a bit of shade to be had, and not a tree higher than a gooseberry-bush.'

'Oh, I don't mind,' she cried; 'I don't mind anything.' She could not bear to hear him talking as lightly as if to-morrow's sun would not rise and find them far apart. Her voice betrayed plainly enough this time that she was suffering, and the knowledge gave him a dull gnawing pain.

'You must take care of yourself,' he said, looking into her grey eyes with a quaking conscience, thankful with a thankfulness that knew no bounds that she had never guessed his secret. He prayed in his heart that she might never know it. 'You don't look up to much now, poor child,' he said tenderly; 'but George and Nellie will take care of you, and cheer you up, and do you a world of good.'

'Yes,' she said, almost gratefully. It was odd how she understood all that was in his thoughts on that last walk they took together.

'You will come back quite strong and well.'

'If I die,' she said suddenly, 'you must marry again soon and be very happy—do you hear?'

'Nonsense!' and he tried to laugh—a sorry sort of laugh. 'You are not going to die; you must not get morbid.'

'I am not morbid,' she said gravely. Then, after a moment's pause, she went on: 'I wish I had been better to you, Teddy, brighter and more companionable, and more lovable—oh, I do!' she cried. 'I would give all the world to have been different.' The last words came almost in a whisper from her trembling lips. He stopped, and with a troubled face answered her earnestly:

'No one in the world could have been better—no one in the world. You are the gentlest woman alive, Millie; I wish I had been worthier of you.'

She could not speak, but for answer she stooped and kissed his coat-sleeve. It was unlike her, but it was the action by which he remembered her through all the after years.

They stopped by the stern for a moment. The wheel-house was there, and behind it, at the extreme end of the ship, there were two raised steps that formed a seat. It was the point from which the log was taken. Mildred looked at the place for a moment, and hesitated; then mounting the steps, looked down at the water beneath. 'I shall come and sit here when it is warm enough,' she said. 'I shall have my face towards home, and my back towards Malta.'

'Don't you want to go?' he asked, hating himself.

'Oh, yes; I couldn't have stayed longer in England.' She sat down on the steps for an instant, and looked out towards the distance.

'You must mind how you sit there,' he said, 'unless it is very calm. If the ship gave a lurch you would go over before you knew where you were, and not a soul have an inkling of it in time to pick you up.'

'Yes,' she answered slowly, 'if the ship gave a lurch I might go over.'

They went for one more turn along the deck, and then it was time for Teddy to go ashore. He turned back as he stood by the gangway.

'I'll send you a line to Gibraltar, though I am not sure that it will get there in time,' he said. 'But at any rate you can post me one from there, and tell me how you are getting on.' She nodded her head, she could not speak, but he understood. He waved his hand, and she stood watching him going farther and farther away. Just before he vanished altogether he turned and made one more sign of farewell.

'Good-bye,' she whispered to herself, 'good-bye,' and looked at the water—at the sea that already divided them.

Gibraltar, 27*th January*

DEAREST TEDDY,

We stay here about six hours, but I am not going ashore. There is no letter from you. They say it is impossible for one to arrive in time. We have had lovely weather since Saturday, warm and soft; and I have gone to the little seat we found behind the wheel-house, and sat with my back to the ship and my face towards England, and watched the long line of foam we left behind as we came through the water. I have thought of you all the time; sometimes I have held out my arms to that long white line stretching and stretching between us, and felt as if I would die gladly for one more look at your dear face. I hope you are very happy, Teddy. I am always hoping that.

I do not know what has come to my fingers, I cannot write. I stop to think of one evening, years ago now—it was very soon after we were married—I met you in the hall, and you held me fast and kissed me. It felt as if I could never get away, as if you loved me. If I had only died then—my darling, my love, my husband, *mine!* Don't think that I have not loved you much or passionately because I have kept my heart hidden and my lips still. No woman has loved you nor ever will love you as I have, not if you live to be a thousand. Good-bye. Be happy, very, very happy. Your happiness is the thing I long for most in the world. Always remember that.

MILDRED

Teddy moved from the little house at Kensington before his second marriage, and took a better one nearer town. It was prettier and cosier as well as grander than the one over which poor Mildred had presided— more like a home to which a man hurries back from his work and is proud to ask his friends. He could not bear to spend an evening away from it; he had almost forgotten the short cuts to the club, he went there so seldom; and sometimes, when he was obliged to work in the evening, brought his papers home, and did it in the pretty drawing-room, while his wife sat near him. Many a time when he was absorbed in some legal problem, or framing some eloquent explanation of a difficult point, it helped him to look up and for a moment to see her face. It was like a gleam of sudden sunshine in a lawyer's office. He told her so once, and she laughed—that little merry laugh that seems to live in a happy life, like a bird in a wood—and said she should never have dreamt of calling him a lawyer's office. People said that she had been a widow, that Teddy had fallen head and ears in love with her, and was a wonderful step-father to her children. He and she laughed at the little deception sometimes. They laughed that night when George's letter came, saying that he was on his way home at last, and should be with them before the month was out.

'I wonder if he will be curious about Mr Grey?' Teddy said. 'I shall say you ill-used him, Mary; do you hear?' She was writing notes at a little table beside the fireplace. Her husband sat pretending to turn over a pile of new books, but in reality looking at her, and at all the prettinesses gathered round her. She had altered little since her interview with Mildred, nearly two years ago now. The idealism of youth still looked out of her eyes, and there was more of the strength and passion of womanhood in the lines of her mouth and the tones of her voice. But she was girl-like still, though the white throat was a shade fuller, the sweet face a little graver, perhaps more thoughtful. She was even prettier—she might almost have been called beautiful. Teddy thought so as he looked at her—his sweetheart, his dear one, his wife of whom he was so proud. She had a knack of making her surroundings pictur-esque, too, and yet most thoroughly comfortable. He had never real-ized the happy restfulness of home till her hands had made one for him. She had raised in his eyes the whole value of women.

'Dear Mr Grey,' she said, holding out her hand to him. 'I wonder what he was like.' He stooped and kissed her fingers.

'A disagreeable sort of fellow, no doubt.'

'That is ungenerous,' she laughed. 'I wonder if he was fond of his wife?'

'Perhaps so, poor fellow.'

'And why poor?'

'No doubt she killed him.'

'Your manners are positively shocking!' she said gaily; 'but I forgive you. I am so happy that I can afford to be generous,' she added, with a touch of gravity.

'Happier than—than before?' he asked.

She clasped her hands together, and answered, with a long sigh of content:

'Oh, a thousand times. I can breathe more freely, and look round and not feel ashamed.'

'Ah, I thought Mr Grey was not so very delightful,' he said, trying to laugh away her seriousness. She understood him—she always did, almost instinctively—and tried to fall in with his humour.

'I was very fond of him,' she laughed. 'He was quite as nice as you are, Mr Vanity. Let us draw his portrait.' She took up a pencil and made a grotesque likeness of Teddy, at which he, leaning over her shoulder, laughed, then he looked down at her head and smoothed her hair.

'My pretty wife,' he said. 'Then you can breathe freely now?'

'Yes, but not altogether—it troubles even now to think of it.'

'Ah, you women put an enormous value on respectability,' he answered. He liked to provoke her a little; he thought his words would do it, and he was right. She got up quickly and looked at him.

'It isn't that,' she flashed—'you know it isn't,' she cried passionately; 'but there are the children. Sometimes when I think of it I feel ashamed to look them in the face—not for what I did, but for what it may yet cause them to suffer.'

He hardly listened. She was so pretty when she was roused, when her cheeks were flushed and her eyes sparkling. She knew how to make herself look pretty, too, and did it always for Teddy. He looked at her bright hair, at her trailing dress, at the lace ruffles at her elbows, leaving the white arms bare. There were some flowers in her bosom—he had brought them home that day—round her throat there was a twist of soft lace, fastened with a diamond arrow. He thought of the day when he had bought it and sold it to her for a kiss, while she had declared it was far too dear.

'My prettiest,' he exclaimed, 'how I love you! Don't think of the children—they can never suffer or know. Don't be foolish, my sweet,' and he caught her in his arms and kissed her. 'If I could only know that you would never hate me for it—Mary, I am a fool about you. I love you so, my darling.'

'Hate you!' she cried, 'how could I? And yet I wish it had been right,' she whispered. 'I usedn't to care, but I do now. I would give anything if we had waited. We called what we did fine names, and I felt them all to be true then; but now I seem to see more clearly how wrong it was. I wish we had waited. I remember reading somewhere once, "All sin is dogged; and though that which follows may lag, it never loses the track." Sometimes I feel as if that which follows were over-taking us. Just when I am happiest its shadow is in my heart.'

'Thank God *she* never knew, my darling.' He sat down on her chair by the writing-table as he spoke, and she kneeling beside him clasped her hands upon his shoulder.

'No, she never knew,' she said, with a sigh of thankfulness; 'but— did it ever strike you what a thin curtain sometimes divides us from the most terrible suffering? If she had known—oh, Teddy, what would she have done?'

'It would have broken her heart, I think,' he said, sadly. Then trying to shake off the subject, he played with the arrow at her throat. 'Sweet, would it break your heart if I were false to you?' he asked. The question was half a joke; for he knew how fast her chains bound him. She looked up. There was none of Mildred's patience in her. She was a woman to win love easily, but not easily to let it go.

'Yes, it would break my heart, too,' she answered. 'But first I would kill you.'

'Kill me! Why not kill her?'

'The woman for whose sake you were false? No, I would kill you. She would suffer more in living.'

'Mary, I am half afraid of you,' he said.

With one of her quick changes of mood she laughed, a happy, triumphant little laugh. She unclasped her hands from his shoulder. 'Are you?' she said. 'Then you are free. Go and love elsewhere, if you will.'

'You know I can't,' he said fervently.

'Nor I,' she whispered. 'I never did or could, right or wrong. But oh, how glad I am that it is right at last,' she added, with a sigh.

'So am I, my own—more thankful than I can say.'

'Teddy,' she whispered, 'I never dared say it before; but I wish that she had died naturally—that she had not been drowned.' He nodded his head. Many and many a time had the same thought come over him too. 'It is so strange, but in the twilight I can often see her face looking up from a grey sea to a grey sky, a dead white face.'

'Nonsense!' he shuddered.

'I am thankful that I never saw her,' she went on, with a little shiver— 'that I never even saw a portrait of her. I could not bear to shape her face, her real face, in my thoughts.'

'You shall never see a portrait of her, my darling,' he said. 'But let us shake this off; we are only making ourselves miserable.'

'I know,' she answered. 'Let us shake it off. If she had only not been drowned—it is what might have happened, had she known? She would not have killed you, as I should?'

'No, she would not have killed me. Yes, it is perhaps what she might have done, had she known.'

'Oh, Teddy! it would have killed me too. I should have shrank away from you for ever afterwards.' And even as she spoke she shuddered and drew back from him. 'I would never have let you kiss me again— never! I should have died too.'

'But she never did know, darling. Let us stop all this painful talk. Are we not happy together, in spite of all we did? And were we not happy even then?'

'Yes, oh yes!' she said; and putting her arms round his neck again she rested her face against his, and was silent for a minute. Then she spoke calmly. 'Teddy, dear,' she said, 'I want to tell you something. It is the only secret I ever had from you. It cost me so much at the time, but I promised not to tell, and a sort of superstition has kept me silent. Besides, I wanted to save you pain. I do not think there has been a day since—hardly an hour—in which I have not thought of it. Wait a minute.' She went back to the writing-table, and kneeling before it, took up her pencil, and began to draw some one from memory—some one in a bonnet, with a veil tied under her chin. Suddenly he, watching, started with an exclamation.

'Great Heaven!' he cried, 'it is Mildred!' She got up and stood facing him, holding out her hands as one blinded, while her lips grew white and trembled.

'Then she knew!' she cried, and stretched out her arms, but they did not reach him. 'She knew! oh, God! she knew!' she cried, shrinking as though she dreaded lest he should touch her. Slowly, with scared faces, they looked at each other, it seemed as if across a great space—as if between them flowed the sea.

He shut the door and locked it, feeling that if any one came near him he should go mad. With a shiver he looked round the chilly empty room, and towards the shadowy corners. Then going to the writing-table, with a hand he vainly tried to make steady he unlocked a drawer, and taking out her letter, read it once again. There was a line under the word '*mine*,' a thick line, blurred, as though a tear had fallen on it. He had wondered when it came—at its passionate tone, at its sadness, at the living something in it that had haunted him many a time since. He remembered the night it had all happened; how he in England had sat through the twilight before the fire talking to Mary. He closed his eyes and groaned as he thought of it; he could see her sitting at the ship's end on the little seat they had looked at together. He remembered that her maid had described how she had not gone down to dinner that night after the ship had left Gibraltar, she had wished to be left alone. He could see her watching the track of the white foam, while the shadows gathered round her, and through the open hatchments came the clink of glasses, the sound of voices, as the passengers dined and laughed in the saloon below. He could feel the cool breeze that swept over her face, could see her hold out her hands to him once more, could feel all the agony in her heart, the bitter, bitter loneliness, and then—ah, God! and the ship went on, and the white line stretched and stretched. And he had sat the while with his arms round another woman.

W. S. GILBERT

An Elixir of Love

CHAPTER I

Ploverleigh was a picturesque little village in Dorsetshire, ten miles from anywhere. It lay in a pretty valley nestling amid clumps of elm trees, and a pleasant little trout stream ran right through it from end to end. The vicar of Ploverleigh was the Hon. and Rev. Mortimer De Becheville, third son of the forty-eighth Earl of Caramel. He was an excellent gentleman, and his living was worth £1,200 a-year. He was a graduate of Cambridge, and held a College Fellowship, besides which his father allowed him £500 a-year. So he was very comfortably 'off'.

Mr De Becheville had a very easy time of it, for he spent eleven-twelfths of the year away from the parish, delegating his duties to the Rev. Stanley Gay, an admirable young curate to whom he paid a stipend of £120 a-year, pocketing by this means a clear annual profit of £1,080. It was said by unkind and ungenerous people, that, as Mr De Becheville had (presumably) been selected for his sacred duties at a high salary on account of his special and exceptional qualifications for their discharge, it was hardly fair to delegate them to a wholly inexperienced young gentleman of two-and-twenty. It was argued that if a colonel, or a stipendiary magistrate, or a superintendent of a county lunatic asylum, or any other person holding a responsible office (outside the Church of England), for which he was handsomely paid, were to do his work by cheap deputy, such a responsible official would be looked upon as a swindler. But this line of reasoning is only applied to the cure of souls by uncharitable and narrow-minded people who never go to church, and consequently can't know anything about it. Besides, who cares what people who never go to church think? If it comes to that, Mr De Becheville was *not* selected (as it happens) on account of his special and exceptional fitness for the cure of souls, inasmuch as the living was a family one, and went to De Becheville because his two elder brothers preferred the Guards. So that argument falls to the ground.

The Rev. Stanley Gay was a Leveller. I don't mean to say that he was a mere I'm-as-good-as-you Radical spouter, who advocated a re-distribution of property from mere sordid motives. Mr Gay was an aesthetic Leveller. He held that as Love is the great bond of union between man and woman, no arbitrary obstacle should be allowed to interfere with its progress. He did not desire to abolish Rank, but he *did* desire that a mere difference in rank should not be an obstacle in the way of making two young people happy. He could prove to you by figures (for he was a famous mathematician) that, rank notwithstand-ing, all men are equal, and this is how he did it.

He began, as a matter of course, with x, because, as he said, x, whether it represents one or one hundred thousand, is always x, and do what you will, you cannot make w or y of it by any known process.

Having made this quite clear to you, he carried on his argument by means of algebra, until he got right through algebra to the 'cases' at the end of the book, and then he slid by gentle and imperceptible degrees into conic sections, where x, although you found it masquerading as the equation to the parabola, was still as much x as ever. Then if you were not too tired to follow him, you found yourself up to the eyes in plane and spherical trigonometry, where x again turned up in a variety of assumed characters, sometimes as 'cos α' sometimes as 'sin β,' but gen-erally with a $\sqrt[3]{}$ over it, and none the less x on that account. This singular character then made its appearance in a quaint binomial disguise, and was eventually run to earth in the very heart of differential and integral calculus, looking less like x, but being, in point of fact, more like x than ever. The force of his argument went to show that, do what you would, you could not stamp x out, and therefore it was better and wiser and more straightforward to call him x at once than to invest him with complicated sham dignities which meant nothing, and only served to bother and perplex people who met him for the first time. It's a very easy problem—anybody can do it.

Mr Gay was, as a matter of course, engaged to be married. He loved a pretty little girl of eighteen, with soft brown eyes, and bright silky brown hair. Her name was Jessie Lightly, and she was the only daugh-ter of Sir Caractacus Lightly, a wealthy baronet who had a large place

in the neighbourhood of Ploverleigh. Sir Caractacus was a very dignified old gentleman, whose wife had died two years after Jessie's birth.
A well-bred, courtly old gentleman, too, with a keen sense of honour.
He was very fond of Mr Gay, though he had no sympathy with his
levelling views.

One beautiful moonlit evening Mr Gay and Jessie were sitting together on Sir Caractacus's lawn. Everything around them was pure and
calm and still, so they grew sentimental.

'Stanley,' said Jessie, 'we are very, very happy, are we not?'

'Unspeakably happy,' said Gay. 'So happy that when I look around
me, and see how many there are whose lives are embittered by disappointment—by envy, by hatred, and by malice' (when he grew ora-
torical he generally lapsed into the Litany) 'I turn to the tranquil and
unruffled calm of my own pure and happy love for you with gratitude
unspeakable.'

He really meant all this, though he expressed himself in rather flatulent
periods.

'I wish with all my heart,' said Jessie, 'that every soul on earth were
as happy as we two.'

'And why are they not?' asked Gay, who hopped on to his hobby
whenever it was, so to speak, brought round to the front door. 'And
why are they not, Jessie? I will tell you why they are not. Because—'

'Yes, darling,' said Jessie, who had often heard his argument before.
'I know why. It's dreadful.'

'It's as simple as possible,' said Gay. 'Take x to represent the abstract
human being—'

'Certainly, dear,' said Jessie, who agreed with his argument heart
and soul, but didn't want to hear it again. 'We took it last night.'

'Then,' said Gay, not heeding the interruption, 'let $x + 1$, $x + 2$,
$x + 3$, represent three grades of high rank.'

'Exactly, it's contemptible,' said Jessie. 'How softly the wind sighs
among the trees.'

'What is a duke?' asked Gay—not for information, but oratorically,
with a view to making a point.

'A mere $x + 3$,' said Jessie. 'Could anything be more hollow. What
a lovely evening!'

'The Duke of Buckingham and Chandos—it sounds well, I grant

you,' continued Gay, 'but call him the $x + 3$ of Buckingham and Chandos, and you reduce him at once to—'

'I know,' said Jessie, 'to his lowest common denominator,' and her little upper lip curled with contempt.

'Nothing of the kind,' said Gay, turning red. 'Either hear me out, or let me drop the subject. At all events don't make ridiculous suggestions.'

'I'm very sorry, dear,' said Jessie, humbly. 'Go on, I'm listening, and I won't interrupt any more.'

But Gay was annoyed and wouldn't go on. So they returned to the house together. It was their first tiff.

CHAPTER II

In St Martin's Lane lived Baylis and Culpepper, magicians, astrologers, and professors of the Black Art. Baylis had sold himself to the Devil at a very early age, and had become remarkably proficient in all kinds of enchantment. Culpepper had been his apprentice, and having also acquired considerable skill as a necromancer, was taken into partnership by the genial old magician, who from the first had taken a liking to the frank and fair-haired boy. Ten years ago (the date of my story) the firm of Baylis and Culpepper stood at the very head of the London family magicians. They did what is known as a pushing trade, but although they advertised largely, and never neglected a chance, it was admitted even by their rivals, that the goods they supplied could be relied on as sound useful articles. They had a special reputation for a class of serviceable family nativity, and they did a very large and increasing business in love philtres, 'The Patent Oxy-Hydrogen Love-at-First-Sight Draught' in bottles at 1s. 1½d. and 2s. 3d. ('our leading article', as Baylis called it) was strong enough in itself to keep the firm going, had all its other resources failed them. But the establishment in St Martin's Lane was also a 'Noted House for Amulets', and if you wanted a neat, well-finished divining-rod, I don't know any place to which I would sooner recommend you. Their Curses at a shilling per dozen were the cheapest things in the trade, and they sold thousands of them in the course of the year. Their Blessings—also very cheap indeed, and quite effective—were not much asked for. 'We always keep a few on hand as curiosities and for completeness, but we don't sell two in the twelvemonth,' said

Mr Baylis. 'A gentleman bought one last week to send to his mother-in-law, but it turned out that he was afflicted in the head, and the persons who had charge of him declined to pay for it, and it's been returned to us. But the sale of penny curses, especially on Saturday nights, is tremendous. We can't turn 'em out fast enough.'

As Baylis and Culpepper were making up their books one evening, just at closing time, a gentle young clergyman with large violet eyes, and a beautiful girl of eighteen, with soft brown hair, and a Madonna-like purity of expression, entered the warehouse. These were Stanley Gay and Jessie Lightly. And this is how it came to pass that they found themselves in London, and in the warehouse of the worthy magicians.

As the reader knows, Stanley Gay and Jessie had for many months given themselves up to the conviction that it was their duty to do all in their power to bring their fellow men and women together in holy matrimony, without regard to distinctions of age or rank. Stanley gave lectures on the subject at mechanics' institutes, and the mechanics were unanimous in their approval of his views. He preached his doctrine in workhouses, in beer-shops, and in lunatic asylums, and his listeners supported him with enthusiasm. He addressed navvies at the roadside on the humanising advantages that would accrue to them if they married refined and wealthy ladies of rank, and not a navvy dissented. In short, he felt more and more convinced every day that he had at last discovered the secret of human happiness. Still he had a formidable battle to fight with class prejudice, and he and Jessie pondered gravely on the difficulties that were before them, and on the best means of overcoming them.

'It's no use disguising the fact, Jessie,' said Mr Gay, 'that the Countesses won't like it.' And little Jessie gave a sigh, and owned that she expected some difficulty with the Countesses. 'We must look these things in the face, Jessie, it won't do to ignore them. We have convinced the humble mechanics and artisans, but the aristocracy hold aloof.'

'The working-man is the true Intelligence after all,' said Jessie.

'He is a noble creature when he is quite sober,' said Gay. 'God bless him.'

Stanley Gay and Jessie were in this frame of mind when they came across Baylis and Culpepper's advertisement in the *Connubial Chronicle*.

'My dear Jessie,' said Gay, 'I see a way out of our difficulty.'

And dear little Jessie's face beamed with hope.

'These Love Philtres that Baylis and Culpepper advertise—they are very cheap indeed, and if we may judge by the testimonials, they are very effective. Listen, darling.'

And Stanley Gay read as follows:—

'From the Earl of Market Harborough. "I am a hideous old man of eighty, and everyone avoided me. I took a family bottle of your philtre, immediately on my accession to the title and estates a fortnight ago, and I can't keep the young women off. Please send me a pipe of it to lay down." '

'From Amelia Orange Blossom.—"I am a very pretty girl of fifteen. For upwards of fourteen years past I have been without a definitely declared admirer. I took a large bottle of your philtre yesterday, and within fourteen hours a young nobleman winked at me in church. Send me a couple of dozen." '

'What can the girl want with a couple of dozen young noblemen, darling?' asked Jessie.

'I don't know—perhaps she took it too strong. Now these men,' said Gay, laying down the paper, 'are benefactors indeed, if they can accomplish all they undertake. I would ennoble these men. They should have statues. I would enthrone them in high places. They would be $x + 3$.'

'My generous darling,' said Jessie, gazing into his eyes in a fervid ecstasy.

'Not at all,' replied Gay. 'They deserve it. We confer peerages on generals who plunge half a nation into mourning—shall we deny them to men who bring a life's happiness home to every door? Always supposing,' added the cautious clergyman, 'that they can really do what they profess.'

The upshot of this conversation was that Gay determined to lay in a stock of philtres for general use among his parishioners. If the effect upon them was satisfactory he would extend the sphere of their operations. So when Sir Caractacus and his daughter went to town for the season, Stanley Gay spent a fortnight with them, and thus it came to pass that he and Jessie went together to Baylis and Culpepper's.

'Have you any fresh Love Philtres to day?' said Gay.

'Plenty, sir,' said Mr Culpepper. 'How many would you like?'

'Well—let me see,' said Gay. 'There are a hundred and forty souls in my parish,—say twelve dozen.'

'I think, dear,' said little Jessie, 'you are better to take a few more than you really want, in case of accidents.'

'In purchasing a large quantity, sir,' said Mr Culpepper, 'we would strongly advise you taking it in the wood, and drawing it off as you happen to want it. We have it in four-and-a-half and nine-gallon casks, and we deduct ten per cent. for cash payments.'

'Then, Mr Culpepper, be good enough to let me have a nine-gallon cask of Love Philtre as soon as possible. Send it to the Rev. Stanley Gay, Ploverleigh.'

He wrote a cheque for the amount, and so the transaction ended.

'Is there any other article?' said Mr Culpepper.

'Nothing to-day. Good afternoon.'

'Have you seen our new wishing-caps? They are lined with silk and very chastely quilted, sir. We sold one to the Archbishop of Canterbury not an hour ago. Allow me to put you up a wishing-cap.'

'I tell you that I want nothing more,' said Gay, going.

'Our Flying Carpets are quite the talk of the town, sir,' said Culpepper, producing a very handsome piece of Persian tapestry. 'You spread it on the ground and sit on it, and then you think of a place and you find yourself there before you can count ten. Our Abudah chests, sir, each chest containing a patent Hag, who comes out and prophesies disasters whenever you touch this spring, are highly spoken of. We can sell the Abudah chest complete for fifteen guineas.'

'I think you tradespeople make a great mistake in worrying people to buy things they don't want,' said Gay.

'You'd be surprised if you knew the quantity of things we get rid of by this means, sir.'

'No doubt, but I think you keep a great many people out of your shop. If x represents the amount you gain by it, and y the amount you lose by it, then if $x/2 = y$ you are clearly out of pocket by it at the end of the year. Think this over. Good evening.'

And Mr Gay left the shop with Jessie.

'Stanley,' said she, 'what a blessing you are to mankind. You do good wherever you go.'

'My dear Jessie,' replied Gay, 'I have had a magnificent education, and if I can show these worthy but half-educated tradesmen that their ignorance of the profounder mathematics is misleading them, I am only dealing as I should deal with the blessings that have been entrusted to my care.'

As Messrs Baylis & Culpepper have nothing more to do with this story, it may be stated at once that Stanley Gay's words had a marked effect upon them. They determined never to push an article again, and within two years of this resolve they retired on ample fortunes, Baylis to a beautiful detached house on Clapham Common, and Culpepper to a handsome château on the Mediterranean, about four miles from Nice.

CHAPTER III

We are once more at Ploverleigh, but this time at the Vicarage. The scene is Mr Gay's handsome library, and in this library three persons are assembled—Mr Gay, Jessie, and old Zorah Clarke. It should be explained that Zorah is Mr Gay's cook and housekeeper, and it is understood between him and Sir Caractacus Lightly that Jessie may call on the curate whenever she likes, on condition that Zorah is present during the whole time of the visit. Zorah is stone deaf and has to be communicated with through the medium of pantomime, so that while she is really no impediment whatever to the free flow of conversation, the chastening influence of her presence would suffice of itself to silence ill-natured comments, if such articles had an existence among the primitive and innocent inhabitants of Ploverleigh.

The nine-gallon cask of Love Philtre had arrived in due course, and Mr Gay had decided that it should be locked up in a cupboard in his library, as he thought it would scarcely be prudent to trust it to Zorah, whose curiosity might get the better of her discretion. Zorah (who believed that the cask contained sherry) was much scandalised at her master's action in keeping it in his library, and looked upon it as an evident and unmistakeable sign that he had deliberately made up his mind to take to a steady course of drinking. However, Mr Gay partly reassured the good old lady by informing her in pantomime (an art of expression in which long practice had made him singularly expert) that the liquid was not intoxicating in the ordinary sense of the word, but that it was a cunning and subtle essence, concocted from innocent herbs by learned gentlemen who had devoted a lifetime to the study of its properties. He added (still in pantomime) that he did not propose to drink a single drop of it himself, but that he intended to distribute it among his parishioners, whom it would benefit socially, mentally, and morally to a considerable extent. Master as he was of the art of expression by gesture, it took two days' hard work to make this clear to her, and even then she had acquired but a faint and feeble idea of its properties, for she always referred to it as sarsaparilla.

'Jessie,' said Gay, 'the question now arises,—How shall we most effectually dispense the great boon we have at our command? Shall we give a party to our friends, and put the Love Philtre on the table in decanters, and allow them to help themselves?'

'We must be very careful, dear,' said Jessie, 'not to allow any married people to taste it.'

'True,' said Gay, 'quite true. I never thought of that. It wouldn't do at all. I am much obliged to you for the suggestion. It would be terrible —quite terrible.'

And Stanley Gay turned quite pale and faint at the very thought of such a *contretemps*.

'Then,' said Jessie, 'there are the engaged couples. I don't think we ought to do anything to interfere with the prospects of those who have already plighted their troth.'

'Quite true,' said Gay, 'we have no right, as you say, to interfere with the arrangements of engaged couples. That narrows our sphere of action very considerably.'

'Then the widows and the widowers of less than one year's standing should be exempted from its influence.'

'Certainly, most certainly. That reflection did not occur to me, I confess. It is clear that the dispensing of the philtre will be a very delicate operation: it will have to be conducted with the utmost tact. Can you think of any more exceptions?'

'Let me see,' said Jessie. 'There's Tibbits, our gardener, who has fits; and there's Williamson, papa's second groom, who drinks, oughtn't to be allowed to marry; and Major Crump, who uses dreadful language before ladies; and Dame Parboy, who is bed-ridden; and the old ladies in the almshouses—and little Tommy, the idiot—and, indeed, all children under—under what age shall we say?'

'All children who have not been confirmed,' said Gay. 'Yes, these exceptions never occurred to me.'

'I don't think we shall ever use the nine gallons, dear,' said Jessie. 'One tablespoonful is a dose.'

'I have just thought of another exception,' said Gay. 'Your papa.'

'Oh! papa *must* marry again! Poor dear old papa! Oh! You *must* let *him* marry.'

'My dear Jessie,' said Gay, 'Heaven has offered me the chance of entering into the married state unencumbered with a mother-in-law. And I am content to accept the blessing as I find it. Indeed, I prefer it so.'

'Papa *does* so want to marry—he is always talking of it,' replied the poor little woman, with a pretty pout. 'O indeed, *indeed*, my new mamma, whoever she may be, shall never interfere with us. Why, how thankless you are! My papa is about to confer upon you the most inestimable treasure in the world, a young, beautiful and devoted wife, and you withhold from him a priceless blessing that you are ready to confer on the very meanest of your parishioners.'

'Jessie,' said Gay, 'you have said enough. Sir Caractacus *shall* marry. I was wrong. If a certain burden to which I will not more particularly refer is to descend upon my shoulders, I will endeavour to bear it without repining.'

It was finally determined that there was only one way in which the philtre could be safely and properly distributed. Mr Gay was to give out that he was much interested in the sale of a very peculiar and curious old Amontillado, and small sample bottles of the wine were to be circulated among such of his parishioners as were decently eligible as brides and bridegrooms. The scheme was put into operation as soon as it was decided upon. Mr Gay sent to the nearest market-town for a gross of two-ounce phials, and Jessie and he spent a long afternoon bottling the elixir into these convenient receptacles. They then rolled them up in papers, and addressed them to the persons who were destined to be operated upon. And when all this was done Jessie returned to her papa, and Mr Gay sat up all night explaining in pantomime to Zorah that a widowed aunt of his, in somewhat straitened circumstances, who resided in a small but picturesque villa in the suburbs of Montilla, had been compelled to take a large quantity of the very finest sherry from a bankrupt wine-merchant, in satisfaction of a year's rent of her second floor, and that he had undertaken to push its sale in Ploverleigh in consideration of a commission of two-and-a-half per cent. on the sales effected—which commission was to be added to the fund for the restoration of the church steeple. He began his explanation at 9 P.M., and at 6 A.M. Zorah thought she began to understand him, and Stanley Gay, quite exhausted with his pantomimic exertions, retired, dead beat, to his chamber.

CHAPTER IV

The next morning as Sir Caractacus Lightly sat at breakfast with Jessie, the footman informed him that Mr Gay's housekeeper wished to speak to him on very particular business. The courtly old Baronet directed that she should be shown into the library, and at once proceeded to ask what she wanted.

'If you please Sir Caractacus, and beggin' your pardon,' said Zorah as he entered, 'I've come with a message from my master.'

'Pray be seated,' said Sir Caractacus. But the poor old lady could not hear him, so he explained his meaning to her in the best dumb show he could command. He pointed to a chair—walked to it—sat down in it—leant back, crossed his legs cosily, got up, and waved his hand to her in a manner that clearly conveyed to her that she was expected to do as he had done.

'My master's compliments and he's gone into the wine trade, and would you accept a sample?'

After all, Mr Gay's exertions had failed to convey his exact meaning to the deaf old lady.

'You astonish me,' said Sir Caractacus; then, finding that she did not understand him, he rumpled his hair, opened his mouth, strained his eye-balls, and threw himself into an attitude of the most horror-struck amazement. Having made his state of mind quite clear to her, he smiled pleasantly, and nodded to her to proceed.

'If you'll kindly taste it, sir, I'll take back any orders with which you may favour me.'

Sir Caractacus rang for a wineglass and proceeded to taste the sample.

'I don't know what it is, but it's not Amontillado,' said he, smacking his lips; 'still it is a pleasant cordial. Taste it.'

The old lady seemed to gather his meaning at once. She nodded, bobbed a curtsey, and emptied the glass.

Baylis and Culpepper had not over-stated the singular effects of the 'Patent Oxy-Hydrogen Love-at-First-Sight Draught'. Sir Caractacus's hard and firmly-set features gradually relaxed as the old lady sipped the contents of her glass. Zorah set it down when she had quite emptied it, and as she did so her eyes met those of the good old Baronet. She blushed under the ardour of his gaze, and a tear trembled on her old eyelid.

'You're a remarkable fine woman,' said Sir Caractacus, 'and singularly well preserved for your age.'

'Alas, kind sir,' said Zorah, 'I'm that hard of hearin' that cannons is whispers.'

Sir Caractacus stood up, stroked his face significantly, smacked his hands together, slapped them both upon his heart, and sank on one knee at her feet. He then got up and nodded smilingly at her to imply that he really meant it.

Zorah turned aside and trembled.

'I ain't no scollard, Sir Caractacus, and I don't rightly know how a poor old 'ooman like me did ought to own her likings for a lordly barrownight—but a true 'art is more precious than diamonds they do say, and a lovin' wife is a crown of gold to her husband. I ain't fashionable, but I'm a respectable old party, and can make you comfortable if nothing else.'

'Zorah, you are the very jewel of my hopes. My dear daughter will soon be taken from me. It lies with you to brighten my desolate old age. Will you be Lady Lightly?'

And he pointed to a picture of his late wife, and went through the pantomime of putting a ring on Zorah's finger. He then indicated the despair that would possess him if she refused to accept his offer. Having achieved these feats of silent eloquence, he smiled and nodded at her reassuringly, and waited for a reply with an interrogative expression of countenance.

'Yes, dearie,' murmured Zorah, as she sank into the Baronet's arms.

After a happy half-hour Zorah felt it was her duty to return to her master, so the lovers took a fond farewell of each other, and Sir Caractacus returned to the breakfast-room.

'Jessie,' said Sir Caractacus, 'I think you really love your poor old father?'

'Indeed, papa, I do.'

'Then you will, I trust, be pleased to hear that my declining years are not unlikely to be solaced by the companionship of a good, virtuous, and companionable woman.'

'My dear papa,' said Jessie, 'do you really mean that—that you are likely to be married?'

'Indeed, Jessie, I think it is more than probable! You know you are going to leave me very soon, and my dear little nurse must be replaced, or what will become of me?'

Jessie's eyes filled with tears—but they were tears of joy.

'I cannot tell you papa—dear, dear, papa—how happy you have made me.'

'And you will, I am sure, accept your new mamma with every feeling of respect and affection.'

'Any wife of yours is a mamma of mine,' said Jessie.

'My darling! Yes, Jessie, before very long I hope to lead to the altar a bride who will love and honour me as I deserve. She is no light and giddy girl, Jessie. She is a woman of sober age and staid demeanour, yet easy and comfortable in her ways. I am going to marry Mr Gay's cook, Zorah.'

'Zorah,' cried Jessie, 'dear, dear old Zorah! Oh, indeed, I am very, very glad and happy!'

'Bless you, my child,' said the Baronet. 'I knew my pet would not blame her poor old father for acting on the impulse of a heart that has never misled him. Yes, I think—nay, I am sure—that I have taken a wise and prudent step. Zorah is not what the world calls beautiful.'

'Zorah is very good, and very clean and honest, and quite, quite sober in her habits,' said Jessie warmly, 'and that is worth more—far more than beauty, dear papa. Beauty will fade and perish, but personal cleanliness is practically undying, for it can be renewed whenever it discovers symptoms of decay. Oh, I am sure you will be happy!' And Jessie hurried off to tell Stanley Gay how nobly the potion had done its work.

'Stanley, dear Stanley,' said she, 'I have such news—Papa and Zorah are engaged!'

W. S. Gilbert

'I am very glad to hear it. She will make him an excellent wife; it is a very auspicious beginning.'

'And have *you* any news to tell me?'

'None, except that all the bottles are distributed, and I am now waiting to see their effect. By the way, the Bishop has arrived unexpectedly, and is stopping at the Rectory, and I have sent him a bottle. I should like to find a nice little wife for the Bishop, for he has Crawleigh in his gift—the present incumbent is at the point of death, and the living is worth £1,800 a year. The duty is extremely light, and the county society unexceptional. I think I could be truly useful in such a sphere of action.'

CHAPTER V

The action of the 'Patent Oxy-Hydrogen Love-at-First-Sight Philtre' was rapid and powerful, and before evening there was scarcely a disengaged person (over thirteen years of age) in Ploverleigh. The Dowager Lady Fitz-Saracen, a fierce old lady of sixty, had betrothed herself to Alfred Creeper, of the 'Three Fiddlers', a very worthy man, who had been engaged in the public trade all his life, and had never yet had a mark on his licence. Colonel Pemberton, of The Grove, had fixed his affections on dear little Bessie Lane, the pupil teacher, and his son Willie (who had returned from Eton only the day before) had given out his engagement to kind old Mrs Partlet, the widow of the late sexton. In point of fact there was only one disengaged person in the village—the good and grave old Bishop. He was in the position of the odd player who can't find a seat in the 'Family Coach'. But, on the whole, Stanley Gay was rather glad of this, as he venerated the good old prelate, and in his opinion there was no one in the village at that time who was really good enough to be a Bishop's wife, except, indeed, the dear little brown-haired, soft-eyed maiden to whom Stanley himself was betrothed.

So far everything had worked admirably, and the unions effected through the agency of the philtre, if they were occasionally ill-assorted as regards the stations in life of the contracting parties, were all that could be desired in every other respect. Good, virtuous, straightforward, and temperate men were engaged to blameless women who were calculated to make admirable wives and mothers, and there was every

258

prospect that Ploverleigh would become celebrated as the only Home of Perfect Happiness. There was but one sad soul in the village. The good old Bishop had drunk freely of the philtre, but there was no one left to love him. It was pitiable to see the poor love-lorn prelate as he wandered disconsolately through the smiling meadows of Ploverleigh, pouring out the accents of his love to an incorporeal abstraction.

'Something must be done for the Bishop,' said Stanley, as he watched him sitting on a stile in the distance. 'The poor old gentleman is wasting to a shadow.'

The next morning as Stanley was carefully reading through the manuscript sermon which had been sent to him by a firm in Paternoster Row for delivery on the ensuing Sabbath, little Jessie entered his library (with Zorah) and threw herself on a sofa, sobbing as if her heart would break.

'Why, Jessie—my own little love,' exclaimed Stanley. 'What in the world is the matter?'

And he put his arms fondly round her waist, and endeavoured to raise her face to his.

'Oh, no—no—Stanley—don't—you musn't—indeed, indeed, you musn't.'

'Why, my pet, what can you mean?'

'Oh, Stanley, Stanley—you will never, never forgive me.'

'Nonsense, child,' said he. 'My dear little Jessie is incapable of an act which is beyond the pale of forgiveness.' And he gently kissed her forehead.

'Stanley, you musn't do it—indeed you musn't.'

'No, you musn't do it, Muster Gay,' said Zorah.

'Why, confound you, what do you mean by interfering?' said Stanley in a rage.

'Ah, it's all very fine, I dare say, but I don't know what you're a-talking about.'

And Stanley, recollecting her infirmity, explained in pantomime the process of confounding a person, and intimated that it would be put into operation upon her if she presumed to cut in with impertinent remarks.

'Stanley—Mr Gay—' said Jessie.

'*Mr* Gay!' ejaculated Stanley.

'I musn't call you Stanley any more.'

'Great Heaven, why not?'

'I'll tell you all about it if you promise not to be violent.'

And Gay, prepared for some terrible news, hid his head in his hands, and sobbed audibly.

'I loved you—oh so, so much—you were my life—my heart,' said the poor little woman. 'By day and by night my thoughts were with you, and the love came from my heart as the water from a well!'

Stanley groaned.

'When I rose in the morning it was to work for your happiness, and when I lay down in my bed at night it was to dream of the love that was to weave itself through my life.'

He kept his head between his hands and moved not.

'My life was for your life—my soul for yours! I drew breath but for one end—to love, to honour, to reverence you.'

He lifted his head at last. His face was ashy pale.

'Come to the point,' he gasped.

'Last night,' said Jessie, 'I was tempted to taste a bottle of the Elixir. It was but a drop I took on the tip of my finger. I went to bed thinking but of you. I rose to-day, still with you in my mind. Immediately after breakfast I left home to call upon you, and as I crossed Bullthorn's meadow I saw the Bishop of Chelsea seated on a stile. At once I became conscious that I had placed myself unwittingly under the influence of the fatal potion. Horrified at my involuntary faithlessness—loathing my miserable weakness—hating myself for the misery I was about to weave around the life of a saint I had so long adored—I could not but own to myself that the love of my heart was given over, for ever, to that solitary and love-lorn prelate. Mr Gay (for by that name I must call you to the end), I have told you nearly all that you need care to know. It is enough to add that my love is, as a matter of course, reciprocated, and, but for the misery I have caused you, I am happy. But, full as my cup of joy may be, it will never be without a bitter after-taste, for I cannot forget that my folly—my wicked folly—has blighted the life of a man who, an hour ago, was dearer to me than the whole world!'

And Jessie fell sobbing on Zorah's bosom.

Stanley Gay, pale and haggard, rose from his chair, and staggered to a side table. He tried to pour out a glass of water, but as he was in the act of doing so the venerable Bishop entered the room.

'Mr Gay, I cannot but feel that I owe you some apology for having gained the affections of a young lady to whom you were attached—Jessie, my love, compose yourself.'

And the Bishop gently removed Jessie's arms from Zorah's neck, and placed them about his own.

'My Lord,' said Mr Gay, 'I am lost in amazement. When I have more fully realized the unparalleled misfortune that has overtaken me I shall perhaps be able to speak and act with calmness. At the present moment I am unable to trust myself to do either. I am stunned—quite, quite stunned.'

'Do not suppose, my dear Mr Gay,' said the Bishop, 'that I came here this morning to add to your reasonable misery by presenting myself before you in the capacity of a successful rival. No. I came to tell you that poor old Mr Chudd, the vicar of Crawleigh has been mercifully removed. He is no more, and as the living is in my gift, I have come to tell you that, if it can compensate in any way for the terrible loss I have been the unintentional means of inflicting upon you, it is entirely at your disposal. It is worth £1,800 per annum—the duty is extremely light, and the local society is unexceptional.'

Stanley Gay pressed the kind old Bishop's hand.

'Eighteen hundred a year will not entirely compensate me for Jessie.'

'For Miss Lightly,' murmured the Bishop, gently.

'For Miss Lightly—but it will go some way towards doing so. I accept your lordship's offer with gratitude.'

'We shall always take an interest in you,' said the Bishop.

'Always—always,' said Jessie. 'And we shall be so glad to see you at the Palace—shall we not Frederick?'

'Well—ha—hum—yes—oh, yes, of course. Always,' said the Bishop. 'That is—oh, yes—always.'

The 14th of February was a great day for Ploverleigh, for on that date all the couples that had been brought together through the agency of the philtre were united in matrimony by the only bachelor in the place, the Rev. Stanley Gay. A week afterwards he took leave of his parishioners in an affecting sermon, and 'read himself in' at Crawleigh. He is still unmarried, and likely to remain so. He has quite got over his early disappointment, and he and the Bishop and Jessie have many a hearty laugh together over the circumstances under which the good old prelate wooed and won the bright-eyed little lady. Sir Caractacus died within a year of his marriage, and Zorah lives with her daughter-in-law at the Palace. The Bishop works hard at the art of pantomimic expression, but as yet with qualified success. He has lately taken to conversing with her through the medium of diagrams, many of which are very spirited in effect, though crude in design. It is not unlikely that they may be published before long. The series of twelve consecutive sketches, by which the Bishop informed his mother-in-law that, if she didn't mind her own business, and refrain from interfering between his wife and himself, he should be under the necessity of requiring her to pack up and be off, is likely to have a very large sale.

OLIVE SCHREINER

In a Far-Off World

There is a world in one of the far-off stars, and things do not happen here as they happen there.

In that world were a man and woman; they had one work, and they walked together side by side on many days, and were friends——and that is a thing that happens now and then in this world also.

But there was something in that star-world that there is not here. There was a thick wood: where the trees grew closest, and the stems were interlocked, and the summer sun never shone, there stood a shrine. In the day all was quiet, but at night, when the stars shone or the moon glinted on the tree-tops, and all was quiet below, if one crept here quite alone and knelt on the steps of the stone altar, and uncovering one's breast, so wounded it that the blood fell down on the altar steps, then whatever he who knelt there wished for was granted him. And all this happens, as I said, because it is a far-off world, and things often happen there as they do not happen here.

Now, the man and woman walked together; and the woman wished well to the man. One night when the moon was shining so that the leaves of all the trees glinted, and the waves of the sea were silvery, the woman walked alone to the forest. It was dark there; the moonlight fell only in little flecks on the dead leaves under her feet, and the branches were knotted tight overhead. Farther in it got darker, not even a fleck of moonlight shone. Then she came to the shrine; she knelt down before it and prayed; there came no answer. Then she uncovered her breast; with a sharp two-edged stone that lay there she wounded it. The drops dripped slowly down on to the stone, and a voice cried, 'What do you seek?'

She answered, 'There is a man; I hold him nearer than anything. I would give him the best of all blessings.'

The voice said, 'What is it?'

263

The girl said, 'I know not, but that which is most good for him I wish him to have.'

The voice said, 'Your prayer is answered; he shall have it.'

Then she stood up. She covered her breast and held the garment tight upon it with her hand, and ran out of the forest, and the dead leaves fluttered under her feet. Out in the moonlight the soft air was blowing, and the sand glittered on the beach. She ran along the smooth shore, then suddenly she stood still. Out across the water there was something moving. She shaded her eyes and looked. It was a boat; it was sliding swiftly over the moonlit water out to sea. One stood upright in it; the face the moonlight did not show, but the figure she knew. It was passing swiftly; it seemed as if no one propelled it; the moonlight's shimmer did not let her see clearly, and the boat was far from shore, but it seemed almost as if there was another figure sitting in the stern. Faster and faster it glided over the water away, away. She ran along the shore; she came no nearer it. The garment she had held closed fluttered open; she stretched out her arms, and the moonlight shone on her long, loose hair.

Then a voice beside her whispered, 'What is it?'

She cried, 'With my blood I bought the best of all gifts for him. I have come to bring it him! He is going from me!'

The voice whispered softly, 'Your prayer was answered. It has been given him.'

She cried, 'What is it?'

The voice answered, 'It is that he might leave you.'

The girl stood still.

Far out at sea the boat was lost to sight beyond the moonlight sheen.

The voice spoke softly, 'Art thou contented?'

She said, 'I am contented.'

At her feet the waves broke in long ripples softly on the shore.

GEORGE EGERTON

A Little Grey Glove

Early-Spring, 1893

The book of life begins with a man and woman in a garden and
ends—with Revelations.

OSCAR WILDE

Yes, most fellows' book of life may be said to begin at the chapter
where woman comes in; mine did. She came in years ago, when
I was a raw undergraduate. With the sober thought of retrospective
analysis, I may say she was not all my fancy painted her; indeed now
that I come to think of it there was no fancy about the vermeil of her
cheeks, rather an artificial reality; she had her bower in the bar of the
Golden Boar, and I was madly in love with her, seriously intent on
lawful wedlock. Luckily for me she threw me over for a neighbouring
pork butcher, but at the time I took it hardly, and it made me sex-shy.
I was a very poor man in those days. One feels one's griefs more keenly
then, one hasn't the wherewithal to buy distraction. Besides, ladies
snubbed me rather, on the rare occasions I met them. Later I fell in for
a legacy, the forerunner of several; indeed, I may say I am beastly rich.
My tastes are simple too, and I haven't any poor relations. I believe
they are of great assistance in getting rid of superfluous capital, wish I
had some! It was after the legacy that women discovered my attractions. They found that there was something superb in my plainness
(before, they said ugliness), something after the style of the late Victor
Emanuel, something infinitely more striking than mere ordinary beauty.
At least so Harding told me his sister said, and she had the reputation
of being a clever girl. Being an only child, I never had the opportunity
other fellows had of studying the undress side of women through familiar intercourse, say with sisters. Their most ordinary belongings were
sacred to me. I had, I used to be told, ridiculous high-flown notions

265

about them (by the way I modified those considerably on closer acquaintance). I ought to study them, nothing like a woman for developing a fellow. So I laid in a stock of books in different languages, mostly novels, in which women played title rôles, in order to get up some definite data before venturing amongst them. I can't say I derived much benefit from this course. There seemed to be as great a diversity of opinion about the female species as, let us say, about the salmonidae.

My friend Ponsonby Smith, who is one of the oldest fly-fishers in the three kingdoms, said to me once: 'Take my word for it, there are only four true salmon; the salar, the trutta, the fario, the ferox; all the rest are just varieties, sub-genuses of the above; stick to that. Some writing fellow divided all the women into good-uns and bad-uns. But as a conscientious stickler for truth, I must say that both in trout as in women, I have found myself faced with most puzzling varieties, that were a tantalising blending of several qualities.' I then resolved to study them on my own account. I pursued the Eternal Feminine in a spirit of purely scientific investigation. I knew you'd laugh sceptically at that, but it's a fact. I was impartial in my selection of subjects for observation,—French, German, Spanish, as well as the home product. Nothing in petticoats escaped me. I devoted myself to the freshest *ingenue* as well as the experienced widow of three departed; and I may as well confess that the more I saw of her, the less I understood her. But I think they understood me. They refused to take me *au sérieux*. When they weren't fleecing me, they were interested in the state of my soul (I preferred the former), but all humbugged me equally, so I gave them up. I took to rod and gun instead, *pro salute animae*; it's decidedly safer. I have scoured every country in the globe; indeed I can say that I have shot and fished in woods and waters where no other white man, perhaps, ever dropped a beast or played a fish before. There is no life like the life of a free wanderer, and no lore like the lore one gleans in the great book of nature. But one must have freed one's spirit from the taint of the town before one can even read the alphabet of its mystic meaning.

What has this to do with the glove? True, not much, and yet it has a connection—it accounts for me.

Well, for twelve years I have followed the impulses of the wandering spirit that dwells in me. I have seen the sun rise in Finland and gild the Devil's Knuckles as he sank behind the Drachensberg. I have caught the barba and the gamer yellow fish in the Vaal river, taken muskelunge and black-bass in Canada, thrown a fly over *guapote* and *cavallo* in Central American lakes, and choked the monster eels of the Mauritius with a cunningly faked-up duckling. But I have been shy as a chub at the shadow of a woman.

Well, it happened last year I came back on business—another confounded legacy; end of June too, just as I was off to Finland. But Messrs Thimble and Rigg, the highly respectable firm who look after my affairs, represented that I owed it to others, whom I kept out of their share of the legacy, to stay near town till affairs were wound up. They told me, with a view to reconcile me perhaps, of a trout stream with a decent inn near it; an unknown stream in Kent. It seems a junior member of the firm is an angler, at least he sometimes catches pike or perch in the Medway some way from the stream where the trout rise in audacious security from artificial lures. I stipulated for a clerk to come down with any papers to be signed, and started at once for Victoria. I decline to tell the name of my find, firstly because the trout are the gamest little fish that ever rose to fly and run to a good two pounds. Secondly, I have paid for all the rooms in the inn for the next year, and I want it to myself. The glove is lying on the table next me as I write. If it isn't in my breast-pocket or under my pillow, it is in some place where I can see it. It has a delicate grey body (Suède, I think they call it) with a whipping of silver round the top, and a darker grey silk tag to fasten it. It is marked $5\frac{3}{4}$ inside, and has a delicious scent about it, to keep off moths, I suppose; naphthaline is better. It reminds me of a 'silver-sedge' tied on a ten hook. I startled the good landlady of the little inn (there is no village fortunately) when I arrived with the only porter of the tiny station laden with traps. She hesitated about a private sitting-room, but eventually we compromised matters, as I was willing to share it with the other visitor. I got into knickerbockers at once, collared a boy to get me worms and minnow for the morrow, and as I felt too lazy to unpack tackle, just sat in the shiny arm-chair (made comfortable by the successive sitting of former occupants) at the open window and looked out. The river, not the trout stream, winds to the right, and the trees cast trembling shadows into its clear depths. The red tiles of a farm roof show between the beeches, and break the monotony of blue sky background. A dusty waggoner is slaking his thirst with a tankard of ale. I am conscious of the strange lonely feeling that a visit to England always gives me. Away in strange lands, even in solitary places, one doesn't feel it somehow. One is filled with the hunter's lust, bent on a 'kill'; but at home in the quiet country, with the smoke curling up from some fireside, the mowers busy laying the hay in swaths, the children tumbling under the trees in the orchards, and a girl singing as she spreads the clothes on the sweetbrier hedge, amidst a scene quick with home sights and sounds, a strange lack creeps in and makes itself felt in a dull, aching way. Oddly enough, too, I had a sense of uneasiness, a 'something going to happen'. I had often experienced it when out alone in a great forest, or on an unknown lake, and it always meant 'ware danger' of some kind. But why should I feel it here? Yet I did, and I couldn't shake it off. I took to examining the room. It was a commonplace one of the usual type. But there was a work-basket on the table, a dainty thing, lined with blue satin. There was a bit of lace stretched over shiny blue linen, with the needle sticking in it; such fairy work, like cobwebs seen from below, spun from a branch against a background of sky. A gold thimble, too, with initials, not the landlady's, I know. What pretty things, too, in the basket! A scissors, a capital shape for fly-making; a little file, and some floss silk and tinsel, the identical colour I want for a new fly I have in my head, one that will be a demon to kill. The northern devil I mean to call him. Some one looks in behind me, and a light step passes up-stairs. I drop the basket, I don't know why. There are some reviews near it. I take up one, and am soon buried in an article on Tasmanian fauna. It is strange, but whenever I do know anything about a subject, I always find these writing fellows either entirely ignorant or damned wrong.

After supper, I took a stroll to see the river. It was a silver grey evening, with just the last lemon and pink streaks of the sunset staining the sky. There had been a shower, and somehow the smell of the dust after rain mingled with the mignonette in the garden brought back vanished scenes of small-boyhood, when I caught minnows in a bottle, and dreamt of a shilling rod as happiness unattainable. I turned aside from the road in accordance with directions, and walked towards the stream. Holloa! some one before me, what a bore! The angler is hidden by an elder-bush, but I can see the fly drop delicately, artistically on the water. Fishing up-stream, too! There is a bit of broken water there, and

the midges dance in myriads; a silver gleam, and the line spins out, and
the fly falls just in the right place. It is growing dusk, but the fellow is
an adept at quick, fine casting—I wonder what fly he has on—why,
he's going to try down-stream now? I hurry forward, and as I near him,
I swerve to the left out of the way. S-s-s-s! a sudden sting in the lobe
of my ear. Hey! I cry as I find I am caught; the tail fly is fast in it. A
slight, grey-clad woman holding the rod lays it carefully down and
comes towards me through the gathering dusk. My first impulse is to
snap the gut and take to my heels, but I am held by something less
tangible but far more powerful than the grip of the Limerick hook in
my ear.

'I am very sorry!' she says in a voice that matched the evening, it was
so quiet and soft; 'but it was exceedingly stupid of you to come behind
like that.'

'I didn't think you threw such a long line; I thought I was safe,' I
stammered.

'Hold this!' she says, giving me a diminutive fly-book, out of which
she has taken a scissors. I obey meekly. She snips the gut.

'Have you a sharp knife? If I strip the hook you can push it through;
it is lucky it isn't in the cartilage.'

I suppose I am an awful idiot, but I only handed her the knife, and
she proceeded as calmly as if stripping a hook in a man's ear were an
everyday occurrence. Her gown is of some soft grey stuff, and her grey
leather belt is silver clasped. Her hands are soft and cool and steady, but
there is a rarely disturbing thrill in their gentle touch. The thought
flashed through my mind that I had just missed that, a woman's voluntary tender touch, not a paid caress, all my life.

'Now you can push it through yourself. I hope it won't hurt much.'
Taking the hook, I push it through, and a drop of blood follows it.
'Oh!' she cries, but I assure her it is nothing, and stick the hook surreptitiously in my coat sleeve. Then we both laugh, and I look at her for
the first time. She has a very white forehead, with little tendrils of hair
blowing round it; under her grey cap, her eyes are grey. I didn't see
that then, I only saw they were steady, smiling eyes that matched her
mouth. Such a mouth, the most maddening mouth a man ever longed
to kiss, above a too pointed chin, soft as a child's; indeed, the whole
face looks soft in the misty light.

'I am sorry I spoilt your sport!' I say.

'Oh, that don't matter, it's time to stop. I got two brace, one a beauty.'

She is winding in her line, and I look in her basket; they *are* beauties, one two-pounder, the rest running from a half to a pound.

'What fly?'

'Yellow dun took that one, but your assailant was a partridge spider.' I sling her basket over my shoulder; she takes it as a matter of course, and we retrace our steps. I feel curiously happy as we walk towards the road; there is a novel delight in her nearness; the feel of woman works subtly and strangely in me; the rustle of her skirt as it brushes the black-heads in the meadow-grass, and the delicate perfume, partly violets, partly herself, that comes to me with each of her movements is a rare pleasure. I am hardly surprised when she turns into the garden of the inn, I think I knew from the first that she would.

'Better bathe that ear of yours, and put a few drops of carbolic in the water.' She takes the basket as she says it, and goes into the kitchen. I hurry over this, and go into the little sitting-room. There is a tray with a glass of milk and some oaten cakes upon the table. I am too disturbed to sit down; I stand at the window and watch the bats flitter in the gathering moonlight, and listen with quivering nerves for her step—perhaps she will send for the tray, and not come after all. What a fool I am to be disturbed by a grey-clad witch with a tantalising mouth! That comes of loafing about doing nothing. I mentally darn the old fool who saved her money instead of spending it. Why the devil should I be bothered? I don't want it anyhow. She comes in as I fume, and I forget everything at her entrance. I push the arm-chair towards the table, and she sinks quietly into it, pulling the tray nearer. She has a wedding ring on, but somehow it never strikes me to wonder if she is married or a widow or who she may be. I am content to watch her break her biscuits. She has the prettiest hands, and a trick of separating her last fingers when she takes hold of anything. They remind me of white orchids I saw somewhere. She led me to talk; about Africa, I think. I liked to watch her eyes glow deeply in the shadow and then catch light as she bent forward to say something in her quick responsive way.

'Long ago when I was a girl,' she said once.

'Long ago?' I echo incredulously, 'surely not?'

'Ah, but yes, you haven't seen me in the daylight,' with a soft little laugh. 'Do you know what the gipsies say? "Never judge a woman or a ribbon by candle-light." They might have said moonlight equally well.'

She rises as she speaks, and I feel an overpowering wish to have her put out her hand. But she does not, she only takes the work-basket and a book, and says good-night with an inclination of her little head.

I go over and stand next her chair; I don't like to sit in it, but I like to put my hand where her head leant, and fancy, if she were there, how she would look up.

I woke next morning with a curious sense of pleasurable excitement. I whistled from very lightness of heart as I dressed. When I got down I found the landlady clearing away her breakfast things. I felt disappointed and resolved to be down earlier in future. I didn't feel inclined to try the minnow. I put them in a tub in the yard and tried to read and listen for her step. I dined alone. The day dragged terribly. I did not like to ask about her, I had a notion she might not like it. I spent the evening on the river. I might have filled a good basket, but I let the beggars rest. After all, I had caught fish enough to stock all the rivers in Great Britain. There are other things than trout in the world. I sit and smoke a pipe where she caught me last night. If I half close my eyes I can see hers, and her mouth in the smoke. That is one of the curious charms of baccy, it helps to reproduce brain pictures. After a bit, I think 'perhaps she has left'. I get quite feverish at the thought and hasten back. I must ask. I look up at the window as I pass; there is surely a gleam of white. I throw down my traps and hasten up. She is leaning with her arms on the window-ledge staring out into the gloom. I could swear I caught a suppressed sob as I entered. I cough, and she turns quickly and bows slightly. A bonnet and gloves and lace affair and a lot of papers are lying on the table. I am awfully afraid she is going. I say—

'Please don't let me drive you away, it is so early yet. I half expected to see you on the river.'

'Nothing so pleasant; I have been up in town (the tears have certainly got into her voice) all day; it was so hot and dusty, I am tired out.'

The little servant brings in the lamp and a tray with a bottle of lemonade.

'Mistress hasn't any lemons, 'm, will this do?'

'Yes,' she says wearily, she is shading her eyes with her hand; 'anything; I am fearfully thirsty.'

'Let me concoct you a drink instead. I have lemons and ice and things. My man sent me down supplies to-day; I leave him in town. I am rather a dab at drinks; learnt it from the Yankees; about the only thing I did learn from them I care to remember. Susan!' The little maid helps me to get the materials, and *she* watches me quietly. When I give it to her she takes it with a smile (she *has* been crying). That is an ample thank-you. She looks quite old. Something more than tiredness called up those lines in her face.

Well, ten days passed, sometimes we met at breakfast, sometimes at supper, sometimes we fished together or sat in the straggling orchard and talked; she neither avoided me nor sought me. She is the most charming mixture of child and woman I ever met. She is a dual creature. Now I never met that in a man. When she is here without getting a letter in the morning or going to town, she seems like a girl. She runs about in her grey gown and little cap and laughs, and seems to throw off all thought like an irresponsible child. She is eager to fish, or pick gooseberries and eat them daintily, or sit under the trees and talk. But when she goes to town—I notice she always goes when she gets a lawyer's letter, there is no mistaking the envelope—she comes home tired and haggard-looking, an old woman of thirty-five. I wonder why. It takes her, even with her elasticity of temperament, nearly a day to get young again. I hate her to go to town; it is extraordinary how I miss her; I can't recall, when she is absent, her saying anything very wonderful, but she converses all the time. She has a gracious way of filling the place with herself, there is an entertaining quality in her very presence. We had one rainy afternoon; she tied me some flies (I shan't use any of them); I watched the lights in her hair as she moved, it is quite golden in some places, and she has a tiny mole near her left ear and another on her left wrist. On the eleventh day she got a letter but she didn't go to town, she stayed up in her room all day; twenty times I felt inclined to send her a line, but I had no excuse. I heard the landlady say as I passed the kitchen window: 'Poor dear! I'm sorry to lose her!' Lose her? I should think not. It has come to this with me that I don't care to face any future without her; and yet I know nothing about her, not even if she is a free woman. I shall find that out the next time I see her. In the evening I catch a glimpse of her gown in the orchard, and I follow her. We sit down near the river. Her left hand is lying gloveless next me in the grass.

'Do you think from what you have seen of me, that I would ask a question out of any mere impertinent curiosity?'

She starts. 'No, I do not!'

I take up her hand and touch the ring. 'Tell me, does this bind you to any one?'

I am conscious of a buzzing in my ears and a dancing blurr of water and sky and trees, as I wait (it seems to me an hour) for her reply. I felt the same sensation once before, when I got drawn into some rapids and had an awfully narrow shave, but of that another time.

The voice is shaking.

'I am not legally bound to any one, at least; but why do you ask?' she looks me square in the face as she speaks, with a touch of haughtiness I never saw in her before.

Perhaps the great relief I feel, the sense of joy at knowing she is free, speaks out of my face, for hers flushes and she drops her eyes, her lips tremble. I don't look at her again, but I can see her all the same. After a while she says—

'I half intended to tell you something about myself this evening, now I *must*. Let us go in. I shall come down to the sitting-room after your supper.' She takes a long look at the river and the inn, as if fixing the place in her memory; it strikes me with a chill that there is a good-bye in her gaze. Her eyes rest on me a moment as they come back, there is a sad look in their grey clearness. She swings her little grey gloves in her hand as we walk back. I can hear her walking up and down overhead; how tired she will be, and how slowly the time goes. I am standing at one side of the window when she enters; she stands at the other, leaning her head against the shutter with her hands clasped before her. I can hear my own heart beating, and, I fancy, hers through the stillness. The suspense is fearful. At length she says—

'You have been a long time out of England; you don't read the papers?'

'No.' A pause. I believe my heart is beating inside my head.

'You asked me if I was a free woman. I don't pretend to misunderstand why you asked me. I am not a beautiful woman, I never was. But there must be something about me, there is in some women, "essential femininity" perhaps, that appeals to all men. What I read in your eyes I have seen in many men's before, but before God I never tried to rouse it. To-day (with a sob), I can say I am free, yesterday morning I could not. Yesterday my husband gained his case and divorced me!' she closes her eyes and draws in her under-lip to stop its quivering. I want to take her in my arms, but I am afraid to.

'I did not ask you any more than if you were free!'

'No, but I am afraid you don't quite take in the meaning. I did not divorce my husband, he divorced *me*, he got a decree *nisi*; do you understand now? (she is speaking with difficulty), do you know what that implies?'

I can't stand her face any longer. I take her hands, they are icy cold, and hold them tightly.

'Yes, I know what it implies, that is, I know the legal and social conclusion to be drawn from it,—if that is what you mean. But I never asked you for that information. I have nothing to do with your past. You did not exist for me before the day we met on the river. I take you from that day and I ask you to marry me.'

I feel her tremble and her hands get suddenly warm. She turns her head and looks at me long and searchingly, then she says—

'Sit down, I want to say something!'

I obey, and she comes and stands next the chair. I can't help it, I reach up my arm, but she puts it gently down.

'No, you must listen without touching me, I shall go back to the window. I don't want to influence you a bit by any personal magnetism I possess. I want you to listen—I have told you he divorced me, the co-respondent was an old friend, a friend of my childhood, of my girlhood. He died just after the first application was made, luckily for me. He would have considered my honour before my happiness. *I* did not defend the case, it wasn't likely—ah, if you knew all? He proved his case; given clever counsel, willing witnesses to whom you make it worth while, and no defence, divorce is always attainable even in England. But remember: I figure as an adulteress in every English-speaking paper. If you buy last week's evening papers—do you remember the day I was in town?'—I nod—'you will see a sketch of me in that day's; some one, perhaps he, must have given it; it was from an old photograph. I bought one at Victoria as I came out; it is funny (with an hysterical laugh) to buy a caricature of one's own poor face at a newsstall. Yet in spite of that I have felt glad. The point for you is that I made no defence to the world, and (with a lifting of her head) I will make no apology, no explanation, no denial to you, now nor ever. I am very desolate and your attention came very warm to me, but I don't love you. Perhaps I could learn to (with a rush of colour), for what you have said to-night, and it is because of that I tell you to weigh what this means. Later, when your care for me will grow into habit, you may chafe at my past. It is from that I would save you.'

I hold out my hands and she comes and puts them aside and takes me by the beard and turns up my face and scans it earnestly. She must have been deceived a good deal. I let her do as she pleases, it is the wisest way with women, and it is good to have her touch me in that way. She seems satisfied. She stands leaning against the arm of the chair and says—

'I must learn first to think of myself as a free woman again, it almost seems wrong to-day to talk like this; can you understand that feeling?'

I nod assent.

'Next time I must be sure, and you must be sure,' she lays her fingers on my mouth as I am about to protest, 'S-sh! You shall have a year to think. If you repeat then what you have said to-day, I shall give you your answer. You must not try to find me. I have money. If I am living, I will come here to you. If I am dead, you will be told of it. In the year between I shall look upon myself as belonging to you, and render an account if you wish of every hour. You will not be influenced by me in any way, and you will be able to reason it out calmly. If you think better of it, don't come.'

I feel there would be no use trying to move her, I simply kiss her hands and say:

'As you will, dear woman, I shall be here.'

We don't say any more; she sits down on a footstool with her head against my knee, and I just smooth it. When the clocks strike ten through the house, she rises and I stand up. I see that she has been crying quietly, poor lonely little soul. I lift her off her feet and kiss her, and stammer out my sorrow at losing her, and she is gone. Next morning the little maid brought me an envelope from the lady, who left by the first train. It held a little grey glove; that is why I carry it always, and why I haunt the inn and never leave it for longer than a week; why I sit and dream in the old chair that has a ghost of her presence always; dream of the spring to come with the May-fly on the wing, and the young summer when midges dance, and the trout are growing fastidious; when she will come to me across the meadow grass, through the silver haze, as she did before; come with her grey eyes shining to exchange herself for her little grey glove.

HUBERT CRACKANTHORPE

A Conflict of Egoisms

I

The sun must have gone down some time ago, for the room was darkening rapidly. Still Oswald Nowell went on writing, covering page after page with a bold, irregular scrawl. Since breakfast he had been there, and large sheets of paper littered the table and the floor around it. In front of him, by the inkstand, was a plate filled with half-burnt cigarettes.

Of a sudden he became aware that the light was very bad; so he laid down his pen, rose and paced up and down impatiently, his canvas shirt unbuttoned at the throat, his coat discoloured, and worn quite threadbare at the elbows, his thin, grey hair dishevelled as after a sleepless night; his eyes with the dull look of brain exhaustion in them.

For some moments he stood blinking thoughtfully down at the sheets on the floor, and passed his fingers roughly across his forehead, and once more sat down at the writing-table; with the reckless pluck of a blood-horse, struggling on for a few minutes longer. But in vain. He was dead beat.

This was how he always worked—a brief spell of magnificent effort following weeks of listless idleness.

For twelve years he had been writing. In all, he had published five novels and a volume of short stories. The work was singularly unequal, now so dreamy and vague as to be almost unintelligible, now grand with largeness of handling and a power of vision that lifted it at once into the front rank. He had learnt nothing from modern methods, neither French nor English; he belonged to no clique, he had no followers, he stood quite alone. He knew nothing of the disputes that were raging in the world of letters around him: when they told him that a popular critic had set him up as a chief of the idealist school, to do battle with an aggressive and prosperous band of young realists, he puckered his eyebrows and smiled a faint, expressionless smile. For in reality, he had grown accustomed to his own ignorance of what was going on around him, and, when people talked to him of such things, he never expected to understand. And so, day by day, his indifference grew more and more impregnable. His books achieved a *succes d'éstime* readily enough, but the figures of their sale were quite mediocre: the last one, however, probably owing to his having been labelled chief of a school, had run through several editions.

All by himself, in a quiet corner of Chelsea, he lived, at the top of a pile of flats overlooking the river. And each year the love of solitude had grown stronger within him, so that now he regularly spent the greater part of the day alone. Not that he had not a considerable circle of acquaintances; but very few of them had he admitted into his life ungrudgingly. This was not from misanthropy, sound or morbid, but rather the accumulated result of years of voluntary isolation. People sometimes surmised that he must have had some great love trouble in his youth from which he had never recovered. But it was not so. In the interminable day-dreams, which had filled so many hours of his life, no woman's image had ever long occupied a place. It was the sex, abstract and generalised, that appealed to him; for he lived as it were too far off to distinguish particular members. In like manner, his whole view of human nature was a generalised, abstract view: he saw no detail, only the broad lights and shades. And, since he started with no preconceived ideas or prejudices concerning the people with whom he came in contact, he accepted them as he found them, absolutely; and this, coupled with the effects of his solitary habits, gave him a supreme tolerance—the tolerance of indifference. This indifference lent a background of strength to his artistic personality. It was for this reason perhaps, and also because no one knew much about him, that every one spoke of him with respect.

Just now his power of work was exhausted: stretching himself on a sofa and shutting his eyes, he loosened the tension which was causing his brain to ache. His thoughts, as if astonished at their sudden liberation, for a minute or two flitted about aimlessly; then sank to rest as he fell into a dull slumber.

II

Below, in a tiny sitting-room, daintily, but inexpensively furnished, a woman, broad-shouldered and large-limbed, was stirring a cup of tea, with the unconstraint of habitual solitude. She sat facing the light, which exposed the faint wrinkle-marks about the eyes and mouth and made her seem several years older than she probably was; and these, coupled with the absence of colour in her cheeks, gave to the whole face a worn look, as if the effort of living had for her been no slight one.

And so indeed it was.

Eight of the best years of her life had slipped away in a hard-fought, all-absorbing struggle for independence. At last, a year and a half ago, it had come, and ever since, the emotional side of her nature, hitherto cramped and undeveloped, had been expanding with a passionateness that was almost painful.

Her childhood and her girlhood till she was nineteen, had been spent with her father, who was sub-editor of a halfpenny evening daily—a joyless, homeless existence, moving from boarding-house to boarding-house. Then one dirty November evening brought the first turning-point in her life. An omnibus knocked down her father as he was crossing the Strand, and the wheels passed over his chest. Death was quite instantaneous. Letty gave way to no explosion of grief, only she uttered a little gasp of horror at the sight of the distorted, dead face.

She had never cared for her father, the outbreaks of whose almost uncontrollable temper were the only dark incidents that relieved the dreariness of her colourless memories; and she had never learnt to pretend what she did not feel.

Old Stephen Moore, thriftless and dissolute all his life, left behind him nothing but a month's unpaid salary.

A couple of days after the funeral, she appeared at the office, and doggedly demanded to be given something to do. The manager peered suspiciously through his glasses at this gawky, overgrown girl and put one or two questions to her. Her apparent friendlessness and her determined spirit touched him; he promised to see what could be done.

The next day, and every day for the following six years, she spent in and out of the narrow, grimy building in Fleet Street, doing all manner of odd jobs, carrying messages, copying and answering letters, after awhile working up paragraphs and even writing leaderettes. Into whatever she was set to do, she threw her whole soul, always bright-faced and quick of intelligence, always eager to learn. And three or four times her salary was raised.

Then the sub-editorship of a ladies weekly was offered her. She accepted it eagerly, for, though it meant but a little more money, there seemed good prospect of promotion. Here, as before, she was indefatigable. Two years later the editor died; the post was at once given to her.

The new sense of authority and of responsibility was a source of great pleasure to her; she liked to recall the old Fleet Street days, when she was at every one's beck and call, to remind herself that no one had helped her, that her exertions alone had done it all. This thought repeated itself constantly, never failing to send through her a warm thrill of self-satisfaction. Hitherto she had had no desire, no interest outside her work; in complete unconsciousness of self, in complete ignorance of her own emotional possibilities, she had lived on, day after day.

Little by little, she began to realise herself in her relation to the corner of the world in which she mixed; insensibly to compare herself with others; dimly to perceive that life had perhaps many things in store for her, that were not included in the daily routine of work. And this process of awakening, once begun, proceeded with a curious rapidity.

Formerly she had always spent the couple of hours between her dinner and bed-time typewriting or doing other light work, making or mending her own clothes.

Now the necessity for this was gone, and at first she found the filling of the daily gap by no means easy, for she had never learnt how to be idle. She could, of course, have found plenty of work for herself in connection with the paper, but when she thought of it, she became aware that somehow the idea was distasteful. In reality an undefinable but growing longing for something—what she knew not—was unsettling her.

One evening the dinginess of her lodgings struck her, and from that moment she took a violent dislike to them. A week later she moved into the rooms she now occupied, half-way up the pile of flats overlooking the river.

The choosing of the furniture gave her a fortnight of excitement, for she set about it, as she set about everything, with an intense seriousness.

Next followed a period of restless arranging and rearranging; directly the dinner was cleared away, hammering in nails and wrenching them out again, pushing chairs and tables from one corner of the room to another, the whole accompanied by protracted consultations with the newly engaged servant-girl.

Sometimes on her way back from the office, it would occur to her that the looking-glass ought to be hung higher or lower, or that the table-cloth on the square table would look better on the round one; hastening home, and without waiting to take off her hat and gloves, she would at once try the effect of the alteration.

And, when everything was done, the clean, new chintzes, the stiff, white muslin curtains, the Japanese fans, and the hundred and one other bright-coloured knick-knacks on the walls, all, instead of delighting her, as she had expected, made her feel awkward and ill at ease. Her well-worn work-a-day clothes seemed out of place in this new interior, which made their deficiencies appear all the more glaring. In her daily work she had of necessity acquired a considerable knowledge of the fashions, but to use that knowledge for the adornment of herself had never occurred to her before.

The new elegancies in her dress led her to self-admiration, and to the delicious discovery of her own beauty. It came one afternoon, through a glimpse caught of the reflection of her own profile in a shop window. She stopped, turned and passed before it five or six times, examining herself anxiously. Then, as she walked on homewards, she found herself eagerly comparing her own appearance, which remained clearly visualised, with that of the passers-by.

About this time, too, she became infected with a passion for reading —chiefly inferior, sentimental novels. A considerable number of these were sent each week to the office for review. One afternoon, when things were slack, she happened to open one of these volumes that was lying on her table. Before long her attention was absorbed, and, in the evening, she carried the book home with her. All through her dinner, and on till nearly twelve o'clock, she pored over it, till the three volumes were finished.

The habit, once set going, rapidly ate its way into her life, so that, soon, she never sat down to a meal without a novel before her. And directly one book was finished, she would start on another; hence she remembered scarcely anything of what they contained, but their incidents, piled up and jumbled together in her mind, inflamed her imagination and brought on inexplicable fits of dissatisfaction and depression. Her thoughts took to dwelling on man's love; vaguely she marvelled that it had always been divorced from her life, that no one had ever whispered softly to her, 'Letty, darling, I love you.'

But surely one day, now that she was well dressed and smart—yes, it seemed that it must be, when she thought of the others, dull and ugly, who were married. And the care with which she dressed herself each morning was for the sake of this unknown new-comer, for whom she was waiting with vague expectation.

This evening however, as she sat over her half-finished cup of tea, her expression—sensitive reflection of all that was passing in her mind —started to fluctuate from radiancy to perplexity, from perplexity to despair.

III

'I beg your pardon,' he said, 'but may I offer you half of my umbrella? It's not quite so bad now.'

The shower had been a fierce one covering the roadway with a thick crop of rain spikes, filling the gutters with rushing rivulets of muddy water; now, through a rift in the ink-coloured clouds, the sunlight was filtering feebly, and the swirl of the downpour had subsided to a gentle patter.

Under a doorway they stood, side by side. Having no umbrella, she had fled there for shelter, when the shower had overtaken her on her way home from the office. And as soon as she had recovered her breath, she saw that he was there too, leaning against the wall, staring absently before him, puffing at a short pipe, his hat pulled over his eyes, his clothes hanging loosely about his large frame. She knew him well by sight from having passed him often on the stairs of the flat; but they had never exchanged a word.

When she had first learnt who he was, she had bought his books, and had set about reading them, not as she usually read, but attentively, almost religiously, because the fact that she was constantly meeting him, and that he lived overhead, gave her an almost personal interest in them. And hence, though there was much in them that she did not understand, they remained distinct in her memory.

She encouraged her servant to repeat to her all sorts of gossip about the inmates of the flats, and in this way she learnt much concerning him. And all that she so learnt, coupled with his picturesque appearance, only set her imagination working the more. So that, insensibly, she slipped into the habit of thinking a great deal about him.

As he spoke, she flushed under her veil, and endeavoured by an anxious scrutiny of the sky to disguise her nervousness.

'Thank you,' she answered. 'Thank you very much; but I think it would be better to wait a few minutes longer. It looks, over there, as if it were going to quite stop.'

Two or three minutes passed. She was waiting for him to speak; but he said nothing. She was growing angry with herself for not having gone with him at once: the silence oppressed her. A dozen different ways of breaking it passed through her mind, but she rejected them all as soon as they occurred to her. Why did he not say something? She glanced at him—back in the listless attitude, gazing vacantly across the street; the sight of this unconsciousness considerably relieved her embarrassment.

Presently he seemed to become aware that she was looking at him; rousing himself, he took the pipe from his mouth and said:

'I think you should be getting home; you ought not to stand here in your wet clothes.' He spoke easily, with a quiet familiarity, as if he had known her for a long time.

They started out together: quite slowly, for in order to keep herself out of the rain, she was obliged to accommodate herself to his pace. And as they strolled along through the drizzle, he clumsily pecked at her hat from time to time with the points of his umbrella. She longed to ask him to walk quicker, or to let her hold the umbrella; but she dared not, on account of his self-possession. He was talking leisurely, questioning her about herself, about her life, with a directness that would have been presumptuous but for the half-disguised indifference of his tone. Then gradually the uncomfortable edge of the strangeness wore off and his calm communicated itself to her.

She was not listening attentively to what he was saying; she was thinking about him as the author of his books, vaguely wondering that he did not talk as she had expected him to talk.

There was a pause; he had done speaking and she had nothing to answer.

Suddenly, almost with surprise, she found herself saying:

'I've read your books.' And immediately she felt a sense of relief flowing through her, as if the weight of some heavy thing had been all at once removed.

He started and answered with a change of tone:

'Which ones?'

'All of them.'

For the first time he seemed embarrassed, uncertain what to say. Surprised at his silence, she looked, and saw that his lips were moving hesitatingly; but he said nothing. Then a crash, just behind her—a heavy dray-horse fell, and lay helplessly floundering on the slimy pavement. They turned and stood watching its vain efforts to rise.

'What a shame not to put down some sand!' she exclaimed.

But he answered:

'Did you like the last—"Kismet"?'

Smiling a little at the irrelevancy of his question, she answered him at first with trite, meaningless phrases; but as she tried to explain how it had affected her, she found herself talking as she had never talked before, as it were inventing ideas that sounded astonishingly clever and well expressed. And, one after another, they rose to her lips.

She was unconsciously charmed by this new pleasure of listening to her own talk; oblivious of all else, she walked on by his side, till the sight of the familiar, red-brick doorway abruptly brought back the sense of reality.

'Good-bye,' she said hurriedly. 'Thank you so much. I hope,'—she wanted to apologise for her outburst of garrulity—she wanted to express a hope that he would come to see her—to tea some afternoon; but somehow she did neither, and without finishing her sentence, mounted the stairs. He waited till she was gone; then filling his pipe again, lit it, and went out slowly, his large figure growing more and more indistinct as it receded down the brown pavement.

The rain was over: the countless little streams that trickled down the roadway gleamed yellow in the sunlight.

IV

On the morrow, as Letty, hastening homewards, approached the spot in the Strand where she had met him yesterday, she became aware of a thrill of expectation; for she was half counting on seeing him leaning against the doorway, his hat pulled over his eyes, his short pipe in the corner of his mouth. She even stopped and looked about her. But the crowd flowed thick on the pavement; there was no sign of him. And, since he was not there, just as she had imagined he would be, her expectation died away, her thoughts drifting to other things.

And so till she was home; then, by the entrance to the flats, she caught sight of him—how she liked the loose way his coat hung from his shoulders!

'Won't you come up and have some tea?' she said nervously.

'Thank you,' he answered, and they mounted the stairs together.

She had been scheming the evening before, as she lay awake in bed, how she should get him to come to tea with her; she had imagined him sitting in her armchair, consulting her about his books, or admiring her yellow silk curtains and the plush hangings behind the door. But with their entry into the room, a constraint seemed to come over both of them. Without even glancing around him, he sat down and drank his tea, awkwardly, obviously not accustomed to holding his cup in his hand. And when he spoke—and he said but little—it was with a slight stammer that she had not noticed before. She, too, was ill at ease: it had been easy enough to talk to him in the street, now she could think of nothing to say. And more and more keenly she resented her disappointment, growing quite indignant with him because it was all so different from what she had expected. So that, when at last he rose to go it was almost a relief, and her petulance was scarcely concealed. And he, noticing her change of manner, gave her a look half-puzzled, half-pained.

During the week that followed, she met him almost every day on her way home: each time it was in the same, absent, almost casual manner that he accosted her. But she knew that he came out expressly to meet her. All day, as she went about her work in her little room at the office, she would look forward to the walk home by his side; in the evening she would sit, as it were, living every incident of it over again. Beyond his books they had found no common interest, so they talked of little else; but this alone seemed to her full of possibilities, indefinable but endless.

One evening she was sorting a bundle of letters she had brought home from the office, when her servant opened the door and he walked in.

'I can't get on with that chapter; I want to talk to you,' he said abruptly.

She saw the yellow look on his face; she noticed, too, that his shirt was unbuttoned at the throat, and that there were inkstains on his fingers; it was as if he had risen from his writing-table and had come straight down to her.

'I can't get on with it at all,' he repeated, half to himself.

There was something in this appeal which, outside her own personal feeling for him, went straight to her heart, and put her quite at her ease.

He began to talk, walking up and down the room, and, in a minute or two, she perceived that he had forgotten all about her. For he was not talking to her, but to himself, thinking aloud; now blurting out headless, tailless phrases, now breaking into long, rhythmical sentences which he recapitulated and corrected as he went along. She was listening, a little impatiently, waiting till he should stop, anxious to turn the conversation. But when at last there was a pause, it seemed impossible for her to break the silence with any other topic, so impregnated did the very air of the room seem with his words.

'And after that, what happens?' she asked, not really wanting to know, but only to hear him speak again.

He gave her a sudden glance, as if surprised that she should have overheard him; then, picking up the thread of his thought, continued as before.

Presently he stopped abruptly, just in front of her.

'Good-night.'

She held out her hand: he took it in both of his.

'Good night,' he repeated absently, 'things are much clearer now.'

'Then I have really helped you?' Her eyes fell on her hand which he still held, and she flushed a little, drawing it away. But he never noticed her movement: he was staring straight in front of him.

'Yes, things are much clearer. I think I'll go up and put them on paper. I'm afraid I've disturbed you,' he added, glancing at the papers on the table. 'It was good of you to listen to me for so long.' And with his hand on the door he continued: 'It is all well marked out in my mind now.'

She stood listening to his footsteps, as they died away up the stair-case. Then glancing down at her right hand, as it hung by her side, she flushed again, more deeply this time, and moved almost impatiently to the chair by the table. She took up the paper again, but it was only for a minute or two. The loneliness of the little room struck her: the knick-knacks that brightened it irritated her, and this for the first time. Her head sunk on her hands.

'I have really helped you?'

'Yes, things are much clearer now.'

The question, the answer, and the faint smile which had accom-panied it were repeating themselves in her mind over and over again.

How long she had been there she did not know, for she was thinking of him, sitting at his writing-table upstairs, putting it all on paper as he had said he would do. What was his room like, she wondered, for she had never seen it. Of a sudden—a step—his step—coming down the stairs. Instinctively she felt that he was coming back to her; so she rose and opened the door. Without a word he walked in, she following him. So continuously had she been thinking of him that the strangeness of his proceeding never struck her: it seemed quite natural that he should return.

'Well?' she said inquiringly, as he did not speak.

'I've done it, it's all come splendidly. Thank you, thank you.'

A pause.

'But I came down again because I want to ask you something, Miss Moore.' He spoke with the slight stammer that she had noticed once already, and he called her by her name, which sounded strange, as if he had never done so before.

'Well? what is it?'

'Would you care to be my wife?' He said it quite easily.

'Yes,' she answered, quite easily also, not realising the situation, but knowing by instinct that there was no other answer possible.

'I haven't much, only a few hundreds a year, about four or five I think. I don't suppose I spend half of it myself. There will be enough for both of us.'

At the sound of this bald statement of the practical side of the matter, she winced; but almost immediately, with a woman's quick intuition, she saw that the words had not come naturally, that he had only said them in a blundering endeavour to rise to the situation.

'I don't see many people,' he went on in the same, clumsy way, 'but I think it would help me having you—with the work, I mean. Would you really care to live with me?'

'Yes.' The word came back through her set teeth with a little hissing sound. Her joy struggled with the disappointment she could not help feeling at the way he had said it, and the struggle hurt her considerably.

He crossed the room and stood quite close to her.

'May I kiss you?'

In answer she held up her face; the light of the lamp fell on it, and there was no colour in it. As he bent down, with a sudden movement she clasped both arms round his neck and dragging his face down to hers, said:

'You will love me, won't you?'

'Yes, of course.'

There was a silence painful to each of them. At last with an evident effort he broke it.

'Good night once more.'

But she had caught his hand and was holding it tightly, looking anxiously into his face.

'Please,' she whispered.

'I—I don't understand.'

The blood rushed to her face.

'Please,' she repeated under her breath.

He understood; and when he had kissed her, he went slowly out. On the landing he stumbled heavily over the mat, for the gas on the stairs had been turned off.

V

Mechanically, in a state of unnatural passivity, drifting on as if impelled by some invisible outside force, she lived through the next few days. Some great thing was about to happen to her, but somehow she shrank from questioning herself concerning it. Outwardly there was little change in her daily life. She went down to the office as usual, for to throw up her situation at a moment's notice was impossible; besides, she clung to the old life instinctively; partly because at the thought that soon it would all be gone, a feeling of dismay, almost of terror, would creep over her; partly because its daily routine enabled her to ignore her own suppressed excitement.

She saw him a good deal oftener now, for every evening he would come down and sit with her. He no longer talked to her about his work since that strange night, now far receded into the past, when he had asked her to marry him; all his fever for it seemed to have passed away. And so, for the first time, their conversation drifted to other things, to the insignificant incidents of their daily existence. Then came the first half-realisation of her ignorance of him, which bewildered her.

For he was quite different now—so different that at times on looking back over the old days she could scarcely believe that he was the same man. The abrupt self-absorption had given way to a simple kindliness, with a trustful look in his eyes, which sent all her love for him leaping up within her. He had no variation of mood, his easy familiarity, at once gentle and respectful, was always the same.

And, as for Letty, her feeling for him, sprung at first out of her own overwrought sentimental imagination, soon began to grow each day in strength and richness. Into this newborn love for him her whole being fused itself in impetuous rebellion against the life of solitude which had cramped it for so long. With a rapidity that at first sight seemed startling, she absorbed every detail concerning him, till the whole perspective of her life veered round, everything being subordinated to its relation to him. And all these new things accumulated themselves within her, till their accumulation was painful to endure. For through his easy kindliness of manner she soon divined his supreme unconsciousness of all that the marriage meant to her, and thus her yearning to bring herself at once quite close to him became anguish; looming in front of her, as it were, she began to dimly perceive the barrier of his own personality, a barrier which was the outcome of years of accumulated habit, and which had grown so natural to him that he ignored its very existence. Yet, following a common paradox of human nature, the further she felt herself from him, the more she loved him.

As the days went by her listlessness concerning practical details became almost wilful, so that he was driven to making most of the arrangements for the marriage, foreign though it all was to his nature. Of course there was to be no ceremony; everything was to be as simple as possible. One morning they were to walk together to the Registrar's office in the King's Road—that was all; and there was no need to hunt for fresh lodgings, for Oswald's flat contained two empty rooms. When he suggested this as he sat with her one evening, she assented without a word of comment. Next, the matter of the moving up of her furniture arose.

'I should think it could all be done in a day,' he murmured, looking vaguely round the room.

'Yes, while we're away.'

He looked up, puzzled.

'Away?' he repeated after her.

'Yes, we're going away, aren't we—for—for—the honeymoon,' and her voice quavered a little.

'Of course—of course,' he answered hurriedly, 'but where?' There was a despairing accent in his voice, so dismayed was he at this new, unforeseen difficulty.

The comic side to it never struck her, only she continued, staring vacantly before her:

'I should like to go where we could walk together under tall pine trees, where the bracken grows high and thick, where there are mossy banks to rest oneself upon, and a little inn by the roadside with a gabled roof.'

'But I don't know where it is,' he said blankly.

'Nor do I,' she answered. 'I must have read about it in some book.'

So they never left London; but on the marriage day, he took her down to Greenwich by steamer instead. And to her that was all the honeymoon.

VI

The crowd, black and restless, swarmed aimlessly round the flaring kiosque, from whence rose and fell the sensuous cadence of a Strauss waltz; behind, amid the trees, winked yellow and sea-green lights, lending an air at once weird and fascinating; while beyond, the buildings of the Exhibition lifted their fire-rimmed roofs.

Oswald and Letty were sitting a little apart from the rest. Since they had come there, the band had played, and ceased, and played and ceased again several times; but, as yet, neither of them had spoken. At last, however, Letty began, realising as she spoke, the length of their silence.

'Look at the people. How silent and sad, all of them! Why is it? Why is every one so sad to-night?'

But not a muscle of his face stirred; he had not heard her.

'Tell me, why is it? Why is every one so sad to-night?' she continued, a shrill note of exasperation in her voice.

Still his lips did not move, and she began moodily to dig up the gravel with the point of her umbrella.

After a pause, with perverse determination to make him speak, she broke out again:

'I wonder if any of them are as unhappy as I am.'

This time at her words he started; he did not know to what she was referring, but the tone of her voice made the anger rise within him. He resented this unhappiness of hers which he saw she was trying to force under his notice. And now he remembered how soon after their marriage it had begun—reproachful generalities, fits of inexplicable irritability, of exacting affection, or of studied coldness. They had been married several weeks; how many he scarcely knew, only the old life seemed to have receded far, far into the past.

Since the night when he had asked her to marry him he had done no work. There was nothing strange in this, for in between the outbreaks of work-fever, he had always been accustomed to spend weeks without once putting pen to paper—unbroken weeks of eventless peace, as it seemed to him to-night. But now she was always there, with her air of suppressed discontent, from which he shrank, never meeting it openly, pretending to ignore it. To arrive at an explanation of it he never attempted. The necessary effort, and a vague dread of consequences were more than sufficient to deter him.

It had been a strange thing this marriage of his—a thing so sudden, so impulsive, that, as he thought, he marvelled at it. This woman by his side, her full-lipped mouth quivering with an expression that he disliked—all at once, she seemed no longer near him; but, from a distance, as it were, he was looking at her as one looks upon a stranger—a stranger who had come into his life and who was changing it all for him.

Back his thoughts drifted to his unfinished book, and the craving for work returned, coming as a great relief. To-morrow morning he would start again. There were passages, especially in the last chapter, that sadly needed revision. Yes, to-night he would begin. And, all at once, a whole multitude of ideas, leaping up, chased one another across his brain. Expressionless his eyes stared out across the crowd, while a wonderful intuition seemed for a moment to lay bare the whole secret of his life. But it was for a moment only, gloriously it all flitted past and was gone.

He rose.

'Shall we go home?' Letty asked. There was a note of penitent tenderness in her voice.

'Yes, I want to look over a manuscript. I'm going to begin work again to-morrow morning. Come, this is the shortest way. We can get a cab at the entrance.'

'Oh! my Oswald,' she exclaimed, 'I *am* glad. You will talk it all over with me, just as you used to do before, in the old days, won't you? That will be splendid. And I will help you—ever so much. Listen, I've thought of something. Do you remember how once you said to me that ideas came to you in talking, but that when you tried to write them down, they all slipped away? Well, you shall talk to me, I will write it all down. I can write quite quickly enough, I'm sure. I used to take down articles like that years ago at the office, when they were in a hurry. That will help you, won't it?'

They had left the gardens and were walking rapidly down the main hall, she, her face lit up to excited radiancy, he, preoccupied, frowning a little.

VII

The next morning, when she awoke, he was already dressed and gone. Should she slip on a dressing-gown and go to him? Not just yet—presently; for she shrank from the reality that awaited her. So she lay on in bed, and closing her eyes, half asleep and half awake, dreamed that they were together on a desert island and that he was loving her in a new, wonderful way. After awhile she awoke more completely, and she grew restlessly curious to find out what he was doing.

Breakfast was ready in the little dining-room, but only a single place was laid.

'Mr Nowell's writing in his room, ma'am, and he said he shouldn't want no breakfast, and that he mustn't be disturbed,' explained the servant.

She sat down; but beyond a cup of tea and half a slice of dry toast, she could eat nothing.

A mental pain, dull at first, growing in intensity as she brooded over it, was settling down upon her. This was the first time that she had breakfasted alone since their marriage: so he did not want her—yet last night, when she had proposed that she should help him—no, it struck her now that he had made no movement of assent. And she had some-how taken for granted that he would like it. How happy the thought of it had made her. For a long while as he slept heavily by her side, she had lain awake thinking of it in a state of excited happiness. 'He mustn't be disturbed'—that was his message. All at once, tumultuously, her wounded pride rose within her. He did not want her—she, who had loved him—ah! how she had loved him. There was nothing she would not have done for him; and he scorned it all—who was he to treat her in this way? She had thrown herself away on him—he did not care for her, not a bit; a dozen small signs of his indifference occurred to her. Why had he married her, then? Oh! why had he made her love him, since he did not care for her? And in bitter, reckless desire for self-inflicted pain, she strove to conjure up all the silly day-dreams she had had about him.

Then, of a sudden, her mood changed. Her love for him, pent up and unsatisfied, cried out in anguish, 'Oswald, Oswald', and big teardrops rolled down her cheeks. 'Come to me, my Oswald, you are the whole world to me.' Yes, she would go to him and tell him all; she would break down this barrier that lay between them. But not now. He was at work. She must not disturb him. He would not like it. Perhaps he would answer her crossly. And, with a rush, her pride broke forth again, fiercer this time. Thus, while the hands of the clock slipped round, they wrangled together, her wounded pride and her wounded love.

'Mr Nowell says you needn't wait lunch for him, ma'am; I've just taken him some coffee and bread-and-butter, and he says he won't want anything more till tea-time.'

Tea-time—so he meant to stop work at tea-time—nearly four hours to wait. A quarter of an hour of it she killed, trying to eat some luncheon. After this she fetched her bonnet and went out, wandering disconsolately down the Embankment. Unconsciously she took the way along which she had walked so often with him. And her thoughts were very bitter.

With Oswald hour after hour was slipping by—only the scratching of the pen, and the tick-tick of the clock. How good he felt, as two or three times he leant back, stretching his arms, back to the regular grind after the nerve-exasperating idleness of the past weeks! Then he would turn to again.

As for Letty, her image never once crossed his mind. Outside the work in which, with the exhilaration of new-found freedom, he was revelling, he had forgotten everything; all things were alike.

When he had finished, he strolled downstairs and out into the street, never looking to see what she was doing. The summer evening was clear and cool, the roadway glowed like a track of beaten gold, and his brain, lazily drinking it all in, sank into a delicious torpor.

About five o'clock he came in. Letty was already drinking her tea; she had not waited for him. She gave him no word of greeting; only a look expressive, as a woman alone can give.

But he noticed nothing; he did not even remember that he had not spoken to her before that day.

'It's been splendid,' he broke out. 'Splendid. I feel a different man.'

'Your tea is getting cold,' she answered in icy exasperation.

'I've written that last chapter from beginning to end, and nearly finished another one,' he went on, taking up the cup, 'there's a real rhythm about the last three pages.'

'The muffin is down by the fire.'

'Look here,' putting down his tea untasted, 'I'll just fetch them and read them.'

In a minute he was back again, the manuscript in his hand.

He walked up and down, trying the sound of the sentences some-times over and over again before passing on to the next, or appealing to her as to the justness of a word or continuing without waiting for her verdict.

The scene in her own old little room underneath, the evening that he had asked her to marry him, came back to Letty. She felt that she could bear it no longer, but, with a last effort, clenching her teeth, she re-strained herself.

When he had finished he turned to her:

'Well?'

But there was no answer from the white, set face.

'Come, say something,' he went on almost roughly.

Slowly her head began to droop, the lips pressed tighter and tighter together, till they were quite bloodless. Suddenly, burying her face in her hands, she burst into a passionate fit of sobbing.

'What on earth's the matter with you?' he exclaimed, making no attempt to conceal his annoyance.

'Can't you see?' she burst out. 'Are you as heartless as that?'

'Heartless! What do you mean? Whatever do you want?'

'Oh! nothing,' she answered in a hard voice, and there the conver-sation ended; a few minutes afterwards he went back to his study.

VIII

After this, in grim serenity, a whole month passed, while the breach between them steadily widened. On Letty's part all signs of the smoul-dering fire within her disappeared beneath a permanent attitude of chilly apathy. By a mutual, tacit understanding neither spoke to the other, beyond attempting now and then some forced commonplace remark, when the tension of silence became especially intolerable. But even this pretence of intercourse was rare, for, except during the evening meal, they were never together. And, as often as not, Letty would sit with an open book before her plate, taking refuge in the old habit of reading, which she had dropped since her marriage.

All this while, the fever of creation was consuming Oswald more rapidly than it had ever done before. In a sort of blind recklessness, fostered, at first, to a considerable extent by an instinctive striving to forget the strain of the daily life with Letty, he would shut himself up in his study every morning, and struggle on till evening, with scarcely any food, till his eyes throbbed and it seemed that endless regiments of heavy soldiers were tramping across his brain. When he had done, he would lie in his armchair, a helpless prey to fits of depression, inexplicable as it seemed to him, but which were in reality the reaction that inevitably followed the long hours of cerebral excitement. The effort required to seat himself each morning at his writing-table grew greater and greater, and the progress achieved was each day less and less. His brain under the continual, accumulated strain, became impotent with exhaustion, and he would sit for hours, feebly grappling with a single sentence.

Letty never appeared to observe that anything was the matter with him; she made no comment when his appetite grew smaller and smaller. Only once, as he furtively glanced across the table at her, he perceived that she was scrutinising him with a strange, searching look that he did not understand.

And, with the acute sensitiveness of an overstrained nervous system, he grew to hate this half-hour face to face with her over the evening meal; in her presence he felt painfully uneasy, as if there were hanging over his head a storm, which, at any moment, might break and overwhelm him. So that every time she began to speak to him, he was conscious of a spasm of alarm; and all through the day, the dread of meeting her was present in his mind.

One evening—he had been working later than usual—when the servant came in to tell him that dinner was ready, and that Letty had already begun, he felt that he could bear it no longer. He waited till the girl was gone back to the kitchen; then crept stealthily along the passage, took down his hat from the peg behind the door, and hurried out down the stairs, into the street.

From the river came a fresh breeze. Before he had walked a dozen yards, his brain began to reel, and a black mist floated before his eyes. He clutched at a railing to steady himself, and crawled on to an eating-house round the corner.

The place was sordid-looking and far from cleanly, and a hot smell of cooking pervaded it. Oswald found his way to one of the narrow tables covered with greasy and yellow oilcloth and sat down. Presently a young man, in his shirt-sleeves, fetched him from the counter at the far end a steaming plateful of hot food. Oswald began to eat feebly, glancing up at the door between each mouthful. Letty! if she should come and find him out here; and he fancied she was standing before him, beckoning to him to follow her. His fork slipped from his hand. He was asleep over his food.

He awoke with a start; some one was shaking him roughly by the shoulders. It was the young man in his shirt-sleeves who had waited upon him. The room was empty, and all the lights but one had been extinguished. With a shiver, Oswald rose and went home, slinking up the stairs of the flats. All was dark; Letty had gone to bed. For the first time since their marriage, he unlocked the door of the room where he had always slept in the old days. And, fetching some blankets from a cupboard, he arranged them, as best he could, on the narrow bedstead.

So that now they were separated day and night.

The next day Letty expressed no surprise at his behaviour, and that evening and each following evening, he went out to the eating-house round the corner, sitting there stupidly over his food, till the young man in his shirt-sleeves turned out the lights.

And as time went on the thought of death began to haunt him till it became a constant obsession. In the daytime, fascinated by it, he would lay down his pen and sit brooding on it; at night, he would lie tossing feverishly from side to side, with the blackness that was awaiting ever before him. And with the sickly light of the early morning, there met him the early relief of having dragged on one day nearer the end.

IX

'Don't go out this evening. I ask you to stay in to dinner. I have a particular reason.'

She was standing in the doorway of his study, on her face a look of infinite pleading, strangely out of harmony with the stiffness of her phrases.

All day he had been writing, squandering in a sort of fierce delight the last desperate rally of his brain, and now that he felt his strength to be running low, goading himself on with pitiless obstinacy.

After she had spoken, there was silence, for he could not immediately transfer his thoughts to what she had said. When at last he did so, it was in savage irritation that he answered:

'I can't—I don't know—I'm busy.'

An hour and a half later the servant came in to tell him that his wife was waiting dinner for him. The phase of irritability was gone. With weary docility he collected the scattered sheets of paper and followed her into the dining-room, the manuscript in his hand.

He was unaware whether the expression with which she greeted him was angry or pained, for he never looked at her. Without a word he walked straight to his place and sat down. Putting the manuscript on his plate, he began mechanically to turn over the pages. In a few minutes he ceased, and leant back wearily in his chair.

A long while, a short while, he knew not which, and consciousness began to return. A white table before him—a half finished pudding. He was alone; she had gone. The manuscript!—surely he had had it in front of him. Where is it?—gone! He looked up, and the first thing that met his glance was Letty, her face half turned away from him, evidently unaware that he was awake, on her lap the manuscript. Presently the crackling sound of crumbling paper, next, the harsh noise of tearing; she was tearing it, slowly, deliberately. Then, again and again; it was with a sort of frenzied fierceness that she was tearing now, and the fragments were fluttering on to the floor. She stood upright, and quickly, without heeding him, went past.

It was dead; she had killed it—this was the end. He picked up some of the fragments, handling them gently, tenderly almost. A wild look came into his face: he followed her out of the room.

Softly he pushed the door open, and stood, in hesitation, on the threshold. From below, through the open window, came the rattle of wheels and an instant after the distant wail of a steam-tug. The room was almost dark, only the dim night-light from outside. Yet he was quite familiar with its arrangement, and this somehow astonished him a little. Almost simultaneously two thoughts occurred to him. That it was a long time since he had been inside the room, and that he had slept there with her many nights. Where was she? Suddenly, quite close to him, so close that he shuddered, the sound of heavy breathing. It was she. He could see her huddled form, shapeless in the dark, crouching by the bedside. The rumble of wheels died away, the noise of her breathing grew in intensity till it filled the whole room.

Holding his breath in dread lest she should discover him, he peered through the obscurity at her. By degrees he perceived that she was kneeling with her head buried between her two arms, which were stretched out straight on the bed in front of her. Then, a queer muffled sound, breaking in upon the stillness—she was speaking, and his fingers closed on the door handle.

'Oh God! Merciful God! Listen to me; hear me. Almighty God! They say that Thou helpest people who are in trouble. Surely it cannot be much to Thee just to help me. Dear God! (here she began to sob) I cannot bear it any longer, indeed I cannot. Bring him back to me, God, just for a moment. I wanted him. Oh, how I wanted him! And I will give up my whole life to Thee. I swear it, my whole life shall be Thine. I have been wicked, very wicked in the past. Give me this one thing, and I will do whatever Thou wishest. Almighty, merciful God, say that Thou wilt help me!'

For a while her sobs choked her utterance. Oswald's fingers pressed tighter and tighter on the door-handle. She broke out again:

'Oswald, my Oswald, come back to me. Oswald, Oswald, my husband, speak to me—oh! speak to me, just one little word. What have I done that you will not speak to me? What is it that has taken you from me? Oh! I want you, I want your love. Oswald, my Oswald, I cannot live without it. Come back to me, come back to me. I cannot bear it any longer. It is killing me. Oh! it is killing me. If only it could be.'

X

He stood in the middle of the suspension bridge, peering down through the iron-work at the river.

A long fall through the air—the water black, cold and slimy, the rush down his throat, the fight for breath, to sink down, down at once, and the yearning for the peace of death swept through him.

Could he crawl through the iron-work? No, it was too small. And some one might see him. He must clamber over, quickly. As he looked round him to see if he were observed, his eyes fell on a heap of flints a few yards off, where the road was under repair. He went up to it, and stooping down, began, with the feeble slowness of an old man, to fill his pockets with the stones. Then he went back to the bridge edge, and gripping the stanchions, prepared to swing himself on to the top of them. As he did so, a blackness filled his eyes; a dull thud; his body dropped back on to the roadway—dead.

An Ugly Little Woman

Felix Tenby stood aside at the crowded barrier to give place to a little nervous flurried woman, who between fear of losing her train, dismay at finding herself unexpectedly in the midst of a noisy crowd, and gratitude to the courteous stranger, became more flurried than ever, got into a muddle with her change, struggled in vain to pick up the slippery ticket with cold, indifferently gloved fingers, and dropped a shower of coppers on the ground.

'Serve you right, Don-Quixote-out-of-date,' said the friend who was seeing Tenby off. 'You have lost your train through your misplaced gallantry.'

The ticket clerk was passing Felix a ticket under another man's arm. He had turned aside from looking after the little flurried woman and laughed.

'Thirty,' he said, 'and plain at that. Misplaced indeed! The women for whom we do these things owe it to us to be pretty.'

She heard, and looked at him. He had not dreamt of that; he had thought she was gone, but she had just risen from picking up the last copper from under the feet of a hurrying commercial traveller, and had heard the laugh and the words. She looked at him just for a second, not angrily or scornfully as such words deserved, but humbly, deprecatingly, remorsefully almost, as if begging forgiveness for her crime of ugliness. Then she turned her little worn brown face away, and hurried on to the platform. Felix felt as if he had struck a child.

His friend hurried him on to the platform. He did not miss the train after all; it had been delayed a little in consequence of the unusual and unexpected rush of passengers. He had even time to get a paper or two and choose a comfortable carriage, which he had all to himself, for the extra passengers were mostly third class, time to say a few more words to his friend, and laugh over a message or two.

Nora Vynne

When the train had started, and he was trying to read, the worn, patient little face came back to him, and reproached him. Had there been tears in the eyes? Had he made this poor little creature cry by his vulgar brutality? After all, his words had meant careless irritation that he had, as he thought, missed his train, more than anything else. What right had he to criticise? He was thirty himself—over thirty, and nothing to boast of in the way of beauty; but, then, he was a man.

Surely it must be bad enough to be a woman without having to be an ugly one. Why had God made ugly women? It would have been just as easy to have made them all beautiful.

What makes the joy of manhood? Strength, the knowledge of what is sweet, the power to win and hold it. And of womanhood? Well, women are never quite happy, but they have their joys too. Love, that makes the man's strength theirs—Love, that makes their weakness their pride because it serves as occasion of a lover's tenderness, the sweetness of being a thing desired—the hope of motherhood. But ugly women, what have they of all this? Good God, to be an ugly woman!

How had he come to forget, for he had known this all along; those sad patient eyes reminded him of so much.

To be an ugly woman—to feel with earliest feeling that one is a blot on a beautiful world—to understand, as soon as understanding unfolds, that one's part in life must be to watch while others enjoy, long while others attain, thirst while others drink.

To be an ugly woman—to be an ugly woman and know it.

And thirty years old too, thirty at least—no youth, and no beauty! An ugly woman!

Not always old, though. Once there had been an ugly child—those heart-broken eyes reminded him of it. An ugly child, pushed out of the way perpetually for her beautiful sisters—a failure, an embarrassment to her family, a superfluity. How bitter it all was!

An ugly girl! he remembered it so well, the hopelessness of it, the flat dulness. Not a clever girl either—not one who could have taken ambition by the hand instead of love, or made the beauty of art her beauty. Just a girl, with a girl's wondering curiosity of life, a girl's strange amaze at the growth of first emotions, and possibilities of emotions, a girl's love of love, a girl's sweet, impossible dreams. Soon with a girl's strange new knowledge that one face was more to her than other faces,

302

one voice quicker to reach her ear than all other voices, that one touch had magic in it. He remembered it all.

Yes, that morning, too, when instead of the ordinary dawn of day there was a new creation. The heavens and the earth were made anew, and one little thin brown girl sitting up wondering in her white bed, with a letter clasped fast in her hand, saw that they were very good.

Very good, oh very good! Life was beautiful, the earth glorious, the heavens very near. The letter had done it all.

It was a wonderful letter, for it said she was loved. It spoke tenderly, passionately, strongly. It told how duty called the writer suddenly away, he must leave without seeing her again, but could not leave without telling her his love. He would not be away long, a year at the most; when he came back he should claim her. And would she not write to him meanwhile? Would she not wait for him? Hold herself his, and welcome him when he returned?

Ah, would she not indeed!

And the letter spoke of her beauty! That was puzzling. The little brown girl dropped back on the pillow and rubbed her eyes with her thin hard hand wondering, and read the words again and again many times, then smiled, and kissed the letter, and held it to her bare breast. He remembered it all.

He remembered that studio in the afternoon, the pictures there— and all the while the sweet secret of that letter kept sacredly—looking at the pictures, talking of them, careless words from careless friends, 'How bright you are to-day.' Ah, it was small wonder, after that letter!

There was a portrait of the artist's wife among the pictures; it was the most beautiful of them all. The artist's wife stood beside it, a vapid commonplace, empty-headed woman, not beautiful at all. The little brown girl looked from her to the portrait, like but glorified, and smiled. 'That is how we look to the men who love us,' and she pressed her hand on her bodice where the letter rested on her heart; he remembered the sharp pleasure as the rough edge of the envelope pressed against the soft flesh.

After that there had been more letters, all wonderful, all sweet, and loving, and hopeful. A year of delight, of love, of beauty; for the lover creates beauty by praising it. Oh that year, that pleasant year, how well he remembered it! And the day of triumph, the day when the lover, the creator, was to return: the neat little room, the open window, the scent of fresh turned earth from the ploughed field across the road, the laughter of the birds in the eaves, the laughter of the leaves as they rustled together! He remembered it all—the trembling lips—the breathless eagerness—the burning face, the steps on the gravel, the ring at the bell, the opening door, the suffocating joy.

'My God! it was your sister I meant.'

Oh it was terrible, terrible, not to be borne; and yet it must be borne; that was the sting of it. The tears rained down his face. Remember? Could such a thing ever be forgotten? The new created earth fell in atoms, the new heavens vanished far out of reach; nothing was left but a little ugly woman, smiling with white lips lest the world should make a mock of her, that such as she had dared to dream of love!

And the days that followed, the long days that followed, they were so burnt into his memory that he doubted if he could forget, even in the ages of eternity; the hourly pain, and the shame of it all. The agony of watching the happy love of sister and lover—the fuss of preparation for the wedding—to sit and sew at wedding clothes that shrouded her own love—to see her lover pouring out his love upon that careless bright girl, who had many lovers, who had not thought of him till now—to hear his friendly praise of herself—as 'such a sensible girl', take his careless greeting and go from the room that the happy lovers might be left together.

And the thoughtless wounding of curious friends. 'Well, my dear, I must say I think you behaved very well about it. And so you gave him up? All a mistake, you say; dear! dear! what a pity! And you don't mind? Now that's so brave of you.'

So brave? yes, but to the weak courage is anguish.

Oh the longing to end it all—to cry out, 'Give me one kiss, and then let me die.'

But pride forbade death, for to die was to confess her unsought love to the world. There was no choice but to endure, endure, endure—always endure.

And the dreariness of it, after the sharp agony of parting, the long pain of loneliness, the days without comfort, the years without hope, the daily death of youth; youth that should die in child-bed, bringing forth to time accomplished hopes, but her youth died sterile.

And the long dull days of life at home, the drudgery of duty uncrowned by love, the thankless service to parents who cared so much less for her unselfish devotion than for the beauty and success of their more fortunate child, and even when they died, were more moved by the brief shallow sorrow of the happy wife than by the long patient watchfulness of the ugly daughter.

And the bitterness of dependence in the house of that fortunate sister, the careless, tolerant pity of the man she had loved—to feel her love die in contempt, and be more desolate for the loss of it—to look on the great sorrow of her life as a thing of shame, of scorn, food for mirth rather than tears; cruel mirth, the tears were less bitter.

The shame of living where she was not wanted, a superfluity in a full life, a discredit, with her plain face and dowdy figure, in a pleasant home!

And the futile efforts to earn her own living, the bitterness of seeing the way made so easy for the young and bright and hopeful, but so hard for her; of seeing the stronger push past her, the fairer chosen before her. The tragic pain of the past was almost sweet, compared with the squalid misery of the present.

There is something in great agony that in itself strengthens us to endurance, but who can endure contempt? In the past she had been wounded and crushed, now every touch was agony, and no one spared her, why should they? What graces had she that should win tenderness, a little faded ugly woman, a mark for the mirth of the young and thoughtless, the dislike of the sensuous, the impatience of the strong? Nothing left her but patience, and she had grown so very weary of patience. Life would have been easier if she could have been angry, but she had no cause for anger. The world loves beauty, and youth, and happiness, and she was old, and sad, and ugly.

The world was full of love, but not for her. The world lives on hope, and she was hopeless; the world is very beautiful, and she was a stain upon it.

'Oh God! to be a woman, and old, and ugly.'

It broke his heart, the pain was too great to be borne, he cried out aloud, and started in his seat.

The little brown-faced woman at the further end of the carriage started too, and shrank into herself; he stared at her, bewildered.

It was so tragic, the gentle pathos of her face, as if she would beg forgiveness for her very existence; as if she would cry out to him not to crush her, as insects are crushed by the strong because they are unsightly.

He passed his hand across his eyes as if to clear his sight, and looked at her, puzzled.

'May I express my deep sympathy with the very sad story you have told me?' he said.

'My story? I have told you no story. I hope I do not disturb you. I have no right here I know; mine is a third-class ticket, but the guard put me in here last time we stopped because the people in the carriage where I was were so noisy.'

'I am amazed, bewildered,' he said; 'certainly you told me your story.'

The little woman had pride; she set her lips firmly, and spoke coldly.

'I do not speak of my affairs to strangers,' she said; 'even if they were of any interest I should not.'

Her pride touched him more than all, it was so impotent, so gentle. He moved along the seat till he was opposite her, looking straight into the patient, proud, pathetic face; he spoke tenderly, gently, and with infinite reverence.

'I am sure, though you have not told me your story, that the story which has in some strange way come within my knowledge is your story, and I want to hear the end. Do you mind telling me where you are going now?'

'I am going to be a drudge among strangers. What is it to you?'

What, indeed? A little plain, faded woman, what did it mean that he, a man in the prime of life, handsome, rich, overburdened with friends, felt the tears rise in his eyes, and a great ache in his heart? She might well look at him in wonder. He stretched out his hands towards her, he could scarcely speak.

'I know it all,' he said, 'I have felt it all. You have suffered so much, you shall not suffer any more. I will make your life so bright to you if you will let me.'

'I don't understand,' she faltered.

'Neither do I,' he cried, 'neither do I, not how I know so much, or why I love you. I only know that I must take you right into my heart and keep you warm there, for I do love you!'

'Oh no! me, impossible!'

But looking in his eyes she saw that it was possible, and true, and she held out her hands, trembling, wondering, questioning. He answered the question with words that seemed to come through him, as if they were a message, and not only his own thought.

'Every human soul is lovable; we could not hold back from loving every soul on earth, could we once see it. But we cannot. Beauty hides the soul equally with deformity. To-day God has been very good to me: I have seen the soul of a woman and loved it.'

FLORENCE HENNIKER

Our Neighbour, Mr Gibson

Two separate divided silences,
Which, brought together, would find loving voice;
Two glances, which, together, would rejoice
In love, now lost like stars beyond dark trees.

It is now just ten years since I retired, possessed of a modest fortune, from my stationery business in Mount-Street, where, I venture to think, I was as much respected as I had long been well-known. Many ladies from Grosvenor Square, and other fashionable quarters, would often come and exchange a few friendly words with me when they went out for a morning's shopping; and I, for my part, was never mistaken as to which wanted 'extra fine cream laid' writing-paper, or 'original blue laid Kent'; or as to whether a fair customer affected my especially good 'charta orientalis', or had a preference for 'Papyrus Regia'. It was perhaps as much owing to this, my accurate memory, as to my unfailing cheerfulness of disposition, that my shop was such a favourite resort. Doubtless my daughter Janet was also a great help to me. She was very pleasant to look upon, with her fresh cheeks like a newly gathered peach, fresh indeed, as those of any country girl, and her thoughtful dusky eyes. Her slight figure, in its neat black cashmere, flitted about deftly and briskly, yet without giving any sense of bustle or restlessness. She spoke pure English, with no trace of a London accent, so I have been told by our respected vicar, Mr Gordon-Curzon, in whose Sunday-school she had been a teacher since she was fifteen. If she had a failing, she was apt to be a little too severe upon her neighbours' faults and weaknesses, a narrowness of mind for which her very careful bringing-up may have been in some degree to blame.

Of course Janet had her admirers, as so pretty and graceful a girl could not fail to have; but she was very demure, I thought, and seemed curiously indifferent to their attentions. There was my nephew, Mr

Abel Coram, who has now succeeded me in my business, for one; a most worthy, if heavy and silent young man; and as a contrast there was a smart city clerk, Mr Wilcox Crisp, who often informed me with a wink 'that *he* hadn't cut his wisdom-teeth yesterday'; and who also used to say that his superiors thought him 'too much of a dog for their taste', both of which expressions seemed to me to savour of vulgarity.

I felt sad at the idea of giving up the old house, and the business in which I had spent so many happy and, fortunately, profitable hours; but I was growing an old man, and Janet had often urged me very prettily to go away and live in the country and rest and enjoy myself during my last days.

'Think, father,' she would say, 'how delicious it would be to have a little garden of our own, with hollyhocks and sweet-williams and stocks, like the one we saw when we were in Surrey! And we might keep chickens and rabbits; and then, in the evenings, you would sit under the porch and smoke, and I would read the *Family Herald* to you.'

It was a tempting picture, and I acquiesced, as I usually do in all that Janet suggests. We had always been in the habit of going into the country for a few weeks each year; and I remembered having been once much attracted by a certain snug little house on a peninsula which juts into the sea that washes our southern coast. It was advertised then 'To be let', and I thought that by a lucky chance it might still be empty. On one side was a wild stretch of golden gorse bushes and broad vistas of green turf, the best golf-links in the neighbourhood, I was told. And ten minutes walk away from the cottage was the ferry, and the sea tamed and imprisoned, for a space, between smooth reaches of yellow sand. It lapped so softly and gently there against the pebbles that one forgot that such things as wrecks and storms could be. And over our heads a thousand larks were singing, I remember, and the light shone upon an old deserted boat with red-brown sails, and over rocks covered with clammy seaweed of a vivid green. A sweet and peaceful place in which to make a home when the stir and fret of life was over, I thought. But for Janet I feared that it might be dull. 'Should you like to go and live in that little far-off house by the sea, if we can get it?' I asked her. And she said she would—she wanted quiet; and the singing of the larks was much better than the chatter of people one didn't want to listen to. By this I think she must have meant young Mr Wilcox Crisp.

It was during the last days of February that we took possession of our new home,—for the house which I have described was still untenanted. There was not quite so much garden belonging to it as I should have liked—a far larger one surrounded an empty cottage about a hundred yards from us, and further from the sea. But then the walks over the springy turf on the common were exhilarating, and if I wanted greater solitude I could pace along the sands and watch a few sleepy little boats dotting the water here and there, and the children playing at the cottage door across the water, where the ferryman lived.

Janet, who, in spite of her quiet manner, is always very popular, soon made friends with the brawny young ferryman and his father and stepmother: and also with a young widow called Mrs Ellery, who was their lodger. *I* thought her a very tiresome woman. To use her own expression she 'enjoyed pore health', but this fact did not seem to prevent her from taking long strolls on the common after sundown with her landlord's handsome son; I often met them when I went for a lonely ramble the while Janet was getting supper ready. The widow's detestable child, Clementina—called 'Clemmie' for short—was always in and out of our house; but Janet said it was a shame to snub the poor little dear, so her visits were never discontinued—until the last days of our stay, at least. One Saturday—it was the end of March now, and a surprisingly hot March it had been—I strolled into the parlour to find Mrs Ellery and Clemmie at tea with Janet. Warm gusts of air floated in, pleasantly tempered with a scent of the sea and the green weeds from the rocks. A flowering currant-bush that almost swept the windowpanes had burst into a cluster of rosy blooms. A few blue hyacinths were shyly peeping their heads over the box border of our garden-path, and Janet had arranged a giant nosegay of daffodils in the old Worcester bowl which belonged to my great-grandmother.

Mrs Ellery, clad in dusty weeds, was stirring the contents of her teacup with a languid hand, which, I could not help observing, ended in rather black finger-nails.

'I was telling Miss Eames,' she remarked in the drawling voice which she considered a mark of gentility, 'as how I 'ad quite a turn this afternoon; I was stepping ashore, Mr Eames, from the ferry-boat, when 'oo should I see a-coming down from the common but a gentleman just like what pore Mr Ellery was before 'is last decline which took him off.

Same figure, Miss Eames, and cut, and style, and a short beard—just like pore Hugh' (she pronounced this patronymic as 'Yew'). The widow here wiped her eyes with a black-bordered handkerchief, and sighed.

'Only think, father,' said Janet, 'that the empty house is taken—by a single gentleman from London, I believe. It will be nice for you, father dear, to have a neighbour to chat and smoke with a bit in the evenings.'

I was not as much interested at this information as the widow and my daughter appeared to be; and neither did I believe in the strange resemblance between the stranger and the late lamented Mr Ellery. I imagined that it had only been discovered with a view to increasing our interest in and respect for the lady whom he had left behind him.

The following day, being Sunday, we walked to the little church, at the further and more wind-swept end of our peninsula. On this particular morning March had chained up his gales, and the soft breeze which lifted the little curls on Janet's forehead had hardly a touch of east in it. The sea was blue, blue as forget-me-nots, the larks sang a chorus over our heads, the little churchyard was turned into a garden, with wreaths of primroses and daffodils. The clergyman, who came over the ferry from a large parish right away on the mainland, perhaps sympathized with our wish to spend most of our day out in the glorious sunlight, among the birds and flowers and white butterflies, for he gave us a shorter sermon than usual.

Mrs Ellery stood awaiting us in the porch. She carried an enormous prayer-book of red plush, and a hymn-book of more sombre hue, containing a large funeral card, and a bookmark worked with the hair of some defunct relative.

'He's *not* come!' she said in a loud and mysterious whisper to Janet.

'Who hasn't come?'

'Why, your neighbour, Mr Gibson. Perhaps he's not Church of England. I saw him in his garden, leaning over the railings. Now I see him closer, he's not got pore Yew's pleasant way with 'im; I'm sure of that. Though I must say *he did* smile when he looked at Clemmie.'

Clementina, whose crimped hair of tow-colour stood out in a bush round her freckled little face, grinned approval.

As Janet and I walked home together we kept up a ceaseless happy chatter, like a boy and girl out for a holiday.

'What an extraordinary March, father! it's as hot as June. Look at that gorse-bush—why, you can hardly see any green; it's like a great ball of gold.' The delicious scent, like ripe apricots filled the air. 'See, too, what dear little pale violets are coming out among the stones at our feet!'

'*How* glad I am we came here!' I said, opening my mouth wide to inhale the invigorating sweetness of the breeze. Then I looked seaward, where the gulls were floating, white and dazzling as the few little wave-crests over which they hovered. On the other side the sails of the broken fishing-boat seemed like a great brown butterfly at rest. Far beyond were the shining roofs of the distant seaport, which seemed such long miles away from this our quiet paradise of gold and green.

We passed the house where our new neighbour had come to live. It stood just above the broad sandy lane leading to our smaller cottage. Leaning over the fence was the new tenant. I did not like to stare at him, and Janet, after one swift glance, looked shyly away at the brown-sailed boat and the ferry-house over the water. He seemed to be a tall man, dressed in well-fitting blue serge. I saw that he had a short beard, and was wearing a straw hat, but I could not make out whether his expression was pleasant, or forbidding, or even how old he might be.

Two days afterwards I was walking home down the dusty road between the rough banks covered with tufts of blooming gorse, when I heard a voice behind me saying, 'I think this must be yours? I found it just now outside the post-office?'

I turned, to see my neighbour holding my shabby old green pocket-book in his hand.

I thanked him, and we walked on together. His voice was singularly well modulated, and I liked the expression of his light blue eyes, which seemed to smile even when his lips did not move. We exchanged a few commonplaces on the wonderful sunshine we had enjoyed before the advent of April, and for a moment we stood still watching two golfers, followed by their attendant boys, going across the green framed in by the belt of sea.

'Have you come here to patronize the game?' I asked my new acquaintance.

'I? Oh, no! I have come for rest and quiet; I have been so much rubbed up against my fellow-creatures for many years of my later life that I don't care to join clubs, or to make many new acquaintances as a rule. But,' he added pleasantly, 'I am glad to have had this opportunity of meeting you, we are such very near neighbours. I am a great gardener, and I was wondering only yesterday if I might send your daughter some of my daffodils? I see your garden has been a little neglected, and so, for the matter of that, has mine, but I fancy the late owner must have taken some trouble with it, and it has possibilities.'

'Thank you very much, Mr Gibson. And if you would ever care to drop in of an evening, and have a smoke and a chat?'

I felt that I was becoming rather red in the face, for it seemed to me that his light blue eyes wore an amused expression.

'Perhaps I ought not to take the liberty—without an introduction,' I stammered lamely.

'Why not? It is very kind of you. I will come and pay my respects to you and your daughter to-morrow.'

I was quite pleased and excited at being able to tell Janet about my interview with Mr Gibson.

'It's easy to see, my dear, that he's a man of education. I have lived long enough in the West End to know a gentleman, I hope, when I meet him.'

The following evening Janet took particular trouble with the arrangement of our modest tea-table. She put little glasses full of green sprays upon the white cloth, and the brown urn was discarded for the one of nickel-plate, which is such a good pattern it might really be mistaken for silver. She also made some little cress-sandwiches, and went herself down to the baker for cakes. At five o'clock Mr Gibson made his appearance. He was perhaps not quite so good-looking without his straw hat, for I noticed that he was growing bald, and that the lines across his forehead were very deep. But Janet seemed to find him attractive. They were soon talking as cheerfully as if they had been old friends, and she answering his most common-place queries with an earnestness and interest that were never displayed during her conversations with my nephew Abel, or young Mr Wilcox Crisp.

'Ah! you lived in Mount Street? That is almost the nicest part of London. I used to be a good deal in that neighbourhood as a boy, for a relation of mine had a house in Grosvenor Street. How I enjoyed rambling about Kensington-Gardens! I always had a love of solitude and the country, and that was the nearest thing I could get to either. I wrote verses, too, in those days; and I remember so well, as if it were yesterday, a horse-chestnut tree under which I usually sat and made the most deplorable rhymes.'

Janet's soft brown eyes were fixed admiringly upon Mr Gibson.

'I love poetry,' she said softly.

'I am sure you do. But I gave up verse-making in disgust after I failed to get the prize poem at Harrow.'

I felt quite impressed when I thought what a superior education Mr Gibson must have received. I remarked that he would have plenty of time for study during his visit to our little solitude by the sea.

'Yes, I mean to go and sit out amongst the gorse-bushes and read in the evenings. Later on, I shall slave at my garden, and I hope astonish the natives with the result. I shall come to you, Miss Eames, for advice.'

A slow tapping at the door was followed by the entrance of Mrs Ellery; her widow's bonnet a little awry, her heated face wearing an apologetic expression.

'I beg pardon, Mr Eames. I didn't know you had company.'

I was convinced that she had watched Mr Gibson's arrival, and taken this opportunity of judging for herself of his personal advantages. I did not ask her to come in, for I own to having felt a little ashamed of the grimy-fingered widow, especially when such a distinguished guest as my new neighbour was good enough to visit us in this friendly fashion.

Clemmie, open-mouthed and wide-eyed, pushed past her mother, and stood staring at Mr Gibson. He smiled, and held out his hand. 'How old are you, little woman? What do you say to getting yourself a box of chocolate? I saw some in the village shop.' And he felt in his pocket for silver.

'Clemmie, you rude child, thank the gentleman at once!' said the widow, in great agitation. Whereupon her daughter bestowed a damp kiss upon Mr Gibson's cheek. He explained that he always liked children, and got on with them; and then he rose to take leave.

As he reached the door he turned round, and I fancied that his gaze rested earnestly on Janet.

'I was thinking,' he said, 'of going in a few days' time quite inland, to hunt for primroses. I find I can get a decent waggonette at the inn. Will you and your daughter, Mr Eames, come with me? We might take a little luncheon, and have a sort of primitive picnic?'

The flush on Janet's cheek, and the shining of her eyes, showed me that she meant me to accept.

I shall never forget the day on which we three drove slowly through the silent dusty lanes into the heart of the green country. The larks sang louder than I had ever heard them, and deadened the twitter of the smaller song-birds wooing their mates in bush and bough. Here and there a stagnant little green pond lay among long grasses, and an abundance of primroses peeped out round its margin, shy and fragrant. Then we would leap out of our carriage, and busy ourselves filling baskets like school-children holiday-making. Mr Gibson, though I suppose he must have been over forty years old, was the most childish of us all, and triumphant if his bunches were the biggest. He looked quite hot and sunburnt by the time that we had found a sheltered place under a bank where we could rest and eat and drink. When the simple luncheon was over he threw himself at Janet's feet, and gazing up at her from under the straw hat tilted over his brows he said:

'What do you say, Miss Eames, to cutting the larks out, and singing us a song? They will go and hide their poor little heads in the longest grass they can find, when once you begin.'

'How did you know I sang?' Janet asked, blushing.

'I saw music on your piano. But I should have known from your face that you were musical.'

I rather wished that he would not look at Janet with such a concentrated gaze. I thought it embarrassed her, for she turned her soft pink cheek away.

Mr Gibson sighed a little, raised himself on one elbow, looked up at a hovering lark then singing in a mad ecstasy above his head, and, to my surprise, himself burst into a song. His voice was not very strong, but pure and sweet. *I* did not care for the words, but Janet admired them, and nothing would satisfy her but to write them out then and there.

Let me once again recall
        Rose Marie,
The crumbling stretch of wall
        By the quay,
Where I sat with you beside,
To watch the ebbing tide,

And the rosy lights that died
On the sea!

Ah you come before me still,
Rose Marie,
Singing, racing down the hill
In your glee,
To your garden-green below,
Where the orchard-blossoms blow,
Blossoms red, and white as snow,
Rose Marie!

But I left you—was it best—
Could it be?
Kissed you, held you to my breast,
Set you free,
Saw you weeping pass away
Through the fragrant groves of May,
Down the aisle of poplars grey,
Rose Marie!

That realm of song and flowers,
Arcady;
Was no brighter world than ours,
Rose Marie—
But, ah me! that age of gold
Was not ours to keep and hold.
You are dead, and I am old,
Rose Marie!

We lingered long in the lanes; the inky shadows spread over the distant common, and the bees ceased humming, and little silvery and dun-coloured moths flitted round our heads, while the gayer butterflies went to sleep with folded wings under the golden shelter of the gorse-clusters. There was a dusky red sky, like the expiring embers of some huge furnace, over the far-off seaport town; and saffron coloured clouds hovering above the chalky line of the distant forts, outlined white and clear as a snow-range. The air blew chilly in our faces as we drove home slowly as before, through the accumulated dust of the silent lanes. Everything smelt dewy and fresh and sweet, and there seemed a whispered promise of even more glorious spring days in the breeze that gently loosened Janet's hair.

The days went past in pleasant monotony, at least as far as I was concerned: but to my daughter there may have been more of change in them than I dreamt of. For one thing I was grateful, and that was the fact of Mrs Ellery being asked in much less often; Janet now went after tea on to the sands, and she said that it was hardly worth while to ask the widow to cross the ferry for the meal merely, unless she could stay on a good while, which now that the evenings were so long and lovely, would have hindered her making the most of them.

During one of my rambles, I came hastily round a corner to find Mrs Ellery and handsome young Jim Andrews, the ferryman, sitting peacefully beneath the shelter of a gorse-bush. I am almost sure that he hastily withdrew his arm from around her shoulders, as she arose, sad and flustered as usual.

'Good evening, Mr Eames! I 'ad come out to take a little fresh air when all of a sudden I come over that faint, I did, that Mr Andrews says, "Mrs Ellery, a lady with your weak health should not walk so far on end," and so we jest set here for a bit till I came round again,' &c.

I paid but little attention to the widow's explanation, for two figures in the far distance, crossing the links, and making for the long stretch of sand opposite the ferry caught my eye and interested me far more. A tall man and a slender woman. They disappeared over the rising ground, and descended the slope of shingle and rough grass which led to the sea. I returned homewards, and walked down to the beach from the opposite direction, turning to my left so as to meet the pair coming from the links. As I half expected, the figures were those of Janet and Mr Gibson. Janet, fresh and sweet in her dark blue gingham, with the earnest trustful look in her eyes that I knew so well; Mr Gibson, tall and well-bred, with a different and a sadder expression on his face, I thought, than it wore some weeks ago. He changed colour a little when he saw me.

'I persuaded your daughter to come for a stroll on the links,' he said. 'I only hope she is not tired. I have been selfish, perhaps, in taking her so far, but the light over the sea was so wonderful, we could not bear to hurry indoors.'

'Janet is a very good walker, sir,' I answered, rather stiffly. 'But I generally like to take her out myself. Come back with me, dear,'—here I assumed my most dignified manner—'I have been waiting for you for the last hour. Good evening, sir.' And we turned our steps homewards, Janet, who looked vexed, keeping silence all the way thither.

My feelings of annoyance towards Mr Gibson were only of a passing nature. I could not help being softened by his kind, refined bearing when we next met. He seemed so anxious to atone for his offence, which, after all, was not a serious one. Then he very amiably sent us some young asparagus, which I knew to be costly, and as Mr Crisp had proposed to come down and spend a day with us this present was all the more welcome. I was well aware of Wilcox's feelings towards Janet, and had not been surprised at his suggestion.

When I saw him swaggering up from the ferry, a scarlet flower in his button-hole, and a new straw hat leaning rakishly over one eye, I must own that I was struck by the vulgarity of his appearance; and—it may have been after my constant intercourse with a gentleman of Mr Gibson's culture and breeding—his manners seemed to me decidedly offensive. I came out of my little sheltered porch.

'Glad to see you, Crisp. It's a quiet place, isn't it? *You* would find it slow; but Janet and I are as happy here as the day is long.'

'It does seem precious quiet. But one might get a gun, and have a go at the seagulls,' said Mr Crisp, taking out a toothpick. 'Ah! there's Miss Janet, fresh as a new pin!'

My daughter shook hands very coldly.

'You're rather badly off for neighbours, I expect, Miss Janet? But I hear you've got quite a swell living over there.' And he pointed to-wards Mr Gibson's house.

Janet frowned and blushed. Then she went to the window and stretched her pretty head out.

'Listen to the larks singing! We ought to go out over the links after dinner, father.'

Mr Crisp observed, with a wink at me, that *he* should have thought this a poor sort of place for larks of any sort. Then we sat down to our roast mutton, and Mr Gibson's asparagus. Our neighbour looked in after luncheon, but I thought he seemed a little vexed to find that we had a guest with us. When he was gone, we went out into our garden, and Mr Wilcox Crisp lighted a huge cigar, and stretched his legs, which were tightly clad in a series of large checks, far out in front of him.

'That's a gloomy-looking dog, that neighbour of yours,' he was pleased to observe. 'And, for a gentleman, he's got as big hands as they make 'em. A leg of mutton's a joke to them.'

'*I* prefer a man who uses his hands for gardening to one who sits all day, with a pen behind his ear, scribbling,' said Janet crossly.

I tried to change the subject; but Mr Crisp would go harping on about our neighbour. What was he doing here? Perhaps he was hiding-up from a wife who wanted him back? At Harrow school, was he? Oh! that was a likely story! And so on.

Janet at last completely lost her temper, and gathering her work together went indoors.

'I'm awfully sorry, Mr Eames. I didn't think Miss Janet would be so gone on a chap like that? But I stick to it. There's something fishy in a fellow of that style coming here. I wonder what the game is?'

'It's perfectly natural that a gentleman who's been all over the world, and had, I daresay, rather a hard life, should like a bit of quiet, Crisp. And you needn't have talked as you did before Janet. Mr Gibson has been very kind to us both, and she naturally doesn't care to see you, who know nothing of him, sitting there and saying spiteful things.'

'Well, he ain't *my* sort,' said Mr Crisp, taking out another huge cigar. 'He looked at me, Mr Eames, quite cheeky, as much as to say, "What business has a sweep like you to come here?" Confound his airs! But, I say, Mr Eames, do go and tell Miss Janet I'm awfully sorry. I wouldn't offend *her* for worlds. Won't she come out again, and make it up with me?'

But Janet would not come back, and Mr Crisp, rather crestfallen, returned to London by an earlier train than the one which he had intended to take.

The following morning little Clemmie Ellery, a square parcel in her hands, made her appearance. She held it very carefully, and the contents of the package fluttered and rustled.

'I've brought you a present, Miss Janet!' she said, her small ugly face crimson with excitement. 'It's from Jim, at the Ferry. He said he knew you liked singing-birds, and here's a live lark for you! There's a bit of grass in his cage, and he'll sing like anything!'

She undid the wrappings, and the little prisoner came in view. Janet was delighted. She insisted upon my hanging him at once outside our parlour-window. But he only fluttered and fluttered and beat his wings against the bars, and would not sing.

'He's shy and strange,' she said.

Presently we saw Mr Gibson strolling down the road towards our house. He had got into the habit now of coming every day.

'See my present?' cried Janet. 'He's such a beauty! I am going to call him Mario. I heard Signor Mario sing the first time I ever went with father to the opera.'

'He don't look much used to his cage,' said Mr Gibson.

'No, but he will be, soon. It's all new to him here, and it's shaken him coming over in the boat.'

'Some birds never take kindly to captivity,' said Mr Gibson, rather sadly.

'Oh! but Mario will. I shall make such a fuss with him.' And she put her pretty red lips near the bars and whistled.

The lark fluttered again, and seemed to shrink further into the corner of his cage.

'Poor little prisoner!' said Mr Gibson. Then he added: 'I don't like to see a caged lark, Miss Janet. Some birds are all right shut up; contented hedge-birds who merely go twittering about in the boughs. But think how high a lark flies! How insignificant we must all seem to him! Can't you fancy how poor little Mario will sit and dream on his perch of the golden gorse, and the bees and green links below, and the dazzling heavens above, in which he could plunge, and bathe, and shake his wings? Will he sing happily then? Just a few inches of turf beneath him, instead of the boundless common and the trackless sea?'

I don't think Janet liked being contradicted. She said nothing, but she left Mario hanging on the wall among the trailing creepers, and went slowly indoors.

We were not allowed to remain in solitude, it seemed, for long. For I was soon afterwards obliged to write to my sister-in-law Mrs Hallowes, of Peckham, and tell her (which was not in the least true) that we were very pleased to hear from her, and that Janet and I hoped that she and her daughter and the little grandson would come down and spend a day or two with us whenever they felt inclined.

Mrs Hallowes is a sister of my late wife. She made a good marriage, and to quote her own mode of speech, has 'got all her own girls off' now. She sometimes says to me, 'Janet's a long time on your hands, Charles. Why not try Dover, or Southsea? That's the kind of place where you get a girl off. And, I'm sure, Janet's as stylish a young woman as Amelia was, and if she don't play the piano so well, she does chalks and water-colours very nicely. And though of course Amelia's waist's smaller, I must say Janet holds herself upright, and always looks neat.'

Mrs Hallowes and Amelia (now Mrs Pye of Tooting), and Master Adolphus Pye, were all sitting at tea with us on one of the very hottest days of this wonderfully hot spring. My idea of my sister-in-law—the picture which instantly comes before me when I think of her—is that of a stout lady, very red in the face, with loosened bonnet-strings of a crude blue framing the crimson cheeks. A rustling black silk dress, an umbrella with a large dog's head in ivory on the stick, fawn-coloured silk gloves; all these were property of Mrs Hallowes. Amelia, a fresh-looking young woman, in a tailor-made suit, was constantly obliged to clutch Master Adolphus by his very short petticoats, and try to prevent him from sallying forth into our small garden. Adolphus was much overweighted by his sailor hat, and was hot and cross.

Mrs Hallowes, who had as she expressed it: 'a sweet tooth', put two more large lumps of sugar into her tea-cup, and spoke.

'Well, Janet, my dear! I saw Mr Crisp the other day, and he blushed when I told him I was coming down here. You really might do worse, my dear girl. Old Crisp, his uncle, is likely to go off, they tell me, quite suddenly, any day, and he's got a great partiality for Wilcox—thinks him such a sharp young fellow. And so he is.'

Our little maid-servant opened the door to admit a visitor. I wished that he had not chosen this moment to come in.

'Mary,' I said, 'this is our neighbour, Mr Gibson.' I should like to have said, *our friend*, but I did not quite think that our degree of intimacy warranted the employment of the term. Besides, the contrast between my relations, Mrs Hallowes and Mrs Pye, and my visitor, struck me forcibly and, I must say, sadly. I realized for the first time, perhaps, the folly of allowing Janet to see so much of a man out of her own class. The Crisps and the Pyes were the sort of people with whom her life would have to be spent. What was the use of disguising this disagreeable fact? It were better that she should feel it too.

Mr Gibson shook hands pleasantly with Mrs Hallowes. But I saw his eyes seeking Janet's, the while she persistently averted hers. I don't think that she spoke a word to him until he rose to go. Then:

'Mario *has* been singing!' she said, triumphantly, lifting her long lashes to look at him for one moment.

He smiled. 'Ah! he must try and pass the time. But I believe he dreams more than he sings. Still, Miss Eames, if he is to be caged, he could not have a kinder gaoler, I am sure. Good-bye.'

She put her hand into his. I am sure that he held it longer than was necessary. Then little Adolphus suddenly ran across the room, and clasped the tall stranger by the knees. Mr Gibson laughed, took the child in his arms, and tossed him up and down in the air, to the boy's unbounded delight. He was cross no longer. Like most people, he seemed attracted by my neighbour's smile and kind blue eyes.

'I never saw the child so took up with anybody,' said Mrs Hallowes, with her mouth half-full of buttered toast. 'One would think you were a family man, Mr Gibson.'

'I am afraid that's the one thing I am never likely to be,' he answered, taking the boy on his shoulder and carrying him to the window. Janet coloured, and pretended to busy herself with fetching more plates.

When my neighbour was gone, Mrs Hallowes, whose face now shone like the setting sun, was loud in his praises.

'One can see that he's a gentleman, Charles. I suppose you don't know his circumstances?'

'You mean, if he's well off? I fancy so, for he seems to buy everything for his house that he wants. And the Vicar tells me he has been very generous about the Church funds.'

'He's a very handsome man, to my taste,' said Mrs Pye. 'Such broad shoulders, and a fine beard. If I were you, Janet,'—here she winked, and giggled—'I should set my cap at your Mr Gibson. I should like him for a cousin. Wouldn't he make a nice nephew, Mar?'

It was a relief when Janet and I were left again in undisturbed enjoyment of our home. But the weather was beginning to break up. The first sign was the change of the wind to the north. Then, towards evening, we saw small flamingo-coloured clouds, skurrying to westward, one after the other, like a procession of migratory birds. Then a mist spread over the common, from which all the gorse bloom had vanished. A day or two afterwards came the rain. First in cold still showers, moistening the links which felt hard as iron to the touch, and laying the swirling dust-heaps on the road to rest. After this it flew in wild scuds over the ferry, and large drops hurled themselves against our window panes. The gusts of wind shook the walls, and beat the laurustinus boughs against the glass. The paths were transformed into ponds, the flowers beaten down and draggled.

'How sad this seems after our gorgeous spring,' said Janet, looking ruefully from the kitchen-window. She was helping our little maid, for Janet is fond of work, and thinks no task too paltry to be well done. Mario's cage was hung up by the fire. He sat sadly on his perch, staring out at the sheets of rain, and the ferry-house half hidden in veils of mist. Was he dreaming of the golden gorse, and the blue sea; of freedom still?

'We ought not to feel aggrieved at the weather,' I said. 'Think what a wonderful March and April and May we have had. Besides, I believe it's really clearing. If I were you, Janet, I would put on my hat, and have a run on the sands before tea. You look a little pale. I have a twinge of my sciatica coming on, and old people are best indoors when it's damp underfoot.'

Mario hopped down on to his few inches of turf, then up to his perch, and began, I suppose, dreaming again.

The rain had passed away, leaving behind it a pure golden sky, and a crimson cloud-streak over the old boat, when Janet came in. Not alone. Mr Gibson was with her. He followed her into our parlour, but did not sit down. The evening light flooded the panes, poured a yellow stream on to the shabby carpet, and lit up Janet's face and hair, all in one glow. I have never forgotten her as she looked then. Mr Gibson took her hand, and moved a step towards me.

'Mr Eames,' he said, in a low, firm voice, 'Will you give me your daughter? The one thing in the world that I desire is to make her my wife.'

I knew, I think, that he loved her profoundly. And I have never doubted it since. But I could not answer for a minute. A pain seemed to grip my throat.

'Darling father!' cried Janet. And she threw her arms round my neck

323

and kissed me. I believe the tears fell from my eyes on her hair. Then I took her hand, and held it in both mine.

'Mr Gibson,' I said, 'it all seems so strange. We have not known each other long. My only child is very precious to me.'

'I know it, I know it,' he answered. 'I can understand all you feel. And so does she. But I swear to you, Mr Eames, I will always love her. She will be as one sacred to me. Trust me, and you shall never repent it.'

'How could you repent it, father?' said she, 'there never was in the whole world anyone as good as he is.'

I think it was the pleading in Janet's eyes and tone, far more than Mr Gibson's words, that won the day. I left them alone together, feeling as if a joy had gone out of my life, and the house were strangely deserted and empty. The sky paled to westward, the crimson sails of the boat turned into a rusty brown, the sheet of sea was grey once more. And though a few last rays flickered brightly on the bars of Mario's cage, and on the square of green turf at his feet, he still sat upon his perch—dreaming; he would not sing.

Our simple preparations for the wedding did not take long to make. Janet was anxious that it should be as quiet a one as possible, and that neither Mrs Hallowes or any other relations should be asked. We went over together, she and I, to the fashionable seaport-town, the shining roofs of which we catch a glimpse of from our quiet house. She ordered a gown of white muslin and lace, one in which she could go away with her husband when the ceremony should be over; for they had arranged to make a little tour on the coast before coming back again to Mr Gibson's house.

I had a talk with my future son-in-law, which I own was satisfactory in every respect.

'You need have no anxiety about Janet's future, Mr Eames,' said he. 'I have an income of fifteen hundred a year, and all can be settled on her and her children, if I should die first. I have no relations living. My last, an old aunt, who left the bulk of her fortune to me, died two years ago.' He sighed as he spoke.

So the settlements were drawn up, and I felt that my child was happily provided for. The sight of her radiant face did much to cheer me in the sadness which, do what I could to prevent it, sometimes threatened to weigh me down.

I was sitting in rather a more melancholy frame of mind than usual one evening by the window, when Janet and Mr Gibson came in. They had been on an expedition to the distant town.

'See, father, what—Vernon has given me!'

She still hesitated a little before she called him by his Christian name.

I took her extended hand in mine.

'What a beautiful ring!' I cried; 'diamonds and sapphires.'

'And look here!'—pointing to the lace frill at her throat, where a brooch of amethysts and more diamonds glittered, in the shape of a heartsease.

'Pansies for thoughts,' said Mr Gibson. 'If I ever have to leave her she will wear this, and it will tell her I am always thinking of her.'

'And now Vernon, what shall I give you?'

She looked into his eyes with that happy, tender expression, that they never—God help her—wear now.

'I don't want you to buy me a present, dear,' he said. 'You have given me quite enough. But stay; you can, if you wish, grant a foolish whim of mine, on our wedding day.'

'What is that?'

'You will laugh. It is to give little Mario the best gift *he* could receive—his freedom. He looks very sad, poor fellow, in his cage still. You know I don't mind your having some song-birds as pets, but *he* is not happy.'

'O Vernon; and I'm so fond of him! But—never mind, I'll do it, if you wish. He shall be allowed to fly away over the links, and join his friends.'

The day before the wedding arrived. The sky had been overcast for many hours, and a cold and most un-summerlike drizzle was falling. My garden was looking sad and draggled by this time, and it was early in July, when it should have been gay with a mass of sweet coloured blossoms. It was so misty over the links that we could barely see the outlines of the church-spire. Janet was flitting about from room to room, putting things in order, she said, before her departure. But I think she stopped too often to think and smile to herself, to do much. Once or twice she looked at the lark in his cage. His feathers were rough and puffy, and he sat huddled on one corner of his perch. He seemed to miss the sun, which had now hidden himself for so many days.

Mrs Ellery, more lachrymose than ever, and clad in damp crape, had been over with Clemmie to say good-bye.

Vernon was to have supper with us this last evening on which my child was to belong to me.

He and I were sitting at the table a few hours later when Janet came in from her walk. We saw by the hardness of her face that something was wrong. I recalled with a feeling of pain the dogged obstinacy of its expression in childhood, when rightly or wrongly she had resented a fancied injury from one of her playmates. But perhaps she would have been too near perfection had her tenderness to the errors of others been proportionate to the strictness of the rule of life which she had laid down for herself.

'I never should have believed it!' she cried.

'What is it?'

'Why, you know, father, my gold locket that belonged to dear mother? I looked for it, to wear it for supper. It was gone! I knew it was not Jemima who took it; and then a horrid idea came into my head that Clemmie had seen me open the box and put it by.'

'I always disliked that child,' I said.

Janet, with crimsoning cheeks, went on, speaking louder.

'It was dreadful to suspect her, because I had been so kind to her, and had her so much in the house. It made me feel sick to think she could deceive me. So I put on my hat, father, an hour ago, and crossed the ferry, and went to find Clemmie. She was frightened, and cried, because she saw by my face something was wrong. Then, Vernon, she confessed to having taken it! And she was coming to the wedding, and all! I can't forgive that kind of thing in a person one has trusted!'

There were tears in Janet's eyes. Mr Gibson said nothing.

'Don't you think it *sickening*, when one has believed in someone?'

'She is very young—' said Mr Gibson.

'But you *can't* excuse it! It would be a fatal mistake to overlook that sort of fault! It shows such a despicable character. I shall never forgive Clemmie.'

'You are a little hard,' said Mr Gibson, speaking with an effort. I suppose he did not like to differ from his betrothed.

'It isn't being hard. It would be weak to forgive such a dishonourable action! I have told Clemmie never to come here again!'

Vernon did not know Janet as I knew her. He had not found out that her faults always were a slight obstinacy, and too great intolerance for sins which she herself had no temptation to commit. He made another attempt to soften her.

'Don't you think on this occasion, dear—when we—when we—are so happy ourselves, you might be persuaded to forgive the child? Perhaps—you don't know—she hardly realized the baseness of what she did? One is always glad, I think, afterwards, to have taken a merciful view of other people's sins. Perhaps you have never been tempted? Perhaps you are strong; and if you were, you would stand firm. But have pity on those who fall!'

He leant his elbow on the table and looked at her with a troubled expression.

'That is all nonsense, Vernon. But don't let us talk of it any more. I am sure I hated having to go and tell the child I had found her out.'

We were all three rather silent after this. At half past nine Mr Gibson rose. He wrung me warmly by the hand, before going with Janet into the porch to say a few last words. The door was ajar, and I could not help hearing.

'I did not know you could be so stern, my darling, as you were to-night. Do you know, you half frighten me. What would become of me if I were to disappoint you—not to come up to what you believe and expect me to be?'

'You silly Vernon! As if I didn't know that you have no faults! You are only too dear and kind to people who are not good like you!'

'O Janet—swear to me that you will always think kindly of me—as you do now!' His voice sounded terribly sad to me.

'My darling—can you ask? How could I ever have cause to think differently of you? I could not even have *cared* for a man who was not like you, honourable, and straightforward, one who has never, I know, done anything to prevent my being proud of him!'

'God bless you, my dear.' And he bent down and kissed her, gravely —once—twice. Then he was gone.

The wind rose, and the rain began to fall, drip, drip, from the porch on to the gravel: drip, drip, from the window ledge on to the sills. The laurustinus boughs swung backwards and forwards against the panes. From a dark abyss of cloud the moon's pale face looked out, fearfully, it seemed to me, as if the blank and rain-driven landscape terrified her. Then she hid herself beneath sombre wrappings of mist.

Janet had gone up to bed. For some time afterwards I heard her moving lightly up and down. I knew that her pretty white frock was hung over the chair facing her bed, so that her eyes might rest upon it when she awoke. I got up from my chair and drew a green baize covering over Mario's cage. In the excitement of our discussion we had forgotten him. I felt strangely disinclined to sleep; so I lit a fire, drew up my cosiest arm-chair beside it, and sat, half dreaming—looking into the future. What would it be to me without my child? What would it bring her in this new life with a man of whom she and I knew so little? Were we wise to entrust our all to him?—our all?

Drip, drip, fell the rain from the bushes on to the gravel. My garden must be soon ruined if this went on. And the wind was still rising. I fancied that I heard a footstep on the soft, slushy path. Then a low tapping, firm and distinct, upon the window. I was surprised. Who could come so late? The clock told me it was after eleven. The tapping was repeated, and I went to the window, and drew aside the curtain. The moon was peering at me from a black hood of cloud, and a shadow, the shadow of a tall man, stretched across the footway as Vernon Gibson's voice spoke.

'Forgive me,' he said, 'for coming at this hour, and in such a mysterious fashion, Mr Eames. But I wanted much to see you. It is important. I *must* have a few words with you. And I did not wish to wake *her*. Your front-door bell rings so loudly.'

'I will let you in at once. How wet you are!'

He had no greatcoat nor umbrella. The rain ran in little streams off his collar and the brim of his hat. I went round to the front-door and let him in. He walked carefully, fearing to wake Janet.

'I will speak low,' he said, coming up to the fire and stretching his hands over the blaze. His clothes smelt damp in the warm room. I noticed that his face was ashy pale, as if he had been suffering great pain.

'I have a short story to tell you, Mr Eames.'

'Sit down, Mr Gibson; you look so cold and wet.'

'Thank you, I will stand here.'

I have never forgotten how he looked. All the details of the room are present to me now as if I were staring at a photograph. I remember that a huge brown moth, which had been sleeping, I suppose, in the window, began flying restlessly round the pictures, flapping his wings against the ceiling, and flitting nearer and nearer to the lamp. Mr Gibson looked at it. The insect hurled itself madly into the flame, and fell, singed and quivering, at his feet.

He stepped forward and crushed it.

'Poor brute, its wing is burnt off. It will never fly again. Better to kill it,' he said.

I looked enquiringly at him.

'You said you had a story to tell me——?'

'Yes,—yes. About a friend of mine. Don't interrupt me, Mr Eames, until I have done. But, I warn you, it is an ugly story.'

For a moment he paused, and I heard only the incessant dripping of the rain.

'There was a young man,' he went on, 'whose name you may remember years ago in connection with a case which made some stir at the time: Arthur Watson-Slade. He had a rich cousin of the same name—it's a well-known firm?' (I nodded assent.) 'This cousin was very good to him, treated him as a son, and when the boy was about twenty he took him into his business. The older man was married to a young and beautiful woman, and the boy, unluckily for him and for her, was much thrown with this lady. She—I believe she loved him, and I *know* that he loved her with the desperate passion of a boy for a woman older than himself, but one possessing the experience of maturity joined to all the graces of girlhood. To please her he spent money, far more than he could afford; not only *on* her; but in living a luxurious life,—an existence which he foolishly thought would impress her, and raise him in her estimation. Then a time came when his liabilities were harassing. To cut a long story short, young Watson-Slade forged his cousin's name for four thousand pounds. He prevailed on the wife to leave her home, and to join him abroad. He escaped for a time, but was tracked and caught after a month had passed. Caught, Mr Eames, and condemned to fifteen years penal servitude. The woman whose life he had ruined wrote to her husband imploring his forgiveness. But he was not a young man, and not strong in health. The ingratitude of the boy whom he had befriended broke his heart. He felt the loss of his wife's love a million times more, I need not say, than the loss of his money. *That* he might have condoned. He was dead before her letter reached him. . . . An ugly story, Mr Eames . . .'

I was silent. A pain like a knife seemed to be stabbing me. I only looked at Mr Gibson stupidly and aimlessly, and stammered out:

'Why do you come and tell me this? The wedding is to-morrow . . .'

'Yes,' he answered: 'to-morrow—it was to have been. Mr Eames, my name is not Vernon Gibson. Do you wish to marry your daughter to Watson-Slade—the ex-convict and forger, the man who seduced his friend's wife, and broke her heart and his?'

No answer. Still the dripping of the rain.

'The wedding is to-morrow—' I said, at last, burying my face in my hands.

He moved a step towards me.

'Mr Eames—You know what *she*, what Janet said about that wretched child who had deceived her. She has no forgiveness for her. Could she ever forgive *me*—to say nothing of those other words, *honour* and *obey*? You would ask'—and he began walking up and down—'why I come *now*, at the eleventh hour—why I waited, why I would have taken her, pure and innocent and beautiful as she is—to my heart? Because I *had* repented, I tell you; because I have suffered as, I pray God, few men can suffer; because I really believed there might be a chance for sinners such as me, in this cursed world, do you hear? But I feel that I was wrong. Ah! Eames, don't I know what you are thinking of now as you look at me? You—and your daughter—you go to church—you read of the ninety and nine sheep, and the one who strayed, and you are full of pity. You shed tears over the prodigal; your heart softens when you hear of the angels who rejoice most over the penitent ones! But how does *your* life bear all this out? She, Janet, so kind, so tender, how does she treat that miserable little girl who has offended? How about the lost sheep there? O God! O God!—and you call yourselves Christians— and yet leave no possible place of repentance for those who have passed through their hell already!'

He sank into a chair by the fire. Ought I to have spoken?—to have taken his hand in mine, and said, 'I do forgive you. This shall be for ever a secret between you and me. Take my child—you love her; and her love, and her prayers offered daily for you, will bring atonement for your terrible past'?—I do not know; sometimes I think that I should.

At last he rose.

'Good-bye, Mr Eames.' His voice was the familiar one now; but with a ring of sadness in it that I cannot forget. 'Good-bye. Only one thing I ask of you. Never, as you hope for mercy, speak to *her*—to my love—my wife that was to have been'—here the words trembled —'of what I have told you to-night. Let me pass away out of her life in silence. Let her think me base, faithless, what you will; but I conjure you, don't take away from me all hope of her forgiveness eternally!'

'I *swear* to you,' I said, 'she shall never know. O my poor little Janet!'

'I will write her one line, telling her that I have to go. That she must never try to find out why. That she must think I am dead, and pray for my despairing soul.'

He crossed over to the door. I did not take his hand; I only felt that the words, 'The wedding day has come', were ringing in my ears. For the clock had struck twelve. I heard his footsteps dying away as the new day was born.

Very early I came downstairs to find the sky blue, and the sun shining over the green slopes. Scarcely a ripple was on the sea. I drew, mechanically, the covering away from Mario's cage. As I did so it struck me that on this, the wedding day of Vernon and Janet, he was to be enjoying his liberty. Ah! sad little lark! It had come indeed, in a better way perhaps than we could give it. He lay huddled up in one corner of his cage, his poor claws pathetically turned upwards, his soft brown head ruffled, and half embedded in the sand. He would never sing, or dream of the gorse and the blue sky any more. And in the midst of my far greater grief, the grief that will, I think, always be mine, I spared a tear for the innocent prisoner who had won his freedom on the day that should have been glad for us too.

When the first shock was over, and those early and most bitter tears of anguish were dried, Janet said to me:

'O father dear, let's go right away from the country! Somewhere where there's no sea, and no flowers and birds!'

I understood her. We took a well-built, hideous little house at Finsbury Park; where I have no garden but my small boxes of geraniums, and pansies (for thoughts); where we hear the trams go night and morning, and the newspaper-boys shouting, and forget that there are such things as wide gorse-grown commons, and larks hymning in the blue above, and brown sails skimming and dancing over the waves. It is better so. It is ten years since we saw those fair sights, and people tell me, truthful people like my sister-in-law Hallowes, that I look very old for my age. Janet is over thirty now. She dresses plainly, and rarely goes out anywhere. She teaches in the Sunday-school, and I believe that if she liked she might marry the curate. But he is a dull young man with a long neck like a stork, and Janet does not think much of him. We live a monotonous life. I take two walks every day, sometimes having tea with a neighbour, but more often returning at six, to prevent Janet feeling too lonely. Then I smoke my pipe, and she reads to me,—not novels or poetry now, because she has ceased to care for these things. I am well aware that we have every reason to be proud of writers such as Gibbon and Macaulay, but there are times when I own that I should like to hear about something more cheerful and trifling than the rise and fall of kings and emperors. But unless I walk to the station and buy myself a gaudily-covered shilling volume, I have no opportunity of indulging my frivolous fancies.

Once or twice I have prevailed upon Janet to come out with me, but on the last occasion when I took her to see her aunt Hallowes, I fear that my well-meant attempts to cheer her ended in failure. Of course it was long ago understood between my sister-in-law and myself that the topic of marriage should not be discussed, before Janet at least; and even when the old lady and I are alone she has almost given up recommending me to try Dover as a happy hunting ground. My daughter and I arrived at Peckham one hot and dusty afternoon to find Mrs Hallowes and Mrs Pye, now also a widow, and as stout as her mother, awaiting us with beaming faces.

'Amelia's just wetted the tea,' observed Mrs Hallowes cheerfully; 'and Sarah's gone round the corner for one of Benson's shilling cakes— nice cakes, too, they are, Charles. I'm sure you're very welcome, both of you. Janet, my dear, you look rather drawn and peaked. The change here 'll do you no end of good!'

Sarah, carrying the cake, and followed by a gentleman in a check suit, burst into the room. From the overdone unconscious way in which Mrs Hallowes exclaimed 'Lor'! Mr Crisp, you *are* a stranger!' I felt sure that she had arranged this meeting between him and Janet, as a last gallant attempt to settle her niece in life.

Mr Crisp was not perhaps quite as much altered as I was in the last ten years. He had the same jaunty air, and waxed moustache; but he was growing fat and decidedly bald. After he had made many futile attempts to attract Janet's attention, and had asked her playfully, 'if there was room for a little one' on the sofa beside her, he suggested to me that he and I should go out into the garden and smoke. Then he confided to me that his prospects were better than they had ever been. Old Uncle Crisp was still living, but on condition that his nephew would give up 'playing the giddy garden-goat'—so Mr Wilcox gracefully expressed it—he would make over the bulk of his fortune to him in his lifetime.

'Including,' said Mr Wilcox, 'as nice a bungalow as you'd wish to see—just ten minutes by train from the little village.' Then he began raking up the gravel with his shiny boot.

'The fact is, Mr Eames, if I'm to settle down, there's only one young lady to suit me. And you know who *that* is.'

'My dear Mr Crisp, Janet will never marry.'

And I sighed as I spoke.

'She *can't* still be thinking of that sweep who went off and left her on her wedding-day?'

I said I feared that she was. And, with a less jaunty bearing, poor Mr Crisp followed me indoors.

Going home that evening I was more than ever a prey to trouble and self-reproachful thoughts. Had I been right? Ought I to have let Vernon Gibson go? Surely he had repented long before we knew him. From his own account I knew that he had lived some years in America, and worked hard. That was after his terrible punishment. Then, would his aunt have left him her money if she had not thought his penitence sincere, and his resolutions to reform likely to bear fruit? And the same torturing fancies haunted me after I had gone to bed—not to sleep. Next door, where Janet slept, I heard low sobs, and moans. They cut me to the quick. I rose, and knocked at her door.

She was sitting, still dressed, by the window, her head bent down over her knees. On a table in front of her was a folded letter, and a case in which I recognized the brooch shaped like a heartsease, shining under the candle. She turned her tear-stricken face to mine. My heart was very sore, as I knelt down by my poor child.

'Darling,' I said—'*do*, do try not to think of him still.'

'How *dare* you say that, father? I *know* he wasn't tired of me! Something—something else kept him away. Oh! father darling,' and she fixed her passionate, sad eyes on me with a terrible earnestness; 'I've sometimes thought it was *my* fault. There may have been that in his past life which he did not like to tell me. He thought me hard and narrow-minded. I've worried and worried myself till I felt almost mad sometimes, thinking that perhaps it was my want of sympathy that came between us. And yet he *must* have known how I cared! how I worshipped him!'

She flung her arms on the table, and I saw the hot tears running down between her fingers on to the ground.

Presently she raised her head.

'Father, do you think if I wait,—and I am always, *always* waiting, we shall hear of him before long? He might come, mightn't he, when we least expect it?'

How could I resist the pleading agony in her voice? If I spoke, on the impulse of the moment, untruthfully, God forgive me!

'Yes, yes, my darling, it's quite possible. We may, of course, have news of him some day; good news!'

But, in my inmost heart, I know that we never shall.

HENRY HARLAND

Flower o' the Quince

I

Theodore Vellan had been out of England for more than thirty years. Thirty odd years ago the set he lived in had been startled and mystified by his sudden flight and disappearance. At that time his position here had seemed a singularly pleasant one. He was young—he was seven- or eight-and-twenty; he was fairly well off—he had something like three thousand a year, indeed; he belonged to an excellent family, the Shropshire Vellans, of whom the titled head, Lord Vellan of Norshingfield, was his uncle; he was good-looking, amiable, amusing, popular; and he had just won a seat in the House of Commons (as junior member for Sheffingham), where, since he was believed to be ambitious as well as clever, it was generally expected that he would go far.

Then, quite suddenly, he had applied for the Chiltern Hundreds, and left England. His motives for this unlikely course he explained to no one. To a few intimate friends he wrote brief letters of farewell. 'I am off for a journey round the world. I shall be gone an indefinite time.' The indefinite time ended by defining itself as upwards of thirty years, for the first twenty of which only his solicitor and his bankers could have given you his address, and they wouldn't. For the last ten he was understood to be living in the island of Porto Rico, and planting sugar. Meanwhile his uncle had died, and his cousin (his uncle's only son) had succeeded to the peerage. But the other day his cousin, too, had died, and died childless, so that the estates and dignities had devolved upon himself. With that, a return to England became an obligation; there were a score of minor beneficiaries under his cousin's will, whose legacies could not, without great delay, be paid unless the new lord was at hand.

II

Mrs Sandryl-Kempton sat before the fire in her wide, airy, faded drawing-room, and thought of the Theodore Vellan of old days, and wondered what the present Lord Vellan would be like. She had got a note from him that morning, despatched from Southampton the day before, announcing, 'I shall be in town to-morrow—at Bowden's Hotel, in Cork Street,' and asking when he might come to her. She had answered by telegraph, 'Come and dine at eight to-night,' to which he had wired back an acceptance. Thereupon, she had told her son that he must dine at his club; and now she was seated before her fire, waiting for Theodore Vellan to arrive, and thinking of thirty years ago.

She was a bride then, and her husband, her brother Paul, and Theodore Vellan were bound in a league of ardent young-mannish friendship, a friendship that dated from the time when they had been undergraduates together at Oxford. She thought of the three handsome, happy, highly-endowed young men, and of the brilliant future she had foreseen for each of them: her husband at the Bar, her brother in the Church, and Vellan—not in politics, she could never understand his political aspirations, they seemed quite at odds with the rest of his character—but in literature, as a poet, for he wrote verse which she considered very unusual and pleasing. She thought of this, and then she remembered that her husband was dead, that her brother was dead, and that Theodore Vellan had been dead to his world, at all events, for thirty years. Not one of them had in any way distinguished himself; not one had in any measure fulfilled the promise of his youth.

Her memories were sweet and bitter; they made her heart glow and ache. Vellan, as she recalled him, had been, before all things, gentle. He was witty, he had humour, he had imagination; but he was, before all things, gentle—with the gentlest voice, the gentlest eyes, the gentlest manners. His gentleness, she told herself, was the chief element of his charm—his gentleness, which was really a phase of his modesty. 'He was very gentle, he was very modest, he was very graceful and kind,' she said; and she remembered a hundred instances of his gentleness, his modesty, his kindness. Oh, but he was no milksop. He had plenty of spirit, plenty of fun; he was boyish, he could romp. And at that, a scene repeated itself to her mind, a scene that had passed in this same drawing-room more than thirty years ago. It was tea-time, and on the tea-table lay a dish of pearl biscuits, and she and her husband and Vellan were alone. Her husband took a handful of pearl biscuits, and tossed them one by one into the air, while Vellan threw back his head, and caught them in his mouth as they came down—that was one of his accomplishments. She smiled as she remembered it, but at the same time she put her handkerchief to her eyes.

'Why did he go away? What could it have been?' she wondered, her old bewilderment at his conduct, her old longing to comprehend it, reviving with something of the old force. 'Could it have been . . .? Could it have been . . .?' And an old guess, an old theory, one she had never spoken to anybody, but had pondered much in silence, again presented itself interrogatively to her mind.

The door opened; the butler mumbled a name; and she saw a tall, white-haired, pale old man smiling at her and holding out his hands. It took her a little while to realise who it was. With an unthinking disallowance for the action of time, she had been expecting a young fellow of eight-and-twenty, brown-haired and ruddy.

Perhaps he, on his side, was taken aback a little to meet a middle-aged lady in a cap.

III

After dinner he would not let her leave him, but returned with her to the drawing-room, and she said that he might smoke. He smoked odd little Cuban cigarettes, whereof the odour was delicate and aromatic. They had talked of everything; they had laughed and sighed over their ancient joys and sorrows. We know how, in the Courts of Memory, Mirth and Melancholy wander hand in hand. She had cried a little when her husband and her brother were first spoken of, but at some comic reminiscence of them, a moment afterwards, she was smiling through her tears. 'Do you remember so-and-so?' and 'What has become of such-a-one?' were types of the questions they asked each other, conjuring up old friends and enemies like ghosts out of the past. Incidentally, he had described Porto Rico and its negroes and its Spaniards, its climate, its fauna and its flora.

In the drawing-room they sat on opposite sides of the fire, and were silent for a bit. Profiting by the permission she had given him, he produced one of his Cuban cigarettes, opened it at its ends, unrolled it, rolled it up again, and lit it.

'Now the time has come for you to tell me what I most want to know,' she said.

'What is that?'

'Why you went away.'

'Oh,' he murmured.

She waited a minute. Then, 'Tell me,' she urged.

'Do you remember Mary Isona?' he asked.

She glanced up at him suddenly, as if startled. 'Mary Isona? Yes, of course.'

'Well, I was in love with her.'

'You were in love with Mary Isona?'

'I was very much in love with her. I have never got over it, I'm afraid.'

She gazed fixedly at the fire. Her lips were compressed. She saw a slender girl, in a plain black frock, with a sensitive, pale face, luminous, sad, dark eyes, and a mass of dark, waving hair—Mary Isona, of Italian parentage, a little music teacher, whose only relation to the world Theodore Vellan lived in was professional. She came into it for an hour or two at a time now and then, to play or to give a music lesson.

'Yes,' he repeated; 'I was in love with her. I have never been in love with any other woman. It seems ridiculous for an old man to say it, but I am in love with her still. An old man? Are we ever really old? Our body grows old, our skin wrinkles, our hair turns white; but the mind, the spirit, the heart? The thing we call "I"? Anyhow, not a day, not an hour, passes, but I think of her, I long for her, I mourn for her. You knew her—you knew what she was. Do you remember her playing? Her wonderful eyes? Her beautiful pale face? And how the hair grew round her forehead? And her talk, her voice, her intelligence! Her taste, her instinct, in literature, in art—it was the finest I have ever met.'

'Yes, yes, yes,' Mrs Kempton said slowly. 'She was a rare woman. I knew her intimately,—better than any one else, I think. I knew all the unhappy circumstances of her life: her horrid, vulgar mother; her poor, dreamy, inefficient father; her poverty, how hard she had to work. You were in love with her. Why didn't you marry her?'

'My love was not returned.'

'Did you ask her?'

'No. It was needless. It went without saying.'

'You never can tell. You ought to have asked her.'

'It was on the tip of my tongue, of course, to do so a hundred times. My life was passed in torturing myself with the question whether I had any chance, in hoping and fearing. But as often as I found myself alone with her I knew it was hopeless. Her manner to me—it was one of frank friendliness. There was no mistaking it. She never thought of loving me.'

'You were wrong not to ask her. One never can be sure. Oh, why didn't you ask her?' His old friend spoke with great feeling.

He looked at her, surprised and eager. 'Do you really think she might have cared for me?'

'Oh, you ought to have told her: you ought to have asked her,' she repeated.

'Well—now you know why I went away.'

'Yes.'

'When I heard of her—her—death'—he could not bring himself to say her suicide—'there was nothing else for me to do. It was so hideous, so unutterable. To go on with my old life, in the old place, among the old people, was quite impossible. I wanted to follow her, to do what she had done. The only alternative was to fly as far from England, as far from myself, as I could.'

'Sometimes,' Mrs Kempton confessed by-and-bye, 'sometimes I wondered whether, possibly, your disappearance could have had any such connection with Mary's death—it followed it so immediately. I wondered sometimes whether, perhaps, you had cared for her. But I couldn't believe it—it was only because the two things happened one upon the other. Oh, why didn't you tell her? It is dreadful, dreadful!'

IV

When he had left her, she sat still for a little while before the fire.

'Life is a chance to make mistakes—a chance to make mistakes. Life is a chance to make mistakes.'

It was a phrase she had met in a book she was reading the other day:

339

then she had smiled at it; now it rang in her ears like the voice of a mocking demon.

'Yes, a chance to make mistakes,' she said, half aloud.

She rose and went to her desk, unlocked a drawer, turned over its contents, and took out a letter—an old letter, for the paper was yellow and the ink was faded. She came back to the fireside, and unfolded the letter and read it. It covered six pages of notepaper, in a small feminine hand. It was a letter Mary Isona had written to her, Margaret Kempton, the night before she died, more than thirty years ago. The writer recounted the many harsh circumstances of her life; but they would all have been bearable, she said, save for one great and terrible secret. She had fallen in love with a man who was scarcely conscious of her existence; she, a little obscure Italian music teacher, had fallen in love with Theodore Vellan. It was as if she had fallen in love with an inhabitant of another planet: the worlds they respectively belonged to were so far apart. She loved him—she loved him—and she knew her love was hopeless, and she could not bear it. Oh, yes; she met him sometimes, here and there, at houses she went to to play, to give lessons. He was civil to her: he was more than civil—he was kind; he talked to her about literature and music. 'He is so gentle, so strong, so wise; but he has never thought of me as a woman—a woman who could love, who could be loved. Why should he? If the moth falls in love with the star, the moth must suffer. . . . I am cowardly; I am weak; I am what you will; but I have more than I can bear. Life is too hard—too hard. Tomorrow I shall be dead. You will be the only person to know why I died, and you will keep my secret.'

'Oh, the pity of it—the pity of it!' murmured Mrs Kempton. 'I wonder whether I ought to have shown him Mary's letter.'

ELLA DARCY

The Pleasure-Pilgrim

I

Campbell was on his way to Schloss Altenau, for a second quiet
season with his work. He had spent three profitable months there
a year ago, and he was hoping now for a repetition of that good fortune. His thoughts outran the train; and long before his arrival at the
Hamelin railway station, he was enjoying his welcome by the Ritterhausens, was revelling in the ease and comfort of the old Castle, and
was contrasting the pleasures of his home-coming—for he looked upon
Schloss Altenau as a sort of temporary home—with his recent cheerless
experiences of lodging-houses in London, hotels in Berlin, and strange
indifferent faces everywhere. He thought with especial satisfaction of
the Maynes, and of the good talks Mayne and he would have together,
late at night, before the great fire in the hall, after the rest of the household had gone to bed. He blessed the adverse circumstances which had
turned Schloss Altenau into a boarding-house, and had reduced the
Freiherr Ritterhausen to eke out his shrunken revenues by the reception, as paying guests, of English and American pleasure-pilgrims.

He rubbed the blurred window-pane with the fringed end of the
strap hanging from it, and, in the snow-covered landscape reeling towards him, began to recognise objects that were familiar. Hamelin could
not be far off. . . . In another ten minutes the train came to a standstill.

He stepped down with a sense of relief from the overheated atmosphere of his compartment into the cold, bright February afternoon, and
saw through the open station doors one of the Ritterhausen carriages
awaiting him, with Gottlieb in his second-best livery on the box. Gottlieb
showed every reasonable consideration for the Baron's boarders, but
had various methods of marking his sense of the immense abyss separating them from the family. The use of his second-best livery was one

341

of these methods. Nevertheless, he turned a friendly German eye up to Campbell, and in response to his cordial 'Guten Tag, Gottlieb. Wie geht's? Und die Herrschaften?' expressed his pleasure at seeing the young man back again.

While Campbell stood at the top of the steps that led down to the carriage and the Platz, looking after the collection of his luggage and its bestowal by Gottlieb's side, he became aware of two persons, ladies, advancing towards him from the direction of the Wartsaal. It was surprising to see any one at any time in Hamelin Station. It was still more surprising when one of these ladies addressed him by name.

'You are Mr Campbell, are you not?' she said. 'We have been waiting for you to go back in the carriage together. When we found this morning that there was only half-an-hour between your train and ours, I told the Baroness it would be perfectly absurd to send to the station twice. I hope you won't mind our company?'

The first impression Campbell received was of the magnificent apparel of the lady before him; it would have been noticeable in Paris or Vienna—it was extravagant here. Next, he perceived that the face beneath the upstanding feathers and the curving hat-brim was that of so very young a girl, as to make the furs and velvets seem more incongruous still. But the sense of incongruity vanished with the intonation of her first phrase, which told him she was an American. He had no standards for American conduct. It was clear that the speaker and her companion were inmates of the Schloss.

He bowed, and murmured the pleasure he did not feel. A true Briton, he was intolerably shy; and his heart sank at the prospect of a three-mile drive with two strangers who evidently had the advantage of knowing all about him, while he was in ignorance of their very names. As he took his place opposite to them in the carriage, he unconsciously assumed a cold, blank stare, pulling nervously at his moustache, as was his habit in moments of discomposure. Had his companions been British also, the ordeal of the drive must have been a terrible one; but these young American ladies showed no sense of embarrassment whatever.

'We've just come back from Hanover,' said the girl who had already spoken to him. 'I go over once a week for a singing lesson, and my little sister comes along to take care of me.'

She turned a narrow, smiling glance from Campbell to her little sister, and then back to Campbell again. She had red hair; freckles on her nose, and the most singular eyes he had ever seen; slit-like eyes, set obliquely in her head, Chinese fashion.

'Yes, Lulie requires a great deal of taking care of,' assented the little sister sedately, though the way in which she said this seemed to imply something less simple than the words themselves. The speaker bore no resemblance to Lulie. She was smaller, thinner, paler. Her features were straight, a trifle peaked; her skin sallow; her hair of a nondescript brown. She was much less gorgeously dressed. There was even a suggestion of shabbiness in her attire, though sundry isolated details of it were handsome too. She was also much less young; or so, at any rate, Campbell began by pronouncing her. Yet presently he wavered. She had a face that defied you to fix her age. Campbell never fixed it to his own satisfaction, but veered in the course of that drive (as he was destined to do during the next few weeks) from point to point up and down the scale from eighteen to thirty-five. She wore a spotted veil, and beneath it a pince-nez, the lenses of which did something to temper the immense amount of humorous meaning which lurked in her gaze. When her pale prominent eyes met Campbell's, it seemed to the young man that they were full of eagerness to add something at his expense to the stores of information they had already garnered up. They chilled him with misgivings; there was more comfort to be found in her sister's shifting, red-brown glances.

'Hanover is a long way to go for lessons,' he observed, forcing himself to be conversational. 'I used to go there myself about once a week, when I first came to Schloss Altenau, for tobacco, or notepaper, or to get my hair cut. But later on I did without, or contented myself with what Hamelin, or even the village, could offer me.'

'Nannie and I,' said the young girl, 'meant to stay only a week at Altenau, on our way to Hanover, where we were going to pass the winter; but the Castle is just too lovely for anything.' She raised her eyelids the least little bit as she looked at him, and such a warm and friendly gaze shot out, that Campbell was suddenly thrilled. Was she pretty, after all? He glanced at Nannie; she, at least, was indubitably plain. 'It's the very first time we've ever stayed in a castle,' Lulie went on; 'and we're going to remain right along now, until we go home in the spring. Just imagine living in a house with a real moat, and a drawbridge, and a Rittersaal, and suits of armour that have been actually worn in battle! And oh, that delightful iron collar and chain! You remember it, Mr Campbell? It hangs right close to the gateway on the courtyard side. And you know, in old days the Ritterhausens used it for the punishment of their serfs. There are horrible stories connected with it. Mr Mayne can tell you them. But just think of being chained up there like a dog! So wonderfully picturesque.'

'For the spectator perhaps,' said Campbell, smiling. 'I doubt if the victim appreciated the picturesque aspect of the case.'

With this Lulie disagreed. 'Oh, I think he must have been interested,' she said. 'It must have made him feel so absolutely part and parcel of the Middle Ages. I persuaded Mr Mayne to fix the collar round my neck the other day; and though it was very uncomfortable, and I had to stand on tiptoe, it seemed to me that all at once the courtyard was filled with knights in armour, and crusaders, and palmers, and things; and there were flags flying and trumpets sounding; and all the dead and gone Ritterhausens had come down from their picture-frames, and were walking about in brocaded gowns and lace ruffles.'

'It seemed to require a good deal of persuasion to get Mr Mayne to unfix the collar again,' said the little sister. 'How at last did you manage it?'

But Lulie replied irrelevantly: 'And the Ritterhausens are such perfectly lovely people, aren't they, Mr Campbell? The old Baron is a perfect dear. He has such a grand manner. When he kisses my hand I feel nothing less than a princess. And the Baroness is such a funny, busy, delicious little round ball of a thing. And she's always playing bagatelle, isn't she? Or else cutting up skeins of wool for carpet-making.' She meditated a moment. 'Some people always *are* cutting things up in order to join them together again,' she announced, in her fresh drawling young voice.

'And some people cut things up, and leave other people to do the reparation,' commented the little sister enigmatically.

And meantime the carriage had been rattling over the cobble-paved streets of the quaint mediaeval town, where the houses stand so near together that you may shake hands with your opposite neighbour; where allegorical figures, strange birds and beasts, are carved and painted over the windows and doors; and where to every distant sound you lean your ear to catch the fairy music of the Pied Piper, and at every street corner you look to see his tatterdemalion form with the frolicking children at his heels.

Then the Weser bridge was crossed, beneath which the ice-floes jostled and ground themselves together, as they forced their way down the river; and the carriage was rolling smoothly along country roads, between vacant snow-decked fields.

Campbell's embarrassment began to wear off. Now that he was getting accustomed to the girls, he found neither of them awe-inspiring. The red-haired one had a simple child-like manner that was charming. Her strange little face, with its piquant irregularity of line, its warmth of colour, began to please him. What though her hair was red, the uncurled wisp which strayed across her white forehead was soft and alluring; he could see soft masses of it tucked up beneath her hat-brim as she turned her head. When she suddenly lifted her red-brown lashes, those queer eyes of hers had a velvety softness too. Decidedly, she struck him as being pretty—in a peculiar way. He felt an immense accession of interest in her. It seemed to him that he was the discoverer of her possibilities. He did not doubt that the rest of the world called her plain; or at least odd-looking. He, at first, had only seen the freckles on her nose, her oblique-set eyes. He wondered now what she thought of herself, how she appeared to Nannie. Probably as a very ordinary little girl; sisters stand too close to see each other's qualities. She was too young to have had much opportunity of hearing flattering truths from strangers; and besides, the average stranger would see nothing in her to call for flattering truths. Her charm was something subtle, out-of-the-common, in defiance of all known rules of beauty. Campbell saw superiority in himself for recognising it, for formulating it; and he was not displeased to be aware that it would always remain caviare to the multitude.

The carriage had driven through the squalid village of Dürrendorf, had passed the great Ritterhausen barns and farm-buildings, on the tie-beams of which are carved Bible texts in old German; had turned in at the wide open gates of Schloss Altenau, where Gottlieb always whipped up his horses to a fast trot. Full of feeling both for the pocket and the dignity of the Ritterhausens, he would not use up his beasts in unnecessary fast driving. But it was to the credit of the family that he should reach the Castle in fine style. And so he thundered across the draw-bridge, and through the great archway pierced in the north wing, and over the stones of the cobbled courtyard, to pull up before the door of the hall, with much clattering of hoofs and a final elaborate whip-flourish.

II

'I'm jolly glad to have you back,' Mayne said, that same evening, when, the rest of the boarders having retired to their rooms, he and Campbell were lingering over the hall-fire for a talk and smoke. 'I've missed you awfully, old chap, and the good times we used to have here. I've often meant to write to you, but you know how one shoves off letter-writing day after day, till at last one is too ashamed of one's indolence to write at all. But tell me—you had a pleasant drive from Hamelin? What do you think of our young ladies?'

'Those American girls? But they're charming,' said Campbell, with enthusiasm. 'The red-haired one is particularly charming.'

At this Mayne laughed so strangely that Campbell questioned him in surprise. 'Isn't she charming?'

'My dear chap,' Mayne told him, 'the red-haired one, as you call her, is the most remarkably charming young person I've ever met or read of. We've had a good many American girls here before now—you remember the good old Choate family, of course—they were here in your time, I think?—but we've never had anything like this Miss Lulie Thayer. She is something altogether unique.'

Campbell was struck with the name. 'Lulie—Lulie Thayer,' he repeated. 'How pretty it is!' And, full of his great discovery, he felt he must confide it to Mayne, at least. 'Do you know,' he went on, '*she* is really very pretty too? I didn't think so at first, but after a bit I discovered that she is positively quite pretty—in an odd sort of way.'

Mayne laughed again. 'Pretty, pretty!' he echoed in derision. 'Why, *lieber Gott im Himmel*, where are your eyes? Pretty! The girl is beautiful, gorgeously beautiful; every trait, every tint, is in complete, in absolute harmony with the whole. But the truth is, of course, we've all grown accustomed to the obvious, the commonplace; to violent contrasts; blue eyes, black eyebrows, yellow hair; the things that shout for recognition. You speak of Miss Thayer's hair as red. What other colour would you have, with that warm, creamy skin? And then, what a red it is! It looks as though it had been steeped in red wine.'

'Ah, what a good description,' said Campbell, appreciatively. 'That's just it—steeped in red wine.'

'Though it's not so much her beauty,' Mayne continued. 'After all, one has met beautiful women before now. It's her wonderful generosity, her complaisance. She doesn't keep her good things to herself. She doesn't condemn you to admire from a distance.'

'How do you mean?' Campbell asked, surprised again.

'Why, she's the most egregious little flirt I've ever met. And yet, she's not exactly a flirt, either. I mean she doesn't flirt in the ordinary way. She doesn't talk much, or laugh, or apparently make the least claims on masculine attention. And so all the women like her. I don't believe there's one, except my wife, who has an inkling as to her true character. The Baroness, as you know, never observes anything. *Seigneur Dieu!* if she knew the things I could tell her about Miss Lulie! For I've had opportunities of studying her. You see, I'm a married man, and not in my first youth, and the looker-on generally gets the best view of the game. But you, who are young and charming and already famous —we've had your book here, by-the-by, and there's good stuff in it—you're going to have no end of pleasant experiences. I can see she means to add you to her ninety-and-nine other spoils; I saw it from the way she looked at you at dinner. She always begins with those velvety red-brown glances. She began that way with March and Prendergast and Willie Anson, and all the men we've had here since her arrival. The next thing she'll do will be to press your hand under the tablecloth.'

'Oh come, Mayne, you're joking,' cried Campbell a little brusquely. He thought such jokes in bad taste. He had a high ideal of Woman, an immense respect for her; he could not endure to hear her belittled, even in jest. 'Miss Thayer is refined and charming. No girl of her class would do such things.'

'But what is her class? Who knows anything about her? All we know is that she and her uncanny little friend—her little sister, as she calls her, though they're no more sisters than you and I are—they're not even related—all we know is, that she and Miss Dodge (that's the little sister's name) arrived here one memorable day last October from the

347

Kronprinz Hotel at Waldeck-Pyrmont. By-the-by, it was the Choates, I believe, who told her of the Castle—hotel acquaintances—you know how travelling Americans always cotton to each other. And we've picked up a few little auto and biographical notes from her and Miss Dodge since. *Zum Beispiel*, she's got a rich father somewhere away back in Michigan, who supplies her with all the money she wants. And she's been travelling about since last May: Paris, Vienna, the Rhine, Düsseldorf, and so on here. She must have had some rich experiences, by Jove, for she's done everything. Cycled in Paris; you should see her in her cycling costume, she wears it when the Baron takes her out shooting—she's an admirable shot by the way, an accomplishment learned, I suppose, from some American cow-boy—then in Berlin she did a month's hospital nursing; and now she's studying the higher branches of the Terpsichorean art. You know she was in Hanover to-day. Did she tell you what she went for?'

'To take a singing lesson,' said Campbell, remembering the reason she had given.

'A singing lesson! Do you sing with your legs? A dancing lesson, *mein lieber*. A dancing lesson from the ballet-master of the Hof Theater. She could deposit a kiss on your forehead with her foot, I don't doubt. I must ask her if she can do the *grand écart* yet.' And when Campbell, in astonishment, wondered why on earth she should wish to learn such things, 'Oh, to extend her opportunities,' Mayne explained, 'and to acquire fresh sensations. She's an adventuress. Yes, an adventuress, but an end-of-the-century one. She doesn't travel for profit, but for pleasure. She has no desire to swindle her neighbour, but to amuse herself. And she's clever; she's read a good deal; she knows how to apply her reading to practical life. Thus, she's learned from Herrick not to be coy; and from Shakespeare that sweet-and-twenty is the time for kissing and being kissed. She honours her masters in the observance. She was not in the least abashed when, one day, I suddenly came upon her teaching that damned idiot, young Anson, two new ways of kissing.'

Campbell's impressions of the girl were readjusting themselves completely, but for the moment he was unconscious of the change. He only knew that he was partly angry, partly incredulous, and inclined to believe that Mayne was chaffing him.

'But, Miss Dodge,' he objected, 'the little sister, she is older; old enough to look after her friend. Surely she could not allow a young girl placed in her charge to behave in such a way——'

'Oh, that little Dodge girl,' said Mayne contemptuously; 'Miss Thayer pays the whole shot, I understand, and Miss Dodge plays gooseberry, sheep-dog, jackal, what you will. She finds her reward in the other's cast-off finery. The silk blouse she was wearing to-night, I've good reason for remembering, belonged to Miss Lulie. For, during a brief season, I must tell you, my young lady had the caprice to show attentions to your humble servant. I suppose my being a married man lent me a factitious fascination. But I didn't see it. That kind of girl doesn't appeal to me. So she employed Miss Dodge to do a little active canvassing. It was really too funny; I was coming in one day after a walk in the woods; my wife was trimming bonnets, or had neuralgia, or something. Anyhow, I was alone, and Miss Dodge contrived to waylay me in the middle of the courtyard. "Don't you find it vurry dull walking all by yourself?" she asked me; and then blinking up in her strange little short-sighted way—she's really the weirdest little creature—"Why don't you make love to Lulie?" she said; "you'd find her vurry charming." It took me a minute or two to recover presence of mind enough to ask her whether Miss Thayer had commissioned her to tell me so. She looked at me with that cryptic smile of hers; "She'd like you to do so, I'm sure," she finally remarked, and pirouetted away. Though it didn't come off, owing to my bashfulness, it was then that Miss Dodge appropriated the silk "waist"; and Providence, taking pity on Miss Thayer's forced inactivity, sent along March, a young fellow reading for the army, with whom she had great doings. She fooled him to the top of his bent; sat on his knee; gave him a lock of her hair, which, having no scissors handy, she burned off with a cigarette taken from his mouth; and got him to offer her marriage. Then she turned round and laughed in his face, and took up with a Dr Weber, a cousin of the Baron's, under the other man's very eyes. You never saw anything like the unblushing coolness with which she would permit March to catch her in Weber's arms.'

'Come,' Campbell protested again, 'aren't you drawing it rather strong?'

'On the contrary, I'm drawing it mild, as you'll discover presently for yourself; and then you'll thank me for forewarning you. For she makes love—desperate love, mind you—to every man she meets. And goodness knows how many she hasn't met in the course of her career, which began presumably at the age of ten, in some "Amur'can" hotel or watering-place. Look at this.' Mayne fetched an alpenstock from a corner of the hall; it was decorated with a long succession of names, which, ribbon-like, were twisted round and round it, carved in the wood. 'Read them,' insisted Mayne, putting the stick in Campbell's hands. 'You'll see they're not the names of the peaks she has climbed, or the towns she has passed through; they're the names of the men she has fooled. And there's room for more; there's still a good deal of space, as you see. There's room for yours.'

Campbell glanced down the alpenstock—reading here a name, there an initial, or just a date—and jerked it impatiently from him on to a couch. He wished with all his heart that Mayne would stop, would talk of something else, would let him get away. The young girl had interested him so much; he had felt himself so drawn towards her; he had thought her so fresh, so innocent. But Mayne, on the contrary, was warming to his subject, was enchanted to have some one to listen to his stories, to discuss his theories, to share his cynical amusement.

'I don't think, mind you,' he said, 'that she is a bit interested herself in the men she flirts with. I don't think she gets any of the usual sensations from it, you know. My theory is, she does it for mere devilry, for a laugh. Or, and this is another theory, she is actuated by some idea of retribution. Perhaps some woman she was fond of—her mother even—who knows?—was badly treated at the hands of a man. Perhaps this girl has constituted herself the Nemesis for her sex, and goes about seeing how many masculine hearts she can break, by way of revenge. Or can it be that she is simply the newest development of the New Woman—she who in England preaches and bores you, and in America practises and pleases? Yes, I believe she's the American edition, and so new that she hasn't yet found her way into fiction. She's the pioneer of the army coming out of the West, that's going to destroy the existing scheme of things, and rebuild it nearer to the heart's desire.'

'Oh, damn it all, Mayne,' cried Campbell, rising abruptly, 'why not say at once that she's a wanton, and have done with it? Who wants to hear your rotten theories?' And he lighted his candle without another word, and went off to bed.

III

It was four o'clock, and the Baron's boarders were drinking their afternoon coffee, drawn up in a semi-circle round the hall fire. All but Campbell, who had carried his cup away to a side-table, and, with a book open beside him, appeared to be reading assiduously. In reality he could not follow a line of what he read; he could not keep his thoughts from Miss Thayer. What Mayne had told him was germinating in his mind. Knowing his friend as he did, he could not on reflection doubt his word. In spite of much superficial cynicism, Mayne was incapable of speaking lightly of any young girl without good cause. It now seemed to Campbell that, instead of exaggerating the case, Mayne had probably understated it. He asked himself with horror, what had this girl not already known, seen, permitted? When now and again his eyes travelled over, perforce, to where she sat, her red head leaning against Miss Dodge's knee, and seeming to attract to, and concentrate upon itself all the glow of the fire, his forehead set itself in frowns, and he returned to his book with an increased sense of irritation.

'I'm just sizzling up, Nannie,' Miss Thayer presently complained, in her child-like, drawling little way; 'this fire is too hot for anything.' She rose and shook straight her loose tea-gown, a marvellous plush and lace garment created in Paris, which would have accused a duchess of wilful extravagance. She stood smiling round a moment, pulling on and off with her right hand a big diamond ring which decorated the left. At the sound of her voice Campbell had looked up, and his cold, unfriendly eyes encountered hers. He glanced rapidly past her, then back to his book. But she, undeterred, with a charming sinuous movement and a frou-frou of trailing silks, crossed over towards him. She slipped into an empty chair next his.

'I'm going to do you the honour of sitting beside you, Mr Campbell,' she said sweetly.

'It's an honour I've done nothing whatever to merit,' he answered, without looking at her, and turned a page.

'The right retort,' she approved; 'but you might have said it a little more cordially.'

'I don't feel cordial.'

'But why not? What has happened? Yesterday you were so nice.'

'Ah, a good deal of water has run under the bridge since yesterday.'

'But still the river remains as full,' she told him, smiling, 'and still the sky is as blue. The thermometer has even risen six degrees.'

'What did you go into Hanover for yesterday?' Campbell suddenly asked her.

She flashed him a comprehending glance from half-shut eyes. 'I think men gossip a great deal more than women,' she observed, 'and they don't understand things either. They try to make all life suit their own pre-conceived theories. And why, after all, should I not wish to learn dancing thoroughly? There's no harm in that.'

'Only, why call it singing?' Campbell enquired.

Miss Thayer smiled. 'Truth is so uninteresting!' she said, and paused. 'Except in books. One likes it there. And I wanted to tell you, I think your books perfectly lovely. I know them, most all. I've read them away home. They're very much thought of in America. Only last night I was saying to Nannie how glad I am to have met you, for I think we're going to be great friends, aren't we, Mr Campbell? At least, I hope so, for you can do me so much good, if you will. Your books always make me feel real good; but you yourself can help me much more.'

She looked up at him with one of her warm, narrow, red-brown glances, which yesterday would have thrilled his blood, and to-day merely stirred it to anger.

'You over-estimate my abilities,' he said coldly; 'and, on the whole, I fear you will find writers a very disappointing race. You see, they put their best into their books. So not to disillusion you too rapidly'—he rose—'will you excuse me? I have some work to do.' And he left her sitting there alone.

But he did no work when he got to his room. Whether Lulie Thayer was actually present or not, it seemed that her influence was equally disturbing to him. His mind was full of her: of her singular eyes, her quaint intonation, her sweet, seductive praise. Twenty-four hours ago such praise would have been delightful to him: what young author is proof against appreciation of his books? Now, Campbell simply told himself that she laid the butter on too thick; that it was in some analogous manner she had flattered up March, Anson, and all the rest of the men that Mayne had spoken of. He supposed it was the first step in the process by which he was to be fooled, twisted round her finger, added to the list of victims who strewed her conquering path. He had a special fear of being fooled. For beneath a somewhat supercilious exterior, the dominant note of his character was timidity, distrust of his own merits; and he knew he was single-minded—one-idea'd almost—if he were to let himself go, to get to care very much for a woman, for such a girl as this girl, for instance, he would lose himself completely, be at her mercy absolutely. Fortunately, Mayne had let him know her character. He could feel nothing but dislike for her—disgust, even; and yet he was conscious how pleasant it would be to believe in her innocence, in her candour. For she was so adorably pretty; her flower-like beauty grew upon him; her head, drooping a little on one side when she looked up, was so like a flower bent by its own weight. The texture of her cheeks, her lips, was delicious as the petals of a flower. He found he could recall with perfect accuracy every detail of her appearance: the manner in which the red hair grew round her temples; the way in which it was loosely and gracefully fastened up behind with just a single tortoise-shell pin. He recollected the suspicion of a dimple that shadowed itself in her cheek when she spoke, and deepened into a delicious reality every time she smiled. He remembered her throat; her hands, of a beautiful whiteness, with pink palms and pointed fingers. It was impossible to write. He speculated long on the ring she wore on her engaged finger. He mentioned this ring to Mayne the next time he saw him.

'Engaged? very much so, I should say. Has got a *fiancé* in every capital of Europe probably. But the ring-man is the *fiancé en titre*. He writes to her by every mail, and is tremendously in love with her. She shows me his letters. When she's had her fling, I suppose she'll go back and marry him. That's what these little American girls do, I'm told; sow their wild oats here with us, and settle down into *bonnes ménagères* over yonder. Meanwhile, are you having any fun with her? Aha, she presses your hand? The "gesegnete Mahlzeit" business after dinner is an excellent institution, isn't it? She'll tell you how much she loves you soon; that's the next move in the game.'

But so far she had done neither of these things, for Campbell gave her no opportunities. He was guarded in the extreme, ungenial; avoiding her even at the cost of civility. Sometimes he was downright rude. That especially occurred when he felt himself inclined to yield to her advances. For she made him all sorts of silent advances, speaking with her eyes, her sad little mouth, her beseeching attitude. And then one evening she went further still. It occurred after dinner in the little green drawing-room. The rest of the company were gathered together in the big drawing-room beyond. The small room has deep embrasures to the windows. Each embrasure holds two old faded green velvet sofas in black oaken frames, and an oaken oblong table stands between them. Campbell had flung himself down on one of these sofas in the corner nearest the window. Miss Thayer, passing through the room, saw him, and sat down opposite. She leaned her elbows on the table, the laces of her sleeves falling away from her round white arms, and clasped her hands.

'Mr Campbell, tell me, what have I done? How have I vexed you? You have hardly spoken two words to me all day. You always try to avoid me.' And when he began to utter evasive banalities, she stopped him with an imploring 'Ah, don't! I love you. You know I love you. I love you so much I can't bear you to put me off with mere phrases.'

Campbell admired the well-simulated passion in her voice, remembered Mayne's prediction, and laughed aloud.

'Oh, you may laugh,' she said, 'but I'm serious. I love you, I love you with my whole soul.' She slipped round the end of the table, and came close beside him. His first impulse was to rise; then he resigned himself to stay. But it was not so much resignation that was required, as self-mastery, cool-headedness. Her close proximity, her fragrance, those wonderful eyes raised so beseechingly to his, made his heart beat.

'Why are you so cold?' she said. 'I love you so, can't you love me a little too?'

'My dear young lady,' said Campbell, gently repelling her, 'what do you take me for? A foolish boy like your friends Anson and March? What you are saying is monstrous, preposterous. Ten days ago you'd never even seen me.'

'What has length of time to do with it?' she said. 'I loved you at first sight.'

'I wonder,' he observed judicially, and again gently removed her hand from his, 'to how many men you have not already said the same thing?'

'I've never meant it before,' she said quite earnestly, and nestled closer to him, and kissed the breast of his coat, and held her mouth up towards his. But he kept his chin resolutely high, and looked over her head.

'How many men have you not already kissed, even since you've been here?'

'But there've not been many here to kiss!' she exclaimed naïvely.

'Well, there was March; you kissed him?'

'No, I'm quite sure I didn't.'

'And young Anson; what about him? Ah, you don't answer! And then the other fellow—what's his name—Prendergast—you've kissed him?'

'But, after all, what is there in a kiss?' she cried ingenuously. 'It means nothing, absolutely nothing. Why, one has to kiss all sorts of people one doesn't care about.'

Campbell remembered how Mayne had said she had probably known strange kisses since the age of ten; and a wave of anger with her, of righteous indignation, rose within him.

'To me,' said he, 'to all right-thinking people, a young girl's kisses are something pure, something sacred, not to be offered indiscriminately to every fellow she meets. Ah, you don't know what you have lost! You have seen a fruit that has been handled, that has lost its bloom? You have seen primroses, spring flowers gathered and thrown away in the dust? And who enjoys the one, or picks up the others? And this is what you remind me of—only you have deliberately, of your own perverse will, tarnished your beauty, and thrown away all the modesty, the reticence, the delicacy, which make a young girl so infinitely dear. You revolt me, you disgust me. I want nothing from you but to be let alone. Kindly take your hands away, and let me go.'

He shook her roughly off and got up, then felt a moment's curiosity to see how she would take the repulse.

Miss Thayer never blushed: had never, he imagined, in her life done so. No faintest trace of colour now stained the warm pallor of her rose-leaf skin; but her eyes filled up with tears, two drops gathered on the under lashes, grew large, trembled an instant, and then rolled unchecked down her cheeks. Those tears somehow put him in the wrong, and he felt he had behaved brutally to her, for the rest of the night.

He began to seek excuses for her: after all, she meant no harm: it was her upbringing, her *genre*: it was a *genre* he loathed; but perhaps he need

355

not have spoken so harshly. He thought he would find a more friendly word for her next morning; and he loitered about the Mahlsaal, where the boarders come in to breakfast as in an hotel just when it suits them, till past eleven; but she did not come. Then, when he was almost tired of waiting, Miss Dodge put in an appearance, in a flannel wrapper, and her front hair twisted up in steel pins.

Campbell judged Miss Dodge with even more severity than he did Miss Thayer; there was nothing in this weird little creature's appearance to temper justice with mercy. It was with difficulty that he brought himself to inquire after her friend.

'Lulie is sick this morning,' she told him. 'I've come down to order her some broth. She couldn't sleep any last night, because of your unkindness to her. She's vurry, vurry unhappy about it.'

'Yes, I'm sorry for what I said. I had no right to speak so strongly, I suppose. But I spoke strongly because I feel strongly. However, there's no reason why my bad manners should make her unhappy.'

'Oh, yes, there's vurry good reason,' said Miss Dodge. 'She's vurry much in love with you.'

Campbell looked at the speaker long and earnestly to try and read her mind; but the prominent blinking eyes, the cryptic physiognomy, told him nothing.

'Look here,' he said brusquely, 'what's your object in trying to fool me like this? I know all about your friend. Mayne has told me. She has cried "Wolf" too often before to expect to be believed now.'

'But, after all,' argued Miss Dodge, blinking more than ever behind her glasses, 'the wolf did really come at last, you know; didn't he? Lulie is really in love this time. We've all made mistakes in our lives, haven't we? But that's no reason for not being right at last. And Lulie has cried herself sick.'

Campbell was a little shaken. He went and repeated the conversation to Mayne, who laughed derisively.

'Capital, capital!' he cried; 'excellently contrived. It quite supports my latest theory about our young friend. She's an actress, a born comédienne. She acts always, and to every one: to you, to me, to the Ritterhausens, to the Dodge girl—even to herself when she is quite alone. And she has a great respect for her art; she'll carry out her rôle, *coûte que coûte*, to the bitter end. She chooses to pose as in love with you; you don't respond; the part now requires that she should sicken and pine. Consequently, she takes to her bed, and sends her confidante to tell you so. Oh, it's colossal, it's *famos!*'

IV

'If you can't really love me,' said Lulie Thayer—'and I know I've been a bad girl and don't deserve that you should—at least, will you allow me to go on loving you?'

She walked by Campbell's side, through the solitary, uncared-for park of Schloss Altenau. It was three weeks later in the year, and the spring feeling in the air stirred the blood. All round were signs and tokens of spring; in the busy gaiety of bird and insect life; in the purple flower-tufts which thickened the boughs of the ash trees; in the young green things pushing up pointed heads from amidst last season's dead leaves and grasses. The snow-wreaths, that had for so long decorated the distant hills, were shrinking perceptibly away beneath the strong March sunshine.

There was every invitation to spend one's time out of doors, and Campbell passed long mornings in the park, or wandering through the woods and the surrounding villages. Miss Thayer often accompanied him. He never invited her to do so, but when she offered him her company, he could not, or at least did not, refuse it.

'May I love you? Say,' she entreated.

' "Wenn ich Dich liebe, was geht's Dich an?" ' he quoted lightly. 'Oh, no, it's nothing to me, of course. Only don't expect me to believe you—that's all.'

This disbelief of his was the recurring decimal of their conversation. No matter on what subject they began, they always ended thus. And the more sceptical he showed himself, the more eager she became. She exhausted herself in endeavours to convince him.

They had reached the corner in the park where the road to the Castle turns off at right angles from the road to Dürrendorf. The ground rises gently on the park-side to within three feet of the top of the boundary wall, although on the other side there is a drop of at least twenty feet. The broad wall-top makes a convenient seat. Campbell and the girl sat down on it. At his last words she wrung her hands together in her lap.

'But how can you disbelieve me?' she cried, 'when I tell you I love you, I adore you? when I swear it to you? And can't you see for yourself? Why, every one at the Castle sees it.'

'Yes, you afford the Castle a good deal of unnecessary amusement; and that shows you don't understand what love really is. Real love is full of delicacy, of reticences, and would feel itself profaned if it became the jest of the servants' hall.'

'It's not so much my love for you, as your rejection of it, which has made me talked about.'

'Isn't it rather on account of the favours you've lavished on all my predecessors?'

She sprang to her feet, and walked up and down in agitation.

'But, after all, surely, mistakes of that sort are not to be counted against us? I did really think I was in love with Mr March. Willie Anson doesn't count. He's an American too, and he understands things. Besides, he is only a boy. And how could I know I should love you before I had met you? And how can I help loving you now I have? You're so different from other men. You're good, you're honourable, you treat women with respect. Oh, I do love you so, I do love you! Ask Nannie if I don't.'

The way in which Campbell shrugged his shoulders clearly expressed the amount of reliance he would place on any testimony from Miss Dodge. He could not forget her 'Why don't you make love to Lulie?' addressed to a married man. Such a want of principle argued an equal want of truth.

Lulie seemed on the brink of weeping.

'I wish I were dead,' she struggled to say; 'life's impossible if you won't believe me. I don't ask you any longer to love me. I know I've been a bad girl, and I don't deserve that you should; but if you won't believe that I love you, I don't want to live any longer.'

Campbell confessed to himself that she acted admirably, but that the damnable iteration of the one idea became monotonous. He sought a change of subject. 'Look there,' he said, 'close by the wall, what's that jolly little blue flower? It's the first I've seen this year.'

He showed her where, at the base of the wall, a solitary blossom rose above a creeping stem and glossy dark green leaves.

Lulie, all smiles again, picked it with childlike pleasure. 'Oh, if that's the first you've seen,' she cried, 'you can take a wish. Only you mustn't speak until some one asks you a question.'

She began to fasten it in his coat. 'It's just as blue as your eyes,' she said. 'You have such blue and boyish eyes, you know. Stop, stop, that's not a question,' and seeing that he was about to speak, she laid her finger across his mouth. 'You'll spoil the charm.'

She stepped back, folded her arms, and seemed to dedicate herself to eternal silence; then relenting suddenly:

'Do you believe me?' she entreated.

'What's become of your ring?' Campbell answered beside the mark. He had noticed its absence from her finger while she had been fixing in the flower.

'Oh, my engagement's broken.'

Campbell asked how the fiancé would like that.

'Oh, he won't mind. He knows I only got engaged because he worried so. And it was always understood between us that I was to be free if I ever met any one I liked better.'

Campbell asked her what sort of fellow this accommodating fiancé was.

'Oh, he's all right. And he's very good too. But he's not a bit clever, and don't let us talk about him. He makes me tired.'

'But you're wrong,' Campbell told her, 'to throw away a good, a sincere affection. If you really want to reform and turn over a new leaf, as you are always telling me you do, I should advise you to go home and marry him.'

'What, when I'm in love with you?' she cried reproachfully. 'Would that be right?'

'It's going to rain,' said Campbell. 'Didn't you feel a drop just then? And it's getting near lunch-time. Shall we go in?'

Their shortest way led through the little cemetery in which the departed Ritterhausens lay at peace, in the shadow of their sometime home.

'When I die the Baron has promised I shall be buried here,' said Lulie pensively; 'just here, next to his first wife. Don't you think it would be lovely to be buried in a beautiful, peaceful, baronial grave-yard instead of in some horrid, crowded city cemetery?'

Mayne met them as they entered the hall. He noticed the flower in his friend's coat. 'Ah, my dear chap, been treading the—periwinkle path of dalliance, I see? How many desirable young men have I not witnessed, led down the same broad way by the same seductive lady! Always the same thing; nothing changes but the flower according to the season.'

When Campbell reached his room he took the poor periwinkle out of his coat, and threw it away into the stove.

And yet, had it not been for Mayne, Miss Thayer might have triumphed after all; might have convinced Campbell of her passion, or have added another victim to her long list. But Mayne had set himself as determinedly to spoil her game, as she was bent on winning it. He had always the cynical word, the apt reminiscence ready, whenever he saw signs on Campbell's part of surrender. He was very fond of Campbell. He did not wish him to fall a prey to the wiles of this little American siren. He had watched her conduct in the past with a dozen different men; he genuinely believed she was only acting in the present.

Campbell, for his part, began to experience an ever-increasing exasperation in the girl's presence. Yet he did not avoid it; he could not well avoid it, she followed him about so persistently: but his speech would overflow with bitterness towards her. He would say the cruellest things; then remembering them when alone, be ashamed of his brutalities. But nothing he said ever altered her sweetness of temper or weakened the tenacity of her purpose. His rebuffs made her beautiful eyes run over with tears, but the harshest of them never elicited the least sign of resentment. There would have been something touching as well as comic in this dog-like humility, which accepted everything as welcome at his hands, had he not been imbued with Mayne's conviction that it was all an admirable piece of acting. Or when for a moment he forgot the histrionic theory, then invariably there would come a chance word in her conversation which would fill him with cold rage. They would be talking of books, travels, sport, what not, and she would drop a reference to this man or to that. So-and-so had taken her to Bullier's, she had learned skating with this other; Duroy, the *prix de Rome* man, had painted her as Hebe, Franz Weber had tried to teach her German by means of Heine's poems. And he got glimpses of long vistas of amourettes played in every state in America, in every country of Europe, since the very beginning, when, as a mere child, elderly men, friends of her father's, had held her on their knee and fed her on sweetmeats and kisses. It was sickening to think of; it was pitiable. So much youth and beauty tarnished; the possibility for so much good thrown away. For if one could only blot out her record, forget it, accept her for what she chose to appear, a more endearing companion no man could desire.

V

It was a wet afternoon; the rain had set in at mid-day, with a gray determination, which gave no hopes of clearing. Nevertheless, Mayne had accompanied his wife and the Baroness into Hamelin. 'To take up a servant's character, and expostulate with a recalcitrant dressmaker,' he explained to Campbell, and wondered what women would do to fill up their days were it not for the perennial crimes of dressmakers and domestic servants. He himself was going to look in at the English Club; wouldn't Campbell come too? There was a fourth seat in the carriage. But Campbell was in no social mood; he felt his temper going all to pieces; a quarter of an hour of Mrs Mayne's society would have brought on an explosion. He thought he must be alone; and yet when he had read for half an hour in his room he wondered vaguely what Lulie was doing; he had not seen her since luncheon. She always gave him her society when he could very well dispense with it, but on a wet day like this, when a little conversation would be tolerable, of course she stayed away. Then there came down the long Rittersaal the tapping of high heels, and a well-known knock at his door.

He went over and opened it. Miss Thayer, in the plush and lace tea-gown, fronted him serenely.

'Am I disturbing you?' she asked; and his mood was so capricious that, now she was standing there on his threshold, he thought he was annoyed at it. 'It's so dull,' she said persuasively: 'Nannie's got a sick headache, and I daren't go downstairs, or the Baron will annex me to play Halma. He always wants to play Halma on wet days.'

'And what do you want to do?' said Campbell, leaning against the doorpost, and letting his eyes rest on the strange piquant face in its setting of red hair.

'To be with you, of course.'

'Well,' said he, coming out and closing the door, 'I'm at your service. What next?'

They strolled together through the room and listened to the falling rain. The Rittersaal occupies all the space on the first floor that the hall and four drawing-rooms do below. Wooden pillars support the ceiling, dividing the apartment lengthwise into a nave and two aisles. Down the middle are long tables, used for ceremonial banquets. Six windows look into the courtyard, and six out over the open country. The centre pane of each window is emblazoned with a Ritterhausen shield. Between the windows hang family portraits, and the sills are broad and low and cushioned in faded velvet.

'How it rains!' said Lulie, stopping before one of the south windows; 'why, you can't see anything for the rain, and there's no sound at all but the rain either. I like it. It makes me feel as though we had the whole world to ourselves.'

Then, 'Say, what would you like to do?' she asked him. 'Shall I fetch over my pistols, and we'll practise with them? You've no notion how well I can shoot. We couldn't hurt anything here, could we?'

Campbell thought they might practise there without inconvenience, and Lulie, bundling up the duchess tea-gown over one arm, danced off in very unduchess-like fashion to fetch the case. It was a charming little box of cedar-wood and mother-o'-pearl, lined with violet velvet; and two tiny revolvers lay inside, hardly more than six inches long, with silver engraved handles.

'I won them in a bet,' she observed complacently, 'with the Hon. Billie Thornton. He's an Englishman, you know, the son of Lord Thornton. I knew him in Washington two years ago last fall. He bet I couldn't hit a three-cent piece at twenty yards and I did. Aren't they perfectly sweet? Now, can't you contrive a target?'

Campbell went back to his room, drew out a rough diagram, and pasted it down on to a piece of cardboard. Then this was fixed up by means of a penknife driven into the wood of one of the pillars, and Campbell, with his walking-stick laid down six successive times, measured off the distance required, and set a chalk mark across the floor. Lulie took the first shot. She held the little weapon up at arm's length above her head, the first finger stretched out along the barrel; then dropping her hand sharply so that the finger pointed straight at the butt, she pulled the trigger with the third. There was the sharp report, the tiny smoke film—and when Campbell went up to examine results, he found she had only missed the very centre by a quarter of an inch.

Lulie was exultant. 'I don't seem to have got out of practice any,' she remarked. 'I'm so glad, for I used to be a very good shot. It was Hiram P. Ladd who taught me. He's the crack shot of Montana. What! you don't know Hiram P.? Why, I should have supposed every one must have heard of him. He had the next ranche to my Uncle Samuel's, where I used to go summers, and he made me do an hour's pistol practice every morning after bathing. It was he who taught me swimming too—in the river.'

'Damnation,' said Campbell under his breath, then shot in his turn, and shot wide. Lulie made another bull's-eye, and after that a white. She urged Campbell to continue, which he sullenly did, and again missed.

'You see I don't come up to your Hiram P. Ladd,' he remarked savagely, and put the pistol down, and walked over to the window. He stood with one foot on the cushioned seat, staring out at the rain, and pulling moodily at his moustache.

Lulie followed him, nestled up to him, lifted the hand that hung passive by his side, put it round her waist and held it there. Campbell lost in thought, let it remain so for a second; then remembered how she had doubtless done this very same thing with other men in this very room. All her apparently spontaneous movements, he told himself, were but the oft-used pieces in the game she played so skilfully.

'Let go,' he said, and flung himself down on the window-seat, looking up at her with darkening eyes.

She sitting meekly in the other corner folded her offending hands in her lap.

'Do you know, your eyes are not a bit nice when you're cross?' she said; 'they seem to become quite black.'

He maintained a discouraging silence.

She looked over at him meditatively.

'I never cared a bit for Hiram P., if that's what you mean,' she remarked presently.

'Do you suppose I care a button if you did?'

'Then why did you leave off shooting, and why won't you talk to me?'

He vouchsafed no reply.

Lulie spent some moments immersed in thought. Then she sighed deeply, and recommenced on a note of pensive regret.

'Ah, if I'd only met you sooner in life, I should be a very different girl.'

The freshness which her quaint, drawling enunciation lent to this time-dishonoured formula, made Campbell smile, till, remembering all its implications, his forehead set in frowns again.

Lulie continued her discourse. 'You see,' said she, 'I never had any one to teach me what was right. My mother died when I was quite a child, and my father has always let me do exactly as I pleased, so long as I didn't bother him. Then I've never had a home, but have always lived around in hotels and places: all winter in New York or Washington, and summers out at Longbranch or Saratoga. It's true we own a house in Detroit, on Lafayette Avenue, that we reckon as home, but we don't ever go there. It's a bad sort of life for a girl, isn't it?' she pleaded.

'Horrible,' he said mechanically. His mind was at work. The loose threads of his angers, his irritations, his desires, were knitting themselves together, weaving themselves into something overmastering and definite.

The young girl meanwhile was moving up towards him along the seat, for the effect which his sharpest rebuke produced on her never lasted more than four minutes. She now again possessed herself of his hand, and holding it between her own, began to caress it in childlike fashion, pulling the fingers apart and closing them again, spreading it palm downwards on her lap, and laying her own little hand over it, to exemplify the differences between them. He let her be; he seemed unconscious of her proceedings.

'And then,' she continued, 'I've always known a lot of young fellows who've liked to take me round; and no one ever objected to my going with them, and so I went. And I enjoyed it, and there wasn't any harm in it, just kissing and making believe, and nonsense. But I never really cared for one of them—I can see that now, when I compare them with you; when I compare what I felt for them with what I feel for you. Oh, I do love you so much,' she murmured; 'don't you believe me?' She lifted his hand to her lips and covered it with kisses.

He pulled it roughly from her. 'I wish you'd give over such fool's play,' he told her, got up, walked to the table, came back again, stood looking at her with sombre eyes and dilating pupils.

'But I do love you,' she repeated, rising and advancing towards him.

'For God's sake, drop that damned rot,' he cried out with sudden fury. 'It wearies me, do you hear? it sickens me. Love, love—my God, what do you know about it? Why, if you really loved me, really loved any man—if you had any conception of what the passion of love is, how beautiful, how fine, how sacred—the mere idea that you could not come to your lover fresh, pure, untouched, as a young girl should— that you had been handled, fondled, and God knows what besides, by this man and the other—would fill you with such horror for yourself, with such supreme disgust—you would feel yourself so unworthy, so polluted . . . that . . . that . . . by God! you would take up that pistol there, and blow your brains out!'

Lulie seemed to find the idea quite entertaining. She picked the pistol up from where it lay in the window, examined it critically, with her pretty head drooping on one side, and then sent one of her long red-brown caressing glances up towards him.

'And suppose I were to,' she asked lightly, 'would you believe me then?'

'Oh, . . . well . . . then, perhaps! If you showed sufficient decency to kill yourself, perhaps I might,' said he, with ironical laughter. His ebullition had relieved him; his nerves were calmed again. 'But nothing short of that would ever make me.'

With her little tragic air, which seemed to him so like a smile disguised, she raised the weapon to the bosom of her gown. There came a sudden, sharp crack, a tiny smoke film. She stood an instant swaying slightly, smiling certainly, distinctly outlined against the background of rain-washed window, of gray falling rain, the top of her head cutting in two the Ritterhausen escutcheon. Then all at once there was nothing at all between him and the window—he saw the coat of arms entire—but a motionless, inert heap of plush and lace, and fallen wine-red hair, lay at his feet upon the floor.

'Child, child, what have you done?' he cried with anguish, and kneeling beside her, lifted her up, and looked into her face.

When from a distance of time and place Campbell was at last able to look back with some degree of calmness on the catastrophe, the element in it which stung him most keenly was this: he could never convince himself that Lulie had really loved him after all. And the only two persons who had known them both, and the circumstances of the case, sufficiently well to have resolved his doubts one way or the other, held diametrically opposite views.

'Well, listen, then, and I'll tell you how it was,' Miss Nannie Dodge had said to him impressively, the day before he left Schloss Altenau for ever. 'Lulie was tremendously, terribly in love with you. And when she found that you wouldn't care about her, she didn't want to live any more. As to the way in which it happened, you don't need to reproach yourself for that. She'd have done it, anyhow. If not then, why later. But it's all the rest of your conduct to her that was so mean. Your cold, cruel, complacent British unresponsiveness. I guess you'll never find another woman to love you as Lulie did. She was just the darlingest, the sweetest, the most loving girl in the world.'

Mayne, on the other hand, summed it up in this way. 'Of course, old chap, it's horrible to think of: horrible, horrible, horrible! I can't tell you how badly I feel about it. For she was a gorgeously beautiful creature. That red hair of hers! Good Lord! You won't come across such hair as that again in a lifetime. But, believe me, she was only fooling with you. Once she had you in her hunting-noose, once her buccaneering instincts satisfied, and she'd have chucked you as she did all the rest. As to her death, I've got three theories—no, two—for the first being that she compassed it in a moment of genuine emotion, we may dismiss, I think, as quite untenable. The second is, that it arose from pure misadventure. You had both been shooting, hadn't you? Well, she took up the pistol and pulled the trigger from mere mischief, to frighten you, and quite forgetting one barrel was still loaded. And the third is, it was just her histrionic sense of the fitness of things. The rôle she had played so long and so well now demanded a sensational finale in the centre of the stage. And it's the third theory I give the preference to. She was the most consummate little actress I ever met.'

LAURENCE ALMA-TADEMA

At the Gates of Paradise

And in the gloom another vision rose before us. It was evening; the room in which we stood was vast and dimly-lighted; the lofty ceiling and distant corners were lost in darkness. Beside the table where the lamp burned, a white-haired man sat in a high-backed chair; he was richly clothed, one of the Council of Ten, maybe; his chin now rested on his breast-bone, for he was asleep; and his long white hand, stranger to toil, lay listless between the pages of the open book upon his knee.

To the right, a four-fold window, whose pointed arches rested upon columns of fine marble, let in a stream of moonlight that lay pale upon the coloured floor; and at this window stood two women.

Both were young, but one was very young, sixteen or thereabouts, a mere girl whose silken dress clung to a slender form, whose soft brown hair escaped in wayward tendrils from the pearl fillet that bound her brow. It was a face more sweet than beautiful, and veiled in a mist of dreams; the face of one who has not yet raised her head to look into the eyes of life.

The other woman was rich in beauty and very woman; as she bent low over the sill her white bosom lay bared to the rays of the moon, and the jewels that decked it glittered with the heaving of her breath. The girl beside her stood upright; so slender was she that her downcast eyes rested on her girdle; in her hands she clasped a crucifix.

There was no sound without save the gentle rub of the water against the posts; within, on the stillness of the air, one heard the measured breathing of the sleeper.

'If he ask for your hand,' said the woman to the girl, 'what answer will you make?'

She waited an instant, then replied:

'Time enough, aunt, when he asks it; and he will not ask.'

The woman, still bending low over the cushioned sill, turned on her elbow and looked up at her niece.

'He will ask it,' she said; 'I feel it, I know it.'

The girl's bosom heaved; she was so spare, one seemed to see the throbbing of her heart, so near it beat to the silken gown. She held the crucifix in both hands, and pressed between her thumbs tremulously that failing head wide-mouthed with grief and death.

'A man,' she replied—and the words came slowly, disjointedly—'a man who does not love a woman, does not ask her to be his wife.'

The other laughed lightly.

'And why should he not love you?'

'If he did,' said the girl with great simplicity, 'I should have felt it before now.'

'Yet he comes here almost daily.'

'He is my uncle's nephew.'

'He always has a smile for you, a pleasant word.'

'He takes me for a child.'

'He gave you that crucifix.'

'He is kind.'

'Yesterday I saw him take your hand at parting—not thumb within thumb, but otherwise—thus, palm to palm.'

The girl's cheek flamed.

'It was mere accident,' said she.

There came a moment's silence; the plash of an oar sounded on the water.

The woman stood up and laid her soft hands, like a necklet, about the girl's throat.

'Up with that head! Up!' said she. 'Are you colder that the moon—or does the chill of the convent cling about your heart?'

And she smiled, probing the girl's dim eyes.

'You love him!'

'No.'

'You love him!'

'No.'

'You love him!'

The maiden's eyes filled with tears; struggling against the soft pressure of the hands at her throat, she bent her head low.

'Perhaps,' she said—'perhaps. . . .'

The door opened and a man entered the room; no mere youth, a man in the pride of his strength, vigorous, handsome, aglow with consciousness of life.

The sleeper awoke and the new-comer was made welcome; he kissed the hand of his uncle's wife and, with a smile upon his lips, made a series of mock bows to the young girl, proclaiming himself the humblest of her servants. She laughed gaily, sweetly, but was too timid to reply as her mood prompted, with feigned dignity; she could only look at him with merry eye and laugh.

Then the women sat; the one near her husband, under the lamp; the other somewhat apart, opposite the young man who stood to the left, leaning against a chest of carved wood. The six eyes were turned upon him; as he looked from face to face he was met by smiles.—There are some such, human magnets who gather to them unfailingly the observance of those around, claiming response.

The girl sat on a low stool before him, slightly in the shade, and looked up into his face; silent she sat, yet the voice of her heart rose louder to our ears than the voice of him that jested there, or the laughter that answered him so easily.

'I love you! I love you!' cried the heart of the girl. 'The first time I beheld you I flew to your bosom as a bird to its nest, and never shall I leave you more. Death may come to tear me from you, death, but no other. Death!—let me die for you! How else shall I prove my submission? What am I that I should aspire to be yours? You shine above me as the sun shines from Heaven; sometimes joy blossoms forth in flowers beneath your gaze; but they wither all, pierced by the thorns of grief. I dare to love you, yet what am I? The jewel on your finger, the chain about your neck, these would I be. Yet am I nothing but a grey pearl without lustre,—and the world holds others, rainbow-touched.'

Here the voice of her heart fell and faded; the young man had ceased speaking, the white head nodded in sleep. Not a breath stirred in the room; without, there was no sound but the far-away cry of a gondolier as he turned some distant corner.

The girl rose and went to the window. 'Go, now,' whispered the woman, and left the room.

Treading lightly, the young man approached the window and bent over the girl.

'Where are your thoughts?' asked he. 'In the moon there behind the chimneys?'

She started, she had not heard him come; he was very near her, she tried to answer, but could not.

The young man then stretched his hand out over her shoulder and laid it on the crucifix, so that his fingers were mingled with hers that held it.

'Madonna,' asked he, 'are you going to turn nun? Why do you carry this all day with you?'

Her fingers trembled under his, she had no strength, poor child, and only half the will to disengage them. It seemed to her an eternity that they stood thus shoulder on shoulder; and something held her at the throat, she could not speak.

'Are you going to turn nun?' asked he again.

The girl shook her head and with great effort answered:

'No, not yet.'

'Not yet? Some day, then?'

'Perhaps.'

His fingers held her closer and closer.

'I dream! I dream!' cried the heart of the girl. 'Let me die now, O God!'

The young man bent so low that his hair touched hers.

'Never!' he whispered. 'The shears shall never approach this head. Give your love to Heaven if you will, but give it first to me.'

The girl with sudden effort freed herself and stood upright beside the window. She looked up into the eyes of her suitor like a frightened child, and flattened the cross against her breast.

'I don't understand,' said she.

He held both hands out.

'I want you for my wife.'

She stared at him an instant dumbly, then her head fell back a little, her eyelids drooped, and her lips parted in a smile of wondrous joy— the smile of a lost spirit that beholds the gates of Paradise.

'Will you?' asked he; and he bent his face towards her.

Sometimes in her dreams she had hovered round such a thought, and dared to wish—without looking the wish in the face, as it were—that some day this, even this, might come to pass. But now a sudden fear seized her, and she drew back.

'Wait—wait,' she said; and she wept, partly for joy, partly for shame of her emotion.

The young man understood the gesture of her outspread hand and left her, treading on tip-toe towards the door; and the girl, bending over the sill once more, and over the crucifix, put forth a wordless prayer unto Him that Gives.

Now this is what we saw.

As the young man reached the door it opened softly, and there behind it stood his uncle's wife.

She raised her eyebrows.

'Well?' said she.

'Well,' said he; and his eyes rested an instant on the jewel that glittered low on her breast, illumined by the lamp that hung on the stairs.

The woman raised her soft hand and tucked a curl behind his ear; then they smiled and, looking into each other's eyes, slowly kissed with parted lip.

ERNEST DOWSON

The Statute of Limitations

During five years of an almost daily association with Michael Garth, in a solitude of Chili, which threw us, men of common speech, though scarcely of common interests, largely on each other's tolerance, I had grown, if not into an intimacy with him, at least into a certain familiarity, through which the salient features of his history, his character reached me. It was a singular character, and an history rich in instruction. So much I gathered from hints, which he let drop long before I had heard the end of it. Unsympathetic as the man was to me, it was impossible not to be interested by it. As our acquaintance advanced, it took (his character I mean) more and more the aspect of a difficult problem in psychology, that I was passionately interested in solving: to study it was my recreation, after watching the fluctuating course of nitrates. So that when I had achieved fortune, and might have started home immediately, my interest induced me to wait more than three months, and return in the same ship with him. It was through this delay that I am enabled to transcribe the issue of my impressions: I found them edifying, if only for their singular irony.

From his own mouth indeed I gleaned but little; although during our voyage home, in those long nights when we paced the deck together under the Southern Cross, his reticence occasionally gave way, and I obtained glimpses of a more intimate knowledge of him than the whole of our juxtaposition on the station had ever afforded me. I guessed more, however, than he told me; and what was lacking I pieced together later, from the talk of the girl to whom I broke the news of his death. He named her to me, for the first time, a day or two before that happened: a piece of confidence so unprecedented, that I must have been blind, indeed, not to have foreseen what it prefaced. I had seen her face the first time I entered his house, where her photograph hung on a conspicuous wall: the charming, oval face of a young girl, little more

372

than a child, with great eyes, that one guessed, one knew not why, to be the colour of violets, looking out with singular wistfulness from a waving cloud of dark hair. Afterwards, he told me that it was the picture of his *fiancée*: but, before that, signs had not been wanting by which I had read a woman in his life.

Iquique is not Paris; it is not even Valparaiso; but it is a city of civilization; and but two days' ride from the pestilential stew, where we nursed our lives doggedly on quinine and hope, the ultimate hope of evasion. The lives of most Englishmen yonder, who superintend works in the interior, are held on the same tenure: you know them by a certain savage, hungry look in their eyes. In the meantime, while they wait for their luck, most of them are glad enough when business calls them down for a day or two to Iquique. There are shops and streets, lit streets through which blackeyed Senoritas pass in their lace mantilas; there are *cafés* too; and faro for those who reck of it; and bull fights, and newspapers younger than six weeks; and in the harbour, taking in their fill of nitrates, many ships, not to be considered without envy, because they are coming, within a limit of days to England. But Iquique had no charm for Michael Garth, and when one of us must go, it was usually I, his subordinate, who being delegated, congratulated myself on his indifference. Hard-earned dollars melted at Iquique; and to Garth, life in Chili had long been solely a matter of amassing them. So he stayed on, in the prickly heat of Agnas Blancas, and grimly counted the days, and the money (although his nature, I believe, was fundamentally generous, in his set concentration of purpose he had grown morbidly avaricious) which should restore him to his beautiful mistress. Morose, reticent, unsociable as he had become, he had still, I discovered by degrees, a leaning towards the humanities, a nice taste, such as could only be the result of much knowledge, in the fine things of literature. His infinitesimal library, a few French novels, an Horace, and some well thumbed volumes of the modern English poets in the familiar edition of Tauchnitz, he put at my disposal, in return for a collection, somewhat similar, although a little larger, of my own. In his rare moments of amiability, he could talk on such matters with *verve* and originality: more usually he preferred to pursue with the bitterest animosity an abstract fetish which he called his 'luck'. He was by temperament an enraged pessimist; and I could believe, that he seriously attributed to

Providence, some quality inconceivably malignant, directed in all things personally against himself. His immense bitterness and his careful avarice, alike, I could explain, and in a measure justify, when I came to understand that he had felt the sharpest stings of poverty, and, moreover, was passionately in love, in love *comme on ne l'est plus*. As to what his previous resources had been, I knew nothing, nor why they had failed him; but I gathered that the crisis had come, just when his life was complicated by the sudden blossoming of an old friendship into love, in his case, at least, to be complete and final. The girl too was poor; they were poorer than most poor persons: how could he refuse the post, which, through the good offices of a friend, was just then unexpectedly offered him? Certainly, it was abroad; it implied five years' solitude in Equatorial America. Separation and change were to be accounted; perhaps, disease and death, and certainly his 'luck', which seemed to include all these. But it also promised, when the term of his exile was up, and there were means of shortening it, a certain competence, and very likely wealth; escaping those other contingencies, marriage. There seemed no other way. The girl was very young: there was no question of an early marriage; there was not even a definite engagement. Garth would take no promise from her: only for himself, he was her bound lover while he breathed; would keep himself free to claim her, when he came back in five years, or ten, or twenty, if she had not chosen better. He would not bind her; but I can imagine how impressive his dark, bitter face must have made this renunciation to the little girl with the violet eyes; how tenderly she repudiated her freedom. She went out as a governess, and sat down to wait. And absence only rivetted faster the chain of her affection: it set Garth more securely on the pedestal of her idea; for in love it is most usually the reverse of that social maxim, *les absents ont toujours tort*, which is true.

Garth, on his side, writing to her, month by month, while her picture smiled on him from the wall, if he was careful always to insist on her perfect freedom, added, in effect, so much more than this, that the renunciation lost its benefit. He lived in a dream of her; and the memory of her eyes and her hair was a perpetual presence with him, less ghostly than the real company among whom he mechanically transacted his daily business. Burnt away and consumed by desire of her living arms, he was counting the hours which still prevented him from them. Yet, when his five years were done, he delayed his return, although his economies had justified it; settled down for another term of five years, which was to be prolonged to seven. Actually, the memory of his old poverty, with its attendant dishonours, was grown a fury, pursuing him ceaselessly with whips. The lust of gain, always for the girl's sake, and so, as it were, sanctified, had become a second nature to him; an intimate madness, which left him no peace. His worst nightmare was to wake with a sudden shock, imagining that he had lost everything, that he was reduced to his former poverty: a cold sweat would break all over him before he had mastered the horror. The recurrence of it, time after time, made him vow grimly, that he would go home a rich man, rich enough to laugh at the fantasies of his luck. Latterly, indeed, this seemed to have changed; so that his vow was fortunately kept. He made money lavishly at last: all his operations were successful, even those which seemed the wildest gambling: and the most forlorn speculations turned round, and shewed a pretty harvest, when Garth meddled with their stock.

And all the time he was waiting there, and scheming, at Agnas Blancas, in a feverish concentration of himself upon his ultimate reunion with the girl at home, the man was growing old: gradually at first, and insensibly; but towards the end, by leaps and starts, with an increasing consciousness of how he aged and altered, which did but feed his black melancholy. It was borne upon him, perhaps, a little brutally, and not by direct self-examination, when there came another photograph from England. A beautiful face still but certainly the face of a woman, who had passed from the grace of girlhood (seven years now separated her from it), to a dignity touched with sadness: a face, upon which life had already written some of its cruelties. For many days after this arrival, Garth was silent and moody, even beyond his wont: then he studiously concealed it. He threw himself again furiously into his economic battle; he had gone back to the inspiration of that other, older portrait: the charming, oval face of a young girl, almost a child, with great eyes, that one guessed, one knew not why, to be the colour of violets.

As the time of our departure approached, a week or two before we had gone down to Valparaiso, where Garth had business to wind up, I was enabled to study more intimately the morbid demon which possessed him. It was the most singular thing in the world: no man had hated the country more, had been more passionately determined for a period of years to escape from it; and now that his chance was come the emotion with which he viewed it was nearer akin to terror than to the joy of a reasonable man who is about to compass the desire of his life. He had kept the covenant which he had made with himself; he was a rich man, richer than he had ever meant to be. Even now he was full of vigour, and not much past the threshold of middle age, and he was going home to the woman whom for the best part of fifteen years he had adored with an unexampled constancy, whose fidelity had been to him all through that exile as the shadow of a rock in a desert land: he was going home to an honourable marriage. But withal he was a man with an incurable sadness; miserable and afraid. It seemed to me at times that he would have been glad if she had kept her troth less well, had only availed herself of that freedom which he gave her, to disregard her promise. And this was the more strange in that I never doubted the strength of his attachment; it remained engrossing and unchanged, the largest part of his life. No alien shadow had ever come between him and the memory of the little girl with the violet eyes, to whom he at least was bound. But a shadow was there; fantastic it seemed to me at first, too grotesque to be met with argument, but in whose very lack of substance, as I came to see, lay its ultimate strength. The notion of the woman, which now she was, came between him and the girl whom he had loved, whom he still loved with passion, and separated them. It was only on our voyage home, when we walked the deck together interminably during the hot, sleepless nights, that he first revealed to me without subterfuge, the slow agony by which this phantom slew him. And his old bitter conviction of the malignity of his luck, which had lain dormant in the first flush of his material prosperity, returned to him. The apparent change in it seemed to him, just then, the last irony of those hostile powers which had pursued him.

'It came to me suddenly,' he said, 'just before I left Agnas, when I had been adding up my pile and saw there was nothing to keep me, that it was all wrong. I had been a blamed fool! I might have gone home years ago. Where is the best of my life? Burnt out, wasted, buried in that cursed oven! Dollars? If I had all the metal in Chili, I couldn't buy one day of youth. Her youth too; that has gone with the rest; that's the worst part!'

Despite all my protests, his despondency increased as the steamer ploughed her way towards England, with the ceaseless throb of her screw, which was like the panting of a great beast. Once, when we had been talking of other matters, of certain living poets whom he favoured, he broke off with a quotation from the 'Prince's Progress' of Miss Rossetti:

> Ten years ago, five years ago,
>   One year ago,
> Even then you had arrived in time,
>   Though somewhat slow;
> Then you had known her living face
>   Which now you cannot know.

He stopped sharply, with a tone in his voice which seemed to intend, in the lines, a personal instance.

'I beg your pardon!' I protested. 'I don't see the analogy. You haven't loitered; you don't come too late. A brave woman has waited for you; you have a fine felicity before you: it should be all the better, because you have won it laboriously. For Heaven's sake, be reasonable!' He shook his head sadly; then added, with a gesture of sudden passion, looking out over the taffrail, at the heaving gray waters: 'It's finished. I haven't any longer the courage.' 'Ah!' I exclaimed impatiently, 'say once for all, outright, that you are tired of her, that you want to back out of it.' 'No,' he said drearily, 'it isn't that. I can't reproach myself with the least wavering. I have had a single passion; I have given my life to it; it is there still, consuming me. Only the girl I loved: it's as if she had died. Yes, she is dead, as dead as Helen: and I have not the consolation of knowing where they have laid her. Our marriage will be a ghastly mockery: a marriage of corpses. Her heart, how can she give it me? She gave it years ago to the man I was, the man who is dead. We, who are left, are nothing to one another, mere strangers.'

One could not argue with a perversity so infatuate: it was useless to point out, that in life a distinction so arbitrary as the one which haunted him does not exist. It was only left me to wait, hoping that in the actual event of their meeting, his malady would be healed. But this meeting, would it ever be compassed? There were moments when his dread of it seemed to have grown so extreme, that he would be capable of any cowardice, any compromise to postpone it, to render it impossible. He was afraid that she would read his revulsion in his eyes, would suspect how time and his very constancy had given her the one rival with whom she could never compete; the memory of her old self, of her gracious girlhood, which was dead. Might not she too, actually, welcome a reprieve; however readily she would have submitted, out of honour or lassitude, to a marriage which could only be a parody of what might have been?

At Lisbon, I hoped that he had settled these questions, had grown reasonable and sane, for he wrote a long letter to her which was subsequently a matter of much curiosity to me; and he wore, for a day or two afterwards, an air almost of assurance which deceived me. I wondered what he had put in that epistle, how far he had explained himself, justified his curious attitude. Or was it simply a *résumé*, a conclusion to those many letters which he had written at Agnas Blancas, the last one which he would ever address to the little girl of the earlier photograph?

Later, I would have given much to decide this, but she herself, the woman who read it, maintained unbroken silence. In return, I kept a secret from her, my private interpretation of the accident of his death. It seemed to me a knowledge tragical enough for her, that he should have died as he did, so nearly in English waters; within a few days of the home coming, which they had passionately expected for years.

It would have been mere brutality to afflict her further, by lifting the veil of obscurity, which hangs over that calm, moonless night, by pointing to the note of intention in it. For it is in my experience, that accidents so opportune do not in real life occur, and I could not forget that, from Garth's point of view, death was certainly a solution. Was it not, moreover, precisely a solution, which so little time before he had the appearance of having found? Indeed when the first shock of his death was past, I could feel that it was after all a solution: with his 'luck' to handicap him, he had perhaps avoided worse things than the death he met. For the luck of such a man, is it not his temperament, his character? Can any one escape from that? May it not have been an escape for the poor devil himself, an escape too for the woman who loved him, that he chose to drop down, fathoms down, into the calm, irrecoverable depths of the Atlantic, when he did, bearing with him at least an unspoilt ideal, and leaving her a memory that experience could never tarnish, nor custom stale?

LAURENCE HOUSMAN

The Story of the Herons

A long time ago there lived a King and a Queen who loved each other dearly. They had both fallen in love at first sight; and as their love began so it went on through all their life. Yet this, which was the cause of all their happiness, was the cause also of all their misfortunes.

In his youth, when he was a beautiful young bachelor, the King had had the ill-luck to attract the heart of a jealous and powerful Fairy; and though he never gave her the least hope or encouragement, when she heard that his love had been won at first sight by a mere mortal, her rage and resentment knew no bounds. She said nothing, however, but bided her time.

After they had been married a year the Queen presented her husband with a little daughter; before she was yet a day old she was the most beautiful object in the world, and life seemed to promise her nothing but fortune and happiness.

The family Fairy came to the blessing of the new-born; and she, looking at it as it lay beautifully asleep in its cradle, and seeing that it had already as much beauty and health as the heart could desire, promised it love as the next best gift it was within her power to offer. The Queen, who knew how much happiness her own love had brought her, was kissing the good Fairy with all the warmth of gratitude, when a black kite came and perched upon the window sill crying: 'And I will give her love at first sight! The first living thing that she sets eyes on she shall love to distraction, whether it be man or monster, prince or pauper, bird, beast or reptile.' And as the wicked Fairy spoke she clapped her wings, and up through the boards of the floor, and out from under the bed, and in through the window, came a crowd of all the ugliest shapes in the world. Thick and fast they came, gathering about the cradle and lifting their heads over the edge of it, waiting for the poor little Princess to wake up and fall in love at first sight with one of them.

Luckily the child was asleep; and the good Fairy, after driving away the black kite and the crowd of beasts it had called to its aid, wrapped the Princess up in a shawl and carried her away to a dark room where no glimmer of light could get in.

She said to the Queen: 'Till I can devise a better way, you must keep her in the dark; and when you take her into the open air you must blindfold her eyes. Some day, when she is of a fit age, I will bring a handsome Prince for her; and only to him shall you unblindfold her at last, and make love safe for her.'

She went, leaving the King and Queen deeply stricken with grief over the harm which had befallen their daughter. They did not dare to present even themselves before her eyes lest love for them, fatal and consuming, should drive her to distraction. In utter darkness the Queen would sit and cherish her daughter, clasping her to her breast, and calling her by all sweet names; but the little face, except by stealth when it was sound asleep, she never dared to see, nor did the baby-Princess know the face of the mother who loved her.

By and by, however, the family Fairy came again, saying: 'Now, I have a plan by which your child may enjoy the delights of seeing, and no ill come of it.' And she caused to be made a large chamber, the whole of one side of which was a mirror. High up in the opposite wall were windows so screened that from below no one could look out of them, but across on to the mirror came all the sweet sights of the world, glimpses of wood and field, and the sun and the moon and the stars, and of every bird as it flew by. So the little Princess was brought and set in a screened place looking towards the mirror, and there her eyes learned gradually all the beautiful things of the world. Over the screen, in the glass before her, she learned to know her mother's face, and to love it dearly in a gentle child-like fashion; and when she could talk she became very wise, understanding all that was told her about the danger of looking at anything alive, except by its reflection in the glass.

When she went out into the open air for her health, she always wore a bandage over her eyes, lest she should look, and love something too well: but in the chamber of the mirror her eyes were free to see whatever they could. The good Fairy, making herself invisible, came and taught her to read and make music, and draw; so that before she was fifteen she was the most charming and accomplished, as well as the most beautiful Princess of her day.

At last the Fairy said that the time was come for her world of reflections to be made real, and she went away to fetch the ideal Prince that the Princess might at first sight fall in love with him.

The very day after she was gone, as the morning was fine, the Princess went out with one of her maids for a walk through the woods. Over her patient eyes she wore a bandage of green silk, through which she felt the sunlight fall pleasantly.

Out of doors the Princess knew most things by their sounds. She passed under rustling leaves, and along by the side of running water; and at last she heard the silence of the water, and knew that she was standing by the great fish-pond in the middle of the wood. Then she said to her waiting-woman, 'Is there not some great bird fishing out there, for I hear the dipping of his bill, and the water falling off it as he draws out the fish?'

And just as she was saying that, the wicked Fairy, who had long bided her time, coming softly up from behind, pushed the waiting-woman off the bank into the deep water of the pond. Then she snatched away the silk bandage, and before the Princess had time to think or close her eyes, she had lost her heart to a great heron, that was standing half-way up to his feathers fishing among the reeds.

The Princess, with her eyes set free, laughed for joy at the sight of him. She stretched out her arms from the bank and cried most musically for the bird to come to her; and he came in grave stately fashion, with trailing legs, and slow sobbing creak of his wings, and settled down on the bank beside her. She drew his slender neck against her white throat, and laughed and cried with her arms round him, loving him so that she forgot all in the world beside. And the heron looked gravely at her with kind eyes, and, bird-like, gave her all the love he could, but not more; and so, presently, casting his grey wings abroad, lifted himself and sailed slowly back to his fishing among the reeds.

The waiting-woman had got herself out of the water, and stood wringing her clothes and her hands beside the Princess. 'O, sweet mistress,' she cried, with lamentation, 'now is all the evil come about which it was our whole aim to avoid! And what, and what will the Queen your mother say?'

But the Princess answered, smiling, 'Foolish girl, I had no thought of what happiness meant till now! See you where my love is gone? and did you notice the bend of his neck, and the exceeding length of his legs, and the stretch of his grey wings as he flew? This pond is his hall of mirrors, wherein he sees the reflection of all his world. Surely I, from my hall of mirrors, am the true mate for him!'

Her maid, seeing how far the evil had gone, and that no worse could now happen, ran back to the palace and curdled all the court's blood with her news. The King and the Queen and all their nobility rushed down, and there they found the Princess with the heron once more in her arms, kissing and fondling it with all the marks of a sweet and maidenly passion. 'Dear mother,' she said, as soon as she saw the Queen, 'the happiness, which you feared would be sorrow, has come; and it is such happiness I have no name for it! And the evil that you so dreaded, see how sweet it is! And how sweet it is to see all the world with my own eyes and you also at last!' And for the first time in her life she kissed her mother's face in the full light of day.

But her mother hung sobbing upon her neck, 'O, my darling, my beautiful,' she wept, 'does your heart belong for ever to this grey bird?'

Her daughter answered, 'He is more than all the world to me! Is he not goodly to look upon? Have you considered the bend of his neck, the length of his legs, and the waving of his wings; his skill also when he fishes: what imagination, what presence of mind!'

'Alas, alas,' sorrowed the Queen, 'dear daughter, is this all true to you?'

'Mother,' cried the Princess, clinging to her with entreaty, 'is all the world blind but me?'

The heron had become quite fond of the Princess; wherever she went it followed her, and, indeed, without it nowhere would she go. Whenever it was near her, the Princess laughed and sang, and when it was out of her sight she became sad as night. All the courtiers wept to see her in such bondage. 'Ah,' said she, 'your eyes have been worn out with looking at things so long; mine have been kept for me in a mirror.'

When the good family Fairy came (for she was at once sent for by the Queen, and told of all that had happened), she said, 'Dear Madam, there are but two things you can do: either you can wring the heron's neck, and leave the Princess to die of grief; or you can make the Princess happy in her own way, by——' Her voice dropped, and she looked from the King to the Queen before she went on. 'At her birth I gave your daughter love for my gift; now it is her's, will you let her keep it?'

The King and the Queen looked softly at each other. 'Do not take love from her,' said they, 'let her keep it!'

'There is but one way,' answered the Fairy.

'Do not tell me the way,' said the Queen weeping, 'only let the way be!'

So they went with the Fairy down to the great pond, and there sat the Princess, with the grey heron against her heart. She smiled as she saw them come. 'I see good in your hearts toward me!' she cried. 'Dear godmother, give me the thing that I want, that my love may be happy!'

Then the Fairy stroked her but once with her wand, and two grey herons suddenly rose up from the bank, and sailed away to a hiding-place in the reeds.

The Fairy said to the Queen, 'You have made your daughter happy; and still she will have her voice and her human heart, and will remember you with love and gratitude; but her greatest love will be to the grey heron, and her home among the reeds.'

So the changed life of the Princess began; every day her mother went down to the pool and called, and the Princess came rising up out of the reeds, and folded her grey wings over her mother's heart. Every day her mother said, 'Daughter of mine, are you happy?'

And the Princess answered her, 'Yes, for I love and am loved.'

Yet each time the mother heard more and more of a note of sadness come into her daughter's voice; and at last one day she said, 'Answer me truly, as the mother who brought you into the world, whether you be happy in your heart of hearts or no?'

Then the heron-Princess laid her head on the Queen's heart, and said, 'Mother, my heart is breaking with love!'

'For whom, then?' asked the Queen astonished.

'For my grey heron, whom I love, and who loves me so much. And yet it is love that divides us, for I am still troubled with a human heart, and often it aches with sorrow because all the love in it can never be fully understood or shared by my heron; and I have my human voice left, and that gives me a hundred things to say all day, for which there is no word in herons' language, and so he cannot understand them. Therefore these things only make a gulf between him and me. For all the other grey herons in the pools there is happiness, but not for me who have too big a heart between my wings.'

Her mother said softly, 'Wait, wait, little heron-daughter, and it shall be well with you!' Then she went to the Fairy and said, 'My daughter's heart is lonely among the reeds, for the grey heron's love covers but half of it. Give her some companions of her own kind that her hours may become merry again!'

So the Fairy took and turned five of the Princess's lady's-maids into herons, and sent them down to the pool.

The five herons stood each on one leg in the shallows of the pool, and cried all day long; and their tears fell down into the water and frightened away the fish that came their way. For they had human hearts that cried out to be let go. 'O, cruel, cruel,' they wept, whenever the heron-Princess approached, 'see what we suffer because of you, and what they have made of us for your sake!'

The Princess came to her mother and said, 'Dear mother, take them away, for their cry wearies me, and the pool is bitter with their tears! They only awake the human part of my heart that wants to sleep; presently, may be, if it is let alone, it will forget itself.'

Her mother said, 'It is my coming every day also that keeps it awake.' The Princess answered, 'This sorrow belongs to my birthright; you must still come; but for the others, let the Fairy take them away.'

So the Fairy came and released the five lady's-maids whom she had changed into herons. And they came up out of the water, stripping themselves of their grey feather-skins and throwing them back into the pool. The Fairy said, 'You foolish maids, you have thrown away a gift that you should have valued; these skins you could have kept and held as heirlooms in your family.'

The five maids answered, 'We want to forget that there are such things as herons in the world!'

After much thought the Queen said to the Fairy, 'You have changed a Princess into a heron, and five maids into herons and back again; cannot you change one heron into a Prince?' But the Fairy answered sadly, 'Our power has limits; we can bring down, but we cannot bring up, if there be no heart to answer our call. The five maids only followed their hearts, that were human, when I called them back; but a heron has only a heron's heart, and unless his heart become too great for a bird and he earn a human one, I cannot change him to a higher form.' 'How can he earn a human one?' asked the Queen. 'Only if he love the Princess so well that his love for her becomes stronger than his life,' answered the Fairy. 'Then he will have earned a human body, and then I can give him the form that his heart suits best. There may be a chance, if we wait for it and are patient, for the Princess's love is great and may work miracles.'

A little while after this, the Queen watching, saw that the two herons were making a nest among the reeds. 'What have you there?' said the mother to her daughter. 'A little hollow place,' answered the heron-Princess, 'and in it the moon lies.' A little while after she said again, 'What have you there, now, little daughter?' And her daughter answered, 'Only a small hollow space; but in it two moons lie.'

The Queen told the family Fairy how in a hollow of the reeds lay two moons. 'Now,' said the Fairy, 'we will wait no longer. If your daughter's love has touched the heron's heart and made it grow larger than a bird's, I can help them both to happiness; but if not, then birds they must still remain.'

Among the reeds the heron said in bird language to his wife, 'Go and stretch your wings for a little while over the water; it is weary work to wait here so long in the reeds.' The heron-Princess looked at him with her bird's eyes, and all the human love in her heart strove, like a fountain that could not get free, to make itself known through them; also her tongue was full of the longing to utter sweet words, but she kept them back, knowing they were beyond the heron's power to understand. So she answered merely in heron's language, 'Come with me, and I will come!'

They rose, wing beating beside wing; and the reflection of their grey breasts slid out under them over the mirror of the pool.

Higher they went and higher, passing over the tree tops, and keeping time together as they flew. All at once the wings of the grey heron flagged, then took a deep beat; he cried to the heron-Princess, 'Turn, and come home, yonder there is danger flying to meet us!' Before them hung a brown blot in the air, that winged and grew large. The two herons turned and flew back. 'Rise,' cried the grey heron, 'we must rise!' and the Princess knew what was behind, and struggled with the whole strength of her wings for escape.

The grey heron was bearing ahead on stronger wing. 'With me, with me!' he cried. 'If it gets above us, one of us is dead!' But the falcon had fixed his eye on the Princess for his quarry, and flew she fast, or flew she slow, there was little chance for her now. Up and up she strained, but still she was behind her mate, and still the falcon gained.

The heron swung back to her side; she saw the anguish and fear of his downward glance as his head ranged by hers. Past her the falcon went, towering for the final swoop.

The Princess cried in heron's language, 'Farewell, dear mate, and farewell, two little moons among the reeds!' But the grey heron only kept closer to her side.

Overhead the falcon closed in its wings and fell like a dead weight out of the clouds. 'Drop!' cried the grey heron to his mate.

At his word she dropped; but he stayed, stretching up his wings, and, passing between the descending falcon and its prey, caught in his own body the death-blow from its beak. Drops of his blood fell upon the heron-Princess.

He stricken in body, she in soul, together they fell down to the margin of the pool. The falcon still clung fleshing its beak in the neck of its prey. The heron-Princess threw back her head, and, darting furiously, struck her own sharp bill deep into the falcon's breast. The bird threw out its wings with a hoarse cry and fell back dead, with a little tuft of the grey heron's feathers still upon its beak.

The heron-Princess crouched down, and covered with her wings the dying form of her mate; in her sorrow she spoke to him in her own tongue, forgetting her bird's language. The grey heron lifted his head, and, gazing tenderly, answered her with a human voice:

'Dear wife,' he said, 'at last I have the happiness so long denied to me of giving utterance in the speech that is your own to the love that you have put into my heart. Often I have heard you speak and have not understood; now something has touched my heart, and changed it, so that I can both speak and understand.'

'O, beloved!' She laid her head down by his. 'The ends of the world belong to us now. Lie down, and die gently by my side, and I will die with you, breaking my heart with happiness.'

'No,' said the grey heron, 'do not die yet! Remember the two little moons that lie in the hollow among the reeds.' Then he laid his head down by hers, being too weak to say more.

They folded their wings over each other, and closed their eyes; nor did they know that the Fairy was standing by them, till she stroked them both softly with her wand, saying to each of them the same words:

'Human heart, and human form, come out of the grey heron!'

And out of the grey heron-skins came two human forms; the one was the Princess restored again to her own shape, but the other was a beautiful youth, with a bird-like look about the eyes, and long slender limbs. The Princess, as she gazed on him, found hardly any change, for love remained the same, binding him close to her heart; and, grey heron or beautiful youth, he was all one to her now.

Then came the Queen, weeping for joy, and embracing them both, and after them, the Fairy. 'O, how good an ending,' she cried, 'has come to that terrible dream! Let it never be remembered or mentioned between us more!' And she began to lead the way back to the palace.

But the youth, to whom the Fairy gave the name of Prince Heron, turned and took up the two heron-skins which he and his wife had let fall, and followed, carrying them upon his arm. And as they came past the bed of reeds, the Princess went aside, and, stooping down in a certain place drew out from thence something which she came carrying, softly wrapped in the folds of her gown.

With what rejoicing the Princess and her husband were welcomed by the King and all the Court needs not to be told. For a whole month the festivities continued; and whenever she showed herself, there was the Princess sitting with two eggs in her lap, and her hands over them to keep them warm. The King was impatient. 'Why cannot you send them down to the poultry yard to be hatched?' he said.

But the Princess replied smiling, 'My moons are my own, and I will keep them to myself.'

'Do you hear?' she said one day, at last; and everybody who listened could hear something going 'tap, tap', inside the shells. Presently the eggs cracked, and out of each, at the same moment, came a little grey heron.

When she saw that they were herons, the Queen wrung her hands. 'O, Fairy,' she cried, 'what a disappointment is this! I had hoped two beautiful babies would have come out of those shells.'

But the Fairy said, 'It is no matter. Half of their hearts are human already; birds' hearts do not beat so. If you wish it, I can change them.' So she stroked them softly with her wand, saying to each, 'Human heart, and human form, come out of the grey heron!'

Yet she had to stroke them three times before they would turn; and she said to the Princess, 'My dear, you were too satisfied with your lot when you laid these eggs. I doubt if more than a quarter of them is human.'

'I was very satisfied,' said the Princess, and she laughed across to her husband.

At last, however, on the third stroke of the wand, the heron's skins dropped off, and they changed into a pair of very small babies, a boy and a girl. But the difference between them and other children was, that instead of hair, their heads were covered with a fluff of downy grey feathers; also they had queer, round, bird-like eyes, and were able to sleep standing.

Now, after this the happiness of the Princess was great; but the Fairy said to her, 'Do not let your husband see the heron-skins again for some while, lest with the memory a longing for his old life should return to him and take him away from you. Only by exchange with another can he ever get back his human form again, if he surrenders it of his own free will. And who is there so poor that he would willingly give up his human form to become a bird?'

So the Princess took the four coats of feather—her own and her husband's and her two children's—and hid them away in a closet of which she alone kept the key. It was a little gold key, and to make it safe she hung it about her neck, and wore it night and day.

The Prince said to her, 'What is that little key that you wear always hung round your neck?'

She answered him, 'It is the key to your happiness and mine. Do not ask more than that!' At that there was a look in his face that made her say, 'You *are* happy, are you not?'

He kissed her, saying, 'Happy indeed! Have I not you to make me so?' Yet though, indeed, he told no untruth, and was happy whenever she was with him, there were times when a restlessness and a longing for wings took hold of him; for, as yet, the life of a man was new and half strange to him, and a taint of his old life still mixed itself with his blood. But to her he was ashamed to say what might seem a complaint against his great fortune; so when she said 'happiness', he thought, 'Is it just the turning of that key that I want before my happiness can be perfect?'

Therefore, one night when the early season of spring made his longing strong in him, he took the key from the Princess while she slept, and opened the little closet in which hung the four feather coats. And when he saw his own, all at once he remembered the great pools of water, and how they lay in the shine and shadow of the moonlight, while the fish rose in rings upon their surface. And at that so great a longing came into him to revisit his old haunts that he reached out his hand and took down the heron-skin from its nail and put it over himself; so that immediately his old life took hold of him, and he flew out of the window in the form of a grey heron.

In the morning the Princess found the key gone from her neck, and her husband's place empty. She went in haste to the closet, and there stood the door wide with the key in it, and only three heron-skins hanging where four had used to be.

Then she came crying to the family Fairy, 'My husband has taken his heron-skin and is gone! Tell me what I can do!'

The Fairy pitied her with all her heart, but could do nothing. 'Only by exchange,' said she, 'can he get back his human shape; and who is there so poor that he would willingly lose his own form to become a bird? Only your children, who are but half human, can put their heron-skins on and off as they like and when they like.'

In deep grief the Princess went to look for her husband down by the pools in the wood. But now his shame and sorrow at having deceived her were so great that as soon as he heard her voice he hid himself among the reeds, for he knew now that, having put on his heron-skin again, he could not take it off unless some one gave him a human form in exchange.

At last, however, so pitiful was the cry of the Princess for him, that he could bear to hear it no more; but rising up from the reeds came trailing to her sadly over the water. 'Ah, dear love!' she said when he was come to her, 'if I had not distrusted you, you would not have deceived me: thus, for my fault we are punished.' So she sorrowed, and he answered her:

'Nay, dear love, for if I had not deceived you, you would not have distrusted me. I thought I was not happy, yet I feared to tell it you.' Thus they sorrowed together, both laying on themselves the blame and the burden.

Then she said to him: 'Be here for me to-night, for now I must go; but then I shall return.'

She went back to the palace, and told her mother of all that had happened. 'And now,' she said, 'you who know where my happiness lies will not forbid me from following it; for my heart is again with the grey heron.' And the Queen wept, but would not say her no.

So that night the Princess went and kissed her children as they slept standing up in their beds, with their funny feather-pates to one side; and then she took down her skin of feathers and put it on, and became changed once more into a grey heron. And again she went up to the two in their cots, and kissed their birdish heads saying: 'They who can change at will, being but half human, they will come and visit us in the great pool by the wood, and bring back word of us here.'

In the morning the Princess was gone, and the two children when they woke looked at each other and said: 'Did we dream last night?'

They both answered each other 'Yes, first we dreamed that our mother came and kissed us; and we liked that. And then we dreamed that a grey heron came and kissed us, and we liked that better still!' They waved their arms up and down. 'Why have we not wings?' they kept asking. All day long they did this, playing that they were birds. If a window were opened, it was with the greatest difficulty that they were kept from trying to fly through.

In the Court they were known as the 'Feather-pates'; nothing could they be taught at all. When they were rebuked they would stand on one leg and sigh with their heads on one side; but no one ever saw tears come out of their birdish eyes.

Now at night they would dream that two grey herons came and stood by their bedsides, kissing them; 'And where in the world,' they said when they woke, '*are* our wings?'

One day, wandering about in the palace, they came upon the closet in which hung the two little feather coats. 'O!!!' they cried, and opened hard bright eyes at each other, nodding, for now they knew what they would do. 'If we told, they would be taken off us,' they said; and they waited till it was night. Then they crept back and took the two little coats from their pegs, and, putting them on, were turned into two young herons.

Through the window they flew, away down to the great fish-pond in the wood. Their father and mother saw them coming, and clapped their wings for joy. 'See,' they said, 'our children come to visit us, and our hearts are left to us to love with. What further happiness can we want?' But when they were not looking at each other they sighed.

All night long the two young herons stayed with their parents; they bathed, and fished, and flew, till they were weary. Then the Princess showed them the nest among the reeds, and told them all the story of their lives.

'But it is much nicer to be herons than to be real people,' said the young ones, sadly, and became very sorrowful when dawn drew on, and their mother told them to go back to the palace and hang up the feather coats again, and be as they had been the day before.

Long, long the day now seemed to them; they hardly waited till it was night before they took down their feather-skins, and, putting them on, flew out and away to the fish-pond in the wood.

So every night they went, when all in the palace were asleep; and in the morning came back before anyone was astir, and were found by their nurses lying demurely between the sheets, just as they had been left the night before.

One day the Queen when she went to see her daughter said to her, 'My child, your two children are growing less like human beings and more like birds every day. Nothing will they learn or do, but stand all day flapping their arms up and down, and saying, "Where are our wings, where are our wings?" The idea of one of them ever coming to the throne makes your father's hair stand on end under his crown.'

'Oh, mother,' said the heron-Princess, 'I have made a sad bed for you and my father to lie on!'

One day the two children said to each other, 'Our father and mother are sad, because they want to be real persons again, instead of having wings and catching fish the way we like to do. Let us give up being real persons, which is all so much trouble, and such a want of exercise, and make them exchange with us!' But when the two young herons went down to the pond and proposed it to them, their parents said, 'You are young; you do not know what you would be giving up.' Nor would they consent to it at all.

Now one morning it happened that the Feather-pates were so late in returning to the palace that the Queen, coming into their chamber, found the two beds empty; and just as she had turned away to search for them elsewhere, she heard a noise of wings and saw the two young herons come flying in through the window. Then she saw them take off their feather-skins and hang them up in the closet, and after that go and lie down in their beds so as to look as if they had been there all night.

The Queen struck her hands together with horror at the sight, but she crept away softly, so that they did not know they had been found out. But as soon as they were out of their beds and at play in another part of the palace, the Queen went to the closet, and setting fire to the two heron-skins where they hung, burnt them till not a feather of them was left, and only a heap of grey ashes remained to tell what had become of them.

At night, when the Feather-pates went to their cupboards and found their skins gone, and saw what had become of them, their grief knew no bounds. They trembled with fear and rage, and tears rained out of their eyes as they beheld themselves deprived of their bird bodies and made into real persons for good and all.

'We won't be real persons!' they cried. But for all their crying they knew no way out of it. They made themselves quite ill with grief; and that night, for the first time since they had found their way to the closet, they stayed where their nurses had put them, and did not even stand up in their beds to go to sleep. There they lay with gasping mouth, and big bird-like eyes all languid with grief, and hollow grey cheeks.

Presently their father and mother came seeking for them, wondering why they had not come down to the fish-pond as they were wont. 'Where are you, my children?' cried the heron-Princess, putting her head in through the window.

'Here we are, both at death's door!' they cried. 'Come and see us die! Our wicked granddam has burnt our feather-skins and made us into real persons for ever and ever, Amen. But we will die rather!'

The parent herons, when they heard that, flew in through the window and bent down over the little ones' beds.

The two children reached up their arms. 'Give us your feathers!' they cried. 'We shall die if you don't! We *will* die if you don't! O, do!' But still the parent birds hesitated, nor knew what to do.

'Bend down, and let me whisper something!' said the boy to his father: and 'Bend down, and whisper!' cried the girl to her mother. And father and mother bent down over the faces of their sick children. Then these, both together, caught hold of them, and crying, 'Human heart, and human form, exchange with the grey heron!' pulled off their parents' feather-skins, and put them upon themselves.

And there once more stood Prince Heron and the Princess in human shape, while the two children had turned into herons in their place.

The young herons laughed and shouted and clapped their wings for joy. 'Are you not happy now?' cried they. And when their parents saw the joy, not only in their children's eyes, but in each other's, and felt their hearts growing glad in the bodies they had regained, then they owned that the Feather-pates had been wise in their generation, and done well according to their lights.

So it came about that the Prince and the Princess lived happily ever after, and the two young herons lived happily also, and were the best-hearted birds the world ever saw.

In course of time the Prince and Princess had other children, who pleased the old King better than the first had done. But the parents loved none better than the two who lived as herons by the great fish-pond in the wood; nor could there be greater love than was found between these and their younger brothers and sisters, whose nature it was to be real persons.

WALTER BESANT

The Shrinking Shoe

I

'Oh you poor dear!' said the two Elder Sisters in duet, 'you've got to stay at home while we go to the ball. Good night, then. We *are* so sorry for you! We did hope that you were going too!'

'Good night, Elder Sisters,' said the youngest, with a tear just showing in either eye, but not rolling down her cheek. 'Go and be happy. If you *should* see the Prince you may tell him that I am waiting for the Fairy and the Pumpkin and the Mice.'

The Elder Sisters fastened the last button—the sixth, was it? or the tenth perhaps—took one last critical, and reassuring, look at the glass, and departed.

When the door shut the Youngest Sister sat down by the fire; and one, two, three tears rolled down her cheeks.

Mind you, she had very good cause to cry. Many girls cry for much less. She was seventeen: she had understood that she would come out at this visit to London. Coming out, to this country girl, meant just this one dance and nothing more. But no—her sisters were invited and she was not. She was left alone in the house. And she sat down by the fire and allowed herself to be filled with gloom and sadness, and with such thoughts as, in certain antiquated histories, used to be called rebellious. In short, she was in a very bad temper indeed. Never before had she been in such a bad temper. As a general rule she was sweet-tempered as the day is long. But—which is a terrible thing to remember—there are always the possibilities of bad temper in every one: even in Katharine —Katie—Kitty, who generally looked as if she could never, never, never show by any outward sign that she was vexed, or cross, or put out, or rebellious. And now, alas! she was in a bad temper. No hope, no sunshine, no future prospects; her life was blasted—her young spring life. Disaster irretrievable had fallen upon her. She could not go to the ball. What made things worse was, that the more angry she grew the louder she heard the dance music, though the band was distant more than a mile. Quite plainly she heard the musicians. They were playing a valse which she knew—a delicious, delirious, dreamy, swinging valse. She saw her sisters among a crowd of the most lovely girls in the world, whirling in the cadence that she loved upon a floor as smooth as ice, with cavaliers gallant and gay. The room was filled with maidens beautifully dressed, like her sisters, and with young men come to meet and greet them on their way. Oh, happy young men! Oh, happy girls! Katie had been brought up with such simplicity that she envied no other girl, whether for her riches or for her dresses; and was always ready to acknowledge the loveliness and the sweetness and the grace of any number of girls—even of her own age. As regards her own sex, indeed, this child of seventeen had but one fault; she considered twenty as already a serious age, and wondered how anybody could possibly laugh after five-and-twenty. And, as many, or most, girls believe, she thought that beauty was entirely a matter of dress; and that, except on state occasions, no one should think of beauty—*i.e.*, of fine dress.

She sat there for half an hour. She began to think that it would be best to go to bed and sleep off her chagrin, when a Rat-tat-tat at the door roused her. Who was that? Could it—could it—could it be the Fairy with the Pumpkin and the Mice?

'My dear Katie'—it was not the Fairy, but it was the Godmother—'how sorry I am! Quick—lay out the things, Ladbrooke.' Ladbrooke was a maid, and she bore a parcel. 'It's not my fault. The stupid people only brought the things just now. It was my little surprise, dear. We will dress her here, Ladbrooke. I was going to bring the things in good time, to surprise you at the last moment. Never mind: you will only be a little late. I hope and trust the things will fit. I got one of your frocks, and Ladbrooke here can, if necessary——There, Katie! What do you think of that for your first ball dress?'

Katie was so astonished that she could say nothing, not even to thank her godmother. Her heart beat and her hands trembled; the maid dressed her and did her hair; her godmother gave her a necklace of pearls and a little bunch of flowers: she put on the most charming pair of white satin shoes: she found in the parcel a pair of white gloves with ever so many buttons, and a white fan with painted flowers. When she looked at the glass she could not understand it at all; for she was transformed. But never was any girl dressed so quickly.

'Oh!' she cried. 'You *are* a Fairy. And you've got a Pumpkin as well?'

'The Pumpkin is at the door with the Mice. Come, dear. I shall be proud of my *débutante*.'

The odd thing was that all the time she was dressing, and all the time she sat in the carriage, Katie heard that valse tune ringing in her ears, and when they entered the ball-room that very same identical valse was being played, and the smooth floor was covered with dancers, gallant young men and lovely maidens—all as she had seen and heard in her vision. Oh! there is something in the world more than coincidence. There must be; else, why did Katie . . .

'Oh, my dear,' said the Elder Sisters, stopping in their dance, 'you have come at last! We knew you were coming, but we couldn't tell. Shall we tell the Prince you are here?'

Then a young gentleman was presented to her. But Katie was too nervous to look up when he bowed and begged. After a little, Katie found that his step went very well with hers. She was then able to consider things a little. Her first partner in her first ball was quite a young man—she had not caught his name, Mr Geoffrey something— a handsome young man, she thought, but rather shy. He began to talk about the usual things.

'I live in the country,' she said, to explain her ignorance. 'And this is my first ball. So, you see, I do not know any people or anything.'

He danced with her again: she was a wonderfully light dancer; she was strangely graceful; he found her, also, sweet to look at; she had soft eyes and a curiously soft voice, which was as if all the sympathy in all the world had been collected together and deposited in that little brain. He had the good fortune to take her in to supper; and, being a young man at that time singularly open to the charms of maidens, he lavished upon her all the attentions possible. Presently he was so far subdued by her winning manner that he committed the foolishness of Samson with his charmer. He told his secret. Just because she showed a little interest in him, and regarded him with eyes of wonder, he told her the great secret of his life—his ambition, the dream of his youth, his purpose. Next morning he felt he had been a fool. The girl would tell other girls, and they would all laugh together. He felt hot and ashamed for a moment. Then he thought of her eyes, and how they lightened when he whispered; and of her voice, and how it sank when she murmured sympathy and hope and faith. No—with such a girl his secret was safe.

So it was. But for her, if you think of it, was promotion indeed! For a girl who a few days before had been at school, under rules and laws, hardly daring to speak—certainly not daring to have an opinion of her own—now receiving deferential homage from a young man at least four years her senior, and actually being entrusted with his secret ambitions! More; there were other young men waiting about, asking for a dance; all treating her as if—well, modern manners do not treat young ladies with the old reverential courtesy—as if she were a person of considerable importance. But she liked the first young man the best. He had such an honest face, this young man. It was a charming supper, and, with her charming companion, Katie talked quite freely and at her ease. How nice to begin with a partner with whom one could be quite at one's ease! But everything at this ball was delightful.

After the young man had told his secret, blushing profoundly, Katie told hers—how she had as nearly as possible missed her first ball; and how her sisters had gone without her and left her in the cinders, crying.

'Fairy Godmother turned up at the last moment, and when I was dressed and we went out,' she laughed merrily, 'we found the Pumpkin and the Mice turned into a lovely carriage and pair.'

'It is a new version of the old story,' said the young man.

'Yes,' she replied thoughtfully, 'and now all I want is to find the Prince.'

The young man raised his eyes quickly. They said, with great humility, 'If I could only be the Prince!' She read those words, and she blushed and became confused, and they talked no more that night.

'It was all lovely,' she said in the carriage going home. 'All but one thing—one thing that I said—oh, such a stupid thing!'

'What was it you said, Katie?'

'No: I could never tell anybody. It was *too* stupid. Oh! To think of it makes me turn red. It almost spoiled the evening. And he saw it too.'

'What was it, Katie?'

But she would not tell the Elder Sisters.

'Who was it,' asked one of them, 'that took Katie in to supper?'

'A young man named Armiger, I believe. Horace told me,' said the
other Elder. Horace was a cousin. 'Horace says he is a cousin of a Sir
Roland Armiger, about whom I know nothing. Horace says he is a
good fellow—very young yet—an undergraduate somewhat. He is a
nice-looking boy.'

Then the Elder Sisters began to talk about matters really serious
—namely, themselves and their own engagements—and Katie was
forgotten.

Two days after the ball there arrived a parcel addressed to the three
sisters collectively—'The Misses De Lisle'. The three sisters opened it
together, with Evelike curiosity.

It contained a white satin shoe; a silver buckle set with pearls adorned
it, and a row of pearls ran round the open part. A most dainty shoe; a
most attractive shoe; a most bewildering shoe.

'This,' said the Elder Sisters, solemnly, 'must be tried on by all of us
in succession.'

The Elder Sisters began: it was too small for either, though they
squeezed and made faces and an effort and a fuss, and everything that
could be made except making the foot go into the shoe. Then Katie
tried it on. Wonderful to relate, the foot slipped in quite easily. Yet
they say that there is nothing but coincidence in the world.

Katie blushed and laughed and blushed again. Then she folded up
the shoe in its silver paper and carried it away; and nobody ever heard
her mention that shoe again. But everybody knew that she kept it, and
the Elder Sisters marvelled because the young prince did not come to
see that shoe tried on. He did not appear. Why not? Well—because he
was too shy to call.

There are six thousand five hundred and sixty-three variants of this
story, as has been discovered through the invaluable researches of the
Folk-Lore Society, and it would be strange if they all ended in the same
way.

II

The young man told his secret; he revealed what he had never before
whispered to any living person; he told his ambition—the most sacred
thing that a young man possesses or can reveal.

There are many kinds of ambition; many of them are laudable; we are mostly ambitious of those things which seem to the lowest imagination to be within our reach—such, for instance, as the saving of money. Those who aspire to things which seem out of reach suffer the pain and the penalty of the common snub. This young man aspired to things which seemed to other people quite beyond his reach; for he had no money, and his otherwise highly respectable family had no political influence, and such a thing had never before been heard of among his people that one of themselves should aspire to greater greatness than the succession to the family title with the family property. As a part of the new Revolution, which is already upon us, there will be few things indeed which an ambitious young man will consider beyond his reach. At the present moment, if I were to declare my ambition to become, when I grow up, Her Britannic Majesty's Ambassador at Paris, the thing would be actually received with derision. My young life would be blasted with contempt. Wait, however, for fifty years: you shall then see to what heights I will reach out my climbing hands.

Geoffrey Armiger would have soared. He saw before him the cases of Canning, of Burke, of Disraeli, of Robert Lowe, and of many others who started without any political influence and with no money, and he said to himself, 'I, too, will become a Statesman.'

That was the secret which he confided into Katie's ear; it was in answer to a question of hers, put quite as he could have wished, as to his future career. 'I have told no one,' he replied in a low voice, and with conscious flush. 'I have never ventured to tell any one, because my people would not understand; they are not easily moved out of the ordinary groove. There is a family living, and I am to have it: that is the fate to which I am condemned. But——' his lips snapped; resolution flamed in his eyes.

'Oh!' cried Katie. 'It is splendid! You must succeed. Oh! To be a great Statesman. Oh! There is only one thing better—to be a great Poet. You might be both.'

Geoffrey replied modestly that, although he had written verse, he hardly expected to accomplish both greatness in poetry and greatness as a legislator. The latter, he declared, would be good enough for him.

That was the secret which this young man confided to the girl. You must own that, for such a young man to reveal such a secret to this girl, on the very first evening that he met her, argues for the maiden the possession of sympathetic qualities quite above the common.

III

Five years change a boy of twenty into a mature man of twenty-five, and a *débutante* of seventeen into an old woman of twenty-two. The acknowledgment of such a fact may save the historian a vast quantity of trouble.

It was five years after the great event of the ball. The family cousin, Horace, of whom mention has been already made, was sitting in his chambers at ten or eleven in the evening. With him sat his friend Sir Geoffrey Armiger, a young man whom you have already met. The death of his cousin had transformed him from a penniless youth into a baronet with a great estate (which might have been in Spain or Ireland for all the good it was), and with a great fortune in stocks. There was now no occasion for him to take the family living: that had gone to a deserving stranger; a clear field lay open for his wildest ambitions. This bad fortune to the cousin, who was still quite young, happened the year after the ball. Of course, therefore, the young man of vast ambition had already both feet on the ladder? You shall see.

'What are you going to do all the summer?' asked the family cousin, Horace.

'I don't know,' Geoffrey replied languidly. 'Take the yacht some-where, I suppose. Into the Baltic, perhaps. Will you come too?'

'Can't. I've got work to do. I shall run over to Switzerland for three weeks perhaps. Better come with me and do some climbing.'

Geoffrey shook his head.

'Man!' cried the other impatiently, 'you want something to do. Doesn't it bore you—just going on day after day, day after day, with nothing to think of but your own amusement?'

Geoffrey yawned. 'The Profession of Amusement,' he said, 'is, in fact, deadly dull.'

'Then why follow it?'

'Because I am so rich. You fellows who've got nothing *must* work.

When a man is not obliged to work, there are a thousand excuses. I don't believe that I *could* work now if I wanted to. Yet I used to have ambitions.'

'You did. When it was difficult to find a way to live while you worked, you had enormous ambitions. "If only I was not obliged to provide for the daily bread"; that was what you used to say. Well, now the daily bread is provided, what excuse have you?'

'I tell you a thousand excuses present themselves the moment I think of doing any work. Besides, the ambitions are dead!'

'Dead! And at five-and-twenty! They can't be dead.'

'They are. Dead and buried. Killed by five years' racket. Profession of Pleasure—Pleasure, I believe they call it. No man can follow more than one profession.'

'Well, old man, if the world's pleasures are already rather dry in the mouth, what will they be when you've been running after them for fifty years?'

'There are cards, I believe. Cards are always left. No,'—he got up and leaned over the mantelshelf,—'I can't say that the fortune has brought much happiness with it. That's the worst of being rich. You see very well that you are not half so happy as the fellows who are making their own way, and yet you can't give up your money and start fair with the rest. I always think of that story of the young man who was told to give up all he had to the poor. He couldn't, you see. He saw very clearly that it would be best for him; but he couldn't. I am that young man. If I was like you, with all the world to conquer, I should be ten times as strong and a hundred times as clever. I know it—yet I cannot give up the money.'

'Nobody wants you to give it up. But surely you could go on like other fellows—as if you hadn't got it, I mean.'

'No—you don't understand. It's like a millstone tied round your neck. It drags you down and keeps you down.'

'Why don't you marry?'

'Why don't I? Well, when I meet the girl I fancy I will marry if she will have me. I suppose I'm constitutionally cold, because as yet—— Who is this girl?' He took up a cabinet photograph which stood on the mantelshelf. 'I seem to know the face. It's a winning kind of face— what they call a beseeching face. Where have I seen it?'

'That? It is the portrait of a cousin of mine. I don't think you can have met her anywhere, because she lives entirely in the country.'

'I have certainly seen her somewhere. Perhaps in a picture. Beatrice, perhaps. It is the face of an angel. Faces sometimes deceive, though: I know a girl in quite the smartest set who can assume the most saintly face when she pleases. She puts it on when she converses with the curate; when she goes to church she becomes simply angelic. At other times——Your cousin does not, however, I should say, follow the Profession of Amusement.'

'Not exactly. She lives in a quiet little seaside place where they've got a convalescent home, and she slaves for the patients.'

'It is a beautiful face,' Geoffrey repeated. 'But I seem to know it.' He looked at the back of the photograph. 'What are these lines written at the back?'

'They are some nonsense rhymes written by herself. There is a little family tradition that Katie is waiting for her Prince—she says so herself —she has refused a good many men. I think she will never marry, because she certainly will not find the man she dreams of.'

'May I read the lines?' He read them aloud:—

> Oh! tell me, Willow-wren and White-throat, beating
>   The sluggish breeze with eager homeward wing,
> Bear you no message for me—not a greeting
>   From him you left behind—my Prince and King?
>
> You come from far—from south and east and west;
>   Somewhere you left him, daring some great thing,
> I know not what, save that it is the best:
>   Somewhere you saw him—saw my Prince and King.
>
> You cannot choose but know him: by the crown
>   They place upon his head—the crown and ring;
> And by the loud and many-voiced renown
>   After the footsteps of my Prince and King.
>
> He speaks, and lo! the listening world obeys;
>   He leads, and all men follow; and they cling,
> And hang around the words and works and ways,
>   As of a Prophet—of my Prince and King.
>
> What matter if he comes not, though I wait?
>   Bear you no greeting for me, birds of spring?

> Again—what matter, since his work is great,
> And greater grows his name—my Prince and King.

'You see,' said the cousin, 'she has set up an ideal man.'

'Yes. Why does she call him her Prince?'

The cousin laughed. 'There is a story about a ball—her first ball—her last too, poor child, because—well, there were losses, you know. Like the landlady, Katie has known better days; and friends died, and so she lives by herself in this little village, and looks after her patient convalescents.'

'What about her first ball?'

'Well, she nearly missed it, because her godmother, who meant to give her a surprise, lost a train or got late somehow. So her Elder Sisters went without her, and she arrived late; and they said that, to complete the story, nothing was wanted but the Prince.'

Geoffrey started and changed colour.

'That's all. She imagined a Prince, and goes on with her dream. She enacts a novel which never comes to an end, and has no situations, and has an invisible hero.'

Geoffrey laid down the photograph. He now remembered everything, including the sending of the slipper. But the cousin had quite forgotten his own part in the story.

'I must go,' he said. 'I think I shall take the yacht somewhere round the coast. You say your cousin lives at——'

'Oh! Yes, she lives at Shellacomb Bay, near Torquay. Sit down again.'

'No. Dull place, Shellacomb Bay: I've been there, I think.' He was rather irresolute, but that was his way. 'I must go. I rather think there are some men coming into my place about this time. There will be nap. All professionals, you know—Professors of Amusement. It's dull work. I say, if your cousin found her Prince, what an awful, awful disappointment it would be!'

IV

At five in the morning Geoffrey was left alone. The night's play was over. He turned back the curtains and opened the windows, letting in the fresh morning air of April. He leaned out and took a deep breath.

Then he returned to the room. The table was littered with packs of cards. There was a smell of a thousand cigarettes. It is an acrid smell, not like the honest downright smell of pipes and cigars; the board was covered with empty soda-water and champagne bottles.

'The Professional Pursuer of Pleasure', he murmured. 'It's a learned profession, I suppose. Quite a close profession. Very costly to get into, and beastly stupid and dull when you are in it. A learned profession, certainly.'

He sat down, and his thoughts returned to the girl who had made for herself a Prince. 'Her Prince!' he said bitterly. And then the words came back to him—

> Daring some great thing,
> I know not what, save that it is the best:
> Somewhere you saw him—saw my Prince and King.

'For one short night I was her Prince and King,' he murmured. 'And I sent her the slipper—was stone-broke a whole term after through buying that slipper. And after all I was afraid to call at the house. Her Prince and King. I wonder——' He looked about him again—looked at the empty bottles. '*What* a Prince and King!' he laughed bitterly.

Then he sprang to his feet; he opened a drawer and took from it a bundle of letters, photographs, cards of invitation which were lying there piled up in confusion. He threw these on the fire in a heap; he opened another drawer and pulled out another bundle of notes and papers. These also he threw on the fire. 'There!' he said resolutely. What he meant I know not, for he did not wait to see them burned, but went into his bedroom and so to bed.

V

Geoffrey spoke no more than the simple truth when he said that Katie De Lisle had a saintly face—the face of an angel. It was a lovely face when he first saw it—the face of a girl passing into womanhood. Five years of tranquil life, undisturbed by strong emotions, devoted to unselfish labours and to meditation, had now made that face saintly indeed. It was true that she had created for herself a Prince, one who was at once a Galahad of romance and a leader of the present day, chivalrous knight and Paladin of Parliament. What she did with her Prince I do not know. Whether she thought of him continually or only seldom, whether she believed in him or only hoped for him, no one can tell. When a man proposed to her—which happened whenever a man was presented to her—she refused him graciously, and told her sisters, who were now matrons, that another person had come representing himself to be the Prince, but that she had detected an impostor, for he was not the Prince. And it really seemed as if she never would find this impossible Prince, which was a great pity, if only because she had a very little income, and the Elder Sisters, who lived in great houses, desired her also to have a great house. Of course, every Prince who regards his own dignity must have a big house of his own.

Now, one afternoon in April, when the sun sets about a quarter-past seven and it is light until eight, Katie was sitting on one of the benches placed on the shore for the convenience of the convalescents, two or three of whom were strolling along the shore. The sun was getting low; a warmth and glow lay upon the bay like an illuminated mist. Katie had a book in her hand, but she let it drop into her lap, and sat watching the beauty and the splendour and the colour of the scene before her. Then there came, rounding the southern headland, a steam yacht, which slowly crept into the bay, and dropped anchor and let off steam: a graceful little craft, with her slender spars and her dainty curves. The girl watched with a little interest. Not often did craft of any kind put into that bay. There were bays to the east and bays to the west, where ships, boats, fishing smacks, and all kind of craft put in; but not in that bay, where there was no quay, or port, or anything but the convalescents, and Katie the volunteer nurse. So she watched, sitting on the bench, with the western sun falling upon her face.

After a little a boat was lowered, and a man and a boy got into it. The boy took the sculls and rowed the man ashore. The man jumped out, stood irresolutely looking about him, observed Katie on the bench, looked at her rather rudely it seemed, and walked quickly towards her. What made her face turn pale? What made her cheek turn red and pale? Nothing less than the appearance of her Prince—her Prince. She knew him at once. Her Prince! It was her Prince come to her at last.

But the Prince did not hold out both hands and cry, 'I have come.' Not at all. He gravely and politely took off his hat. 'Miss De Lisle,' he said. 'I cannot hope that you remember me. I only met you once. But I—I heard that you were here, and I remembered your face at once.'

'I seldom forget people,' she replied, rising and giving him her hand. 'You are Mr Geoffrey Armiger. We danced together one night. I remember it especially, because it was my first ball.'

'Which you nearly missed, and were left at home like Cinderella, till the fairy godmother came. I—I am cruising about here. I learned that you were living here from your cousin in the Temple, and—and I thought that, if we put in here, I might, perhaps, venture to call.'

'Certainly. I shall be very glad to see you, Mr Armiger. It is seven o'clock now. Will you come to tea to-morrow afternoon?'

'With the greatest pleasure. May I walk with you—in your direction?'

The situation was delicate. What Geoffrey wanted to convey was this: 'You once received the confidences of a young man who hoped to do great things in the world. You have gone on believing that he would do great things. You have built up an ideal man, before whom all other men are small creatures. Well, that ideal must be totally disconnected with the young fellow who started it, because he has gone to the bad. He is only a Professor of Amusement, an idle killer of time, a man who wastes all his gifts and powers.' A difficult thing to say, because it involved charging the girl with, or telling her he knew that she had been, actually thinking of him for five years.

That evening he got very little way. He reminded her again of the ball. He said that she had altered very little, which was true; for at twenty-two Katie preserved much the same ethereal beauty that she had at seventeen. That done, his jaws stuck, to use a classical phrase. He could say no more. He left her at the door of her cottage,—she lived in a cottage in the midst of tree fuchsias and covered with roses,—and went back to his yacht, where he had a solitary dinner and passed a morose evening.

At five o'clock in the afternoon next day he called again. Miss De Lisle was at the Home, but would come back immediately. The books on the girl's table betrayed the character of her mind. Katie's books showed the level of her thoughts and the standard of her ideals. They were the books of a girl who meditates. There are such people, even in this busy and noisy age. Geoffrey took them up with a sinking heart. Professors of Amusement never read such books.

Then she came in, quiet, serene; and they sat down, and the tea was brought in.

'Now, tell me,' she said abruptly. 'I see by your card that you have a title. What did you do to get it?'

'Nothing. I succeeded.'

'Oh!' Her face fell a little. 'When I saw you—the only time that I saw you—I remember that you had great ambitions. What have you done?'

'Nothing. Nothing at all. I have wasted my time. I have lived a life of what they call pleasure. I don't know that I ought to have called upon you at all.'

'Is it possible? Oh! Can it be possible? Only a life of pleasure? And you—you with your noble dreams? Oh! Is it possible?'

'It is possible. It is quite true. I am the prodigal son, who has so much money that he cannot get through it. But do you remember the silly things I said? Why, you see, what happened was, that when the temptation came all the noble dream vanished?'

'Is it possible?' she repeated. 'Oh! I am so very, very sorry!'—in fact, the tears came into her eyes. 'You have destroyed the one illusion that I nourished.' Every one thinks that he has only one illusion and a clear eye for everything else. That is the Great, the Merciful, Illusion. 'I thought that there was one true man at least in the world, fighting for the right. I had been honoured as a girl with the noble ambitions of that man when he was quite young. I thought I should hear of him from time to time winning recognition, power, and authority. It was a beautiful dream. It made me feel almost as if I were myself taking part in that great career, even from this obscure corner in the country. No one knows the pleasure that a woman has in watching the career of a brave and wise man. And now it is gone. I am sorry you called,'—her voice became stony and her eyes hard: even an angel or a saint has moments of righteous indignation,—'I am very sorry, Sir Geoffrey Armiger, that you took the trouble to call.'

Her visitor rose. 'I am also very sorry,' he said, 'that I have said or done anything to pain you. Forgive me: I will go.'

But he lingered. He took up a paper-knife, and considered it as if it were something rare and curious. He laid it down. Then he laughed a little short laugh, and turned to Katie with smiling lips and solemn eyes.

'Did that slipper fit?' he asked, abruptly.

She blushed. But she answered him.

'It was too small for my Elder Sisters, but it fitted me.'

'Will you try it on again?'

She went out of the room and presently returned with the pretty, jewelled, little slipper. She took off her shoe, sat down, and tried it on.

'You see,' she said, 'it is now too small for my foot. Oh! my foot has not changed in the least. It has grown too small.'

'Try again.' The Prince looked on anxiously. 'Perhaps, with a little effort, a little goodwill——'

'No; it is quite hopeless. The slipper has shrunk; you can see for yourself, if you remember what it was like when you bought it. See, it is ever so much smaller than it was, Sir Geoffrey.' She looked up, gravely. 'See for yourself. And the silver buckle is black, and even the pearls are tarnished. See!' There was a world of meaning in her words. 'Think what it was five years ago.'

He took it from her hand and turned it round and round disconsolately.

'You remember it—five years ago—when it was new?' the girl asked again.

'I remember. Oh! yes, I remember. A pretty thing it was then, wasn't it? A world of promise in it, I remember. Hope, and courage, and——and all kinds of possibilities. Pity—silver gone black, pearls tarnished, colour faded, the thing itself shrunken. Yes.' He gave it back to her. 'I'm glad you've kept it.'

'Of course I kept it.'

'Yes, of course. Will you go on keeping it?'

'I think so. One likes to remember a time of promise, and of hope, and courage, and, as you say, all kinds of possibilities.'

He sighed.

'Slippers are so. There are untold sympathies in slippers. I call this the Oracle of the slipper. Not that I am in the least surprised. I came here, in fact, on purpose to ascertain, if I could, the amount of shrinkage. It would be interesting to return every five years or so, just to see how much it shrinks every year. Next time it would be a doll's shoe, for instance. Well, now'—again he fell back upon the paper-knife—'there was something else I had to say; something else——' He dropped his eyes and examined the paper-knife closely. 'The other day in your cousin's rooms I saw your photograph; and I remembered the kind of young fellow I was when we talked about ambitions and you sympathised with me. I think I should like to take up those ambitions again, if it is not too late. I am sick and weary of the Profession of Pleasure. I have wasted five good years, but perhaps they can be retrieved. Let me, if possible, burnish up that silver, expand the shrinking shoe, renew those dreams.'

'Do you mean it? Are you strong enough? Oh! You have fallen so low. Are you strong enough to rise?'

'I don't know. If the event should prove—if that slipper should enlarge again—if it should once more fit your foot——'

'If! Oh! how can a man say *if*, when he ought to say *shall*?'

'The slipper *shall* enlarge,' he said quietly, but with as much determination as one can expect from an Emeritus Professor of Pleasure.

'When it does, then come again. Till then, do not, if you please, seek me out in my obscurity. It would only be the final destruction of a renewed hope. Farewell, Sir Geoffrey.'

'*Au revoir*. Not farewell.'

He stooped and kissed her hand and left her.

MARY ANGELA DICKENS

An Idyll of an Omnibus

She was sitting in one of the corners of the omnibus next the door, and the November sun shone full upon her. She was a mere child, not more than seventeen. The contour of the cheeks was soft and round; the full red lips, a little rebellious in expression, were not yet set; the great grey eyes flashed out on the world the unrestrained and undisguised ill-temper of undisciplined youth. It was this very youthfulness which gave so striking a touch of pitifulness to the tawdry picturesqueness of her attire. She wore a bright blue pelisse, made of some cheap material; it was open at the throat, and exposed a shabby black under dress, cut low at the neck to show a throat (encircled by a narrow band of cheap black velvet) beautifully moulded, which should also have been beautifully white. Her hat was a large black straw, with a gracefully curved brim; it was trimmed with yellow marguerites, and on the bright brown, curly, hair—unbrushed, unwashed, and ruffled into a systematic disorder—there rested another spray of the same flower. On the soft young cheeks was a perceptible touch of artificial colour. There was nothing about her that was fresh or good of its kind, nothing about her that was not arranged for effect; and the result produced was rather pathetic in its suggestiveness.

The young man in the corner opposite was conscious of the result, though he hardly knew how it was produced. He was a pale, dark-haired man, noticeable only for a pleasant pair of eyes, at once humorous and sympathetic; and for a good forehead. He was a gentleman, obviously. His keen eyes had scanned his opposite neighbour quite unobtrusively; and he had listened to the music-school gossip she carried on with her companion—an unwashed boy, who carried a musical instrument—with a twinkle of amusement. It was the meanest possible kind of art-gossip—gossip in which the names of great masterpieces seemed only the tools for a petty rivalry, strife, and envying;

the background of the whole was a hopelessly low and self-satisfied standard, and the amusement in the young man's eyes developed before long into a sympathetic compassion.

The unwashed boy got snubbed at last, and silence ensued. The omnibus had rolled well into Hammersmith, when the girl burst into speech again. Family affairs, connected with the arrival of an unwelcome visitor, seemed to be the topic—conversation not interesting to an outsider in itself, but rendered piquant by the unrestrained indignation of the high-pitched, childish voice.

'Says he wants to make friends with his relations!' were the first consecutive words the young man caught. 'What rubbish! He can't afford to stay at a hotel, I expect. Did I tell you what he said about Christmas?'

A noisy piece of road rendered her voice inaudible, and when her words again reached the young man's ear she had passed apparently to another branch of the same subject.

'Like?' she was saying scornfully. 'Oh yes, I know just what he'll be like! A sentimental German, don't you know,—flabby and affectionate.'

She had been noticing the progress of the omnibus as she spoke, and as she laughed indignantly she signalled to the conductor to stop, and got out with a careless nod to the boy. The conductor's eyes suddenly fell on the young man.

'Didn't you say Roland Crescent, sir? Here you are! On the left.'

It was not a particularly inviting outlook which opened on the left, as the young man stood upon the pavement. It was a shabby little road, with untidy poverty written in large letters all over the small houses. The only bit of colour to be seen was the blue pelisse fluttering down the left-hand side of it.

'Poor little girl!' the young man said to himself, and again a twinkle, half-amused, half-sympathetic, lighted up his eyes. Then he glanced at the street critically, and raised his eyes doubtfully to the 'Roland Crescent' painted on a house just above him. He lowered them again just in time to see the blue pelisse disappear into the dirtiest and shabbiest house in the road.

'Hullo!' he said. 'Lives hereabouts! Perhaps they'll know something about her. Now, then, where's number twelve? Even numbers left-hand side, apparently.' He crossed the road, and in two minutes more stood confronted with number twelve as the house into which the blue pelisse had disappeared.

There was a low whistle of amazement; an expression of blank astonishment, developing into dismay, made its appearance on the young man's countenance; and he stood apparently transfixed in contemplation of the undesirable edifice before him. Then he turned away, and walked to the end of Roland Crescent, and out into the Hammersmith Road again.

Half-an-hour had passed before he again presented himself at number twelve, and this time he rang the bell. His eyes were full of a rather rueful fun, and there was a certain comic, 'go-through-with-it-and-get-it-over' air about him. The door was opened by a very slatternly servant.

'Is Mr Baldwyn in?' said the young man. 'He expects me, I believe —Mr John Glendinning.'

It was a narrow little passage into which Mr John Glendinning was admitted, and it smelt strongly of cooking. A door was opened, and he advanced into a dingy sitting-room, as a dilapidated and rather red-nosed man rose from an arm-chair by the fire.

It is given to most of us to have unknown relatives. It is given to many of us to have undesirable relatives. It was given to John Glendinning, on this November afternoon, to discover the latter in the former.

John Glendinning had come from Dresden, not solely with a view to making the acquaintance of the gentleman with whom he was now confronted, but with that object in the foreground of his thoughts. He was visiting his native country for the first time for ten years. Eighteen months before, his mother, between whom and himself there had existed that perfect union which dual solitude sometimes engenders, had died, leaving him alone in their Dresden home. Brought face to face with his second lonely Christmas, an instinct arose in him—partly the outcome of his own nature, partly the creation of that tender German sentiment which makes Christmas pre-eminently the season of domestic happiness—towards the only human beings whom he knew as kindred. These were the family of his mother's long-dead sister. An old quarrel between the sisters, and Mrs Glendinning's residence abroad, had prevented any intercourse between the families. Glendinning knew only one fact about his relatives, and this one fact served as a passport to his favour. His uncle by marriage, Mr Baldwyn, was understood by him to belong to the musical profession—and music was Glendinning's own profession and passion.

He hunted out their address with difficulty, and wrote, proposing to pay them a visit. He had received a gushing response, and had proceeded to carry his proposition into effect.

'I am charmed to see you, my dear boy! Your letter was such a pleasure as not often befalls me. A very hearty welcome!'

Mr Baldwyn's slippers were down at heel, Mr Baldwyn's smoking-jacket was frayed at the cuffs, and his linen was far from spotless; but even these attributes did not render Mr Baldwyn's greeting so indescribably incongruous to Glendinning, in connection with himself, as did his general expression and tone of voice—the former squalid, the latter cringing. A keen sense of humour in the young man produced a reply which was an excellent imitation of the response which a less impossible relation would have drawn from him; and just as he finished speaking a folding-door behind him opened, and Mr Baldwyn hastened to say loudly, 'The elder of your two cousins, my dear boy!—Nellie, your cousin John!'

John Glendinning advanced to meet a girl of four-and-twenty, pretty in a dark, common style, and showily dressed in red.

His cousin Nellie's eyes rested upon the well-bred and well-appointed figure thus presented to her with a stare of astonishment; and a touch of embarrassment did not add to the attraction of a loud and pert manner.

'Our dinner hour,' said Mr Baldwyn airily, 'is five. Our engagements claim our presence at half-past seven. Nellie and myself are assisting at present in the production of the new opera; she is in the chorus, I in the orchestra. Gwendoline's engagements—Ah! here is Gwendoline—Gwen, as we call her.'

The folding-door opened again, with a kind of reluctant snatch. John Glendinning turned quickly. There in the opening stood his opposite neighbour in the omnibus, the wearer of the blue pelisse. She was wearing a brown plush frock, indescribably shabby and dirty, and she looked lovelier than ever. She came across the room, hardly looking at the stranger, and held out her hand to him with an ill-tempered thrust, and in silence.

'How do you do?' said John Glendinning politely.

As he spoke the girl started violently. She raised her eyes to his face, and a wonderful colour rushed over her soft cheeks. She looked at him for a moment, unconscious in her surprise that her hand still rested in his. He met her eyes and smiled.

The next instant she had wrenched her hand away, and rushed out of the room, banging the door after her.

The meal which presently ensued, John Glendinning never forgot. The food, appointments, and the manners alike made it for him an occasion which was only rendered endurable by a keen sense of the ridiculous. Glendinning faced the situation as he had sometimes faced an unsuccessful picnic party—talking, laughing, ignoring. He would find himself recalled to Dresden on the very next day, that was a fore-gone conclusion. But it was an odd coincidence, that whenever he found himself mentally arranging for this summons he should find the scorn-ful eyes of his cousin Gwen fixed upon him.

'By Jove!' he said to himself afterwards, 'she looked as if she knew what I was thinking. What eyes she's got! Poor little girl!'

He was sitting alone when this reflection occurred to him; Mr Baldwyn and Nellie having departed to their 'engagements'. And he started as a touch fell on the door. Then he recollected that Gwen was in the house, and the next instant she stood on the threshold.

John Glendinning rose, and stood with his cigarette between his fingers.

'Your sister gave me leave to smoke,' he said, by way of saying something. 'I hope it doesn't annoy you?'

His cousin's reply was characterized by energy and little elegance. Gwen's eyes were flashing, and the rebellious mouth was set into pas-sionate curves.

'Don't talk rubbish!' she said. 'Do you think I'm a fool? Do you think I don't see that you're just putting up with us? Why don't you say we're not good enough, and go? That's what I've come to ask you!'

Through all the child's vulgarity of exterior, phrase, and tone there rang a fierce intensity of resentment, a sensitive passion of perception.

'If it's to pay me out for what I said in the omnibus,' she went on vehemently, 'I shouldn't have thought that any man could be so mean! I don't remember what I did say exactly, but of course I know the kind of thing. I knew I should hate you, but I never supposed you'd be as hateful as you are! Is it to pay me out, I want to know?'

Her slender figure was quivering with unrestrained passion, and as Glendinning looked at her his eyes had grown very gentle and conciliating.

'Of course it isn't,' he said. 'I don't know what you mean. Don't distress yourself about what happened in the omnibus. It didn't apply, don't you see? I'm not a German; I hope I'm not flabby; and I don't seem likely—' The irrepressible twinkle had reappeared in his eyes, and Gwen stamped her foot fiercely.

'Don't!' she cried. 'You shan't laugh at me! Well, why don't you go, then? You know by this time why father was so glad to have you! And Nellie and I don't want you!'

A transference of coin of the realm which had taken place before Mr Baldwyn's departure had certainly enlightened Glendinning as to that gentleman's views; and the undisguised scorn of her father which rang in the girlish tones touched his ready sympathies to the quick.

'That's very likely,' he said gently, answering her last statement. 'It is I who—'

Whether a sudden realization of the circumstances of the case made him hesitate, or whether she really interrupted him, John Glendinning did not know.

'You don't want us!' she said, with a bitter laugh. 'We're not good enough for you!' She paused, and then flashed out on him suddenly. 'What's the matter with us?' she cried. 'We're all right. What makes you treat us like this?'

It was the desperate repudiation of a suddenly awakened doubt; which was not to be acknowledged; which came as a climax on years of child-ish discontent and rebellion, only to be hurled passionately away. The note of defiance was eloquent to Glendinning, and his voice and move-ments were a little uncertain as he hurriedly turned a chair to the fire for her.

'Don't let us quarrel,' he said. 'Look here, let us sit down and talk.'

But before the words were fairly uttered Gwen had dashed out of the room.

John Glendinning was not recalled to Dresden on the following day. All the half-humorous, half-pitying kindliness of his nature was arrayed against the thought of leaving Gwen with that bitter passion of resentment unassuaged in her heart. Exactly what course of action he proposed to himself when he decided to stay in Roland Crescent for another day he hardly knew. It was useless, he saw plainly, to try and undo the effect that he had produced on the girl. Even if he could have uttered the disclaimer that the conventionalities of the situation demanded, Gwen would not have been deceived. Her perceptions were far too keen and sensitive.

It was perhaps the realization of this truth that first created in Glendinning's mind the conception of possibilities in the poor little undisciplined girl; possibilities which might, were there a hand to touch and train them, be developed into something very different; possibilities over which he smiled or sighed, according as the humorous or sympathetic side of his nature was uppermost. And though he himself scarcely understood the reason, it was simply because of this realization that he let his stay in Roland Crescent lengthen itself day after day—to Mr Baldwyn's effusively expressed satisfaction.

That Gwen's temper at this time was perfectly abominable was a fact that nobody living in the house with her attempted to deny. No one could come in contact with her without being, as the rough servant expressed it, 'scarified'. And of all the people subjected to the 'scarifying' process the most frequent victim was Glendinning. It seemed as if the girl could not be for five minutes in her cousin's presence without, to use her own phrase, 'flying out at him'. Nothing he said, nothing he did, was too great or too small for Gwen to take exception to. Sometimes it was as if not only his presence, but his very personality, threw her into a sullen white heat of wrath.

But the worst apple of discord between the two, the culminating point of their dissension, was Gwen's music. Glendinning was a musician to his finger-tips. He had made rapid strides in his profession, and one of the objects of his visit to London had been the making acquaintance with certain English musicians to whom he had introductions. His attitude towards Gwen as a musician was typical of his attitude towards her whole personality. If she had been destitute of talent, her utter lack of knowledge and her pleasure in what was inferior, would have affected him not at all. But behind all her professional deficiencies there burnt a little spark of the fire of genius, and all the artist in her cousin tingled to give that spark fair play. On the occasion, when Gwen forced from him the fact that he did not admire her playing, they had the battle royal which established them in the relative positions of mentor and pupil—the mentor, half earnest, half amused; the pupil, fierce, defiant, rebellious, and yet voluntary.

They were thrown a great deal together. If Glendinning was out during the day, he dropped into the habit of being in Roland Crescent during the evening. If he were out in the evening, he would see something of Gwen during the day. And every day, at some time or other, they would find time to assume their strange relations. Not that their artistic intercourse was by any means of a more equable nature than their ordinary contact. On three evenings out of four, Gwen's frame of mind would be such that only a dogged obstinacy on Glendinning's part, a sheer determination to vindicate his faith in those strange possibilities in her, held him to his patient, half-amused compassion for her. Then on the fourth evening, perhaps, he would see her in another aspect; bitter, rebellious, defiant; full of the passionate misery of a creature at war with her world, and only dimly and most wretchedly conscious of the existence of any other.

Three weeks had come and gone in this fashion, and it was within a week of Christmas. Gwen had been at her worst for two days past, and Glendinning, sitting by the fire with a cigar in the evening, was wondering idly and a little sadly whether it was of any use to try and influence her, after all. He did not hear her come into the room, and he started slightly, when he looked up, to find her standing by the fireplace looking down into the fire. He looked at her for a moment, wondering what was the improvement in her appearance, of which he was vaguely conscious. Gwen, as if aware of his gaze, moved uneasily, and coloured crimson; but she need not have feared—or hoped. His masculine eyes were unaware that they rested on her lovely hair properly brushed and neatly dressed for the first time.

'Well,' she said, letting herself fall into a low chair, and resting her chin on her hand as she stared into the fire, 'and what do you think about Christmas here?'

The voice was bitter and derisive, but there was a suggestion of restless unhappiness about it which gave it a less combative sound than usual.

'I think what I've always thought about it, Gwen,' he said.

'What! all that—that nonsense about its being a happy time—made gladder by family affection, and so on?'

The young man coloured. They had differed on the subject of Christmas sentiment early in their acquaintance, and the mocking voice gave a colour to his previously expressed opinions under which he would have liked to disown them. But he stood to his flag like a man.

'Yes,' he said, 'I do. Of course I know there has been a heap of cant talked about Christmas; one can't strike that out too thoroughly. But it's an awful mistake to strike out the truth as well. Look here, Gwen,' he went on earnestly and diffidently, 'I'm not a parson; I don't want to go in to what makes the Christmas spirit, only I've a strong notion that there is such a thing. It's not the kind of thing men create for themselves, and they make clumsy work enough with it, I don't deny. But they're the better for it, I believe; and theirs is a baddish way when they can't feel it.'

He stopped, and took a long pull at his cigar. There was a pause, and then Gwen said, with a harsh laugh;

'Then I'm in a baddish way, I can tell you. I hate Christmas, and that's all about it. I've always hated it more than any other time of the year!'

To Glendinning's intense astonishment, he saw that her eyelashes were wet. While he was trying to account for a curious pain that the sight created in him, she went on in the same tone:

'I should like to know why I shouldn't hate it? Or what happiness it brings to me? We shall dine at six instead of five, and father will get drunk—that's all that will happen.'

She tried to laugh, but her voice was ringing with feeling. There was a defiant sense, in her speech, of the potentialities of Christmas withheld from her; and it was to this sense that Glendinning, striving to collect his attributes as mentor, addressed his reply.

'That's the other side of the Christmas spirit,' he said in rather a low voice. 'That's what makes you hate it. It makes you feel you want something you haven't got—that there's a lot you might have if you chose——'

'If I chose?' she interrupted him scornfully. 'What has my choosing got to do with it?' She stopped, and then turned suddenly upon him, springing to her feet, her eyes flashing. 'I don't want anything that I haven't got! I'm satisfied with everything—myself and all! What did you ever come here for, to make me miserable? Oh, I hate you! I wish I'd never seen you!'

She stood looking down upon him, her lovely face aglow, her childish figure quivering with passionate emotion. And as if some electrical current had passed from her to him, Glendinning sprang up also, his face flushed and agitated.

'Gwen!' he cried,—'Gwen! you don't mean that? You don't mean that?'

The last words echoed in an empty room, for Gwen was gone.

For some time John Glendinning stood where she had left him, as though rooted to the spot. Then the colour faded out of his face, and he sat down with something very like a groan. He had prided himself on his powers of perception; he had admired his realization of the incongruity between Gwen's manners and her deeper nature; he had flattered himself that he was undertaking a gratuitous and disinterested work in trying to develop her. And all the time there had been developing in himself, entirely unsuspected, an incongruity before which the other was as nothing. He, John Glendinning, his vulgar little cousin's mentor, patron, and superior, had been learning, while he instructed, the old, old lesson of love. Glendinning did not attempt to argue the matter with himself. He loved Gwen; loved her with all her faults and failings; loved the struggling artist nature, the half-dormant woman's soul, which he himself had rendered sentient. It would not serve him to deny the fact. For the time being he could only sit and stare at it in blank dismay. Then he began to think about the future. What was he to do?

If Glendinning could have believed that he had unwittingly taught Gwen the lesson which he himself had learned, a sense of honour would have acted as compulsion, and he might have asked her to be his wife with that semi-reluctance which compulsion engenders. But during the three days that followed the evening of his discovery, Glendinning became convinced that Gwen did indeed hate him. If speech with him was by any means to be avoided she did not speak to him at all; if it was inevitable, her observations were almost savage. All that was worst in her, in thought, manner, and speech—characteristics which had softened during the previous three weeks—seemed to be accentuated now, deliberately, until there were times when his love for her seemed to the young man to be little short of insanity. And yet, in spite of the rough nature of the soil in which it was set, that love grew and flourished. Demonstrations of the futility of his position were all in vain, and Glendinning was indescribably wretched.

On Christmas Eve there was to be a charity concert at one of the smaller halls, for which both Glendinning and Gwen were engaged. Gwen was to appear as one of a string quartette consisting of girl musicians of the same calibre as herself, who added to the attractions of their performance by dressing alike in fancy costume. Glendinning's name had been added to the programme only a week before, and the circumstance had made an odd little bond of union between the two. Now, however, this bond of union seemed to be transformed into an inexhaustible source of bitterness. Gwen refused, fiercely, to accompany Glendinning when he practised; she substituted a showy piece of music for the graceful old gavotte that he had persuaded her to play; she absolutely flaunted all the preparations for the fancy dress that she knew he disliked; and utterly declined his escort to the concert-room. She would go with the other girls, she said, and then he needn't recognize her if he didn't like her dress. He could amuse himself with the friends who were good enough for him.

The friends thus bitingly alluded to were a young pianist and his sister, in whose hands the arrangement of the concert had chiefly lain, and who had asked Glendinning to sing. They were well-bred, clever, and enthusiastic; they had taken a fancy to Glendinning; and thus it happened that when Gwen and her companions entered the artists' room her cousin was talking and laughing with Miss Marchant. Gwen cast in their direction one flashing glance, in which her miserable, scornful eyes seemed to take in every detail of the other woman's dainty dress, and then she turned sharply away and dragged off her own cloak, revealing the tawdry, theatrical finery underneath.

The quartette appeared almost immediately, and during the intervals before and after Glendinning's song she entirely ignored his presence, laughing and talking with her companions with a persistency that almost entirely frustrated his intention of speaking to her. Her own solo came late in the programme, just after a song by Miss Marchant.

Glendinning, miserable beyond words, was enthusiastically discussing the song's merits with the singer, as Gwen left the room; and she passed them with her childish face oddly flushed and set. The door of the artists' room was open, and as the first notes of the violin floated down, Miss Marchant started.

'Who is that?' she said. 'What a tone! Let us go and listen, Mr Glendinning.'

It was the gavotte, after all; and Gwen was playing, as Glendinning had never heard her play yet, with a passionate feeling and a wild, erratic power that took the audience by storm. She ran down the few steps when she had finished amid a tumult of applause; and as she passed the pair who had been listening to her, Miss Marchant said excitedly, 'Who is she, Mr Glendinning? I saw you speak to her some time ago. Introduce me to her.'

Gwen, fumbling blindly for her cloak, heard the words, and faced round sharply, her eyes on Glendinning. To the young man their tempestuous glance conveyed a flat defiance. It seemed to him that Gwen was absolutely forbidding him to introduce her.

He hesitated. He saw Gwen's eyes change. He saw something leap up in them that he had never seen in their depths before. Then he realized that she had thrown her cloak around her and had dashed out of the room, and that he was following her involuntarily and instinctively, his heart throbbing wildly. As though impelled by an irresistible impulse, she ran down the stairs, and ran on, even when she was in the street, making instinctively, as Glendinning understood, for the corner from which her omnibus would start. An insane belief that if she escaped him now he would never again see the Gwen into whose eyes he had looked for that one moment, literally possessed him. He saw her rush across the road and jump into an empty omnibus. Regardless of horses and vehicles, he rushed across after her and jumped into the same omnibus just as it moved on. With the same odd impulse that had dictated her flight through the streets, she had buried herself in the farther corner of the dim vehicle, crouching back against the cushions. She did not look up at his entrance—evidently she had been unconscious of his pursuit. He made a progress towards her, rendered less graceful than might have been wished by the jolting of the omnibus. Then he sat down by her side.

'Gwen!' he said breathlessly. 'You don't really hate me?'

It was just as well that the omnibus was empty. In that most uncelestial conveyance Gwen and Glendinning were jolted on towards a future life together, in which love—as strange a love, surely, as ever blossomed out of stony soil—was justified of both her children.

A. ST JOHN ADCOCK

Bob Harris's Deputy

It was not an ordinary love affair, and the tenants of Filter's Rents laughed when they first heard about it, yet laughed good-naturedly, too. The male element of the tenantry was divided in its admiration of his cheek and her devotion; the feminine element said openly that, though nobody could blame him, poor fellow, she was a fool, but said it half-heartedly, and, in secret, cherished a sympathetic interest in both of them. Only the very young were puzzled because they could not fathom her motives, for only the very young expect to understand a woman or look for a reason in everything or anything she may do.

There cannot be less than two chief actors in any love story; in this there were three, and the odd one was a man. One roof covered them all. The woman, who was still under five and twenty, lived alone in a front room on a second floor; one of the men, Dave Kirk, occupied the back room opening on to the same landing; and the other, Bob Harris, resided, with his aged mother, down in the basement.

Perhaps the most unusual circumstance in connection with this episode was that Dave Kirk had no legs; he lost them four years before in the explosion of a gas retort, at the works where he had been employed. But he was a man of an independent, self-reliant spirit, and on his discharge from hospital was, by his own wish, carried back to his old room in Filter's Rents, resolute to resume the task of earning his own living.

Without being parsimonious, he had always been rationally careful of his money, and drawing now on his small capital in the savings bank, he fitted himself out with a specially-constructed wooden trolley on four small wheels, and set up in business as a shoe black. The trolley was low enough for him to be able to reach the ground easily, and paddle himself to and fro with his hands, whilst a long iron handle, hinged on at the front, supplied a ready means of traction, when a casual friend was disposed to oblige him by pulling.

There were inconveniences, of course, in such systems of life and locomotion, but Dave was wise enough to accommodate himself to the inevitable, and so by degrees recovered much of his former cheerfulness of demeanour, and discovered that existence without legs was not only bearable, but even to be enjoyed. Since he could no longer climb into bed, he realised the bedstead and disposed his mattress on the floor. His table and chairs being practically inaccessible heights, he sawed their legs off short, and dwarfed all his furniture.

'If I can't get up to them,' he said, cheerily, 'I can bring them down to me, an' they look as tidy on their stumps as I do on mine, an' chance it!'

For an infinitesimal salary, he retained the services of an able-bodied moucher to look after his trolley, and carry him up and down stairs; and finding that his business was liberally patronised, and, moreover, that he could not mount or descend the kerbs unaided, he presently increased the stipend of this menial, on condition that he drew him daily to and from his pitch by Dalston Station.

To this coming and going in state there was but one objection. The menial, though he rarely possessed visible means, had a tendency to get miraculously drunk quite early in the day, and hence could not be depended upon to draw the trolley home at night, in anything like a direct line. He generally tacked along the pavement, from side to side, as if the vehicle were a preposterous yacht making headway in the teeth of a gale, and this practice grew upon him, until twice he went too far in one direction, and, the wheels of the trolley slipping off the edge of the kerb, Dave was deposited in the road.

After the second of these mishaps, Dave began to look about him for a new and more reliable man; and was luckier in finding one than he had expected to be.

It was just about this time that Bob Harris and his mother arrived in the basement of the house in Filter's Rents, and Bob, in particular, took an immediate and friendly interest in the crippled lodger on the second floor back. He came up of evenings to chat with him, and hearing of the moucher's imperfections, generously volunteered to replace him. He was a warehouse porter, and passed Dalston Station every morning and evening on his way to the City and back.

'Why not?' he urged, when Dave demurred. 'I go right by the very place. It's no trouble to me, y'see, an' it'll save you a bit—eh?'

He was so persistent that, satisfied he was in earnest, Dave gratefully availed himself of the offer.

And for the next eighteen months he did his daily travelling in perfect safety, the friendship between him and Bob Harris thriving apace. There were evenings when Dave was invited down to tea in the basement, and evenings when he shone as a host, and Bob Harris and his mother came up and sat on the reduced chairs about his undersized table. And on these latter occasions Nell Wyatt, the occupant of the adjoining room, was one of the party, having, as a matter of fact, with her own hands got the tea ready before she came to it.

For, you must know, there was not a girl in Filter's Rents—no, not in all London, nor in all the world—more kindly-hearted, truer, gentler, or more compassionate than was Nell. She was not beautiful; her dress was poor and coarse, her hands were rough with work, but the purity of her heart, the womanly sweetness of her whole nature so lit up her eyes and her quiet, homely features that the worst of men were softened by the influence of her presence, so that if there had been any incorrigible beast in the court who could have offered her an indignity, there would have been no lack of honester hands to break his head extemporaneously, and pitch him into the street.

Nell was no natural denizen of Filter's Rents; she had come there from the country, some time before Dave knew her, a dainty maiden enough, with the roses in her cheeks, and in her eyes a light gathered from brighter skies and clearer air. The roses were faded now, but the light was still undimmed.

The aunt she came to live with died during Dave's absence in hospital, and when he returned home he found her, as she had no other relation to go to, living on there by herself. A pleasant acquaintance had sprung up betwixt her and Dave during the six months preceding his accident, and now she was not long in proving herself the best and staunchest friend he had.

She had cried at first for very pity, seeing him so maimed and helpless; but her sympathies were eminently practical, and ever after she had met him with a cheerful face and voice and sought in every way she could to lighten the burden of his affliction.

It was Nell who kept his room so clean and neatly ordered. It was Nell who, every morning shortly before seven, knocked on his door to know if he was up, and carried in his breakfast all ready on a tray; and it was Nell—who else could it be?—that of an evening had his tea laid on the table, and, in winter weather, the fire lighted against his home coming.

If in the early days of his calamity Dave had fretted over some unspoken hope that was now become an impossible dream of the past, he had striven with himself so manfully that no word of his despair ever found its way to his lips until one memorable evening—the most memorable of any he had ever known.

There was nothing exceptional about the evening itself, as Dave sat by Dalston Station drumming tunes on his box with the blacking-brush, shouting the cry of his trade to passers-by, with an incessant jangle of tram-bells and rumble of traffic all around him, and the lantern he hung after dark on the end of the trolley-handle, a mere blot of yellow in the grey mist that had been thickening since sunset. Business had been slack, he was cold and hungry, and more than commonly thankful, at last, when Bob Harris attached himself to the handle and the trolley went rattling along homewards.

The kettle was singing on a ruddy fire in his room, the tea-things were on the table, and Bob Harris, who was as thoughtful as if he had something on his mind, invited himself to sit down and have a cup.

'I want to hev a private chat with you, Dave,' he began by and by. 'I've been a-wanting to a long while. If you ain't guessed it—an' I shouldn't wonder if you had—I'm a-goin' to let you into a secret.'

'Oh?'

'Yes.' Bob Harris blushed nervously, and wriggled his neck as if his collar was strangling him. He was a tall, thin, colourless fellow, Bob was; younger than Dave, but older looking by reason of his shrunken, melancholy countenance. 'Yes,' he said, 'I'm—I'm fair in love—that's straight!'

Dave regarded him dubiously.

'I haven't told her yet—'

'Told who?' Dave interrupted sharply.

Bob Harris winked, without the least appearance of mirth or slyness.

'Why, Nell Wyatt, o'course. I thought you'd ha' noticed.'

'Noticed what?' demanded Dave, gruffly.

'Oh—I dunno! I've loved that gal, though, ever since I fust see 'er. I was fair struck all of a heap right off. I ain't talked about it—it—well, it seems rather silly like, don't it? I ain't a lady's man neither, I ain't. But I made sure you'd ha' noticed it.'

Dave shook his head without speaking.

'D'yer think she's guessed it? I suppose she ain't never give you no hint, like? No? I rather fancy she has guessed, though, an'—sometimes I think it's all right, and sometimes I think she don't care no more for me than a brass farden. She—she's never arst you nothing about me?'

Dave shook his head again and said 'No', and Bob Harris was too self-absorbed to be startled by the tone in which he said it.

'She thinks a deal o'you, Dave,' Bob resumed, 'an' she praised me once, she did, because she said I was a decent sort of cove to you; something like that. I've come up with her odd times when she's bin takin' her work 'ome, but she won't never let me carry it, though I've walked aside of her an' talked. It's always bin about you, too; I s'pose I started it, 'cos I didn't know what else to talk of. She's downright sorry for you, old chap; she says she feels as if you was her own brother. "So do I," says I. An' that seemed to make us sort o' related, as it might be, an' yet I hadn't got the pluck to say what I wanted to, even then.' He fell into a gloomier mood and went on, 'If I was to speak up an' she says "No," I reckon it 'ud break my 'art. Sounds silly, don't it? But if you'd ever bin in love you'd know what I mean. Was you ever in love, Dave?'

Dave hesitated.

'Once,' he said abruptly.

'And how did you tell 'er? If you could give me the tip, like—'

'I never told 'er,' Dave cut in, irritably.

'P'raps you found out she didn't cotton to you, an'—'

'Look here!' growled Dave. 'Is it likely I was goin' to be such a tomfool as to go and trouble her after that?' He pointed impatiently to his maimed limbs. 'Very well, then!'

Bob Harris was contrite for five minutes.

'Another thing I was a-thinkin' of,' he pursued, 'I told you Nell Wyatt thought a deal o' your opinions, an' so on. Well, you can talk confidential to her, same as if she really was your own sister, an' I thought, p'raps, you wouldn't mind doin' me a turn by sayin' a good word for me an' lettin' me know 'ow she takes it?'

Dave did not reply immediately; yet Bob Harris had done him many friendly services, and he was not ungrateful.

'I doubt—whether it would be much use,' he faltered, huskily. 'Hadn't you better—speak to her—yourself?'

'I ain't got the pluck, that's a fact,' cried Bob. 'If I knew it was all right, then I'd do it like a shot. But if she ain't got to care for me yet, it 'ud be best to wait a bit longer afore I tries my luck. If she was to say "No", it 'ud break my 'art; it would that!'

'If you think anything I could say—'

'That's it. She thinks a deal o' you. I'd like you to say to her like this: "Miss Wyatt," says you, "I happen to know a young bloke what's fonder of a particular gal I know than any other gal on earth. He's fair struck." Put it delicate, like that. "Oh?" says she. "Yes," says you, "he's been 'ankerin' after her for a rare long while, but 'e ain't got the pluck to tell her." Then if she blushes an' looks pleased, you can bet it's all right. "He said 'e was sure you'd guessed it," says you. "Who is he?" says she. "It's Bob 'Arris downstairs," says you; "I know 'im well for a steady-goin' chap as any man need be, I do." Something nice, like that. "If he was to arst you," says you, confidential, "what d' yer think of him?" You can let me know what she says, an' I can speak out or shut up according. See?' Dave was a little ashamed of his own ungraciousness, he was so long in replying and so grudgingly gave the promise that was required of him.

'Will you try it this evening? I dessay you'll have a chance when she looks in to clear away the tea things,' Bob observed eagerly. 'Anyhow, I'll nip up a bit later an' see if she's said anything. Eh?'

Dave nodded mechanically, and was glad to be left alone.

He felt it was the wildest folly to be hankering wistfully, as he was, after those unforgotten whisperings of his heart which it would, mayhap, have been happier for him if he had never heard. He had taken refuge in a dull resignation; he had told himself a thousand times that there was not, there could not be hope for him any longer, and yet now—

'I thought I heard Mr Harris go down.'

Nell was looking in upon him from the doorway. He threw off his depression and assumed an air of gaiety that was but too obviously forced.

'Nell,' he cried, bent upon carrying out his undertaking without allowing himself further time for thought or uncertainty; 'I have got something very particular to say to you.'

She put her filled tray back on the table, and stood waiting for him to continue.

'I wanted to tell you;' his voice was not so steady as he had meant it to be; a strange bewilderment came upon him suddenly, and it was only by fortifying himself with a reminiscence of Bob Harris's ideal dialogue that he avoided breaking down at the very outset; 'there's a young fellow I know—who—who thinks the world of—of a girl that's—that's known to me too, but he—well, he daren't tell her so.'

Nell caught her breath, and the colour left her face and then came tingling back again, but she did not speak.

'He daren't tell her,' Dave stammered, awkwardly, 'because if she— she—if he found she cared nothing for him, he says, it would break his heart, Nell.'

Her lip quivered, and as he ventured to glance up at her their eyes met, and he saw that her's were full of tears. Flurried, and feeling that his advocacy was succeeding only too well, he went on confusedly:

'You don't ask who he is or she is, Nell, but—but he thought perhaps you—you might guess at it . . .'

She was down on her knees beside him; her arms were about his neck, her face hidden close against his, so that he could not see how the roses had blown again in her cheeks and that the light of a divine compassion was shining in her eyes with a radiance caught from no heaven that ever spanned this motley earth.

'Oh, she guessed it, Dave—she did guess it long ago,' she sobbed, 'but she wanted to be sure, and she waited—waited until now. She guessed it, though you tried to hide it from her, and shrank from asking her to share your life with you because you were so crippled and helpless, but—oh, Dave! she loved you before that, and—and it grieved her sometimes to think you could fancy she didn't love you now—now when you need her love far more than ever.'

What could he say? All he had desired was his, when he was fearing it was wholly lost to him; he had blindly accepted despair and it had changed to hope as he grasped it, and he was not stoical and unselfish enough to relinquish it again.

'But I am a mere wreck,' he faltered, feebly, 'and nigh helpless—'

'The more you'll need my help.'

'I shall never be fit for other work than I'm doing, and I—I doubt if what I can earn—'

'I can earn more than sufficient for myself, Dave—never think of that any more.'

Her womanly pity, her fearless and self-sacrificing love for him filled him with wonder and intense thankfulness. He could not understand it, he could scarcely even believe the reality of his own happiness.

'I don't deserve it,' he said, 'I can never deserve it—'

But she placed her hand upon his lips, and would hear no more.

Later, when they were both calm, he told her of Bob Harris, and frankly confessed what had led him to speak to her as he had done, and how, in pleading Bob's cause, he had involuntarily pleaded his own.

'And the only thing that troubles me,' he concluded, 'is that I must tell him the truth, Nell—I feel almost as if I had wronged him, and— he said it would break his heart.'

'You have not wronged him, Dave, for I never should have cared for him,' she said gravely. 'I am sorry for him too; but, dear, one had to be broken—which would you rather it was, his heart or mine?'

ELLEN T. FOWLER

An Old Wife's Tale

Though harps be dumb and crowns be dim,
I care not, if I comfort him.

Not Forsaken

'Rachel, my love,' said old Mr Weatherley, 'perhaps Ethel would take a dish of tea with us, if we could induce our hyperpunctual handmaid to bring it before the appointed time.'

Mrs Weatherley smiled. 'I will ring, dear, and see what we can do,' she replied in her gentle voice; 'but, as you know, our good Martha cannot endure an irregularity.'

'Oh! the land of bondage that we live in—we unfortunate men whose homes are ruled by women,' cried the dear old gentleman, gleefully rubbing his hands together.

But here I chimed in. 'Please don't order tea any earlier on my account, Mrs Weatherley, for I really am not in the slightest hurry. I was only afraid you might find the "linked sweetness" of my visitation "drawn out" a little too long, and that is why I made attempts at departure.'

'Sit down, my dear Ethel, sit down,' cried Mr Weatherley; 'do we ever find the sunset comes too late even on the longest day?'

'That is very pretty of you!' I replied; 'now I shall stay and enjoy myself. But what a pity that you rang to order tea earlier!'

'Not at all, not at all! It will not make a shadow of difference. My wife may order the tea—as King Canute ordered the tide—at whatsoever hour seemeth good to her; but the tea and the tide will still come in at the time appointed to them by Nature and Martha respectively. Great laws, my dear young lady, are not set aside to please every careless petitioner.'

I laughed. 'You knock-under shockingly to Martha,' I said.

'Nay; I wisely submit to the inevitable, and bow before a power greater than myself. And so does my wife. We never dare to defy Martha, do we dear?' he said, taking Mrs Weatherley's withered hand in his.

Mrs Weatherley smiled without speaking. She never spoke unless she was compelled to do so; but the cheerful, garrulous old gentleman talked enough for both.

I do not think I ever saw a more devoted couple than the Weatherleys. Fortunatus Weatherley was still a handsome man, and must have been a perfect demigod in his youth; but, alas! an accident, which occurred shortly before his marriage, had rendered him stone blind. His wife was a gentle, faded, elegant woman, whose whole nature seemed to be absorbed by her intense passion for her husband. Verily she was eyes to the blind; for she read to him, listened to him, tended him, with unceasing care. And although she was so quiet, one felt it was not because she had nothing to say. She was one of the women who remind one of Elise's shop window: not much show, but any amount of prestige. There was nothing modern about the Weatherleys—they would have scorned the idea; he cared for Addison and old port, and she for real lace and gardening; but, above all, they cared for each other—perhaps an equally old-fashioned taste.

Reading aloud to Mr Weatherley was a liberal education to me, who, alas! in those days was terribly up-to-date. He would not listen to modern novels, which were as meat and drink to my intellectual palate; he preferred style to plot, and good English to mental analysis. He would rather discover the origin of a word than vivisect a woman's feelings; and he appeared to regard the fathers and schoolmen as greater authorities than the leader-writers of the daily papers. He was a most cultured old gentleman.

'Do you ever wonder what people's minds would look like if you could see inside them?' I asked one day.

'No, my dear, no; what a very peculiar idea!'

'Well, I know what yours is like,' I continued.

'Do you indeed? Pray tell me,' he requested politely.

'Your mind is exactly like an old library; it is full of books bound in vellum and written in Latin, and its air is the atmosphere of culture and refinement. But it is just a bit—a very little bit—stuffy, don't you know?

It wants to have its windows opened to let in the fresh breezes of to-day.'

Mr Weatherley laughed. 'Very good, very good indeed! Now shall I tell you what your mind is like, my dear young lady?'

'Certainly; I am dying to hear.'

'It is like a newspaper stall: here a bit of news, and there a piece of gossip; here the review of some fresh book, and there the description of some fashionable costume; first one thing and then another, and the whole superstructure new every day.'

'You are rather hard on me, Mr Weatherley!'

'No, my dear, I am not. Remember that, nowadays, for one man that reads a book fifty read the newspaper; so you are on the winning side.'

'Now Mrs Weatherley's mind,' I continued thoughtfully, 'is like a picture-gallery in some grand old château; but when one comes to examine the pictures they are all portraits of you.'

'Very neat, my dear, very neat indeed. You have a wonderful power of observation, Ethel, and a most happy gift of putting that which you see into words; a gift, my child, which is no less a source of pleasure to yourself than to those who have the privilege of enjoying your friendship, I should imagine.'

'I'm glad that my chatter amuses you, Mr Weatherley.'

'It does so to a very great extent. I have always felt a sincere interest in young people; and as I have never had a child of my own, I delight to surround myself with young persons not of my own household. My quarrel with the young people of to-day is that they are not young enough.'

'Do you think that we are too advanced?'

'Quite so, quite so. Nowadays young women are always bothering their pretty heads about abstruse social problems or the higher mathematics; but when I was young they had more important things to think of—such as their latest sweethearts and their newest bonnets.'

'But we still have bonnets and sweethearts, as well as social problems and higher mathematics,' I argued. 'We may love Rome more than we used to do, but not Caesar less.'

'Perhaps so, perhaps so, my dear. You doubtless still go in for bonnets and sweethearts, but what bonnets!—and what sweethearts!—compared with those the girls had in my young days.'

'Do you think them so very inferior?'

'Inferior beyond expression! Of course I cannot see these things for myself; but my Rachel reads to me descriptions of the same now and again in some modern book or newspaper, and they make me feel positively unwell.'

I laughed.

'When I was young,' continued Mr Weatherley, 'a bonnet was— well, a bonnet; and I can assure you that it placed an almost insurmountable barrier betwixt one's self and the young woman concealed in the depths of it.'

'Like Truth at the bottom of a well.'

'Precisely. To-day, as far as I can gather, an impossible butterfly makes a nest of lace under the shadow of an artificial rose; and there is your bonnet!'

'It seems like a falling off, I confess,' I said. 'And what about the sweethearts?'

'There, my dear Ethel, the decadence is even more lamentable. In my time a young man fell in love with a young woman, and never rested till he had made a suitable home for her. Now a young man makes— at his leisure—a suitable home; and then, when he is middle-aged, furnishes it with the woman of his acquaintance who bores him the least.'

'What an awful description!'

'But,' he continued, 'to make up for not feeling love, modern people talk about it; just as they indulge in senseless conversation about medical science to make up for their lack of health and strength. We have more love stories than we used to have, but less love; just as we have more dentists than we used to have, but fewer teeth.'

'Tell me your love story, please,' I coaxed.

'Oh! that is an old story, Ethel, a very old story; but it is always new to me.'

'I do *so* want to hear it,' I urged.

'Then, my dear, I will tell it to you with pleasure. When I was very young I went to Canada, and there met two most charming orphan sisters, Naomi and Rachel Lestrange. Naomi, the elder, was a quiet, unobtrusive woman, with nothing distinctive about either her character or her appearance; but Rachel was the most beautiful and loveable creature I ever saw in my life.'

434

And the old man smiled with tender pride as he recalled the love of his youth.

'I daresay,' he continued, 'that now it is difficult for you to realize how very lovely my wife was when she was young. I have never seen her since, so she is still beautiful Rachel Lestrange to me; but I suppose her pretty hair is grey, and her dear face aged now.'

'Her hair is grey and her face worn,' I admitted; 'but she is still a most elegant woman, with a wonderful air of distinction.'

'She always had that,' he said, looking pleased. 'It was a characteristic of all the Lestranges that they had the grand air, I believe. She is very proud of her family, you know; it was one of the best French families in Canada.'

'She always shows by every movement that she is well-born,' I replied; 'but please go on with your story.'

'Well, of course I fell over head and ears in love with Rachel as soon as I set eyes on her; and to let you into an open secret, my dear, I have been in that state ever since. But before I dared to ask her to be my wife, the great catastrophe of my life occurred.'

'What was that?'

'One bitter winter's night the Lestranges' house caught fire, and was burnt to the ground. Fire, as you know, spreads very rapidly in that dry climate, and is most difficult to extinguish. When I appeared on the scene the staircase had already fallen in ruins, and the two sisters were standing at their bedroom window shrieking for help.'

'How terrible!' I exclaimed.

'Quick as thought,' continued Mr Weatherley, 'I placed a ladder against the wall of the burning house, and ascended it; though already the walls scorched my hands, and the smoke was so dense that I could hardly see. On reaching the sisters' room I seized Rachel—who happened to be nearest to the window—in my arms, carried her down the ladder, and resigned her to the crowd of friendly hands below. Then I reascended the ladder in order to save Naomi; but, alas! ere I was half-way up, the side of the house fell in, and I was precipitated into the burning ruins. Poor Naomi, of course, perished in the flames; but I was saved, though as by a miracle.'

'Were you much hurt?' I asked in breathless interest.

'Terribly. For many weeks I hung between life and death; and when at last I did recover, it was to the sad consciousness that I should be hopelessly blind to the end of my life.'

'How sad!' I whispered.

'Through all that long illness my Rachel nursed me with indefatigable skill and unwearying tenderness, and it was to her care that I really owed my recovery. Of course I felt that a blind man, such as I then found myself, had no right to ask any woman to link her lot with his; nor should I ever have done such a thing.'

'Not even if you knew she loved you?'

'No; her love would be no excuse for my selfishness.'

'But,' I argued, 'a woman, who really loved you, would only love you the more for your blindness; women are made like that.'

'I know they are, my dear, and men are made like this. But there was no need for me to ask Rachel anything, for during my illness—as I learnt afterwards—her name was ever on my lips, and I told her over and over again the story of my love for her.'

'And, when you were well enough to listen to her, she told you the story of her love for you, I suppose.'

'She did, bless her! she did. And I have been well enough for that ever since, thank Heaven! and have found increasing pleasure in the exercise.'

'And were you married soon afterwards?'

'Immediately that I was able to be moved, Rachel brought me to Halifax, away from the scene of our great catastrophe: there we were quietly married, and thence we sailed for England as soon as I was strong enough for the voyage.'

'Poor Mrs Weatherley! Did she feel her sister's death very much?' I asked.

'Sadly, my dear, sadly! In fact, I do not think she has ever been the same woman since. They were the most devoted pair of sisters I ever saw; but, between ourselves, I used to think that Naomi was just a little hard and severe on my sweet, loving Rachel, and domineered over her too much. But you, who have seen something of my darling's intensely sensitive and loving nature, can understand that a cold and stern and unsympathetic woman, such as Naomi was, might easily wound her without knowing it.'

'That is very likely,' I said; 'for I think it is quite impossible for those cold, calm natures to enter into the feelings of so passionately loving a woman as Mrs Weatherley.'

'But what distressed my poor Rachel so much,' added he, 'was that she felt that her sister's life had been, so to speak, sacrificed for hers; and she has an idea that perhaps she ought to have made me save Naomi first and then come back for her.'

'But in that case Rachel would have been burnt to death.'

'Of course she would. One of them must have perished anyhow, and I cannot cease to feel thankful that the one that was spared was my darling wife. But Rachel was always so utterly unselfish—as you see she is now in all her dealings with me—that she would rather suffer herself to any extent than let suffering fall on those whom she loved. As I hinted to you before, I think that poor Naomi—who was the elder and the least affectionate—sometimes took advantage of this; but I would not suggest such a thing to Rachel for worlds. She would not allow me—even in Naomi's lifetime—to suggest to her that there was a flaw in her idolized elder sister; and I should not be likely to do such a thing now that the poor woman has been in her grave these forty years and more.'

'It seems to me that Mrs Weatherley has a perfect genius for loving,' I said softly.

'She has, my dear, she has; but I sometimes fear that it takes too much out of her. Her body is so frail, and her heart so strong.'

Life passed on like an old-world dream in the quiet home of Fortunatus Weatherley. It was a perfect idyl to see these two old sweethearts together, and to guess at the love beyond all words which existed between them. But it grieved me to perceive that they both grew feebler as the days went by, and that their years were beginning to tell upon them.

'Ethel,' said Mrs Weatherley to me one day when her husband was out of earshot, 'don't you think that Fortunatus is looking less vigorous than he did some time ago?'

'You see, dear Mrs Weatherley, the weather is rather trying just now,' I replied evasively.

She gave a sad little laugh. 'Think of any weather's being trying to my Fortunatus! Why, Ethel, he has always been so splendidly strong that he never knew if the days were cold or hot, and he has never allowed a thermometer inside his house; he regarded them as what he calls modern medical rubbish.'

'But don't you think he is well?'

'No, I don't. I have shut my eyes to it as long as I could, but now they will not keep shut any longer. I can't help seeing it, though it almost kills me to do so.'

'Dear Mrs Weatherley,' I said, kissing her, because I did not know what else to say; and I find, in my dealings with my own sex, that kisses are as useful as asterisks in filling up inconvenient spaces.

'My child,' she said tenderly, her large blue eyes filling with tears, 'I hope you will fall in love some day, for no woman can be happy until she does. But pray that you may never love as much as I do! It is killing work.'

'Yet it means great joy.'

'And great sorrow. Surely the woman who feels "within her eyes the tears of two" has more than her share of weeping.'

'But she has the smiles of two as well.'

'Perhaps. And, Ethel, also pray that you and your sister may never fall in love with the same man. That is what I and my sister did, and it was the first cloud that ever came between us. The servant who described a cloud of the size of a man's hand as only a small cloud was very young and inexperienced, for a cloud of that size and shape is large enough to throw an unlifting shadow over the lives of countless women.'

'And did your sister love him very much?' I asked in youthful curiosity.

'I think she loved him as much as she was capable of loving anybody. But she had not the intense and concentrated power of loving, nor of feeling, nor of suffering, that I have. I have loved Fortunatus too much, Ethel; it would have been better for him and better for me if I had widened the circle of our life, and taken in more friends and broader interests. I see it all, now that it is too late.'

'Dear Mrs Weatherley, you are wrong.'

'No, child, I am right. Being a woman, the man I loved was quite enough for me, and filled every crevice of my life. But men are different. No woman—however much he loves her—is enough to fill a man's life and be his whole world, in the same way that men are everything to us. And I ought to have remembered this, seeing that my Fortunatus was blind, and could not make fresh interests for himself.'

'Yet he has been very happy,' I urged.

'Yes, he has; but he would have been happier had he lived in a larger world, and his hold on life would have been stronger. People who are moped die more easily than people who have plenty of interests.'

'But you did it because you loved much,' I said by way of comfort.

'Surely,' she answered with her sad smile, 'that plea for forgiveness can always be mine, whatever sins, negligences, and ignorances are brought up against me.'

Mrs Weatherley was right. Fortunatus was breaking up. Day by day he grew frailer and frailer, and even his wife's great love could not hold him back from the unknown bourne, whither he was journeying so quickly. Within a few months of my conversation with Mrs Weatherley, Fortunatus was dead; he died holding his wife's hand, and the last word he said was 'Rachel.'

But—to everyone's surprise, her own included—the blow did not kill Mrs Weatherley. Those slim, fragile creatures have often more latent strength than their robuster sisters, and it was so in her case. Strong, hearty women in the village fell ill and died, and still the thin, delicate-looking old lady lived on and on at the Manor House, not caring for her life in the very least. I never saw Mrs Weatherley smile after her husband's death, and I do not believe anyone else ever did. Poor old Martha finished her work and went to her place, but her mistress lived on and on, taking no notice of anything or anybody.

One day, when she was very old indeed, Mrs Weatherley said to me—

'Ethel, now that my life is over I see that it has all been a mistake.'

'How?' I asked.

'I cannot forgive myself for letting Fortunatus save me, and leave my poor sister to be burnt to death.'

'But, dear Mrs Weatherley,' I argued, 'you did not know that he would not be able to come back and fetch her also.'

'Of course, child, I did not. Had I thought so, nothing would have induced me not to stay behind. But, though it was all unintentional, my life really was saved at the sacrifice of my sister's.'

'But otherwise hers would have been saved at the expense of yours, which comes to the same thing. And if that had been the case, and she had lived and you had died, think what a difference it would have made to your husband!'

'I know; I have often thought of that, and it is my one comfort. Even had they married each other (which is doubtful, as my sister had a great horror of anyone with a physical infirmity), she could never have loved and cared for Fortunatus as I have done; it wasn't in her. And suppose —which is far more likely—that they had not married each other, what woman could have ever been to Fortunatus what I was?'

'No one, I am sure.'

'My sister loved him then because she always adored strength and beauty; but she would not have had the patience to wait on a blind man all her life, which to me was perfect bliss,' continued the old lady.

'Don't be unhappy about it, dear,' I said, trying in vain to soothe her.

She took no notice of me, but went on: 'You see, Ethel, it was all done in such a hurry I had not time to think. Fortunatus appeared at the window, and took me in his arms and carried me down through the blinding smoke, before I had time to realize what was happening. If I had known my sister would die I would never have left her, never. We had better have died together; though that would have been dreary for Fortunatus.'

'It would indeed. He could not have lived without you, Mrs Weatherley. Believe me, it is all for the best. I am sure that Naomi herself would forgive you, and understand.'

She looked at me with sorrowful eyes. 'I am Naomi,' she said; 'but he never found it out.'

De Amicitia

I

They were walking home from the theatre.

'Well, Mr White,' said Valentia, 'I think it was just fine.'

'It was magnificent!' replied Mr White.

And they were separated for a moment by the crowd, streaming up from the Français towards the Opera and the Boulevards.

'I think, if you don't mind,' she said, 'I'll take your arm, so that we shouldn't get lost.'

He gave her his arm, and they walked through the Louvre and over the river on their way to the Latin Quarter.

Valentia was an art student and Ferdinand White was a poet. Ferdinand considered Valentia the only woman who had ever been able to paint, and Valentia told Ferdinand that he was the only man she had met who knew anything about Art without being himself an artist. On her arrival in Paris, a year before, she had immediately inscribed herself, at the offices of the *New York Herald*, Valentia Stewart, Cincinnati, Ohio, U.S.A. She settled down in a respectable *pension*, and within a week was painting vigorously. Ferdinand White arrived from Oxford at about the same time, hired a dirty room in a shabby hotel, ate his meals at cheap restaurants in the Boulevard St Michel, read Stephen Mallarmé, and flattered himself that he was leading '*la vie de Bohême*'.

After two months, the Fates brought the pair together, and Ferdinand began to take his meals at Valentia's *pension*. They went to the museums together; and in the Sculpture Gallery at the Louvre, Ferdinand would discourse on ancient Greece in general and on Plato in particular, while among the pictures Valentia would lecture on tones and values and chiaroscuro. Ferdinand renounced Ruskin and all his works; Valentia read the Symposium. Frequently in the evening they went to

441

the theatre; sometimes to the Français, but more often to the Odéon; and after the performance they would discuss the play, its art, its technique—above all, its ethics. Ferdinand explained the piece he had in contemplation, and Valentia talked of the picture she meant to paint for next year's Salon; and the lady told her friends that her companion was the cleverest man she had met in her life, while he told his that she was the only really sympathetic and intelligent girl he had ever known. Thus were united in bonds of amity, Great Britain on the one side and the United States of America and Ireland on the other.

But when Ferdinand spoke of Valentia to the few Frenchmen he knew, they asked him,—

'But this Miss Stewart—is she pretty?'

'Certainly—in her American way; a long face, with the hair parted in the middle and hanging over the nape of the neck. Her mouth is quite classic.'

'And have you never kissed the classic mouth?'

'I? Never!'

'Has she a good figure?'

'Admirable!'

'And yet—Oh, you English!' And they smiled and shrugged their shoulders as they said, 'How English!'

'But, my good fellow,' cried Ferdinand, in execrable French, 'you don't understand. We are friends, the best of friends.'

They shrugged their shoulders more despairingly than ever.

II

They stood on the bridge and looked at the water and the dark masses of the houses on the Latin side, with the twin towers of Notre Dame rising dimly behind them. Ferdinand thought of the Thames at night, with the barges gliding slowly down, and the twinkling of the lights along the Embankment.

'It must be a little like that in Holland,' she said, 'but without the lights and with greater stillness.'

'When do you start?'

She had been making preparations for spending the summer in a little village near Amsterdam, to paint.

'I can't go now,' cried Valentia. 'Corrie Sayles is going home, and there's no one else I can go with. And I can't go alone. Where are you going?'

'I? I have no plans. . . . I never make plans.'

They paused, looking at the reflections in the water. Then she said,—

'I don't see why you shouldn't come to Holland with me!'

He did not know what to think; he knew she had been reading the Symposium.

'After all,' she said, 'there's no reason why one shouldn't go away with a man as well as with a woman.'

His French friends would have suggested that there were many reasons why one should go away with a woman rather than a man; but, like his companion, Ferdinand looked at it in the light of pure friendship.

'When one comes to think of it, I really don't see why we shouldn't. And the mere fact of staying at the same hotel can make no difference to either of us. We shall both have our work—you your painting, and I my play.'

As they considered it, the idea was distinctly pleasing; they wondered that it had not occurred to them before. Sauntering homewards, they discussed the details, and in half an hour had decided on the plan of their journey, the date and the train.

Next day Valentia went to say good-bye to the old French painter whom all the American girls called Popper. She found him in a capacious dressing-gown, smoking cigarettes.

'Well, my dear,' he said, 'what news?'

'I'm going to Holland to paint windmills.'

'A very laudable ambition. With your mother?'

'My good Popper, my mother's in Cincinnati. I'm going with Mr White.'

'With Mr White?' He raised his eyebrows. 'You are very frank about it.'

'Why—what do you mean?'

He put on his glasses and looked at her carefully.

'Does it not seem to you a rather—curious thing for a young girl of your age to go away with a young man of the age of Mr Ferdinand White?'

'Good gracious me! One would think I was doing something that had never been done before!'

'Oh, many a young man has gone travelling with a young woman, but they generally start by a night train, and arrive at the station in different cabs.'

'But surely, Popper, you don't mean to insinuate—Mr White and I are going to Holland as friends.'

'Friends!'

He looked at her more curiously than ever.

'One can have a man friend as well as a girl friend,' she continued. 'And I don't see why he shouldn't be just as good a friend.'

'The danger is that he become too good.'

'You misunderstand me entirely, Popper; we are friends, and nothing but friends.'

'You are entirely off your head, my child.'

'Ah! you're a Frenchman, you can't understand these things. We are different.'

'I imagine that you are human beings, even though England and America respectively had the intense good fortune of seeing your birth.'

'We're human beings—and more than that, we're nineteenth century human beings. Love is not everything. It is a part of one—perhaps the lower part—an accessory to man's life, needful for the continuation of the species.'

'You use such difficult words, my dear.'

'There is something higher and nobler and purer than love—there is friendship. Ferdinand White is my friend. I have the amplest confidence in him. I am certain that no unclean thought has ever entered his head.'

She spoke quite heatedly, and as she flushed up, the old painter thought her astonishingly handsome. Then she added as an afterthought,—

'We despise passion. Passion is ugly; it is grotesque.'

The painter stroked his imperial and faintly smiled.

'My child, you must permit me to tell you that you are foolish. Passion is the most lovely thing in the world; without it we should not paint beautiful pictures. It is passion that makes a woman of a society lady; it is passion that makes a man even of—an art critic.'

'We do not want it,' she said. 'We worship Venus Urania. We are all spirit and soul.'

'You have been reading Plato; soon you will read Zola.'

He smiled again, and lit another cigarette.

444

'Do you disapprove of my going?' she asked after a little silence.

He paused and looked at her. Then he shrugged his shoulders.

'On the contrary, I approve. It is foolish, but that is no reason why you should not do it. After all, folly is the great attribute of man. No judge is as grave as an owl; no soldier fighting for his country flies as rapidly as the hare. You may be strong, but you are not so strong as a horse; you may be gluttonous, but you cannot eat like a boa-constrictor. But there is no beast that can be as foolish as man. And since one should always do what one can do best—be foolish. Strive for folly above all things. Let the height of your ambition be the pointed cap with the golden bells. So, *bon voyage*! I will come and see you off to-morrow.'

The painter arrived at the station with a box of sweets, which he handed to Valentia with a smile. He shook Ferdinand's hand warmly and muttered under his breath,—

'Silly fool! he's thinking of friendship, too!'

Then, as the train steamed out, he waved his hand and cried,—

'Be foolish! Be foolish!'

He walked slowly out of the station, and sat down at a *café*. He lit a cigarette, and, sipping his absinthe, said,—

'Imbeciles!'

III

They arrived at Amsterdam in the evening, and, after dinner, gathered together their belongings and crossed the Ij as the moon shone over the waters; then they got into the little steam tram and started for Monnickendam. They stood side by side on the platform of the carriage and watched the broad meadows bathed in moonlight, the formless shapes of the cattle lying on the grass, and the black outlines of the mills; they passed by a long, sleeping canal, and they stopped at little, silent villages. At last they entered the dead town, and the tram put them down at the hotel door.

Next morning, when she was half dressed, Valentia threw open the window of her room, and looked out into the garden. Ferdinand was walking about, dressed as befitted the place and season—in flannels—with a huge white hat on his head. She could not help thinking him very handsome—and she took off the blue skirt she had intended to work in, and put on a dress of muslin all bespattered with coloured flowers, and she took in her hand a flat straw hat with red ribbons.

'You look like a Dresden shepherdess,' he said, as they met.

They had breakfast in the garden beneath the trees; and as she poured out his tea, she laughed, and with the American accent which he was beginning to think made English so harmonious, said,—

'I reckon this about takes the shine out of Paris.'

They had agreed to start work at once, losing no time, for they wanted to have a lot to show on their return to France, that their scheme might justify itself. Ferdinand wished to accompany Valentia on her search for the picturesque, but she would not let him; so, after breakfast, he sat himself down in the summer-house, and spread out all round him his nice white paper, lit his pipe, cut his quills, and proceeded to the evolution of a masterpiece. Valentia tied the red strings of her sunbonnet under her chin, selected a sketchbook, and sallied forth.

At luncheon they met, and Valentia told of a little bit of canal, with an old windmill on one side of it, which she had decided to paint, while Ferdinand announced that he had settled on the names of his *dramatis personae*. In the afternoon they returned to their work, and at night, tired with the previous day's travelling, went to bed soon after dinner.

So passed the second day; and the third day, and the fourth; till the end of the week came, and they had worked diligently. They were both of them rather surprised at the ease with which they became accustomed to their life.

'How absurd all this fuss is,' said Valentia, 'that people make about the differences of the sexes! I am sure it is only habit.'

'We have ourselves to prove that there is nothing in it,' he replied. 'You know, it is an interesting experiment that we are making.'

She had not looked at it in that light before.

'Perhaps it is. We may be the forerunners of a new era.'

'The Edisons of a new communion!'

'I shall write and tell Monsieur Rollo all about it.'

In the course of the letter, she said,—

Sex is a morbid instinct. Out here, in the calmness of the canal and the broad meadows, it never enters one's head. I do not think of Ferdinand as a man—

She looked up at him as she wrote the words. He was reading a book and she saw him in profile, with the head bent down. Through the leaves the sun lit up his face with a soft light that was almost green, and it occurred to her that it would be interesting to paint him.

I do not think of Ferdinand as a man; to me he is a companion. He has a wider experience than a woman, and he talks of different things. Otherwise I see no difference. On his part, the idea of my sex never occurs to him, and far from being annoyed as an ordinary woman might be, I am proud of it. It shows me that, when I chose a companion, I chose well. To him I am not a woman; I am a man.

And she finished with a repetition of Ferdinand's remark,—
'We are the Edisons of a new communion!'
When Valentia began to paint her companion's portrait, they were naturally much more together. And they never grew tired of sitting in the pleasant garden under the trees, while she worked at her canvas and green shadows fell on the profile of Ferdinand White. They talked of many things. After a while they became less reserved about their private concerns. Valentia told Ferdinand about her home in Ohio, and about her people; and Ferdinand spoke of the country parsonage in which he had spent his childhood, and the public school, and lastly of Oxford and the strange, happy days when he had learnt to read Plato and Walter Pater. . . .
At last Valentia threw aside her brushes and leant back with a sigh.
'It is finished!'
Ferdinand rose and stretched himself, and went to look at his portrait. He stood before it for a while, and then he placed his hand on Valentia's shoulder.
'You are a genius, Miss Stewart.'
She looked up at him.
'Ah, Mr White, I was inspired by you. It is more your work than mine.'

IV

In the evening they went out for a stroll. They wandered through the silent street; in the darkness they lost the quaintness of the red brick houses, contrasting with the bright yellow of the paving, but it was even quieter than by day. The street was very broad, and it wound about from east to west and from west to east, and at last it took them to the tiny harbour. Two fishing smacks were basking on the water, moored to the side, and the Zuyder Zee was covered with the innumerable reflections of the stars. On one of the boats a man was sitting at the prow, fishing, and now and then, through the darkness, one saw the red glow of his pipe; by his side, huddled up on a sail, lay a sleeping boy. The other boat seemed deserted. Ferdinand and Valentia stood for a long time watching the fisher, and he was so still that they wondered whether he too were sleeping. They looked across the sea, and in the distance saw the dim lights of Marken, the island of fishers. They wandered on again through the street, and now the lights in the windows were extinguished one by one, and sleep came over the town; and the quietness was even greater than before. They walked on, and their footsteps made no sound. They felt themselves alone in the dead city, and they did not speak.

At length they came to a canal gliding towards the sea; they followed it inland, and here the darkness was equal to the silence. Great trees that had been planted when William of Orange was king in England threw their shade over the water, shutting out the stars. They wandered along on the soft earth, they could not hear themselves walk—and they did not speak.

They came to a bridge over the canal and stood on it, looking at the water and the trees above them, and the water and the trees below them—and they did not speak.

Then out of the darkness came another darkness, and gradually loomed forth the heaviness of a barge. Noiselessly it glided down the stream, very slowly; at the end of it a boy stood at the tiller, steering; and it passed beneath them and beyond, till it lost itself in the night, and again they were alone.

They stood side by side, leaning against the parapet, looking down at the water. . . . And from the water rose up Love, and Love fluttered down from the trees, and Love was borne along upon the night air. Ferdinand did not know what was happening to him; he felt Valentia by his side, and he drew closer to her, till her dress touched his legs and the silk of her sleeve rubbed against his arm. It was so dark that he could not see her face; he wondered of what she was thinking. She made a little movement and to him came a faint wave of the scent she wore. Presently two forms passed by on the bank and they saw a lover with his arm round a girl's waist, and then they too were hidden in the darkness. Ferdinand trembled as he spoke.

'Only Love is waking!'

'And we!' she said.

'And—you!'

He wondered why she said nothing. Did she understand? He put his hand on her arm.

'Valentia!'

He had never called her by her Christian name before. She turned her face towards him.

'What do you mean?'

'Oh, Valentia, I love you! I can't help it.'

A sob burst from her.

'Didn't you understand,' he said, 'all those hours that I sat for you while you painted, and these long nights in which we wandered by the water?'

'I thought you were my friend.'

'I thought so too. When I sat before you and watched you paint, and looked at your beautiful hair and your eyes, I thought I was your friend. And I looked at the lines of your body beneath your dress. And when it pleased me to carry your easel and walk with you, I thought it was friendship. Only to-night I know I am in love. Oh, Valentia, I am so glad!'

She could not keep back her tears. Her bosom heaved, and she wept.

'You are a woman,' he said. 'Did you not see?'

'I am so sorry,' she said, her voice all broken. 'I thought we were such good friends. I was so happy. And now you have spoilt it all.'

'Valentia, I love you.'

'I thought our friendship was so good and pure. And I felt so strong in it. It seemed to me so beautiful.'

'Did you think I was less a man than the fisherman you see walking beneath the trees at night?'

'It is all over now,' she sighed.

'What do you mean?'

449

'I can't stay here with you alone.'

'You're not going away?'

'Before, there was no harm in our being together at the hotel; but now—'

'Oh, Valentia, don't leave me. I can't—I can't live without you.'

She heard the unhappiness in his voice. She turned to him again and laid her two hands on his shoulders.

'Why can't you forget it all, and let us be good friends again? Forget that you are a man. A woman can remain with a man for ever, and always be content to walk and read and talk with him, and never think of anything else. Can you forget it, Ferdinand? You will make me so happy.'

He did not answer, and for a long time they stood on the bridge in silence. At last he sighed—a heartbroken sigh.

'Perhaps you're right. It may be better to pretend that we are friends. If you like, we will forget all this.'

Her heart was too full; she could not answer; but she held out her hands to him. He took them in his own, and, bending down, kissed them.

Then they walked home, side by side, without speaking.

V

Next morning Valentia received M. Rollo's answer to her letter. He apologised for his delay in answering. 'You are a philosopher,' he said—she could see the little snigger with which he had written the words—

You are a philosopher, and I was afraid lest my reply should disturb the course of your reflections on friendship. I confess that I did not entirely understand your letter, but I gathered that the sentiments were correct, and it gave me great pleasure to know that your experiment has had such excellent results. I gather that you have not yet discovered that there is more than a verbal connection between Friendship and Love.

The reference is to the French equivalents of those states of mind.

But to speak seriously, dear child. You are young and beautiful now, but not so very many years shall pass before your lovely skin becomes coarse and muddy, and your teeth yellow, and the wrinkles appear about your mouth and eyes. You have not so very many years before you in which to collect sensations, and the recollection of one's loves is, perhaps, the greatest pleasure left to one's old age. To be virtuous, my dear, is admirable, but there are so many interpretations of virtue. For myself, I can say that I have never regretted the temptations to which I succumbed, but often the temptations I have resisted. Therefore, love, love, love! And remember that if love at sixty in a man is sometimes pathetic, in a woman at forty it is always ridiculous. Therefore, take your youth in both hands and say to yourself, 'Life is short, but let me live before I die!'

She did not show the letter to Ferdinand.

Next day it rained. Valentia retired to a room at the top of the house and began to paint, but the incessant patter on the roof got on her nerves; the painting bored her, and she threw aside the brushes in disgust. She came downstairs and found Ferdinand in the dining-room, standing at the window looking at the rain. It came down in one continual steady pour, and the water ran off the raised brickwork of the middle of the street to the gutters by the side, running along in a swift and murky rivulet. The red brick of the opposite house looked cold and cheerless in the wet. . . . He did not turn or speak to her as she came in. She remarked that it did not look like leaving off. He made no answer. She drew a chair to the second window and tried to read, but she could not understand what she was reading. And she looked out at the pouring rain and the red brick house opposite. She wondered why he had not answered.

The innkeeper brought them their luncheon. Ferdinand took no notice of the preparations.

'Will you come to luncheon, Mr White?' she said to him. 'It is quite ready.'

'I beg your pardon,' he said gravely, as he took his seat.

He looked at her quickly, and then immediately dropping his eyes, began eating. She wished he would not look so sad; she was very sorry for him.

She made an observation and he appeared to rouse himself. He replied and they began talking, very calmly and coldly, as if they had not known one another five minutes. They talked of Art with the biggest of A's, and they compared Dutch painting with Italian; they spoke of Rembrandt and his life.

'Rembrandt had passion,' said Ferdinand, bitterly, 'and therefore he was unhappy. It is only the sexless, passionless. creature, the block of ice, that can be happy in this world.'

She blushed and did not answer.

The afternoon Valentia spent in her room, pretending to write letters, and she wondered whether Ferdinand was wishing her downstairs.

At dinner they sought refuge in abstractions. They talked of dykes and windmills and cigars, the history of Holland and its constitution, the constitution of the United States and the edifying spectacle of the politics of that blessed country. They talked of political economy and pessimism and cattle rearing, the state of agriculture in England, the foreign policy of the day, Anarchism, the President of the French Republic. They would have talked of bi-metallism if they could. People hearing them would have thought them very learned and extraordinarily staid.

At last they separated, and as she undressed Valentia told herself that Ferdinand had kept his promise. Everything was just as it had been before, and the only change was that he used her Christian name. And she rather liked him to call her Valentia.

But next day Ferdinand did not seem able to command himself. When Valentia addressed him, he answered in monosyllables, with eyes averted; but when she had her back turned, she felt that he was looking at her. After breakfast she went away painting haystacks, and was late for luncheon.

She apologised.

'It is of no consequence,' he said, keeping his eyes on the ground. And those were the only words he spoke to her during the remainder of the day. Once, when he was looking at her surreptitiously, and she suddenly turned round, their eyes met, and for a moment he gazed straight at her, then walked away. She wished he would not look so sad. As she was going to bed, she held out her hand to him to say goodnight, and she added,—

'I don't want to make you unhappy, Mr White. I'm very sorry.'

'It's not your fault,' he said. 'You can't help it, if you're a stock and a stone.'

He went away without taking the proffered hand. Valentia cried that night.

In the morning she found a note outside her door:—

Pardon me if I was rude, but I was not master of myself. I am going to Volendam; I hate Monnickendam.

VI

Ferdinand arrived at Volendam. It was a fishing village, only three miles across country from Monnickendam, but the route, by steam tram and canal, was so circuitous, that, with luggage, it took one two hours to get from place to place. He had walked over there with Valentia, and it had almost tempted them to desert Monnickendam. Ferdinand took a room at the hotel and walked out, trying to distract himself. The village consisted of a couple of score of houses, built round a semi-circular dyke against the sea, and in the semi-circle lay the fleet of fishing boats. Men and women were sitting at their doors mending nets. He looked at the fishermen, great, sturdy fellows, with rough, weather-beaten faces, huge earrings dangling from their ears. He took note of their quaint costume—black stockings and breeches, the latter more baggy than a Turk's, and the crushed strawberry of their high jackets, cut close to the body. He remembered how he had looked at them with Valentia, and the group of boys and men that she had sketched. He remembered how they walked along, peeping into the houses, where everything was spick and span, as only a Dutch cottage can be, with old Delft plates hanging on the walls, and pots and pans of polished brass. And he looked over the sea to the island of Marken, with its masts crowded together, like a forest without leaf or branch. Coming to the end of the little town he saw the church of Monnickendam, the red steeple half-hidden by the trees. He wondered where Valentia was—what she was doing.

But he turned back resolutely, and, going to his room, opened his books and began reading. He rubbed his eyes and frowned, in order to fix his attention, but the book said nothing but Valentia. At last he threw it aside and took his Plato and his dictionary, commencing to translate a difficult passage, word for word. But whenever he looked up a word he could only see Valentia, and he could not make head or tail of the Greek. He threw it aside also, and set out walking. He walked as hard as he could—away from Monnickendam.

The second day was not quite so difficult, and he read till his mind was dazed, and then he wrote letters home and told them he was enjoying himself tremendously, and he walked till he felt his legs dropping off.

Next morning it occurred to him that Valentia might have written. Trembling with excitement, he watched the postman coming down the street—but he had no letter for Ferdinand. There would be no more post that day.

But the next day Ferdinand felt sure there would be a letter for him; the postman passed by the hotel door without stopping. Ferdinand thought he should go mad. All day he walked up and down his room, thinking only of Valentia. Why did she not write?

The night fell and he could see from his window the moon shining over the clump of trees about Monnickendam church—he could stand it no longer. He put on his hat and walked across country; the three miles were endless; the church and the trees seemed to grow no nearer, and at last, when he thought himself close, he found he had a bay to walk round, and it appeared further away than ever.

He came to the mouth of the canal along which he and Valentia had so often walked. He looked about, but he could see no one. His heart beat as he approached the little bridge, but Valentia was not there. Of course she would not come out alone. He ran to the hotel and asked for her. They told him she was not in. He walked through the town; not a soul was to be seen. He came to the church; he walked round, and then—right at the edge of the trees—he saw a figure sitting on a bench.

She was dressed in the same flowered dress which she had worn when he likened her to a Dresden shepherdess; she was looking towards Volendam.

He went up to her silently. She sprang up with a little shriek.

'Ferdinand!'

'Oh, Valentia, I cannot help it. I could not remain away any longer. I could do nothing but think of you all day, all night. If you knew how I loved you! Oh, Valentia, have pity on me! I cannot be your friend. It's all nonsense about friendship; I hate it. I can only love you. I love you with all my heart and soul, Valentia.'

She was frightened.

'Oh! how can you stand there so coldly and watch my agony? Don't you see? How can you be so cold?'

'I am not cold, Ferdinand,' she said, trembling. 'Do you think I have been happy while you were away?'

'Valentia!'

'I thought of you, too, Ferdinand, all day, all night. And I longed for you to come back. I did not know till you went that—I loved you.'

'Oh, Valentia!'

He took her in his arms and pressed her passionately to him.

'No, for God's sake!'

She tore herself away. But again he took her in his arms, and this time he kissed her on the mouth. She tried to turn her face away.

'I shall kill myself, Ferdinand!'

'What do you mean?'

'In those long hours that I sat here looking towards you, I felt I loved you—I loved you as passionately as you said you loved me. But if you came back, and—anything happened—I swore that I would throw myself in the canal.'

He looked at her.

'I could not—live afterwards,' she said hoarsely. 'It would be too horrible. I should be—oh, I can't think of it!'

He took her in his arms again and kissed her.

'Have mercy on me!' she cried.

'You love me, Valentia.'

'Oh, it is nothing to you. Afterwards you will be just the same as before. Why cannot men love peacefully like women? I should be so happy to remain always as we are now, and never change. I tell you I shall kill myself.'

'I will do as you do, Valentia.'

'You?'

'If anything happens, Valentia,' he said gravely, 'we will go down to the canal together.'

She was horrified at the idea; but it fascinated her.

'I should like to die in your arms,' she said.

For the second time he bent down and took her hands and kissed them. Then she went alone into the silent church, and prayed.

455

VII

They went home. Ferdinand was so pleased to be at the hotel again, near her. His bed seemed so comfortable; he was so happy, and he slept, dreaming of Valentia.

The following night they went for their walk, arm in arm; and they came to the canal. From the bridge they looked at the water. It was very dark; they could not hear it flow. No stars were reflected in it, and the trees by its side made the depth seem endless. Valentia shuddered. Perhaps in a little while their bodies would be lying deep down in the water. And they would be in one another's arms, and they would never be separated. Oh, what a price it was to pay! She looked tearfully at Ferdinand, but he was looking down at the darkness beneath them, and he was intensely grave.

And they wandered there by day and looked at the black reflection of the trees. And in the heat it seemed so cool and restful. . . .

They abandoned their work. What did pictures and books matter now? They sauntered about the meadows, along shady roads; they watched the black and white cows sleepily browsing, sometimes coming to the water's edge to drink, and looking at themselves, amazed. They saw the huge-limbed milkmaids come along with their little stools and their pails, deftly tying the cow's hind legs that it might not kick. And the steaming milk frothed into the pails and was poured into huge barrels, and as each cow was freed, she shook herself a little and recommenced to browse.

And they loved their life as they had never loved it before.

One evening they went again to the canal and looked at the water, but they seemed to have lost their emotions before it. They were no longer afraid. Ferdinand sat on the parapet and Valentia leaned against him. He bent his head so that his face might touch her hair. She looked at him and smiled, and she almost lifted her lips. He kissed them.

'Do you love me, Ferdinand?'

He gave the answer without words.

Their faces were touching now, and he was holding her hands. They were both very happy.

'You know, Ferdinand,' she whispered, 'we are very foolish.'

'I don't care.'

'Monsieur Rollo said that folly was the chief attribute of man.'

'What did he say of love?'

'I forget.'

Then, after a pause, he whispered in her ear,—

'I love you!'

And she held up her lips to him again.

'After all,' she said, 'we're only human beings. We can't help it. I think—'

She hesitated; what she was going to say had something of the anti-climax in it.

'I think—it would be very silly if—if we threw ourselves in the horrid canal.'

'Valentia, do you mean—?'

She smiled charmingly as she answered,—

'What you will, Ferdinand.'

Again he took both her hands, and, bending down, kissed them. . . . But this time she lifted him up to her and kissed him on the lips.

VIII

One night after dinner I told this story to my aunt.

'But why on earth didn't they get married?' she asked, when I had finished.

'Good Heavens!' I cried. 'It never occurred to me.'

'Well, I think they ought,' she said.

'Oh, I have no doubt they did. I expect they got on their bikes and rode off to the Consulate at Amsterdam there and then. I'm sure it would have been his first thought.'

'Of course, some girls are very queer,' said my aunt.

CHARLOTTE MEW

Some Ways of Love

I

*Les âmes sont presque impénétrables les unes aux autres, et c'est
ce qui vous montre le néant cruel de l'amour.*

(Souls are almost impenetrable to each other, and it is this which
demonstrates to you the cruel nothingness of love.)

'And so you send me away unanswered?' said the young man, rising
reluctantly, taking his gloves from the table and glancing meanwhile at the obdurate little lady on the sofa, who witnessed his distress
with that quizzical kindness, which distracted him, in her clear, rather
humorous blue eyes.

'I will give you an answer if you wish it.'

'I would rather hope,—you do give me a ray of hope?'

'Just a ray', she admitted, laughing, with the same disturbing air of
indulgence. 'But don't magnify it—one has a habit, I know, of magni-
fying "rays"—and I don't want you to come back—if you do come
back—with a whole blazing sun.'

'You are very frank, and a little cruel.'

'I am afraid I mean to be—both. It is so much better for you.' She
was twisting the rings round her small fingers while she spoke, as if the
interview were becoming slightly wearisome.

'You treat me like a boy', he broke out, with youthful bitterness.

'Ah! the cruellest treatment one can give to boys', she answered,
looking up at him with her hovering brilliant, vexatious smile. But
meeting his clouded glance she paused, and abandoned temporarily the
lighter line of argument.

'Forgive me, Captain Henley——'

He scanned the treacherous face to see if the appellation so sedately

458

uttered were not designedly malicious, but her next words reassured
him.

'I will be more serious. See,—frankly, cruelly perhaps,—I do not
know my heart.' She did not falter over the studied phrase. 'You are not
the first', observing his troubled features ruefully, as she dealt the innocent blow. 'You may not be—the last.'

It left her lips a little labouredly, despite its apparent levity, but he
was too much absorbed to notice fine shades of accent, and she went
on,—'I am not so charming as you think me, but that's a foregone
conclusion. Shall I say, not so charming as I seem? At eighteen I made—
I will not suggest I was led into—a loveless marriage. It was a failure,
of course. I do not want to make another. I shrink from helping, shall
we say, you? to a similar mistake. You must pardon me if I admit I do
look upon you as—young; for years, you know, are deceptive things,—
even with women.'

His boyish face expressed annoyance.

'Ah! I meant you to smile, and you are frowning. I should not be
outraged if any one offered me the indignity you resent so foolishly;
but then I am not—fortunately or unfortunately—so young as you.
Come, be reasonable', she urged, with a singular sweetness of persuasion: 'if I do not know my mind, is it so strange in me to suppose that
yours may change? Again forgive me if I anticipate you. I have been
glib enough with "nevers" and "for evers" in my day; but I shun them.
I listen to them with more caution now. "Never", "for ever",' she repeated, and mused for a moment over the words. 'I sometimes imagine
one is only safe in speaking them on the threshold of another life than
this. It is a fancy of mine we should not use them now. Please humour it.'

'I am not so diffident, doubtful, nor possibly so cynical', he began;
but she interposed with the wave of a little glittering hand.

'Precisely; therefore I warn you. Why,' she proceeded, with an unmistakable note of tenderness, which he did not catch, 'you are even
younger than I thought. I am glad—heartily—that you are going to the
front. Cut up as many rascals as you can,—a little fighting will bring
you a lot of wisdom, and—oh yes! I know what a brute I am!—you
want it badly. Come back in a year with your V.C. or without it:
anyhow, with an ounce or two of experience in your pocket, and, if you

do come back to me'—he winced at the repetition of the 'if' and the doubt implied by it—'I promise to treat you like a man.'

'And give me my answer?'

'Yes.' She pronounced it with sudden softness.

'Meanwhile?'

'Meanwhile, husband the "ray" if you like, but don't extend it; and remember it pledges us both to nothing. You'—she rapidly substituted 'we—are free.'

'You are free of course, Lady Hopedene', he agreed, with becoming solemnity. 'I shall always consider myself bound. I—I—should like you to know that I do not consider myself free.'

'As it please you', she yielded, with a flash of amusement shot at the melancholy countenance.

'It will be my only consolation', he returned, with ponderous sadness.

'So be it, then: I mustn't rob you of that. But remember, if the occasion calls, that I acquit you absolutely from reappearance at this bar.'

A slight break in her voice reminded her that the time had come for his dismissal, and she proceeded promptly: 'Now we must say Good-bye.'

'Only *au revoir*.'

'You are very literal; I like the old phrase best.' She rose and took his hand, holding it longer than usual; and he looked down at her perturbedly. 'Am I to have only a frown to keep?'

'Keep that', he cried, suddenly stooping to kiss the frail white fingers in his palm.

Then he turned away quickly, went out and closed the door, missing, behind it, that curious fragrance of her presence, fresh and keen like morning air in meadows, subtler and sweeter than the faint perfume that hung about her person.

She stood motionless, tasting his departure: the smile which she had given him leave to take had faded from her eyes, and they were staring blankly at the door.

'Have I done well—for him?' she asked herself. 'He may—he will—surely meet other women perhaps less scrupulous than I. And for myself?' She went towards a mirror set between the windows, and studied critically the reflexion that faced her there. It showed a diminutive, delicately-tinted face, beneath the childishly fair hair waved carefully above it, and for the moment, robbed of its insouciance, it looked wistful and a little wan. 'I can spare a year,' she decided, after a pause of close regard, 'and at any rate my conscience is delightfully clear. My heart—"I do not know my heart."' She laughed unsteadily. 'He swallowed that absurdity; he might have read—bah', she cried, throwing her hands out with a gesture caught abroad, sometimes recurring with other un-English tricks of manner. 'He is too young to read anything without a stammer yet. A woman has no right to take advantage of such a boy's first fancy. Assuredly I have done well.'

She went back to the sofa and rested her head among the vivid cushions. When at length she raised it, the gay blue eyes were dim.

II

The *Nubia* was homeward bound, and her passengers were experiencing the inconveniences incidental to a passage through the Red Sea. Now and then the picturesque figure of a lascar darted across the semi-darkness. The stewards were throwing the mattresses upon the deck under a starlit sky. The captain and his first officer had just surprised a *tête-à-tête* taking place in a quiet corner of the ship, with diversified feelings of annoyance.

'Is Henley serious?' the former inquired irritably. 'Because it's a deuced awkward business. Miss Playfair is in my charge, and it isn't the first time I have had trouble over little affairs of the kind. Relatives are always unreasonable—even other people's relatives—but, by Jove, I think the attractive objects of their solicitude are worse.'

'They met in India, so I suppose it's all right', returned the young man curtly, disinclined to discuss a situation which inspired him personally with a sensation of despair.

'I shall be glad to see Plymouth and the last of such an embarrassing cargo', returned the captain, turning on his heel.

'*Moi aussi*', muttered the young lieutenant sulkily.

But the subjects of this brief discourse did not apparently share these sentiments of relief at the prospect of gaining port.

'In spite of this awful heat, I wish it would never end', a deep voice proclaimed from the darkness. 'It's ideal! The sea and the sky, this glorious sense of solitude, and you and I the only people on earth, it seems, in the midst of it. Say'—in a lower key—'you wish it might never end.'

'What is the good of wishing, when you persist that it must end when we go ashore?'

'The gods may be merciful.'

'You mean Lady Hopedene may be—cold?'

'She is always cold; a lovely little piece of ice. She never cared a hang for me, Mildred, or don't you think she must have betrayed it then?'

'I suppose she wanted to see what stuff you were made of. Why did she give you the chance of going back?'

'It was only a manner (she has a charming manner) of saying "No". Women'—he pronounced it with an air of profundity—'don't try experiments on the men they love.'

'Then why go back at all? It is only inviting humiliation, if that's your view of it.' Her tone, usually languorous, took a brisker note.

'I must, dearest: I gave my word.'

'But you say she insisted upon not pledging you?'

'I pledged myself.'

'You are too quixotic. Suppose you find her consoled?'

'Let us suppose it,'—he seized her hands,—'the other possibility stuns me, let us forget it. Tonight, tomorrow, and still tomorrow are ours. Mildred—'

She released herself. 'How can we forget it? It poisons today, it blunts tomorrow. It makes a farce of—of everything.'

'I ought not to have spoken,' he said remorsefully, 'and, but for that other fellow, I should have waited till I was free. Do you forgive me?'

'I do not know.'

'Whatever happens, the world will never hold any woman for me but you.'

'You have possibly said that before?'

'I was a young fool—she told me so; and, good heavens! I know it now.'

'Tell me', she said; 'let us walk about. What is this other woman like?'

'Let us forget her', he pleaded.

'I want to know.'

'Very small and fair; remarkably fair and witty and—well, I hardly know how to put it, courageous: it was the kind of fine unfeminine courage she seemed to have, that—that trapped my fancy. It struck me as an uncommon trait; if she had been a man she would have been cut out for a soldier. You see it was not love, darling; it began with a sort of impersonal admiration, and that's what it has come back to now.'

'She will marry you', the girl assented conclusively. 'I think I understand her better than you.'

'And you will hate my memory?'

'Yes, for a time; and then—then I suppose I shall marry some one else.'

'If I were you, I would rather spend my life alone.'

'It is not so easy for women to talk or think of loneliness; but I love you, Alan', she ended passionately.

They bade each other a troubled and subdued good-night.

III

   . . . tandis que, dans le lointain, le cloche de la paroisse—emplissait l'air de vibrations douces, protectrices, conseillères de bon sommeil à ceux qui ont encore des lendemains——

   (. . . while, in the distance, the parish bell—filled the air with soft, protective vibrations, counsellors of a good sleep to those for whom tomorrow will still come——)

Lady Hopedene closed the book brusquely, with the little recurrent foreign gesture of impatience.

'I must avoid this man; he is deplorably enervating.' The china clock on the opposite wall struck four, and, summoned by its chime, the rejected phrase returned, to be rapidly dismissed again. *Ceux qui ont encore des lendemains.*

She passed a hand across her eyes, and pushed back the brilliant cushions against which her head rested uneasily. They framed the gold hair superbly, but seemed to have chased the delicate flush, once sweetly permanent, from the childish face. It looked out now from them nearly colourless and a little drawn.

The door opened, and a mechanical voice announced, 'Captain Henley'.

She did not rise, and he advanced towards her.

'Alan!' The name escaped her, poignant, even piteous in the sudden-
ness and intensity of its utterance. A long succession of days, of weeks—
a weight of waiting—seemed to be visibly thrust before him, painted
on the wing of that swift cry.

And something more: behind it lurked a note of anguish, faint, but
clashing audibly against its joy.

Insensibly he recoiled before the unfamiliar greeting. It was unlike
her, unlike anything he had heard before. But in a moment the blue
eyes, so strangely lit, resumed their old expression of half-bantering
welcome; and she beckoned him forward, with the well-known wave of
a small commanding hand.

'Come here, you wonderful apparition; I want to assure my senses,
test my sanity. Is it actually *you*?'

'Unmistakably. I have come for my answer', he began briefly, hurriedly: aware that she had given it, before his question, in that startling
and involuntary utterance of his name.

'You speak as if you were presenting a bill,' she responded, laughing, 'and the demand sounds somewhat peremptory, when I have been
wondering if I should ever have to meet it. Oh, there are long arrears,
I know', she added, taking his hand as he stood beside her. 'Sit here.'
She made a place for him, and looked frankly, earnestly, at his slightly
matured face.

'Why,' she said, drawing back in mock alarm, 'it *is* a man I have to
deal with!' And then, with a quick and winning sweetness, 'shall I tell
you a secret, Captain Henley? I am rather disappointed, for—for—as
a fact I loved the boy.'

'Then why did you play with him?' he broke out, hardly able to
control his bitterness, and returning her close gaze intently. 'Your
whim'—he spoke the truth baldly, careless, for the moment, whether or
not she caught his meaning—'your whim has cost me much an honest
answer would have saved me.'

'You have a right, knowing so little, to reproach me. I will tell you',
she returned gently. 'It was after all, I suppose, mere egotism, because
I cared for you more than myself. Your happiness was, is, will always,
so I fancy, be more to me than mine.'

An impulse came to him to put the truth before her, to tell his story plainly. For this woman whom he had loved inspired him strongly still with trust. Her mind, he knew, was sounder than the minds of other women he had met, and he could not fail to trust the heart that shone so clearly, straightly, through the blue eyes regarding him. He might have yielded to that momentary impulse, had she not broken in too hastily upon his wavering thought.

'I chose the most effectual lie that I could frame that day—do you remember?—when I told you that you were not the first, you might not be the last. You *are* the first'—her glance fell suddenly upon the yellow volume which had slipped, at his entrance, from the sofa to the floor— 'you will be certainly the last. Lying always disgusts me. I pray you forgive my first and only lie.'

He offered no response, but rose and stood silently, awkwardly beside her, loth to return her honesty with artificial protestation, knowing that speech was required of him, painfully seeking words.

She laughed, remembering him sometimes dumb of old, and went on with a trace of hesitation in her tone.

'My openness surprises you; but look at this', and she spread out before him a denuded, shrunken hand.

'How bare it is!' he said, taking it quietly in his own. 'Where are the old adornments? Why have you forsaken them?'

She replied ruefully, 'They have forsaken me. Perhaps'—she pointed lightly to her cheeks—'you have remarked that other adornments have turned traitors too. Sooner or later I must tell you: why not now? My physicians'—she pronounced the words with a mock pomposity, and punctuated them with a slight grimace—'give me a year, or not so long perhaps, for the pomps and vanities of this delightfully wicked world. And so, you see, out of pure consideration, the pomps and vanities are withdrawing gradually in preparation for their final exit.'

She relinquished the accent of raillery, and began hurriedly and anxiously to caress his detaining hand. He seized her wrists and bent an incredulous glance upon her.

'It is some wretched jest. I do not believe you serious.'

'Just now I am as serious as I shall ever be.'

'You do not mean. . . .' He could not achieve the obvious question, and stood holding the small fingers closely—stammering—silenced.

'Yes, truly, I have got marching orders, with a respite. There is a year for speech, for folly, for wisdom—if it were not so dull—and a year, my dear, for love.'

'My G——!' he cried. 'You have stunned me, Ella. You are here; I can see and hear you; but I can't manage to understand. It is like a nightmare. It isn't *true*?'

She released and laid her hands upon his arm, and checking his outburst with the flicker of a smile, protested,—'You do not meet the enemy like a soldier.'

'I have not your nerve', he answered. 'Surely,' he ventured, 'some other man will give you hope or time.'

She shook her head, and quoted lightly,—' "If we die today, if we die tomorrow, there is little to choose. No man may speak when once the Fates have spoken." '

Her eyes were challenging his to courage. 'You loved your life far more than most of us', he said, immediately wishing the words back.

'I adored—I adore it. You link me with the past tense too readily. We will have no future nor subjunctive moods, only the present and imperative. *Je t'aime—aime-toi, par example.*'

'Ella,' he cried, 'for God's sake be serious. I don't know how long you have known what you have told me. Remember it is new to me.'

'It is passably new to me.' She flashed a swift rebuke towards him from the brave blue eyes. 'Do you wish me to play the coward?'

'You could not', he asserted brokenly. 'You are a good soldier spoiled.'

'The finest, if the clumsiest, compliment you have ever paid me.'

'It is not that', he said almost roughly. 'You shame me heart and soul; I feel like a deserter.'

'They are cut after another pattern', she observed, with sweet decision. 'We were neither of us made to turn our backs upon what lies before us or pull long faces at a foe. Through this long year—I will confess to a weary year—it never occurred to me as a reality that you would fail. I thought you might—I did not fear you *would*; but if you had, I should have faced it, and it would have been harder to face than death.'

'I will never fail you', he said determinately; and as the 'never' left his lips, he recalled her little speech upon the employment of that far-reaching term; only safely to be spoken, she had said, as now he spoke it, upon the threshold of the grave. And then it flashed across him how that interview had been a curious prototype of this. Then they had touched on death and laughter, and looked forth, too, upon the passage of a year. This was the ending to that unreal dream. But he was not to view its empty structure; she should not spend last hours picking up the petals of his fallen love.

'I will not fail you', he repeated passionately.

She listened with some wonder to the reiterated phrase.

'My dear, I do not doubt you.'

'I have not said what I came to say, Ella. Will you be my wife?'

He asked the question foreseeing its consequences, but impelled to it by something deeper and more grave than pity. For a moment, she did not reply. She had been standing by him, but now sat down and began to finger the embroidered cushion, while she framed her answer. It came at last, but slowly from so quick a speaker.

'Love,' she said, 'though we don't often think of it, has an extensive wardrobe. Everyone cannot wear his richest garment,—we cannot, you and I. Let us be glad he offers us any, for without his charity we must indeed go bare. We can be comrades, you and I, and only that, I think. It is the sanest, the best compact possible, since lovers end as we may not. You will keep watch with me, as if we were both good friends, good soldiers, till the enemy strikes, and he *will* strike, you know.'

'That is a cold night's watch', he forced himself to say, remembering her cry of greeting, and wondering how she kept such guard upon her heart.

'Warm enough', she said; 'much warmer than the dawn which is to end it. You will wait and keep this watch with me?'

'I will do anything you bid me.'

'Then I bid you cultivate a smile for all weathers, and not to shiver yet.' She took his hand again and led him to the window, where the lamps were being lit beside the railings of the park. 'It is spring outside; I noticed the trees in bud this morning. The Fates have not been too unkind. They have lent us all the seasons; summer, my favourite, is coming, and—you have come.'

He stooped and caught and kissed the little fingers loosely clasping his.

'Your last kiss has found a friend', she whispered; 'it has lain for a long while lonely there.'

'Give me your rings', he suggested; 'I will get them altered. I like to see you wearing them.'

'Yes', she agreed, 'it is stupid to give them up. I will send—no, I will fetch them myself, if you will excuse me.'

Loosing his hand, she crossed the darkening room and left him there alone, confronting the first great problem of his life.

IV

Mildred Playfair rose and left her seat by the window to stand beside the fire. She was renewing, without much display of friendliness, her acquaintance with an English spring. Henley was standing by the mantelpiece, and her movement brought them face to face. She lifted her dark eyes to his, and remarked, with the lingering intonation habitual to her, 'There seems to be nothing more to say; I almost wonder why you came.'

'Because you sent for me. I have put everything before you—the case as it stands, as it must stand for me. Perhaps it was better to come and tell you myself.'

'You need not have waited for my summons.'

'I meant to write. I thought it would be less painful for us both. It wasn't an easy matter, though. I was making a bungling attempt at an explanation on paper when your letter came.'

'The explanation that you were going to relinquish me for a poetic and almost feminine fancy?'

'I had no choice.'

'I did not know that men went in for this kind of thing. I imagined they were more—definite.'

'I did not know myself that I could have done it a month ago; but women—a good woman—can turn a man inside out sometimes, and show him what he can and cannot do.'

She had been holding her hands towards the fire, but now she turned and took from a table an Indian paper-knife and began slipping it in and out the uncut pages of a magazine.

'The fact is that you love this other woman still.'

He hesitated, experiencing an almost Puritan desire to speak the barest truth.

'Not in the way you mean. I have learned this week that there are many ways of love.'

'Is that original?' she asked, running a finger up and down the carved blade in her hand. 'Are you sure you are not echoing a phrase of hers?'

'Perhaps. Mildred,' he cried, 'you make things even harder than they were. If you saw my heart, you would know I am not a traitor—at least to you.'

To that other, he did not feel that he was playing altogether an untreacherous part.

'Your intricacies elude me. I admit I do not understand your way— your "ways".'

'Not after I have told you everything: when I have begged you to wait for me, as perhaps I ought not, as I surely should not have done if I did not care for you so much, dread losing you so terribly?'

'You must have known I should not consent to see you implicitly the lover of another woman.'

'I am not her lover', he said briefly.

'Another fine distinction which I cannot grasp.'

'If you could see my heart—' he began again; but she broke in.

'I can see enough of it to know it is not wholly mine.'

'Do you want protestations?' he asked heavily, but without bitterness. 'How can I make them now, with your refusal—with the vanity of hope—before me, with nothing but good-bye to say?'

'If you cared, you would not say it!'

Again he repeated, 'I have no choice.'

'Because you have chosen.'

'In my heart, in my soul, I have chosen you.'

'And yet you are going back to some one else?'

'For a year, and possibly less than that. Cannot you look at it as I do? We have life before us, but there is death in her eyes—death already, as I saw it, upon her lips. There is the grave between us', he urged, and ended with a new note of sadness. 'Isn't that space enough?'

'It is invisible,' she returned, 'so do not blame me if I cannot see it. I can see only that there is a woman, or her shadow, between you and me.'

'Is that your last word?' he asked, almost at that moment hoping it might be, aware that words had availed them little—brought no illumination and no relief.

'No', she broke forth suddenly, doffing the coldness and the calmness of her attitude petulantly, like an overweighted garment. 'My last word is that I love you, Alan, and that by your own admission you belong to me.' She crossed the room and threw herself upon him,—'I cannot and I will not let you go.'

He caught her with a short, familiar cry of welcome, and held her for a second; then releasing her, he rested a hand upon her dark and slightly ruffled hair.

'So you will wait?'

He spoke simply his first thought; but at its utterance she sprang away.

'No, not that—not that.'

'What, then?' he asked bewilderedly. 'You will not trust me?'

'*She* trusted you', the girl exclaimed, letting through her lips, in this last moment of distraction, the reminder which had hovered behind them once or twice before. '*She* let you go; and though she does not know it, you have failed her, or so you say; indeed, I do not know what to believe of you.'

'That is true', he said. 'God knows that I have failed her; *that* is true.'

'Give me a pledge that you will not fail *me*.'

'What pledge?' he asked; and added passionately; 'any, any I can give is yours.'

'Give me the only credible one,' she urged, 'and stay with me.'

He paused,—perplexed, dubious, stung; swaying upon a second choice. To which woman did he owe most? They seemed, as he stood there irresolute, both stationed before his vision, calling upon him that he should not fail. The one more distant, miniature and frail, a form of fading loveliness, in the posture of halting life; the other—she who stood beside him—vigorous, beautiful, distinct and dear, her feet strongly planted upon the stair of youth. The physical contrast struck him forcibly, and yet it was not that which brought conclusion to his contending thought. It was a sentence, spoken sweetly by a decisive voice proceeding from a chamber, which to his view was dimmer than the room wherein he stood—'We were neither of us made to turn our backs upon what lies before us or pull long faces at a foe.'

With that in his ears he faced the tacit foe before him urging mutely in counter-claim.

'You will not trust me?' he asked again, this time with a dull accent of humility that might not have missed an older heart.

'I cannot', she replied rebelliously.

He met the dark, unyielding eyes, to find they stated an unyielding fact.

The woman who compelled it could not hear his answer; she would have understood it.

'And I,' he said simply, with a regret that reached beyond the passion of the moment, 'I cannot stay.'

Georgie Porgie

Georgie Porgie, pudding and pie,
Kissed the girls and made them cry.
When the boys came out to play
Georgie Porgie ran away.

If you will admit that a man has no right to enter his drawing-room early in the morning, when the housemaid is setting things right and clearing away the dust, you will concede that civilised people who eat out of China and own card-cases have no right to apply their standard of right and wrong to an unsettled land. When the place is made fit for their reception, by those men who are told off to the work, they can come up, bringing in their trunks their own society and the Decalogue, and all the other apparatus. Where the Queen's Law does not carry, it is irrational to expect an observance of other and weaker rules. The men who run ahead of the cars of Decency and Propriety, and make the jungle ways straight, cannot be judged in the same manner as the stay-at-home folk of the ranks of the regular *Tchin*.

Not many months ago the Queen's Law stopped a few miles north of Thayetmyo on the Irrawaddy. There was no very strong Public Opinion up to that limit, but it existed to keep men in order. When the Government said that the Queen's Law must carry up to Bhamo and the Chinese border the order was given, and some men whose desire was to be ever a little in advance of the rush of Respectability flocked forward with the troops. These were the men who could never pass examinations, and would have been too pronounced in their ideas for the administration of bureau-worked Provinces. The Supreme Government stepped in as soon as might be, with codes and regulations, and all but reduced New Burma to the dead Indian level; but there was a short time during which strong men were necessary and ploughed a field for themselves.

Among the forerunners of Civilisation was Georgie Porgie, reckoned by all who knew him a strong man. He held an appointment in Lower Burma when the order came to break the Frontier, and his friends called him Georgie Porgie because of the singularly Burmese-like manner in which he sang a song whose first line is something like the words 'Georgie Porgie'. Most men who have been in Burma will know the song. It means: 'Puff, puff, puff, puff, great steamboat!' Georgie sang it to his banjo, and his friends shouted with delight, so that you could hear them far away in the teak-forest.

When he went to Upper Burma he had no special regard for God or Man, but he knew how to make himself respected, and to carry out the mixed Military-Civil duties that fell to most men's share in those months. He did his office work and entertained, now and again, the detachments of fever-shaken soldiers who blundered through his part of the world in search of a flying party of dacoits. Sometimes he turned out and dressed down dacoits on his own account; for the country was still smouldering and would blaze when least expected. He enjoyed these charivaris, but the dacoits were not so amused. All the officials who came in contact with him departed with the idea that Georgie Porgie was a valuable person, well able to take care of himself, and, on that belief, he was left to his own devices.

At the end of a few months he wearied of his solitude, and cast about for company and refinement. The Queen's Law had hardly begun to be felt in the country, and Public Opinion, which is more powerful than the Queen's Law, had yet to come. Also, there was a custom in the country which allowed a white man to take to himself a wife of the Daughters of Heth upon due payment. The marriage was not quite so binding as is the *nikkah* ceremony among Mahomedans, but the wife was very pleasant.

When all our troops are back from Burma there will be a proverb in their mouths, 'As thrifty as a Burmese wife', and pretty English ladies will wonder what in the world it means.

The headman of the village next to Georgie Porgie's post had a fair daughter who had seen Georgie Porgie and loved him from afar. When news went abroad that the Englishman with the heavy hand who lived in the stockade was looking for a housekeeper, the headman came in and explained that, for five hundred rupees down, he would entrust his daughter to Georgie Porgie's keeping, to be maintained in all honour, respect, and comfort, with pretty dresses, according to the custom of the country. This thing was done, and Georgie Porgie never repented it.

He found his rough-and-tumble house put straight and made comfortable, his hitherto unchecked expenses cut down by one-half, and himself petted and made much of by his new acquisition, who sat at the head of his table and sang songs to him and ordered his Madrassee servants about, and was in every way as sweet and merry and honest and winning a little woman as the most exacting of bachelors could have desired. No race, men say who know, produces such good wives and heads of households as the Burmese. When the next detachment tramped by on the war-path the Subaltern in command found at Georgie Porgie's table a hostess to be deferential to, a woman to be treated in every way as one occupying an assured position. When he gathered his men together next dawn and replunged into the jungle he thought regretfully of the nice little dinner and the pretty face, and envied Georgie Porgie from the bottom of his heart. Yet *he* was engaged to a girl at Home, and that is how some men are constructed.

The Burmese girl's name was not a pretty one; but as she was promptly christened Georgina by Georgie Porgie, the blemish did not matter. Georgie Porgie thought well of the petting and the general comfort, and vowed that he had never spent five hundred rupees to a better end.

After three months of domestic life a great idea struck him. Matrimony —English matrimony—could not be such a bad thing after all. If he were so thoroughly comfortable at the Back of Beyond with this Burmese girl who smoked cheroots, how much more comfortable would he be with a sweet English maiden who would not smoke cheroots, and would play upon a piano instead of a banjo? Also he had a desire to return to his kind, to hear a Band once more, and to feel how it felt to wear a dress-suit again. Decidedly, Matrimony would be a very good thing. He thought the matter out at length of evenings, while Georgina sang to him, or asked him why he was so silent, and whether she had done anything to offend him. As he thought, he smoked, and as he smoked he looked at Georgina, and in his fancy turned her into a fair, thrifty, amusing, merry, little English girl, with hair coming low down on her forehead, and perhaps a cigarette between her lips. Certainly, not a big, thick, Burma cheroot, of the brand that Georgina smoked. He would wed a girl with Georgina's eyes and most of her ways. But not all. She could be improved upon. Then he blew thick smoke-wreaths through his nostrils and stretched himself. He would taste marriage. Georgina had helped him to save money, and there were six months' leave due to him.

'See here, little woman,' he said, 'we must put by more money for these next three months. I want it.' That was a direct slur on Georgina's housekeeping; for she prided herself on her thrift; but since her God wanted money she would do her best.

'You want money?' she said with a little laugh. 'I *have* money. Look!' She ran to her own room and fetched out a small bag of rupees. 'Of all that you give me, I keep back some. See! One hundred and seven rupees. Can you want more money than that? Take it. It is my pleasure if you use it.' She spread out the money on the table and pushed it towards him with her quick, little, pale yellow fingers.

Georgie Porgie never referred to economy in the household again.

Three months later, after the dispatch and receipt of several mysterious letters which Georgina could not understand, and hated for that reason, Georgie Porgie said that he was going away, and she must return to her father's house and stay there.

Georgina wept. She would go with her God from the world's end to the world's end. Why should she leave him? She loved him.

'I am only going to Rangoon,' said Georgie Porgie. 'I shall be back in a month, but it is safer to stay with your father. I will leave you two hundred rupees.'

'If you go for a month, what need of two hundred? Fifty are more than enough. There is some evil here. Do not go, or at least let me go with you.'

Georgie Porgie does not like to remember that scene even at this date. In the end he got rid of Georgina by a compromise of seventy-five rupees. She would not take more. Then he went by steamer and rail to Rangoon.

The mysterious letters had granted him six months' leave. The actual flight and an idea that he might have been treacherous hurt severely at the time, but as soon as the big steamer was well out into the blue, things were easier, and Georgina's face, and the queer little stockaded house, and the memory of the rushes of shouting dacoits by night, the cry and struggle of the first man that he had ever killed with his own hand, and a hundred other more intimate things, faded and faded out of Georgie Porgie's heart, and the vision of approaching England took its place. The steamer was full of men on leave, all rampantly jovial souls who had shaken off the dust and sweat of Upper Burma and were as merry as schoolboys. They helped Georgie Porgie to forget.

Then came England with its luxuries and decencies and comforts, and Georgie Porgie walked in a pleasant dream upon pavements of which he had nearly forgotten the ring, wondering why men in their senses ever left Town. He accepted his keen delight in his furlough as the reward of his services. Providence further arranged for him another and greater delight—all the pleasures of a quiet English wooing, quite different from the brazen businesses of the East, when half the community stand back and bet on the result, and the other half wonder what Mrs So-and-So will say to it.

It was a pleasant girl and a perfect summer, and a big country-house near Petworth where there are acres and acres of purple heather and high-grassed water-meadows to wander through. Georgie Porgie felt that he had at last found something worth the living for, and naturally assumed that the next thing to do was to ask the girl to share his life in India. She, in her ignorance, was willing to go. On this occasion there was no bartering with a village headman. There was a fine middle-class wedding in the country, with a stout Papa and a weeping Mamma, and a best-man in purple and fine linen, and six snub-nosed girls from the Sunday School to throw roses on the path between the tombstones up to the Church door. The local paper described the affair at great length, even down to giving the hymns in full. But that was because the Direction were starving for want of material.

Then came a honeymoon at Arundel, and the Mamma wept copiously before she allowed her one daughter to sail away to India under the care of Georgie Porgie the Bridegroom. Beyond any question, Georgie Porgie was immensely fond of his wife, and she was devoted to him as the best and greatest man in the world. When he reported himself at Bombay he felt justified in demanding a good station for his wife's sake; and, because he had made a little mark in Burma and was beginning to be appreciated, they allowed him nearly all that he asked for, and posted him to a station which we will call Sutrain. It stood upon several hills, and was styled officially a 'Sanitarium', for the good reason that the drainage was utterly neglected. Here Georgie Porgie settled down, and found married life come very naturally to him. He did not rave, as do many bridegrooms, over the strangeness and delight of seeing his own true love sitting down to breakfast with him every morning 'as though it were the most natural thing in the world'. 'He had been there before,' as the Americans say, and, checking the merits of his own present Grace by those of Georgina, he was more and more inclined to think that he had done well.

But there was no peace or comfort across the Bay of Bengal, under the teak-trees where Georgina lived with her father, waiting for Georgie Porgie to return. The headman was old, and remembered the war of '51. He had been to Rangoon, and knew something of the ways of the *Kullahs*. Sitting in front of his door in the evenings, he taught Georgina a dry philosophy which did not console her in the least.

The trouble was that she loved Georgie Porgie just as much as the French girl in the English History books loved the priest whose head was broken by the King's bullies. One day she disappeared from the village, with all the rupees that Georgie Porgie had given her, and a very small smattering of English—also gained from Georgie Porgie.

The headman was angry at first, but lit a fresh cheroot and said something uncomplimentary about the sex in general. Georgina had started on a search for Georgie Porgie, who might be in Rangoon, or across the Black Water, or dead, for aught that she knew. Chance favoured her. An old Sikh policeman told her that Georgie Porgie had crossed the Black Water. She took a steerage-passage from Rangoon and went to Calcutta, keeping the secret of her search to herself.

In India every trace of her was lost for six weeks, and no one knows what trouble of heart she must have undergone.

She reappeared, four hundred miles north of Calcutta, steadily heading northwards, very worn and haggard, but very fixed in her determination to find Georgie Porgie. She could not understand the language of the people; but India is infinitely charitable, and the women-folk along the Grand Trunk gave her food. Something made her believe that Georgie Porgie was to be found at the end of that pitiless road. She may have seen a sepoy who knew him in Burma, but of this no one can be certain. At last, she found a regiment on the line of march, and met there one of the many subalterns whom Georgie Porgie had invited to dinner in the far off, old days of the dacoit-hunting. There was a certain amount of amusement among the tents when Georgina threw herself at the man's feet and began to cry. There was no amusement when her story was told; but a collection was made, and that was more to the point. One of the subalterns knew of Georgie Porgie's whereabouts, but not of his marriage. So he told Georgina and she went her way joyfully to the north, in a railway carriage where there was rest for tired feet and shade for a dusty little head. The marches from the train through the hills into Sutrain were trying, but Georgina had money, and families journeying in bullock-carts gave her help. It was an almost miraculous journey, and Georgina felt sure that the good spirits of Burma were looking after her. The hill-road to Sutrain is a chilly stretch, and Georgina caught a bad cold. Still there was Georgie Porgie at the end of all the trouble to take her up in his arms and pet her, as he used to do in the old days when the stockade was shut for the night and he had approved of the evening meal. Georgina went forward as fast as she could; and her good spirits did her one last favour.

An Englishman stopped her, in the twilight, just at the turn of the road into Sutrain, saying, 'Good Heavens! What are you doing here?'

He was Gillis, the man who had been Georgie Porgie's assistant in Upper Burma, and who occupied the next post to Georgie Porgie's in the jungle. Georgie Porgie had applied to have him to work with at Sutrain because he liked him.

'I have come,' said Georgina simply. 'It was such a long way, and I have been months in coming. Where is his house?'

Gillis gasped. He had seen enough of Georgina in the old times to know that explanations would be useless. You cannot explain things to the Oriental. You must show.

'I'll take you there,' said Gillis, and he led Georgina off the road, up the cliff, by a little pathway, to the back of a house set on a platform cut into the hillside.

The lamps were just lit, but the curtains were not drawn. 'Now look,' said Gillis, stopping in front of the drawing-room window. Georgina looked and saw Georgie Porgie and the Bride.

She put her hand up to her hair, which had come out of its top-knot and was straggling about her face. She tried to set her ragged dress in order, but the dress was past pulling straight, and she coughed a queer little cough, for she really had taken a very bad cold. Gillis looked, too, but while Georgina only looked at the Bride once, turning her eyes always on Georgie Porgie, Gillis looked at the Bride all the time.

'What are you going to do?' said Gillis, who held Georgina by the wrist, in case of any unexpected rush into the lamplight. 'Will you go in and tell that English woman that you lived with her husband?'

'No,' said Georgina faintly. 'Let me go. I am going away. I swear that I am going away.' She twisted herself free and ran off into the dark.

'Poor little beast!' said Gillis, dropping on to the main road. 'I'd ha' given her something to get back to Burma with. What a narrow shave though! And that angel would never have forgiven it.'

This seems to prove that the devotion of Gillis was not entirely due to his affection for Georgie Porgie.

The Bride and the Bridegroom came out into the verandah after dinner, in order that the smoke of Georgie Porgie's cheroots might not hang in the new drawing-room curtains.

'What is that noise down there?' said the Bride. Both listened.

'Oh,' said Georgie Porgie, 'I suppose some brute of a hillman has been beating his wife.'

'Beating—his—wife! How ghastly!' said the Bride. 'Fancy *your* beating *me*!' She slipped an arm round her husband's waist, and, leaning her head against his shoulder, looked out across the cloud-filled valley in deep content and security.

But it was Georgina crying, all by herself, down the hillside, among the stones of the watercourse where the washermen wash the clothes.

FLORA ANNIE STEEL

Uma Himāvutee

I

Uma-devi was sitting on a heap of yellow wheat, which showed golden against the silvery surface of her husband's threshing-floor. She was a tall woman, of about five-and-twenty, with a fair, fine-cut face, set in a perfect oval above the massive column of her throat. She was a Brâhmani of the Suruswutee tribe—in other words, a member of perhaps the most ancient Aryan colony in India, which long ages back settled down to cultivate the Hurreana, or 'green country'; so called, no doubt, before its sacred river, the Suruswutee, lost itself in the dry deserts west of Delhi; a member, therefore, of a community older than Brâhmanism itself, which clings oddly to older faiths, older ways, and older gods. So Uma-devi, who was on the rack of that jealousy which comes to most women, whether they be ignorant or cultured, had the advantage over most of the latter: she could look back through the ages to a more inspiring and stimulating progenitrix than Mother Eve. For, despite the pharisaical little hymn of Western infancy bidding us thank goodness for our birth and inheritance of knowledge, one can scarcely be grateful for a typical woman simpering over an apple, or subsequently sighing over the difficulties of dress. The fact being that our story of Creation only begins when humanity, fairly started on the Rake's Progress, felt the necessity for bolstering up its self-respect by the theory of original sin.

But this woman could dimly, through the numb pain of her heart, feel the influence of a nobler Earth-mother in Uma Himāvutee—Uma her namesake—Uma of the Himalayas, birthplace of all sacred things—Uma of the sunny yet snowy peaks, emblem at once of perfect wifehood, motherhood, and that mystical virginity which, in Eve-ridden faiths, finds its worship in Mariolatry.

That she could even dimly recognise the beauty of this conception came, partly from the simple yet ascetic teachings of her race, partly because there are some natures, East and West, which turn instinctively to Uma Himāvutee, and this woman among yellow corn was of that goodly company.

Yet a sharp throb of sheer animal jealousy—the jealousy which in most civilised communities is considered a virtue when sanctified by the bonds of matrimony—seemed to tear her heart as her hands paused in her patient darning of gold-coloured silk on dull madder-red stuff, and her eyes sought the figure of a man outlined against the dull red horizon.

It was Shiv-deo, her husband, returning from his work in the fields.

She folded up her work methodically, leaving the needle with its pennant of floss still twined deftly in and out of the threads as a mark to show where to take up the appointed pattern once more. For Uma-devi's work was quaintly illustrative of her life, being done from the back of the stuff and going on laboriously, conscientiously, trustfully, without reference to the unseen golden diaper slowly growing to beauty on the other side of the cloth. That remained as a reward to tired eyes and fingers when the toil was over, and the time came to piece the whole web into a garment—a wedding veil, perchance, for her daughter, had she had one. But Uma was childless.

Yet there was no reproach, no discontent in her husband's fine beardless face as he came up to her; for he happened—despite the barbarous marriage customs of his race—to love his wife as she loved him.

They were a handsome pair truly, much of an age, tall, strong, yet of a type as refined-looking as any in the world. At their feet lay the heaps of wheat; beyond them, around them, that limitless plain which once seen holds the imagination captive for ever, whether the recollection be of a sea of corn, or, as now, of stretches of brown earth bare of all save the dead sources of a gathered harvest. To one side, a mile or so away, the piled mud village was girdled by a golden haze of dust which sprang from the feet of the homing cattle.

'I saw one with thee but now,' he said, as, half-mechanically, he stooped to gather up a handful of the wheat and test it between finger and thumb. 'Gossip Râdha by her bulk—and by thy face, wife. What new crime hath the village committed? what new calamity befallen the part-owners? Sure, even her tongue could say nought against the harvest!'

'Nought! thanks be to the Lord!' replied Uma briefly. 'Now, since thou hast come to watch, I will go bring the water and see *Baba-jee* hath his dinner. I will return ere long and set thee free.'

'Thou hast a busy life,' he said suddenly, as if the fact struck him newly. 'There are too few of us for the work.'

The woman turned from him suddenly to look out to the horizon beyond the level fields.

'Ay! there are too few of us,' she echoed with an effort, 'but I will be back ere the light goes.'

Too few! Yes, too few. She had known that for some time; and if it were so in their youth and strength, what would it be in the old age which must come upon them as it had upon the *Baba-jee*, who, as she passed in to the wide courtyard in order to fetch the big brazen water-vessel, nodded kindly, asking where his son had lingered.

'He watches the corn-heaps till I return. It must be so, since there are so few of us.'

The nod changed to a shake, and the cheerful old voice trembled a little over the echo.

'Ay! there are few of us.'

All the way down to the shallow tank, set, as it were, in a crackle-edge of a sun-baked mud, the phrase re-echoed again and again in Uma-devi's brain till it seemed written large through her own eyes in the faces of the village women passing to and fro with their water-pots. They knew it also; they said it to themselves, though as yet none had dared—save Mai Râdha, with her cowardly hints—to say to *her* that the time had come when the few ought to be made more. Ah! if Shivdeo's younger brother had not died before his child-wife was of age to be brought home, this need not have been. Though, even then, a virtuous woman for her husband's sake ought——

Uma-devi, down by the water-edge, as if to escape from her own thoughts, turned hastily to spread the corner of her veil over the wide mouth of the brazen pot, and with a smaller cup began to ladle the muddy water on to the strainer. But the thought was passionate, insistent. Ought! What was the use of prating about ought? She could not, she would not let Shivo take another woman by the hand. How could they ask her, still young, still beautiful, still beloved, to give him another bride? Why, it would be her part to lift the veil from

482

the new beauty, as she lifted it from the now brimming water-pot—
so——

Uma Himāvutee! what did she see? Her own face reflected in the brass-ringed water, as in a mirror set in a golden frame! Clear as in any mirror her own beauty—the lips Shivo had kissed—the eyes which held him so dear; all, all, unchanged. Ah! but it was impossible! That was what the pious old folk preached—what the pious young folk pretended. She poised the brazen vessel on her head, telling herself passionately it was impossible. Yet the sight of the wide courtyard, empty save for *Baba-jee* creeping about to feed the milch kine and do what he could of woman's work, revived that refrain of self-reproach, 'There are too few of us.' Shivo himself had said it—for the first time, it is true, but would it be the last? Wherefore? since it was true. She set down the water pot and began to rekindle the ashes on the hearth, thinking stupidly of that reflection of her own face. But water was like a man's heart; it could hold more faces than one.

'*Ari, hai!* sister,' called Mai Râdha, pausing at the open doorway to look in and see the house-mistress clapping unleavened bread between her palms with the hot haste of one hard pressed for time. 'Thou hast no rest; but one woman is lost in these courts. I mind when thy mother-in-law lived and there were young things growing up in each corner. That is as it should be.'

A slow flush darkened Uma's face. 'Young things come quick enough when folks will,' she retorted passionately. 'Give me but a year's grace, gossip, and I, Uma-devi, will fill the yard too—if I wish it filled. Ay! and without asking thy help either.'

It was intolerable that this woman with her yearly, endless babies should come and crow over the childless hearth. Yet she was right; and again the old sickening sense of failure replaced the flash of indignant forgetfulness.

'Heed not my food, daughter,' came the cheerful, contented old voice. 'I can cook mine own, and Shivo must need his after the day's toil. If thou take it to him at the threshing-floor 'twill save time; when hands are few the minutes are as jewels, and it grows dark already. Thou wilt need a cresset for safety from the snakes.'

Once more the woman winced. That was true also; yet had she been doing her duty and bringing sons to the hearth it would not have been so, for the glory of coming motherhood would have driven the serpents from her path.*

She paused at the doorstep to give a backward glance, to see the old man already at his woman's work, and her heart smote her again. Was it seemly work for the most learned man in the village who had taught his son to be so good, so kind? Yet Shivo of himself would never say the word, neither would the old man. That was the worst of it; for it would have been easier to have kicked against the pricks.

She passed swiftly to the fields, the brass platter—glittering under the flicker of the cresset and piled with dough cakes and a green leaf of curds—poised gracefully on her right palm, the brass *lotah* of drinking-water hanging from her left hand, the heavy folds of her gold and madder draperies swaying as she walked. It was not yet quite dark. A streak of red light lingered in the horizon, though overhead the stars began to twinkle, matched in the dim stretch of shadowy plain by the twinkling lights showing one by one from the threshing-floors. But Shiv-deo's was still dark, because there had been no one to bring him a lamp. She gave an angry laugh, set her teeth and stepped quicker. If it came to that, she had better speak at once; speak now—to-night—before Mai Râdha or some one else had a chance—speak out in the open where there were no spies to see—to hear!

It was a clear night, she thought, for sure, and, despite the red warning, giving promise of a clear dawn. One of those dawns, may be, when, like a pearl-edged cloud, the far-distant Himalayas would hang on the northern horizon during the brief twilight and vanish before the glare of day. *Ai!* Mai Uma must be cold up there in the snows!

And Shivo must be hungry by this time; watching, perhaps, the twinkling light she carried come nearer and nearer.

The thought pleased her, soothing her simple heart, and the placid routine of her life came to aid her as she set the platter before her husband reverently with the signs of worship she would have yielded a god. Were they not, she and Shivo, indissolubly joined together for this world and the next? Was not a good woman redemption's source to her husband? *Baba-jee* had read that many times from his old books.

* A common belief in India.

So she felt no degradation as she set the water silently by Shivo's right hand, scooped a hollow in the yellow wheat for the flickering cresset, and then drew apart into the shadows, leaving the man alone to perform the ritual in that little circle of light. He was her husband; that was enough.

With her chin upon both her hands she crouched on another pile of corn and watched him with sad eyes. Far and near all was soft, silent darkness save for those twinkling stars shining in heaven and matched on earth. Far and near familiar peace, familiar certainty. Even that pain at her heart, had not others felt it and set it aside? The calm endurance of her world, its disregard of pain, seemed to change her own smart to a dull ache, as her eyes followed every movement of the man who loved her.

'Thou art silent, wife,' he said, kind wonder in his tone, when, the need for silence being over, she still sat without a word.

That roused her. Silent! yea! silent for too long.

She rose suddenly and stood before him, tall and straight in the circle of light. Then her voice came clear without a tremble——

'There are too few of us in the house, husband. We must have more. We must have young hands when ours are old.'

He stood up in his turn stretching his hands towards her.

'Uma! say not so,' he faltered, 'I want no more.'

She shook her head.

'The fields want them; and even thou——' Then her calm broke, dissolved, disappeared, like a child's sand barrier before the tide. She flung her arms skyward and her voice came like a cry——

'Ask her—ask thy sister—let her do all. I cannot. And she—*she* must come from afar, Shivo, from far! Not from here—lest Mai Râdha——'

She broke off, turned and flung herself face down in the corn silently, clutching at it with her hand.

Shiv-deo stood looking out over the shadowy fields.

'They need them surely,' he said softly after a time, 'and my father has a right——'

He paused, stooped, and laid a timid touch on the woman's shoulder.

'Yea! she shall come from far, wife, from far.'

Then there was silence, far and near.

II

There was no lack of life now in the wide courtyards, though the year claimed by Uma's pride had scarcely gone by. And there was more to come ere the sunset, if the gossips said sooth as they passed in and out, setting the iron knife (suspended on a string above the inner door) a-swinging as they elbowed it aside. From within came a babel of voices, striving to speak softly, and so sinking into a sort of sibilant hiss, broken by one querulous cry of intermittent complaint. Without, in the bigger courtyard, was a cackle and clamour, joyfully excited, round a platter of sugar-drops set for due refreshment of the neighbours. It would be a boy, for sure, they said, the omens being all propitious and *Purmeshwar** well aware of the worthiness of the household. But, good lack! what ways foreign women had! There was the girl's mother, disregarding *this* old custom, performing *that* new mummery as if there were no canon of right and wrong; yet they were—those town women—of the race, doubtless of the same race! It was passing strange; nevertheless Uma herself did bravely, having always been of the wise sort. She had given the word back keenly but now to Mai Râdha, who, as usual, had her pestle in the mortar, and must needs join in the strange woman's hints that the first wife was better away from the sufferer's sight. *Puramesh!* what an idea! She had spoken sharp and fair, as was right, seeing that it was hard above the common on Uma—so young, so handsome, so well-beloved! Many a pious one in her place, with no mother-in-law to deal with—only two soft-hearted, soft-tongued men—would have closed the door on another wedding yet a while, and bided on Providence longer. Small blame either. It was not ten years since those two had come together; while as for affection——

The rush of words slackened as the object of it set the swinging knife aside, and came forward to see that nought was lacking to the hospitality of the house. With those strange women within, lording it over all by virtue of their relationship to the expectant mother, it behoved her honour to see that there was no possible ground for complaint. It was a year since Uma had flung herself face down upon the wheat, and now the yellow corn once more lay in heaps upon the white threshing-floor.

* The Universal God.

Another harvest had been sown and watered and reaped; but Uma was waiting for hers. And her mind was in a tumult of jealous fear. Shivo, with all his goodness, his kindness to her, could scarcely help loving the mother of his child better than the woman who had failed to bring him one. How could she take that other woman's son in her arms and hold it up for the father's first look? Yet that would be her part.

The strain of the thought showed in her face as she moved about seeing to this and that, speaking to those other women serenely, cheerfully. Her pride ensured so much.

Within, the coming grandmother heaved a very purposeful sigh of relief at her absence. The patient would be better now that those glowering eyes were away. Whereat Mai Râdha, the time-server, nodded her head sagely; but the girlish voice from the bed, set round with lamps and flowers, rose in fretful denial.

'Hold thy peace, mother. Thou canst not understand, being of the town. It is different here in the village.'

The mother giggled, nudging her neighbour. 'Nine to credit, ten to debit! That's true of a first wife, town and country. But think as thou wilt, honey! Trust me to see she throws no evil eye on thee or the child. She shall not even see it till the fateful days be over.'

The village midwife, an old crone sitting smoking a pipe at the foot of the bed, laughed.

'Thou art out there, mother! 'Tis her part, her right, to show the babe to its father. That is old fashion, and we hold to it.'

'Show it to its father! Good lack! Heard one ever the like,' shrilled the indignant grandmother to be. 'Why, with us he must not see it for days. Is it not so, friends?'

The town-bred contingent clamoured shocked assent; the midwife and her cronies stood firm. Uma, appealed to by a deputation, met the quarrel coldly.

'I care not,' she said; 'settle it as you please. I am ready to hold the child or not.'

So a compromise was effected between the disputants within, before the beating of brass trays announced the happy birth of a son, and they came trooping into the outer court full of words and explanations. But Uma heard nothing and saw nothing except the crying frog-like morsel of humanity they thrust into her unwilling arms. So that was Shivo's child! How ugly, and what an ill-tempered little thing! Suddenly the gurgling cry ceased, as instinctively she folded her veil about the struggling, naked limbs.

'So! So!' cried the gossips, pushing and pulling joyfully, excitedly. 'Yonder is the master! All is ready.'

She set her teeth for the ordeal and let herself be thrust towards Shivo, who was seated by the door, his back towards her. She had not seen him since the advent of the gossips at dawn had driven the men-kind from the homestead. And now the sun was setting redly as on that evening a year ago when she had told him they were too few for the house. Well, there were more now. And this was the worst. Now she was to see love grow to his face for the child which was not hers, knowing that love for its mother must grow also unseen in his heart.

'So! So!' cried the busy, unsympathetic voices intent on their own plans. 'Hold the child so, sister, above his shoulders, and bid him take his first look at a son.'

The old dogged determination to leave nothing undone which should be done strengthened her to raise the baby as she was bid, stoop with it over Shivo's shoulder and say, almost coldly—

'I bring thee thy son, husband. Look on it, and take its image to thine heart.'

Then she gave a quick, incredulous cry; for, as she stooped, she saw her own face reflected in the brass-ringed mirror formed by the wide mouth of the brimming water-pot, which was set on the floor before Shiv-deo!

'Higher! sister! higher,' cried the groups, 'let him see the babe in the water for luck's sake. So! *Ari!* father, is not that a son indeed! *Wah!* the sweetest doll.'

Sweet enough, in truth, looked the reflection of that tiny face where her own had been. She let it stay there for a second or two; then a sudden curiosity came to her and she drew aside almost roughly, still keeping her eyes on the water-mirror. Ah! there was her husband's face now, with a look in it that she had never seen before—the look of fatherhood.

Without a word she thrust her burden back into other arms, asking impatiently if that were all, or if they needed more of her services.

'More indeed,' muttered the grandmother tartly as she disappeared again, intent on sugar and spices, behind the swinging knife. 'Sure some folk had small labour or pains over this day's good work. Lucky for the master that there be other women in the world.'

Uma looked after her silently, beset by a great impatience of the noise and the congratulations. She wanted to get away from it all, from those whispers and giggles heard from within, and interrupted every now and then by that new gurgling cry. The excitement was over, the gossips were departing one by one, Shivo and his father were being dragged off to the village square for a pipe of peace and thanksgiving. No one wanted her now; her part in the house was done, and out yonder in the gathering twilight the heaps of corn were alone, as she was. She could at least see to their safety for a while and have time to remember those faces—hers, and the child's, and Shivo's.

Well! it was all over now. No wonder they did not need her any more since she had done all—yea! she had done her duty to the uttermost!

A sort of passionate resentment at her own virtue filled her mind as, wearied out with the physical strain, she lay down to rest upon the yielding yellow wheat. How soft it was, how cool! She nestled into it, head, hands, feet, gaining a certain consolation from the mere comfort to her tired body. And as she looked out over her husband's fields, the very knowledge that the harvest had been reaped and gathered soothed her; besides, in the years to come there would be other hands for other harvests. That was also as it should be. And yet? She turned her face down into the wheat.

'Shivo! Shivo!' she sobbed into the fruits of the harvest which she had helped to sow and gather. 'Shivo! Shivo!'

But to her creed marriage had for its object the preservation of the hearth fire, not the fire of passion, and the jealousy which is a virtue to the civilised, was a crime to this barbarian.

So, as she lay half hidden in the harvested corn the thought of the baby's face, and hers, and Shivo's—all, all in the water-mirror—brought her in a confused half-comprehending way a certain comfort from their very companionship. So, by degrees, the strain passed from mind and body leaving her asleep, with slackened curves, upon the heap of corn. Asleep peacefully until a hand touched her shoulder gently, and in the soft grey dawn she saw her husband standing beside her.

She rose slowly, drawing her veil closer with a shiver, for the air was chill.

'I have been seeking thee since nightfall, wife,' he said in gentle reproach, with a ring of relief in his voice; 'I feared—I know not what—that thou hadst thought me churlish, perhaps, because I did not thank thee for—for thy son.'

His hand sought hers and found it, as they stood side by side looking out over the fields with the eyes of those whose lives are spent in sowing and reaping, looking out over the wide sweep of bare earth and beyond it, on the northern horizon, the dim dawn-lit peaks of the Himalayas.

'He favours her in the face, husband,' she said quietly, 'but he hath thy form. That is as it should be, for thou art strong and she is fair.'

So, as they went homeward through the lightening fields,—she a dutiful step behind the man—the printing-presses over at the other side of the world were busy, amid flaring gas-jets and the clamour of marvellous machinery, in discussing in a thousand ways the dreary old problems of whether marriage is a failure or not.

It was not so to Uma-devi.

OSCAR WILDE

The Nightingale and the Rose

'She said that she would dance with me if I brought her red roses,' cried the young Student, 'but in all my garden there is no red rose.'

From her nest in the holm-oak tree the Nightingale heard him, and she looked out through the leaves and wondered.

'No red rose in all my garden!' he cried, and his beautiful eyes filled with tears. 'Ah, on what little things does happiness depend! I have read all that the wise men have written, and all the secrets of philosophy are mine, yet for want of a red rose is my life made wretched.'

'Here at last is a true lover,' said the Nightingale. 'Night after night have I sung of him, though I knew him not: night after night have I told his story to the stars and now I see him. His hair is dark as the hyacinth-blossom, and his lips are red as the rose of his desire; but passion has made his face like pale ivory, and sorrow has set her seal upon his brow.'

'The Prince gives a ball to-morrow night,' murmured the young student, 'and my love will be of the company. If I bring her a red rose she will dance with me till dawn. If I bring her a red rose, I shall hold her in my arms, and she will lean her head upon my shoulder, and her hand will be clasped in mine. But there is no red rose in my garden, so I shall sit lonely, and she will pass me by. She will have no heed of me, and my heart will break.'

'Here, indeed, is the true lover,' said the Nightingale. 'What I sing of, he suffers: what is joy to me, to him is pain. Surely love is a wonderful thing. It is more precious than emeralds, and dearer than fine opals. Pearls and pomegranates cannot buy it, nor is it set forth in the market-place. It may not be purchased of the merchants, nor can it be weighed out in the balance for gold.'

'The musicians will sit in their gallery,' said the young Student, 'and play upon their stringed instruments, and my love will dance to the sound of the harp and the violin. She will dance so lightly that her feet will not touch the floor, and the courtiers in their gay dresses will throng round her. But with me she will not dance, for I have no red rose to give her'; and he flung himself down on the grass, and buried his face in his hands, and wept.

'Why is he weeping?' asked a little Green Lizard, as he ran past him with his tail in the air.

'Why, indeed?' said a Butterfly, who was fluttering about after a sunbeam.

'Why, indeed?' whispered a Daisy to his neighbour, in a soft, low voice.

'He is weeping for a red rose,' said the Nightingale.

'For a red rose?' they cried; 'how very ridiculous!' and the little Lizard, who was something of a cynic, laughed outright.

But the Nightingale understood the secret of the Student's sorrow, and she sat silent in the oak-tree, and thought about the mystery of Love.

Suddenly she spread her brown wings for flight, and soared into the air. She passed through the grove like a shadow and like a shadow she sailed across the garden.

In the centre of the grass-plot was standing a beautiful Rose-tree, and when she saw it she flew over to it, and lit upon a spray.

'Give me a red rose,' she cried, 'and I will sing you my sweetest song.'

But the Tree shook its head.

'My roses are white,' it answered; 'as white as the foam of the sea, and whiter than the snow upon the mountain. But go to my brother who grows round the old sun-dial, and perhaps he will give you what you want.'

So the Nightingale flew over to the Rose-tree that was growing round the old sun-dial.

'Give me a red rose,' she cried, 'and I will sing you my sweetest song.'

But the Tree shook its head.

'My roses are yellow,' it answered; 'as yellow as the hair of the mermaiden who sits upon an amber throne, and yellower than the daffodil that blooms in the meadow before the mower comes with his scythe. But go to my brother who grows beneath the Student's window, and perhaps he will give you what you want.'

So the Nightingale flew over to the Rose-tree that was growing beneath the Student's window.

'Give me a red rose,' she cried, 'and I will sing you my sweetest song.'

But the Tree shook its head.

'My roses are red,' it answered, 'as red as the feet of the dove, and redder than the great fans of coral that wave and wave in the ocean-cavern. But the winter has chilled my veins, and the frost has nipped my buds, and the storm has broken my branches, and I shall have no roses at all this year.'

'One red rose is all I want,' cried the Nightingale, 'only one red rose! Is there no way by which I can get it?'

'There is a way,' answered the Tree; 'but it is so terrible that I dare not tell it to you.'

'Tell it to me,' said the Nightingale, 'I am not afraid.'

'If you want a red rose,' said the Tree, 'you must build it out of music by moonlight, and stain it with your own heart's-blood. You must sing to me with your breast against a thorn. All night long you must sing to me, and the thorn must pierce your heart, and your life-blood must flow into my veins, and become mine.'

'Death is a great price to pay for a red rose,' cried the Nightingale, 'and Life is very dear to all. It is pleasant to sit in the green wood, and to watch the Sun in his chariot of gold, and the Moon in her chariot of pearl. Sweet is the scent of the hawthorn, and sweet are the bluebells that hide in the valley, and the heather that blows on the hill. Yet Love is better than Life, and what is the heart of a bird compared to the heart of a man?'

So she spread her brown wings for flight, and soared into the air. She swept over the garden like a shadow, and like a shadow she sailed through the grove.

The young Student was still lying on the grass, where she had left him, and the tears were not yet dry in his beautiful eyes.

'Be happy,' cried the Nightingale, 'be happy; you shall have your red rose. I will build it out of music by moonlight, and stain it with my own heart's-blood. All that I ask of you in return is that you will be a true lover, for Love is wiser than Philosophy, though he is wise, and mightier than Power, though he is mighty. Flame-coloured are his wings, and coloured like flame is his body. His lips are sweet as honey, and his breath is like frankincense.'

The Student looked up from the grass, and listened, but he could not understand what the Nightingale was saying to him, for he only knew the things that are written down in books.

But the Oak-tree understood, and felt sad, for he was very fond of the little Nightingale, who had built her nest in his branches.

'Sing me one last song,' he whispered; 'I shall feel lonely when you are gone.'

So the Nightingale sang to the Oak-tree, and her voice was like water bubbling from a silver jar.

When she had finished her song, the Student got up, and pulled a note-book and a lead-pencil out of his pocket.

'She has form,' he said to himself, as he walked away through the grove— 'that cannot be denied to her; but has she got feeling? I am afraid not. In fact, she is like most artists; she is all style without any sincerity. She would not sacrifice herself for others. She thinks merely of music, and everybody knows that the arts are selfish. Still, it must be admitted that she has some beautiful notes in her voice. What a pity it is that they do not mean anything, or do any practical good!' And he went into his room, and lay down on his little pallet-bed, and began to think of his love; and, after a time, he fell asleep.

And when the moon shone in the heavens the Nightingale flew to the Rose-tree, and set her breast against the thorn. All night long she sang, with her breast against the thorn, and the cold crystal Moon leaned down and listened. All night long she sang, and the thorn went deeper and deeper into her breast, and her life-blood ebbed away from her.

She sang first of the birth of love in the heart of a boy and a girl. And on the topmost spray of the Rose-tree there blossomed a marvellous rose, petal following petal, as song followed song. Pale was it, at first, as the mist that hangs over the river—pale as the feet of the morning, and silver as the wings of the dawn. As the shadow of a rose in a mirror of silver, as the shadow of a rose in a water-pool, so was the rose that blossomed on the topmost spray of the Tree.

But the Tree cried to the Nightingale to press closer against the thorn. 'Press closer, little Nightingale,' cried the Tree, 'or the Day will come before the rose is finished.'

So the Nightingale pressed closer against the thorn, and louder and louder grew her song, for she sang of the birth of passion in the soul of a man and a maid.

And a delicate flush of pink came into the leaves of the rose, like the flush in the face of the bridegroom when he kisses the lips of the bride. But the thorn had not yet reached her heart, so the rose's heart remained white, for only a Nightingale's heart's-blood can crimson the heart of a rose.

And the Tree cried to the Nightingale to press closer against the thorn. 'Press closer, little Nightingale,' cried the Tree, 'or the Day will come before the rose is finished.'

So the Nightingale pressed closer against the thorn, and the thorn touched her heart, and a fierce pang of pain shot through her. Bitter, bitter was the pain, and wilder and wilder grew her song, for she sang of the Love that is perfected by Death, of the Love that dies not in the tomb.

And the marvellous rose became crimson, like the rose of the eastern sky. Crimson was the girdle of petals, and crimson as a ruby was the heart.

But the Nightingale's voice grew fainter, and her little wings began to beat, and a film came over her eyes. Fainter and fainter grew her song, and she felt something choking her in her throat.

Then she gave one last burst of music. The white Moon heard it, and she forgot the dawn, and lingered on in the sky. The red rose heard it, and it trembled all over with ecstasy, and opened its petals to the cold morning air. Echo bore it to her purple cavern in the hills, and woke the sleeping shepherds from their dreams. It floated through the reeds of the river, and they carried its message to the sea.

'Look, look!' cried the Tree, 'the rose is finished now;' but the Nightingale made no answer, for she was lying dead in the long grass, with the thorn in her heart.

And at noon the Student opened his window and looked out.

'Why, what a wonderful piece of luck!' he cried; 'here is a red rose! I have never seen any rose like it in all my life. It is so beautiful that I am sure it has a long Latin name;' and he leaned down and plucked it.

Then he put on his hat, and ran up to the Professor's house with the rose in his hand.

The daughter of the Professor was sitting in the doorway winding blue silk on a reel, and her little dog was lying at her feet.

'You said that you would dance with me if I brought you a red rose,' cried the Student. 'Here is the reddest rose in all the world. You will wear it to-night next your heart, and as we dance together it will tell you how I love you.'

But the girl frowned.

'I am afraid it will not go with my dress,' she answered; 'and, besides, the Chamberlain's nephew has sent me some real jewels, and everybody knows that jewels cost far more than flowers.'

'Well, upon my word, you are very ungrateful,' said the Student angrily; and he threw the rose into the street, where it fell into the gutter, and a cartwheel went over it.

'Ungrateful!' said the girl. 'I tell you what, you are very rude; and, after all, who are you? Only a Student. Why, I don't believe you have even got silver buckles to your shoes as the Chamberlain's nephew has'; and she got up from her chair and went into the house.

'What a silly thing Love is!' said the Student as he walked away. 'It is not half as useful as Logic, for it does not prove anything, and it is always telling one of things that are not going to happen, and making one believe things that are not true. In fact, it is quite unpractical, and, as in this age to be practical is everything, I shall go back to Philosophy and study Metaphysics.'

So he returned to his room and pulled out a great dusty book, and began to read.

BIOGRAPHICAL NOTES

GRACE AGUILAR, 1816–47. Writer on Jewish issues, and author of seven novels, including *Home Influence: A Tale For Mothers and Daughters* (1847) and *A Mother's Recompense* (1850). 'The Authoress' was first published in *Home Scenes and Heart Studies* (Groombridge & Sons, 1853).

ELIZABETH GASKELL, 1810–65. Novelist, particularly known for her treatment of social problems (*Mary Barton*, 1848; *Ruth*, 1853; *North and South*, 1855) and provincial society (*Cranford*, 1851–3; *Wives and Daughters*, 1864). Biographer of Charlotte Brontë. 'Right at Last' appeared in Dickens's magazine, *Household Words* (27 November 1858), as 'The Sin of a Father'; it was reprinted in *Right at Last, and Other Tales* (Sampson Low, 1860).

WILLIAM MORRIS, 1834–96. Poet, political writer, and promoter of the arts and crafts movement; author of a number of utopian fictions (including *News from Nowhere*, 1890) and prose romances (such as *The Roots of the Mountains*, 1889; *The Well at the World's End*, 1896). Co-founder of the *Oxford and Cambridge Magazine*, in which 'Frank's Sealed Letter' was published in April 1856.

ANTHONY TROLLOPE, 1815–82. Prolific novelist, whose works include *Barchester Towers* (1857), *Can You Forgive Her?* (1864), *The Last Chronicle of Barset* (1867), *The Way We Live Now* (1875), and *The Prime Minister* (1876). 'Malachi's Cove' was published in *Good Words* (1864), and reprinted in *Lotta Schmidt and Other Stories* (Strahan, 1867).

HENRY JAMES, 1843–1916. Author of some twenty novels, including *Washington Square* (1881), *The Portrait of a Lady* (1881), *The Wings of the Dove* (1902), *The Ambassadors* (1903), and *The Golden Bowl* (1904), and a prolific short-story writer and critic. 'A Day of Days' was first published in *Galaxy*, 1 (1866); it was reprinted in *Stories Revived* (Macmillan & Co., 1885).

WILKIE COLLINS, 1824–89. Mystery and sensation novelist, producing such works as *The Woman in White* (1860), *Armadale* (1866), *The Moonstone* (1868), and *The Law and the Lady* (1875). 'The Captain's Last Love' was published under that title in *The Spirit of the Times* (1876), and reprinted, with the title 'Mr Captain and the Nymph', in *Little Novels* (Chatto & Windus, 1887).

CHRISTIANA FRASER-TYTLER, 1848–1927. Poet and novelist, best known for the sensational *Jasmine Leigh* (1871), which deals with abduction and forced

497

marriage. 'Margaret' was first published in *Sweet Violet, and Other Stories* (Hatchards, 1869).

CHRISTINA ROSSETTI, 1830–94. Poet, writing on religious themes and on largely melancholy topics; writer of devotional prose, children's verses and short fiction, and short stories. 'Hero' was first published in *Commonplace and Other Short Stories* (F. S. Ellis, 1870).

MARY BRADDON, 1835–1915. Sensational novelist, best known for *Lady Audley's Secret* (1862) and *Aurora Floyd* (1863), and prolific writer of magazine fiction. Edited *Temple Bar* and *Belgravia*. 'Her Last Appearance' was first published in volume form in *Weavers and Weft and Other Tales* (3 vols., John Maxwell, 1877).

AMELIA B. EDWARDS, 1831–92. Novelist, journalist, and Egyptologist. Worked on the *Saturday Review* and the *Morning Post*, and produced eight novels, including the popular *Barbara's History* (1864). 'The Story of Salome' was first published in *Monsieur Maurice, A New Novelette; and Other Tales* (3 vols., Hurst & Blackett, 1873).

THOMAS HARDY, 1840–1928. Novelist, poet, and short-story writer, especially associated with 'Wessex', the Dorsetshire context of such novels as *Under the Greenwood Tree* (1872), *Far From the Madding Crowd* (1874), *The Return of the Native* (1876), *The Mayor of Casterbridge* (1886), *Tess of the d'Urbervilles* (1891), and *Jude the Obscure* (1895). 'The Son's Veto' was first published in the *Illustrated London News*, Christmas number (1891); it was reprinted in *Life's Little Ironies* (Osgood, McIlvaine & Co., 1894).

LUCY CLIFFORD, 1853–1929. Novelist, short-story writer, and dramatist, best known for the controversial *Mrs Keith's Crime* (1882) about a dying mother who poisons her sick child, and for the dramatic version of 'The End of Her Journey', *The Likeness of the Night* (1900). 'The End of Her Journey' was first published in *Temple Bar* (June/July, 1887).

W. S. GILBERT, 1836–1911. Best known as a dramatist, librettist, and writer of light verse; collaborated with Sir Arthur Sullivan for D'Oyly Carte's opera company in a long series of comic operas. 'An Elixir of Love' was first published in *Foggerty's Fairy and Other Tales* (George Routledge & Sons, 1890).

OLIVE SCHREINER, 1855–1920. Born in Basutoland, Schreiner moved to England in 1881, publishing *The Story of an African Farm* in 1883. She returned to South Africa in 1889: her major feminist study, *Women and Labour*, appeared in 1911. 'In a Far-Off World' was first published in *Dreams* (T. Fisher Unwin, 1894).

GEORGE EGERTON (Mary Chavelita Bright, née Dunne), 1859–1945. Short-story writer, associated with 'new woman' fiction, her best-known collections being *Keynotes* (1893) and *Discords* (1894). 'A Little Grey Glove' was first published in *Keynotes* (E. Mathews and J. Lane, 1893).

HUBERT CRACKANTHORPE, 1870–96. Short-story writer, associated with the aesthetic and decadent movements, and influenced by Maupassant and other French realists: committed suicide. Published three volumes of rather bleak stories: *Wreckage: Seven Studies* (1893), *Sentimental Studies* (1895), and *Vignettes* (1896). 'A Conflict of Egoisms' was first published in *Wreckage* (Heinemann, 1893).

NORA VYNNE, ?1870–1914. Journalist, novelist (including *The Priest's Marriage* (1899), a story of obsessive love), dramatic critic, and political writer. 'An Ugly Little Woman', was first published in volume form in *The Blind Artist's Pictures; and Other Stories* (Jarrold & Sons, 1893).

FLORENCE HENNIKER, 1855–1923. Novelist and short-story writer, specializing in fiction (including *Sir George*, 1891; *Foiled*, 1892) dealing with failed or unhappy relationships. 'Our Neighbour, Mr Gibson' was first published in *Outlines* (Hutchinson, 1894).

HENRY HARLAND, 1861–1905. Born in St Petersburg, and educated in Europe and the USA, Harland moved to London in 1890. Having written sensational novels such as *Mrs Peixada* (1886) up to that date, he came to concentrate on psychological fiction and the short story. He was literary editor of *The Yellow Book* from 1894 to 1897. 'Flower o' the Quince' was first published in volume form in *Grey Roses* (John Lane, 1895).

ELLA DARCY, 1851–?1937. Short-story writer, and assistant editor of the *Yellow Book* in the mid-1890s. 'The Pleasure-Pilgrim' was first published in *Monochromes* (John Lane, 1895).

LAURENCE ALMA-TADEMA, 1864/7–1940. Daughter of the painter Sir Lawrence Alma-Tadema; poet, novelist, short-story writer and dramatist, and regular contributor to the *Yellow Book*. *Love's Martyr* (1886), deals with the intense pain of misplaced love. 'At the Gates of Paradise' was first published in volume form in *The Crucifix: A Venetian Phantasy, and Other Tales* (Osgood, 1895).

ERNEST DOWSON, 1867–1900. Poet and novelist; translator of Balzac and Zola. *A Comedy of Masks* (1893) gives a picture of Bohemian London. 'The Statute of Limitations' was first published in volume form in *Dilemmas* (Elkin Mathews, 1895).

Biographical Notes

LAURENCE HOUSMAN, 1865–1959. Poet, art critic, essayist, and novelist, best known for the controversial *An English Woman's Love Letters* (1900). 'The Story of the Herons' was first published in *The House of Joy* (Kegan Paul Trübner, 1895).

WALTER BESANT, 1836–1901. Man of letters, philanthropist, and prolific fiction writer (many works written in collaboration with James Rice); particularly known for novels dealing with the East End of London, such as *All Sorts and Conditions of Men* (1882) and *Children of Gibeon* (1886). 'The Shrinking Shoe' was first published in volume form in *In Deacon's Orders* (Chatto & Windus, 1895).

MARY ANGELA DICKENS, ?1863–1948. Eldest grandchild of Charles Dickens; novelist dealing with sensational and controversial topics in such works as *A Valiant Ignorance* (1894) and *Prisoners of Silence* (1895). 'An Idyll of an Omnibus' was first published in volume form in *Some Women's Ways* (Jarrold & Sons, 1896).

A. ST JOHN ADCOCK, 1864–1930. Short-story writer, specializing in stories of Bohemian life and vignettes of London slum life, in *An Unfinished Martyrdom and Other Stories* (1894), *East End Idylls* (1897), and *In the Image of God* (1898); produced two Boer War novels in 1900. 'Bob Harris's Deputy' was first published in *East End Idylls* (James Bowden, 1897).

ELLEN T. FOWLER, 1860–1929. Poet and novelist, best known for the bestselling *Concerning Isabel Carnaby* (1898), which describes a romance between an upper-class girl and her nonconformist tutor. 'An Old Wife's Tale' was first published in volume form in *Cupid's Garden* (Cassell, 1897).

SOMERSET MAUGHAM, 1874–1965. A prolific novelist, whose reputation largely belongs with such twentieth-century novels as *Of Human Bondage* (1915); his earliest fiction, *Liza of Lambeth* (1897), is a work of Zolaesque realism. 'De Amicitia' was first published in volume form in *Orientations* (T. F. Unwin, 1899), and is reprinted by permission of A. P. Watt Ltd. on behalf of the Royal Literary Fund.

CHARLOTTE MEW, 1869–1928. Poet and short-story writer who tended to choose depressing themes; *Yellow Book* contributor. 'Some Ways of Love' was first published in *Pall Mall Magazine* (1901).

RUDYARD KIPLING, 1865–1936. Born in India, the setting for many of his short stories (starting with *Plain Tales from the Hills*, 1888) and his best-known novel, *Kim* (1901). Some of his most powerful works, such as the *Jungle Books*

(1894–5), are intended for children. 'Georgie Porgie' was first published in *The Week's News* (1888); it was reprinted in *Life's Handicap* (Macmillan, 1891).

FLORA ANNIE STEEL, 1847–1929. Travelled with her Civil Servant husband to India in 1869, where she became extremely interested in the lives of the Indian people, especially women. Most of her fiction, including the very successful novel of the Mutiny, *On the Face of the Waters* (1896), is set in India. 'Uma Himāvutee' was first published in *In the Permanent Way, and Other Stories* (Heinemann, 1898).

OSCAR WILDE, 1854–1900. Wit, dramatist, journalist, novelist (*The Picture of Dorian Gray*, 1891), poet, and short-story writer. 'The Nightingale and the Rose' was first published in *The Happy Prince and Other Tales* (David Nutt, 1888).